ANCIENT HISTORIOGRAPHY AND ITS CONTEXTS

Ancient Historiography and Its Contexts

Studies in Honour of A. J. Woodman

Edited by
CHRISTINA S. KRAUS, JOHN MARINCOLA,
AND CHRISTOPHER PELLING

OXFORD
UNIVERSITY PRESS

OXFORD

UNIVERSITY PRESS

Great Clarendon Street, Oxford OX2 6DP

Oxford University Press is a department of the University of Oxford.
It furthers the University's objective of excellence in research, scholarship,
and education by publishing worldwide in

Oxford New York

Auckland Cape Town Dar es Salaam Hong Kong Karachi
Kuala Lumpur Madrid Melbourne Mexico City Nairobi
New Delhi Shanghai Taipei Toronto

With offices in

Argentina Austria Brazil Chile Czech Republic France Greece
Guatemala Hungary Italy Japan Poland Portugal Singapore
South Korea Switzerland Thailand Turkey Ukraine Vietnam

Oxford is a registered trade mark of Oxford University Press
in the UK and in certain other countries

Published in the United States
by Oxford University Press Inc., New York

British Library Cataloguing in Publication Data
Data available

Library of Congress Cataloging in Publication Data
Data available

Typeset by SPI Publisher Services, Pondicherry, India
Printed in Great Britain
on acid-free paper by
CPI Antony Rowe, Chippenham, Wiltshire

ISBN 978–0–19–955868–1

1 3 5 7 9 10 8 6 4 2

Preface

It is hard to imagine how one might repay the kind of attention, intellectual stimulus, and friendship that Tony Woodman has given so many of us for so long. This volume is intended as a mark of admiration and—we hope!—as a stimulus for continuing discussion and debate. The editors would like to thank Hilary O'Shea and the OUP team for their help and efficiency; John F. Miller for supplying essential information; Laurel Fulkerson for assistance in reading the proofs; John Woodman for the cover image; and the whole Woodman family for helping to keep the secret. We greatly regret that Ronald Martin did not live to see the publication, about which he was very enthusiastic, including his projected piece on 'Tacitus and Cicero'.

As Elizabeth Rawson once said of another ancient historiographer: 'He is still a young man. It will be fascinating to see what he does next.' Since Tony continues to publish at an astounding rate, and to diversify and deepen his scholarly interests, we have not included a bibliography of his published works; it would be out of date before this volume appeared. We would, however, like to thank him for his (unwitting) patience with many of us, who delayed projects for which he has been waiting while we worked on these *antidora*.

C.S.K., J.M., C.B.R.P.
July 2009

New Haven, Tallahassee, Oxford

Contents

PART III: POETRY AND POLITICS

PART IV: TACITUS REVIEWED

List of Contributors

RHIANNON ASH teaches Classics at Merton College, Oxford University. She has published various books and articles on Tacitus and Roman historiography, including *Ordering Anarchy: Armies and Leaders in Tacitus'* Histories (1999) and a commentary, *Tacitus:* Histories Book II (2007). Her next major project is a commentary on Tacitus *Annals* 15.

FRANCIS CAIRNS has taught at the universities of Edinburgh, Liverpool, and Leeds and is now Professor of Classical Languages at The Florida State University. He is the author of several books on Greek and Roman poetry, the latest of which is *Sextus Propertius: the Augustan Elegist* (2006).

ANNA CHAHOUD is Professor of Latin at Trinity College Dublin. She is the author of *C. Lucilii Reliquiarum Concordantiae* (1998), of articles on Republican Latin and the grammatical tradition, and co-editor (with E. Dickey) of *Colloquial and Literary Latin* (forthcoming). She is a member of the editorial board of the *Bryn Mawr Classical Review.*

JANE CHAPLIN was educated at Brown, Oxford, and Princeton She has been on the faculty of Middlebury College since 1992. Previous publications include *Livy's Exemplary History* (2000) and *Rome's Mediterranean Empire*, a translation of Livy 41–5 and the *Periochae* (2007).

EDWARD COURTNEY has held professorships at King's College London and at Stanford University, and was until his retirement in 2002 the first Gildersleeve Professor of Classics at the University of Virginia. His publications include *A Commentary on the Satires of Juvenal* (1980), *The Fragmentary Latin Poets* (1993; with addenda, 2003), and critical editions of Ovid's *Fasti* (1997) and Statius' *Silvae* (1989).

CYNTHIA DAMON is Professor of Classical Studies at the University of Pennsylvania. She is the author of *The Mask of the Parasite* (1997), a commentary on Tacitus, *Histories* 1 (2003), and, with Will Batstone, *Caesar's Civil War* (2006). Current projects include a co-edited edition of and commentary on Caesar's *Bellum Civile*, and a translation of Tacitus' *Annals* (where she aims for a version *brevior, haud melior* than that of Woodman).

DENIS FEENEY is Giger Professor of Latin at Princeton University. He is the author of *The Gods in Epic: Poets and Critics of the Classical Tradition* (1991), *Literature and Religion at Rome: Cultures, Contexts, and Beliefs* (1998), and *Caesar's Calendar: Ancient Time and the Beginnings of History* (2007).

ELIZABETH KEITEL has taught classics for many years at the University of Massachusetts Amherst. She has written many articles on Tacitus and other aspects of ancient historiography.

CHRISTINA S. KRAUS is Professor of Classics at Yale University; she first met Tony in 1988 and her life has not been the same since. She works on Roman historiography and Latin prose style, with sidelines in the theory and form of commentaries and (in a former life) puns and narrative form in Greek tragedy.

D. S. LEVENE is Professor of Classics at New York University. He is the author of *Religion in Livy* (1993) and *Livy on the Hannibalic War* (2010), and editor of *Tacitus: The Histories* (1997). His other works include a variety of articles on Latin prose authors such as Cicero, Sallust, and Tacitus.

JOHN MARINCOLA is Leon Golden Professor of Classics at The Florida State University. His publications include *Authority and Tradition in Ancient Historiography* (1997), and *Greek Historians* (2001), and, as editor, *A Companion to Greek & Roman Historiography* (2007). He is currently working on a book on Hellenistic historiography.

ELIZABETH MEYER is Associate Professor of History at the University of Virginia. Author of *Legitimacy and Law in the Roman World*: Tabulae *in Roman Belief and Practice* (2004) and two forthcoming works on Greek epigraphy and history, she has also written articles on Greek and Roman history, epigraphy, and historiography.

J. L. MOLES is Professor of Latin at Newcastle University. He is the author of an edition of Plutarch, *Life of Cicero* (1988) and of numerous articles on Latin poetry, Greek and Roman philosophy, and Greek and Roman historiography.

DAMIEN NELIS is Professor of Latin in the University of Geneva. He works mainly on Augustan Latin poetry. His publications include *Vergil's* Aeneid *and the* Argonautica *of Apollonius Rhodius* (2001). He is currently writing a book on Vergil's *Georgics*.

STEPHEN OAKLEY has taught Classics at the Universities of Cambridge and Reading; he is currently Kennedy Professor of Latin at the University of Cambridge and Fellow of Emmanuel College. His publications include *The Hill-Forts of the Samnites* (1995) and *A Commentary on Livy, Books VI–X* (1997–2005).

CHRISTOPHER PELLING is Regius Professor of Greek at Oxford University. His books include a commentary on Plutarch, *Life of Antony* (1988), *Literary Texts and the Greek Historian* (2000), and *Plutarch and History* (2002). His commentary on Plutarch's *Life of Caesar* is shortly to appear in the Clarendon Ancient History series.

JONATHAN G. F. POWELL was Lecturer in Classics at the University of Newcastle upon Tyne 1984–92, Professor of Latin at Newcastle 1992–2001, and is now Professor of Latin at Royal Holloway, University of London. He has published mainly on Cicero, the Latin language, and Roman satire, and has a particular interest in Roman rhetoric and advocacy.

RICHARD RUTHERFORD has been Tutor in Greek and Latin Literature at Christ Church, Oxford, since 1982. Among his publications are *The Meditations of Marcus Aurelius: A Study* (1989), a commentary on Books 19 and 20 of Homer's *Odyssey* (1992), and *Classical Literature: A Concise History* (2005). He has a long-standing interest in the border areas between historiography and other genres.

ROBIN SEAGER was born in Plymouth in 1940 and educated at Lincoln and Oriel Colleges, Oxford. He spent his entire academic career at the University of Liverpool, with visiting appointments at the University of Illinois at Urbana-Champaign, the University of New England (Armidale), and the Florida State University.

DAVID WEST has taught at the universities of Sheffield and Edinburgh and was Professor of Latin at Newcastle upon Tyne from 1969 to 1992. His publications include *Reading Horace* (1967), *The Imagery and Poetry of Lucretius* (1969), and three volumes of translation and commentary on Horace's *Odes* I–III (1995, 1998, 2002).

T. P. WISEMAN is Emeritus Professor of Classics and Ancient History at the University of Exeter, and a Fellow of the British Academy. His most recent books are *The Myths of Rome* (2004), which won the American Philological Association's Goodwin Award of Merit, *Unwritten Rome* (2008), and *Remembering the Roman People* (2009).

Abbreviations

Abbreviations of ancient authors follow the generally accepted conventions as found in Liddell–Scott–Jones or *OLD*. Periodicals are cited according to *L'Année philologique*, with the usual modifications in English. Frequently cited modern works are abbreviated as follows.

ANRW	W. Haase and H. Temporini, edd., *Aufstieg und Niedergang der römischen Welt* (Berlin and New York, 1971–).
CAH²	*Cambridge Ancient History*, 2nd edn.
CIL	*Corpus Inscriptionum Latinarum* (Berlin, 1863–).
EJ	V. Ehrenberg and A. H. M. Jones, *Documents Illustrating the Reigns of Augustus and Tiberius*, 2nd edn. with addenda by D. L. Stockton (Oxford, 1976).
FGrHist	F. Jacoby, et al., *Die Fragmente der griechischen Historiker* (Berlin and Leiden, 1923–58; Leiden, 1994–).
FRH	H. Beck and U. Walter, *Die frühen römischen Historiker*, 2 vols. (Darmstadt, vol. 1, 2nd edn., 2005; vol. 2, 2004).
HCT	A. W. Gomme, A. Andrewes and K. J. Dover, *A Historical Commentary on Thucydides*, 5 vols. (Oxford, 1945–80).
Hornblower, *Comm.*	S. Hornblower, *A Commentary on Thucydides*, 3 vols. (Oxford, 1991–2008).
HRR	H. Peter, *Historicorum Romanorum Reliquiae*, 2 vols. (Stuttgart, 1906–14).
Oakley, *Comm.*	S. P. Oakley, *A Commentary on Livy, Books VI–X*, 4 vols. (Oxford, 1997–2005).
OLD	P. G. W. Glare, ed., *Oxford Latin Dictionary* (Oxford, 1982).
ORF	H. Malcovati, ed., *Oratorum Romanorum Fragmenta Liberae Rei Publicae*, 2 vols., 4th edn. (Turin, 1967).
PIR²	*Prosopographia imperii romani saec. I, II, III, Edita consilio et auctoritate Academiae litterarum borussicae* (Berlin and Leipzig, 1933–).
PMG	D. L. Page, ed., *Poetae Melici Graeci* (Oxford, 1962).
RE	A. von Pauly, G. Wissowa, and W. Kroll, edd., *Realencyclopädie der classischen Altertumswissenschaft*, 84 vols. (Stuttgart, 1893–1980).

SH   H. Lloyd-Jones and P. Parsons, edd., *Supplementum Helle-*
                      nisticum (Berlin, 1983).

TLL   *Thesaurus Linguae Latinae* (Munich, 1900–).

Introduction

I

One of the earliest articles published by A. J. Woodman was a study of the influence of Sallust on Velleius Paterculus.[1] In it were already revealed many of the characteristics that would define his scholarship in the decades to follow: a close attention to the details of language; an interest in making connexions across different literary works; a strong concern with the relationship between language and ideas; an independent assessment of the evidence and its meaning and importance; and—related to this last—a willingness to take on established literary judgements and accepted scholarly truths.[2] For some forty years now, Woodman has published studies of Latin and Greek literature that have stimulated, energized, and (at times) enraged. He has directed his critical gaze most often towards the poets Catullus and Horace, and the prose writers Cicero, Sallust, Livy, Velleius, and Tacitus; but as with all great Latinists he is continually aware of Greek influence both on individuals and on genres and traditions as a whole. It is not our intention in this Introduction to give a detailed analysis of Woodman's scholarship, but rather to summarize briefly some of the characteristics of his work, and then to situate the papers gathered in this volume within the larger interests and approaches of the honorand.

Woodman's interest in the importance of language runs throughout all of his work. Early in his career, the choice of Velleius Paterculus as a subject for commentary necessitated an engagement with traditional textual criticism, since Velleius' text is one of the most corrupt and problematic from antiquity. Woodman's method was, characteristically, one in which each reading had to be judged independently: the editor needed, above all, to make sense of the text—'difficulties', he said, 'should be no argument in favour of adopting a

---

[1] Woodman (1969).

[2] The young Woodman here took on no less a luminary than Syme: see Woodman (1969), 786; cf. Woodman (1977), 45, and esp. 55–6, where Woodman boldly quotes Syme on Ammianus and then claims for Velleius' account of Tiberius (a particular target of Syme's disgust) the same qualities that Syme had claimed for Ammianus.

"conservative" approach'—but must also at times admit defeat by recognizing the 'numerous occasions when conjecture seems to reach nowhere near the truth'.[3] Woodman has continued textual criticism throughout his career, both in his editions with commentary and in his translations.

Establishing the text of an ancient author, however essential, could be seen only as a first step. It is then necessary to subject what the author had written to the most detailed and exacting analysis, for, as Woodman has maintained repeatedly, it is only by careful study of the language of Greek and Roman writers that we can fully appreciate and understand their complex thought.[4] The ability to analyse classical texts is dependent not only on close reading, of course, but also and especially on a knowledge of the precepts of ancient rhetorical training, for these formed the basis of ancient criticism and guided writers in all fields of literary endeavour. Structure, argument, elaboration—these were inculcated in the writer by his rhetorical training, the uniformity of which meant that authors shared many of the same concerns and methods, whether they were writing oratory, poetry, or history.

For Woodman, structure especially is key to understanding ancient literary works, since it is structure that imparts meaning. In an essay on Horace's *Odes* 3.1, for example, he was convinced that earlier critics had understood 'neither the form nor the argument of the poem'. Once it was recognized that Horace was speaking as a priest and therefore used features that were 'characteristic of the oracular manner of composition', the form of the poem became clear, as did its meaning. Not coincidentally, Woodman was able to show important points of contact between the opening of the ode (judged troublesome by some scholars) and the *Rhetorica ad Herennium*, which helped to explain how Horace had constructed the poem.[5]

Such a reliance on details of language and structure hardly raises issues of principle when applied to a Horatian ode. But Woodman's belief in the overarching influence of rhetoric became more controversial when it was applied to genres such as historiography, where 'rhetorical' had long been used as a pejorative term to designate a historian as less 'serious' in his approach to the past; if, moreover, the same historian were to betray an interest in poetical techniques, he would similarly be judged as less concerned (or not concerned at all) with 'truth'. Yet Woodman's analyses of

---

[3] Woodman cautioned against a too great reliance on emendations, since they had led some scholars to create historical reconstructions on what was nothing more than sand. Discussion at Woodman (1977), 26 (where both quotations will be found).

[4] The argument that a knowledge of the ancient languages is essential to any form of analysis of classical texts runs throughout Woodman's work, but see particularly Woodman (1983), 18–9, and more fully (and more polemically) Woodman (2007).

[5] See, respectively, Woodman (1984), 83, 84, 92.

historiographical texts (and of texts that discussed historiography) followed the same methods as he employed for poetry. In his treatment of the opening of Thucydides' history, for example, Woodman argued—amongst other things—that the failure by scholars to recognize the structure of argument in Thucydides' 'Archaeology', and in particular the way in which the historian used ring-composition to set off the various parts of his work, led them to attribute to Thucydides a 'methodology' and approach to the past that were unwarranted.[6] Similarly, in his detailed analysis of the discussion of historiography in Book 2 of Cicero's *de Oratore*, he argued that scholars had selectively chosen individual remarks from Cicero without regard for their context, i.e., for their place within the entire argument. Proceeding carefully through the structure of the discussion by Antonius and Crassus, Woodman argued that previous scholars had ignored the structure of the discussion (marked off, again, by ring-composition) and the careful distinctions made by the speakers in the individual parts of the dialogue, and that they had thus failed to see how closely connected were Cicero's remarks on the writing of history to the prescriptions of rhetorical teaching on *inuentio*. The result, he argued, was that (as with Thucydides) scholars attributed to Cicero beliefs about the writing of history that Cicero would not have endorsed.[7]

Woodman has maintained throughout that the importance of rhetoric to the writing of history no less than for other genres in the ancient world was paramount. He was not the first to do this, of course, but his work has brought home how for the ancients the attention to *exaedificatio*, the arrangement and adornment of the text, was—perhaps paradoxically for us—the very mark of the seriousness of historiography as a genre, a seriousness not necessarily to be found in the same places that a modern might look. Already in the first volume of his commentary on Velleius, Woodman posited a significant divide between ancient and modern practitioners of history, warning of the dangers inherent in the facile assumption that the two groups have the same aims or the same methods:

To the ancients the writing of history was a literary process directly comparable with oratory or poetry: ... [the ancient historians] aimed at embellishing and inflating their subject matter, and at surpassing their predecessors in stylistic achievement. They had no conception of scientific history, which is mainly a nineteenth-century notion, with the result that the modern historian, to whom historical research is scientific, needs to keep these considerations continually in mind.[8]

---

[6] Woodman (1988), 1–69, esp. 5–32.
[7] Woodman (1988), 70–116; cf. Woodman (2008) for answers to recent critics.
[8] Woodman (1977), 35.

Woodman's approach to classical historiography has the great merit of argu-ing for a consistent attitude amongst ancient historians from first to last, a largely unified viewpoint of the aims and purposes of history held no less by Thucydides[9] than by Tacitus.[10] A consequence of this is that he rejects a very common bifurcation of ancient historiography by modern scholarship, in which certain historians are designated as representative of a 'mainstream', while others (usually those *we* find more problematic) are demoted or deemed atypical or unrepresentative.[11] Moreover, because Woodman con-siders the conventions of ancient historiography as not fundamentally differ-ent from other types of creative writing in antiquity, he has always seen a close integration amongst all the literary genres of antiquity, poetic, and prose.

In that regard, he has consistently sought to illuminate the meaning of historiographical texts by studying their intertextuality and intratextuality, just as one would do with epic or lyric. The careful literary composition practised by the ancients demands that we examine carefully the ways in which they invoke their predecessors—whether these be historians, orators, or poets. For Woodman, then, it is no surprise that Thucydides persistently refers to Homer, Velleius frequently alludes to Cicero, and Tacitus regularly invokes Livy and Virgil. Imitation can include 'self-imitation' as well: in an article with important consequences for Tacitus' historiographical method, Woodman argued that the detailed account of Germanicus' visit to the Teutoburg Forest in *Annals* 1 was closely modelled on Tacitus' own earlier account in *Histories* 2 of Vitellius' visit to the site of the battle of Cremona.[12] Just as important as intertextual elements are topoi, or 'commonplaces', the familiar themes, scenes, and images with which ancient authors thought and described. So, for example, recognizing that the collapse of the Fidenae amphitheatre is narrated in terms conventional for an *expugnatio urbis*, he enhances our understanding of the Tacitean Tiberius as one who turns on his own people.[13]

Movement between genres or within an author's own work played an important role in the engagement and manipulation of audience expectations,

---

[9] Here he differed from Wiseman's very influential *Clio's Cosmetics* (Wiseman 1979), in which the largely rhetorical nature of ancient historiography is similarly maintained, but Thucydides is seen as the great exception.

[10] Note e.g. Woodman (1979), 153 where the belief that historical events will recur unites Thucydides and Tacitus.

[11] It must have raised more than one eyebrow when Woodman wrote in the first volume of his Velleius commentary (1977), 40 that Velleius was 'an integral part' of the Roman historio-graphical tradition between Livy and Tacitus.

[12] Woodman (1979) = (1998), 70–85.

[13] Woodman (1989), 232–6.

as authors felt free not only to invoke their predecessors but also to exploit particular genres or sub-genres in different parts of their works. Just as Horace could employ 'vatic' discourse in his poetry, so historians could deploy the conventions of paradoxography, ethnography, or tragedy.[14] Such invocations, moreover, were not done only for entertainment or 'rhetorical' effect[15] but also to indicate something of importance in the world itself, as, for example, when the 'amateur dramatics' at the court of Nero indicate 'a world of unreality from which almost no one is immune', and where 'the few realists . . . are betrayed and overwhelmed'.[16] It should also be emphasized that for Woodman intertextuality is a two-way street, as when, for example, he argued that Virgil, in describing several scenes on the shield of Aeneas, consciously echoed the language of Livy Book 1, and, by employing *oppositio in imitatione*, consistently minimized or ignored Livy's rationalizations.[17] Woodman's conclusion that they were engaged in literary *aemulatio*, and that 'both Virgil and Livy were using similar means for similar ends',[18] shows once again his belief in the essential unity of ancient literary creation.

Finally, we should mention that despite his belief that the great writers of classical antiquity must be approached through their own language, Woodman also recognizes that increasing numbers of people have contact with Greece and Rome only through translations. To that end he has recently offered translations of Tacitus' *Annals* and Sallust's *Catiline* and *Jugurtha*.[19] The former must be considered an astonishing achievement. Woodman's purpose 'was to produce as exact a rendering of Tacitus' Latin as lay within my power'.[20] He fulfilled this not only by translating the Latin into accurate English—a tall enough order for any translator, particularly when the Latin is Tacitus'—but also by reproducing in English the effects of what he calls Tacitus' 'linguistic power', a power that resides in the historian's metaphors, archaisms, remarkable variation in vocabulary, and wordplay.[21] In trying to convey the masterful work to an audience without Latin, Woodman was not perturbed if the resultant work seemed difficult or strange, since a translation

---

[14] See e.g. Woodman (1992) on paradoxography and history, and (1993) on tragedy and history.

[15] The possibility of entertainment is not to be discounted, of course (see the quotation above at n. 10), but for Woodman rhetoric is never merely about 'effects', but much more importantly about structure, arrangement, argumentation, and presentation. For the impossibility of separating 'style' from content, see Woodman (2007), 141–4.

[16] Woodman (1998), 216.

[17] Woodman (1989).

[18] Woodman (1989), 140.

[19] Woodman (2004) and (2007) respectively.

[20] Woodman (2004), p. vii.

[21] Woodman (2004), p. xxii.

is 'grossly misleading if it lulls readers into minimizing the differences between our society and that of the early Roman empire. On the contrary, it
is positively valuable to be reminded constantly that ancient Rome was an
alien world.'[22]

II

The reader familiar with Woodman's scholarship will note that we have used
the titles of some of his best-known volumes as subsections in this collection.
We do this simply as a fond acknowledgement of the importance and influence of his work. Apart from this rather broad organization, we left it to
our contributors to decide what type of work made the best offering to
Woodman. Unsurprisingly, different contributors have responded to different
strands in his scholarship. Nonetheless, it has struck the editors how many of
the contributions cannot fit neatly into one single category of response, itself a
tribute to the way that the varied aspects of Woodman's approach to literature
are mutually complementary and mutually enriching. Rather than proceeding
through the papers individually, then, we here draw together briefly some of
the themes that recur in the volume.

   Woodman's passion for language and close textual analysis is mirrored in
a number of the contributions. Edward Courtney's examination and emendation of seven passages in the *Annals* is an obvious example; he echoes
Woodman's demands of the textual critic in his warning that 'Tacitean
brevity' is not the same thing as 'authorial confusion of thought and expression' (the latter being what is sometimes offered in the standard texts). In his
most extended discussion, Courtney carefully examines the language of *Ann.*
15.63.3 (a text Woodman had already found troublesome), arguing that
the most important issue revolves around the meaning of *inuertere*: whereas
previous scholars were forced to employ a meaning that the word has
nowhere else in Latin, Courtney's solution—to delete the word—restores
sense to the passage. Anna Chahoud examines how Cicero engaged in self-
construction through the deployment of precise verbal devices, reconfiguring
his champions of the past by combining different aspects of their humour so
as to construct a unified model of verbal wit. Damien Nelis, in an analysis of
linguistic phenomena and verbal echoing and wordplay in *Georgics* 1, examines how Virgil 'writes himself into the didactic tradition'. David West focuses

---

[22] Woodman (2004), p. xxvi.

on the rhetorical expertise and verbal dexterity of the first five poems of Ovid's *Amores* 1. Moving from literature to ancient scholarship, Francis Cairns's treatment of the 'secret name' of Rome demonstrates via a close analysis of the language of the ancient texts the flaws and contradictions evident in them, calling into question their evidentiary value and—in a very Woodmanesque move—effectively eliminating them as reliable sources. John Moles offers a Thucydides who dazzles by persistent wordplay, punning, and the use of significant names, and shows how subtle developments in the use of the same or similar words underpin important interpretative strands in the *History*. Robin Seager, examining an incident in Ammianus' history, closely examines a Latin phrase of the historian's on which much depends, and on the proper interpretation of which historical reconstruction can be employed.

Many of the contributors emphasize the importance of structure in the interpretation of texts. Moles's detailed exposition of the structure of Book I shows how proper appreciation of the structure carries with it insight into Thucydides' notions of cause and pretext, as well as into his establishment of paradigmatic figures. Christina Kraus points out the close correlation in Caesar's *Bellum Gallicum* 7 between Caesar the historical character, focused on *aedificatio*, and Caesar the historical narrator, focused on *exaedificatio*; she details how Caesar's arrangement of major episodes in this book allows him 'to organize complex historical information around a limited number of significant moments'. Nelis explores the structural and thematic coherence of *Georgics* 1 by examining its metaphors of *uia* and *cursus*, arguing that the poem offers 'a body of knowledge which is expounded in close relation to a narrative trajectory related to the preservation of the Roman state at a time of crisis'. West shows how the carefully structured first five poems of *Amores* 1 mark a progression in the portrait of the poet: he begins as the helpless, love-struck victim of Cupid struggling against the god's powers, but then decides to win over the girl through persuasion, conspires with her in the presence of her husband, and finally emerges victorious, in 1.5, as the successful seducer.

The value of contextualized reading is of great importance to a number of the contributors. T. P. Wiseman looks at Velleius' 'Archaeology' in an attempt to illuminate the historian's interests in the lacunose early part of his work, observing that Hercules is an important recurring figure: Wiseman suggests that Hercules, the 'guarantor of civilization', might well have furnished the starting point for Velleius. Denis Feeney's examination of the Manlii Torquati in Catullus and Horace argues that both poets draw on a rich historical tradition surrounding the family, knowledge of which deepens and enriches our understanding of the poems, and brings out the ambiguity and tensions inherent in Catullus' exhortation to Manlius to be like his father (in a family whose most famous father put his son to death), or Horace's traditional encouragement to an addressee of this same family who is the last of his line. Like Feeney, Jonathan Powell offers a historical contextualization of Juvenal's *Satire* 2, exploiting the texts of Quintilian and Martial to argue that a *delator* is not, as is often asserted, an 'informer' but rather has the precise legal meaning of 'lead prosecutor' (a recognition that in turn illuminates other texts). Cairns argues against the modern tendency to amalgamate disparate texts on the 'secret name' of Rome into a homogeneous ancient view, noting instead that a contextual reading of each of the passages rules out such a procedure, and that even those texts often adduced to demonstrate a culture of secrecy in Roman religion, if read in context, prove no such thing.

Not surprisingly, intertextual and intratextual readings abound. It will be clear throughout this collection that the contributors share Woodman's belief that different genres, whether in verse or prose, far from being in their own separate worlds, mutually illuminate one another. Jane Chaplin's examination of an incident in Livy Book 26, where Scipio Africanus refuses to violate a beautiful war captive, links the event both intratextually with the rape of Lucretia in Book 1 and intertextually with the earlier historiographic tradition on (especially) Alexander the Great. Elizabeth Meyer focuses on the relationship between Pompey's letter to the Senate in Sallust's *Histories* and Nicias' to the Athenians in Thucydides' Book 7. She examines how intertextuality, by exploiting both similarities and contrasts, deepens our interpretation of Pompey, but also has the benefit of making the close reader of Sallust into a better reader of Thucydides as well. Stephen Oakley's comparison of Dionysius of Halicarnassus' account of the triple combat of the Horatii and the Curiatii with that of Livy demonstrates how Dionysius echoes earlier historians and poets; he also shows how the narratives of both historians, though sharing a strong visual component, differ in their emphases, with Dionysius taking his metaphors largely from the realm of tragic drama, while Livy, more interested in portraying individual and crowd psychology, uses as a frame of reference the *spectaculum* of gladiatorial combat. West details Ovid's humorous intertextual engagement with his elegiac predecessors and with the conventions of other poetry, including epic and hymn. John Marincola looks at the second half of the *Aeneid* and uses the historical texts of Diodorus and Sallust to argue that the Social War of 91–88 BC was an ordering paradigm for the war that Virgil portrays in Books 7–12. Powell's conclusions about the meaning of *delator* illuminate in a way not previously appreciated the emperor Tiberius' defence of the legal system at *Ann.* 4.30. Rhiannon Ash examines a puzzling minor incident in Tacitus' *Agricola*, the mutiny of the Usipi, whose escape and voyage around the coast of Britain end in cannibalism and enslavement; she shows the close intratextual relationship of this passage to Agricola's own attempt at circumnavigating Britain and to the use of the Usipi later on as an *exemplum*. David Levene explores the role that Pompeius Trogus' world-view had on Tacitus, arguing that the monarchy-centred beginning of the *Annals* is in intertextual engagement with Trogus' history, as Tacitus is likely to be 'reworking Trogus' account of the development of world history through monarchy'. Richard Rutherford looks at the speeches of Calgacus and Agricola in the *Agricola* and those of Civilis and Cerialis in *Histories* 4. He notes that Calgacus' forceful criticisms of Roman greed are not answered by Agricola; in the more expansive *Histories*, he goes on to argue, Tacitus omits the simple structure of an *agōn*, replacing two competing speeches with those of several characters in direct and indirect discourse, 'polyphonic' texts that dissect Roman imperialism from different viewpoints. Christopher Pelling, in his analysis of Tiberius' rejection of divine honours in *Annals* 4, notes that the criticisms of Tiberius that are voiced there must be considered within their intratextual context, since Tiberius' supposed lack of concern with posterity is undermined by (among other things) the recently narrated trial of Cremutius Cordus and the following narrative in which Sejanus fawns on the emperor as almost divine.

Woodman's emphasis on the rhetorical nature of all literary work in antiquity is seen not least in his discussion of topoi, also a recurrent interest in these contributions. Kraus points out that Caesar describes the wall at Avaricum as 'typical', and she connects this with type-scenes and the use of imitative repetition, the exploitation and manipulation of topoi that feature so prominently in classical historiography. We mentioned above the topos of the 'beautiful captive' examined by Chaplin in her study of Livy. Oakley as well examines the use of topoi by Dionysius and Livy. Ash shows that Tacitus challenges and revises ethnographical topoi, portraying the Usipi not simply as irrational barbarians but as people who display calculation, efficiency, and daring. Levene connects Tacitus' portrait of Tiberius as an invader in his own country (a topos that has been developed by Woodman) to Trogus' strong insistence that 'the key vulnerability of the Roman empire lay not on its borders but closer to home', concluding that Tacitus has reworked this Trogan theme to portray Tiberius as 'the internal enemy by whose strength alone Rome can be undermined'. Elizabeth Keitel examines the appearance and use of disaster scenes in Tacitus' works, scenes that exploit various topoi: the *urbs capta* motif (the fire at Rome in AD 64); the besieged city motif (Galba in 69); or even, as in the sack of Cremona, the 'portable, endlessly repeatable last night of Troy'. She argues that Tacitus uses these topoi to bring home the brutality and horror of civil war. Cynthia Damon in her study of scenes of *enargeia* shows how Tacitus takes a particular historiographical topos—that of the historian's 'movement' through his narrative—and varies it to create a strikingly new metaphor of presence, where both republican and imperial historians 'take up metaphorical residence in their chosen periods'.

Finally, a number of contributors explore the relationship between literature and the political world in which poets and prose writers worked, with a special focus on the careful reader's active role in interpretation. Kraus argues that Caesar's use of imitation and familiar topoi tie his individual campaigns into the whole project of Roman imperialistic historiography—and with the problem of 'writing the Roman empire'—while Caesar's own rhetoricizing narrative forms part of his wider rhetoric of self-projection. Chaplin shows how a small incident from the Second Punic War contains powerful resonances with Livy's own time, as the historian implicitly (and prospectively) sketches a contrast between Scipio, the man who refused well-deserved honours and rewards, and the big men of the late Republic who showed no such restraint in either their personal or political lives. Wiseman contends that the importance of Hercules in Velleius' early history is not accidental, but is meant to summon up the hero's battle against the Giants, who were associated in the first century AD with the murderers of Julius Caesar. Chahoud delineates how Cicero's notion of political humour owed much to the tradition of satire at Rome, but also how the orator could not adopt wholesale the conventions or persona of the satirist, with the result that Cicero's self-construction engages with and exploits the satiric genre while nevertheless modulating political invective in accordance with the *dignitas* and *auctoritas* appropriate to the orator. Meyer observes that Pompey's letter shows not only the 'huge and distorting egotism' of Pompey himself, but also that these qualities are mirrored in the self-centredness and self-seeking of the Roman Senate. Nelis and Marincola both show a Virgil very much engaged with the political issues of his time, not least the debate about moral decline and the construction of an idealized past. Powell tries to win from Juvenal's *Satire* 2 a clearer understanding of the role that *delatores* played in the Roman legal system and the qualities that they displayed which most offended the satirist and his contemporaries. Ash proposes that we are meant to link the Usipi's cannibalism with Domitian's draining-off of the state's lifeblood, and that paradoxically barbarians can display greater integrity than a Roman *princeps*. Rutherford's examination of Tacitus' polyphonic treatment of Roman imperialism observes that by such a procedure Tacitus' work 'contains and engenders voices of resistance'. Pelling emphasizes the importance, but also the uncertainty, of memory and glory, observing that although Tiberius' critics are unfair, one can nevertheless sympathize with their viewpoint: the reader's engagement in understanding the mentality of these critics, then, can promote understanding both of Tiberius' dilemma and of how his own actions actually made things worse.

In his inaugural lecture at the University of Durham in 1985,[23] Woodman spoke of his early training in Latin, generously acknowledging the inspiration he had found from an inspiring teacher and model. It will be clear from the following studies that we contributors have found equal inspiration in the example set by Tony himself, and we are happy to offer this volume to him as a token of our friendship and esteem.

[23] Woodman (1985).

Part I

Author and Audience

1

Narrative and Speech Problems in Thucydides Book I

John Moles

Beginnings and endings are notoriously difficult.[1] Thucydides solved the latter with summary brilliance: he died.[2] I focus on beginnings, but also say things about endings and 'closure'.

The narrative of Thucydides I has attracted more attention than any other book's. A bad reason for this is 'the *Iliad* 1 syndrome' (that Homeric book being the most referenced by ancients and moderns). But there are good reasons too. The book *appears* to be unified by its focus on causes and events before the war.[3] It is a 'pre-write' (23.5) within the total 'writing-up' (1.1),[4] and the programmatic character of the prefatory material (1–23) extends into the narratives, which herald many of *the* Thucydides questions. Moreover, the intuition that *Iliad* 1 has extensive resonance is richly fulfilled.[5] These narratives also pose their own, juicy problems, which have produced very different interpretations, including radical claims of profound disunity, different compositional strata, and authorial changes of mind.[6] Badian's revival of Schwartz's thesis that the narrative is systematically skewed against Sparta has further energized debate, especially regarding narrative

'Hoc tibi, quod potui . . .' Snow prevented Tony's presence at this paper's first outing (Leeds, 16 April 1999). Progressively elaborated versions were given over the years at Newcastle and Columbia. I gratefully thank Chris Pelling as 'nurse'. Space circumscribes bibliography.

[1] Arist. *Poet.* 7.1450b26–31; White (1987), 44; Roberts, Dunn, and Fowler (1997).

[2] Even Canfora's (2006a) radical rewrite of Thucydides' biography concedes untimely death.

[3] The non-Thucydidean book-divisions and problematics of 2.1 (e.g. Price (2001), 277–82) here matter little.

[4] Immaterial here the nuances of ξυγγράφω argued by Bakker (2006).

[5] Bowie (1993).

[6] Surveys: *HCT* V.379–82; 405–23; Pelling (2000), 82 ff.; Stahl (2003) 37–64; (2006), 301–20; Zagorin (2005), 40–56.

omissions and displacements.[7] These have also inspired sophisticated narratology.[8]

Despite important advances by Walker, Stahl, Stadter, Rood, Pelling, Price, and others,[9] there remain things to say.

The book may be summarized as follows, with 'l'=linking passages; 'n'=immediate pre-war narrative; and 'r'=retrospective narratives. The latter are usually styled 'digressions' or 'excursuses': not unreasonably and not un-Thucydideanly (cf. 97.2). But to reconstruct the past is to 'look back' (1.3); and 'sight', extending to 'insight', is fundamental to Thucydidean historiography:[10] 'retrospective narratives' reflects this essential focus. I translate *archē* (and cognates) in the sense of 'beginning' as 'first-beginning', and *archē* (and cognates) in the sense of 'rule' or 'empire' as 'first-rule', to allow possible punning.

1–23		Extended proem
	2–19	(r) The 'Archaeology'/'Account of ancient/first-beginning things'
	20–1	Historical method *re* 'Archaeology'
	22–3	Historical method *re* Peloponnesian War
	23.5–6	(l) T. distinguishes between the *aitiai* and the *prophasis* of the war and will first relate the *aitiai* that induced the two sides to undo the treaty and go to war.
24–55		(n) Corcyra narrative (first *aitia* of the war)
56–66		(n) Potidaea narrative (second *aitia* of the war)
67–88		(n) First Conference at Sparta
88		(l) Spartans decide the treaty undone and they must go to war, 'not so much persuaded by the *logoi* of their allies as fearing the Athenians, lest they get greater power, seeing that the greater part of Greece was already under their hands'.

---

[7] Schwartz (1929), 154–67; Badian (1990) (with other 'anti-Thucydides essays); positive responses: Hornblower, *Comm.* I.65, 84; id. (1994), 131–66, esp. 140–5; id. (1997), 270–2; negative: Stadter (1993); Moles (1995); Pritchett (1995); Cawkwell (1997), 34–7; Meyer (1997); Rood (1998), 215–19, 221–2.

[8] Hornblower (1994); Rood (1998); Gribble (1998); *contra* Stahl (2006), 329–33.

[9] Walker (1957); Stahl (2003), 37–64; Stadter (1993); Rood (1998), 205–48; Pelling (2000), 82–111; Price (2001), 127–31; 147–55; 161–4; 171–8; 191–5; 274–6; 333–71; recently: Stahl (2006), 301–20; Kallet (2006), 345–50; Dewald (2005) omits Book I as narratologically untypical (25).

[10] Moles (2001), 213–17; Greenwood (2006), 19–41.

89–117		(r) The *Pentecontaetia*
	89.1	(l) 'The Athenians came to the situation in which they grew [to power] in the following way'.
	89–95	(1) Athenian rise to *hegemonia*
	96–7	(2) Establishment of Delian League; transition to empire
	97.2	(l) 'I wrote these things and made this diversion from my *logos* for this reason, namely that this place was left out by all those before me and either they put together Hellenic things before the Median things or the Median things themselves. But the one who indeed touched on these things in his *Attic Writing-up*, Hellanicus, recalled them both briefly and not accurately in his timings. And they also contain a demonstration of the manner in which the Athenian first-rule was established.'
	98–117	(3) Development of Athenian first-rule
118–25		(n) Second Conference at Sparta
126–8		(n) Spartan and Athenian embassies demanding expulsion of curses
126–8		(r) Curse of Cylon
128–35		(r) Curse of Taenarum ('triggering' Pausanias retrospect)
135–8		(r) Themistocles retrospect ('trigger': accusation of medizing along with Pausanias)
138.3		Themistocles' obituary
139		(n) Further Spartan embassies
140–4		(n) Pericles' speech
145–6		(n) Athenians stand firm; peace broken.

I treat: (1) the *aitia-prophasis* distinction of 23.5–6 and its consequences; (2) the *Pentecontaetia* retrospect; and (3) the Pausanias-Themistocles retrospects. I cover the usual questions. How does the *aitiai-prophasis* distinction work? Is it coherent? Why are the retrospects placed where they are? What is Thucydides' relationship to his predecessors? How good is his historical judgement? Is there a 'composition-question'? Are Badian's claims tenable? Above all, is Thucydides' text, or at least this part, 'open' or 'closed'? Pelling judges: 'Where Herodotus opens questions up, Thucydides' tendency is to close them down, to impose a single "monologic" view imperiously on his readers. His causal questions have answers, and he cares that his audience should get them right'.[11]

[11] Pelling (2000), 83; *contra* (somewhat) Morrison (2006), 254 and Bakker (2006) (both stressing the reader's responsibility to make connexions).

I

23.4–6 runs:

The Athenians and Peloponnesians first-began . . . [the war] after undoing the thirty years' truce which they had made after the capture of Euboea. [5] As to why they undid it, I pre-wrote first the causes [*aitiai*] and the differences [*diaphorai*], so that no one need seek from what so great a war as this came upon the Greeks. [6] The truest pre-cause [*alethestate prophasis*], though most un-apparent in speech, I hold to have been the fact that the Athenians, becoming great and making the Peloponnesians fearful, compelled them towards going to war. But the causes said in the open on each side were as follows, from which they undid the truce and came to the war.

I consistently render *diaphorai* and cognates by 'difference', as (1) implying estrangement and rifts; (2) cognate (via the Latin) with the Greek; and (3) most conducive to Thucydidean wordplay. I consistently render *aitia* and cognates by 'cause'. This perhaps underplays the 'grievance' element,[12] but any choice involves trade-offs; 'cause' *can* have negative implications; it is important to reproduce 'double causality'; and maintenance of consistent vocabulary is thoroughly desirable.

It is vital to read 23.4–6 as integral to chapters 22–3 (though space—or ennui—precludes discussion of that section)[13] and, indeed, to chapters 1–23, or, at least, to test its integrality, since some scholars hold it a late addition.

The salient points are these:

(a) 23.4–6 combines the main thrusts of 23.1–3 ($\pi\alpha\theta\dot{\eta}\mu\alpha\tau\alpha$ as implying both passivity and emotion)[14] and of 22.1–23.1 (action and speech aspiring towards 'reason') into *emotional reaction to pressure.*

(b) 23.5–6's focus on causation corresponds to the last clause of Herodotus' *Preface* ('for what cause they went to war against one another').[15]

(c) 23.5–6 echoes Herodotus' 'resumed preface' (1.5.3): 'This is what the Persians and Phoenicians say. But I am not going to say that these things happened this way or otherwise, rather I shall indicate the man whom I myself know to have begun unjust deeds towards the Greeks'. Naturally, Thucydides' much more complex formulation implies a much more complex causality.

---

[12] Cf. also n. 24.

[13] Moles (2001), 199–218.

[14] 23.1–3 not merely 'rhetorical': Moles (2001), 205, 211–12, *contra* Woodman (1988), 28–32; Hornblower, *Comm.* I.63; 'suffering' in Book I: Stadter (1993), 61–2; Rood (1998), 8, 57; Price (2001), 359–61.

[15] General imitation of Herodotus: Moles (1993), 98–114.

(d) 23.4–5 'first-began . . . [the war] . . . I pre-wrote first', picking up on 1.1 'I wrote up . . . first-beginning', echoes Hesiod's *Theogony* (1, 115) in paralleling the author's 'beginning' with his theme of 'beginnings'.

(e) 23.5–6 exemplifies 22.1–2's distinction between *logoi* and *erga*, again implying that the former are less solid historically.

(f) Since 23.4–6 entails a narrative not only about the war's beginning and progression but also about its *pre*-beginnings, its causes, *and* its responsibilities, the *spatium historicum*, austerely confined in 21.1–2 and 22.2 to contemporary, or near-contemporary, history, is now somewhat extended, although Thucydides cannot be as committed to the factual truth of the *Pentecontaetia* as to that of the main war narrative from 2.1.

(g) This 'pre'-narrative corresponds structurally to the 'Archaeology', whose close (18.2–19) sketches the Peloponnesian-Athenian dissension which will be treated at length in 89–117. This constant narrative regressiveness again imitates Herodotus.

(h) Thucydides already conceives of ἀρχή ('first-beginning') in a very complex way, cf. the verbal interactions beween ἤρξαντο, δι' ὅ τι, τὰς αἰτίας, προύγραψα πρῶτον, ζητῆσαί . . . ἐξ ὅτου and 1.1 ξυνέγραψε and ἀρξάμενος. Like Herodotus (*Praef.*; 1.1.1) and the Hippocratics, he views ἀρχή and *aitia* as interlinked. Like Herodotus (1.5.3), he sees *aitia* as covering both objective causality and human blameworthiness.

(i) The distinction between *aitiai/diaphorai* and *prophasis* entails careful and multiple calibration. It is not simply polar: the characterization of the *prophasis* as 'truest' indicates that the *aitiai* contain *some* truth—that there is indeed a level on which there is *no* distinction between *aitia* and *prophasis* as words (they can be synonyms). But *aitiai* also includes 'allegations, complaints' (as shown by the partly epexegetic *diaphorai* and by the emphasis on their being *said*); there is also a temporal distinction between *aitiai* as specific causes and *prophasis* as a protracted *process*; this temporal distinction is underlined by the interaction between πρόφασιν and προύγραψα: the *prophasis* is a 'pre'-cause (hence ἡγοῦμαι is particularly good for 'think'). The emphasis, consistent with 1.22's concern with the interaction between specifics and generals,[16] already anticipates the *Pentecontaetia*. Importantly, also, the *prophasis* is a *psychological* pre-cause.

(j) The distinction between different sorts and levels of causality should be read as Hippocratic, hence the available Hippocratic colouring of *prophasis* also becomes active.[17] But the Hippocratics characteristically use the

---

[16] Moles (2001), 209–19.
[17] Moles (2001), 210 n. 57, with bibliography.

terms *prophasis* and *aitia* the other way round, and *prophasis* commonly means 'excuse'. Thus Thucydides is challenging the linguistic
expectations both of medical language[18] and of ordinary usage (as
also, implicitly, the Hippocratics' 'diagnostic' skills).[19]

(k) Discussion of *aitiai* often neglects διαφοράς. Partly epexegetic of *aitiai*,
the word also has positive implications: (1) in the *Archaeology* (18.2–3)
δια-compounds convey the 'split' between Athenians and Spartans after
the Persian wars. (2) 23.5 reworks *Il.* 1.6–7 'from what [time] Atreides
king of men and divine Achilles first stood apart in strife', διαφοράς
glossing διαστήτην. Thus διαφοράς and πρόφασιν echo chapter 22's
important horizontal/spatial and vertical/chronological concerns.[20] (3)
It is Herodotean (1.1.1). These implications extend the range of *diaphorai* into the physical.

(l) Debate whether πρόφασις comes from προφαίνω or πρόφημι is otiose,
because πρόφασιν interacts *both* with ἀφανεστάτην/φανερόν *and* with
ἀφανεστάτην/λόγῳ/λεγόμεναι. Thucydides again emphasizes the insta-
bility of language and the inadequacy of *logos* or *logoi* (as in 22.1 on
the speeches): his formulation is challenging, paradoxical, problematic.
Significantly, also, *prophasis* itself embodies both the spatial and temporal: both saying or showing *forth* and *fore*-saying or -showing.

(m) The language of the *aitiai/diaphorai-prophasis* distinction implies larger
contrasts: between appearance, or words, and reality; between concealment and openness; between subtlety and crudity; and between specific
contexts and longer time frames (again like chapter 22).

Thus 23.4–6 creates an extraordinarily rich discourse, and one thoroughly
embedded in chapters 22–3 and 1–23.

The narrative material falls into the following categories:[21]

(a) use of *aitiai/diaphorai* vocabulary in relation to the immediate context.
The asyndetic 24.1 makes the Corcyra affair the first 'cause'; the narrative
contains speeches wherein that 'cause' is 'said' and closes summarily (55.2):
'this was the first cause'. Then the Potidaea affair is introduced: 56.1
'after this immediately these things also happened to the Athenians and
Peloponnesians as a difference impelling towards warring'. 57.2 notes that
the Corinthians were already 'quite apparently at difference', in contrast to the

---

[18] Pelling (2000), 268 n. 9; Moles (2001), 210.
[19] Jouanna (2005), 21–2 sees nothing of this.
[20] Moles (2001), 207–8; Greenwood (2006), 42–56.
[21] For economy, I omit the 'charges' (*egklemata*), which overlap with, and sometimes gloss, *aitiai/diaphorai* (26.1, 34.2, 42.3, 67.4, 68.2, 72.1, 73.1, 78.1, 79.1, 82.5–6, 121.1, 126.1, 140.2, 145).

'most un-apparent' 'truest cause'. The narrative closes (66): 'the Athenians and the Peloponnesians had had these causes against each other', and notes that the Athenians had fought 'quite apparently'. The debate at Sparta (67–88) focuses on the *aitiai*. In 67.4 the Megarians 'show not small differences', especially that of the Megarian Decree. 68.2–3 alludes to 'differences' and to the Athenians' not being 'un-apparent' in their unjust behaviour. Similarly, the end of the Athenian ambassadors' speech (78.4) proposes arbitration of 'the differences'. The Spartan king Archidamus speaks of 'advancing causes' against the Athenians. The Corinthians find no further 'cause' to blame the Spartans (120.1): this example, with others, illustrates how the lexicon of 23.5–6 can naturally be extended into intra-alliance relations. They then argue that their 'differences' with the Athenians are not merely as between individual states (122.2). The book ends (146) with the summarizing 'these were the causes and differences for both sides before the war, first-beginning immediately from the events in Epidamnus and Corcyra'. The reference to the Megarians at 67.4 is picked up in the Spartan ultimatum of 139.1, whose chief point and 'clearest forth-saying' was that the rescinding of the Decree would avert war. But Pericles argues (140.4) that the Athenians would be wrong to regard it, 'which [the Spartans] hold forth most', as a slight 'cause'.

While this category is dense, its relationship to 23.4–6 is unproblematic.

(b) use of *prophasis* of the larger context and of the process.
At 60.1 the Corinthians are 'fearful for the place and consider the danger their own' (a description repeated at 67.1): this reaction foreshadows, indeed influences, the eventual Spartan fear that *their* interests are directly threatened. The same applies to the description of the Aeginetans at 67.2, who 'did not send an embassy apparently, fearing the Athenians, but secretly drove on the war in company with the Corinthians'. This category too fulfils the programme of 23.4–6 unproblematically.

(c) the two editorial passages linking *aitiai/diaphorai* and *prophasis*.
88 has already been quoted.[22]
At 118 the Spartans, not previously having gone to war, unless pressured to do so (an allusion to the *prophasis*), decide that the Athenians have clearly become so powerful and are laying hands on their alliance (an allusion to the *aitiai*), that they must go to war.

This category reiterates the overt programme.

(d) allusions to the *prophasis* in *speeches*.
The Corcyraeans (33.3): 'if any of you thinks that the war . . . will not happen, he errs in judgement and does not perceive that the Spartans want to go to war through fear of you'.

---

[22] p. 16, above.

Sthenelaidas the ephor (86.5): 'do not let the Athenians become greater'.
This category *seems* to conflict with the programme.

On 33.3, Hornblower comments: 'the...passage shows that, whatever
ἀφανεστάτην...λόγῳ means, it cannot mean that the "true [*sic*] cause" was
not mentioned at Athens'.[23] Now, many scholars have speculated that the
truest cause may or may not have been said in Athens or Sparta or Timbuktu,
but such speculations smack of 'How many children had Lady Macbeth?', or
'What time was it when Aeneas left the Underworld?' Moreover, the allusion
only 'shows' what Hornblower claims, *if* it is historical. It has, of course, often
been claimed that, since 'most un-apparent in speech' (23.6) does not necessarily entail 'no mention at all', allusions to the *prophasis* in the speeches are
not necessarily unhistorical. But it is a narrative surprise when the 'truest'
prophasis 'most un-apparent in speech' is so prominently flagged in the first
formal speech. Yet, if the τὰ δέοντα element ('the necessary things') in the
speeches is fictional, as Thucydides himself states (22.1),[24] the Corcyraean
remark is no problem: it exemplifies τὰ δέοντα as supplied by Thucydides. It is
indeed so counter-realistic as to re-emphasize the fictionality of that element.[25] The same applies to Sthenelaidas. Note that, since τὰ δέοντα are
fictional, unhistorical allusions to the *prophasis* in the speeches are actually
required.

Other cases where speech material alludes to the *prophasis*, though the
credibility gap is less, are 36.1, where the Corcyraeans argue that 'fear [of
breaking the treaty] which acquires strength [derived from alliance between
Athens and Corcyra] will cause fear rather to our opponents';[26] 40.5, where
the Corinthians claim to the Athenians that 'we spoke against it [the proposal
that the Peloponnesians help Samos against Athens] quite apparently'; 68.3,
where they reject the notion that the Athenians 'were wronging Greece un-
apparently'; and 123.1, where they claim that the rest of Greece will fight
alongside the Peloponnesians 'through fear' (cf. also 141.1 [below, (f)]), and
77.6, where the Athenians allude to the fear they inspire).

(e) use in speeches of *aitiai/diaphorai* terminology in ways that extend
their reference and blur the distinction of 23.4–6.

At 68.2, the Corinthians say that, when they repeatedly warned the Spartans
of prospective harm from the Athenians, the Spartans imputed the warnings
'to their own private differences'; at 69.1, that the Spartans are 'the cause'

---

23 Hornblower, *Comm.* I.78.
24 Moles (2001), 207–8.
25 Moles (2001), 210–11; Stahl (2003), 61 n. 7.
26 Discussion: Price (2001), 84–5; *HCT* I.170–1 (better).

of Athenian imperial expansion since the Persian Wars; at 69.6, that they are criticizing the Spartans 'not for enmity but for a cause'; and at 70.1, that 'the differences [between Spartans and Athens] are great . . . the contest will be against those wholly different from you'. Similarly, the Athenians at 75.4: 'you Spartans no longer being friends with us but at difference'. 'Difference' is thus brought within a general debate about ethnic characteristics, whose validity is denied by Archidamus (84.4: 'one must not consider that a human being differs much from another human being'). At 123.1 'cause' vocabulary links past and present.

The 'blurring' problem is compounded by the fact that many of these allusions interact with themes and events treated in the *Pentecontaetia*, whose explicit purpose is to explain not only how the Athenians became great and subjugated most of Greece to their empire but also the growth of Spartan fear, which eventually compelled them to war (88).

(f) Application of *prophasis* vocabulary to the immediate causes. Thucydides himself twice seems to 'misapply' the distinction of 23.4–6:
118.1: 'After this already happened not many years later the aforesaid things: the Corcyra and Potidaea affairs and all the things which were established as a *prophasis* of this war'.

146: 'these were the causes and differences for both sides before the war, first-beginning immediately from the events in Epidamnus and Corcyra [so far so good] . . . for the things that were happening were the annulment of the truce and the *prophasis* of the going to war'.

Prophasis is also twice so 'misapplied' by the participants. At 126.1 the Spartans make continual charges 'in order that they might have the greatest *prophasis* of going to war'. At 141.1 Pericles urges resistance 'whether the *prophasis* [of the Spartans] be great or small', and discourages the Athenians' from holding what they have 'in fear'. The first element uses *prophasis* in the sense of 'pretext'; the second integrates 'fear' into Athenian motivation as well as Spartan. The general effect is to reinforce the problematics of 23.5–6.

These difficulties cannot be resolved separately from the *Pentecontaetia*.

II

Literary interpreters such as Walker, Stahl, Heath, Stadter, Rood, and Pelling emphasize that the composite formulation of 88 explains why the Spartans found Corcyra and Potidaea so threatening; why the *Pentecontaetia* comes here in the narrative; and why it exhibits the selectivity, emphases, and

(Spartan) focalization that it does.[27] Their excellent discussions, however, do not fully gauge the intensity of Thucydides' punning, and hence of his analysis of causality, or the significance either of the interaction of *aitia* and *prophasis* in this section or of the interaction, throughout Book I, between the three different narrative modes: narrative, speech, and retrospective narrative.

After the Persian defeat, when the Athenians under Themistocles prepare to rebuild their walls, the Spartans try to frustrate them, largely incited by their allies, who were 'fearing . . . the number of their fleet, which before did not exist/first-begin' (90.1). Here is the first case of Peloponnesian 'fear', though felt not by the Spartans but by their allies. The punning ὑπῆρχε is noteworthy (effectively prefiguring the Athenian ἀρχή). Themistocles goes to Sparta for deceptive diplomatic ends (the incident pre-plays the negotiations of 432, when the Athenians made representations at Sparta): 'he did not go to the "first-rulers" but . . . kept putting forward pre-causes' (προυφασίζετο [90.5]). The verb recalls the cognate *prophasis*. Themistocles' 'pre-texts' contribute to that *prophasis* but also here avert any outright rift. Again we see interaction between the ideas of 'beginning' and 'ruling'. In all the talk of ἀρχή and *aitia* etc. in the first half of the book, the book's ἀρχή, Thucydides never uses ἀρχή and cognates of the Athenian empire, until the Athenians do so in their speech at Sparta in 75–8: in the narrative context immediately preceding the *Pente-contaetia*. Now Thucydides himself pointedly brings the two senses into conjunction and conflict, thereby further deepening the already very complex causal analysis of 23.4–6. In this, as in much else, he is building elaborate structures from a Herodotean basis (1.5–6; 8.142.2).[28]

91.3 ('Themistocles sent secretly to the Athenians telling them to keep them [the Spartan informants] not in the least apparently . . . he feared that the Spartans, when they heard clearly, would not let them [the Athenian ambassadors] go') and 4 ('Themistocles said quite apparently that their city was already walled') maintain *prophasis* vocabulary, though the 'fear' element is again displaced from the Spartans. After the rebuilding, 'the Spartans did not make their anger apparent to the Athenians . . . but they secretly took it hard' (92.1): this is the first-beginning of the 'un-apparent' *prophasis*.

Then Themistocles promotes the building of the Piraeus, which 'had been first-begun before in his first-rule which he first-ruled for a year over the Athenians, considering that . . . they having themselves become naval people would greatly progress (προφέρειν) towards the acquisition of power (for he was the first to dare to say of the sea that it was necessary to lay hold of it), and

---

[27] Walker (1957); Heath (1986); Stadter (1993); Rood (1998), 225–48; Pelling (2000), 90; Price (2001), 346–63; Stahl (2006).

[28] Moles (2002a), 35–6; 43.

he straightaway helped in equipping the ἀρχή' (93.3–4). The punning here (largely unregistered by commentators) is peculiarly insistent. Not only is there an initial association between 'beginning' and 'ruling', but προφέρειν recalls διαφέρειν: the Athenians' becoming naval people constitutes a decisive 'difference' which 'profers' their acquisition of power.[29]

Further, Hornblower among others[30] debates whether ἀρχή means 'beginning of the work' or 'empire' and chooses the latter. But *both* are meant: the ἀρχή of the building eventually produces, but also proleptically describes, the foundation of empire (the conceptual and temporal 'slide' eased by that nifty 'straightaway'). Themistocles' archonship was the ἀρχή of the ἀρχή of the ἀρχή (and the ultimate ἀρχή of the war). And, *pace* Hornblower and others,[31] to deny that Themistocles foresaw that his ἀρχή (in however many senses) was the ἀρχή of the empire is an interpretative failure unimaginable by Themistocles himself,[32] whom in 90.5 *we* have already seen pre-echoing the Peloponnesian War, and whose unparalleled foresight his obituary will emphasize (138.3).

94–5 trace the Athenians' advance to hegemony, 96–7 the beginning of their ἀρχή. Like Themistocles at 90.5, like the Spartans before the Peloponnesian war (126.1), the Athenians (96.1) make a 'pre-text' (πρόσχημα) for the ἀρχή of their ἀρχή. And 'the Greek treasurers were then first established to/ for/by (ambiguous dative) the Athenians as an ἀρχή' (96.2). More paradox: an all-Greek office is an Athenian one: this is a further ἀρχή (in two senses) in the establishment of the Athenian ἀρχή. These treasurers 'received the tribute/ φόρος'. Tribute is the marker of empire, and the notice recalls that the Athenian φόρος succeeded those of Croesus and Persia, as in Hdt. 1.6.2: 'Croesus... subjugated some of the Greeks to payment of *phoros*'. And this Athenian φόρος supposedly a sign of Panhellenic 'togetherness' (note the three ξυν-compounds) signifies *separation* (διαχειρίσει) (97.1): cf. the δια-compounds marking the separation of Athenians and Spartans in the *Archae-ology* (18.2–3). Or, in the terms of 23.4–6, this φόρος is a crucial διαφορά and a διαφορά at once spatial/territorial, temporal, and textual.

Hence, at precisely the right point, Thucydides' 'showing forth' (ἀπόδειξις) of the Athenian ἀρχή (97.2). The Herodotean echo (*Praef.*) marks the point at which Thucydides' narrative road (cf. 'diversion') takes over from Herodotus' (e.g. 1.5.3), which stopped in 478. The echo is an act of aggressive

---

[29] Thucydides here sharpens the generalized 18.2–3 of the Archaeology, which, as noted, uses δια-compounds.

[30] Hornblower, *Comm.* I.140.

[31] e.g. Price (2001), 350.

[32] Here, as throughout, I mean the *Thucydidean representation*, not the *historical agent*.

appropriation, with a further pointed implication: whereas Herodotus frequently alludes to the Athenian empire, he generally does so covertly, as, precisely, in 1.6.2 on Croesus' φόρος.[33] Contrarily, Thucydides can discuss that empire *openly*, and this openness allows him to trump Herodotus' ἀπόδειξις of causality with the power, precision, complexity, and explicitness (relative, of course) of his own.

This play on openness and covertness itself replays the contrasts of 23.5–6. But the allusion to Hellanicus by name (97.2) is a breach of decorum that contrasts with the silent allusion to Herodotus. The effect is even more polemical. As it begins the story of empire, Thucydides' imperialist text captures the last remaining literary 'place', zapping his only faint rival for it, who had the cheek to write an 'Attic writing-up' and call himself 'Victor of Greece'. Here narrative space maps territorial space and temporal space, and the paradoxical 'this space was left out' reinforces the sense of confusion of chronology: as if previous writers left out this place without ever occupying it. Thucydides' 'conquest' of Herodotus and Hellanicus is ingenious and absolute (though, naturally, very tendentious).

The remainder of the *Pentecontaetia* maintains the lexicon of 23.5–6. Allies' failures to meet contributions were the 'greatest causes' of revolts (99.1); the allies themselves 'caused' Athenian expansion (99.3). The Spartans 'secretly' promised the Thasians military support (101.1). From the joint campaign against Ithome occurred 'an apparent difference for the first time' (102.3), with the Spartans 'fearing' Athenian daring and innovativeness. About the same time, the Athenians 'first-began' the Long Walls (107.1), following Themistocles' lead (90–1). Then at 118.2 Thucydides sharply juxtaposes the two clashing senses of *arche*: 'All these things which the Greeks did towards each other and the barbarian (note the renewed 'trumping' of Herodotus; ~ *Praef.*) happened in fifty years more or less between the retreat of Xerxes and the first-beginning of this war; in which years the Athenians established their first-rule as stronger . . .'. As often, the ancient writer pats his reader on the back for decoding an interpretative problem.

My conclusions so far, therefore, are as follows:

1) The distinction between *aitiai/diaphorai* and *prophasis* is organic to the narrative: *pace* scholars such as Andrewes and Cawkwell,[34] there is no case for 23.6's being a later insertion. The *Pentecontaetia*, presaged at 23.6, is also organic. No support here for different compositional strata.

[33] Moles (1996); (2002a), 33 ff.
[34] Andrewes (1959); Cawkwell (1997), 20–1.

2) The distinction *does*, however, pose problems, *pace* Dover: *aitiai* and *prophasis* are 'harmoniously interconnected throughout book I'.[35]

3) Since the *prophasis* is a *process* and Thucydides' analysis of the war's causes extends right back to the archonship of Themistocles and involves many complexities, the *prophasis* is the agglomeration of *all* the *archai, aitiai, diaphorai,* and 'fears' documented all the way from 493 down to 432. This explains the apparently paradoxical application of *aitiai* and *diaphorai* terminology to the concerns of the *prophasis*. These individual cases are part of the total package—but only part. It is important to see that the formulation of the *prophasis* in 23.6 is itself a brachylogy, requiring interpretative teasing out by readers and both fragmentation and expansion by Thucydides.

4) Since the *prophasis* is a process that starts in 493 and culminates only in 432, the arguments and behaviour of the Corinthians and other Peloponnesians at that time constitute *part* of the *prophasis*; their allies pressurize the Spartans, who already feel pressurized by the Athenians; the Athenian ambassadors at the first conference up the pressure, because in order to deter the Spartans from war they emphasize the greatness of their power, fear of which is precisely the pre-cause for the Spartans' considering war; Pericles piles on further pressure (127.3).

5) It is therefore reasonable for Thucydides *both* to distinguish between *aitiai* and *prophasis* and to some extent to assimilate them.

6) Since the *prophasis* is the long and complex process that it is, Thucydides can rightly describe it as 'most un-apparent in speech'.

7) His own 'apparently' contradictory application of *prophasis* to the immediate *aitiai* of 432 serves to emphasize the inadequacy of those short-term analyses in contrast to his own. The flipping of categories, returning *prophasis* to normal usage, underlines sameness and difference: Thucydides uses the same terminology as others but does so with proper discrimination (23.5–6), yet without technical pedantry (118.1; 146). Granted language's slipperiness (23.5–6), it can still do analytical work.

8) His characterization of the *prophasis* as 'most un-apparent in speech' is slyly self-referential: the only *logos* (including all modern discussions) that propounds the *prophasis* in all its complexity is Thucydides' own *logos* and even then largely through a deceptive ἐκβολὴ τοῦ λόγου, characterized as an ἀπόδειξις (an ἀπόδειξις which from another focalization is ἀφανεστάτη— Thucydides keeps testing our perception). He can characterize the *prophasis* as 'least apparent', not only because no one else had ever set it out, but because the correct interpretation of 23.4–6 and of its working-out in the narrative requires interpretative discernment and penetration.

---

[35] *HCT* V.423.

9) Thucydides can, however, still say that his documentation of the specific *aitiai* will free his readers from searching for causes because *these aitiai* provide an *immediate* explanation. But that sort of 'search' remains relatively trivial (so much for interminable disquisitions on 'The Causes of the Peloponnesian War').

10) By contrast, the interpretative search required by the *prophasis* requires readers to probe the gaps and spaces within words, between words, between causes and pre-causes, between speeches and narratives, between narratives and retrospects, and between different places and times: in short, to probe causality in all its aspects. Thus literary penetration promotes political understanding.

11) Formally speaking, the straight narrative plus the speeches puts the reader in a preliminary unmediated *mimesis* posture;[36] but because the question of causality is so complex, he needs additional help: first, the unhistorical allusions to the *prophasis* within the speeches, second, the full-scale analysis of causality in the *Pentecontaetia* retrospect; the combination of these three modes puts the reader at the critical intersection of spatial/horizontal and chronological/vertical which enables himself to understand everything and himself to face the question faced by the Spartans and Athenians at the time: what to do *now*?

12) The criticism voiced by historians and conceded by some literary interpreters[37] that Thucydides says insufficient about Megara and Aegina is misconceived: 67.2 subsumes Aegina under the *prophasis*, and the pressure exerted on the Spartans both by the Megarians and by the Aeginetans is part of the general pressure which compelled the Spartans to war. It accords with the programme of 23.5–6 that they get the attention they do: it is important and sufficient. Historians' criticisms of the *Pentecontaetia* similarly misconceive its purpose.

13) The allusion to Hellanicus in the *Pentecontaetia* is integral.[38] But the integrality of the *Pentecontaetia itself* within the architecture of the *prophasis* analysis and the intensity of its exploration of causality preclude the hypothesis that Thucydides wrote the *Pentecontaetia primarily* to correct Hellanicus.

14) The *Pentecontaetia* promotes detailed understanding of the complexities of causality in 432 by taking the reader all the way back to 493; within the retrospect the reader finds that in 493 Themistocles had already seen all

---

[36] Fundamental to Thucydides' historiographical model: Moles (2001), 212–13; Greenwood (2006), 19–41.

[37] Rood (1998), 214–15; Price (2001), 274–5.

[38] *Pace* many, e.g. (even) Price (2001), 356 n. 49.

the way *forward* to 431. Already in the *Pentecontaetia* Themistocles exemplifies political insight and foresight: he is a sort of ideal reader translated into ideal judgement and ideal action.[39] Many other elements in the retrospect have two-way force, both retrospective/explanatory *and* prospective/anticipatory.[40]

15) Thucydides' investigations of causality are influenced by Homer, Herodotus, and the Hippocratics. But inasmuch as these investigations zigzag through narrative, space, and time, I sense (again)[41] the influence also of one of the deepest thinkers of *all* Thucydides' literary predecessors: Hesiod, though the transcendental principle of Thucydides' causality narrative is not Zeus ∼ διά in the sense of 'throughness' (*Theog.* 465), or Zeus as supreme power (*Il.* 1.5), but διά in the sense of 'separation'.

16) The intensity, complexity, and 'th(o)roughness' of this analysis leave little space for modern notions that Thucydides is trivially 'taking sides' in contemporary debates, especially as (13) he *does* give proper weight to Megara and Aegina, still less for Badian's uncontextualized accusations of pro-Athenian bias.[42]

17) All these narratives, but especially the *Pentecontaetia*, substantiate Thucydides' claim to better Herodotus' analysis of causality.

18) They make Thucydides' an 'imperialist' text, not only in that it centrally concerns Athenian imperialism, or that it 'orders' its readers 'around',[43] or that it sometimes applies imperialist language to its own procedures (97.2), but that it absorbs and 'conquers' all possible rivals (97.2).[44]

19) Thucydides' use of language is intensely creative.

20) The *aitia/prophasis* distinction and its intricate working-out in the narrative is a *pro*paedeutic for understanding causality in the rest of the *History*, notably in Books 5 and 6,[45] but everywhere else too.

21) Internally (irrespective of the question of 'historical omissions'), these narratives could hardly better fulfil Aristotelian criteria of organic unity (*Poet.* 7.1450b26–31), although, piquantly, this unity consists in 'separation' ((15) above).[46]

---

[39] Moles (2001), 215, 217; p. 34 below.

[40] e.g. the Corinthian (106) and Athenian disasters (109); Stadter (1993), 61–2.

[41] Cf. Moles (2001), 206 on the play on αἰεί in 21–22 as ∼ *Theog.* 31–4.

[42] On 'the Peace of Callias' see p. 36 below.

[43] Cf. Pelling on p. 17 above.

[44] Further: Moles (2001), 206–7; more generally, Marincola (1997), esp. 3–12; Corcella (2006), 52–6; for 'imperialist' texts cf. esp. Virg. *Geo.* 3.9–36.

[45] 5.25; 6.6.1; Rawlings (1981).

[46] This as Thucydides' 'master narrative': Price (2001), esp. 344 ff. (very interestingly).

22) It is important to register a judgement of quality. Thucydides' causality narrative is a work of towering and intimidating brilliance. It is also, of course, supremely arrogant, but sometimes arrogance can be both justified and inspiring.

If, of the *aitia-prophasis* analysis and the *Pentecontaetia*, we ask whether Thucydides' text is 'open' or 'closed', the answer is that, while it is very difficult and makes great demands of the reader, it is not ultimately 'open'.

III

The paired Pausanias and Themistocles retrospects raise similar questions. How relevant are they? Is their inclusion source-driven[47] (Thucydides inertly following an earlier source or writing to correct one)?[48] Is he just taking time out to 'do a Herodotus', or, again, to 'do Herodotus in'?[49] Are these retrospects even his own first steps in historiography, subsequently pasted in? What of his political and historical judgement? Is he simply more naive than Herodotus (5.32) in accepting Pausanias' medism (95.5; 128.3)? Does he underestimate the significance of Persia? This is a real question,[50] yet there are mentions of Persia throughout Book I: in the *Archaeology* (the synchronization between Greek navies and Persian kings in 13–14), chapter 23 (23.1), the speeches, the *Pentecontaetia* (which begins with the Persian defeat, records many clashes between Athens and Persia or her allies, and ends [118.2] with a formula evocative of Herodotus' *Preface*), and the Pausanias–Themistocles retrospects themselves. Archidamus' allusion to possible recourse to barbarian subventions (82.1) is particularly telling, precisely because it is veiled. This narrative does not 'fore-ground' Persia, it 'back-grounds' Persia, but that background is very substantial. Pericles' obituary (2.65) registers the Persian role in Athens' defeat. And in the second half of the work there is much on Persians, not only explicitly, in Book 8, but also implicitly, in Books 6 and 7, which create parallels between the Athenian expedition against Sicily and the Persian against Greece, and sporadically in other books.[51] The usual

---

[47] Westlake (1977/1989).
[48] Carawan (1989).
[49] Cf. Hornblower, *Comm.* I.214.
[50] Variously: Andrewes (1961); Hornblower, *Comm.* I.179–81; Cawkwell (1997), 15–16, 46–9; Rood (1998) 153–4; 229 n. 14; 239–40; 268–9; Price (2001), 363–71; Wiesehoefer (2006).
[51] Rood (1999); Rogkotis (2006); Price (2001), 364–9.

assumption that Thucydides and his characters are largely uninterested in Persia seems dubious. I shall return to this.

In terms of narrative architecture, the Herodotean parallel is again striking and itself indicative of organic unity. Hornblower writes:[52] 'Like Hdt. in *his* first book (i. 59–68, the Lycurgan and Pisistratid digressions), Th. is here introducing [*sic*] us to the two great protagonists, Sparta and Athens, via a sketch of a great citizen of each ... But it is also significant that, like some of the prominent individuals on both sides in the Peloponnesian War itself, these two commanding personalities fell foul of their fellow-citizens'. So: questions of difference of national character (yet again) and the relations between prominent individuals and their societies and political structures (both also almost kingly figures, to be compared and contrasted with Archidamus, Spartan king; Cylon, would-be tyrant within what would become the tyrant-city (122.3; 124.3); and Pericles, virtual monarch of Athens, as Book II will further reveal (2.65.9), but already experiencing his own difficulties with his people). Both are also eventual eastern-looking medizers (though the nature of their respective medizing requires scrutiny). It was at least convenient for Thucydides to accept Pausanias' medizing: not political *naïveté*, then, but a tactical decision promoting the investigation of wider historical issues. In serious ancient historiography there is Truth and Truth.[53]

The Herodotean parallel can be developed, since, in his Book I, the corresponding elements, the Lycurgus-Pisistratus and Sparta-Athens inserts, bear not only on the fifth century's reception of the sixth but also on the sixth century's anticipation of the fifth.[54] Further, in Herodotus Croesus and Lydia stand not only for Croesus and Lydia but also for Pericles, the Alcmaeonids, and the Athenian empire.[55] By analogy, therefore, in Thucydides Pausanias and Themistocles prequel Lysander and Alcibiades, with many fruitful parallels and contrasts prefigured.

Further literary structures accrue. At the beginning of *his* Book I (23.5), Thucydides pluralizes Homer's διαστήτην of two great individuals, Achilles and Agamemnon, into the *diaphorai* between two great peoples, Athenians and Peloponnesians (*diaphorai* which correspond to Herodotus' *diaphora* between Greeks and barbarians [1.1.1]); towards the end of the Book those plural peoples dissolve again into two great individuals, Pausanias and Themistocles. Pausanias should correspond to the east-corrupted Agamemnon:

---

[52] Hornblower, *Comm.* I.211–12; other thematic readings: Schwartz (1929), 154–62; Rood (1998) 138.

[53] Moles (1993).

[54] Gray (1997), 1.

[55] Moles (1996), 260–70; (2002a), 35–6.

a correspondence seemingly already suggested in Aeschylus.[56] Themistocles
cannot evoke Achilles: from the points of view both of Herodotus' pre-
existent treatment and of contemporary perception (he was nicknamed
Odysseus), he evokes that mythical paragon of intelligence and adaptability
(*Od.* 1.1, 83; 21.274).[57]

Who, then, in this epic drama plays unreconstructed *bia*, as opposed to
Odyssean *metis*? In Book III, obviously, Cleon, 'the most *violent* of the
citizens' (36.6). In Book I, *not* the Spartans en masse, whose hesitant, intro-
spective, intelligence Thucydides, like Herodotus, respects. Nor *Archi*damus,
their king, the intelligence (79.2) of whose *rule* over his *people* manifests itself
in his advice *not* to *begin* the war (82.1 [further play on ἀρχή]). But Archidamus' ἀρχή (or non- ἀρχή) is sabotaged by the forceful *Sthen*elaidas, *bia* writ
large (85.3). Also representative of *bia* are the Athenian ambassadors, whose
appeal to their own *power* (72.1) so stupidly misreads Spartan psychology:[58]
not like the subtle, Odyssean Themistocles, who in a like situation
προυφασίζετο (90.5) and averted hostilities.

This intensely detailed and circumstantial historical narrative is under-
pinned by archetypal and timeless mythic figures and elemental mythic
struggles[59] between force and cunning, the unadaptable and the flexible: the
never-ending dialectic between the transcendental αἰεί and the αἰεί of the
particular (21.2; 22.1; 22.4).[60] Given these mythic universals: again, what to
do *now*?

Concretely, Pausanias and Themistocles illustrate how to handle (or not)
politics and diplomacy, especially in relation to Persians. Pausanias begins
intrigue with the Persian king by deceptive and secret actions (128.3, 5),
which recall the Herodotean Themistocles and find analogies in Thucydides'
account of Themistocles' intrigues with Persian kings (137.3–138.2), but, on
receiving proof of Xerxes' goodwill, he becomes corrupted and arrogant,
hence 'he showed *forth/pre*-showed his intentions': προυδήλου (130.1): the
verb evoking the distinctions of 23.5–6.

Contrariwise, Themistocles keeps showing foresight (136.1) and keeps
learning—even from a woman (136.3)—big concession from the sexist Thucydides.[61] He learns—something that some men never learn—how to hold a

---

[56] Crane (1993), 124–5 (unnecessarily diffident); cf. Sophocles, fr. 887.

[57] Moles (2002a), 48; Plut. *De Malign. Herod.* 869f; Detienne and Vernant (1978), 313–14;
p. 34 below.

[58] Similarly Price (2001), 194–5.

[59] Another case of Herodotean influence (Boedeker 2002), although, pointedly, without
religious underpinning.

[60] Moles (2001), 206; n. 43 above.

[61] Wiedemann (1983).

baby; how to treat with kings, even Persian kings; how to conciliate former enemies (136.2; 137.4); how to speak the Persian tongue (138.1). With the Molossians (136.2ff.), Themistocles goes back in time to 'old Greece', but is he going back in time? Is this leisurely Homeric and Herodotean—even Xenophontic!—narrative (complete with tragic supplication and nod towards *Telephus*)[62] a different narrative, or is it part of the same multi-layered, multi-literary, multi-temporal, story? Themistocles' supplication of Admetus prefigures his supplication of Artaxerxes, son of Xerxes and new king of Persia. When he journeys west, he stops first at Corcyra (source of the first *aitia* of the Peloponnesian War). His journey from west to east brings him to Naxos (137.2), first allied city to be enslaved (98.4), already besieged by the Athenians; he secretly and perilously intersects again with his own architectural role in the *archai* of the *arche*.[63] He keeps learning and foreseeing, keeps reorientating himself in space and time and across the generations. And when Thucydides notes that Themistocles' standing with Artaxerxes (138.2) depended partly on his 'pre-existing/pre-eminent worthiness', no qualifier could be more eloquent.

At the end, in an arresting narrative displacement, his obituary comes not after his death but before it (138.3):

Themistocles most securely *revealed* the strength of natural ability and *differently* and more than any other man was *worthy* to be admired in this respect; for by his native intelligence and neither having learned anything in advance towards it nor having learned afterwards, he was both the *best knower of things present* by means of the least deliberation, and the best conjecturer of *the things that were going to happen*, to the greatest extent of *what would be*; and the things which he took in hand he was able to expound and the things of which he had no experience he did not fall short of *judging* appositely; and the better or worse course in what was yet *un-apparent* he *foresaw* the most. To say the whole: by power of natural ability and by brevity of study this was the best man at *improvising the necessary things*.

From several aspects,[64] this obituary is brilliantly positioned and expressed. 'Cued' by Themistocles' 'pre-existing/pre-eminent worthiness', it provides a confirmatory filter for our 'reading' of Themistocles, alike in the *Pentecontaetia* and in the Themistocles excursus. Besides the explicit generalizations, the emphasis on difference brings out the facts that, as an individual, Themistocles really 'made a difference', and that this 'difference' contributed greatly to the 'truest pre-cause' of the Peloponnesian War. The implicit

---

[62] Hornblower, *Comm.* I.221.
[63] On the text: Hornblower, *Comm.* I.221–2; 'Naxos' makes far better literary (as well as nautical) sense.
[64] Inchoately, Moles (2001), 215.

contrast between Themistocles and two mythical figures, *Pro-metheus* and *Epi-metheus* ('neither having learned anything in advance towards it (προμαθών) nor having learned afterwards' (ἐπιμαθών), confirms alike the general importance of Hesiod to Book I's literary texture, the mythical patterning that underpins the narrative, and the inference that Themistocles exhibits Odysseus' *true metis* (∼ '-metheus').

Coming near the close of the book, the obituary confirms both how Thucydides' historiographical programme is to be understood and how completely Themistocles fulfils it. He exhibits understanding, judgement, forethought, excellence both in speech and action, and the ability to bring different time scales and contexts into the right perspective and thus at any given moment to 'improvise the necessary things' (αὐτοσχεδιάζειν τὰ δέοντα). Themistocles is Thucydides' ideal statesman, even—in rich paradox—his ideal reader. Along with others, this highly 'meta'- passage disposes of ideas that the 'usefulness' of Thucydides' work is purely intellectual.[65] Further, since 'improvise' applies *both* as a metaphor to action *and*, literally, to *speech*, we find confirmation of the interpretation of τὰ δέοντα (22.1) as 'the best arguments', supplied paradigmatically by Thucydides himself and superimposed on a basic historical core of 'what truly was said' ('the best arguments', that is, for the particular historical position of the particular speaker), and of the consequent interpretations of crucial speeches in Book I.[66]

But if Themistocles is Thucydides' ideal statesman, where does this leave Pericles, fellow Athenian, and dominant individual at the actual close of the book?

Thucydides' overall judgement of Pericles seems highly positive. There are significant parallels between Themistocles' and Pericles' policies and strategies, here emphasized by the obituary's juxtaposition with the formal introduction of Pericles, characterized as 'most able at speaking and also at acting' (139.4 ∼ 138.3). Nevertheless, elements in the Themistocles retrospect, in the obituary, and in the *Pentecontaetia* might suggest *some* negatives.

Initially, if Themistocles was 'more than any other man worthy to be admired' for revelation of natural brilliance (138.3), he would seem to be Pericles' superior, at least in this respect. Their very names invite speculation. Herodotus had punned on 'Themistocles' as 'Rightly-famed'/'Famed for his rightness', thereby underwriting his highly favourable estimate of Themistocles' political and strategic abilities.[67] He had also punned on 'Pericles', as

---

[65] 7.42.3; 3.38.3–7; de Ste Croix (1972), 29–33; Moles (2001), 216–18.
[66] p. 22 above.
[67] Moles (2002a), 44–5; cf. main text.

meaning 'Exceedingly famous', thereby underwriting his subtle denigration of Pericles and the Alcmeonids.[68] Such punning would not be alien to Thucydides' narrative, with its many intricate verbal plays; nor to the evocation, in the Themistocles obituary, of Prometheus and Epimetheus; nor to the constant competitiveness with Herodotus, especially in the *Pentecontaetia* but also in the Themistocles obituary, 'corrective' of Herodotus not in its high estimate of Themistocles' abilities (which is essentially the same as Herodotus')[69] but in its powerful economy and resolute exclusion of moral issues; nor to the narrative juxtaposition of the two men.

Thucydides, indeed, seems to pun on Themistocles' 'narrative partner', Pausanias (= 'Stopper'), as a man who could not 'stop himself', cf. 130.1 οὐκέτι ἐδύνατο . . . κατέχειν τὴν διάνοιαν οὐκ ἐδύνατο. And two passages suggest active punning on Themistocles. Thucydides' account of his initial soundings of Artaxerxes (137.3)—'the king Artaxerxes, the son of Xerxes, who was *newly* king'—looks to rework Herodotus' punning (7.143): 'there was a certain man of the Athenians who had *newly* advanced into the first men, whose name was Themistocles ("Rightly-named"/"Famed for his rightness"), but he was called the son of Neocles ("New-name")'. Parallel are the repeated 'newly', the similarity of the names of father and son; and the punning relationships between 'newly' and 'new-name' and 'newly' and 'Artaxerxes' (where Ἀρτ- (~ ἄρτι) seems to interact with νεωστί: Artaxerxes is the 'new' Xerxes). Not only is Herodotus' pun referenced: there is an implicit contrast between the beginning and end of Themistocles' career: a contrast both poignant and positive (he is still displaying resourceful intelligence). And when Themistocles' high standing with Artaxerxes is partly explained by his 'pre-existing worthiness/*reputation*' and Thucydides immediately begins his obituary with the *name* of Themistocles (138.2–3), the pun, surely active, serves the same validating function as in Herodotus. But all this only intensifies the question: how does *Pericles*' 'fame' compare with *Themistocles*'?

Further, if, in this epic drama, Themistocles plays Odysseus and Pausanias Agamemnon, who is Achilles? In Book III Pericles certainly plays Achilles to Cleon's Thersites,[70] and this Achilles analogy extends back to Book I because of the verbal parallels between Cleon's speech (3.38.1) and Pericles' first speech (140.1). When the contrast is with Thersites, the Achilles figure is admirable, but is the same true in Book I? Thucydides does not conceal—he emphasizes—that the majority of the Spartans wanted peace and it was

---

[68] Hdt. 6.125.1, 131.1–2; Moles (2002a), 40–1.
[69] Moles (2002a), 43–8; Baragwanath (2008), 289–322.
[70] Cairns (1982).

Pericles who blocked the Spartan embassies (127.3)[71]—even the only demand on which the Spartans unequivocally insisted, repeal of the Megarian Decree (139.1–3), intoning 'I *always* hold on to the same purpose, *not to yield* to the Peloponnesians' (140.1, cf. 127.3). Should one sense an evocation of the Achilles who, unlike Meleager (*Il.* 9.598), did not 'yield' and rejected the Greek embassy, and of that Achilles' most marked characteristic (stubborn immutability), and a contrast with the subtle, Odyssean Themistocles, who in a like situation προυφασίζετο (90.5) and averted war, and who could conciliate former enemies?

Another important question is: what are we expected to make, within the work as a whole, of Pausanias' and Themistocles' medizing? Their examples— especially given Themistocles' unparalleled foresight, which extended down to the Peloponnesian War—must bear on the question of the Persians' role in that war.

One obvious sub-question is that of Greek commanders' competence in soliciting Persians, whose subventions greatly affected the war's outcome, as Thucydides himself notes in his obituary of Pericles (2.65.12). Themistocles shows how to do it, Pausanias how not to do it, just as later Lysander handled the Persians well, Callicratidas badly,[72] and Alcibiades a mixture of the two.

But there seems to be a much more radical sub-question: did it remain a real possibility, even after the defeat of their attempt in 481–79 to 'enslave' Greece (18.2), that the Persians could 'enslave' Greece, and did they effectively do so by 404? Was this one of the things that Themistocles' unparalleled foresight foresaw? Might this question explain Thucydides' notorious omission from the *Pentecontaetia* retrospect of Athens' peace with Persia? That peace seems historical, whether or not formalized in a 'Peace (or two) of Callias', and must certainly have contributed to Spartan 'fear' of an Athens that no longer bothered to justify 'first-rule' by any Persian threat.[73] Omission of the peace would, however, extend the story of Persian hostility to Greece to the end of the Peloponnesian War and thus keep it in play as a major factor, uniting that end with Thucydides' 'pre-writing' in Book I. With great perspicuity, though little acclaim, the Persian historian A. T. E. Olmstead adjudged:

---

[71] Tritle (2006), 476; Price (2001), 172 misinterprets 126.1 ('that they might have the greatest *prophasis* of going to war') as window dressing by irredeemably bellicose Peloponnesians, ignoring the qualification: 'if they [the Athenians] did not listen to them in any respect'. Contrariwise, Price (2001), 177, 186, 189, 279 detects (I think, rightly) some Thucydidean 'sapping' of Pericles' strategic, civic, and Hellenic visions.

[72] Moles (1994).

[73] Cawkwell (1997), 38—a factor ignored in the apologies of Stadter (1993), 66; Rood (1998) 229; Price (2001), 368–9.

'Persia had won the second great war with the European Greeks'.[74] That verdict would not have seemed absurd in 404, still less in 387, with the Persian-imposed Peace of Antalcidas. By then, presumably, Thucydides himself was dead, but death is no excuse for the suspension of foresight, as Themistocles strikingly demonstrated in relation to the Peloponnesian War itself. The verdict is actually reached at the beginning of the second century AD by Dio Chrysostom, *inter multa alia* one of the better ancient literary critics, in a speech that registers Thucydidean influence, including Book I.[75]

Admittedly, Thucydides' text poses further ticklish sub-questions. For example, Pausanias promised the Persian king enslavement of Greece (128.3, 7), but what of Themistocles? In one of the versions of his death, 'some say that he died willingly by poison, considering it impossible to fulfil what he had promised the King' (138.4). On the other hand, Thucydides himself has stated: 'he ended his life after falling ill'. But he makes Themistocles say something to the Persian king about enslavement of Greece: 'he became great by his side and as no Hellene had never been because of his pre-existing worthiness and the expectation concerning Greece which he suggested to him of his enslaving it, but most of all from his showing himself intelligent when he gave proof' (138.2). On the other hand, this element is given less importance than others, and should we anyway understand Themistocles as in this respect merely stringing Artaxerxes along, rather as he explicitly lied to him about his role in the Greeks' not-cutting the bridges over the Hellespont (137.4)? Again, although Thucydides stresses Themistocles' sumptuous estate in Magnesia (138.5), he ends with his relatives' claim that his bones were, on his orders, secretly buried in Attica (138.6). On the other hand, when the Spartan ambassadors accuse Themistocles of medism, in consequence of their enquiries about Pausanias (135.2), there is no implication that they are acting mistakenly or duplicitously. In regard, then, to this sub-question Thucydides seems to equivocate. Naturally, the historical Themistocles might very well have so equivocated to his Persian master.

Again, what is the effect of the displacement of Themistocles' obituary to before his actual death? Is it to deflect attention from Themistocles' unsuccessful 'suggestion', or is it on the contrary to allow *Thucydides* to 'suggest' that Themistocles' 'story'—including his dealings with Persia—continued after his death, just as Pericles' own story is going to continue for most of the work? How truly 'closural' is the closural 'the things concerning Pausanias the Lacedaemonian and Themistocles the Athenian, who were the most brilliant of the Greeks of their time, ended in this way' (138.6)? Does it

---

[74] Olmstead (1948), 371.
[75] D. Chr. 13.25; Moles (2005), 114–15, 132 n. 187, 134.

imply: that was then, what matters now is Pericles, 'the first man of the Athenians at *that* time' (139.4), that of the Peloponnesian War?

Nevertheless, although Thucydides dangles these imponderables, on the principle of 'proportional meaning'[76] Pausanias and Themistocles do raise questions of continuing relevance, including that of Greek 'enslavement'.

How do this question and its apparent answer (as foreshadowed by Pausanias and Themistocles) relate to Pericles' strategic vision? Are Themistoclean and Periclean forethought in conflict? It would appear so. Pericles' allusion to his *'expectation of* successful survival' in the Peloponnesian War (144.1) even echoes *'the expectation* concerning Greece which [Themistocles] suggested to [Artaxerxes] *of* his enslaving it' (138.2). And, as argued, the interaction between the *Pentecontaetia* and the immediate pre-war narrative also raises the possibility that Pericles was too inflexible, too like Achilles, in rebuffing the continual Spartan embassies. Was his 'expectation', then, too 'previous'?

Despite all this, Thucydides' elaborate obituary of Pericles in 2.65 (paralleling his obituary of Themistocles at 1.138) decisively endorses Pericles' war strategy.[77] The Persian factor is only one of many. The Athenians were only defeated with immense difficulty, after many years and because of their own errors and *differences* (here internalized within Athens). In sum: 'so *exceedingly* abundant (ἐπερίσσευσε) at that time to "*Exceedingly* famous" (Περικλεῖ) were the resources from which he foresaw that the city would altogether easily *successfully survive* (περιγενέσθαι) against the Peloponnesians themselves in the war' (65.13, cf. 65.7, echoing Pericles at 1.144.1). The punning (predictably ignored by commentators) is clamorous. The 'hanging' question of Book I—how to evaluate Pericles' name?—is resolved, and suggestions of conflict between Themistoclean and Periclean foresight, and between Themistoclean flexibility and Periclean immutability, are engulfed in this post-war imprimatur.

Readers, however, can always argue with their text. Periclean strategy was (arguably) untenable;[78] certainly, 'altogether easily' exaggerates. This, however, is not the same as a text's being 'open'. With Pericles' obituary, Thucydides shuts down the competing 'foresights' of the two greatest Athenians. Yet there is a specific issue: 'themselves' (65.13) re-emphasizes that Pericles' strategy would have contained the conflict to the original combatants. But the question of whether the Persians could have been kept out is one that Thucydides

---

[76] Moles (2007), 260.
[77] Subsequent narrative 'deconstructions' (Hornblower, *Comm.* I.341–2) are few and minor, especially on 'proportional meaning'.
[78] Tritle (2006), 478–9; Cawkwell (1997), 45.

himself had opened up in Book I, just as he himself had also there provided grounds for reservations about Pericles. In that sense, the text itself allows readers to disagree with its conclusions. In so doing, readers themselves will be responding to the challenge of choosing whether to follow Themistocles or Pericles. There is an important sense in which even the 'imperious' Thucydides cannot 'close' his text (this, surely, being one of the main reasons why it will 'always' be 'useful'). But that is not a point that Thucydides himself would yield. In the end, he and Pericles were too alike.

2

Divide and Conquer: Caesar, *De Bello Gallico* 7

Christina Shuttleworth Kraus

Caesar . . . having defeated the Ancient Britons by unfair means, such as battering-rams, tortoises, hippocausts, centipedes, axes, and bundles, set the memorable Latin sentence, 'Veni, Vidi, Vici', which the Romans, who were all very well educated, construed correctly. The Britons, however, who of course still used the old pronunciation, understanding him to have called them 'Weeny, Weedy, and Weaky', lost heart and gave up the struggle, thinking that he had already divided them All into Three Parts.

Sellar and Yeatman, *1066 and All That*

I. DIVIDE

In his memoirs of the great declaimers, Seneca the Elder devotes intensive critique to the *diuisio*, the art of making correct distinctions among the essential points of a *controuersia* that marks rhetorical expertise and, consequently, controls the kind of persuasive discourse proper to an elite male.[1] The way things are, or can be, divided is a primary concern of those Roman men who in the first century BC were engaged in codifying conquest by articulating their empire through centuriation, mapping, apportionment,

---

Improbably, Tony commented on this paper when I first wrote it; that it has been sitting in a drawer since is at least partly because he pointed out (in the nicest possible way) that it was an incoherent mess. ('Chris, I'm baffled.') His reading proved, as usual, invaluable: any merit the piece might now have is due to his sharp eyes. He is owed many thanks, for this and for all his years of unstintingly generous help, wisdom, and care. I am grateful as well to Hans Aili, John Jacobs, Christopher Krebs, John Marincola, Debbie Nousek, Fredrick Oldsjö, and Chris Pelling, for comments and encouragement.

[1] For an introduction see Habinek (2005), 60–71, 118 (further reading); on divisions in rhetoric see Heath (1997) and for Seneca see Fairweather (1981), 152–65 and Huelsenbeck (2009).

and confiscation of land, and by identifying distinct parts of a territory for purposes of military conscription.[2] Finally, *diuisio*, considered both in terms of textual and of real space, is a particular concern of Caesar in his *Bellum Gallicum*, whose Gallia is first and foremost marked by great divides: *Gallia est omnis diuisa in partes tres* (*BG* 1.1.1).[3] Those famous opening words align the *BG* with the tradition of geographical *commentarii*;[4] as Caesar continues, by revealing geographical knowledge and designating hierarchical relationships within this foreign territory he pre-emptively insinuates that it is already marked out ready for conquest.[5]

Though clear textual segmentation was a historiographical habit, connecting the *res* written about and the written *res*, as well as the passage of time with the stages of written time,[6] Caesar's interest in division is marked even among historians. This may be a function of his chosen genre, the *commentarius*, which tends towards the schematic: a kind of writing that emphasizes the anecdotal or the list form, so far as we can tell, it probably avoided large-scale connected narrative.[7] It may also reflect a tendency of Caesar's own personality, which shows a penchant for dividing things—be they peoples, actions, grammatical elements, or sentences—into clear and distinct groups.[8] Whatever their ultimate origin, as reflections of rhetorical expertise, cultural attitudes, and personal style, Caesarian sections are worth a closer look.

The macro-divisions of the *BG* are, of course, its bookrolls, which correspond to campaign years.[9] Within these, Caesar shapes and structures events

---

[2] On maps and the division of conquered territory see the wide-ranging discussion of Nicolet (1991) with Wiseman (1992), 22–42, Mattern (1999), 24–80, and Riggsby (2006), 32–45 on surveying and the possession of Gaul. Moatti (1997), 57–95 explores Rome's categorization of the world in its 'archives of conquest' (67); see also 217–54 on the development of typologies of thought in the late Republic.

[3] I cite Caesar throughout from Hering's 1987 Teubner edition of the *Bellum Gallicum*; all translations are from Hammond (1996) with modifications. References to the *BG* without book number are to Book 7.

[4] Rüpke (1992), 212–14; on space in Caesar see n. 31 below.

[5] On the rhetoric of division and conquest in the *BG* see Torigian (1998), Krebs (2006), and cf. Braund (1996), 158.

[6] On *res gestae* see (e.g.) Kraus (1994a), 18; on marking chronological stages in narrative (*primo, deinde,* etc.) see McDonald (1957), 169; Kraus (1994a), 143–4; for discussion of significant divisions in earlier historiographers see Immerwahr (1966) on Herodotus, Walbank (1975) on Polybius.

[7] Riggsby (2006), 133–56 with extensive bibliography; the matter continues to be debated.

[8] One can start from the (in)famous '*ueni uidi uici*', Caesar's triumphal *titulus* after the Pontic campaign. On Caesar's use of syntactical division in the interest of clarity see Eden (1962), 104–6; on his sentences see Spilman (1932); on the *De analogia*—which seems to have been at least partly concerned with dividing words into categories—see Fantham (2009).

[9] Not, however, to calendar years (Adcock (1956), 35; Wiseman (1998), 5). Six *commentarii* end with a movement either away from Gallia Comata (1.54.3, 2.35.4, 6.44.3) or into *hiberna* (3.29.3, 4.38.4, 7.90.7); the exception is 5, which nevertheless suggests withdrawal from military

into episodes by various means—deploying unities of space, time, action, or combinations thereof—and links these together with 'clichés de liaison' (*dum haec geruntur, his rebus gestis*, etc.).[10] Correspondences among otherwise separate scenes are brought out by linking repetition, either of language (more common than one might expect in this 'simple' text[11]), of design, or of character.[12] In particular, topoi are strong connective devices, both intra and intertextually. A topos may serve as shorthand for a particular famous scene—the most widely diffused is Troy, but one also finds Sardis (itself a reflection of Achilles' heel, e.g. at Sall. *BJ* 93, Livy 5.47) and the battle in Syracuse harbour (e.g. Polyb. 1.44.4–5, Sall. *BJ* 60.3–4)—or for a type of scene (e.g., cannibalism in a besieged town); both kinds can forge links between parts of a narrative, and across narratives.[13] Finally, Caesar builds objects into his text—particularly defensive and offensive *opera*—that serve as focal points and structural markers, aiding in the construction of a properly organized (divided) text. In this paper, I explore elements of the three great siege narratives of *Bellum Gallicum* 7, paying special attention to Caesar's use of structure, especially (but not exclusively) the meta-narrative use of physical objects.[14] These echoes, of material both repeating and contrasting, put disparate parts of the text in communication with one another, using the observing reader as a conduit of meaning and interpretation.

I read *BG* 7 as falling into three major segments articulated by its three major siege-battles. Each of these receives emphasis from the amount of text devoted to it, and in each Caesar turns topography and space to compositional advantage, marking the episodes off from the surrounding narrative. The three episodes are joined by an introductory section in which the Gallic rebellion takes shape and Caesar and Vercingetorix take each other's measure (1–13); and by a slightly longer section featuring Labienus in the environs of

activity: 'all the forces of the Eburones and Nervii which had mustered dispersed, and soon after Caesar commanded [*habuit*] a quieter Gaul' (5.58.7).

[10] Chausserie-Laprée (1969), 61–108 for their function in historiographical narrative.

[11] See Batstone and Damon (2006), esp. ch. 3 on Caesar's characterization of others in the *BC* via repeated words, and ch. 5 on his style.

[12] In this Caesar simply behaves like any ancient author of extended narrative. For linkages by repetition of language see Moskalew (1982) (on Virgil), Martin (1955) (Tacitus); for repeating elements of design see Vasaly (2002) (Livy); of character, Griffin (1985), 183–97.

[13] For the former, cf. *BG* 7.12.5–6 (*oppidani* turning suddenly from surrender to exhortation, threat to centurions, etc.) which looks forward to Gergovia, itself explicitly linked to Avaricum (see below). On the 'portability' of topoi see Hinds (1998), 34–7; Keitel, ch. 19 in this volume; on Troy see Paul (1982), 147–8 and Rossi (2004a), ch. 1.

[14] Two important treatments of physical objects in Latin historiography are Konstan (1986) and Jaeger (1997), 94–131; on built objects in Caesar see Dodington (1980), Scarola (1997), and Kraus (2007).

Paris (54–67). The overall modulation is that of a tricolon with a smaller central unit and extended third:[15]

Part 1(12.5 1–13 introductory moves: 1–5 C. in Italy, Gallic plotting;
Teubner pages) 6–13 C. and V., skirmishes

  13.3 C. arrives at Avaricum; V. follows

  14–31 AVARICUM (Romans victorious)

  32.1 C. refits army at Avaricum, departs; 34.2 arrives at Gergovia

Part 2 (9 32–53 GERGOVIA (Romans withdraw)
Teubner pages) 53.4 C. withdraws from Gergovia

Part 3(16.5 54–67 interlude: C.'s regrouping, 57–62 Labienus without
Teubner pages) C., 63–7 skirmishes

  68 V., followed by C., arrives at Alesia

  68–90 ALESIA (Romans victorious)

Gergovia follows immediately from Avaricum and leads on to Alesia. Much of the fighting at Gergovia should not have happened at all: since 43.4, when he learns that his chief allies have joined the Gallic rebellion, Caesar has been looking for a way to leave the area without losing face. The battle that eventually takes place does so largely without either his leadership or the obedience of his normally disciplined soldiers. The attempt to storm the besieged *oppidum* marks the moment at which Caesar moves from being *uictor* to (all but) *uictus*, a shift effected partly by strong, ironic echoes of elements from the (victorious) Avaricum narrative. The Alesia narrative, in turn, will pick up on elements from the two earlier ones, in the process of turning Caesar from *uictus* to *uictor* once more.

This narrative economy has distinct advantages. It allows Caesar to organize complex historical information around a limited number of significant moments; to showcase his army in slow motion, as it were, in the epic drama of the stationary siege narrative;[16] and, by thus slowing the narrative down for speeches and sieges, to hold the spotlight on himself and Vercingetorix for

---

[15] On the thematic modulation in *BG* see Nousek (2004); on tricolon shapes see Kraus (1994a), 23–4. There are arguably other ways to divide this narrative: textual segmentation is an interpretative act and as such, contestable. On the issues involved in dividing a text see Fowler (1995), Kraus (2002).

[16] Kraus (2009), 172. 'Epic', like 'tragic' and 'dramatic', is an overused term in historiographical analysis; by it I mean, that a siege looks back to epic precursors (above, n. 13).

long periods.[17] But even as sketchy a structural model as this raises potential difficulties for historical interpretation. If we accept Caesar's invitation to concentrate on the triad of set pieces, this has at least one significant result for our understanding of what happened on the ground: by tucking its narrative into a less emphatically presented section, Caesar minimizes the importance of the cavalry battle at 7.66–7, whose loss forces Vercingetorix to make the disastrous decision to retreat to Alesia.[18] Structure imports meaning, in this case by sidelining a causally important event.

Structure imports meaning, as well, by inviting comparison and contrast. More so even than in the earlier books, in *BG* 7 characters and action alike are repeatedly doubled, mirrored, or split, a multiplicity enacted by recurring narrative elements.[19] The most obvious example is the presence of not one but two charismatic commanders, Caesar and Vercingetorix. Pairing himself with (or against) a barbarian leader is a technique Caesar introduces early on, in his depiction of the German leader Ariovistus in *BG* 1.[20] But it is in Book 7 where the device is exploited most fully. Vercingetorix enters the book's Gallic narrative in person (at 4.1) before the character Caesar does (at 6.1), and functions throughout as a fully articulated second focal point. The rivalry between the evenly matched commanders tropes the fight for control of Gallia Comata, which is also—and not incidentally—a fight for control of the narrative.

II. BARRING MISFORTUNE

The episodes of Avaricum and Alesia contain physical structures specifically designed to block movement: respectively, a Gallic wall and Roman siege works. From the start, Avaricum is seen as a reflection of its defences. Having burned the neighbouring towns to deny the Romans refuge or food, the Gallic freedom fighters spare Avaricum at the tearful request of its citizens. From Caesar's point

---

[17] Interesting discussions of the varied use of time in (Greek) historiographical narrative are found in de Jong and Nünlist (2007), ch. 7–10 and 13; an influential treatment of narrative speed and duration is Genette (1980), 86–112.

[18] I owe this point to Chris Pelling; on the battle see Rice Holmes (1911), 790–801 and Stevens (1952), 17–18.

[19] On recurrent events in Caesar's narratives see Damon (1994), and cf. n. 12 above; on structure as argument see Batstone and Damon (2006), ch. 3.

[20] Christ (1974). Ariovistus and Vercingetorix are strongly linked in Caesar's large-scale narrative, as are—consequently—Books 1 and 7; so too (less often remarked) are Orgetorix (the first opponent: *BG* 1.2–4) and Vercingetorix; see Torigian (1998), 56–8.

of view, it is the largest, the best fortified, and most fertile of local settlements; from the Bituriges', the most beautiful in all Gaul:

13.3 Caesar ad oppidum Auaricum, quod erat maximum munitissimumque **in finibus Biturigum** atque agri fertilissima regione, profectus est
Caesar set off for Avaricum, a very large and well-fortified town in the territory of the Bituriges, and in a very fertile area of the territory

15.4 procumbunt omnibus Gallis ad pedes Bituriges, ne pulcherrimam **prope totius Galliae** urbem, quae et praesidio et ornamento sit ciuitati, suis manibus succendere cogantur. facile se loci natura defensuros dicunt
the Bituriges fell at the feet of all the Gauls, lest they be compelled to burn down with their own hands the most beautiful city in nearly the whole of Gaul, which both protected and adorned their nation. They claimed that owing to the nature of the site they would easily defend it

The Bituriges put equal weight on Avaricum's value as a defensive fortress (*praesidium*) and a decoration (*ornamentum*); they add that it is 'easily' (*facile*) defensible—but in this text such claims typically mark enemy over-confidence.[21] These two complementary passages with their balancing super-latives pit Caesar's practicality and restraint (he considers military and logistical matters, and avoids making global claims) against Gallic fondness for adornment and tendency towards overdone rhetoric.[22]

The Bituriges are right that Avaricum is naturally defended (17.1), but wrong about the ease of keeping Caesar at bay. Once the Romans invest the *oppidum*, narrative attention focuses on its wall, to which Caesar devotes an extended, ekphrastic description (22.3–24.2):

totum autem murum ex omni parte turribus contabulauerant atque has coriis intex-erant. tum crebris diurnis nocturnisque eruptionibus aut aggeri ignem inferebant aut milites occupatos in opere adoriebantur, et nostrarum turrium altitudinem, quantum has cotidianus agger expresserat, commissis suarum turrium malis adaequabant et apertos cuniculos praeusta et praeacuta materia et pice feruefacta et maximi ponderis saxis morabantur moenibusque adpropinquare prohibebant. [23] Muri autem omnes Gallici hac fere forma sunt. trabes derectae perpetuae in longitudinem paribus inter-uallis, distantes inter se binos pedes, in solo conlocantur. hae reuinciuntur introrsus et

---

[21] In *BG* 7 alone, the claim occurs also at 1.7, 14.3, and 64.2. The very first resistance, led by Orgetorix, has similar confidence (1.2.2 *perfacile esse... totius Galliae imperio potiri*); see Torigian (1998), 55. On 'easily' in historiographical narrative see Rood (1998), 34 n. 30; on the *locus a facultate* (feasibility, including ease) see Heath (1997), 111.

[22] Among other things, their use of *urbs* instead of *oppidum* suggests grandeur; for *urbs* in *BG* see Bedon (1994). The Gauls were famous for talking and fighting (the two quintessential strengths of a hero: Hom. *Il.* 9.443 μύθων τε ῥητῆρ' ἔμεναι πρηκτῆρά τε ἔργων): cf. Cato *Orig.*, *HRR* F 34: *rem militarem et argute loqui* with Williams (2001), 79–80.

multo aggere uestiuntur, ea autem, quae diximus, interualla grandibus in fronte saxis effarciuntur. his conlocatis et coagmentatis alius insuper ordo additur, ut idem illud interuallum seruetur, neque inter se contingant trabes, sed paribus intermissis spatiis singulae singulis saxis interiectis arte contineantur. sic deinceps omne opus contexitur, dum iusta muri altitudo expleatur. hoc cum in speciem uarietatemque opus deforme non est alternis trabibus ac saxis, quae rectis lineis suos ordines seruant, tum ad utilitatem et defensionem urbium summam habet opportunitatem, quod et ab incendio lapis et ab ariete materia defendit, quae perpetuis trabibus pedes quadragenos plerumque introrsus reuincta neque perrumpi neque distrahi potest. [24] His tot rebus impedita oppugnatione milites, cum toto tempore frigore[23] et adsiduis imbribus tardarentur, tamen continenti labore omnia haec superauerunt et diebus XXV aggerem latum pedes CCCXXX, altum pedes LXXX exstruxerunt. <u>cum is murum hostium paene contingeret</u> . . .

They had covered every section of their wall with towers and overlaid these with hides. Now with frequent sorties by day and night, they tried to set fire to the earthwork or attack our soldiers while they were working on the siege. They kept equalling the height of our towers (which increased daily as the earthwork was raised higher and higher) by extending the scaffolding on their own towers. They sabotaged the progress of the mines which we had driven by the use of timbers tempered and sharpened at the end, boiling pitch, and very heavy rocks. <u>In this way they prevented us from coming close to the walls of the town</u>. [23] All Gallic walls follow approximately this same pattern: at right angles to the wall, along its entire length, beams are placed in the ground at equal intervals, with a distance between them of two feet. These are secured firmly from the inside, and then clothed with large amounts of rubble; the gaps we mentioned between them are stuffed with large rocks at the front. Once the beams are laid and joined, another level is added on top in such a way that the gap remains the same; nor does the second set of beams touch the first, but, because the spaces between the beams are the same, each one is firmly kept separate by single stones placed between them. The whole construction is built in this manner until the appropriate height of the wall is complete. The finished edifice is not unattractive in appearance or variety, with the alternating beams and rocks in straight lines preserving their own formation; moreover, it offers an excellent chance for the practical defence of cities, since the stone gives protection from fire and the timber from the ram—for continuous beams, usually forty feet long and secured on the inside, can neither be broken through nor torn apart. [24] All these factors hindered the siege operation, but our soldiers, despite continually being obstructed also by the cold and constant rain, by unremitting effort still overcame every obstacle and within 25 days had built an earthwork 330 feet wide and 80 feet high. <u>When this was almost touching the wall</u> . . . [the Gauls set fire to the *agger*].

---

[23] Hering prints O. Wagner's <*so*>*luto frigore*, but that figurative expression does not recur before Amm. Marc. 17.8.1; *faute de mieux*, I accept the OCT's reading here.

Even as the wall takes shape before our eyes, this passage neutralizes it. First, Caesar notes that the wall is typical ('*all* Gallic walls follow *approximately* this same pattern'): that is, this is not (necessarily) a description of the particular wall blocking Caesar's soldiers, but is a kind of 'standard Gallic wall', resembling a description one might find, for instance, in a treatise on building.[24] In this very rhetoricized scene, the typicality becomes another element inviting us to see the wall as belonging to a plausible, not an actual, world.[25] Second, the passage displays both the technical virtuosity required to construct the wall and that needed to write its description,[26] reflecting the Bituriges' delight in Avaricum as an adornment—this wall is, after all, a complex and attractive creation (23.5 *hoc... in speciem uarietatemque opus deforme non est*)—but also Caesar's ability to understand, and hence, inevitably, to defeat, the Gallic *munimenta*.[27] Third, in its apparent clarity but actual difficulty of reproduction, the description renders the wall useless because practically unbuildable.[28] Far from presenting an obstacle, it is the act of portraying those walls that allows the Romans to progress from the difficulties of 22.5 (*moenibusque adpropinquare prohibebant*) to the success of 24.1–2 (*omnia haec superauerunt... murum hostium paene contingeret*). Instead of constituting a barrier, then, the textual wall opens up a breach.

Framing this description of the *muri Gallici* are two notices of admirable Gallic action, staged on and further enhancing the thematic significance of Avaricum's wall. The first gives a general overview of their skills (22.1–3):

Against the extraordinary bravery of our soldiers the Gauls used every kind of ingenuity, being an extremely resourceful people, and particularly talented at copying and putting into practice everything they receive from anyone. [*Singulari militum*

---

[24] e.g. Vitruvius 1.3.2, 2.8 (Scarola (1997), 195, 199–200). On the real thing, see Dehn (1960); on Caesar's description as an *ekphrasis*, see Dodington (1980), Scarola (1997).

[25] For plausibility as a criterion in historiographical narrative see the essential arguments of Woodman (1988), 231 (General Index).

[26] Caesar emphasizes the process of creation, not the object itself (Dodington (1980), 76, with an interesting comparison to Homer, *Od.* 5.243 ff., Odysseus' raft). Damien Nelis points out to me the density of words in 7.23 that are also at home in discussions of rhetorical construction (so *trabes, ordo, singulae singulis, opus, species, uarietas, materia*): Caesar is clearly playing with the idea of literary as well as defensive *aedificatio*. In both cases, Roman mastery is unaffected by foreign 'expertise'.

[27] For the relationship between knowledge and power in Roman ethnography see the items cited in n. 5 above. Scarola (1997), 193 notes that after the wall, the topographical space at Gergovia becomes 'tactical'—that is, Caesar can use it.

[28] See Rice Holmes (1911), 746–8, esp. 747 'Now Caesar does not guarantee the absolute and invariable accuracy of his description. He only professes to describe the general principles of construction'; Dodington (1980), 3 'The main problem with the assumption that [the engineering] passages function as historical descriptions is that they accomplish this task so poorly.' For one possible (re)construction see Winbolt (1910), 54, 55.

nostrorum uirtuti consilia cuiusque modi Gallorum occurrebant, ut est summae genus sollertiae atque ad omnia imitanda et efficienda, quae ab quoque traduntur, aptissimum.] For they turned our grappling hooks aside with nooses; once these were made secure, they dragged them inside the walls with ropes. They also started tunnelling beneath our earthwork to undermine it: this was all the more skilfully done because they have [*quod apud eos*] many iron mines, and so are practised experts in every kind [*omne genus*] of tunnel.

The second zooms in on a particular act performed by particular Gauls (25):

The night was now at an end, yet fighting continued everywhere... [The Gauls] believed that at that very moment the salvation of Gaul hung in that moment [*uestigio*] of time; and there then occurred, before our very eyes, something which, being worth remembering, we believed should not be passed over [*accidit inspectantibus nobis, quod dignum memoria uisum praetereundum non existimauimus*]. A Gaul stood before the town gate, opposite our tower, and was throwing lumps of tallow and pitch—passed from hand to hand—into the fire; he was wounded in the right side by a dart from an artillery machine, breathed his last, and fell. One of the Gauls nearby stepped across the man as he lay there and carried on with the same task; when he was killed in a similar manner by a dart a third man took over, and likewise a fourth succeeded him. Nor was that position abandoned by their defenders before... the fighting was at an end.

Each of these passages is marked as worthy of note, the first by the emphatically fronted *singulari* and the subsequent ethnographical note on Gallic imitative excellence (continued by the information that 'they have' and are experienced with 'every type' of tunnelling); the second by one of Caesar's rare first-person references, in which he puts one foot outside the narrative to function simultaneously as *dux* and as ethnographer/observer.[29] These flags point us towards these cases of remarkable action. On closer attention, however, they turn out—like the wall—to be no more particular to this moment than they are typical of this kind of story. The Gallic *consilia* that match the 'unique' Roman *uirtus* are 'characteristic' (*ut est...*): these enemies can copy anything (*omnia...quae ab quoque traduntur*). The story that Caesar relates of the brave Gauls guarding the gate (*ante portam*) partakes of a topos stretching as far back as *Iliad* 12.[30] In both cases, the idea of

---

[29] In this case he adopts the stance of the observing historian who deploys a typical historiographical justification for his selection of material. On *dignum memoria* and related expressions see Marincola (1997), 34–43; on *singularis* and the observer here see Kraus (2009), 161, 162.

[30] Guardians of the gates: Hom. *Il.* 12.127–94 (Polypoites and Leontes), cf. Virg. *Aen.* 9.677–8 (Pandarus and Bitias), Sil. It. *Pun.* 13.191–205 (Numitor, Laurens, Taburnus, cf. 199 *tertius aptabat flammis ac sulphure taedas*); live defenders replacing dead: Jos. *BJ* 3.23, Paus. 10.19.10 (Gauls); see Miniconi (1951), 175.

imitative repetition pulls the narrative towards the typical. In both cases, too, Caesar resists that pull to conventionality by insisting on the 'unique' (*singulari...occurrebant*) and remarkable nature of these actions. That resistance ensures our close attention to this rhetoricized historical 'record' staged on the remarkable structure of the *muri Gallici*. Thus a narrativized structure, Avaricum's defensive works, becomes both the backdrop and the emotional centre of that siege.

The counterpoised narrative of Alesia boasts no fewer than three points of emotional heightening, but each is associated, like the Avaricum wall, with a strongly marked place:[31] (1) the centre of the *oppidum*, in which Critognatus makes his modest proposal to cannibalize the weak (77.1 'But those who were besieged in Alesia'); (2) the space between the hill fort and the Roman siege works, in which women and the aged are exposed to die (78.2–5; the space is used again for a disastrous sortie at 81–2); and (3) the Roman *opera* themselves, which demonstrate Caesar's ingenuity, planning, and capacity for endurance (built at 72–4, narratively deployed at 81–2). These three distinct *loci* in which vital actions happen are united by their concentric focus on the citadel itself. Here again, physical structures and spaces contribute to narrative *exaedificatio*. Furthermore, each (physical) *locus* is an instantiation of a (literary) topos: cannibalism in a besiged town;[32] the contested space before a besieged city, a motif that begins with Troy; and *opera* which, like the *murus Gallicus*, suggest technical descriptions.[33] At both Avaricum and Alesia, then, division and recombination of often typical narrative elements structure and focus Caesar's history.

III. CONQUER?

In the central panel of *BG* 7 (32–53) Caesar narrates his unsuccessful attack on Gergovia. In contrast to Avaricum and Alesia, both the physical and emotional focuses of Gergovia are markedly diffused. Though its defensive struc-

[31] For an introduction to the importance of place and space in literature see Mitchell (1980); for space in Latin historiography see Jaeger (1997), esp. ch. 1; in Caesar, see Rambaud (1974), Riggsby (2006), 24–45 and (on Alesia) Scarola (1984–5).
[32] See Cipriani (1986), 1–41 (a study of Alesia, concentrating on Critognatus and parallels to his speech), and on the motif see Stramaglia (2003), 17–23.
[33] Special emphasis is put on the pit-traps, whose description—highlighted by the presence of three examples of (rare) *sermo castrensis* (7.73.4, 8, 9: Mosci Sassi (1983), 72, 77, 84)— balances the Avaricum wall. Like the wall, these have inspired recreations; see (e.g.) Bond and Walpole (1901), 52 and on the *opera* as a whole see Dodington (1980), 55–6.

tures play an important part in the story, there is no ekphrastic description corresponding to the *murus Gallicus* or the Roman *opera*. Gergovia's *murus* provides a platform for conventional siege action (see below), but the main story focuses on Caesar's trying to get away from the area, not on its capture.[34]

Rather than concentrating on the fate of the *oppidum* (as with Avaricum) or on the concentric circles of besiegers and besieged (as with Alesia), in this episode the diffused narrative focus distracts from the Roman defeat. Two plots—Gergovia [1] and the Aeduan rebellion [2]—are articulated by repetitions of the phrase (*ad/ab*) *Gergouia*(*m*) (34.2, 36.1, 37.1, 38.1, 40.7, 41.1, 42.1, 43.5, 45.4). Our attention (qua readers) shifts from storyline to storyline—as indicated by the bold numbers in the list below—following each one's various permutations:

1+2	ch. 32–34.1	Decision to move from Avaricum [1]; war plans interrupted by need to arbitrate among Aeduan royal claimants [2]
1	34.2–36	March to Gergovia, on river Elaver; misgivings about nature of attack; seizure of hill, building of second *castra*
2	37–40	Aeduan rebellion; C. removes some troops from *oppidum* + departs for Aedui; Litaviccus flees to Gergovia
1	41.1–5	C. returns to Gergovia, rescues harassed troops
2	41.6–43	Aedui continue rebellion; C. decides to leave Gergovia
1	44–51	Roman ruse to distract enemy; hidden *insignia*, 45; mismanaged attack; misread *insignia*, 50
1	52–3	C.'s rebuke of troops; withdraws across river Elaver
2	54–6	Litaviccus & Convictolitavis, progress of Aeduan rebellion; C. departs to join Labienus

Interwoven narratives are a feature of historiography, often efficiently presenting simultaneous action in parallel theatres of war.[35] At Gergovia, however, the idea of 'two' takes over as both a thematic and a structuring principle: there are not only two storylines, but two commanders, two Aeduan *uergobrets*, two young Aeduan noblemen, two Roman camps, two manoeuvres with *insignia*, two centurions, two scenes with Gallic *matronae*, two Gallic shouts, two parts of town—etc.

---

[34] At 36.1, C. despairs of *expugnatio* and wants to defer *obsessio*; 43.5, plans to leave Gergovia however he can; 47.1 calls for retreat from walls; 53.1, still desires departure; 53.3–4 eventually decamps.

[35] See Walbank (1975), developed by Clarke (1999).

One storyline ([2]) follows the split of the Aeduan *ciuitas* between loyal and disloyal factions.[36] It begins with two men competing for the position of chief magistrate; their trouble causes Caesar's narrative to take a new tack, and the general himself literally to veer off his main road, after only a sentence introducing storyline [1]. Calculated repetition of vocabulary (indicated typographically below) puts the two movements in close parallel (32.2, 33.1, 2):

Winter was almost over; and though at this very time of year [*ipso* anni **tempore**] he was called to wage war [***uocaretur***] and had decided to set out against the enemy [*ad hostem proficisci constituisset*] . . . the leaders of the Aedui came to him as envoys to beg him to help their people in a time of dire necessity [*maxime necessario* **tempore**]. [33] Despite [*Caesar etsi*] believing that it would be to his disadvantage to leave the path [*discedere*] of the war and the enemy . . . he decided to set out in person [*ipse*] for Aeduan territory [*in Haeduos proficisci statuit*] and summoned [***euocauit***] their whole senate . . . to him.[37]

The doubling of *uergobrets* is later mirrored by the introduction of two noblemen, Eporedorix and Viridomarus, who—though each supporting one of the rival claimants—work together against the splitting of the Aedui as a whole from Caesar's cause (37–41).[38] Even after Caesar physically returns to Gergovia the second time (41.1) the Aeduan problem continues to provoke narrative digression via messages (42.1, 43.1, 43.4), eventually becoming the driving force behind Vercingetorix's final push (63.1). Storyline [2], initially interwoven with the Gergovia narrative, therefore generates continuous narrative pressure, mirroring/mirrored by the military pressure on Caesar to move from one place to another as the Gallic rebellion grows. Downplaying the cavalry battle that causes Vercingetorix to retreat to Alesia (66–7, above) contributes to the sense of pressure: though that victory materially contributes to the ultimate Gallic defeat, Caesar chooses instead to emphasize growing Gallic strength.

---

[36] On the Aeduan relationship with Rome see Woolf (2000), 290 (Index); I follow most scholars in referring to this episode as a 'rebellion', though see Dyson (1971) for a nuanced treatment. Chris Pelling points out that Aeduan adherence to Rome is a serious issue in *BG* 1 as well, forming yet another link between the books, and (in 7) helping close the narrative ring.

[37] The Aeduan situation causes Caesar to digress from his main plot both at 33.1 and at 40.1. For *discedere* of narrative transition, see *OLD*, 6c; for the phrase *Caesar etsi*, which often 'initiates the reader into Caesar's complex thinking', see Batstone (1990; quotation from 352).

[38] Like many such episodes in Caesar, the story of the Aedui both confirms and questions the stereotype of the disunified, quarrelsome Gauls. So here the avaricious, duplicitous Litaviccus is a fair representative of the stereotype, while Eporedorix and Viridomarus are not. On the stereotype see Jervis (2001); Williams (2001), 85, 90–3.

The battle of Gergovia (storyline [1]) is itself constructed around doublets. These give the episode a coherence that is otherwise threatened by the Aeduan digressions; in addition, they provide communicative and structuring links with the book's earlier episodes. The repeated elements show clearly:

34.2–36		March to Gergovia, on river Elaver; ruse at crossing. Misgivings about nature of attack; Gallic skirmishes; C. seizes hill, builds second camp
37–40 [2]		Aeduan rebellion
41.1–5		C. returns to Gergovia, rescues harassed troops there
41.6–43 [2]		Aeduan rebellion
43.5		C. decides to leave Gergovia
44–51		Roman ruse to distract enemy; mismanaged attack on *oppidum*
	45	hidden *insignia*
	47.5	women pleading ($\sim$ 7.28.4)
	47.7	Fabius the centurion climbs onto wall ($\sim$ 7.27.2–3)
	48	women encouraging ($\sim$ 7.26.3–4)
	48.3	death of Fabius
	50.2	misread *insignia*
	50.4–6	Petronius the centurion dies in gate to save men ($\sim$ 7.28.3 *portarum* ... *portis*)
52–3		C. rebukes troops ($\sim$ 7.29); skirmishes to save face (53.2–3); withdraws across river Elaver

Once Caesar can engage with his interrupted plan (32.2 *ad hostem proficisci constituisset*), he sends Labienus north and leads his legions *ad oppidum Gergouiam*,[39] a hill fort separated from him by a river. In the build-up to the main action the narrator stages two stratagems, each of which combines topographical knowledge and the manipulation of appearances. The first involves a standoff between Caesar and Vercingetorix for control of a river crossing (35.2–5). In the end Caesar successfully fools his opponent into misjudging the number and location of his men, a feint enabling him to cross over.[40] Now, in Caesarian narrative, topography can seem to blend into a kind of indistinct background, an impression aided in no small degree by

---

[39] This disposition of troops at 34.2 $\sim$ 32.2 *siue [hostem] ex paludibus siluisque elicere siue obsidione premere posset* ('to see whether he could lure the enemy out of the marshes and woods, or could oppress him with a siege'): Labienus gets the *paludes* (57.1–58.2), Caesar the *obsessio* (36.1). The subsequent expansion of the 'table of contents' at 34.2 is chiastic (Kraus (1994a), 22).

[40] Other such manipulations of the visual field are collected at Front. *Strat.* 1.5.

Caesar's deliberately restricted vocabulary. Yet sometimes a *flumen* is not just a *flumen*.[41] At 5.4–5, for example, the Loire graphically represents the split in loyalty—and the resultant possibility of treachery—between neighbouring tribes: 'When they had reached the Loire (<u>the river [*flumen*] separating the Bituriges from the Aedui</u>) . . . they returned and reported to our legates that they had turned back fearing treachery on the part of the Bituriges.' Though these tribes have featured earlier in his narrative, Caesar has reserved this particular topographical information until this point—a common ancient narrative technique which here enhances the symbolic use of the geographical feature.[42] Readers of Caesar also know from the disaster at Cenabum (11.7–8), where a narrow bridge helps cause a massacre, that control of river crossings is essential. When Caesar and Vercingetorix play their bridge game in 7.35, then, the flatness of the narrative belies the importance of the ability successfully to use topography.[43]

During the investment of Gergovia it will become abundantly clear that—as always in Caesar—topographical knowledge and control are vital to success. Caesar is ultimately defeated more by his legions' lack of them than by Gallic superiority in tactics or strength. His successful manipulation of the Elaver crossing will contrast with the Roman failure to conquer the uneven topography of the *oppidum* itself. Conversely, the scene at the Elaver foreshadows a more serious failure of the Gallic general to make his own specialized knowledge work for him: Vercingetorix is taken in by appearances here (35.3 *uti numerus legionum constare uideretur*), as he will soon be again in the more consequential matter of the high ground outside Gergovia (to which I now turn).[44]

This second stratagem involves a more complicated manipulation of the enemy's visual field (45.1–6):

Caesar sent a number of cavalry squadrons to the place; at midnight he ordered them to range in every direction rather noisily [*tumultuosius*]. At first light he commanded a large number of pack-horses and mules to be led out of camp . . . and the muleteers, wearing helmets so as to look and act [*specie ac simulatione*] like cavalry, to ride

---

[41] On *flumina*, see Guillaumin (1987); for Caesar's preferred words see Richter (1977), 180–90. Any ancient military historiography can produce a similar effect, not least because topographical features tend to be described in conventional terms (Horsfall 1982, 1987).

[42] On rivers in Latin literature see Jones (2005), with extensive further bibliography, and cf. Munson (2001), 9–12 and nn.; for the symbolic use of them in military narrative see esp. Masters (1992), 150–78, and on objects in Latin literature see works cited in n. 14 above.

[43] When Caesar crosses the Elaver again (without incident) at 53.4, that neatly signals the end of the episode.

[44] For the fighting at Gergovia and the topographical problems involved see Rice Holmes (1911), 754–67 and Noché (1974); for Gergovia's afterlife see Dietler (1998).

around the hill. To these he added a few cavalry to range about, for the sake of the show [*ostentationis causa*[45]].... All these activities were seen [*uidebantur*] from far off in the town, for there was a view from Gergovia down into the camp; but at such long range it was impossible to find out anything for sure [*neque tanto spatio certi quid esset explorari poterat*[46]]. Caesar sent one of his legions to the same high ground ... and concealed it in the woods. Gallic suspicion grew, and their whole force transferred to the place to fortify it.

The narrator stresses the distance from the Roman camps to the town: paradoxically, a straight line of vision (*ut erat a Gergouia despectus in castra*) does not allow for adequate interpretation of what is seen. As long as the Romans are in the ascendant, Caesar and his men control that interpretation—the muleteers successfully impersonate *equites*, and the mules, horses. The stratagem succeeds in drawing the Gauls away from the town, giving Caesar the chance to make a face-saving attack and withdraw quickly before the growing rebellion traps him there (45.7–9):

Seeing that the enemy camp was unoccupied, Caesar had his men cover up their *insignia* and conceal their military standards; then he took the soldiers in small groups—so as not to attract attention from the town—from the larger camp to the smaller one. He explained to his legates (to each of whom he had given command of a legion) what he wanted done [*quid fieri uelit*]. In particular he warned them to keep their soldiers under control, lest in an eagerness to fight or in hope of booty they advance too far. He also set out [*proponit*] the disadvantage of unequal ground [*iniquitas loci*]. This could be avoided by speed alone: this was a moment for seizing an opportunity, not fighting a full-scale battle [*hoc una celeritate posse uitare: occasionis esse rem, non proeli*].

What he orders is topsy-turvy—moving quickly with unexcited soldiers, a smash-and-grab raid on a well-fortified town—but wholly in line with his deceptive stratagems.[47] At first all is well, as the legions with amazing speed (*tanta ... celeritate*) overtake the Gallic *castra*, even surprising a sleeping king (46.5).[48] This is Caesar's chosen end point: *consecutus id quod animo propo-*

---

[45]   The Roman show here is countered by Gallic *ostentatio* at 53.3; I hope to explore elsewhere this interplay of showmanship and *species* in Caesar.

[46]   This is the language of autopsy: cf. Liv. 6.1.1 res *cum uetustate nimia obscuras uelut quae magno ex interuallo loci uix cernuntur* with my note (Kraus 1994a). The Romans are also misled by appearances (*similitudine*), at 50.2.

[47]   Caesar goes out of his way at *BC* 3.92.4–5 to stress the importance of charging with excited soldiers; his *cohortatio* at 45.7–9, albeit delivered to commanders, not to the rank and file, is remarkable for the ways in which it negates the norms of exhortation. On these see Yellin (2008), esp. ch. 1; Melchior (forthcoming) discusses Caesar's manipulation of the *cohortatio* form.

[48]   Exact parallels at Liv. 24.40.12–13, Plut. *Demetr.* 9; for the narrow escape by a single leader cf. *BG* 1.53.2 (Ariovistus), Sall. *BJ* 101.9 (Jugurtha) *solus inter tela hostium uitabundus erumpit* (both similarly ending the battle narrative), Tac. *Ann.* 3.39.2 *regisque opportuna eruptione*.

*suerat, Caesar receptui cani iussit legionique decimae... continuo signa consti-
tuit* (47.1 'Having achieved what he intended, Caesar ordered the retreat to be
sounded; the Tenth legion... halted at once').[49] Overwhelmed by their success, however, the other legions go on autopilot—and once again, the narrative takes off in a new direction.

That direction brings us to a cluster of scenes familiar to readers of epic and
history. With the clustering comes also a set of specific references back to the
siege of Avaricum—inviting us, once again, to measure a description of
experience against one mediated by parallels and topoi. Two scenes of
Roman centurions are interwoven with emotive scenes of Gallic women.
Women and children first:

47.5–6 The married women began to throw clothing and money from the wall; baring
their breasts and leaning forward with outstretched hands they pleaded with the
Romans to spare them, not to act as they had at Avaricum, when they did not even
refrain from taking the lives of the women and children. Some let themselves down
hand by hand from the wall and gave themselves to the soldiers.

48.3 When a large host [of Gauls] had gathered, the married women, who had just
now been holding their hands out to the Romans, started to call upon their men and,
in Gallic fashion, to unbind and display their hair, and bring their children forward
into view.

Their quick transition from pleading for mercy to encouragement tracks the
evolving military fortunes of the Gauls, from defensive (47.4) to offensive
(48) mode. The town's topography is intimately involved: walls switch from a
place of exchange (*de muro... iactabant; de muris per manus demissae*) that
the Romans can scale (47.7 *murum ascendit; in murum extulit*), to a defensible
obstacle (48.2 *sub muro consistebat;* 50.3 *de muro* [sc. *Romani*] *praecipitaban-
tur*) that is at the same time a venue for spectacular exhortation (48.3
ostentare).

The women's actions are further marked by details that by referring
outside the story identify the passages as part of a larger narrative. In their
appeal for pity, the *matronae* hark back to the earlier episode at Avaricum
(47.6).[50] When describing their subsequent encouragement of their men, the
narrator explains that the women are acting *more Gallico* (48.3). As with the

---

For the topos—which does not always involve a king—see Hardie's nn. on Virg. *Aen.* 9.189 and
314–66, and Martin–Woodman (1989) on Tac. *Ann.* 4.48.1.

[49] Historians are not entirely sure what, in fact, he wanted; but 47.1 *proposuerat* ~ 45.9
proponit clinches the impression that his design has indeed been completed.

[50] That battle serves as an explicit reference point at 47.6, 47.7, and 52.2; see also parallels
given in the outline, p. 52, above.

descriptions of brave Gallic action discussed in Section II, this material draws attention to the narrative's artificiality: these women—breasts, hair, babies, and all—are typical elements of a siege narrative designed to ratchet up the emotional quotient of the moment.[51]

Following each of these scenes is a vignette with a centurion, whose actions are similarly conventional:

47.7 It became apparent [*constabat*] that Lucius Fabius, a centurion from Legion VIII, had declared among his men that he was stirred by the prospect of Avaricum-like rewards and was not going to enable someone else to scale the wall first. He grabbed three of his fellow soldiers, got them to hoist him up, and climbed the wall; grasping hold of each of them, he in turn hauled them up on to the wall.[52]

50.4–6 Marcus Petronius, a centurion from the same legion, had tried to break down the gates, but was overwhelmed by the enemy host and abandoned hope of saving himself. Gravely wounded, he called to his soldiers who had followed him: 'Since', he said, 'I cannot save myself along with you, I shall at least take care to secure your survival—for it was my desire for glory which made me lead you into danger. When I give you your chance, watch out for yourselves.' At the same time he plunged into the midst of the enemy, killing two and forcing the rest a little way back from the gates. To his men, who tried to come to his assistance, he said, 'In vain you are trying to preserve my life; already my blood and strength fail me. Get away while you can, and return to the legion.' Fighting in this way he fell not long afterwards and proved the saviour of his men.

Centurions are Caesar's favourite actors. They focus action, wield significant objects, are granted rare direct speech, and generally serve as the stylized representatives of his legions, who through their leaders speak in (largely) ultra-brave, ultra-Roman, ultra-loyal voices. Like the Gallic women,[53] Fabius and Petronius are studies in contrast explicitly flagged as *comparandi*: they are introduced in precisely the same way; Petronius is *eiusdem legionis* (50.4); and his story is activated only after Fabius' body is expelled from the town (50.3 'at the same time the centurion Lucius Fabius and those who had scaled

---

[51] On the women in this episode, with many parallels, see Cipriani (1986), 43–73; the link with *BG* 1.51.3 'there they placed their women, who, with outstretched hands and weeping, begged the men setting out into battle not to hand them over into Roman slavery', is another part of the 1 ∼ 7 ring (above, n. 36).

[52] The triple repetition of *murum* closely centres our attention; see Konstan (1986) and Jacobs (2009), ch. 4 on thematically significant walls in historiography and epic.

[53] In their case, Caesar points us directly towards the previous vignette with 48.3 '[*matronae*] who had just now been holding their hands out to the Romans'; this shift from defensive to offensive action is picked up instantly in the narrative, which applies to the besieged adjectives proper to the besieger (48.4): 'For the Romans it was an unfair contest, in terms of both ground and numbers. Tired by their climb and the duration of the fighting, it was not easy to withstand [Gauls] who were fresh and unscathed [*recentes atque integros*]', cf. *BG* 5.16.4, Liv. 26.45.6, and cf. 6.4.10 with Oakley's n.

the wall with him were surrounded, killed, and thrown headlong from the wall').[54] It is Petronius who, in sacrificing himself to save his men, is the spiritual descendant of Cato's military tribune[55] and the immediate forerunner of Lucan's—and Caesar's—Scaeva (*BC* 3.53.4–5, Luc. 6.138–262); it is also he who, as a double for the failed Fabius, redeems his mistake. His is the last voice we hear in this battle, which ends swiftly thereafter.

By positioning Petronius where he does, and by recalling such narrative precedents as Cato's tribune, Caesar does not so much mitigate the Roman defeat as recast it in the mode of sacrificial glory, turning our attention away from the disaster towards the memorialization of it through historiography: this is a type of story with which we are very familiar. It is perhaps, then, churlish to note that Petronius' presence is utterly unprepared for. This is not, in a way, surprising, given Caesar's laconic style, and his tendency to provide information only when it is needed. But since one named centurion (Fabius) does go over the wall at 47.7, it is somewhat unexpected that it is not he, but another centurion (pointedly 'of the same legion') who directly following Fabius' death at 50.3 receives this aggrandizing notice. The effect—again via doubling—is once more to highlight ostentatiously the rhetoricity of the scene—perhaps even more, given that the scene partakes of the same topos as the Gauls in the gate earlier: one centurion seamlessly replaces another.[56]

The third prominently doubled scene in the Gergovia narrative reaches outside that storyline, capping the episode's intratextual relationship with Avaricum (nn. 13, 50 above). Caesar's rebuke to his soldiers after their retreat mirrors by its position and its rhetoric Vercingetorix's consolatory rebuke to the Gauls after Avaricum:

52.1–2, 53.1 The following day Caesar summoned an assembly and upbraided the soldiers for their imprudence and over-eagerness. He explained the significance of disadvantageous ground, which he himself had sensed at Avaricum . . . However admirable their courage . . . they deserved reproach for their lack of discipline . . . [53] He finished his speech by encouraging [*confirmatis*] the soldiers not to be disturbed because of these events, and not to attribute what had resulted from unfair ground to bravery [*uirtuti*] on the enemy's part.

29.1–5 The following day Vercingetorix summoned an assembly, spoke words of comfort [*consolatus*], and urged them not to be too down-hearted or anxious over

---

[54] For the attacker's body thrown over the walls, see *B. Hisp.* 15.6 (where it is identified as a barbarian custom), Liv. 41.11.5, Val. Max. 9.2.4, Jos. *BJ* 7.3.23.

[55] He leads a small group that sustains the charge of the enemy, allowing the main Roman army to escape (Cato, *Orig.*, HRR F 83).

[56] I owe this point to Chris Pelling. These two centurions also form a pendant with the duelling pair in Book 5; on them see Brown (2004).

this setback. After all, he said, the Romans had not won because of their bravery [*uirtute*] or in open battle, but rather by means of trickery and siegecraft in which they themselves were inexperienced. Anyone who expected all outcomes in time of war to be favourable was mistaken; he himself had never wanted a defence of Avaricum, and they were witness to the fact. . . . He would, however, swiftly repair the situation with some more significant advances.

Both generals speak after a defeat, using indirect speech introduced with similar formulae (*Postero die Caesar contione aduocata* ∼ *Postero die concilio conuocato*); both combine criticism with encouragement, praising their fighters' *uirtus* despite their loss. Both leaders exculpate themselves by arguments drawn from history: Vercingetorix had not wanted to defend Avaricum; Caesar had learned at Avaricum of the dangers of unequal ground. Yet the differences, too, are palpable. Caesar's speech is critical of the legions' *licentia* and *adrogantia*; Vercingetorix's, while criticizing the Bituriges' *imprudentia*, praises the power and might of the Gallic union. Caesar is more critical than Vercingetorix: perhaps an indication of his greater realism, and hence of his greater abilities as a general. Nor must he resort to encomium to maintain the unity of his troops.

The correspondence of these speeches underscores the differences between the generals, to the Roman's advantage. Yet it also, obviously, suggests their similarity, especially in defeat. It is conventional to say that Roman literature magnifies the person and power of significant enemies so as to magnify the Roman victories over them: so Sallust on Jugurtha, Horace on Cleopatra, Livy on Hannibal, Tacitus on Arminius, and everyone on Catiline. That modality is certainly operative here: the more Vercingetorix resembles Caesar, the more difficult and hence glorious Caesar's victory will seem. Furthermore, a defeat in the middle of the book sets up and acts as foil to the greater victory at the end. Caesar was in no way obliged to devote as much time or artistry to what he could easily have presented as a minor skirmish at an unknown *oppidum*, or indeed left out altogether: this pattern of a triad with a central low point recurs too often in Caesar's presentation of events to be simply a reflection of 'the way things really were' (above, n. 15). Yet one could also take Vercingetorix's resemblance to a Roman commander as indicative of a larger anxiety about Roman imperial ideology and its effects on 'barbarians'. So at the opening of *BG* 7 the Gauls may use ultra-Republican, Ciceronian jargon not just for the sake of parody (both of Gallic aspirations and of Cicero, one suspects), but also to suggest that Gallic freedom fighters have some degree of right on their sides.[57] And again, we are sent back to *BC* 1, where Ariovistus'

---

[57] The ultra-Ciceronian rhetoric occurs at 1.5 *communem . . . fortunam*, 2.1 *communis salutis causa*, 4.4 *communis libertatis causa arma capiant. c. fortuna* occurs as often in Cicero as in the rest of extant Latin; *communis salus*, lacking in Sall. and Tac. (and only twice in Liv., at 32.20.5, 22.6), is

long speech (1.44) scores important points against Rome's treatment of its 'friends'.[58]

Sympathy with the enemy does not, of course, require one to respect their political integrity. Nor do the similarities traced by repeated structures and diction between Caesar and his Gallo-German opponents necessarily reduce his military *auctoritas*. But the preceding exploration has shown, I hope, that Caesar's sophisticated deployment of topoi, narrated structures, and repeated elements of all sorts makes Book 7 not only the cap of the *Bellum Gallicum*, but also an eloquent representation of the continually challenging work of writing the Roman empire.

an emotive phrase (47 times in Cicero, 39 in speeches); with *BG* 7.4.4 cf. Cic. *Rab. Per.* 27 *qui tum arma pro communi libertate ceperunt*, *Phil.* 10.8 *non sunt...innumerabiles qui pro communi libertate arma capiant.*

[58] This kind of self-reflection on Roman imperialism is found repeatedly in Latin historiography: a famous example is Calgacus' speech in Tacitus' *Agricola*, but it dates well back, to Cato's *Origines* and his own speech on behalf of the Rhodians included therein (*HRR* 95). See Fuchs (1938), Adler (2005-6), and Levene (Ch. 17 in this volume).

3

Scipio the Matchmaker

Jane D. Chaplin

The narrative of Lucretia's exemplary domesticity, rape, suicide, and vindication in Livy Book 1 establishes a paradigm that subsequent episodes draw on, once explicitly, more often implicitly.[1] A key component of Lucretia's story is the connexion between violation of a woman and political disruption: to assault a woman's chastity is to trigger 'regime change'.[2] The present paper, by contrast, focuses on an episode that illustrates the converse: after his victory at New Carthage, Scipio Africanus refrains from violating a woman and thereby stabilizes political relations with Spanish leaders. This paper examines how Livy modifies Lucretia's paradigm in that case and argues that the element of containment Livy saw in Scipio's political career made him, in the historian's eyes, an ideal person to diverge from the topos by rejecting tyrannical behaviour.

I. SCIPIO AND THE SPANISH MAIDEN

Livy devotes the final portion of Book 26 to Scipio Africanus' successful assault on New Carthage and its aftermath (26.41.1–51.14). After the city falls, the Romans gain control of the Carthaginians' hostages, who are prominent members of local communities. In Livy's version, the captives are dealt with in three phases, narrated in increasing detail. With the first and largest group, Scipio learns their places of citizenship and sends messengers to these places so that the captives can be retrieved by their fellow citizens; those individuals fortunate enough to have a representative on the spot are turned

This paper has benefited considerably from the suggestions and constructive criticism of the editors and David Levene. It has the novel distinction of being my first professional endeavour undertaken and completed without the knowledge or assistance of Tony Woodman, whose staunch friendship has made a world of difference to me not just professionally, but also personally.
   [1] The explicit reference introduces the attempted violation of Verginia (3.44.1; see Ogilvie (1965), *ad* 3.44–9); implicit paralleling is found with, e.g., the Maid of Ardea (Ogilvie (1970), *ad* 4.9.4), the younger Fabia (Kraus 1991), and Orgiago's wife (Moore 1998).
   [2] e.g. Phillips (1979), Haberman (1980), and Joshel (1992).

over to them immediately, while the rest are entrusted to the *quaestor* Gaius Flaminius. The second group is comprised of women, all young and beautiful, who are being supervised by the wife of Mandonius (the brother of Indibilis, leader of the Ilergeti); she dramatically throws herself at Scipio's feet and begs him to take extra measures to ensure the maidens' well-being. Scipio entrusts them to a man of proven character with instructions to treat them with as much respect and propriety as he would the wives and mothers of guests. Third and last, his soldiers bring in a young woman so beautiful that, like the girl from Ipanema in the song, she draws all eyes wherever she goes. After inquiring about her *patria* and parents, Scipio has both them and her fiancé fetched. In a private conference with the latter, a young man named Allucius, Scipio offers assurances that his fiancée is untouched; in exchange for her safe return, he asks Allucius for friendship and a good opinion of the Romans. Allucius happily agrees, and Scipio turns over the maiden; Allucius praises Scipio to his countrymen and returns with a band of cavalry.

The story of Allucius' fiancée corresponds to the Lucretia narrative, with the crucial difference that instead of raping the girl and destroying political structures, Scipio preserves her chastity and builds relations with Spanish communities. Before considering why the core story takes this particular turn here, it is worth noting that the Scipionic version is itself a variant on another topos: the victor and the beautiful captive.[3] This was a standard element in the biography of Alexander the Great, in particular. After Issus, the women of Darius' household fall into the hands of the Macedonians. Alexander refuses even to meet with the women (lest he be tempted by their beauty), lets them go, and deliberately refuses any compensation from Darius.[4] Early in Book 26 Livy adverts to the tradition that Scipio was believed to have assimilated himself to Alexander (cf. 26.19.6–7), and in this instance he shows Scipio modulating Alexander's strategy by meeting the beautiful captive and deliberately turning the situation to diplomatic advantage.

The encounter between Scipio and the maiden is an exceptionally rich opportunity to observe how Livy handles material from his sources because, unusually, the accounts of two predecessors—Polybius and Valerius Antias—

---

[3] The phrase is borrowed from de Romilly (1988). She looks at three instances where a beautiful female falls into the power of the enemy (Cyrus and Pantheia in the *Cyropaedia*, Alexander and Darius' wife and mother, and Scipio and the Spanish maiden), comparing them and considering how one influenced the other. Unfortunately for the present discussion her treatment of Scipio is based on Polybius, with Livy serving only as a supplement. Trethewey (2002), 110–13 has a recent comparison of the versions in Polybius and Livy.

[4] Multiple versions of the story were in circulation, but they have in common Alexander's restrained and respectful treatment of the women (e.g. Plut. *Alex.* 21–2 and 30 and Arr. *An.* 2.12.3–8).

are extant. According to Gellius, Antias contradicts all other sources in reporting that Scipio did not return the girl, but kept her as a sexual plaything.[5] This version differs radically, especially in the outcome, from both Polybius and Livy, but Antias' Scipio shares one important feature with Polybius': sexual appetite. In Antias this takes the form of Scipio's treatment of the girl; in Polybius, Scipio's soldiers bring her to him because they know that he is φιλογύνης (10.19.3). The Greek historian's version, however, turns on the fact that although Scipio appreciates the girl's beauty, he believes that as a soldier in time of war he should abstain from the pleasures of the flesh (10.19.4–5). Further, Polybius shapes the story to illustrate the nobility of Scipio's character; his ἐγκράτεια and μετριότης are showcased, making the episode into an object lesson both for the young men and for Polybius' readers.[6] Scipio is the only named actor, and the story is pared to its essentials: soldiers find girl and bring her to Scipio; Scipio rejects girl and gives her to father for suitable marriage. The woman, her father, and her eventual husband are as incidental as they can be. The focus is on the interaction between Scipio and his troops: the soldiers present the maiden to him; then they hear his thinking and applaud his conduct.[7]

While Livy follows Polybius and does not even acknowledge Antias' alternative version,[8] he departs from both in making no reference to Scipio's partiality for women, and shapes the episode to feature not the general's restraint, but his political acumen. To begin with the first of those two points: there is no suggestion in the text that Scipio himself finds Allucius' fiancée attractive; in three swift sentences she is introduced and her beauty noted, Scipio inquires where she is from and learns in addition about her fiancé and, while they are being fetched, discovers that Allucius is passionately in love with her (26.50.1–4). Further, Livy has Scipio articulate the relationship between young men and pleasure rather differently from the version in Polybius. The sentiment there is directed at Scipio's men; the corresponding passage in Livy is embedded in Scipio's speech to Allucius:

----

[5] Gell. 7.8.6 = *FRH* 15 F 26 = *HRR* F 25.

[6] Walbank (2004), 240–1 argues that Polybius prefers lessons to be political rather than moral; if so, this is a notable exception. Kowalewski (2002), 215–16 also notes Polybius' narrow focus on Scipio Africanus as a model of self-control and the absence of a political motive; for her reading see further below.

[7] This presentation of the episode accords with Polybius' view that women and sexual desire pose a danger for young men and that marriage is the best defence. See Eckstein (1995), 150–7, though his discussion does not include this episode.

[8] The silence is noteworthy because Livy frequently notes conflicts and variants in his sources for Scipio Africanus: e.g. 21.46.10 (Coelius Antipater), 34.48.1 (*alii...alii*), 35.2.8 (Antias), 35.14.5–12 (Claudius Quadrigarius, following Acilius), 37.34.5–6 (*alii...alii*), and 37.48.1–7 (Antias).

'Iuuenis' inquit 'iuuenem appello, quo minor sit huius inter nos sermonis uerecundia. ego cum sponsa tua capta a militibus nostris ad me ducta esset, audiremque tibi eam cordi esse et forma faceret fidem, quia ipse, si frui liceret ludo aetatis praesertim in recto et legitimo amore et non res publica animum nostrum occupasset, ueniam mihi dari sponsam impensius amanti uellem, tuo cuius possum amori faueo. fuit sponsa tua apud me eadem qua apud soceros tuos parentesque suos uerecundia; seruata tibi est, ut inuiolatum et dignum me teque dari tibi donum posset. hanc mercedem unam pro eo munere paciscor: amicus populo Romano sis, et si me uirum bonum credis esse quales patrem patruumque meum iam ante hae gentes norant, scias multos nostri similes in ciuitate Romana esse, nec ullum in terris hodie populum dici posse quem minus tibi hostem tuisque esse uelis aut amicum magis.' (26.50.4–8)

'I address you as one young man to another,' he said, 'so that this conversation can entail less embarrassment between us. When your captive fiancée was brought before me by my soldiers and I heard that you loved her—and her appearance served as a guarantee—because I myself would want mercy to be forgiven for loving a fiancée excessively—if there were time to enjoy the pleasures of youth, especially proper and legitimate love, and if the public welfare had not demanded my attention—I lend my support where I can, to your love. In my care your fiancée had the same respect she would in the care of your parents-in-law and her parents; she was protected for you so that she could be given to you as a gift, inviolate and worthy of both you and me. I stipulate this single payment for that gift: be an ally of the Roman people and, if you believe that I am a good man, such as my father and uncle, whom your peoples cultivated previously, wish that no people on earth today be less an enemy to you and yours or more an ally.'

Scipio presents himself not as denying the potential pleasure afforded by this particular beautiful captive, but as empathizing with the couple's situation and acting as he would want another to do if he were in comparable circumstances. He glosses *ludo aetatis* with *praesertim recto et legitimo amore*. The implication is that, if his public duties permitted, he would be starting a family, not painting the town red.

If Livy is not telling the story to highlight Scipio's self-control, what purpose does it serve? As Kowalewski argues, the part played by Allucius distinguishes Livy's account both from that of Polybius and from those of other, later sources.[9] In her view, his absence from Polybius limits the Greek historian's ability to extract moral implications from the story. Certainly by making the fiancé rather than Scipio's soldiers the audience for his response, Livy personalizes it. The point of the commonality that Scipio establishes between Allucius and himself (*iuuenis ~ iuuenem*), however, seems calculatedly political rather than moral. After depicting Allucius and himself as equals who just happen to have found themselves in the current, unbalanced

---

[9] Kowalewski (2002), 216–17.

situation, Scipio seeks a concrete return for his high-minded treatment of the woman (*hanc mercedem unam pro eo munere paciscor*). In exchange for preserving her chastity, Scipio wants Allucius to be an *amicus*, to regard him with the same high opinion that his father and uncle enjoyed, and to choose alliance rather than enmity with the Romans. In short, a woman's virginity is being traded for an alliance with her fiancée's people, and the reward for not forcing a sexual union is the willing formation of a political one.[10] In addition, Scipio graciously converts the ransom money brought by the woman's parents into a wedding present to Allucius. The latter enthusiastically accepts the terms, ecstatically broadcasts Scipio's good name, raises troops among his dependents, and returns a few days later with a 1,400-strong band of cavalry (26.50.7–14). In short, Scipio's decorousness yields a political alliance that in turn strengthens his military hand.[11]

The comparison with Antias and Polybius thus brings out the emphasis of Livy's version: namely, the diplomatic rewards of abstinence. This message resonates all the more because up to this point the *Ab Vrbe Condita* has trained the reader to expect conflict when a man has power over a woman. Livy illuminates Scipio's shrewd thinking precisely by reversing the expectation created by previous iterations of the powerful man and the sexually vulnerable female: if, twenty-six books into the monumental history, we have come to understand that violating a woman's chastity leads to political upheaval, Scipio allows us to see that the converse also is true.

Livy's resurrection of the story later in the Second Punic War suggests that he considered it important for the conception of Scipio's character that he wanted to convey to his audience (30.11.1–15.12). During the African campaign, after Masinissa and Laelius defeat Syphax in a pitched battle, they agree that Masinissa will go on alone to Cirta. There he meets Syphax's temptress of a Carthaginian wife, Sophoniba. Seeking to save her life, she seduces Masinissa, who impetuously marries her to put her under his protection.[12]

---

[10] It is only fair to note that the alliances Scipio made in Spain did not prove especially durable. Although there is no further mention of Allucius, Mandonius and Indibilis subsequently prove unreliable, and Livy has Fabius Cunctator attack Scipio on this point in their debate over the African invasion (28.42.8). Nonetheless, the episode here seems to fit with the pattern of Scipio's 'personal diplomacy' traced by McDonald (1938).

[11] Smethurst (1950), 84–5 contrasts Scipio's model behaviour here with Antiochus' abandonment of his military duties for an extended honeymoon.

[12] Later sources report some kind of relationship between Sophoniba and Masinissa predating her marriage to Syphax, whether an engagement (App. *Pun.* 10 and 27 and Dio 17.57.51 with Zon. 9.11) or an actual marriage (Diod. 27.7). As Haley (1989), 174 points out, 'Livy's omission of such a relationship emphasizes Sophoniba's persuasive skills and Masinissa's impetuosity. Inclusion of it in the later authors diminishes these traits and serves as a justification for Masinissa's actions'. See also Kowalewski (2002), 225. Since Masinissa and Scipio are foils for each other in this episode, the rash conduct of the one heightens the sober behaviour of the other (and vice versa).

Laelius arrives just after the nuptials and tries to call Masinissa to task, but eventually succumbs to the latter's urgent pleadings and allows the matter to await Scipio's arrival. Before confronting Masinissa, Scipio has a conversation with Syphax that colours his understanding of the danger Sophoniba presents. When he meets with Masinissa, he rebukes him for his poor and hasty judgement and reminds him that as war booty, Sophoniba belongs to the Roman people. Masinissa gives Sophoniba poison, and she commits suicide. Scipio then recognizes Masinissa's services by awarding him the symbols of a curule magistracy (30.12.19–22).

Masinissa's heedless union triggers an extended revisiting of Scipio's chaste encounter with the Spanish maiden. Syphax tells Scipio that his marriage to Sophoniba was the source of all his misguided conduct. Inflamed with passion for her, he had lost sight of both his personal guest-friend relationship with Scipio and his official ties. Syphax goes on to warn Scipio that Masinissa's youth makes him, if anything, more susceptible to Sophoniba's dangerous charms. Syphax's passionate views trouble Scipio; the precipitate wedding gives them credence; and Scipio mentally compares Masinissa's rash behaviour on this occasion with his own behaviour in Spain. He finds Masinissa's course of action all the more deplorable because he himself had not succumbed to any woman's attractiveness there: *et eo foediora haec uidebantur Scipioni quod ipsum in Hispania iuuenem nullius forma pepulerat captiuae* (30.14.3).

In his subsequent conversation with Masinissa, Scipio spells out his own, apparently instinctive, grasp of the value of self-control (30.14.4–10):

'Aliqua te existimo, Masinissa, intuentem in me bona et principio in Hispania ad iungendam mecum amicitiam uenisse, et postea in Africa te ipsum spesque omnes tuas in fidem meam commisisse. atqui nulla earum uirtus est propter quas tibi appetendus uisus sim qua ego aeque ac temperantia et continentia libidinum gloriatus fuerim. hanc te quoque ad ceteras tuas eximias uirtutes, Masinissa, adiecisse uelim. non est, non, mihi crede, tantum ab hostibus armatis aetati nostrae periculi quantum ab circumfusis undique uoluptatibus. qui eas temperantia sua frenauit ac domuit multo maius decus maioremque uictoriam sibi peperit quam nos Syphace uicto habemus. quae me absente strenue ac fortiter fecisti, libenter et commemoraui et memini: cetera te ipsum reputare tecum quam me dicente erubescere malo. Syphax populi Romani auspiciis uictus captusque est. itaque ipse coniunx regnum ager oppida homines qui colunt, quicquid denique Syphacis fuit praeda populi Romani est. et regem coniugemque eius, etiamsi non ciuis Carthaginiensis esset, etiamsi non patrem eius imperatorem hostium uideremus, Romam oporteret mitti, ac senatus populique Romani de ea iudicium atque arbitrium esse, quae regem socium nobis alienasse atque in arma egisse praecipitem dicatur'.

'I think, Masinissa, that it was because you saw some virtues in me initially in Spain that you came to ally with me and that afterwards in Africa you entrusted yourself and all your hopes to my bond. And yet of those virtues on account of which I seemed to you worth seeking out would I plume myself on none more than my self-control and abstinence from lust. I would like you also, Masinissa, to have added this to the rest of your fine virtues. Trust me: at our age there is not more danger from armed enemies than from the pleasures surrounding us on all sides. He who has reined these in with his self-control and mastered them has gained for himself a greater distinction and a greater victory than we have in the defeat of Syphax. I have willingly comme-morated and recalled what you have accomplished vigorously and bravely in my absence: the other matters I prefer you to think over with yourself rather than to blush at my saying them aloud. Syphax was defeated and captured under the auspices of the Roman people. Accordingly, he, his wife, his kingdom, his land, his cities, the men who occupy them, whatever, that is, was Syphax's, is the prize of the Roman people; further, it would be appropriate for the king and his wife—even if she were not a Carthaginian citizen, even if we did not look upon her father as an enemy commander—to be sent to Rome, and for the Senate and people of Rome to deliber-ate and decide about a woman who is said to have alienated an allied king from us and to have driven him into war.'

There is a great deal going on in this passage, not all of which can be discussed here. It is worth noting that Livy gives Scipio the same inclination towards identifying and modelling moral qualities—self-restraint and moderation in particular—that Polybius does at New Carthage. But Livy's Scipio goes beyond pointing out his upright nature to apply those virtues to the same political understanding that he showed in Book 26. *Temperantia* and *con-tinentia libidinum* are not good simply in and of themselves; they count when they are marshalled to the ends of war and diplomacy. Further, Scipio seems to recognize the private–public dichotomy that Polybius' Scipio introduced at New Carthage (i.e. the contrast between his preferences as an individual soldier and as a general)[13] and extrapolates its relevance to Masinissa's misconduct. The ability to control one's desires is more important than defeating Syphax because the individual's mastery over his personal wishes strengthens his official position. What Scipio knows intuitively, he must teach to Masinissa. The latter, represented as a man who follows his emotions rather than reason,[14] needs the meaning of his actions explained to him. Masinissa

---

[13] See n. 6 above.

[14] A Roman–barbarian dichotomy is operating here between the cool-headed Roman and the soft-hearted Numidian: Livy attributes Masinissa's near-instantaneous passion for Sophoniba to his Numidian nature (30.12.18). On the stereotyping of Numidians as passionate, see Haley (1990).

failed to appreciate that marrying Sophoniba was a public action, not a private one. Scipio has to tell him that as the wife of a defeated enemy she becomes the property of the *populus Romanus* and that her fate, because she interfered in affairs of state (Syphax's alliance with the Romans) and of war (his decision to take up arms against them), is now properly in the hands of the Roman Senate and people.

Scipio's citing of his behaviour in Spain for Masinissa's benefit has the further effect of reminding the reader of earlier events. Scipio eschews sex with an attractive woman and makes a productive alliance. Masinissa falls into the arms of a seductress and makes a private relationship that conflicts with public ones, such as his alliance with Rome and the state of war between Rome and Carthage. The link between the two narratives is Scipio's understanding that the public always trumps the personal and that every action matters first and foremost for its political consequences.

II. SCIPIO: THE WARLORD WHO WASN'T

To return to my starting point: Scipio manifestly reverses the paradigm of the powerful man whose exploitation of a vulnerable female triggers political change. The characters are the same, but not the plot: by substituting self-restraint for self-indulgence, Scipio lays a foundation for diplomatic stability at a time when the political situation in Spain is fluid. Given the number of times and ways the Lucretia narrative resurfaces in Livy, why did he pick Scipio Africanus to demonstrate that, while forced sex undermines the existing order, sexual restraint can forge alliances? The answer has to do with Livy's exploration of Scipio as a prototype—but only a prototype—of the first-century strongman. At least part of Scipio's fascination for Livy is that his military success was not parleyed into the kind of political power that the warlords of the late Republic sought and, in more than one case, achieved.[15]

As the concluding sentences of the third decade make explicit, Livy regarded Scipio as being in the same category as those warlords: *Africani cognomen militaris prius favor an popularis aura celebrauerit, an, sicuti Felicis Sullae Magnique Pompei patrum memoria, coeptum ab adsentatione familiari sit, parum compertum habeo. primus certe hic imperator nomine uictae ab se gentis est nobilitatus; exemplo deinde huius nequaquam uictoria pares insignes*

---

[15] Livy's attitude towards Scipio Africanus is a rich and complex subject that I hope to explore elsewhere.

imaginum titulos claraque cognomina familiarum fecerunt.[16] Scipio's career exhibits both the military accomplishments and the exceptional or extra-constitutional honours and responsibilities characteristic of first-century leaders: saving his father's life in battle, preventing mutiny after Cannae, proconsular *imperium* and the command in Spain when he was still in his twenties, defeating Hannibal in Africa and ending the war, election to the censorship in his thirties, a second consulship eleven years after the first, and service as an unelected aide to his brother in the campaign against Antiochus.[17]

Focusing on the parallels between Scipio and Hannibal, Rossi offers one way to understand Scipio's ominous role in Livy's text. She argues that in the early stages of his career Scipio embodies the nobility of Rome's past while Hannibal, with whom Livy pairs him and who is partly modelled on Sallust's Catiline, represents the debased Rome of the first century. In the process of defeating Hannibal, Scipio starts to lose the ability to put *patria* first that differentiated him from the Carthaginian. As Rossi notes, Scipio's transformation is detectable as early as the debate over the African command, but his 'ambivalent legacy' is encapsulated in the differing versions of his trial.[18]

Indeed, Livy's most sustained exploration of the ways Scipio anticipates the kind of leader the historian knew from his own lifetime comes in the stories that swirled around the end of Scipio's life. The 'trials of the Scipios' is a notoriously convoluted part of Livy's text. Leaving aside any attempt to untangle it completely, it is still clear that part of the difficulty arises precisely from the contradictory assessments of Scipio on offer.[19] These are summarized at the beginning of the episode, via anonymous reactions to the news of the accusation brought against Scipio (38.50.6–9). Some people reproach not the Petillii, the tribunes of the plebs accusing Scipio, but the entire city, for ingratitude towards a *princeps*; for them, Rome compares unfavourably with Carthage since at least it was in defeat that the latter exiled the *princeps* who was the architect of the defeat, while it is victorious Rome that is turning

---

[16] Liv. 30.45.6–7: 'Whether the goodwill of the army or popular favour first made current the cognomen "Africanus" or, as with Sulla Felix and Pompeius Magnus in our fathers' memories, it arose from the adulation of his inmost circle, I have scarcely been able to ascertain. He definitely was the first general to have become known by the name of the people he conquered; subsequently by his precedent men by no means comparable in their victories achieved distinguished inscriptions for their *imagines* and glorious cognomina for their families.'

[17] See Balsdon (1972) for the argument that Africanus was an embarrassment and a hindrance to his brother throughout the latter's career.

[18] Rossi (2004b); quotation from p. 379.

[19] Jaeger (1997), ch. 5 argues that Livy's intricate use of sources and contradictory portrayal of Scipio in this section correspond to the difficulty the historian has in making sense of such a complex figure.

on the victor. The opposing view is that no citizen should become so important that he is above the law and that the possibility of prosecution is the best guarantee of liberty. Holders of this position pose the following question: if there is no rendering of accounts, can anything, let alone the Republic, be safely entrusted to anyone? As a whole, the passage addresses a conundrum of particular urgency in the late Republic. Is prosecuting a *princeps* an act of shameful ingratitude? Does any citizen merit special treatment?

The account of Scipio's trial(s) that follows this passage repeatedly foregrounds the latent threat of tyranny he presents. At every stage and in every version, he disregards the accusation laid against him. When he is first brought to trial, he responds by ignoring the charges and describing his accomplishments in a speech considered the best and most accurate account of his career ever given (38.50.11). At the next session, he points out that it is the anniversary of Zama, and leads everyone first to the Capitol and then around the city to thank the gods who enabled him to look after the Republic as well as he did (38.51.7–11). When the trial is convened yet again, Scipio goes to Liternum and refuses to appear in Rome: his spirit and character are too great and too accustomed to better fortune for him to undergo the abasement of a trial (38.52.1–2). The stories about his behaviour at his brother's trial feature equal lawlessness: in one account he tears up the account books containing the financial records for the campaign against Antiochus right before the eyes of the Senate (38.55.11); in the other, he drives off the man taking his brother into custody, and then attacks the tribunes who are ordered to restrain him (38.56.10).

This last incident triggers, in Livy's account, a speech of prescriptive praise from Tiberius Gracchus highlighting the difference between Scipio and his first-century counterparts (38.56.11–57.1):

Sed ita hanc unam impotentem eius iniuriam inuidia onerat ut increpando, quod degenerarit tantum a se ipse, cumulatas ei ueteres laudes moderationis et temperantiae pro reprehensione praesenti reddat: castigatum enim quondam ab eo populum ait quod eum perpetuum consulem et dictatorem uellet facere; prohibuisse statuas sibi in comitio, in rostris, in curia, in Capitolio, in cella Iouis poni; prohibuisse ne decerneretur ut imago sua triumphali ornatu e templo Iouis optimi maximi exiret. haec uel in laudatione posita ingentem magnitudinem animi moderantis ad ciuilem habitum honoribus significarent, quae exprobrando inimicus fatetur.

But he [Gracchus] freights this single unrestrained transgressive act of Scipio's with blame in such a way that, by reproaching Scipio because he had fallen so short of his own standards, Gracchus repays him for the censure on that occasion because he heaps him with praises from the past for his moderation and self-control. He says that Scipio once chastised the People for wanting to make him consul and dictator for life; that he forbade statues to be erected to him in the comitium, on the rostra, in the curia, on the Capitol, or inside the temple of Jupiter; that he forbade the passing of a decree that his image in triumphal garb go forth from the temple of Jupiter Optimus Maximus. Even included in a eulogy, these statements would convey Scipio's tremendous greatness of mind, restricting honours to what was within constitutional bounds; but they were made by a personal enemy who was upbraiding him!

As many readers have seen, this catalogue of honours rejected has a Caesarian context and an anti-Caesarian message.[20] In Tiberius' characterization, Scipio's greatness lies not in the accomplishments he retails and revives in the versions of his trial, but rather with his moderation and restraint, as manifested by the marks of singular influence that he refuses. The key words here are *moderationis et temperantiae*, these being the signature virtues that Scipio brought to Masinissa's attention in Book 30.

What distinguishes Scipio from the first-century warlords, then, is that he did not or could not cash in his war record. The reason for his failure to do so matters less than the fact of it.[21] Livy offers no overt explanation, instead colouring Scipio's actions with tension and ambiguity right up to the end. His obituary for Scipio simply lays out the paradoxical juxtaposition of the military hero and the unspectacular politician.[22] The categories of evaluation are the same ones that Livy applies to Marius: where Scipio is *uir memorabilis*,

---

[20] See Briscoe (2008), *ad loc.*

[21] There is no consensus about Scipio's remarkably unremarkable civilian career. So e.g. McDonald (1938) sees him as an exceptional personality thwarted by the collective will of the senate; Scullard (1970), despite the title of his book, sees the question as uninteresting (p. 238); Gruen (1995) attempts to mitigate the 'fall' of the Scipio brothers by putting their careers in the context of senatorial politics in the decades after the Hannibalic war.

[22] Livy 38.53.9–11: *uir memorabilis, bellicis tamen quam pacis artibus memorabilior. <nobilior> prima pars uitae quam postrema fuit, quia in iuuenta bella adsidue gesta, cum senecta res quoque defloruere, nec praebita est materia ingenio. quid ad primum consulatum secundus, etiam si censuram adicias? quid Asiatica legatio, et ualetudine aduersa inutilis et filii casu deformata, et post reditum necessitate aut subeundi iudicii aut simul cum patria deserendi? Punici tamen belli perpetrati, quo nullum <neque> maius neque periculosius Romani gessere, unus praecipuam gloriam tulit.* ('A remarkable man, but more remarkable for his martial talents than for those of peacetime. The first part of his life was more glorious than the last since his youth was spent in constant wars while in his mature years his affairs wilted and no opportunity presented itself to his intellect. What did the second consulship add to the first, even if you throw in the censorship? What did the Asian lieutenancy, useless because of his ill health and wrecked by the fate of his son, and after his return by the necessity of undergoing trial or, equally, abandoning his fatherland? Still, he alone bears the glory of having ended the Punic war, which was the greatest and most dangerous the Romans ever fought.') On Livy's death notices, see Pomeroy (1988) and (1991).

bellicis tamen quam pacis artibus memorabilior, Marius is *uir, cuius si exam-inentur cum uirtutibus uitia, haud facile sit dictu utrum bello melior an pace perniciosior fuerit.*[23] Thus whether through his *cognomen,* the honours he rejected, or the gap between his military and political careers, in Livy's view Scipio belongs with Marius, Sulla, Pompey, and Caesar.[24] The vital distinction is that his latent tyrannical capacities never translate into actions injurious to civil order. For all his influence, Scipio did not hold an unprecedented string of consulships, a solo consulship, or a dictatorship. He did not lead an army against the city of Rome or break the grip of senatorial authority. In short, he did not trigger regime change. Who better, then, to invert the paradigm of sexual violence and political change, or to underscore it when a trusted ally does not understand the rules? Scipio was the perfect vehicle for this version of Lucretia's story, the one where the guy gets the girl and gives her to someone else in exchange for alliance and arms.

III. CONCLUSION

Scipio was famous for another arranged marriage: the betrothal of his daughter Cornelia to Tiberius Sempronius Gracchus, who as tribune saved him from the wrath of the senate. Livy reports two versions of the engagement (38.57.2–8). In one, the engagement and marriage occur after Scipio's death. In the other, recounted second and at much greater length (and thus presumably preferred by Livy), Gracchus intervenes as Lucius Scipio is being hauled off to prison; over dinner that same night, Gracchus' and Scipio's senatorial colleagues insist that the former be affianced to the daughter of the latter. Back at home, Scipio's wife indignantly declares that she would not acquiesce in her exclusion from this decision even if Tiberius Gracchus were the man in question; Scipio delightedly responds that Tiberius is the very one. Thus

---

[23] *Per.* 80: 'a man who, if his vices were scrutinized alongside his virtues, by no means would it be easy to say whether he was more effective in war or dangerous in peace'. As usual, there is no way to know how strictly the epitomator is following Livy; Hine (1978) 85–6 makes a persuasive case for close adherence.

[24] Also relevant here is Seneca's *Naturales Quaestiones* 5.18.4 which has been taken to refer to Julius Caesar but may be about Marius (see Hine (1978) for the latter argument): *Nunc, quod de Caesare maiore uulgo dictatum est et a Tito Liuio positum in incerto esse utrum illum magis nasci an non nasci reipublicae profuerit...* ('Now, what was commonly said about the older Caesar and put in writing by Titus Livius, that it was unclear whether it was better for the republic for him to have been born or not...'). Regardless of the referent, the general sentiment fits the pattern: a man capable of great public service may inflict equally great damage on the state.

Scipio rounds off his career with yet another foray into matchmaking. This time, it is part of a domestic political alliance and an intriguing demonstration of the law of unintended consequences: two men from this union trigger the breakdown of senatorial authority that stood between their grandfather and the tyrannical behaviour of the first-century warlords.[25]

[25] Cicero offers as an example of a wildly improbable argument the case that Scipio is responsible for the upheaval his grandsons caused because of Cornelia's marriage to Gracchus and the birth of Tiberius and Gracchus (*de Inv.* 1.91).

4

Velleius Mythistoricus

T. P. Wiseman

Velleius Paterculus' history consists of two books, the second of which covers Roman history from the destruction of Carthage to the reign of Tiberius. Most of the first book is lost: what survives of it (to describe the phenomena in an appropriately preposterous manner) is the last part, covering Roman history from the third Macedonian war; a fragment quoted by Priscian, referring to the fifth-century Athenian Cimon son of Miltiades; and a narrative of quasi-historical events from the aftermath of the Trojan War to the reign of Romulus. It is this *archaeologia* that I shall try to elucidate,[1] in the rash hope of finding something to say about Velleius that may have escaped Tony Woodman's magisterial exposition.

The extant text begins in mid-sentence, in a list of where the various returning heroes of the Trojan War finished up. But where did Velleius begin, and why? Joseph Hellegouarc'h in the Budé edition assumes that the stories of the *nostoi* were in fact where he began:

Il manque probablement le *prooemium* et la mention de quelques-uns des héros les plus marquants de la guerre de Troie, Ulysse, Ménélas, Diomède principalement.

If the wanderings of Aeneas were included as well, that might indeed be one way of beginning a history of Rome.[2]

But Velleius' history is not just a history of Rome,[3] and even in the surviving text there are indications that for this early period his interests ranged much more widely. For instance, the period covered by the surviving narrative (chapters 1–8), from the fall of Troy to Romulus, is exactly that of the Alban kings in Virgil's and Livy's conception of the prehistory of Rome;

---

[1] There are excellent discussions of Book 1 in Schmitzer (2000), 37–71 and Kramer (2005).

[2] Hellegouarc'h (1982), p.xxii. Cf. also Starr (1981), 163, who assumes he started with the Trojan War; rightly disputed by Kramer (2005), 145–6.

[3] See e.g. Sumner (1970), 282: 'It seems clear enough that what Velleius set out to write was a kind of miniature universal history'. Kramer (2005), 146–50 argues that he began with the Assyrian empire (cf. 1.16.1).

Velleius, however, shows no interest in that. Among the themes that interest him are the foundations of cities and colonies and the succession of monarchical power (*imperium*) in Greece and Asia.[4] Although the lack of a preface makes it hard to discern the logic of his choice of events to narrate, it does at least seem clear that he began before the Trojan War.

Let us summarize what the narrative gives us. The list of *nostoi* results in Epeus founding Metapontum and Teucer founding Cypriot Salamis; Pyrrhus occupied Epirus, Phidippus occupied Ephyra in Thesprotia; Agamemnon was driven by the storm to Crete, where he founded three cities (called Mycenae, Tegea, and Pergamum) before returning home.[5]

Agamemnon is described as *rex regum*, king of kings, and the narrative now turns to the succession of *imperium*. After the murder of Agamemnon, Aegisthus had control of the kingdom for seven years until he in turn was killed by Orestes, who ruled for seventy years and died aged 90. After Orestes' death, his sons Penthilus and Tisamenus ruled for three years.[6]

tum fere anno octagesimo post Troiam captam, centesimo et uicesimo quam Hercules ad deos excesserat, Pelopis progenies, quae omni hoc tempore pulsis Heraclidis Peloponnesi imperium obtinuerat, ab Herculis progenie expellitur. duces recuperandi imperii fuere Temenus Cresphontes Aristodemus, quorum abauus fuerat.

Then, in about the eightieth year after the fall of Troy, and the hundred and twentieth since Hercules had ascended to the gods, the descendants of Pelops, who had expelled Hercules' sons and held power in the Peloponnese for all this time, were expelled by the descendants of Hercules. The leaders in the recapture of power were Temenus, Cresphontes, and Aristodemus, whose great-great-grandfather he had been.

Orestes' children wandered in exile for fifteen years before finding a home in the region 'around the isle of Lesbos'.[7]

There were great movements of peoples in Greece as a consequence: the Achaeans were driven out of Laconia and occupied the land now named after them; the Pelasgians migrated en masse to Athens; the Thesprotians under Thessalus conquered the land of the Myrmidones and named it Thessaly after

---

[4] For the *translatio imperii* theme, see Schmitzer (2000), 66–71; Suerbaum (2002), 427–8; Kramer (2005), 148–9.

[5] 1.1.1–2.

[6] 1.1.3–4, including a short digression: about that time (*per haec tempora*), Tyrrhenus came to Italy from Lydia and gave his name to Tyrrhenia (Etruria) and its inhabitants, and to the Tyrrhenian Sea.

[7] 1.2.1–3, including digressions: about that time (*eodem fere tempore*) the Athenian kingship came to an end with the self-sacrifice of Codrus, and Athens was ruled by archons; the Peloponnesians founded Megara; and a Tyrian fleet founded Gades, and a few years later also Utica in Africa.

their leader.[8] Meanwhile Aletes, 'the sixth from Hercules', founded Corinth on the Isthmus.[9] The Athenians colonized Chalcis and Eretria in Euboea, the Spartans Magnesia in Asia; not long afterwards the Chalcidians founded Cumae in Italy.[10] At a later date (*subsequenti tempore*) the huge migration of Ionians from Athens resulted in the foundation of Ephesus, Miletus, Colophon, Priene, Lebedus, Myus, Erythrae, Clazomenae, and Phocaea, and of Samos, Chios, Andros, Tenos, Paros, Delos, and other cities in the Aegean islands; after that (*mox*) a similar migration of Aeolians led to the foundation of Smyrna, Cyme, Larissa, Myrina, and Mytilene and other cities on Lesbos.[11]

From this point on (*deinde*) 'the celebrated genius of Homer shone out'. In this, the first of his insertions on cultural history,[12] Velleius is concerned to refute the view that Homer's epics belong to a period close to that of the events he describes—'for he flourished about 950 years ago, and was born less than a thousand years ago'.[13] This view of Homer's *floruit* as about 920 BC is comparable with that of Cornelius Nepos, whose *Chronica* put it 'about 160 years before the foundation of Rome'.[14]

'In the following period [*insequenti tempore*], about 870 years ago, power in Asia passed from the Assyrians, who had held it for 1070 years, to the Medes.'[15] That (*ea aetate*) was also the *floruit* of Lycurgus of Sparta; in the same period (*hoc tractu temporis*), sixty-five years before the foundation of Rome, Elissa, called Dido, founded Carthage; about the same time (*circa quod tempus*), Caranus, 'the sixteenth from Hercules', left Argos to take over Macedonia.[16]

---

[8] 1.3.1–2, including a digression refuting the idea that Thessaly was named after Thessalus son of Hercules.

[9] 1.3.3, including a digression on Homer's supposedly anachronistic reference to the city at *Iliad* 2.570.

[10] 1.4.1–2, including a digression on the Cumaeans' subsequent colonization of Naples, the fidelity of both cities to Rome, and the size of their walls as evidence for their ancient strength; see further below on Velleius' Campanian patriotism.

[11] 1.4.3–4.

[12] 1.5.1–2; see also 1.16–18 (*eminentissima cuiusque professionis ingenia*, 16.3), 2.9, 2.36; and cf. 2.34.3 and 66.4–5 on Cicero. Detailed discussion in Schmitzer (2000), 72–100.

[13] 1.5.3, appealing to Homer's own consciousness of the difference between his own time and the age of heroes (*Il.* 5.304, 12.383), and rejecting as absurd the idea that Homer was born blind.

[14] Corn. Nep. *Chron.* fr. 2P (Gell. 17.21.3); cf. fr. 3P (Solin. 1.27) for Nepos' date for the foundation (751 BC).

[15] 1.6.1–2, on Sardanapalus in the 33rd generation from the founders of Babylon, Ninus and Semiramis. 1.6.6 is the interpolated quotation from Aemilius Sura's *De annis populi Romani* on the passage of the *summa imperii* from the Assyrians to the Medes to the Persians to the Macedonians to the Roman People; see n. 4 above.

[16] 1.6.3–5, adding that Alexander, as 'seventeenth from him', was descended from Hercules on his father's side as well as from Achilles on his mother's.

A second cultural excursus deals briefly with Hesiod, about 120 years after Homer's time,[17] which brings us down to about 800 BC. Now Velleius turns to the history of his own land (*incidi in rem domesticam*): Capua and Nola are said to have been founded by the Etruscans about this time (*huius temporis tractu*), approximately 830 years before the time of writing.[18] According to Cato Capua had existed for only 260 years before its capture by the Romans in 211,[19] but Velleius politely declines to believe that so great a city could have flourished and fallen in so short a time.

The institution of the Olympic games is reported next, with a date evidently corrupted in transmission: '823 years before you entered your consulship, Marcus Vinicius', i.e. 792 BC. But then follows an unexpected note:[20]

hoc sacrum eodem loco instituisse fertur abhinc annos ferme MCCL Atreus, cum Pelopi patri funebres ludos faceret: quo quidem in ludicro omnisque generis certaminum Hercules uictor extitit.

This ritual is said to have been instituted at the same place by Atreus about 1,250 years ago, when he put on funerary games for his father Pelops. At those games Hercules came out the winner in every category of competition.

Velleius has already told us that Hercules ascended to the gods forty years before the fall of Troy; that his sons were driven out by the Pelopids, who thus inherited the *Peloponnesi imperium*; that the Heraclids returned after 120 years to reclaim their power; that the 'sixth from Hercules' was Aletes the founder of Corinth; and that the 'sixteenth from Hercules' was Caranus, who established the kingdom of Macedon.[21] It seems clear that for some reason Hercules was important to him.

After a note on the Athenians' introduction of a ten-year limit for the archonship, a system that lasted seventy years before annual magistracies were introduced,[22] Velleius comes to the foundation of Rome. It is dated with appropriate thoroughness, apparently to 755–754 BC:[23]

sexta Olympiade, post duo et uiginti annos quam prima constituta fuerat, Romulus Martis filius, ultus inurias aui, Romam urbem Parilibus in Palatio condidit. a quo

---

[17] 1.7.1.

[18] 1.7.2; Capua and Nola were cities known to Hecataeus of Miletus (*FGrHist* 1 FF 61–2).

[19] Cato *Orig.*, *HRR* F 69.

[20] 1.8.1–2. Velleius was interested in *ludi*: see e.g. 1.14.8, 2.27.6, 2.79.6, 2.93.1.

[21] 1.2.1, 1.3.3, 1.6.5.

[22] 1.8.3, cf. 1.2.2 (n. 7 above).

[23] 1.8.4. Both the Loeb and the Budé texts print Laurentius' emendation *DCCLXXXI* for the corrupt numeral; that would give a foundation date of 750 BC, the third year of the seventh Olympiad.

tempore ad uos consules anni sunt †DCCCCLXXXL†: id actum post Troiam captam annis CCCCXXXVII.

In the sixth Olympiad, twenty-two years after the first was instituted, Romulus son of Mars avenged the wrongs of his grandfather and founded Rome on the Palatine on 21 April. From that time to your consulship . . . years have elapsed; it happened 437 years after the fall of Troy.

This is the only example in Velleius of a dating by Olympiads; the closest parallel is perhaps Solinus' list of rival dates for the foundation (evidently taken from Varro, since Varro's own preferred date is not included), all of which are expressed in Olympiad years.[24] More important for Velleius' own chronology is the use of *Troia capta* as a fixed point, as in his dating of the return of the Heraclids, quoted above (p. 74).

Velleius has a particular point to make about Romulus: he commanded only an unwarlike following of shepherds (even though he strengthened it with arrivals to the *asylum*), and therefore couldn't hope to establish a new city in the face of hostility from the Etruscans, especially Veii, and the Sabines. He must have had help, and Velleius follows those authorities who say that it came from 'his grandfather's Latin legions'.[25] Once established, Romulus picked a hundred *patres* as a sort of public council, from whom the patricians derive their title, and provoked the war with the Sabines by his abduction of their women. At which point, the text is lost again.

What can we make of all this? As far as chronology is concerned, not very much. Velleius' text is notoriously corrupt, and numerals are particularly likely to be wrongly transmitted. As we have seen, the date for the first Olympiad can hardly be right, and seems to be inconsistent with the Olympiad date given immediately afterwards for the foundation of Rome.[26] Similarly, the fall of Carthage in 146 BC is correctly dated as '177 years ago' (*abhinc annos CLXXVII* in *B*; in *P* the figure is *CCLXXVII*); but we are also told that Carthage stood for 666 years (*annis DCLXVI* in *A*; in *P* the figure is

---

[24] Solin. 1.27: Cincius Alimentus, Olympiad 12; Fabius Pictor, Olympiad 8; Nepos and Lutatius (following Eratosthenes and Apollodorus), Olympiad 7.2 [751 BC]; Atticus and Cicero, Olympiad 6.3 [754 BC]. Solinus himself prefers the beginning of Olympiad 7 (presumably 752 BC), 'in the 433rd year after the fall of Troy'.

[25] 1.8.5, *adiutus legionibus Latinis aui sui,* where I accept Lipsius' emendation. The transmitted reading *Latini* implies that Velleius' Romulus was the son of Lavinia—a possible variant of the legend (cf. Dion. Hal. *A.R.* 1.73.1–2 for unidentified Roman sources who made the twins the sons of Aeneas), but not one likely to be found in a Latin author writing after Livy and Virgil.

[26] 1.8.1 and 4.

DCLXVII), and that it was founded sixty-five years before Rome.[27] That should mean that Rome was founded 666 − 65 + 177 = 778 years before the time of writing, i.e. 749 BC, inconsistent both with the Olympiad date for the foundation and with the corrupt and meaningless figure for 'before Vinicius' consulship'.

More useful, perhaps, are the fixed markers Velleius uses for anchoring his dates. Either he counts back from the supposed time of writing, M. Vinicius' entry to the consulship in January AD 30,[28] or he uses a particular date from which to count forward. Twice in the extant text he uses the fall of Troy, four times the foundation of the city, once the sack of Rome by the Gauls, twice the fall of Carthage.[29] Those are all predictable choices, but there is one other chronological marker which is much more unexpected: the apotheosis of Hercules.[30]

The apotheosis of Hercules is certainly relevant to Roman history, since poets and historians alike report that his altar at Rome, the *ara maxima*, was set up at the time of the hero's visit to Evander's settlement with the cattle of Geryon.[31] It was evidently something that mattered to the Romans as early as the sixth century BC, as indicated by the terracotta statue group of Hercules and Minerva from the roof of the archaic temple in the Forum Boarium.[32] But what did it mean to Velleius? Let's look first at the lengthy account in Diodorus Siculus 4.8–39 of Hercules as a quasi-historical figure.

Diodorus makes it clear from the start that immortality was to be the reward for Hercules' completion of the Labours.[33] That was the deal Zeus struck with Hera, and Apollo confirmed it to Hercules himself when the hero consulted his oracle at Delphi.[34] But it is noticeable that Diodorus refers to this long-term reward most frequently in the course of the tenth Labour, and in particular during the return of Hercules with the cattle of Geryon.

---

[27] 1.12.5, cf. 6.4. *A*: Bonifacius Amerbach's copy of (a copy of) the lost Murbach codex, 1516. *B*: J. A. Burer's collation of the Murbach codex, 1520. *P*: Beatus Rhenanus' *editio princeps*, 1520.

[28] Fourteen times in Book 1: 1.5.3, 6.1, 7.2, 7.4, 8.1, 8.4, 12.5, 12.6, 14.3, 14.6, 15.2, 15.3, 15.4, 15.5.

[29] Troy: 1.2.1, 8.4. Foundation: 1.6.4, 2.49.1 (start of civil war, 49 BC), 2.56.5 (Octavian's first consulship, 43 BC), 2.103.3 (adoption of Tiberius, AD 4). Sack: 1.14.1 (starting point for list of Roman colonies). Carthage: 1.13.1 (death of Cato, sack of Corinth).

[30] 1.2.1, quoted at p. 74 above.

[31] Varro *ap*. Macr. *Sat*. 3.6.17 (founded either by Hercules himself or by those he left at Pallantion when he moved on); Livy 1.7.10–11, Dion. Hal. *A.R.* 1.40.2, Strabo 5.3.3, cf. Virg. *Aen*. 8.269–72, Tac. *Ann*. 15.41.1 (founded by Evander on the strength of his mother's prophecy); Livy 9.34.18, Prop. 4.9.67–8, Ovid *Fasti* 1.581–2 (founded by Hercules himself).

[32] Cristofani (1990), 115–30, esp. 119–20 and tav. IX; cf. Wiseman (1995), 39–42 (where unfortunately fig. 4 is printed in reverse).

[33] Diod. 4.8.1 (ἔπαθλον ἦν ἡ ἀθανασία), cf. 8.5.

[34] Diod. 4.9.5, 10.7; cf. Apollod. *Bibl*. 2.4.12.

Arriving at Pallantion, the site of the future Rome, Hercules is hospitably received by Evander's people and tells them that after his apotheosis they will achieve a happy life if they offer a tithe of their property at his altar.[35] Moving on to Sicily, he fights Eryx in a land dispute and stakes the cattle on the outcome, explaining that if he loses them he will lose his immortality too; at Agyrium (Diodorus' home town) he accepts divine sacrifice, in the belief that with ten Labours completed he already has some measure of immortality.[36]

After the final Labour is completed, Hercules expects Apollo's prophecy to be fulfilled, but there is more that the gods want him to do before his apotheosis.[37] Diodorus then goes on to narrate all the hero's 'non-Labour' exploits, with no mention of immortality until after his cremation on Oeta, when Iolaus and his companions, finding no bones among the ashes, conclude that Hercules has gone to join the gods, as the prophecies foretold.[38]

Diodorus' account of the awkwardly proleptic cult of Hercules at Agyrium is very similar to what Dionysius reports of Evander at Pallantion:[39]

Εὔανδρος δὲ παλαίτερον ἔτι τῆς Θέμιδος ἀκηκοὼς διεξιούσης, ὅτι πεπρωμένον εἴη τὸν ἐκ Διὸς καὶ Ἀλκμήνης γενόμενον Ἡρακλέα διαμείψαντα τὴν θνητὴν φύσιν ἀθάνατον γενέσθαι δι᾽ ἀρετήν, ἐπειδὴ τάχιστα ὅστις ἦν ἐπύθετο, φθάσαι βουλόμενος ἅπαντας ἀνθρώπους Ἡρακλέα θεῶν τιμαῖς πρῶτος ἱλασάμενος, βωμὸν αὐτοσχέδιον ὑπὸ σπουδῆς ἱδρύεται καὶ δάμαλιν ἄζυγα θύει πρὸς αὐτῷ, τὸ θέσφατον ὑφηγούμενος Ἡρακλεῖ καὶ δεηθεὶς τῶν ἱερῶν κατάρξασθαι.

Since Evander even earlier had heard [his mother] Themis relate that it was fated for Hercules, son of Jupiter and Alcmene, to change his mortal nature and become immortal by reason of his virtue, as soon as he discovered who he was, he resolved to be the first of all men to appease Hercules with divine honours. He hurriedly set up an improvised altar, and having related the oracle to Hercules and asked him to begin the rites, sacrificed on it a heifer that had never been yoked.

Dionysius goes on to mention that Hercules is worshipped as a god in many other places in Italy, 'both in cities and along roads'.[40] Those cult sites no doubt reflected the extensive mythography of Hercules' travels with the cattle in Italy and Sicily, which must go back at least to Stesichorus' *Geryoneis*.[41]

---

[35] Diod. 4.21.3. For the tithe, see e.g. Dion. Hal., *A.R.* 1.40.3 and 6, Plut. *Crass.* 2.2, Macr. *Sat.* 3.6.11.

[36] Diod. 4.23.2, 24.1–2.

[37] Diod. 2.26.4, 29.1.

[38] Diod. 4.38.5 (ὑπέλαβον τὸν Ἡρακλέα τοῖς χρησμοῖς ἀκολούθως ἐξ ἀνθρώπων εἰς θεοὺς μεθεστάσθαι); cf. 21.3 for the μετάστασις.

[39] Dion. Hal., *A.R.* 1.40.2. Virgil's Evander regards Hercules as already a god when he first comes to Pallantion (Virg. *Aen.* 8.201).

[40] Dion. Hal., *A.R.* 1.40.6. The 'roads' should perhaps be thought of as transhumance trails (*calles publicae*): see van Wonterghem (1973), Di Niro (1977).

[41] Leigh (2000). Stesichorus certainly mentioned Pallantion (*PMG* 182 = Paus. 8.3.2).

The Herculean legends are particularly frequent in Campania. The hero founded not only Herculaneum but also Bauli, Pompeii, and even Naples,[42] and he built the causeway across the Lucrine bay.[43] The tusks of the Erymanthian boar were preserved in the temple of Apollo at Cumae;[44] alas, we don't know how they were supposed to have ended up there. But the most famous of Hercules' Campanian exploits is directly associated with his apotheosis.

When Pindar in the first of his *Nemean Odes* tells the tale of the honorand's ancestor Hercules, he makes Tiresias' prophecy about Amphitryon's son end with an account of his deification:[45]

> καὶ γὰρ ὅταν θεοὶ ἐν
>   πεδίῳ Φλέγρας Γιγάντεσσιν μάχαν
> ἀντιάζωσιν, βελέων ὑπὸ ῥι-
>   παῖσι κείνου φαιδίμαν γαίᾳ πεφύρσεσθαι κόμαν
> ἔνεπεν· αὐτὸν μὰν ἐν εἰρή-
>   νᾳ τὸν ἅπαντα χρόνον <ἐν> σχερῷ
> ἡσυχίαν καμάτων μεγάλων
>   ποινὰν λαχόντ' ἐξαίρετον
> ὀλβίοις ἐν δώμασι, δεξάμενον
>   θαλερὰν Ἥβαν ἄκοιτιν καὶ γάμον
> δαίσαντα, πὰρ Δὶ Κρονίδᾳ,
>   σεμνὸν αἰνήσειν νόμον.

For he also said that when the gods joined battle with the Giants in the plain of Phlegra, [the Giants] would have their bright hair soiled with earth beneath his flying missiles; but he, in continual peace that lasts for ever, gaining tranquillity in blessed mansions as his longed-for recompense for great labours, receiving youthful Hebe as his bride and celebrating the marriage feast, in the presence of Zeus the son of Kronos would praise his august law.

Where was the plain of Phlegra? Some said it was in Pallene, the western peninsula of Chalkidike, and that Hercules had fought the Giants on the way back from his capture of Troy;[46] others put it in Campania, where the volcanic

---

[42] Herculaneum: Dion. Hal., *A.R.* 1.44.1, Strabo 5.4.8 (247). Bauli and Pompeii: Serv. *ad Aen.* 7.662. Naples: Diod. *ap.* Tzetzes on Lycophron *Alex.* 717.

[43] Diod. 4.22.2, Prop. 3.18.4, Strabo 5.4.6 (245), Sil. It. *Pun.* 12.116–19. Caligula no doubt had Hercules' exploit in mind when he described his own bridge of boats as 'road building appropriate to a god' (Jos. *Ant.* 19.6).

[44] Paus. 8.24.5.

[45] Pind. *Nem.* 1.67–72.

[46] Ephorus, *FGrHist* 70 F 34, Apollod. *Bibl.* 1.6.1, 2.7.1, etc; cf. Diod. 5.71.4, who assumes one battle in Pallene and another in Campania.

Solfatara betrayed the restlessness of the buried Giants.[47] For a Sicilian patron, Chromios of Aitna, we may imagine Pindar had the second version in mind.

Diodorus inserts the battle with the Giants into Hercules' passage through Italy after the tenth Labour, but his attribution of it to 'certain mythologists, whom Timaeus the historian also follows', shows that it is an intrusion inconsistent with his main theme.[48] Since his narrative depends on Hercules' immortality being the reward for the completion of the Labours, Diodorus cannot associate it with the victory over the Giants. Pindar, on the other hand, makes precisely that link; and since the aetiology of the *ara maxima* at Rome does not fit comfortably into Diodorus' narrative either, I think it is legitimate to infer that among the western legends of Hercules there were some that had him deified while still in Italy.

To return to our question: where did Velleius begin, and why? He used the apotheosis of Hercules as a chronological marker, but not necessarily in connexion with the Labours, as in Diodorus. It may be more likely that Velleius followed 'those who have narrated the deeds of Hercules in the form of history',[49] and began with the hero as the guarantor of civilization.

As Dionysius puts it, Hercules was the greatest commander of his time, who led a large army throughout the lands of the West, destroying harmful tyrannies and murderous bands of outlaws, and establishing humane and lawful governments in their place; he built cities, opened roads, controlled rivers, and reconciled the Greek colonists on the coast with the native peoples of the hinterland.[50] At Pallantion, he killed the evil Cacus and abolished the custom of human sacrifice.[51] In Campania, he defeated those 'mighty men notorious for lawlessness' who were called the Giants.[52] Having thus 'sorted out everything in Italy as he wanted', he received divine honours from all its inhabitants.[53]

---

[47] Ar. *Meteor.* 368b30, Timaeus, *FGrHist* 566 F 89, Prop. 1.20.9, Strabo 5.4.4 and 6 (243, 245); cf. Pol. 2.17.1, 3.91.7 for the Campanian plain of Phlegra.

[48] Diod. 4.21.7.

[49] Dion. Hal. 1.41.1: ὁ δ' ἀληθέστερος, ᾧ πολλοὶ τῶν ἐν ἱστορίας σχήματι τὰς πράξεις αὐτοῦ διηγησαμένων, τοιόσδε.

[50] Dion. Hal., *A.R.* 1.41.1, cf. Virg. *Aen.* 8.275 (*communis deus*), ps.-Sen. *Herc. Oet.* 1–7 (bringer of peace). See Morgan (2005) for this aspect of Hercules as applied to Augustus in Hor. *Odes* 3.14.

[51] Cacus as barbarous δυνάστης: Dion. Hal., *A.R.* 1.42.2, cf. Livy 1.7.5 (*ferox uiribus*). Human sacrifice (aetiology of *Argei*): Dion. Hal., *A.R.* 1.38.2, Ovid *Fasti* 5.625–32, Plut. *Mor.* 272b (*Q.R.* 32).

[52] Diod. 4.21.3: ἄνδρας ... ταῖς τε ῥώμαις προέχοντας καὶ ἐπὶ παρανομίᾳ διωνομάσμενους.

[53] Dion. Hal. 1.44.1: ἐπεὶ τά τε κατὰ τὴν Ἰταλίαν ἄπαντα ὡς ἐβούλετο κατεστήσατο ... τιμῶν ἰσοθέων παρὰ πᾶσι τοῖς οἰκοῦσιν ἐν Ἰταλίᾳ τυχών.

Velleius was a Campanian. That is clear from his phraseology in two places: he
calls the foundation of Capua and Nola a *res domestica*, and he describes his
grandfather C. Velleius as *uir nulli secundus in Campania*.[54] His own sons
(presumably) were the C. and L. Vellei Paterculi who were suffect consuls in
AD 60 and 61;[55] it is possible that their younger contemporary Silius Italicus
(consul in AD 68) had them in mind in his narrative of Capua's punishment
in 211 BC:[56]

> ueniet quondam felicior aetas
> cum pia Campano gaudebit consule Roma
> et per bella diu fasces perque arma negatos
> ultro ad magnanimos referet secura nepotes.

One day will come a happier age, when faithful Rome will rejoice in a Campanian
consul, and the fasces she long denied them through war and arms she will hand, safe
and willing, to their proud descendants.

Velleius' patron M. Vinicius came from the same area; his home town was
Cales, the Latin colony established in 334 BC about ten miles north of
Capua.[57]

  In fact, the Vinicii were prominent in Campania long before the colony was
founded. A bronze jug found in a tomb in Capua in the nineteenth century
(now in the Hermitage Museum in St Petersburg) carries an Oscan inscription written in Etruscan script: *uinuχs ueneliis peracis estam tetet uenelei
uiniciiu*, 'Vinuchs Peracis son of Venel gave this to Venel Vinicius'.[58] It is
dated to the second quarter of the fifth century BC, about the time when
Pindar, just across the water in Syracuse, was singing the story of Hercules'
battle with the Giants and consequent deification. The same story may well
have been told, or sung, at the aristocratic symposia where that jug was used.

  By the time Velleius was celebrating the consulship of Venel Vinicius'
distant descendant, there was another reason why Hercules in Italy might
seem a good way to start a universal history. In the first century AD the Giants,
impious and arrogant, could be read as a metaphor for the murderers of
Divus Iulius. Ovid takes the parallel for granted, and so does Lucan.[59] In

---

    [54] 1.7.2 (n. 18 above); 2.76.1, with Rawson (1991), 232–3.
    [55] AD 60: *AE* 1929.161, Sen. *Quaest. nat.* 7.28.3 (cf. Tac. *Ann.* 14.22.1 for the date). AD 61: *CIL*
4.5518, 16.4 (misdated to 60). See *PIR*² M140, P201 (their respective colleagues).
    [56] Sil. It. *Pun.* 11.123–6.
    [57] 1.14.3 (foundation date); Tac. *Ann.* 6.15.1 (Vinicius *Calibus ortus*).
    [58] Crawford (2010); Anon. (1988), 189, B 7.24; M. Cristofani, in Anon. (1994), 379–80;
Cerchiai (1995), 189–90 (I am very grateful to David Ridgway for guiding me to this bibliography).
    [59] Ovid *Fasti* 5.555 and 569–78, cf. 3.705–8 (*nefas ausi*); Lucan 1.33–45, esp. 36 (*saeuorum
bella gigantum*). For the Gigantomachy theme in general, see Hardie (1986), 85–90, 125–43.

Velleius' time the very names of Brutus and Cassius were marked with pious horror; to write about them like a historian of the free republic was to invite a charge of treason.[60] Velleius himself takes good care to report that his uncle took part in the prosecution of Cassius for Caesar's murder.[61] If Philippi was the equivalent in modern times of the battle in the plain of Phlegra (and this time too the reward of the victor was to become a god), a tactful historian might well take Hercules' victory as his starting point.

[60] Cassius: *numquam sine praefatione publici parricidii nominandus* (Val. Max. 1.8.8, cf. 3.1.3, 6.8.4). Brutus: *omnem nominis sui memoriam inexpiabili detestatione perfudit* (Val. Max. 6.4.5, cf. 1.5.7). Treason: Tac. *Ann.* 4.34–5, Dio 57.24.3 (Cremutius Cordus, AD 25).

[61] 2.69.5: *quo tempore Capito patruus meus, uir ordinis senatorii, Agrippae subscripsit in C. Cassium.*

Part II

Quality and Pleasure

5

Romani ueteres atque urbani sales:
A Note on Cicero *De Oratore* 2.262
and Lucilius 173M

Anna Chahoud

labore alieno magno partam gloriam uerbis saepe in se transmouet qui
habet salem

With his tongue a man who has wit often transfers to himself the praise
that someone else has earned with much labour

Ter. Eun. 400

Through the speaking voice of Julius Caesar Strabo, the wittiest orator of his
own times,[1] Cicero declares himself unable to tell the difference between the
refined humour (*lepos*) of eminent orators and the sharp wit (*dicacitas*) of
individuals of lower rank (*De Orat.* 2.244):

qui igitur distinguemus a Crasso, a Catulo, a ceteris familiarem uestrum Granium aut
Vargulam amicum meum? Non mehercule in mentem mihi quidem uenit: sunt enim
dicaces; Granio quidem nemo dicacior.

How are we then to distinguish your friend Granius, or my friend Vargula, from
Crassus, Catulus and all the others? For the life of me I can't think of a way; for they do
have a ready tongue—no one more so than Granius.

---

[1] Cic. *Off.* 1.108: *sale uero et facetiis Caesar, Catuli patris frater, uicit omnes* ('Caesar, the
brother of Catulus' father, had no rival in his wit and humour'); *Brut.* 177: *festiuitate igitur et
facetiis, inquam, C. Iulius L. f. et superioribus et aequalibus suis omnibus praestitit oratorque fuit
minime ille quidem uehemens, sed nemo umquam urbanitate, nemo lepore, nemo suauitate
conditior* ('in his wit and humour C. Julius, the son of Lucius, surpassed all his predecessors
and contemporaries, and as an orator he was indeed everything but impetuous, but no one was
better seasoned with elegance, charm and pleasantness than him'); *Tusc.* 5.55: *in quo mihi
uidetur specimen fuisse humanitatis salis suauitatis leporis* ('it seems to me that he was endowed
with a true model of elegance, wit, pleasantness, and charm). On C. Julius Caesar Strabo
Vopiscus (born *c*.131 BC), half-brother of Q. Lutatius Catulus (cos. 102), cf. *ORF,* no. 73;
Sumner (1973), 105–6; Fantham (2004), 139 n. 22 and 186–208.

In the last of his rhetorical works to touch upon the subject of *ridiculum*, Cicero will eventually resolve the tension between the two types of humour— which is also one between acquired skills (*ars*) and inborn talent (*ingenium*)[2]—by recommending both techniques, providing that the latter be moderated by the sense of decorum which alone distinguishes the orator from a buffoon (*scurra*) or a comedian of the lowest type (*mimicus*).[3] The danger is one of wit turning into banter (*cauillatio*), the professional stuff of the parasite.[4] Drawing on Cicero for his systematic treatment of the topic, Quintilian equally advises the would-be orator against giving the impression of Atellan farce or vulgar vituperation by indulging in distasteful jokes, especially those based on ambiguity (*amphibolia*).[5]

Cicero's model, here as elsewhere, is the elegant combination of dignity (*grauitas*) and humour (*lepos*) of Licinius Crassus.[6] In the same year that saw

---

[2] Cf. Cicero's remark on Demosthenes at *Orat.* 90: *quo quidem mihi nihil uidetur urbanius, sed non tam dicax fuit quam facetus; est autem illud acrioris ingeni, hoc maioris artis* ('it seems to me that no greater elegance can be found elsewhere, but he was not as witty as he was humorous; the former quality is a matter of sharper talent, the latter of greater skill'); cf. Quint. *Inst.* 6.3.21.

[3] Cic. *De Orat.* 2.239: *uitandum est oratori utrumque, ne aut scurrilis iocus sit aut mimicus* ('the orator should steer clear from the jokes of the buffoon and of the farce comedian); 2.244: *scurrilis oratori dicacitas magnopere fugienda est* ('the orator must avoid especially the sharp wit of the buffoon'); 2.247: *dicacitatis moderatio . . . distinguit oratorem a scurra* ('moderation in the use of sharp wit marks the difference between the orator and the buffoon'); *Orat.* 88: *illud admonemus tamen ridiculo sic usurum oratorem ut nec nimis frequenti ne scurrile sit, nec subobsceno ne mimicum . . . haec enim ad illud indecorum referuntur* ('my advice, however, is that jokes in oratory should be used sparingly, so as to keep away from buffoonery, and with no trace of indecency, to keep away from farce . . . for these faults suggest impropriety'). On these two types of wit and Panaetius' theory of decorum cf. *Off.* 1.104, with Dyck (1996), ad loc.; see also Krostenko (2001), 220–1.

[4] Plaut. *Stich.* 228–9: *cauillationes, adsentatiunculas | ac peiieratiunculas parasiticas* (the offensive jokes, petty flattery, and perjury of a parasite); *Truc.* 685: synon. *ridicularia* 'jests'; Paul. Fest. 39 L (= 45 M): *cauillatio est iocosa calumniatio* 'banter is funny accusation'; Don. Ter. *Eun.* prol. 6: *dicaces dicuntur qui iocosis salibus maledicunt* ('those who use witty jokes to abuse are called *dicaces* "sharp-witted" '). See Fantham (2004), 194 n. 151; cf. Corbett (1986), 5–26.

[5] Quint. *Inst.* 6.3.29: *dicacitas etiam scurrilis et scaenica huic* [scil. *oratori*] *personae alienissima est* ('buffoonish and farcical wit is also extremely inappropriate in oratory'); 6.3.46–7: *cum sint autem loci plures ex quibus dicta ridicula ducantur, repetendum est mihi non omnis eos oratoribus conuenire, in primis ex amphibolia, neque illa obscura quae Atellano more captant, nec qualia uulgo iactantur a uilissimo quoque, conuersa in maledictum fere ambiguitate* ('while there are many topics from which jokes may be drawn, I must repeat that not all of them are suitable in oratory—first of all the remarks based on *double entendre*, such as the obscurely offensive jests of Atellan farce, or such common jokes as are cracked by the lowest type of people, where ambiguity serves the purpose of abuse').

[6] Cic. *Brut.* 143: *erat cum grauitate iunctus facetiarum et urbanitatis oratorius, non scurrilis lepos* ('the dignity of his eloquence was combined with the charming quality of elegant humour that characterizes the orator, not the buffoon'); cf. *De Orat.* 3.29. On this and related passages see Krostenko (2001), 212.

the publication of the *Orator*, Cicero addresses a letter to his learned friend Papirius Paetus (*Fam.* 9.15=196 SB), crediting him with a pleasantness (*iucunditas*) that arises from the 'true old city style of wit' (*Romani ueteres atque urbani sales*). Cicero's nostalgic reminiscence views Paetus as the survivor of a genuinely Roman quality:

itaque, te cum uideo, omnes mihi Granios, omnes Lucilios—uere ut dicam—Crassos quoque et Laelios uidere uideor: moriar, si praeter te quemquam reliquum habeo, in quo possim imaginem antiquae et uernaculae festiuitatis agnoscere.

And so, when I see you, it feels as though I am seeing the likes of Granius and Lucilius—to tell you the truth, the likes of Crassus and Laelius as well. I'll be damned if I have anyone left except you to conjure up the image of our old-day native humour.

Rather than a sentimental comment, the use of the word *imago* with reference to an exemplary past recalls the paradigmatic value associated with portraits of one's ancestors in Roman aristocratic culture.[7] In Cicero's eyes, Paetus is the living 'likeness' of Granius and Lucilius, of Crassus and Laelius: again we are presented with four names (two of which were already in Strabo's comment at *De Orat.* 2.244), and again a distinction is apparently made within the spirit these names all stand for. The contrast is one of style—the sharp wit of the *dicaces* Granius and Lucilius, and the elegant humour of the *nobiles* Laelius and Crassus[8]—and one of birth—the Campanian flavour of the speech of two natives (Lucilius from Suessa Aurunca, Granius from Puteoli) and the more refined quality of two Romans who owned property there.[9]

Both passages project us back to a time past in which we are invited to recognize the foundation and justification of Cicero's own practice as an orator. The modest aim of this note is the illustration of two passages that bring Cicero's champions together in a unified model of verbal wit (*De Orat.* 2.218 *in dicto ridiculum*), in which the element of theatrical mockery combines with irony to find an acceptable place and function even in the stylized prose of speakers praised for their *grauitas*.

---

[7] Flower (1996), with semantic study at 33–5. For an instance of this motif in Cicero's excursus see *De Orat.* 2.225–6.

[8] So Krostenko (2001), 208–9.

[9] A Campanian connexion for all the named paradigms of the 'spirit of the old-day Rome' was most appropriate in an address to Paetus, a regular resident of Naples: this acute observation of Cicero's powers of accommodation belongs to D'arms (1967), 200–2 (revised in D'Arms (1970), 22); see also Shackleton Bailey ad loc. For Laelius' villa at Puteoli see D'Arms (1970), 7–8.

I. CRASSUS AP. CIC. *DE ORAT.* 2.262: *PULCHELLUS PUER*

The bons mots (*dicta*) of the Campanian auctioneer C. Granius, *praeco dicacissimus* (cf. Schol. Cic. Bob. p. 134.2)[10] and an intimate friend of Licinius Crassus, won the repeated praise of his contemporary Lucilius (411–12M, 1181M) and, later, of Cicero and his friend Atticus (*Planc.* 33; *Brut.* 160 and 172; *Att.* 2.8.1, 6.3.7);[11] the discussion in *De oratore* presents Granius as a master of ambiguity (2.253) and incongruity (2.280–2), a feature of wit that Cicero qualifies as 'neat' (*bellum*). Not so his illustrious friend Licinius Crassus, whose characteristic *grauitas* has been regarded as incompatible with expressions of wit *in uerbo*: 'a search for Crassus' jokes in the *De Oratore* would produce no results'.[12] This is not exactly true. Cicero reports the case of a public occasion in which Crassus snapped at one L. Aelius Lamia who kept interrupting him (*De Orat.* 2.262 = Crass. *orat.*, *ORF* 66.44):[13]

inuertuntur autem uerba ut Crassus apud M. Perpernam iudicem pro Aculeone cum diceret, aderat contra Aculeonem Gratidiano L. Aelius Lamia, deformis, ut nostis; qui cum interpellaret odiose, 'audiamus' inquit 'pulchellum puerum' Crassus; cum esset arrisum, 'non potui mihi' inquit Lamia 'formam ipse fingere, ingenium potui', tum hic 'audiamus' inquit 'disertum': multo etiam arrisum est uehementius.

A case of irony is like when Crassus spoke on behalf of Aculeo before the judge M. Perperna, and L. Aelius Lamia—who was disfigured, as you know—pleaded for Gratidianus against Aculeo. As Lamia kept annoying him with repeated interruptions, Crassus said, 'Let's hear the pretty boy'. After the general laughter, Lamia replied, 'It was not in my power to shape my appearance, but my skills, it was indeed,' at which Crassus, 'Let's hear the skilled speaker'—the laughter was even louder.

---

[10] And note Schol. Cic. Bob. 134.18: *haec dicacitas praeconis istius non minus urbanitatis habuisse uidetur quam asperitatis* ('the sharp wit possessed by this auctioneer was, it seems, no less elegant than harsh').

[11] On the historical and literary figure of Granius see Barbieri (1987) and Perruccio (2002), *passim*; Rauh (1989), 455–6; Goldberg (2005), 146 and 170. My own brief discussion, Chahoud (2007), 47–8, is concerned with Granius' 'Roman accent' in Cicero's construct of urban Latin (*Brut.* 172).

[12] 'Invano si cercherebbero [facezie di Crasso] nel *De Oratore*': Martinelli (1963), 8.

[13] This individual is not known; but the Aelii Lamiae of Formia were on good terms with Cicero, who owned a villa there; and the hearing reported at *De Orat.* 2.262 involved two relatives of Cicero's, Aculeo and Marius Gratidianus: see Treggiari (1973), 247–53 (with discussion of this passage at 247).

The anecdote serves as an illustration of the comic effects of irony, defined here in terms of *inuersio*, 'the use of words to convey something other than their overt meaning'.[14] Crassus' address is ostensibly ironic, for the young man was everything but 'pretty' (*deformis*);[15] the choice of the diminutive *pulchellus*, however, is significant. The form, natural enough for the address to a *puer*, may originate from a colloquial usage,[16] but the formal context of the occurrence (a court hearing) calls for a motivation.

The stylized prose of early orators employs contemptuous diminutives for vividness. In the speech *On his consulship* of 191/0 BC, the elder Cato produces a disparaging list of unprecedented formations of comic and/or colloquial flavour: Cato, *orat.*, *ORF* 8.43 (=12 SC) *ridibundum magistratum gerere, pauculos homines, mediocriculum exercitum obuium duci* ('it was a ludicrous office I held, a tiny little bunch of people, an insignificant little army that marched against me').[17] In a famous invective incorporated in his speech against Ti. Gracchus' legislation of 129 BC (*orat.* 21.30 M), Scipio Aemilianus condemns the practice of allowing young *ingenui* to mix with debauched dancers: *cum cinaedulis... eunt in ludum saltatorium... eunt, inquam, in ludum saltatorium inter cinaedos* ('in the company of pathics... they go to dance school... they go, I say, to dance school, among pathics'), where Courtney (1999), 123 notes, along with the emphatic chiastic repetition, that 'the diminutive here reinforces the scorn'. Leeman (1963), 53 finds a 'satirical tinge' and a 'more colloquial' flavour in this passage than in any other attributed to Scipio, who, just like Crassus, was best known for the extremely refined (*perelegans*) combination of wit and dignity (*cum*

---

[14] *OLD*, s.v. *inuersio* 2; *TLL* VII.2 163.64 ff.; cf. *Rhet. Her.* 1.6.10 *ab aliqua re* (sc. *exordiemur*) *quae risum moueri possit, ab... imitatione deprauata, inuersione, ambiguo* ('the speech should open with something that may raise a laugh, such as... caricature, irony, ambiguity'); Fronto 48.16 van den Hout *inuersa oratio*; on *inuersio* as a special type of allegory (Quint. 8.6.44) see Leeman (1963), 38. Cicero's broader definition of irony as a trope is 'elegant pretence', *urbana dissimulatio* (Cic. *De Orat.* 2.269–271; 3.203 *periucunda* 'very pleasant'), cf. Quint. *Inst.* 9.2.44; Gell. 18.4.1 (*facetissima* 'extremely humorous'). See *TLL* VII.2.381.79–382.24 (*ironia*); 423.19–40 (*irrisio*); Wilkins on *De Orat.* 2.270; Leeman–Pinkster–Rabbie (1989), 183–8; Wisse–Winterbottom–Fantham (2008), 315; Douglas on *Brut.* 292; Hoffman–Szantyr (1965), 837= (2002), 257; extensive treatment of irony in Cicero in Canter (1936); Haury (1955), esp. 7–29; Krostenko (2001), 220 n. 59.

[15] On physical defects as a stock-in-trade of invective see Corbeill (1996), 37–9.

[16] Hofmann (2003), 299; Pasetti (2007), 39. Classic discussions of the various connotations and functions of diminutives in literary Latin are Ernout (1954), 189–92 (in poetic diction Ernout 1957: 82–6) and Hofmann–Szantyr (1965), 772–7 = (2002), 143–50.

[17] Often found in comedy, *pauculus* is attested with reference to persons for the first time here, and again in Sulp. Ruf. ap. Cic. *Fam.* 4.13.3; *mediocriculus* is unparalleled: see Sblendorio Cugusi (1982), 156–7. For *ridibundus* (cf. Pl. *Epid.* 413) and unparalleled formations in –*bundus* in Cato see Quint. *Inst.* 1.6.42; Sblendorio Cugusi (1982), 155. On Cato's humorous coinages as 'invective weapons' see Till (1968), 126–31.

grauitate salsum) resulting from his chief quality, irony (*De Orat.* 2.270 *ironia dissimulantiaque*).[18]

In Crassus' alliterative phrase *pulchellum puerum* the diminutive is the marked word, coming before the noun *puerum*; readers of Cicero in the mid-50s would already be familiar with Cicero's practice of mocking Clodius' physical degradation by labelling him *pulchellus puer* (*Att.* 1.16.10 of 61 BC), or simply *pulchellus* (*Att.* 2.1.4, 2.18.3; 2.22.1, all 59 BC).[19] In the trial against Caelius Rufus, L. Sempronius Atratinus apparently called Caelius *pulchellum Iasonem* 'pretty Jason' (*orat.* 171.7M).[20] Crassus' address to the disfigured Lamia is the earliest example of this diminutive; but we owe the example to Cicero. All the Republican records of *pulchellus* belong to Cicero and his world, and, except for Cic. *Fam.* 7.23.2 (*pulchellae* statues), all are scornful references to young men. This is the sense, if not the tone, in which the word resurfaces, in explicitly ironic and homoerotic context, in Apuleius, *Met.* 8.26 (with reference to a slave) and, more notably, *Met.* 9.27 *tam uenustum tamque pulchellum puellum* ('such an attractive and pretty boy'),[21] where the rhyming double diminutive adds comic flavour to Cicero's nickname for Clodius, *pulchellus puer*.[22]

II. LUCILIUS 173M: *DIGNUS PUELLUS*

cumque hic tam formosus homo ac te dignus puellus

and when he, such a fine fellow, and, indeed, a cute boy worthy of you

The line comes with neither main clause nor indication of context, nor can the addressee be identified.[23] The qualification, however, is not a flattering

---

[18] The historian Fannius, *HRR* F 7 called Scipio the same name that Aristophanes (*Nub.* 449) used for Socrates, εἴρων 'one who says less than he thinks': Cic. *Off.* 1.108 with Dyck (1996), ad loc.; cf. *Acad.* 2.15; *De Orat.* 3.28. On the relation between *grauitas* and irony see Reitzenstein (1901), 149.

[19] Cf. Shackleton Bailey on *Att.* 1.16.10; Scott (1969), 27; Skinner (1982), 202; Crawford (1994), 256–7 on Cic. *In P. Clodium et Curionem*, fr. 24; Corbeill (1996), 79–80; Krostenko (2001), 229–32.

[20] The fragment is preserved as illustration of metaphor by Chir. Fortunat. 3.7 p. 124 Halm.

[21] Cf. Bechtle (1995), 123.

[22] See Traina (1999), 115–16, comparing Plaut. *Asin.* 694 *passerculum putillum* ('a tiny little sparrow'); Pasetti (2007), 39. On combination of diminutives as 'emotional phrases' see Hanssen (1952), 126. A notable double diminutive is the *molliculus adulescentulus* whom Titinius portrays as 'speaking like a woman' in a comedy, according to Char. *gramm.* 258.4B: see the synonymous phrase *tener . . . puellus* in Lucil. 425M below.

[23] All sources are grammatical: Non. 233L; Fest. 292.1L; Suet. ap. Prisc. *gramm.* II.232.1.

one, recalling in structure Lucilius' description of one Quintus Opimius at 419M *formosus fuit homo et famosus* 'graceful in form and graceless in fame'.[24] This individual is mockingly addressed as 'one of those disreputable women' (*famosae*) in an anecdote that, while constructed in Cicero's typical fashion,[25] is most probably drawn from Lucilius (*De Orat.* 2.277).[26] Lucilius' homo-ioteleuton *formosus/famosus* at 419M finds notable oratorical parallels in Cato's derogatory reference to a male prostitute *famosus et suspiciosus* 'notorious and dubious' (*orat.* 8.212M)[27] and in Scipio Aemilianus' vivid depiction of Publius Sulpicius Galus as *adulescentulus... non modo uinosus sed uirosus quoque* 'not only fond of wine, but also fond of men' (*ORF* 21.17 = 20 Astin), where the diminutive has a colloquial if not comic ring to it,[28] and the rhyming adjectives are further connected through alliteration, assonance, and possibly wordplay.[29] In Lucilius the connotation of contempt is carried by a specialized used of the adjective *formosus* and emphasized by the diminutive *puellus* in the punchline. I discuss these two features in reverse order.

While diminutive noun-formations with reference to 'younger people' (*puellus, puella, adulescentulus*) reflect a tendency of spoken language,[30] the connotation of such forms in any given context is anything but uniform. Just as the frequent use of *adulescentulus* in Plautus and Terence gives the word a comic flavour, *puellus* has a literary history of its own. The homoerotic connotation may already have been in Plautus (fr. 89 *dolet huic puello sese uenum ducier*, 'it grieves him (?) to have been sold to this boy'); Lucilius has the first certain attestations of it as a substitute for the lower (and cretic) word *pusio* 'lover boy', in our passage and at 425M, *inde uenit Romam tener ipse etiam atque puellus*, 'then he came to Rome—a delicate fellow he was, yes, a

---

[24] Warmington's translation, fr. 450–2. For the force of *famosus* 'talked about, i.e. infamous' in comedy see *OLD*, s.v., 2b, *TLL* VI.1.257.14 'propter impuritatem, lasciuiam' ('on account of dishonourable, lustful behaviour').

[25] See Gotoff (1981), 294–6 'structural formula': identification of the speaker, circumstances, dictum.

[26] A well-known passage: see Leeman–Pinkster–Rabbie (1989), 201; Corbeill (1996), 151–2; Krostenko (2001), 205 and n. 7. This anecdote is said to refer to a 'mid first-century BC aristocrat' by Richlin (1993), 541. For the substitution of feminine for masculine with reference to *pathici* (e.g. Pompon. *Com.* 151 R.; Cic. *Att.* 1.14.5; Hor. *Sat.* 1.8.39) see Buchheit (1962), 253; Williams (1999), 300 n. 98.

[27] Cic. *De Orat.* 2.256 recalls a comparable example of suggestive wordplay in Cato, *si tu et aduersus et auersus impudicus es*, 'if you have no shame in either of your parts, front and back' (= *Dictum* 67 p. 109 Jordan), where the two terms allude to *fellatio* and *pedicatio*; see Leeman–Pinkster–Rabbie (1989), ad loc.

[28] Cf. Plaut. *Cist.* 157 f. *adulescentulus... uinolentus* ('drunk'); for *adulescentulus* in erotic contexts see also e.g. Ter. *Ad.* 101; Petron. 134.

[29] Courtney (1999), 119–20. On this famous passage of Scipio see also Corbeill (1996), 136–7; Krostenko (2001), 292 n. 7.

[30] See Maltby (1979), 144–5; Adams (1980), 282–3.

boy'.[31] That the force of *puellus* was more often than not a suggestive one is indicated by the erotic context of most other Republican examples (Var. *Men.* 540 of Adon *puellus Veneris* 'Venus' boy', 485 *me puellum inpuberem cepisti,* 'you took me when I was a mere boy') and of all Apuleius' recoveries of the diminutive long after it had long gone out of currency:[32] along with *Met.* 9.27 *pulchellum puellum* (above), *Met.* 7.21 *seu scitula mulier seu uirgo nubilis seu tener puellus,* 'whether a pretty lady or a young girl or a delicate boy' (a possible imitation of Lucil. 425M),[33] 10.29 *puelli puellaeque... forma conspicui* ('boys and girls... striking in their looks'), and most probably also *Carm.* p. 139 Morel = p. 396 Courtney *meum puellum sauior* ('I kiss my boy').[34]

Lucilius has the earliest attestations of *formosus* 'handsome, fine' in references to men, whereas Plautus restricted the usage to the 'well-built' body of animals and Terence once used it in a direct address to Thais in *Eun.* 730; the adjective would come to acquire an erotic connotation (of a *puer* or a *puella*) in later poetry, esp. elegy,[35] and a pejorative one in Ciceronian political invective (= *mollis*, e.g. *Verr.* 5.63).[36] In four out of five examples, Lucilius uses the adjective in mockery:[37] in a playful allusion to the Stoic paradox 'only the wise man is handsome' at 1225–6M *nondum etiam qui omnia habebit,* | *formosus diues liber rex solus feretur* ('not even he who has everything will alone be spoken of as a handsome fellow, rich and free-born, a king');[38] in an ironic concession to the interlocutor's point of view at 1026M *omnes formosi, fortes tibi, ego improbus: esto* ('all fine and decent fellows in your view, I'm the bad one—all right'); and in the alliterative pair *formosus... famosus* discussed

[31] Metrical convenience already recommended *puellus* in hexametrical line-ending to Ennius, *Ann.* 214 Sk; cf. Lucr. 4.1252: see Skutsch (1985), ad loc. All hexametrical occurrences (including Lucilius) are at the end of the line. On the low register of *pusio* see Quint. *Inst.* 8.3.22; Austin (1960), on Cic. *Cael.* 36.

[32] The archaic usage is confirmed by Suet. *Cal.* 8.3, *quod antiqui etiam puellas pueras, sicut et pueros puellos dictitarent* ('because in the old days people would also use the word *puera* for 'girl' as well as the word *puellus* for 'boy').

[33] Cf. Hijmans (1995), ad loc.

[34] An erotic poem attributed by Gellius (19.11.3) to an 'African friend': for the identification of this author with Apuleius see most recently Harrison (1992), 88; Holford-Strevens (2003), 23 n. 59; Courtney (2003), 395–7.

[35] Cf. Pichon (1902), 153–4; Monteil (1964), 58–9; Knox (1986), 97–101; on the physical sense of *formosus* = *pulcher* see Ernout (1957), 78–82.

[36] Cf. Monteil (1964), 47–8.

[37] The reference to the '(not so) fine' form of a horse at 467M is an almost technical use of *formosus* for the 'well-built' body of animals (cf. Var. *Rust.* 2.7.4; Chir. 754): see *TLL* VI.1.111125–36; Monteil (1964), 44.

[38] The quoting source warns that the poet's Stoic tenet is not to be taken seriously: Porph. Hor. *Sat.* 1.3.124 *tamen poeta non simpliciter hoc sed per derisum Stoicorum dicit* ('the poet, however, is not speaking literally but is mocking the Stoics'); cf. Var. *Men.* 245.

above (419M). The phrase *formosus homo* 'fine fellow' is also an instance of irony, as is made clear by the pairing with *te dignus puellus* in the second half of the line.

Lucilius' use of *dignus* brings us back once more to Cicero's *excursus de ridiculis*. At *De Orat.* 2.286 we are told that Laelius replied to a man of lower birth who had accused him of behaviour unworthy of his ancestors, by retorting *at hercule, inquit, tu tuis dignus* 'but hey, you're sure worthy of yours' (*orat.* 20.24M).[39] Laelius' response, just like Lucilius' comment at 1026M (*omnes formosi... ego improbus—esto*), is an example of ironic pretence (*concessio*).[40] It is also a reversal of the topos of the *nobilis* 'worthy of his ancestors', a favourite of Cicero's.[41] And just like Lucilius 173M, Cicero would also extend the theme to invective, in sarcastic representations of individuals 'suited to' one another, notably Sextus Cloelius, whose sexual vices matched those of his associate Clodius (*Sest.* 133 *homo iis dignissimus, quibuscumque uiuit* 'thoroughly worthy of every individual he consorted with'), and Piso with him (*Pis.* 8 *hominem inpurum ac non modo facie, sed etiam osculo tuo dignissimum*, 'a foul fellow, and thoroughly worthy not only of your look, but also of your kiss')—incidentally, both Cloelius and Piso were ugly.[42]

Cicero's notion of political humour draws on a tradition in which the orator and the satirist share stylistic choices and rhetorical devices, refining, rather than discarding, elements of comic or altogether farcical mockery.[43] When he describes the brand of his own 'salt mines' in a letter to Volumnius Eutrapelos (*Fam.* 7.32.1 = 113SB *salinarum mearum*), Cicero contrasts his *uenustas* with the lack of charm (ἀκύθηρον) that nowadays 'would please anyone in Rome, full of scum as it is'; Cicero's characteristic techniques are 'sharp, elegant,

---

[39] Possibly a fragment of speech, rather than a *dictum*: see *ORF* 122 n. What little else remains from the oratory of Laelius belongs to his funerary *laudatio* of Scipio (pp. 121–2 *ORF*), where no display of the man's characteristic *hilaritas* 'light-heartedness' (Cic. *Off.* 1.108) could reasonably be expected: see Leeman (1963), 49–50; Kierdorf (1980), 21–33. Lucilius 'reports' an attack of Laelius on the glutton Gallonius (1238–40M), a passage to which Cicero alludes in *Att.* 13.52.1.

[40] Cicero's specific topic at *De Orat.* 2.286; on *concessio* see also Quint. *Inst.* 9.2.51 (a form of irony) and 6.3.81 (a feature of elegant wit, *multum habet urbanitatis*).

[41] Cf. e.g. *Flacc.* 101 *se... dignum suis maioribus praestitit* ('his conduct showed him worthy of his ancestors'); *Fam.* 2.18.3; *Sest.* 21; *Fam.* 13.34 *dignum et patre et auo* 'worthy of his father and grandfather' (cf. Sall. *Jug.* 9.2 *te atque auo* '(worthy) of you and of your grandfather'). On reversal as a technique in *refutatio*, with Laelius' reply as an example, see Riggsby (1995), 250 n. 21.

[42] See Nisbet (1961), ad loc., also on the emendation *osculo* for *oculo*. On the worthiness theme see Kaster (2006), on Cic. *Sest.* 133; in invective: Corbeill (1996), 112–24.

[43] See e.g. Petrone (1971), 7–9 on *Italum acetum* (Hor. *Sat.* 1.7.32); Fantham (2004), 194 on the dramatic nature of oratorical skills, 'derived from Graeco-Roman comedy, with an element of fine-tuned mimicry'.

neat', and he lists them—note the modifiers: ambiguity (*acuta ἀμφιβολία*), hyperbole (*elegans ὑπερβολή*), pun (*παράγραμμα bellum*), unexpected punch-line (*ridiculum παρὰ προσδοκίαν*);[44] his secret is the artfulness of his jokes (*ἔντεχνα et arguta*).[45] Lucilius, *doctus et perurbanus* (*De Orat.* 1.72, 2.25), has a notable precedent for such a rhetorical self-evaluation, in a verse epistle addressed to someone who calls his use of wordplay and sound effect 'without art' (189M *ἄτεχνον*); the passage is praised by the quoting source as written *facetissime* and *festiuiter* (Gell. 18.8.2). Cicero's relation to his addressee is vice versa one of mutual understanding, if he means his praise for Volumnius' style at the end of the letter (7.32.3 *litterae facetae elegantesque*). Cicero uses exactly the same adjectives to qualify Socratic irony (*ironiam . . . facetam et elegantem puto* 'I regard irony as humorous and elegant') in *Brut.* 292, which technique he describes as the mark of a man 'not at all lacking in judgement, and with a sense of humour as well' (*et minime inepti hominis et eiusdem etiam faceti*).

[44] Shackleton Bailey notes that Cicero freely uses Greek rhetorical terminology in informal conversation with a Greek-speaking friend, while he would have recourse to Latin equivalents or to explanatory glosses in a theoretical discussion. Such a case is the excursus in *De Orat.*: ambiguity: 2.253 *ambiguum* (=ἀμφιβολία); pun: 2.256 *uerbi immutationem, quod . . . Graeci uocant παρονομασίαν* (=παράγραμμα); surprise effect: 2.250 *praeter expectationem*, 2.289 *expectationibus decipiendis* (=παρὰ προσδοκίαν). See also Petrone 1971: 9–10.

[45] Discussion of this letter in relation to Cicero's own reputation as a wit (with humorous or hostile references to him as a *scurra*, cf. Macr. *Sat.* 2.1.12) in Krostenko (2001), 223–4; for ancient collections of 'Ciceronian' jokes, as preserved in Quintilian, Plutarch, and Macrobius, see Kelsey (1907); McLaren (1966), 193.

6

Allusion and Contrast in the Letters of Nicias (Thuc. 7.11–15) and Pompey (Sall. *Hist.* 2.98M)

Elizabeth A. Meyer

Fronto, seeking yet another way to praise the emperor Lucius Verus, declares a letter of the latter superior to Thucydides' letter from Nicias to the Athenians, Sallust's of Mithridates, Pompey, and Adherbal, and a celebrated actual letter of the consular Catulus.[1] 'Yours', he says, 'is eloquent, as of an orator; direct, as of a military leader; weighty, as to the senate; and not over-full of military matters'.[2] These superseded exemplars were famous, competition worthy of imperial emulation and imperial victory: Fronto calls Nicias' letter in particular *nobilissima*, 'most notable' or 'well-known',[3] and it was no doubt famous in Sallust's time as well, for Sallust certainly knew it.[4] That Sallust made

I offer my thanks to John Dillery, J. E. Lendon, Hunter Rawlings III, and the editors, all of whom read and improved this piece, and who are not to be blamed for its deficiencies. In order to maintain the secrecy of the *Festschrift* I could not have Tony actually read this in draft, and so offer it to him in some trepidation—but above all in gratitude for the unstinting friendship he offered me from the moment we met.

I have used the Maurenbrecher (1891–3) text of the fragments of Sallust's *Histories*, as well as his numbering of the fragments, with the numbering of McGushin (1992) and (1994) in brackets as [McG.] where useful; the Jones and Powell (1942) text of Thucydides; and the van den Hout (1988) text and numbering of Fronto's letters. Translations are my own but have been heavily influenced (in the case of Sallust) by Woodman (2007) and (in the case of Thucydides) Crawley.

[1] Fronto *ad L. Verum* 2.1.15. Nicias, Thuc. 7.11–16; Mithridates, Sall. *Hist.* 4.69 [4.67 McG.], Pompey, Sall. *Hist.* 2.98 [2.82 McG.], Adherbal, Sall. *Jug.* 24; Catulus, no longer extant, but Cic. *Brut.* 132 refers to Catulus' *de consulatu et de rebus gestis suis*.

[2] *tuae litterae et eloquentes sunt ut oratoris, strenuae ut ducis, graues ut ad senatum, ut de re militari non redundantes*, Fronto *ad Verum* 2.1.16; Hornblower, *Comm.* III.558 notes that this last is not, strictly speaking, true of Nicias' letter.

[3] Fronto *ad Verum* 2.1.15.

[4] Patzer ((1941), 110), Sallust read the entirety of Thucydides, not an epitome; Avenarius (1957), 49–52, Sallust made use in particular of Thucydides Bks. 1–3 and 7. Thucydides was an author who had recently become popular again in Sallust's time, Cic. *Or.* 30 and 32 and *Brut.* 287–8, with Scanlon (1998), 193.

literary use of that letter has been thought less certain, although Sallust's debt to Thucydides is generally acknowledged,[5] and parallels of context—generals in need writing home, amidst parlous circumstances in the distant West— have been noted.[6] But in fact the parallels go further than those of circumstance, for the complaints and fears voiced by both leaders are also similar, and there are verbal parallels between the two letters.[7] Thus content as well as context link the two letters and reveal Sallust's 'allusive imitation'.[8]

But to what end? In order, first, to sharpen the contrast that emerges from the comparison: these similarities help to highlight which differences in the characters of the two letter-writers as well as which differences in their respective audiences will be most important. This in turn points to a second goal of allusive imitation in the letter of Sallust's Pompey. For just as some of the specific ways in which Sallust's Pompey is made to differ from Nicias reveal Pompey as surprisingly akin to Thucydides' Alcibiades and thereby point to ways in which both men were harmful to their polities, so Pompey's allusion to Thucydides' methodological vocabulary—present also in Nicias' letter—points to Sallust's adaptation of Thucydides' thematic association of lack of clarity, poor decision-making, the deterioration of language, and fatal civil strife. Behind the emphatic contrasts, Sallust's allusions suggest, a terribly similar dynamic is at work. Thus although Pompey, the Roman Senate, and the Roman Republic are only too different from Nicias and the Athenian democrats, the linguistic deceptions and disordered doom into which their polities were eventually to fall were the consequence of the same evil, civil strife.

The historical and historiographical context in which the two letters were written can be deduced from the contents of the letters themselves, and

[5] Noted in antiquity, Vell. 2.36.2; Sen. *Suas.* 6.21; Quint. *Inst.* 10.1.101 and 10.2.17. Modern studies include Patzer (1941); Perrochat (1949); Scanlon (1980), 11–19, 31–48, with further references; Woodman (1986), 126–8; Nicols (1999), 331–2; Schmal (2001), 148–53; and Grethlein (2006), who focuses on 'un-Thucydidean' aspects but presents a helpful comparison of Sallust, Thucydides, and Herodotus.

[6] Avenarius (1957), 51, '[d]ie Situation is hier ähnlich'; Scanlon (1980), 203; at (1980), 191 he notes that Sallust has inserted a Thucydidean *logos-ergon* contrast in Pompey's letter at *Hist.* 2.98.6 and 10. For Canfora (2006b), 739, the similarity consists in two generals asking for more troops, and he considers Sallust's letter an 'out-and-out copy' of that in Thucydides. Katz (1982), 75–6 n. 6 thought that the 'accepted fact that Sallust's Letter of Pompey echoes the Letter of Nicias ... deepens the ... insult to Pompey', showing the depth of Sallust's animosity to Pompey. 'Pompey', he concludes, 'surely, would *not* have appreciated the parallel!'

[7] *Contra* Scanlon (1980), 203, who thought that Pompey's letter 'contain[ed] no specific verbal parallels to Thucydides'.

[8] 'An allusive imitation is that which intends to make a conscious allusion to an event or individual described in Thucydides, and thus it serves to enrich Sallust's narrative by reminding the reader of Thucydides' description and its context', Scanlon (1980), 97, reinforced by Renehan (2000), who emphasizes the significance of Sallust's use of context-to-context allusion.

indeed in the case of Pompey's letter must be so deduced, since the letter itself is preserved only as an excerpt from the larger, and very fragmentary, *Histories*. When they write, Nicias has been in Sicily a year and a half (summer 415 – winter 414/13), Pompey in Spain a year and a half to two years (late 77 – winter 75), although for part of a year in Gaul before that (77). The sequence of events that Nicias narrates is the same as that given in Thucydides' own narrative;[9] the sequence of Pompey's actions, at least in taking his army to Spain across the Alps and through Gaul, as well as the facts of the battles at Lauro ('the first onslaught'), Sucro, Turia, and Valentia, are plausibly accurate as he narrates them.[10] At the moment the letter was written, Nicias was the only commander of the Athenian forces in Sicily (Alcibiades had fled to Sparta [6.61.6–7] and Lamachus had died [6.101.6]); Pompey when he wrote was the only commander of *his* army, although he was ostensibly sent to Spain to assist Q. Caecilius Metellus Pius. Both felt they were, or claimed to be, facing disaster: in Thucydides' narrative, Nicias judged that the Athenians were 'facing horrors' and that without reinforcement there would be 'no salvation' (νομίζων ἐν δεινοῖς τε εἶναι καὶ ... οὐδεμίαν εἶναι σωτηρίαν, 7.8.1), while the horror Pompey sketched was that of a ravening—starved—army falling upon Italy, with the man who had previously been the source of Rome's 'salvation' (*salus*), Pompey himself, as hungry and driven to extreme action as the army itself (*Hist.* 2.98.1, 8). Hence both wrote letters—to the Athenians and to the Roman Senate—that were read out in midwinter, when the messengers carrying them arrived at their respective destinations; and to both letters the response was 'yes'.[11]

---

[9] Noted by Zuretti (1922), 3–4. The order in Thucydides' narrative (as in Nicias' letter, 7.11.2–3) is: the Athenians defeat the Syracusans in most of their engagements (6.69–70, 6.94.2, 6.97.4, 6.98.4, 6.100.2–3, 6.101.4–6.102.4); build siege-works (6.97.5, 6.98.2, 6.99.1, 6.101.1, 6.103.1, 7.2.4, 7.4.2–3, 7.4.5); Gylippus arrives (7.2.1); Gylippus and Syracusans lose their first engagement with the Athenians (7.5.2–3); Syracusans then victorious (7.6.2–3) and build a single wall across Athenian lines (7.6.4, 7.7.1).

[10] The precise order of events has been debated on the basis of later sources: see discussion in Greenhalgh (1981), 237 and Konrad (1995); the latter also argues (182–6) for Pompey's arrival in Spain by September 77. Carolsfeld and Syme thought Pompey indulged in mendacious telescoping of the time Pompey took, as well as in bold misrepresentation of who was truly responsible for victory: see Carolsfeld (1888), 67, 'falschen Angaben und Lügen', making victories out of draws and appropriating others' victories for himself, and Syme (1964), 201, it took more than forty days to raise an army and chase 'Rome's enemies all the way from the Alps to Spain'; Afranius and Metellus Pius, not Pompey, were responsible for the success at the Sucro. They are followed also by Pasoli (1966), 48–9, Büchner (1982), 220, and Schmal (2001), 87 n. 46.

[11] τοῦ δ' ἐπιγιγνομένου χειμῶνος ... [and the Athenians sent in response one general] εὐθὺς περὶ ἡλίου τροπὰς τὰς χειμερινάς ... (7.10.1 and 7.16.2); *hae litterae principio sequentis anni recitatae in senatu, Hist.* 2.98.10. Responses: Thuc. 7.16.1, *Hist.* 2.98.10 (but see below).

The similarities of content are numerous. Both Nicias and Pompey note that they have sent letters and messengers before, a fact that draws attention to the historians' choice of this letter as the one to quote, and strengthens the possibility that Sallust (who did not have to include a letter at all) intentionally inserted Pompey's letter in allusion to Thucydides.[12] For Nicias, communication by messenger raised painful issues of whether the perilous state of the Athenian expeditionary force could be accurately conveyed to Athenians by speech alone, and so he himself writes this time, 'judging that the Athenians would in this way learn, in particular, his own considered opinion' (ἔγραψεν ἐπιστολήν, νομίζων οὕτως ἂν μάλιστα τὴν αὑτοῦ γνώμην ... μαθόντας τοὺς Ἀθηναίους ..., 7.8.2).[13] For Pompey, past communication—of both types—was a matter of frustration that had compelled him to exhaust his own 'resources' and even his 'hopes' ('tired of writing and sending legates, I have used up all my resources and private hopes', *fessus scribendo mittendoque legatos omnis opes et spes priuatas meas consumpsi, Hist.* 2.98.2), so this time he used his letter to 'speak' (*fateor, Hist.* 2.98.4), and in this way conveyed, too, his own considered opinion.[14] Nicias assumed, or could assume, that the Athenians had at least learned something from many previous letters (ἐν ἄλλαις πολλαῖς ἐπιστολαῖς ἴστε, 7.11.1); Pompey, too, knew that the recipients of his messages had learned important information from his previous communications. He insists, however, that his recipients had deliberately chosen to ignore the implications of what they had learned, for despite the fact that the reported successes of the army were 'sufficiently clear to you' (*satis clara uobis sunt*) these reports had not inspired reciprocal, grateful funding (*Hist.* 2.98.6). Both also implied that this would be their last letter,

[12] Letters are referred to only two other times in what survives of the *Histories*, at 1.110 [1.102 McG.], where numbers are reported *per litteras*, and 3.33 [3.19 McG.], where a letter is seized and hurled into a camp by means of a catapult—neither a letter likely to be extensive or quoted in its entirety; so the chances that Pompey's letter is singular, and its inclusion singularly emphatic, are increased.

[13] Zuretti (1922), 3; Gomme et al., *HCT* IV.385, on 7.8.2: '... ἔγραψεν is emphatic: "he composed a message in writing"', and they therefore deduce that most generals' messages were verbal: 'Thucydides makes it sound as if it were unusual for a general to write home', and therefore 'by ἐπιστολή [in 7.11.1] Thucydides means "message"'—that all previous communications with the Athenians had been conveyed orally—and that this letter is the first that Nicias has written; see also Hornblower, *Comm.* III.555). With τὴν αὑτοῦ γνώμην, Dover (1965), 6 notes the emphasis on Nicias' *personal* opinion'. Messengers with letters could also convey additional messages orally, of course.

[14] A metaphorical parallel between the two generals might also be intended, in that Pompey is 'tired' and has spent his 'private *opes*' ('personal strength' is a fundamental meaning of *ops*, see *OLD* s.v. 1b), while Nicias has spent his own body in the service of his *polis*, since he suffers from kidney disease (7.15.1) and therefore is exhausted and without any further 'reserves' or 'resources'.

Nicias because he hoped to be recalled (7.15.1–2), Pompey because an inadequate response from the Senate would ensure that his next visit would be in person (*Hist.* 2.98.8, 10).

Both also gave a history of their army's achievements, Nicias in half a sentence at 7.11.2 (since the Athenians had indeed already learned τὰ μὲν πρότερον πραχθέντα from earlier letters, 7.11.1), Pompey in four lengthier sentences (*Hist.* 2.98.4–6). Both then used their letters to convey the situation in which their respective armies now found themselves, Nicias at great length and with extensive detail (7.11.3–7.14.2)—this is where most of his narrative and analysis are—Pompey by writing, '[t]hus the condition of my army and that of the enemy is the same: for neither is paid, and each, if victorious, is able to march into Italy' (*itaque meo et hostium exercitui par conditio est; namque stipendium neutri datur, uictor uterque in Italiam uenire potest*, 2.98.7). Both, strikingly, mentioned that the supply of food is or will shortly be a problem. Nicias warned that were the Italians to notice that the Athenians were not sending further assistance, the 'lands that nourish us' (τὰ τρέφοντα ἡμᾶς χωρία) would go over to the enemy and the Athenians in Sicily would be driven out without a blow (7.14.3); Pompey claimed that the Senate, by not paying or supplying the army, has inflicted 'starvation, the most miserable death of all' (*fame, miserrima omnium morte*) on men and general alike (*Hist.* 2.98.1; also 3, 6, 9), itself an allusion to a phrase in Thucydides' speech of the Plataeans (3.59.3) and, beyond that, to the *Odyssey*.[15] Both, finally, ended with suggestions. Nicias counselled that the Athenians either recall the expeditionary force or reinforce it with an army and a fleet as large as those initially sent out, along with a large sum of money and a new commander to replace Nicias (7.15.1); Pompey noted that 'you'—the Senate—'are all that remains', and that the senate must help (*reliqui uos estis... subuenitis, Hist.* 2.98.10), for without this help the Senate is likely to find both army and commander back in Italy very shortly.

Thus, in 'last' letters that arrived in midwinter, after the sole commanders of expeditions to the West had been away for at least a year and a half, salvation (σωτηρία, *salus*) is requested (and Pompey indeed reminds his audience that he has been a source of *salus* in the past), while starvation (*fames*) is feared or claimed; attention is drawn to the fact of previous communication; writing is used to convey considered opinions, in Nicias' case by stressing the role of writing as different and better than speaking, in Pompey's by emphasizing speaking through writing; narratives of achievements already known to the recipients are reprised, and the current situation

---

[15] *Od.* 12.342, as noted by Gomme, *HCT* II.345–6, relying on Stahl and Poppo (1875), 108, who also cited imitations by Livy at 21.41.11 and 27.44.8.

described; and suggestions for action given, both of which include the return of the commanders. The emphasis on these particular parallels of structure and situation is surely not coincidental. Sallust could have written a letter for Pompey in which he complained only about money, mentioned *salus* and *fames* not at all, made no reference to previous communications, and gave a very different summary of events, or indeed no summary at all: Pompey's situation did not demand that these aspects be included. By including them, Sallust made Pompey's letter an allusion to Nicias', shaping and sprinkling the letter with details designed to bring the earlier letter, and earlier situation, to mind.

But is Spain a second Sicily, Pompey another Nicias? What exactly is to be brought to mind, and why? A comparison of the two letters also shows some significant differences, differences highlighted precisely by the ways in which the letters and their contexts seem so similar: knowledge of both letters helps a reader to see what Sallust is emphasizing as different and points to why these differences are important. Thus the situations of the armies are, despite the generic similarity of 'disaster' asserted by their leaders, different: Nicias' army and navy have suffered reverses and have been driven to adopt defensive positions, while Pompey's army has been successful and is still on the offensive—or could be, if his soldiers had enough to eat. The very survival of Nicias' force is (he judged, or claimed) in doubt, while Pompey's army is still strong, just very hungry and unpaid. What the two men end up asking for, beyond 'salvation', is also different, for Nicias requested either that the expedition be recalled or that more men, ships, and money be sent, and in any event petitions, himself, to be allowed to go home, while Pompey wanted only money, and his return to Rome was adduced as a threat, not a desired end. In short, the gap between the assertion of 'disaster' and what seems to have been true in their respective situations, which the allusive similarities invite the reader to compare, differs. Nicias' narrative (which follows that of Thucydides) is presented as accurate, and his assessment seems to follow plausibly from it, even if that assessment is not necessarily correct and is certainly, and prematurely, gloomy;[16] Pompey's narrative and assessment, especially in

[16] For Thucydides' narrative, see above n. 10. Westlake (1968), 192 and *HCT* IV.386 (no events 'prepare the reader fully for the tone of hopelessness which pervades this letter') noted Nicias' unwarranted gloom; Zadorojnyi (1998), 300–1 argued that this 'puzzling pessimism' was the consequence of Thucydides' assimilation of Nicias to Agamemnon in Book 2 of the *Iliad*: like Agamemnon, Nicias is adopting a 'provocative strategy' to make the Athenians take a 'decision that might change the campaign to the better . . . That is what Nicias really wants, not permission to withdraw from Sicily'. But the Nicias of the letter may not be capable of the crude plotting of the Nicias who demanded a large fleet at the beginning of Book 6 in hopes of scuttling the entire expedition: this later Nicias is indeed sick (6.102.2), and his prematurely

contrast, seem distorted and exaggerated, although the absence of surviving narrative makes it impossible to judge the extent of his distortions and exaggerations. Similarly, Nicias' requests appear to correspond well to his assessment even if those requests are not necessarily wise, while Pompey's reflect a reduction of his and his army's needs into one apparently over-simplified demand, without even asking for reinforcements and supplies of the sort that Nicias had thought the Athenians in Sicily needed.[17] Because the two situations, and two requests, differ from each other not only in broad outline but also in the extent to which they correspond to their generals' initial assertions of their seriousness, these differences highlight the contrast in the assessments made, and thereby direct attention to the qualities of the two men themselves.

This hint of Sallust's, that Pompey (in contrast to the pessimistic restraint of Nicias) has a penchant for distorting exaggeration, is confirmed by the vivid way Sallust has written his letter. For Pompey's letter, unlike Nicias', begins with a long and complex contrary-to-fact sentence that is both an over-the-top expostulation and a complaint (2.98.1):

Si aduersus uos patriamque et deos penatis tot labores et pericula suscepissem, quotiens a prima adulescentia ductu meo scelestissimi hostes fusi et uobis salus quaesita est, nihil amplius in absentem me statuissetis, quam adhuc agitis, patres conscripti!

If it had been against you and our fatherland and our household gods that I had undertaken so many toils and dangers on the many occasions from my early adolescence when, under my leadership, the most wicked enemies were routed and your salvation was secured, you could not have decreed more severe measures against me in my absence than your actions hitherto, conscript fathers!

This is not the calm reminder that the Athenians 'know' (ἴστε) the previous deeds of the expeditionary force to Sicily with which Nicias began his letter, although Nicias did *end* his letter with a polite, even pathetic assertion that he had been of service to the Athenians (7.15.2). Pompey's opening sentence roars in at an entirely different register, denunciatory and exaggerated, starting with a shout rather than a salute. In keeping with the rhetorically excited level of the letter that the opening sentence so dramatically conveys, Sallust's

gloomy assessment is more likely to derive from this newer (Hornblower, *Comm.* III.568–9), illness-tainted view of the world than from the provocative high-stakes bluffing to be expected from a general at the top of his game.

[17] Although the earlier speech of Cotta (*Hist.* 2.47.6 [2.44 McG.]) made clear that they had been asked for before: 'the commanders in Spain are demanding pay, soldiers, arm, and grain' (*imperatores Hispaniae stipendium, milites, arma, frumentum poscunt*), and see Hillman (1990), 446.

Pompey also indulges in rhetorical questions and exclamations in the body of the letter. 'Was it with this hope that the Roman people sent its sons to war?' 'Are these the rewards for wounds, and for blood spilled so often on behalf of the *res publica*?' 'By the immortal gods, do you judge me to be a stand-in for the treasury, or to be able to keep an army without grain and pay?' 'Why should I enumerate battles or winter expeditions or the towns we have destroyed or captured?' (*Hist.* 2.98.2, 3, 6). 'I am tired of writing and sending legates . . . while meanwhile scarcely one year's expenditure has been given by you for a three-year period!' he cries. '. . . O grateful fathers', he exclaims sarcastically, 'you repay us with destitution and famine!' (*Hist.* 2.98.2, 6). There are no such rhetorical expressions of indignation in Nicias' letter, the tone of which is cool, factual, and obscurely sad; Nicias' rhetorical strategy is one of enumeration, reporting, and concession, with a concentration on the interrelated components of the disaster that looms over the army emphasized by connectives between clauses and sentences (οὖν, ὥστε, and especially γάρ).[18] By itself, Pompey's letter, with its thunderous declarative statements, single meaningless concession, and few connectives, might merely suggest that he is a loud and tiresome blowhard.[19] When compared to Nicias', however, Pompey's letter cues its reader to see distortion and exaggeration as substituting for analysis, and as characteristic vices of the letter's author: Sallust's Pompey is not trying to make connexions or persuade through reason, but proceeds by determined and noisy misrepresentation.

Although both generals claimed that disaster threatened them, Pompey's opening sentence also announces a very different and exaggeratedly self-centred set of parameters in his description of the disaster. Instead of the assessment of strategic position, enemy strength, and fleet readiness that Nicias offered, Pompey's letter is about Pompey, about the Senate's financial treatment of Pompey (and the army he commands), and the Senate's lack of gratitude to Pompey (and the army). The army in Spain finds itself in a situation in which its commander, solicitous of its interests, has been trifled with, and compelled to pay the army with his own money, hopes, and credit (*Hist.* 2.98.2, 9). Where Nicias repeatedly wrote of what 'we' did, reserving expressions in the first-person singular for his own observations on the

---

[18] Tompkins (1972), 187 ranks the letter fifth (out of sixth) of Nicias' speeches in 'complexity'; the letter also (192) has a characteristically Nician passage (7.14.2–15) employing abstract terms or impersonal verbs with the infinitive, and displays (194, 196–7) Nicias' 'insistence on talking about himself, and his tendency to admit concessions that weaken his argument', seen in his other speeches as well.

[19] Concessive: only *equidem fateor* (2.98.4), 'I admit I set off for this war with more enthusiasm than good sense' (but look how brilliantly I've done!); connectives, only *quippe* (2.98.4) and *itaque* (2.98.7).

situation (ὡς ἐγὼ πυνθάνομαι, 7.12.2; ὑμῖν γράφω, 7.14.1; ἐγὼ ἡδίω μὲν ἂν εἶχον ὑμῖν ἕτερα ἐπιστέλλειν, 7.14.4) and on his own weaknesses (7.14.2, on his inability to remedy the naval problems; ἀδύνατός εἰμι ... ἀξιῶ δ᾽ ὑμῶν ξυγγνώμης τυγχάνειν, 7.15.1–2), Pompey wrote about 'me' (*Hist.* 2.98.1, 3, 8), what 'I' have done (*Hist.* 2.98.2, 4–5, 9), and 'my' army (2.98.7). One of his first-person utterances is, notably, a threat (*ego uos moneo quaesoque,* 2.98.8), while another, a final observation on the situation of his Spanish army, is his 'reluctant prediction' that his army will invade Italy (*inuito et praedicente me, Hist.* 2.98.10). Nicias mentioned his own kidney disease with almost quavering diffidence, at the end of his letter, and his request for recall on the basis of this infirmity would be a favour the Athenians would do him in recompense for all the good service he did for them in his prime (7.15.1–2). But a self-serving, even pathetic request for a favour can be (and will be) brushed aside, while a menacing demand for reciprocal recompense is harder to ignore, especially from Pompey.[20] For Pompey, it is all about Pompey, all the time, and Pompey will no longer be overlooked. Again, a reading of Pompey's letter by itself conveys perfectly well the sense that the man is deafening, wearisome, and self-centred. But if Nicias' letter with its quiet if despairing strengths is brought in as a comparison, then Pompey's unremitting focus on himself takes on a much more sinister hue: this man is not just self-centred but a pathological egomaniac. Everything is about him, overshadowing the situation in Spain, the situation of the army, even the Roman Republic itself; everything will take second place to his own needs and desires, and this will make him very dangerous indeed.

The contrast between the specifically highlighted qualities of the two men, which focuses a spotlight on Pompey's huge and distorting egotism, is emphasized when the two letters are set side by side, for both authors are using letters in the same way—to exemplify a man's characteristics. Nicias' letter was thus a way for Thucydides to demonstrate the man's self-protective timidity and over-cautious intellect, to show him as a man inferior to Pericles, like all of Pericles' other Athenian successors.[21] Sallust, however, was perhaps using the letter as a way of sharpening a portrait that he had so far sketched only in general terms. Earlier in Book 2 he had referred to Pompey as

---

[20] *Contra* Pasoli (1966), 49, Hillman (1990), 448 n. 19 argues that it is 'wilful to see a threat of violence here', and that Pompey is only stating the facts. The sentence alone could be read that way, but only if one believes that Pompey did not control his army; and the broader context of the heightened tone of the letter itself, with its angry outrage, suggests that the register is dropping to quiet menace, not to the quiet statement of fact.

[21] On Thucydides' characterization of Nicias elsewhere, see (e.g.) Westlake (1968), 95, 172, 185, 193–4, 210, 'no suggestion ... that he believed Nicias to have been lacking in intelligence', and Rood (1998), 185–92; successors, 2.65.10.

'moderate in all things, except in seeking domination' (*modestus ad alia omnia, nisi ad dominationem, Hist.* 2.17 [McG. 2.18]) and 'shameless of spirit' (*animo inuerecundo, Hist.* 2.16 [McG. 2.17]);[22] in the letter, the displays of noisy misrepresentation and egotism are by no means moderate, and therefore must be considered tools or engines of Pompey's shameless drive for power. What is specifically learned about Pompey from the contrast within the linked letters contributes significant and ominous details to Sallust's character-portrait, and suggests that the letter is showing that character in aggressive action, driving to dominate rather than attempting, as Nicias had, to inform, to persuade, and to protect himself.

Sallust not only used the literary device of the letter in a more active and significant way than Thucydides had, and not only linked the letters to make the contrasts between the two men more specific and emphatic, but used one further allusion, to another Thucydidean character, to push the reader beyond the contrasting personalities of Pompey and Nicias and into the question of harm done to the polities where the letters were received. How? One last contrast that Sallust had drawn was to the different spirits in which the expeditions had been undertaken. Nicias had judged the expedition a bad idea in the first place, and had been unwilling to go on it (ἀκούσιος ... νομίζων, 6.8.4), while Pompey in his letter admits that he 'had set off for this war with more enthusiasm than thought' (*fateor me ad hoc bellum maiore studio quam consilio profectum, Hist.* 2.98.4). One might think Pompey's attitude merely one of boyish imprudence if one read the letter in isolation. But thanks to this pointed and allusive contrast on Sallust's part, the reader can see that Pompey's excited thoughtlessness is specifically and diametrically opposed to Nicias' unenthusiastic good judgement: Nicias thinks too much, and lacks all enthusiasm, while Pompey thinks too little, and has been over-enthusiastic. In Nicias' case, this attitude has ominous implications for the expedition itself. In Pompey's case, on the other hand, there is no hint that his attitude will be bad for the expedition, and no suggestion (from other sources) that the expedition was harmed by Pompey's *maiore studio quam consilio.*

---

[22] Pompey also 'believed that he would be the equal of king Alexander' (*similem fore se credens Alexandro regi, Hist.* 3.88 [3.84 McG.]). On Sallust's characterization of Pompey in the *Histories*, see Syme (1964), 201, 'chill ambition, boasting, menace and mendacity'; Scanlon (1980), 195; McGushin (1992), 17–18; and Kraus and Woodman (1997), 36–7, 'Pompey's letter captures his ambition, talent, and self-importance' (*contra* Earl (1966), 109, who thought that 'there appears to be no trace of the "animus inverecundus" which Sallust saw as his chief characteristic'!); on Sallust's use of speeches and letters to bear out or subvert characterizations in the narrative, see Scanlon (1980), 151 and (sceptical) Büchner (1982), 241.

Instead, this contrast constitutes an allusion of its own, and thereby points to where Pompey's impact will most be felt; for Pompey in his heedless bravado is not only unlike Nicias, but much like Nicias' opponent Alcibiades, characterized by Nicias in the Sicilian debates as 'youthful' and acting 'hastily' (νεωτέρῳ... καὶ ὀξέως, 6.12.5). Indeed, the parallels with Alcibiades are more extensive than this, and neatly match several details of Pompey's letter: Alcibiades too had started the speech Thucydides gives him at 6.16–6.18 with ruthless assertions of his own self-importance and frank claims to special treatment (6.16.1–6); he had discounted obstacles (6.17.2–6) while overlooking many of Nicias' objections (6.10.1–6.11.7); he had asserted the value of benefitting not only himself but also the city with his 'private resources' (τοῖς ἰδίοις τέλεσι μὴ ἑαυτὸν μόνον ἀλλὰ καὶ τὴν πόλιν ὠφελῇ, 6.16.3) because Nicias had warned against men who 'injure the public fortune while they spend their own' (τοὺς τοιούτους τὰ μὲν δημοσίᾳ ἀδικεῖν, τὰ δὲ ἴδια ἀναλοῦν, 6.12.2)—one of Pompey's complaints was that he was spending his own resources to no benefit (*Hist.* 2.98.2); and Alcibiades had himself stressed his youth (νεότης, 6.17.1), as Pompey did (*Hist.* 2.98.1). Elsewhere in Thucydides Alcibiades had also displayed the same qualities.[23] The reckless boldness, and indeed arrogance, of youth contrasted with the hesitations and equivocations of age: this was Alcibiades versus Nicias, but also Pompey versus Nicias. The reader is led first to compare Pompey with Nicias, but also then, by the pointed contrasts between the two, to look for a more appropriate parallel, and so to recall Alcibiades, whose most memorable action in the Peloponnesian War was his defection from Athens to enemy Sparta. That Pompey is not Nicias is a point driven home by the contrasts between the two letters. Where that contrast will have its greatest impact, however, is foreshadowed only by a full understanding of Sallust's allusion to Alcibiades, the opponent of Nicias and the man most similar to Pompey: only one of the two (Pompey and Nicias) will actually and intentionally harm his own city, and by reading through Nicias to Alcibiades, the reader knows which.

---

[23] For example, the first paragraph of Alcibiades' speech to the Spartans is also all about himself (6.89); when Alcibiades was first introduced in Thucydides, his youth was again stressed (5.43.2); see also Macleod (1975), 70–5 and Gribble (1999), 205–13. The parallel with Pompey is not perfect—the Athenians certainly did not believe Alcibiades to be 'moderate in all things except in seeking domination' (see 6.15.4)—but many details overlap. Stylistically, Alcibiades and Pompey also speak in a paratactic way, although the paratactic effect is achieved differently. Tompkins (1972), 204–14 emphasizes the way in which Alcibiades' use of καί in his speeches reduces complexity and antithesis: 'the ultimate effect of this practice is to give an impression of clarity and simplicity' (209), and it is as if 'there were no call for discussion of nuances and no need for subordination of thought'. Pompey uses no such device; his clarity and simplicity are much more the products of his direct statements and exclamations, a kind of 'because I say so' style.

How harm will come, whether to expedition or polity, is eventually made clear by the contrasting reception given to the two letters, and thus, at a more fundamental level, by the contrast between the audiences themselves—Athenian democrats and Roman senators—to whom the letters are written. Just as the linking of the letters through allusion prompted a comparison of situations and characters, so too that linking prompts a comparison of the letters' recipients and reception. Again, the elements of the contrast that Sallust most wishes to emphasize are brought out by setting the recipients, and the strategies undertaken to approach them, side by side. Nicias was writing to the prickly Athenian democrats, who must be persuaded and who can be difficult to persuade. Nicias, indeed, thought the Athenians intimidated messengers, who therefore did not report 'what is' (τὰ ὄντα) because 'they wished to ingratiate themselves with the multitude' (τῷ ὄχλῳ πρὸς χάριν τι λέγοντες, 7.8.2). He therefore wrote in his own hand, to give his message special emphasis and to lay out exactly what he wished the Athenians to learn, and told the Athenians a few home truths about themselves in his letter.[24] For 'I know your nature', he wrote, 'you who wish to hear the most pleasant things but who cast blame later, if something you were told by others does not turn out to be the case' (τὰς φύσεις ἐπιστάμενος ὑμῶν, βουλομένων μὲν τὰ ἥδιστα ἀκούειν, αἰτιωμένων δὲ ὕστερον, ἤν τι ὑμῖν ἀπ᾽ αὐτῶν μὴ ὁμοῖον ἐκβῇ, 7.14.4). Nicias' rhetorical strategy is for the most part in keeping with the directness of this comment rather than with the shrewdness of this observation, for he did not attempt to manipulate the Athenians with what they want to hear—good news—but instead told them what he wanted them to know. He explained what he has written by saying, 'I might have written you other information, more pleasant than this—but indeed nothing more useful, since it is necessary for you to decide matters here on the basis of clear knowledge' (τούτων ἐγὼ ἡδίω μὲν ἂν εἶχον ὑμῖν ἕτερα ἐπιστέλλειν, οὐ μέντοι χρησιμώτερά γε, εἰ δεῖ σαφῶς εἰδότας τὰ ἐνθάδε βουλεύσασθαι, 7.14.4). He aimed to be clear so he could be useful, and therefore did not adjust his rhetorical strategy to accommodate the predilections of his listeners.

Except, fatally, at the end of the letter. For here he concluded by giving the Athenians more than one option, to recall the expedition *or* to send more men, ships, and money, and more than one option about his own return, presenting it as a favour rather than a necessity. Indeed, contrary to his own principle of telling his audience what his audience needs to know, he has in fact given the Athenians no useful information *about himself* except the one bald, late, and unsupported statement of kidney disease, and his pathetic

---

[24] As Rood (1998), 190 (with further references) notes, Nicias' observations about the Athenians' nature 'are variously confirmed elsewhere'.

appeal to the Athenians' ξυγγνώμη, indulgence, is a lapse into emollient and timidly obfuscating sentimentality. He therefore failed to persuade the Athenians of perhaps the most important and only unequivocal point, that he himself should be recalled.[25] Nicias wavered from his persuasive strategy here at the end of his letter, giving the Athenians choices about what to do while himself sliding into ingratiating appeal, and therefore did not persuade the Athenians to make all the right decisions. His rhetorical strategy, itself a response to his perceptions of his audience, shaped his letter, but so too did his own character. Both allowed his audience of Athenians to make a decision that would, in the end, harm the expedition.

Pompey's letter is itself also the product of his perceptions of his audience and his character, although it is the linking of the letters and the concomitant comparison with Nicias that especially make the reader see that Pompey's distorting egotism is not just a revelation of his character but a tactic designed to work on this particular audience—that it too is a rhetorical strategy, albeit one that makes the most of Pompey's natural inclinations. For Pompey's audience was the Roman Senate, which, in striking contrast to Nicias' Athenians (and indeed to what a reader might expect), had here in the mid-seventies none of the corporate capacity to intimidate that the Athenian *demos* of Nicias' time so clearly possessed; indeed, despite the way Sulla had strengthened it and purged all the opposition, the mighty Roman Senate could itself be intimidated.[26] This is the assessment that Pompey's rhetorical strategy demonstrates, for the letter aims not to persuade but, through abuse and threats and yelling, to break the Senate's will: this audience was weak, not strong. This was a weighty letter,[27] for the new consuls of the new year, 'struck heavily' by it (*grauiter perculsi, Hist.* 2.98.10), as a consequence push hard to provide Pompey with pay and reinforcements 'both because the situation was critical and because they were afraid that, if he led an army into Italy, they

---

[25] Diodotus had already pointed out the danger of valuing the pursuit of χάρις from the audience over the speaker's γνώμη (3.42.5–6), and this is the trap Nicias here falls into. As Rood (1998), 190 also notes, Nicias' 'appeal to his past services...reflects the state of mind which militates against his overcoming the assembly's limitations'. Westlake (1968), 194 argues that Thucydides 'implies that [the Athenians'] refusal to relieve Nicias of his command was an act of folly, since...the indecision of Nicias proved ultimately disastrous'.

[26] Philippus notes that Lepidus has intimidated the senate and has made himself 'a man to be feared' (*metuendum effecit*), while the senators detract from their own *dignitas* by passing *mollitia decretorum* (*Hist.* 1.77.3 [1.67 McG.]), and those who continued to negotiate did so because they 'sought peace out of fear' (*metu pacem repetentes, Hist.* 1.77.5); so perhaps even their own self-image was not strong.

[27] Fronto (*ad L. Verum* 2.1.15) referred to this letter as *litterae...graues* (*Cn. Pompeii ad senatum de stipendio litterae graues*), which, as his praise of Verus makes clear, is an appropriate characteristic of a letter written to the senate; but *graues* can also simply mean 'weighty'.

themselves would have neither praise nor dignity' (*cum summae rei gratia tum, ne exercitu in Italiam deducto neque laus sua neque dignitas esset, Hist.* 2.98.10). Nicias must persuade, but is not entirely successful; Pompey can intimidate, and is entirely successful. His character, and his rhetorical strategy, compelled the Senate to make a decision that would help the expedition but would, in the end, harm Rome and their own pre-eminence within it.

The Athenians, as Nicias depicted them, were strong but had one weakness, a desire to hear only good news. As the contrast between the letters' rhetorical strategies—based on the (correct) perceptions of their authors—emphasizes, the Roman Senate is, unexpectedly, much weaker. These differences then play out in how the letters are received. For where the Athenians took swift and united action in response to Nicias' letter (7.16.1),[28] the response of the Roman Senate to Pompey was, this time, different: on this occasion, instead of ignoring the letter (as the senators had ignored previous letters for a year and a half), there was a reaction, but it was sadly undignified and patently self-centred. The first action of the senators after the reading of the letter was not to respond to the crisis, but rather to make the apportionment, between the two outgoing consuls, of the two proconsular provinces that had been designated by the Senate for that year—a selfish or business-as-usual (non-) response, the impropriety of which Sallust emphasizes by using the conjunctive *sed* to begin the sentence (*Hist.* 2.98.10). Only after this did the two new consuls respond to Pompey's letter and push to send him assistance. They were strongly supported in this by the nobility (*adnitente maxime nobilitate*), of whom 'many now followed their ferocity with speech and words with deeds' (*cuius plerique iam tum lingua ferociam suam et dicta factis seque<bantur>, Hist.* 2.98.10), perhaps meaning that this group of the nobility first felt ferocious, then said ferocious things, and finally undertook ferocious actions.[29] *Ferocia* is uncontrolled fury, 'berserker' behaviour, characteristic of barbarians and the young—but deeply inappropriate in the nobility of Rome, for whom self-control should have been the most striking

---

[28] Westlake (1968), 194 speculates that Thucydides 'may be intentionally contrasting the Athenians with Nicias by showing that they at least had no difficulty in making decisions, whether right or wrong'.

[29] The text here is problematic: as Maurenbrecher (1891–3), 103 notes, *postremae incertae*. It was Hauler who supplied *sequebantur*; Diggle (1983), 60 emends to *aequabant*, which Reynolds (1991), 183 considers 'possibly correct' (*fort. recte*), although the latter is conservative and prints only *seque****. If Diggle is correct, the translation would then be 'provided speech equal to their ferocity and deeds equal to the words'. Diggle also, however, considers this phrase praise of the *nobiles*, and since he (following a suggestion of Shackleton Bailey) thinks this unlikely, he also follows Shackleton Bailey in emending *et* to *nec*, thus 'provided speech equal to their ferocity but not deeds equal to the words'; McGushin (1992), 247 argues that Antonius' actions against the pirates renders this suggestion 'untenable'.

characteristic.[30] The response to the letter is, in short, depicted as wrong and fractured, moving from proconsuls to new consuls to nobility to a majority of the nobility, with an emphasis on personal motivations and bad behaviour rather than on statesmanship and group strength: which province do *I* get? what about *my* praise and *dignitas*? how do *I* feel? Rome was full of individuals thinking about themselves and acting 'ferociously', without self-control; this weakened both Senate and city, and a 'weighty' letter full of anger and threat was therefore most effective: Pompey's letter is like a blow from a club falling heavily on a weakened and cracking table. Nicias' persuasion caused his usually fractious audience to unite in what might even have been a public-spirited manner, while Pompey's threats caused the internal fragmentation of his audience into selfishness and vice to become only that much more apparent.

Both the Athenian and the Roman responses are a surprise. Beyond the contrasts between the audiences and their reactions—the swift and unified response of the Athenians, the delayed, multiple, self-centred, and unbecoming reactions of the Senate—is an underlying similarity, a parallel defeat of expectation. Thucydides, for example, has depicted an Athenian assembly regularly given to the enraged punishment of generals who have disappointed;[31] but here Nicias is neither punished nor even recalled. Thucydides has also depicted the Athenians in assembly as regularly split by debate and often slow to take action, but at their worst when they act quickly and in a fit of passion.[32] Here, however, no debate or delay is reported, but no anger or

---

[30] *Ferocia* as a primitive and reckless quality, characteristic of youth, barbarians, Roman kings (in Livy), and Turnus: see Traub (1953), 252–3, daring and excitable insolence, contrasted with *uirtus* and *pudor*; Eckert (1970) wild fighting in defiant disregard of the consequences; Morel (1976), 674–5, with further references, esp. to Dumézil; and Michel (1981), 522–5 and Penella (1990), 211–13 on *ferocia* in the early books of Livy, especially Romulus, Tullus Hostilius, and Horatius.

[31] e.g. Pericles (2.65.3); Eurymedon and his colleagues (4.65.4); and Thucydides himself (5.26.5).

[32] Thucydides depicts disagreements and debates occurring regularly in the Athenian assembly, see 1.32.1–1.44.2 (two separate assemblies, with different opinions, on the matter of the Corcyraean alliance); 1.139.3–1.145.1 (on the Spartan ultimatum); 3.36.2–3.49.2 (the debates over the fate of the Mytilenians); 4.27–8 (Nicias, Cleon, and Pylos); 5.45.3–5.46.1 (Alcibiades and Nicias spar over the Argive alliance and the Spartans); 6.6.2–3 (response to Egestans debated in a number of assemblies); 6.8–6.26 (debate over Sicily, after an initial agreement many others speak, and Nicias tries to derail the expedition). Disagreements and changing their minds are considered by Cleon a characteristic weakness of Athenian democracy (3.37.3), by Diodotus a strength (3.42.1); on the basis of Thucydides' depiction of the Athenians' passion against Pericles (2.59.2 and 2.65.3), the initial Mytilenean decision ('in the fury of the moment', 3.36.2), the response to the Spartans in 425 (4.21.2–4.22.2), and the Athenians' actions in the second half of their investigation of the Mysteries (6.60.1–6.61.5, with Meyer (2008)), it is tempting to conclude that Thucydides himself, like Diodotus, thought speedy and undebated unity dangerous as well as rare (and usually the consequence of passion rather than deliberation).

passion either, when one would have expected both: dispassionate and helpful speed is instead implied. Indeed, this is strikingly contrary to what Thucydides has specifically encouraged the reader to expect of the Athenian assembly during the Sicilian expedition, for he stated prospectively (at 2.65.11) not only that the Athenians did not 'take subsequent decisions in the best interests' of the Sicilian expedition, but that they instead 'occupied themselves with private squabbles... by which they first introduced civil discord at home'.[33] Here, however, there was no time-consuming 'squabbling' reported: the Athenians were united, swift, and apparently public-spirited in their support of the expedition, a self-contradictory and dangerous marvel.

Similarly, although Sallust's depictions of the Senate in the *Histories* do not describe a tower of dignified strength in the Roman state, the senators had in the past been able to overcome internal divisions and torpor to pull together and make decisions.[34] In the past, too, they had decided to ignore Pompey and his demands. Now, suddenly, they changed their minds, but their response was characterized by multiple self-centred and unworthy views. The contrast emphasized by parallel defeats of expectation underlines that both polities are in danger, albeit for different reasons: the Athenians because instant unity makes their unconsidered support of what should have been a

---

[33] Thuc. 2.65.11: οἱ ἐκπέμψαντες οὐ τὰ πρόσφορα τοῖς οἰχομένοις ἐπιγιγνώσκοντες, ἀλλὰ κατὰ τὰς ἰδίας διαβολὰς... καὶ τὰ περὶ τὴν πόλιν πρῶτον ἐν ἀλλήλοις ἐταράχθησαν. I stress the contradiction created by the end of the sentence, while most historians have focused on the contradiction apparently created by the first clause. Gomme, *HCT* II.196, for example, thought this statement 'inconsistent with Thucydides' own narrative; for on each occasion that Nikias asked for them, supplies and reinforcements were sent, and in good measure, and, comparatively, with little or no delay. In fact, οἱ ἐκπέμψαντες, after Alkibiades' recall, play little part in the expedition, and what they do, they apparently do well'. Gomme's judgement assumes, however, that sending what Nicias asked for was in the expedition's best interests when in fact the mistake may have been precisely in sending reinforcements. Hornblower, *Comm.* I.348, whom I have also followed in translating τὰ πρόσφορα, instead interprets these disadvantageous decisions as 'above all the recall of Alcibiades, probably also the failure to recall Nikias; and just possibly the support of Amorges'. In *Comm.* III.28–31, 559–60, Hornblower also notes that Thucydides has over-emphasized the role of the Assembly and downplayed the role of the *boulē*.

[34] The Senate could still vote the *senatus consultum ultimum* after Philippus' speech in 78 BC roused them from their lethargy (*socordia*), delaying (*cunctando*), and paralysis (*torpedo*; *Hist.* 1.77.11 and 21, 17, 19 [1.67 McG.]); that speech suggested divisions in the senate already, between those who strove to appease Lepidus and those who did not (*Hist.* 1.77.5), between supporters of Lepidus and supporters of Catulus (*Hist.* 1.77.6), and both groups together 'corrupted the deliberations of the Senate' (*consilium publicum corruperunt*); but these divisions were not signalled by Sallust as based on self-interest, and did not prevent unified action. For subsequently, when roused to it, senators were still capable of corporate action, and that continues, in 1.84 (*patres* [1.73 McG.]), 2.41 (*senatus* [2.39 McG.]), and 2.46 (*patribus* [2.43 McG.]). The verbal echoes of Cotta's speech (*Hist.* 2.47 [2.44 McG.]) in Pompey's letter (*Hist.* 2.47.2, 4/ *Hist.* 2.98.1) are perhaps also clues to the reader to remember that Cotta too would warn of the atomized self-seeking of the nobility and the dangers it posed to the *res publica* (*Cat.* 38.3).

difficult and debated decision that much more powerful, the Romans because bad behaviour and selfishness diminish the senators' corporate power, as well as Rome's, to control generals like Pompey as well as their own members in Rome. Without the contrast provided by comparing letter to letter, audience to audience, and response to response, a reader would not appreciate how unexpected both responses were, and the extent of the danger these unexpected responses represented. Only with the contrast, and the parallel visible behind the contrast, do Roman indifference, fear, and ferocity become not just historical facts but razor-sharp shards of a mirror that should have been whole, the reflection on its unshattered surface that of a single, powerful entity capable of blinding its challengers.

The letters' parallels, underlined by their similarities and their allusions from one to the other, emphasize the contrasts (of personalities, judgement, rhetoric, audience, and response), which in their particulars, and again through allusion, suggest new and ominous parallels (of capacity to do harm, and in particular of making the writers' audiences do what they should least want to do). A further and even more ominous parallel is, finally, suggested through a direct verbal allusion. Although he wavered and failed in his last paragraph, Nicias' strategy for most of his letter had been to send the Athenians written information that they would be able to grasp 'clearly' (σαφῶς): his factual, and written, presentation, carefully interlaced with explanation, was designed 'to show the truth' (τὸ ἀληθὲς δηλῶσαι, 7.14.4), to give the Athenians the clear information he thought they needed to 'make their decisions about truth' (βουλεύσασθαι περὶ τῆς ἀληθείας, 7.8.2). Nicias' observations on the Athenians, on presenting information σαφῶς, on the desired end of ἀλήθεια, even on the unreliability of messengers because of incapacity or failures of memory (τὴν τοῦ λέγειν ἀδυνασίαν ἢ καὶ μνήμης ἐλλιπεῖς, 7.8.2), are all couched in language that calls to mind the Thucydidean language of historical interpretation and historical methodology (especially 1.22); this echoing implies that Nicias came very close to presenting the facts in a 'clear' and perfect Thucydidean way.[35] For in Thucydides, the way in

---

[35] See Marincola (1997), 67–8, Meyer (1997), 42–6, Allison (1997), 206–37, Scanlon (2002), Grethlein (2005), 67, and Meyer (2008), 32–4, all with further references; such intentional echoes may also help to explain some parallels between Nicias' way of discussing Sicily (6.9–6.11) and Thucydides' narration of what happens. Also, Nicias, after 'perceiving' (αἰσθόμενος) and 'seeing' (ὁρῶν), then, as emphasized (noted above n. 14), 'wrote' (ἔγραψεν) a letter (7.8.1–2). Writing is important, for it permits Nicias to set down his own opinion 'with nothing "made to disappear" in the telling' (τὴν αὑτοῦ γνώμην μηδὲν ἐν τῷ ἀγγέλῳ ἀφανισθεῖσαν, 7.8.2), and the stress apparently placed on Nicias' act of writing may be paralleled by the historian's stress on his own activity of writing in 1.1.1 (ξυνέγραψε) and 1.22.2 (ἠξίωσα γράφειν), both with Loraux (1986), 148–50, and the way that writing can signify 'truth', Allison (1997), 227–30.

which cities, and particularly the Athenians, make decisions—on the basis of what knowledge, with what level of care and attention, with what degree of emotion and memory—is a recurrent theme, and probably would have played an important role in his account of the end of the war and why Athens lost. His exploration of the dynamics and problems of Athenian decision-making would have been rendered more complex by the descent into, return from, and renewed descent of Athenian democracy into *stasis* in the last eight years of the war, if Thucydides' account of what happened in Corcyra in 427 can be taken as paradigmatic (as Thucydides surely intended it to be) for what happens to the clarity of language, the rule of law, and thoughtful decision-making when any city falls into *stasis*. Nicias' failure of nerve—his offer of choices and his lapse into sentimentality at the end of his letter—is therefore all the more agonizing when the reader recognizes just what role the Athenian decision here probably played in Thucydides' history of the war. Nicias' presentation was *almost* completely σαφῶς, and therefore could *almost* produce the right decision and allow his audience to come to ἀλήθεια—but not quite. And so another small step down the path to destruction was taken.

Pompey, too, makes reference to this complex of ideas in his letter, although—since so little of Sallust's *Histories* survives—it is harder to place Pompey's letter among the larger themes of the work in the same way.[36] Yet Sallust's themes were also Thucydidean. For although the fragments of Sallust's *Histories* that survive show little of Thucydides' obsession with types of knowledge, levels of understanding, or the need to explain decisions that were wrong,[37] Pompey nonetheless is found declaring in this letter that his achievements have been made 'sufficiently clear' (*satis clara, Hist.* 2.98.6) to the Senate, the only use of *clarus* in the sense of σαφῶς in the surviving portions of the *Histories*.[38] Similarly, as Sallust notes in his prologue, 'truth' is also one of his aims in writing, as ἀλήθεια was for Thucydides (*neque me diuersa pars in ciuilibus armis mouit a uero, Hist.* 1.6 [McG. 1.7]).[39] *Clara* here in the letter

---

[36] Earl (1966), 109, for example, saw 'no hidden significance in the letter of Pompey' and no connexion with what he judged were the wider themes of the work.

[37] Syme (1964), 248 n. 49: 'Sallust . . . seems hardly aware of the difficulty of establishing facts', although as Marincola (1997), 78 notes, 'the absence of such [methodological] remarks in Sallust . . . should not be seen as evidence for a [Roman] de-emphasis on inquiry and autopsy' in establishing facts, since Sallust 'was attempting to forge a new persona'. Yet even so, no ancient historian (including Sallust) seems to have subjected the epistemological foundation of inquiry to the scrutiny that Thucydides did.

[38] *Clarus* in the sense of 'clear' (rather than 'brilliant' or 'distinguished') is used only here in the *Histories*, and not (to my knowledge) in the other monographs, as consultation of Rapsch and Najock (1991), 249–50 reveals.

[39] 'Truth' as the historian's goal also appears at *Cat.* 4.3 (*quam uerissume potero paucis absoluam*). The 'truth' that Sallust seeks, however, is, according to Büchner (1963), 249–52,

and *uerum* there in the prologue, in the context of the civil war of Sallust's own time (*ciuilibus armis*), encourage the reader to recall Thucydides' complex intertwinings of the failure of understanding and the failure of cities.

Indeed, the fragments of the prologue of the *Histories*, which are famously in intertextual dialogue with Thucydides' account of the Corcyraean *stasis*, convey the sense that Rome (like Sallust himself) is already enmeshed in civil war, or very close to it, an impression that Pompey's letter will strengthen.[40] In the *stasis* at Corcyra, words were not only subject to re-evaluation[41] but bold action and violence trumped debate and discussion (one side τολμηρῶς πρὸς τὰ ἔργα ἐχώρουν . . . while the other ἔργῳ οὐδὲν δεῖν λαμβάνειν, 3.83.3–4); Pompey's words in his letter are still used in a customary way, but his letter is short, to the point, and intolerant, for he has already made his point 'clearly' and has been ignored. 'Clarity' was important but, as with Nicias and his attempt to present his views σαφῶς, has not had the desired effect, so Pompey is losing patience with words. Instead, 'actions are so much stronger than words' (*quando res plus ualet quam uerba*, *Hist.* 2.98.6) was his minatory observation, while words followed by deeds are what most of the nobility, having expressed their *ferocitas*, will offer him in return. In Rome, decision-making based on discussion or even speeches—on any form of words—is almost over.[42] Pompey's spoken words in this written letter do finally produce

'contextual' and does not give us guides to human behaviour in past or future; Scanlon (1998), 223 argues that 'Sallust conceived of his own project as one of revealing the often complex and hidden truths behind events'. As so often in ancient historians (Woodman (1988), 70–4; Marincola (1997), 158–70), Sallust's achievement of truth is asserted by an avowal of impartiality (*eo magis quod mihi a spe metu partibus rei publicae animus liber erat*, *Cat.* 4.3), whereas Thucydides' construction of the concept of 'truth' (although his historical efforts are also buttressed by a non-specific statement of impartiality, οὐδ᾽ ὡς ἐμοὶ ἐδόκει, 1.22.2) is considerably more epistemologically complex; see above n. 36.

[40] See Avenarius (1957), 52–3; Büchner (1982), 335–6, 339–42; Scanlon (1980), 168–9, 172–4, 196–9, 202 on *Hist.* 1.7 and Thuc. 3.82.2; Funari (1996), 14–15; Schmal (2001), 149; Pelling (forthcoming, b) argues that even loose Thucydidean 'texturing' gives 'resonance' in Greek authors writing about Rome: 'to be reminded of Thucydides is to be reminded of that whole hard-edged political and military world that Thucydides described, where words were so often at odds with deeds . . . and where . . . stasis, civil conflict, provided the prism through which the most brutal and unsettling aspects of warfare became particularly visible and stark'. Thucydides' treatment of *stasis* at Corcyra was a Sallustian favourite, alluded to or imitated perhaps as many as fourteen times in Sallust's extant work, see Perrochat (1949), 9, 15–16; Avenarius (1957), 51; Büchner (1982), 336–42, fourteen times; Syme (1964), 246, twelve times.

[41] See, for a discussion of this interpretation of Thuc. 3.82.4, Hornblower, *Comm.* I.483, with further references.

[42] C. Licinius Macer, speaking to the people in Book 3, warns them (in language that echoes that of Pompey in his letter) not to 'change the names of things in the light of your own cowardice, calling slavery "leisure" ' (*ego uos moneo quaesoque, ut animaduertatis neu nomina rerum ad ignauiam mutantes otium pro seruitio appellatis*, *Hist.* 3.48.13 [3.34 McG.]), and begins his peroration to them with 'and thus, enough words have been said!' (*itaque uerborum satis*

the results he demands, but civil war, with actions deciding results, is almost upon all of them, and Pompey—as his prominence in the fragments of the _Histories_ shows—is a major cause of it.[43] Complex Thucydidean musings on language and knowledge have virtually no role in the Rome of (what survives of) Sallust's _Histories_, but only because in Rome people are shouting, words are rapidly coming to be revalued, and actions are trumping speech: the Rome of the _Histories_ has _already_ proceeded much further down the path to ruinous civil war than Thucydides' Athens had. Two allusions in Pompey's letter therefore can be seen to point to a Thucydidean theme and, with it, a world of Thucydidean trouble signalled in the proem of the _Histories_ itself; this in turn permits the reader to place Pompey's letter in its proper context, that of looming _stasis_, and to recognize that the letter itself is an element in a chain of causation. Sallust is conveying the grim reality of what Thucydides would have described had the latter finished his work, and Pompey's letter is one clear step along the way.

A comparison of the letters of Nicias and Pompey thus reveals a productive mix of similarities and contrasts: enough similarities to establish that Sallust intended an allusion to Nicias' 'most famous' or 'noble' letter, and enough pointed and wide-reaching contrasts, and further allusions, to invite the reader to observe how different the men themselves were, and then to read through these differences to note the similarities between Pompey and Nicias' rival Alcibiades, who turned against his own city. The contrast between the two recipients of the letters and their responses—Athenian democrats and Roman senators and nobles—was (through Sallust's emphasis) even more extreme, the first (apparently) united, strong, and public-spirited, the second fracturing, weak, and self-centred. These revelations about the nature of each through their response were unexpected, a similarity that suggests that these moments of reaction to the letters were in both cases a turning point in the larger narrative of downward spiral. That there was a downward spiral in Rome is, finally, made clear by Sallust's allusions (through _clara_ to σαφῶς) to Thucydides' association of clarity and decision-making, and (through actions trumping words) to Thucydides' understanding of the failure of language as a symptom of the disintegration caused by civil strife, which make the reader

---

dictum est, Hist. 3.48.25). This Thucydidean theme of the value and use of words changing in civil war is also found in a Sallustian speech of 63 BC, _Cat._ 52.11, where Cato claims that 'we have long since lost the true designations of things' (_iam pridem equidem nos uera uocabula rerum amisimus_); at _BJ_ 41.9; and in the proem to the _Histories_, _Hist._ 1.12; all with Scanlon (1980), 79–82 and (1998), 203–4 and n. 72.

[43] As McGushin (1992), 17–18 also thinks highly likely; Scanlon (1980), 215 notes Sallust's focus on 'crucial points in Rome's decline', and this breaking of the Senate by Pompey may have been one (of many).

(again) read through the contrast to discover the underlying similarities between Athens and Rome. The close reader of Sallust thereby becomes a better reader of Thucydides as well, understanding more clearly just what a fatal flaw Thucydides thought the Athenians' addiction to 'pleasantness' was, and how dangerous speedy and unreflective action taken by a strong Athens could be. In the end, similarities and verbal allusions between the letters prompt a comparison, and the contrast that emerges from that comparison then suggests, through allusion, a fundamental parallel—the impending death of language, descent into ferocious action, and doom of civil war. Once again.

7

Dionysius of Halicarnassus and Livy on the Horatii and the Curiatii

S. P. Oakley

This essay in comparison has three aims: to illustrate the skill with which both Dionysius of Halicarnassus and Livy tell the tale of the triple combat of the Horatii and the Curiatii and the subsequent trial of Horatius;[1] to show how they shaped in different ways the similar material that they inherited from the Roman annalistic tradition;[2] and to make some observations on the wider historiographical significance of their techniques.

Dionysius' self-consciousness stands out even among the self-absorbed ancient historians; and he frames no tale more self-consciously than this. Before the combat comes:

3.18.1 Since my subject demands that I expound precisely (ἀκριβῶς) both the nature of the battle and the calamities resembling the reversals in the theatre (θεατρικαῖς ἐοικότα περιπετείαις) that occurred after the battle, I shall endeavour to offer an exposition not without diligence (ἀκριβείας) and to speak about each of these things with precision, so far as it is within my power.

Long ago I spoke on this subject, at Tony Woodman's invitation, to the Department of Classics in the University of Durham; I am grateful to those present, and esp. to Prof. D. A. West, for their observations. For helpful criticism of this greatly changed published version I thank Professors C. S. Kraus, D. S. Levene, and C. B. R. Pelling.

[1] Earlier discussions of Livy's account of the Horatii and the Curiatii include Burck (1964), 150–3, Ogilvie (1965), 105–17 (esp. 106 and 109), Solodow (1979) = (2009), Fries (1985), 67–87, and Feldherr (1998), 123–44; most say something also about Dionysius' narrative, of which Walker (1993), 363–70 offers a fuller discussion. Burck's book offers the classic general comparison of Dionysius and Livy.

[2] Since there is very little reason to believe that a triple combat between the Horatii and Curiatii ever took place, that there was ever an important settlement at Alba Longa, or that reliable information survived from the 7th cent. BC into the Roman annalistic tradition, the entire narratives of this episode in both writers must ultimately be the product of free composition. However, the loss of all earlier annalistic accounts means that we can neither document the stages by which the tale grew nor prove that any particular detail is owed to the imagination of Dionysius or Livy.

After the trial comes:

3.21.10 This was the outcome of the affairs of the family of the Horatii, which involved remarkable and sudden reversals of fortune (θαυμαστὰς καὶ παραδόξους περιπετείας).

As the Greek words show, any reading of the episode needs to touch on three issues important for the wider understanding of Greek historiography: the relationship of history and tragedy; the attitude of the historians to the marvellous; and the meaning of ἀκρίβεια.

The influence of the themes and techniques of tragedy on the ancient historians from Herodotus onwards does not require another full exposition;[3] I note merely that, since no tale in ancient historical writing is painted in more self-consciously tragic colours than ours, it is a pity that those writing on the topic have taken little notice of it—not least because Dionysius rarely plays the tragic historian. Writing about marvels, too, goes back in historiography to Herodotus, but, again, our episode is exceptional in Dionysius, who is in general restrained with regard to the marvellous and paradoxical[4] and less interested than Livy in pointing reversals of fortune.[5]

By contrast, ἀκρίβεια ('precision') was very important to him.[6] His fullest discussions of his belief that historical narrative should be detailed are found in two programmatic passages.[7] At 7.66.1–5, which occurs after Coriolanus' conviction, he explains that ἀκρίβεια in political narrative demands the full exposition of the speeches made by the leading participants; and he seems to imply that its equivalent in battle-narrative are topographical description, description of arms and tactics, and exhortations of generals. At 11.1, in his account of the fall of the Decemvirate, he again (§3) makes the point that a proper history needs the full exposition of arguments used in politics, but his justification goes further than in the earlier passage, and beyond the defence of speeches. For history to be a suitable instrument for teaching, and for it to give pleasure, it needs to offer a full and convincing account of important events themselves and (with a deep bow to Thucydides) of their causes.[8]

---

[3] For recent discussion see Rutherford (2007); Walbank (1960), 224–41 is the classic older treatment. On tragic and other emotions in the historians see Marincola (2003).

[4] But see e.g. 5.8.6 (on Brutus) and 6.13.4 (on the epiphany of Dioscuri at Regillus).

[5] μεταβολή ('change') features little in his narrative and, apart from the two instances quoted, he uses περιπέτεια ('reversal') only twice: at *Thuc.* 5 the θεατρικαὶ περιπέτειαι are in the derogatory context of tales told by such writers as Hellanicus; at *AR* 2.6.4 the context is generalized.

[6] Fantasia (2004), which includes extensive bibliography and citation of key ancient texts, supersedes previous synoptic treatments. For Dionysius see also Schultze (1986), 126–7.

[7] Other important passages are 1.5.2, 1.5.4, 1.6.3, 1.23.1, and 2.61.3.

[8] ἀκριβῶς ('in detail') appears at 7.66.3 and 11.1.4.

What in practice this ἀκρίβεια entailed, both in description of battle and in speeches that outline the causes of battle, is illustrated nicely by the preliminaries to the story of the Horatii and the Curiatii, which occupy most of the opening of Book 3 and may be summarized chapter by chapter. If to some even this summary seems excessively long, then this response illustrates the risk Dionysius took in writing at such length.

Chapters 1–3. Dionysius introduces the reign of Tullus Hostilius, turning swiftly to Tullus' martial affairs: the ruler of Alba Longa, Cluilius, becomes jealous of Rome's prosperity and persuades some poor Albans to raid Rome, hoping that the inevitable Roman reprisal will make the Albans think that the Romans started the war. However, he first sends an embassy to Rome to demand satisfaction. Tullus, conjecturing rightly that the embassy has been sent in the hope that the Romans will reject its claims and thereby incur the blame for starting a war against their mother-city, delays receiving the embassy until he has sent a counter-embassy. Its claims are duly rejected by the Albans themselves, who imagine incorrectly that the Romans had already placed themselves in the wrong. **4–5.** Both sides go out to fight, but when they see the powerful array of the other army they do not come to blows. Tired with the delay, and generally regarded as responsible for the war, Cluilius prepares to fight but dies that night. The Albans conjecture several reasons for his sudden death, some point to divine πρόνοια ('foresight') and wrath because of his guilt in bringing the war, others to poisoning by political opponents, others to his committing suicide because his plans had failed, and others to the natural end of his life. Mettius Fufetius succeeds Cluilius; he delays battle on seeing his own people's lack of enthusiasm and unpropitious sacrifices. When he heard about a conspiracy of the Veientines and Fidenates against both cities, he decided to make the first move towards peace. **6.** These two towns, tired of being subject to Rome, plan to fall on the victorious army after the Albans and Romans had fought, but the delay in the fighting between Alba and Rome allows their plans to be revealed. **7.** The Romans, too, had heard of the conspiracy and agree to parley. Fufetius makes clear that his request for a truce was not a sign of weakness; rather, he had been looking for a way to end the hostilities since coming to power, regarding the ties that bound the two countries as far more potent than their differences. He admits to the Romans his difficulties with his own people and in making propitious sacrifices. However, he urges Rome, as the daughter-city, to respect Alba, and he makes plain the danger from the Veientes and Fidenates. **8.** Mettius reveals his information about their conspiracy to Tullus, having letters read and an informer expound his knowledge. He then renews his appeal for peace to Rome. **9.** Tullus then states that the Romans likewise regarded the war as futile but had not thought it right first to sue for peace since Cluilius had begun the war. He argues that the two nations should make lasting peace and combine their resources, preferably with Rome as the recognized capital. **10.** After consulting his advisory council Fufetius tells Tullus that the Albans agreed to the pooling of resources but not the abandoning of their old city. Discussion follows as to which city should have primacy. Dionysius says that much was spoken on both sides, but gives the first speech to Fufetius. He supports Alba's claim largely from its antiquity and the fact that it had not sullied its constitution by giving citizenship to aliens. **11.** Tullus responds that daughter-cities did sometimes dominate mother cities and defends Roman practice with regard to citizenship, to the satisfactory results of which he points. He suggests that the two cities should resolve their differences in a way traditional to the Greeks, by having a portion of the army fight another portion. **12.** Peace is agreed but the two sides differ as to how many men should fight: Tullus is in favour of as few men fighting as possible, and prefers a single combat, with himself as the Roman champion; Fufetius prefers a larger number. Finally they settle on three champions for each side. **13.** There is remarkable enthusiasm (§1 θαυμαστή...φιλοτιμία) on each side, but divine foresight (§3 θεία τις πρόνοια) had prepared champions of birth 'remarkable because of its extraordinary nature' (θαυμαστῆς διὰ τὸ παράδοξον): an Alban Sicinius had married twin daughters to a Roman called Horatius and an Alban called Curiatius; each daughter became pregnant with triplets at the same time and the two nations cherished these triplets as a good omen. **14.** Fufetius suggests to Tullus that they should use divine providence and ask the two sets of triplets to be champions. He too uses language like that of the narrator: (§1) θαυμασιώτατον ('most remarkable'); θαυμαστῇ τινι καὶ θείᾳ...εὐεργεσίᾳ ('a remarkable and divine...beneficence'), §3 θεία τις ...τύχη ('a divine chance'). **15.** Tullus agrees, referring to θαυμαστὴ... τις...τύχη ('a remarkable chance'), but worries that the young men may not wish to fight relatives with whom they had grown up. Fufetius responds that he likewise had thought of this but had checked first with the Curiatii themselves, and the young men had displayed remarkable enthusiasm (θαυμαστῇ προθυμίᾳ). **16.** Tullus consults the Horatii, saying that there is no shame in refusing to fight kin. They consult their father, who is delighted at their respect for paternal authority but gives them a free choice. Since the Curiatii had earlier banished ties of kinship to second place, they choose to fight. The Romans tell the Albans this news.

Even this brief summary shows that in these chapters Dionysius maintains his generally pro-Roman attitude: Cluilius and the Albans are responsible for the war;[9] Fufetius is disingenuous in his speeches; Tullus, unlike Fufetius, shows his own bravery in being willing to fight on behalf of his people; and Tullus and the Romans are more concerned than Fufetius and the Albans (who first suggest the idea) about the dangers of having cousins fight each other in triple combat. Two of his particular themes are lightly touched on: his notion that the Romans were really of Greek descent is supported by the references to Greek precedents and analogies in the numerous speeches;[10] and his notion that the Romans for long avoided violence in their politics is implicit in Tullus' praise of his city's political arrangements. As for ἀκρίβεια, plainly it is found not only in the frame surrounding the climax of the tale but throughout: Dionysius provides a classic illustration of his doctrine (see esp. 11.1.3) of the importance of giving a proper account of the causes of a major event; he does not state merely that it was decided to fight a triple combat but gives an exhaustive account of the prior manoeuvres and speeches spoken on each side.[11]

Yet an astonishing wealth of detail is indeed a main characteristic of the climax of Dionysius' account. For example, he finds space in chapter 18 to describe how the triplets were dressed and their embrace before the battle, in chapter 21 for speeches made by Horatia and Horatius to each other, and in the fighting for a precise description of the wounds that afflicted the fallen triplets: note the close focus on the groin at 19.4, the neck at 19.5, the bowel and thigh at 19.6, and the dismembering of a hand at 20.3.[12]

In structure Dionysius' account of the main story falls into two parts of contrasting tone. The first deals with the triple combat, and in both subject and style it recalls epic in general and the *Iliad* in particular, a poem in which duels are frequent and warriors are dispatched with notably graphic detail and vividness.[13]

---

[9] Note esp. 3.2.1 αἴτιος: Dionysius' ἀκρίβεια has a Thucydidean obsession with causation, and this episode regularly recalls important scenes in Thucydides; see the thorough discussion of Fox (1996), 82–92.

[10] See 3.10.3, 11.2, 11.4, and 11.10. For the theme see e.g. Schultze (1986), 128–33 (with further bibliography at n. 78), Gabba (1991), 107–18.

[11] However, his habit of having speeches repeat narrative has not always been welcomed; see 7.4, 14.1, 15.2, with Schultze (1986), 128.

[12] I make explicit what Burck (1964), 152 leaves implicit ('Verwundungen!').

[13] I observe only that several of the parts of the anatomy pierced in the triple combat are similarly stricken in the *Iliad*: see e.g. 4.492 (βουβών 'groin'), 5.40 (μετάφρενον 'back'), 13.212 (ἰγνύη 'ham-string'), and 20.479 (ἀγκών 'forearm'). No parallel needs to be cited for the 'loosening of the limbs' of the Roman at 19.4. Livy's account likewise recalls epic (several parallels noted below), as do subsequent instances of single combat that he describes (see esp.

The second recalls Graeco-Roman tragedy. Dionysius has earlier stressed the role of Τύχη throughout both the preliminaries to his tale (14.3, 15.1)[14] and his account of the triple combat itself; in the latter, by making a Roman die first (19.4), then an Alban (19.5), then another Roman (19.6), and finally two Albans (20.3), he is able to draw attention to her favouring now one side, now the other (19.6, 20.3); and as if to underline the point, the cognate verb τυγχάνω is prominent in the narrative of the fighting (19.4, 19.5). Now, however, this theme of the mutability of fortune immediately takes centre-stage (21.1):

Ἔδει δὲ ἄρα καὶ τοῦτον ἄνθρωπον ὄντα μὴ πάντα διευτυχεῖν, ἀλλ᾽ ἀπολαῦσαί τι τοῦ φθονεροῦ δαίμονος. ὃς αὐτὸν ἐκ μικροῦ μέγαν ἐν ὀλίγῳ θεὶς χρόνῳ καὶ εἰς ἐπιφάνειαν θαυμαστὴν καὶ παράδοξον ἐξάρας κατέβαλε φέρων αὐθημερὸν εἰς ἄχαριν συμφορὰν ἀδελφοκτόνον.

Nevertheless, since he was but human, it was ordained that he should not live happily in all respects but should experience something of the envious divinity, who, having changed him in a short time from being of no consequence into a great man and having raised him up to a remarkable and surprising fame, on the same day cast him down to the pitiable calamity of being his sister's killer.

This sentence is packed with Herodotean echoes.[15] Above all, the narrative voice recalls Greek historiography's earliest and most famous warning-figure and its first great tragic tale, when Solon advised Croesus on the mutability of fortune (Hdt. 1.32.1–4):

Ὦ Κροῖσε, ἐπιστάμενόν με τὸ θεῖον πᾶν ἐὸν φθονερόν τε καὶ ταραχῶδες ἐπειρωτᾷς ἀνθρωπηίων πρηγμάτων πέρι. (2) ἐν γὰρ τῷ μακρῷ χρόνῳ πολλὰ μὲν ἔστι ἰδεῖν τὰ μή τις ἐθέλει, πολλὰ δὲ καὶ παθεῖν ... (4) πᾶν ἐστι ἄνθρωπος συμφορή.

Croesus, you consult me about human affairs when I know that all the divine is envious and prone to disturbance. For over a long time there is much to see, much to suffer that one would rather not.... Man is altogether contingency.[16]

However, it recalls also several other passages of Herodotus in which the mutability of human fortune is stressed, most obviously those dealing with

---

7.9–10, with which compare Quadrig., *HRR* F 10b, and on which see e.g. Oakley, *Comm.* II.113–48 and Feldherr (1998), 92–111.

[14] Note too the reference to divine beneficence at 14.1.

[15] All noted by Ek (1942), 94–7. I differ only in drawing more attention to my first passage, following Pelling (2007), 255–6.

[16] φθονερός is not common in either author, each using it only three times. Dionysius' ἐν ὀλίγῳ ... χρόνῳ reverses Herodotus' ἐν ... τῷ μακρῷ χρόνῳ (for a similar reversal, see below, p. 125) as well as echoing 7.14. Solon's ponderous counting of days is dispensed with by αὐθημερόν. In recalling Solon here, Dionysius looks back to 2.56.5, where Numa exemplifies the Solonian ideal of felicity; see Pelling loc. cit.

the letter of Amasis to Polycrates (3.40.2–3), the rich Aminocles of Magnesia (7.190),[17] the warning in a dream to Xerxes not to campaign against Greece (7.14), and Pausanias' response to Lampo (9.78.1).[18]

In underlining so heavily the tragic mode of this tale Dionysius, as we have seen, breaks with his usual practice; the extraordinary number of Herodotean echoes, almost all of passages dealing with reversals of fortune, adds to the programmatic weight of this introduction to its second part.

The scene in which the surviving Horatius confronts and kills his sister evokes the domestic difficulties put on stage in most surviving tragedies, both Greek and Roman. Dionysius now tells us much about Horatia, including details not found in Livy: her appearance outside the gates of Rome was surprising for a young unmarried woman (21.2); she was betrothed to one of her cousins (21.3); she carried herself like a demented bacchante when she heard of his death (21.3), and all the more so when she saw carried as spoil the cloak that she and her mother had woven for him (21.4). The short speeches with which Horatius and Horatia confront each other (21.5–6) recall a tragic *agon*, and their main theme, the conflicting duties owed to family and country,[19] resembles that of several tragedies. All this reinforces the theatrical reference in the opening frame.

Both Dionysius and Livy make much of the soldiers watching the triple combat, Dionysius referring to them at 18.3, 19.1–3 (the longest reference, whose length may be regarded as a further manifestation of his concern for ἀκρίβεια), 19.5, 19.6, and 20.3. The theme is implicit also in the reference to the theatre in his frame.

In employing this theme the two authors are influenced by two related traditions: ever since *Iliad* 3.342–3 onlookers and their emotions had had a traditional place in descriptions of duels, in both poetry and prose;[20] and Thucydides' celebrated account (7.71.1–4) of the Athenians watching the decisive battle in the harbour of Syracuse in 413 provided future historians with an example for emulation.[21] The description of emotions offered the opportunity for psychologizing, in Dionysius most perceptively when he points out (19.1) that what is suspected for the future is often feared as much as current danger.

---

[17] The compound ἀδελφοκτόνον recalls the compound παιδοφόνος.

[18] Add too that ἔδει occurs in several passages of Herodotus in which stress is laid on coming evil (2.161.3, 4.79.1, 5.92δ.1, 8.53.1, and 9.109.2).

[19] The theme is introduced at 17.4–5 but is developed more strongly here.

[20] See Oakley, *Comm.* II.120 (where the *Iliad* passage was missed); note also the presence of spectators, divine as well as human, for Achilles' killing of Hector at *Il.* 22.1–515.

[21] See esp. Walker (1993).

Dionysius, a Greek and a literary critic who had written a treatise on Thucydides in which this very passage is commended,[22] engages more directly than Livy with the Thucydidean precedent. With his more frequent references to the spectators than Thucydides (who has just one), he is probably trying to surpass him.[23] Thucydides divided his Athenian spectators up into three groups: those who saw Athenian ships successful at sea; those who saw Athenian ships losing; and those who saw fighting of which the outcome was unclear. As Walker observes, Dionysius places his main description of the spectators at the point in the fighting that makes, of Thucydides' three groups, those who were uncertain of the outcome the main focus of his imitation; doubtless he saw that uncertainty offered the best prospects for emotional description. In Thucydides their lack of clarity and differing reactions came from their proximity to the fighting (δι' ὀλίγου γὰρ οὔσης τῆς θέας 'for the spectacle was close at hand'). In Dionysius, by deliberate contrast, it has the reverse explanation (19.2 ἥ τε γὰρ ὄψις ἐκ πολλοῦ διαστήματος γινομένη 'for their viewing took place at a great interval'); he differs, too, in describing the emotions of both sides, and at 19.3, where he states that many watching on each side wished themselves to fight, he develops Thucydides' idea (71.3) that those watching Athenian reverses suffered more than the contestants.

To describe the emotions of those watching a battle or a spectacle is to make especially self-conscious provision of an internal audience for the narrative. As is well known,[24] readers are thereby invited to ponder how far the viewpoint of the spectators either offers an interpretation that they may wish to share or is to be equated with the perspective of the narrative voice itself. Livy's text offers more possibilities for the former move (see below), Dionysius' for the latter. His spectators feel the immediate tensions of the triple combat itself, its fluctuations, and the difficulty of discerning what is happening. Their concern with the fluctuating fortunes (note esp. 20.3 τῶν δ' ὀδυρομένων ὡς οὐκ ἂν ἔτι τῆς τύχης σφᾶς διαναστησομένης 'the Romans lamenting that Fortune would not restore them') mirrors the concerns of the authorial voice itself, which in the frame and elsewhere has emphasized reversals of fortune. And when the difficulties of the spectators are described with the words (20.2) 'both the frequent advances and retreats of the combatants and the many and quickly changing counter-movements removed any

---

[22] *Thuc.* 26.

[23] But Livy, too, has similarly frequent references; note also Liv. 7.9–10.

[24] For the exploration of these issues in the historians see e.g. Davidson (1991), Walker (1993), Feldherr (1998), and Levene (2006).

prospect of a precise understanding (τὸ ἀκριβὲς τῆς γνώμης)[25], the invitation to match the spectators' reported quest for ἀκρίβεια with that of the narrative voice itself is hard to resist.[25]

Livy's first book divides naturally into segments bounded by the reigns of the seven kings of Rome, Tullus Hostilius' being recounted at 22.1–31.8. This segment may be divided into six separate scenes or episodes: in the first (22.1–23.10) we are introduced to Tullus, and the causes of the dispute between Rome and Alba are outlined;[26] in the second (24.1–9) we meet the Horatii and the Curiatii and read the treaty by which it was agreed that they would resolve the dispute; in the third (25.1–14) comes the triple combat itself; in the fourth (26.1–14) the surviving Horatius kills his sister and stands trial;[27] in the fifth (27.1–28.11) Mettius Fufetius betrays Rome and is punished; and in the sixth (29.1–6) Alba Longa is destroyed. Livy thus builds up the story episode by episode; but these episodes interlock to form a powerful organic unity.[28] Livy regularly moulded the material presented by his sources to create individual episodes of this kind, and it has long been realized that

[25] It is not resisted by Walker (1993), 371–2. Dionysius' self-consciousness makes him a particularly attractive recipient of such readings; even more inviting than our passage are those in speeches where Dionysius' characters express a concern for ἀκρίβεια (e.g. 4.47.6, 4.81.4, 6.15.3, 10.10.1, 10.51.1, 19.15.1) and 3.5.1–2, where the Albans behave like an historian in looking for an explanation of Cluilius' death; note too Thuc. 6.91.1, 6.91.6, Pol. 4.85.5, 8.17.6. In general, speeches in histories quite often reflect metahistorically the concerns of the authorial voice: note the theological interests of Herodotus' Solon (1.32.1–9, with discussion and full bibliography at Pelling (2006), 143 n. 6), the obsession with power displayed by Thucydides' speakers, and the self-conscious exemplarity of Livy's characters (Oakley, *Comm.* I.116, Chaplin (2000), 168–9).

[26] Mensching (1966), esp. 103–6 argues, against Erb (1963), 15–17, that Livy avoided placing the blame on either side, and esp. on Rome and Tullus; he is not entirely successful in explaining away 22.2, *undique materiam excitandi belli quaerebat* ('[Tullus] was looking everywhere for the means of stirring up a war').

[27] Solodow (1979), 252–4 = (2009), 299–301 rightly notes that 'the duel abroad and the trial at home' form sharply contrasting scenes in Livy; his implication that they do not in Dionysius is a little unfair; though Dionysius writes more diffusely, both fall within his frame. Solodow further notes that some verbal echoes bind the two scenes: *ferox* (discussed below), *increpo* (25.4, 26.3, but see below), *horror* and *horrendus* (25.4, 26.6), *defigo* and *transfigo* (25.12, 26.3), and *corruo* (25.5, 26.14); add *minime gratus* and *ingratus* (25.2 and 26.5, both of those watching events) and *par* (25.7, 11, 26.12).

[28] Livy's material did not allow him to maintain such a high degree of integration in 30.1–31.8. This falls into four separate scenes: the integration of Rome and Alba (30.1–3), the defeat of the Sabines (30.4–10), the prodigy on the Alban Mount (31.1–4), and the pestilence and death of Tullus Hostilius (31.5–8). Nevertheless, the frequent references to Alba and the Albans (30.1, 2, 3, 6, 31.1, 3, 4) provide some thematic unity, and the references to Numa (31.7–8) and religion (31.6–8) round off the reign of Tullus with effective ring-composition. On such integrated compositions, see Oakley, *Comm.* I.126.

scenes of this kind are central to his narrative art.[29] I shall discuss the three relating to Horatius, although offering a full reading only of the third.

At the end of the first scene Livy reports that Tullus and Fufetius agreed that the two cities should settle their differences without full-scale conflict. Dionysius presents a very extended exposition of how the two sides agreed that the Horatii and Curiatii should be asked to settle the matter. Livy writes this (23.10–24.2):

quaerentibus utrimque ratio initur cui et fortuna ipsa praebuit materiam. (§1) forte in duobus tum exercitibus erant trigemini fratres nec aetate nec uiribus dispares. Horatios Curiatiosque fuisse satis constat . . . (§2) cum trigeminis agunt reges ut pro sua quisque patria dimicent ferro; ibi imperium fore unde uictoria fuerit. nihil recusatur; tempus et locus conuenit.

With both sides seeking a solution, a plan is hatched for which Fortune herself provided the opportunity. There were then by chance in each army triplets, not unmatched in age and strength. It is generally agreed that they were called the Horatii and Curiatii . . . The kings arrange with the triplets that they should fight with swords on behalf of their country: sovereignty would come to that side from which victory had come. They do not refuse; a time and a place is arranged.

This is an excellent example of Livy's extreme abbreviation of annalistic material, which often elsewhere in Books 1–2 gives his narrative a note of detached irony. Read against Dionysius' more extended narrative, each clause may be seen trenchantly to summarize what there often comprises a chapter or a paragraph. Dionysius would perhaps have criticized Livy's account for not giving an adequate explanation of why the extraordinary triple combat took place, but Livy will keep his expansion for what (we may conjecture) he thought really mattered: the fighting itself and not unimportant preliminaries. Despite Livy's brevity, there are some telling details: *forte*, which picks up *fortuna* in 23.10, strikingly introduces the second scene in the tale: Livy, like Dionysius, emphasizes the importance of fortune to the final outcome, but does so with more restraint;[30] *dispar* prepares for the gladiatorial imagery of the next scene; *imperium*, the concept that lay at the heart of all Roman thinking on the power of their city and its magistrates, mattered much to him: it (or its cognates) have been used already three times in 23.7–9, and other instances will follow;[31] and in its understated way *nihil recusatur; tempus*

---

[29] See e.g. Witte (1910) (the classic demonstration), Walsh (1961), 178–81, Burck (1964), 182–95, Ogilvie (1965), 18–19, Oakley, *Comm.* I.126–8.

[30] The ensuing discussion (omitted from my quotation) as to whether the Horatii were Roman and the Curiatii Alban, or vice versa, may seem artistically intrusive to a modern reader; but Livy could not employ footnotes.

[31] Though perfectly well aware of what was at stake in the triple combat, Dionysius chose not to emphasize it thematically. See also Fries (1985), 79, 81.

et locus conuenit emphasizes the patriotism of the triplets: they will do what their cities want.[32]

Livy does dilate by including an account of the rituals by which the treaty and triple combat were agreed (§§3–8), a passage that dominates the whole episode. However, this fulfils several artistic purposes: it brings Tullus Hostilius to the centre of the action, reminding the reader that the triplets were fighting at the behest of their kings; it emphasizes the solemnity of the agreement which the Albans were soon to break; it provides a dramatic pause before the triple combat;[33] and its elaborate archaizing language makes a strong contrast with the surrounding episodes.[34] The passage also has a wider significance beyond this particular tale: the evocation of old rituals in archaic language is an important theme of Book 1;[35] and sometimes, as here (§3), Livy makes clear that his long description is paradigmatic for later occurrences.[36] He ends the episode by noting that the Albans carried out similar rituals of their own: (§9) *sua item carmina Albani suumque ius iurandum per suum dictatorem suosque sacerdotes peregerunt* 'likewise the Albans conducted their own solemn utterances and their own oath through their own dictator and their own priests'. The fourfold repetition of *suus* is pointed; soon the Albans were to have no sacred language of their own, no oaths, no dictator, and no priests.

The third episode, devoted to the triple combat itself, begins at 25.1, with a sentence only seven words long. The ablative absolute *foedere icto* ('the treaty having been agreed') links it with what has just been recounted in chapter 24; *sicut conuenerat* ('just as had been agreed') looks back to 24.2 *conuenit*, thereby closing by ring-composition the description of the making of the treaty;[37] and *capiunt* is in the historic present tense, which in Livy, as in several other Latin writers, underlines a more exciting phase of the action (the preceding main verbs in chapter 24 (§9 *percussit, peregerunt* were in the past tense).[38]

In the next sentence, each side exhorts its own champions to fight to the best of their abilities. This is Livy's first explicit reference to the spectators,

---

[32] See Fries (1985), 68.

[33] Compare the remarks of Fries (1985), 69.

[34] Space does not permit an analysis of this language; but Ogilvie (1965), 110 was right to term it 'mock-archaic' rather than to regard it as a genuine survival.

[35] Cf. 17.10 (on the creation of the king), 32.6–14 (fetial law), and 38.2 (*deditio*).

[36] Here Dionysius (18.1–2) is briefer, merely recording that the two sides made an agreement. This may seem surprising in view of the very substantial amount of antiquarianism elsewhere in his work, but his writing in Greek precluded quotation of archaizing Latin: he reports customs and rituals practices, not verbal formulae. See also Burck (1964), 151.

[37] For ring-composition in Livy see Ogilvie (1965), 769, Kraus (1994a), 350, and Oakley, *Comm.* I.788.

[38] This well-known technique hardly needs illustration, but numerous instances may be found by consulting the four indexes of Oakley, *Comm.*, s.v. 'present (tense), historic'.

who reappear in §§2, 3, 4, 6, 9, and 13.[39] As we have seen, his spectators appear more conscious than those of Dionysius of what is at stake in the triple combat and are used more obviously to offer interpretations of it. Here, when they tell the combatants that their *di patrii, patria, parentes, quicquid ciuium domi*, and *quicquid ciuium in exercitu sit*—'the ancestral gods, the fatherland, their parents, whatever of the citizen-body is at home . . . whatever is in the army'—all *intueri manus* 'are watching their hands', they make plain both that their own spectating is a substitute for that of everyone, human and divine, connected with their two states and that the contest concerns the future of their very states. The sentence maintains the urgency established by its predecessor, taking the form of a small period with a striking *cum*-clause leading up to a main clause. This *cum*-clause is expanded to twenty-two words so as to contain the report of what each side said. The emotional power of the exhortations recorded in it is enhanced by Livy's rhetorical language: the subject of *intueri* at first appears to be *deos patrios, patriam ac parentes*, a tricolon linked by etymology and alliteration, but then becomes a pentacolon, with anaphora of *quicquid* heightening the tone and adding urgency; then more urgency is imparted by another anaphoric pair (*illorum . . . illorum*), as emotive stress is laid on the arms and hands of the combatants.[40] As often in Livy, these arms and hands, details seemingly casually introduced, will become important later. He regularly describes the psychology of the main protagonists in any given episode: here we are told that the champions came out into the middle *feroces et suopte ingenio et pleni adhortantium uocibus* ('both pugnacious by their own nature and filled with the words of those encouraging'). *adhortantium* looks back to *adhortarentur* ('were encouraging') twenty-five words earlier: well might the six young men be said to be *pleni* after receiving the contents of such a weighty *cum*-clause. *feroces*, which here appears to mean 'pugnacious', will turn out to require a more suble interpretation and to have considerable thematic importance. With *in medium inter duas acies procedunt* ('they march out between the two lines into the middle'), Livy begins to set the scene for the combat, with characteristic care; these words recall Homer's ἐς μέσ(σ)ον, perhaps especially ἐς μέσσον Τρώων καὶ Ἀχαιῶν ἐστιχόωντο ('they marched out to the ground

---

[39] On Livy's use of the spectators see Solodow (1979), 277–8 = (2009) 306–7, who rightly compares his very similar use of spectators at 7.9–10 (on which see now Oakley, *Comm.* II.119–20).

[40] On Livy's periodic sentences and the expressiveness of his sentence-structure see, respectively Oakley, *Comm.* I.128–36 (with further bibliography) and ibid. I.141–2 and Coleman (1995).

between the Trojans and the Achaeans') (*Il.* 3.341, of Paris and Menelaus), giving epic colour to the scene in Book 1 most reminiscent of epic.[41]

§2 is introduced by *consederant* ('had sat down'), placed in the emphatic initial position and juxtaposed in a typically Livian manner to *procedunt*;[42] the juxtaposition of the two plural verbs with differing subjects (champions, spectators) draws attention to the links between the two. When the two spectating armies sit down outside their respective camps, the careful scene-setting combines again with epic colour: Homer's Greeks and Trojans had done the same (*Il.* 3.326, 7.56–66, 115).[43] The Romans' and Albans' anxiety is explained by *quippe imperium agebatur in tam paucorum uirtute atque fortuna positum* ('for sovereignty, entrusted to the bravery and fortune of so few men, was at stake'), words which should be viewed as the explanation of both the spectators themselves and the narrative voice, and which therefore constitute a notable merging of the two perspectives. Livy again gives prominence to the *imperium* that was at stake and to the role of fortune, to which he makes his third reference in this tale. In *itaque ergo erecti suspensique in minime gratum spectaculum animo intenduntur* ('accordingly then, upright and rapt, they are focused in mind on a hardly pleasant sight'), the weightily pleonastic *itaque ergo*, though found four times elsewhere in Livy,[44] was perhaps occasioned on this, his first use of it, by the weighty significance of the occasion. *Erecti* suggests that the men were sitting with straight, upright backs, *suspensi* that they craned their necks, rapt of mind;[45] this close coupling is rare, and the weight given by it follows suitably on from the particles and makes a sharper oxymoron with *minime gratum*. Dionysius refers to the theatre but Livy to a *spectaculum* (cf. §5),[46] which suggests more obviously a gladiatorial show—an image that is particularly appropriate in the context of duelling.[47]

---

[41] See Ogilvie (1965), 112. More parallels at Oakley, *Comm.* II.240 (where these two passages were culpably omitted). Similar expressions in the Latin historians (e.g. *in medium campi* at 4.18.3 and elsewhere) are less close to Homer.

[42] See further Chausserie-Laprée (1969), 355–6 and Oakley, *Comm.* II.121.

[43] Ogilvie (1965), 112 adduced the first passage.

[44] See Oakley, *Comm.* III.414.

[45] For the coupling of the two words (but not with this close juxtaposition) cf. esp. Cic. *Brut.* 200; also Tac. *Ann.* 14.57.2. On their own they are found often in Livy.

[46] Earlier Livy (23.9) had made Fufetius use the image of the spectacle to help convey the significance of the war between Alba and Rome. When an all-out contest seems likely, he warns that the two battle lines will be *spectaculo*, implicitly to the Etruscans, who encircle Alban and Roman territory, as the spectators will soon encircle the triplets. Behind the parochial squabble between Rome and Alba, this conflict has a deeper importance, we learn, for the balance of power in Italy.

[47] The gladiatorial image is enhanced by *fauentium* in § 9: *faueo, fautor,* and their cognates are used regularly in the contexts of partisans of actors, gladiators, and others appearing at the *ludi*.

§3 begins with another juxtaposition of verbs, *intenduntur* being followed by *datur signum* ('the signal is given'). Then we return to the triplets themselves. *uelut acies* ('like a line of battle') points to the spectacle provided by their advancing: just as in a full-scale battle there has been a signal (presumably on the trumpet), so the triplets advance like real lines of battle; but the image reminds us, too, that they were offering their lives in place of whole armies. Since they are described as *magnorum exercituum* <u>animos</u> *gerentes* ('carrying the minds of great armies'), it is not surprising that their own attitude, reported in *nec his nec illis periculum suum, publicum imperium seruitiumque obuersatur* <u>animo</u> *futuraque ea deinde patriae fortuna quam ipsi fecissent* ('for neither side does their own danger cross their minds—only the sovereignty or slavery of their people and that they would determine the fortune of the fatherland'), is in striking symbiosis with that displayed in §1 by these *magni exercitus*. This comment idealizes the Horatii and the Curiatii, by making them appear (at least at this stage) as paragons of selfless patriotism.[48] Note how *suum* and *publicum* are emphasized by chiasmus and adversative asyndeton,[49] and the appearance again of the themes of *imperium* and fortune.

The fighting proper begins in §4. Whereas Dionysius aims for precision, describing the manoevures of the combatants and the feelings of the onlookers in full detail, Livy is more incisive, conveying in a few words the impact of the fighting. As so often, he divides the action up into stages,[50] this first stage (which ends before the six men have grappled with each other) being signalled by *primo... concursu* ('at the first rush') and lasting for just one sentence. Its opening *ut*-clause describes the initial clank of arms and creates a vivid effect by using words suggestive of noise (*concrepuere* 'crashed') and gleaming light (*micantes* 'flickering', *fulsere* 'gleamed').[51] Its double main-clause de-

---

Note that four passages (Plin. *N.H.* 7.186, Sil. It. *Pun.* 16.419, 483, Sidon. *Carm.* 23.376) of the ten cited with ours at *TLL* 6.1.377.63–9 for the substantival use of the present participle *fauens* concern partisan spectators. For earlier interpreters who rightly understood *fauentium*, see Fleckinger (1921). On the gladiatorial connotations of *par*, see below. Detection of some of the gladiatorial imagery goes back at least to German commentators in the 19th cent.; Fries (1985), 72 n. 2 unwisely denies it.

[48] And so the five men who die in the triple combat remain, the selfless patriotism of the Curiatii as well as the Horatii being subsumed into the character of the new, united nation that emerges from this conflict. For the moral ambiguity of the survivor, see below.

[49] See further Solodow (1979), 254 = (2009), 301–2. For chiasmus in Livy see Kraus (1994a), 22 and 353.

[50] See Oakley, *Comm.* I.127, with parallels and further bibliography.

[51] Ogilvie (1965), 113 calls the language 'highly coloured', but his discussion needs qualification. He implies that *fulsere gladii* is poetical, citing Virg. *Aen.* 6.217 and 490, but in these passages *fulgens* qualifies *arma* not *gladius*. In fact, *fulgeo* is used with *gladius* in prose at e.g. Cic. *Tusc.* 2.59, 5.62, Sen. *Epist.* 48.11, and Apul. *Met.* 8.13 (only the last cited by Ogilvie); it is one of

scribes the effect of this on the spectators: with neither side in the ascendant (*neutro inclinata spe*), a great fear had seized them, and their voices and *spiritus* all but failed.[52] *spiritus* could mean either 'breath' (literal) or 'spirit' (figurative). The former may be suggested by the coupling with *uox* ('voice') and by the fact that the spectators were not obviously lacking in mettle. Yet *minime gratum spectaculum* in §2 suggests that the latter should not be ruled out: when this fight began, the spectators had no stomach for it. The torpid silence will make a contrast with what follows.[53] Livy's variation in tenses in this section deserves close attention: the pasts *increpuere* ('crashed') and *fulsere* ('gleamed') in the *ubi*-clause depict completed, momentary actions; the historic present *perstringit* ('grips') vividly underlines the spectators' collective seizure; and the imperfect *torpebat* ('were growing numb') shows the continuing ongoing consequence of this.

The next stage of the fighting is introduced by *consertis deinde manibus* (§5). This should not be translated loosely ('then, when the close combat started . . . ') but literally ('then, when their hands grappled . . . '): we remember that in §1 the armies were watching the *manus* and the *arma* (about to be mentioned) of the six men. This stage is recounted in a magnificent periodic sentence, and the *cum*-clause which follows this opening ablative absolute demands more attention. Expanded by a *non . . . tantum . . . sed . . . quoque . . .* ('not only . . . but also') structure, it conveys by means of its size—seventeen words—the length and intensity of the initial fighting: *motus . . . corporum*

the Latin verbs that most aptly describes a gleaming sword. Ogilvie notes correctly that *increpuere arma* (offered by the MSS) is found only here; since the banging of shields would make a *crepitus*, and since some not dissimilar passages are cited at *TLL* 7.1.1051.15–36, this could be what Livy wrote. However, the corruption of one prefix into another is exceptionally common in Latin mss; *concrepo* is the verb expected in this context (*TLL* 4.93.82–4, 94.30–2: *con*- is the prefix appropriate for a collision); and H. J. Müller's *concrepuere arma*, very well paralleled at 6.24.1 *simul primo concursu concrepuere arma*, should probably be accepted and certainly not dismissed without discussion. The argument of Solodow (1979), 253=(2009), 300, that Livy uses here the unusual *increpuere* so that it may be picked up by 26.3 *increpans*, is an optimistic defence of odd Latin.

[52] *horror . . . perstringit* is a striking expression that seems to be exactly paralleled only at Val. Flac. 7.81 (well cited by Ogilvie), although Curt. 5.9.1 *praesentis periculi species omnium simul corda animosque horrore perstrinxerat*, cited by Weissenborn and Müller, is a very close analogy. It has a rich range of meaning. *horror* often means 'dread' (so our passage is classified at *OLD* 6a), and it is found in the context of *torpor* ('numbness') also at e.g. Virg. *Aen.* 12.867 and Sen. *Med.* 926; but it may be used of sounds (see e.g. Virg. *Aen.* 2.301 *clarescunt sonitus armorumque ingruit horror, OLD* 3). *perstringo* (literally 'make tight') may likewise be used of sounds (*OLD* 4), but more regularly of lightly wounding (*OLD* 2a). Therefore Livy's expression suggests not only the emotional numbness of the spectators but also physical injury to them, enhancing the idea of their being in symbiosis with the contestants.

[53] Livy excelled in describing both silence and *torpor*: see, respectively, Oakley, *Comm.* II.130 and III.62 (for silences also Dutoit (1948) and Ogilvie (1965), 486).

('movement of their bodies') and *agitatioque anceps telorum armorumque* ('indeterminate brandishing of weapons and armour') look back to the theme of the previous sentence and economically convey the movements of the contestants; *uolnera . . . et sanguis* ('wounds . . . and blood') introduce a new development; and *spectaculo* ('spectacle') makes us glance once again at the onlookers. But the real glory of the sentence is its second half, where, after the long build-up in the *cum*-clause, the action is suddenly brought to a point of crisis: all three Albans are wounded (this looks back to the *cum*-clause), but, in a new development, two of the Romans are killed. Particularly impressive is the compressed *uolneratis tribus Albanis* ('after the three Albans had been wounded'), an ablative absolute whose full significance becomes apparent in §§7–12, and the movement of the whole sentence to a climax with the final and emphatic *corruerunt* ('collapsed'). At this point (§6) Livy glances yet again at the effect which the action had on the onlookers: now, in contrast to the previous silence, the Albans cheer with joy and, since (in a particularly deft piece of psychologizing) all hope (*spes*) had deserted the Romans but not yet all worry (*cura*, looking back to §2), we presume that they stay silent.[54] This is the first time that Livy has separated the spectators into two sides. *exanimes uicem unius* ('faint on behalf of the one') again emphasizes the bond between spectators and contestant(s).[55] Unlike Dionysius, he leaves the surviving Horatius to face three Curiatii. His victory therefore involves a greater reversal, in which the Horatius has to dispatch more opponents.

The narrative now (§7) reaches its περιπέτεια, which, as several times elsewhere, Livy introduces with *forte* ('by chance'),[56] thereby giving renewed prominence to the theme of chance and fortune. In the rest of §7 Livy takes stock of the situation. First, largely from the narrator's perspective he notes that Horatius could not manage to fight the Curiatii together (*ut uniuersis solus nequaquam par* 'although alone in no way a match for them together': the juxtaposition of the second and third words reinforces the point) but could handle them individually (*aduersus singulos ferox* 'pugnacious against them as equals'). *par* ('equal') activates the image latent in 24.1 *dispares*: it is a word used regularly in the context of pairs of fighting gladiators,[57] and the surviving Horatius is to fight what, in effect, are three single gladiatorial combats. Livy will use it again in §11 before the climactic duel. *Ferox*, too, continues an important theme. Then, largely from Horatius' perspective, and

---

[54] Dionysius, too, starts with silence (3.19.1) but his gradations of noise are less subtle than Livy's.

[55] *Exanimes*, too, is perhaps poetical: see *TLL* 5.2.1172.46–73 on its distribution.

[56] See e.g. 2.33.6, 6.3.3, and 7.15.1; further discussion at Oakley, *Comm.* I.416 and 664.

[57] See Oakley, *Comm.* II.140.

by means of what was to become the favoured device of a clause introduced by
ratus ('thinking'),[58] he reveals Horatius' plan to split up his three opponents.
In §8 Horatius puts his stratagem into practice; we should note *unum*, which
picks up §7 *singulos* and is emphasized both by its initial position in its colon
and its asyndetic juxtaposition to *sequentes*. A short sentence (§9 *in eum
magno impetu rediit* 'against him he returned with a great charge') now
marks the quickening pulse of the action, as Horatius charges against the
first Curiatius. The next sentence, in which this man is killed, provides a
classic instance of Livy's periodic artistry: with extraordinary power and
brevity we are swept from the exhortations of the Albans, to the death of
the first Curiatius, and to the attack on the second. With *caeso hoste* ('after he
had killed his opponent') Livy once again makes excellent use of the opportunities offered by the ablative absolute construction;[59] and once again he
thrusts the reaction of the onlookers on our attention. Now at last the
Romans cheer (*clamore* 'shout' is in tension with the earlier *inclamat* 'shout
at' and with §6 *conclamasset* 'cried aloud'),[60] and Livy, again with deft
psychological point, describes this cheering as the kind of noise that a
group of supporters at the games makes when things go its way after an
unexpected event.[61] *Suum* ('their own'), in the emphatic final position of the
sentence, again underlines the bond between watching Romans and their
champion. As the pulse quickens we come at the end of §9, in §10, and at
the beginning of §11 to a series of short sentences and historic presents
(*adiuuant, festinat, conficit*).

The final denouement is now in sight, but just as in many a 'Western' the
camera lingers on the two duellists about to make the final shoot-out, so here
Livy slows down the pace of the narrative in order to describe the state of
mind of the two survivors (§11). The one is exultant; the other tired and
despondent. *nec spe nec uiribus pares* ('not evenly matched in hope or
strength') contrasts strongly with 24.1 *nec aetate nec uiribus dispares* and
shows how far circumstances have changed. With *fessum... fessum* ('tired...
tired') repeated in anaphora and then yielding to the play *uictus... uictori*
('conquered... victor'), the syntax mirrors the Alban's tired yielding to his
foe.[62] *Fratrum ante se strage* reminds us of the earlier careful delineation of the
scene: this last Curiatius had been behind his brothers, and had watched them

[58] See Oakley, *Comm.* I.134; other instances in Book 1 are 8.2, 19.2, 22.2, 32.2, 36.2, 37.5.
[59] See also Fries (1985), 75.
[60] Very obviously in tension if one interprets *inclamat* as 'abuse' (*OLD* 3) and *clamore* as
'applause' (*OLD* 1c; Nisbet–Rudd (2004), 290); but neither translation is the only one possible.
[61] For this translation of *ex insperato*, see Fleckinger (1921) and Ogilvie (1965), 113.
inclamat, therefore, evokes the cheering of a rival group of supporters.
[62] Compare the remarks of Fries (1985), 76.

die.[63] Livy was a master at varying the lengths of his sentences and now prefigures the outcome of the duel with a sentence of incisive brevity: (§11) *nec illud proelium fuit* ('nor was that a contest'). Equally characteristically, he brings the episode to its climax in §12 with a short burst of direct speech:[64]

Romanus exsultans 'Duos' inquit 'fratrum manibus dedi; tertium causae belli huiusce, ut Romanus Albano imperet, dabo.'

The Roman was jubilant saying, 'I have presented two men to the shades of my brothers; I shall present this third to the reason for this war, so that the Romans may rule the Albans.'

Not *Horatius* but *Romanus*: the triplets have been fighting on behalf of their nations; now Roman dominion over Alba Longa will be secured; and, with *Romanus* used by both the narrator's and Horatius' voices, the identification of Horatius with his nation is underlined. Note too the thematically important *imperet*. The contrast between *Duos* and *tertium*, each at the head of its colon, is the most prominent instance of plays with numbers that have been frequent throughout this episode.[65]

Curiatius is swiftly dispatched,[66] and Livy returns once more to the Roman spectators, who now display the joy that had once belonged to the Albans, *eo maiore cum gaudio, quo prope metum res fuerat* ('with joy all the greater because the affair had nearly induced panic') being another instance of Livy's perceptive psychologizing. Livy describes the burial of the dead thus:

ad sepulturam inde suorum nequaquam paribus animis uertuntur, quippe imperio alteri aucti, alteri dicionis alienae facti.

Then they turn to the burial of their own folk, with spirits that were not at all evenly matched, since one side possessed more sovereignty, the other was made subject.

Paribus, used here of the spectators, varies the image present twice earlier and reinforces the point that the contest was on behalf of the two cities; in Livy's explanation for the differing emotional states of the two sides, *imperio* (which echoes *paribus* by assonance) reiterates the central point of the episode.

Livy took great care over the closure of his scenes, and in §14, to finish the tale of the triple combat, he uses his favoured device of a reference to

---

[63] *strage* is another, very appropriate, poeticism: see Oakley, *Comm.* II.223.

[64] Compare e.g. 1.41.3, 2.10.11, 2.40.5–9; further references at Oakley, *Comm.* I.119.

[65] Most obviously at 25.5 *duo . . . tribus* and 11 *geminata . . . tertium*; but note the stress on three at 24.2 and 25.3.

[66] On the poetical tone of *gladium . . . iugulo defigit*, see Ogilvie (1965), 113.

something still extant that came into being as a consequence of the episode just related, in this instance the five tombs said to be those of the Horatii and Curiatii.[67]

The next scene begins at 26.1, and our analysis will be brief, limiting itself largely to the differences between Livy and Dionysius.[68] Unlike Dionysius Livy (perhaps surprisingly) takes much less interest in the reversal of fortune that Horatius undergoes, giving it prominence only in the speech of Horatius' father in §10. He takes less interest also in the tragic aspects of the story, eschewing many of the domestic details with which Dionysius had bedecked his account and avoiding a verbal confrontation between brother and sister.[69] Rather, his main concerns are the consequences for the public body of Horatius' rash act, and in particular his two trials, the first by the duumvirs, and second, after *prouocatio* ('appeal'), before the people.[70] In the late Republic *prouocatio* was a symbol of popular liberty, and Livy here assigns it an origin in the earliest days of Roman history. The speech of Horatius' father emphasizes even more than Dionysius had managed the dominance of *patria potestas* ('a father's power') in Roman society, and this, too, is thereby placed in the myths of Rome's foundation.

Throughout the scene Livy again makes use of the views of characters and spectators inside his text; but whereas in the previous chapter the reactions on display were uncomplicated (everyone supported their own side), now the perspectives are different, and each offers a position that readers are invited to consider. The people (§5) view Horatius' murdering of his sister as *atrox* ('dire') but excusable by his recent good deed; Tullus (§5) as requiring some kind of conviction, however unwelcome that may be;[71] the duumvirs (§§6–7), whose view is emphasized by being placed in direct speech, as an example of clear guilt; and Horatius' father (§§9–11), whose view is again emphasized by direct speech, as an instance of justifiable homicide (see esp. §9 *iure caesa* 'justly killed'). He reworks the visual themes so prominent in the earlier scene, reminding (§10) the people that they watched Horatius' triumph and imply-

---

[67] On the aetiologies here see further Solodow (1979), 261–5 = (2009), 310–15; further examples, which include 1.13.5, 26.13–14, 36.5, and 48.7, are listed at Oakley, *Comm.* I.128.

[68] I note in passing the strong emphasis in the first sentence on the theme of *imperium* and in the final sentence (§14) the use once again of a monument to provide closure.

[69] Burck (1964), 153 well observed that, unlike Dionysius', Livy's Horatius thinks largely of his country and hardly of his own slighted pride, thereby heightening the moral dilemma of the tale.

[70] Dionysius' failure to mention these *duumuiri* may be explained either as another instance of his lack of interest in Roman legal formulae or by the whole notion of the *duumuiri* having only a slender hold in the annalistic tradition (Oakley, *Comm.* I.563–5).

[71] On the reasoning of Tullus and the people compare the remarks of Solodow (1979), 255 and 257–8 = (2009), 305–6 and 302–3.

ing that the *spectaculum* of the triple combat, already *minime gratum* even before it had started, is in danger of becoming the *spectaculum* of an execution, *deforme* ('ugly') even to the Albans.

These differing viewpoints underline the moral complexity of the case and prepare for the ambiguous verdict of the narrative voice itself, which states that acquittal comes (§12) *admiratione magis uirtutis quam iure causae* ('more through approval of his bravery than the rightness of his case'), where *iure* contrasts strongly with its appearance in §9.[72] All this allows an obvious moral reading of the tale: when miscreants are popular, justice is not always carried out. *Ferocia*, too, has turned out to be an attribute of moral ambiguity: usefully *ferox* against his opponents (25.7), Horatius is unwisely *ferox* (26.3) towards his sister. This is not the only occasion in Livy or other writers in which the man who is *ferox* turns out, though brave, to be impulsive and lacking in judgement: in Horatius' case we see that qualities of character that serve well in war do not always make for comfortable coexistence in domestic life.[73] As for Horatius, father and son, Livy here shows early in his history that he was no unqualified admirer of old-fashioned severity. Though not explicit, he allows his readers to ponder whether Roman private morality has developed beyond the primitive attitudes found in this and some other episodes in his early books.[74] The ambiguity of Horatius' case, and Livy's refusal to let his narrative voice draw an easy conclusion from it, shows that his moralizing is often more subtle than that for which he was once given credit.[75]

Dionysius' history has much to interest modern students of the Greek classics, who should read more of him: he is one of only three Greek historians writing between Xenophon and the Flavians whose work has survived in any quantity; he is one of only two surviving Greek or Latin authors who wrote both history and theoretical treatises;[76] he views Augustan Rome from the perspective of a

---

[72] For Livy's use of an internal audience to reflect his moralizing concerns, see Levene (2006), esp. 101–6.

[73] For further discussion of *ferocia* see Solodow (1979), 253, 254–5 = (2009), 299–300, 302, Fries (1985), 236–8, Penella (1990), 210–12, and Oakley, *Comm.* I.586. For ferocity leading to lack of judgement see e.g. Liv. 5.36.1 (Roman legates), 6.23.3 (L. Furius), 8.7.8 (the young Torquatus) and, above all, Germanicus' enemy Piso (esp. Tac. *Ann.* 2.43.2). Penella shows how Horatius mirrors the *ferocia* of his king (on which see also e.g. Ogilvie (1965), 105): Tullus' own attitudes beget the most difficult internal problem of his reign.

[74] Compare above all 8.7.22 and 8.36.5–7. Dionysius (3.21.7) suggests this developmental view (note, too, 5.8.1, on Brutus and his sons).

[75] For this view of Livy see Solodow (1979), 259–60 = (2009), 308–10 (who makes some of these points more fully) and Levene (2007), 285. Only for a few characters who make brief appearances does Livy's narrative suggest a morally uncomplicated interpretation of their behaviour (e.g. Marcus Curtius 7.6.3–5).

[76] The other is Tacitus.

contemporary Greek intellectual; he often represents the Roman annalistic tradition more faithfully than any extant Latin writers; his history tells us much about ancient political theory and practice; and his prose style is unfailingly elegant.[77] Yet he lacked a more precious gift, the ability to produce a work of creative art of the first rank. Too often (but especially in his accounts of Coriolanus and the Decemvirate) his love of ἀκρίβεια leads him to lose any sense of proportion, and some may find this failing in his account of the Horatii and Curiatii. By contrast, Livy, almost certainly a much less learned man, was granted the gift of writing with verve, imagination, and a concentration of language that repays careful analysis. The pages that we have been studying, the best that he had yet managed in the *ab urbe condita*, are among the first indications that a great classic was in the making.

---

[77] Livy would have admired many of his periods, including that at 3.21.4 from the portion discussed here.

8

Amores 1.1–5

David West

For the elegance, facility, and golden cadence of poesy . . . Ovidius Naso
was the man

Holofernes in Love's Labour's Lost 4.2.122–4

When we were colleagues in Newcastle University in a different world,
I derived huge pleasure and inspiration from the man along the corridor,
and I offer him this essay as a token of gratitude. In those days we taught Latin
poetry to beginners, and they seemed to take to Ovid. Part of the reason was
that they enjoyed his prodigious ingenuity. The first book of the *Amores* is full
of it, and in 1973 there was Barsby's excellent commentary and a brilliant
essay by Ian Du Quesnay, followed by the massively learned commentary by
J. C. McKeown.[1] They all have keen eyes for Ovid's *lumina ingenii* (particularly Du Quesnay on 1.11 and 12), but there may be some other *scintillae*, and
the object of this essay is to look for them in the first five poems.

Ovid was 17 years old when he began the *Amores* in about 25 BC. The first
publication was in five books, but what we now possess is a three-book
edition which came out some time after 16 BC. This is a young man's work,
bursting with ingenuity, high spirits, and a huge delight in his own genius.
The first line shows that he did not suffer from modesty:

> arma graui numero uiolentaque bella paraui
>   edere, materia conueniente modis.
> par erat inferior uersus; risisse Cupido
>   dicitur, atque unum surripuisse pedem.
> quis tibi, saeue puer, dedit hoc in carmina iuris?
>   Pieridum uates, non tua turba sumus.

> On arms and violent wars I prepared
>   to sound forth, measures matching matter.

---

[1] Barsby (1973); Du Quesnay (1973); McKeown (1987–), i–ii.

My second line was equal to the first. Cupid laughed,
  so they say, and stole a foot.
'You young savage, who gave you this jurisdiction over poetry?
  We are not your retinue, but priests of the Pierides.'

War and arms are the very stuff of epic, and Ovid (and Propertius 3.34.63–4) knew the *Aeneid*. He had the voice for it, *et satis oris erat* (*Amores* 2.1.11–12). That voice is heard here in the second line with *edere*, 'to utter solemnly, pronounce (an oracle etc.)' *OLD* 6b, a tone heard when Aeneas prayed to Jupiter at *Aeneid* 5.693, *uix haec ediderat*, and also when Ilia, ravished by Mars, 'tore her hair and with trembling lips uttered these bitter sounds', *edidit indignos ore tremente sonos* (*Amores* 3.6.71–2) to her rescuer the *lubricus* River Anio.

There is more. The elegiac couplet is a straitjacket, with little scope for metrical variety, and restricted also by the convention that each couplet is self-contained. As Kenney says in his introduction to Melville's translation, 'True enjambment between couplets is rare, in Ovid virtually unheard of though within the couplet it is freely and effectively used.'[2] Here the run-on *bella parabam | edere*, is an effective contribution to the mock-epic utterance. This nuance is maintained when the god replies, *risisse Cupido | dicitur*, and continued in 11–12, *quis acuta cuspide Phoebum | instruat*, when Ovid turns his attention to Apollo and Mars. Ovid enjoyed declaiming his poems. He would have enjoyed inflating *edere, materia conueniente modis*, this and 3.13 being the only four-word pentameters in the first five poems of this book.

Three points remain to be made about *risisse Cupido dicitur*. Commentators refer to previous poets from Hesiod to the Latin elegists where Apollo or Muses appear to the poet beginning a work and give him instructions. The poet always obeys, but in *Amores* 1 the epiphany is not Apollo or a Muse and not even Venus, but the boy Cupid, and Ovid, being a brash teenager, does not obey, but launches without preamble into a tirade. The second point is that the most important word in the poem is *risisse*. Other divine advisers did not laugh, but here Cupid does. It is a category error to interpret this poetry seriously. Serious scholars are charged with the responsibility to laugh with the god, not to suffer the anxiety about love or influences or anything else. The last smile to be extracted from these three words lurks in *dicitur*. This is nonsense. Ovid is reporting a private conversation between Cupid and himself. How can it make sense to say that Cupid *is said* to have laughed? He either laughed or did not laugh, and Ovid knew. The explanation is that *dicitur* is epic parody, as in 5.12. When Virgil tells a tale he tends to disclaim responsibility by attributing it to hearsay. This '*fama* evasion' is

---

[2] Kenney (1990), p. xxv.

common in the *Aeneid*, for example at 6.107 and 7.409. Here it demonstrates the absurdity of the tale, and immediately in the same line Cupid amputates one of Ovid's feet.

The first theme in Ovid's protest is that Cupid is encroaching on the territory of other gods. *Pieridum vates, non tua turba sumus*, says Ovid with contempt. 'We are priests of the Muses, not your rabble' (editors add a strange comma after *tua*). Ovid is still in full cry at 15–20:

> 'an quod ubique, tuum est? tua sunt Heliconia tempe?
> vix etiam Phoebo iam lyra tuta sua est?
> cum bene surrexit uersu noua pagina primo,
> attenuat neruos proximus ille meos.
> nec mihi materia est numeris leuioribus apta,
> aut puer aut longas compta puella comas.'

> 'Is everything, no matter where, yours? Are the groves of Helicon yours?
> Can't even Apollo call the lyre his own these days?
> After my new page rises nicely with my first verse,
> the one beneath shrinks my spirits,
> and I don't have the material for light verse,
> neither boy nor girl with lovely long hair.'

The translation of 15–16 carries much less anger than Ovid's Latin with its assonances and alliterations in *tuumst tua sunt tempe tuta sua est*, sharpened by a metrical variation. In *tuum* and *tua*, -*u*- is short, whereas in *tuta* it is long and completes a crescendo of sarcasm. Ascending tricolon with anaphora is a standard rhetorical figure, as employed by Churchill in June 1940, 'We shall fight on the beaches, we shall fight on the landing grounds, we shall fight in the fields and in the streets' where the order is not only rhetorical but also topographical. Ovid was steeped in rhetoric and here he plays a variation on the figure. The tricolon is there in the three questions, the ascension in the increasing size of the three cola, and the building blocks for anaphora in *tuum tua tuta*, but anaphora would require that each began its colon. Ovid, however, postpones *tuum est* and rams it home by juxtaposition *tuum est? tua sunt*. Besides, in the third element *tuta sua est*, *tuta* is a totally different word which sounds similar, making a pseudo-anaphora, all sharpened by the insult in the word *turba*, a gang of villains in 1.2.36. This is a cold analysis but the rhetoric is ablaze with anger, false of course. Cupid is still laughing.

In 17–18 there is a glimmer of a risqué undertone. McKeown cites five examples of *neruus* meaning penis and might have added *Amores* 3.7.35 before *latus* in 36, and *surgere* occurs in a sexual sense in 2.15.25–6, *sed puto, te nuda, mea membra libidine surgent*. There may also be a sexual undertone in 19–20. The girl seems to have the lovely long hair, but boy lovers are highly esteemed for it, for example Ligurinus, with his locks floating over his shoulders in Horace *Odes* 4.11.3, *umeris inuolitant.* Here in Ovid the lovely hair is best seen as gracing both *puer* and *puella. Capillati* are boy lovers.

Ovid's *Phaedra* won him measured praise from Tacitus in *Dialogus* 12.6, and frosty approval from Quintilian ('ille uir', 10.1.98). His dramatic gifts are deployed in lines 21–6:

> questus eram, pharetra cum protinus ille soluta
> > legit in exitium spicula facta meum,
> lunauitque genu sinuosum fortiter arcum
> > 'quod'que 'canas, uates, accipe' dixit 'opus.'
> me miserum! certas habuit puer ille sagittas:
> > uror et in uacuo pectore regnat Amor.

> I had just finished my complaint when he immediately opened his quiver,
> > picked out arrows with my name on them,
> bent his crescent bow on his knee using his strength, and said,
> > 'I'll give you something to sing, priest. Take that.'
> Poor me! The rascal had arrows that don't miss:
> > I burn and Amor reigns in my empty breast.

Protinus is the crucial word. Amor's response began the moment Ovid had finished his tirade, and then the narrative slows down and spreads, unusually, over two couplets. Amor selects arrows which had been made specially for Ovid, and bends his bow *fortiter.* He has to press the base of it against the inside of his knee, and needs his strength—after all, he is just a boy. And as he shoots, he speaks in a line of six words all accented on the first syllable, 'quód'que 'cánas, uátes, áccipe' díxit 'ópus.' It hurt, and not only the wound, but also the word, *uates.* So much for *Pieridum uates* (6).

Quintilian's view of Ovid is that he was too much in love with his own genius, *nimium amator ingenii sui* (10.1.88), and there is no doubt that he enjoyed abundance. But he could also shape a scene and structure a narrative. This shows here in the ring-composition, where the words italicized repeat or recall words in the first four lines (27–30):

> > *sex* mihi surgat opus *numeris,* in *quinque* residat.
> > > ferrea cum uestris *bella* ualete *modis.*
> > cingere litorea flauentia tempora myrto,
> > > Musa per *und*enos *emod*ulanda *pedes.*

> > Let my work rise in six numbers and settle in five.
> > > Farewell, iron wars and your measures too.
> > Gird your golden brow with seashore myrtle, my Muse,
> > > demodulated to eleven feet.

On *emodulanda* (a word occurring only here in surviving Latin) McKeown collects eight verbs 'compounded with -e- occurring first or only in Ovid'. Literally the word suggests something like 'requiring to be tuned <to sound> through 11 feet', but that ignores the precious prefix -e-, which normally indicates removal or reduction, 'away from'. Ovid probably coined the word for fun, and the prefix should therefore be taken seriously. Hence 'demodulated <by one foot>'.

The Latin hexameter is sometimes shaped as two adjectives, verb, and two nouns with which the adjectives agree, AAVNN. This is the golden line and it usually adds elevation or intensity, as when the ploughman will some day wonder at huge bones he turns up in old battle fields in Virgil *Georgics* 1.497, *grandiaque effossis mirabitur ossa sepulchris.* That is a strict definition, but the same effect is produced by other arrangements of the same elements, in line 29, VAANN, and perhaps also in 28, AANVN, not golden, but perhaps 'golden type'. Line 30 is not dissimilar. A similar sequence occurs also in *Georgics* 1.494–6, all golden-type lines. Ovid is stirred to reverential dignity in addressing his Muse.

AMORES 1.2

The vignette of 1.21–6 demonstrates Ovid's gifts as a dramatist. The next poem begins with a dramatic soliloquy, a stream of consciousness:

> Esse quid hoc dicam, quod tam mihi dura uidentur
>   strata, neque in lecto pallia nostra sedent,
> et uacuus somno noctem, quam longa, peregi,
>   lassaque uersati corporis ossa dolent?
> nam, puto, sentirem, si quo temptarer amore –
>   an subit et tecta callidus arte nocet?
> sic erit: haeserunt tenues in corde sagittae,
>   et possessa ferus pectora uersat Amor.
> cedimus? an subitum luctando accendimus ignem?
>   cedamus: leue fit quod bene fertur onus.

> What is all this? Why does my mattress seem
>   so hard and the blankets not stay on the bed?
> Why have I spent the night without sleep, the whole night?
>   Why are my weary bones sore with tossing and turning?
> For I'd know, I think, if some love were attacking me –
>   or does it creep up stealthily and wound with cunning art?

> That's what it will be. There are sharp arrows stuck in my heart,
>   and Amor has taken possession of my breast.
> Are we to yield? Or ignite a sudden blaze by resisting?
>   Let us yield: a burden becomes light if carried properly.

Ovid's first cunning art is the run-on of *dura uidentur | strata*, a device seen already in 1.2, 4, and 12. Nine times out of ten the end of the hexameter is marked by punctuation. In this fraught introspection, the line-by-line movement is slightly disturbed at the end of line 1, and the jolting effect is confirmed in the early breaks in lines 7, 9, and 10. The only other such breaks in this poem are in lines 26 and 40.

The book began on a high mock-epic note. Now the subject matter is mundane, domestic almost, and the language is correspondingly simple. The opening words seem to be totally natural (Catullus speaks in the same tone of voice in 22.12, *hoc quid putemus esse?* and in 80.1–2), and the trouble with bedclothes in a sleepless night is something we all know, but few poets evoke. 'I have spent the night' (the prefix in *peregi* makes it more like 'endured'), and the strange *quam longa* is almost an exclamation, 'how long it was!' Line 4 (golden type) is a vivid description of his suffering 'the (very) bones of my body are weary with turning'. He can't understand it, *nam, puto, sentirem, si quo temptabar amore*. This, of course, is all persiflage, a fiction to introduce Ovid's version of elegiac. In 1 Cupid made him write love poems; in 2 he has no one to love.

Sic erit in line 7 is again natural speech (*sic certe est* in Catullus 80.7), and the colon after the first dactyl is not a feature Ovid uses lightly. The intensity continues with the verb *haeserunt* in emphatic position. Arrows have lodged in his breast, and <he didn't realize it because> they were slender, *tenuis*. We translators try but fail with 'subtle, invisible, phantom, sharp'. The last word of the couplet is the crucial realization. It is pitiless Amor who has seized possession of his breast and is churning it, *uersat*, picking up *uersati corporis* from line 2.

The internal debate continues as the royal 'we' sets up a conversation between two parts of himself, sharpened by the broken lines 9 (the question mark after *cedimus* is mine) and 10, and by the indicative where the subjunctive would be expected, a 'traditional usage of spoken language'.[3] He promptly capitulates and justifies his decision by an Ovidian simplification of Horace's words of sad comfort in *Odes* 1.4.19–20, *leuius fit patientia | quidquid corrigere est nefas*. Ovid's version sounds like proverbial wisdom, *léue fit quod béne fértur*.

---

[3] Horsfall (2006), 101.

Lines 6–10 give a detailed account of an attack upon a citadel—the stealthy approach in 6, bombardment by arrows in 7, capture in 8, forcing the defenders to choose whether to capitulate or resist and die in their burning buildings. They capitulate and now follows the triumphal procession (19–26), with two more broken lines, 19 and 21:

> en ego confiteor: tua sum noua praeda, Cupido.
>> porrigimus uictas ad tua iura manus.
> nil opus est bello: pacem ueniamque rogamus,
>> nec tibi laus armis uictus inermis ero.
> necte comam myrto, maternas iunge columbas;
>> qui deceant currus uitricus ipse dabit,
> inque dato curru, populo clamante triumphum,
>> stabis et adiunctas arte mouebis aues.

> There, I admit it: I am your latest prize, Cupid.
>> We stretch forth our hands to accept your justice.
> There's no need for war: we ask for peace and pardon.
>> It will do no honour to your arms to defeat the unarmed.
> Weave myrtle in your hair, and yoke your mother's doves,
>> your stepfather himself will provide a worthy chariot,
> and there you will stand on the chariot provided, and skilfully
>> steer your birds while the people hail your triumph.

A vital ingredient in these poems, as later in the *Metamorphoses*, is the fun Ovid derives from treating gods as though they were mortals. Here Cupid is to drive his mother's chariot, but he has to yoke it first, and yoking birds is no easy task even for a god with wings, but steering a team or even a pair of birds, for all Cupid's skill (26), would be as difficult as herding cats. Nor would it be an easy matter for doves to lift Mars' mighty war chariot with gilded wheels (42) off the ground, let alone manoeuvre it in mid-air. In 24 the chariot will be provided by Cupid's stepfather. This could be Vulcan, but Mars is referred to as Cupid's *uitricus* in *Amores* 2.9.48 and *Remedia* 27. Venus' matrimonial arrangements are not simple. If Stesichorus is to be believed (*PMG* 575), Eros was the son of Aphrodite by Ares, perhaps as a result of the incident in *Odyssey* 8.266–366 where Hephaestus traps her in Ares' arms. Ares lent her his chariot in an amusing scene in Homer *Iliad* 5.355, a sound precedent for this loan to her son.

The description of Cupid's triumphal procession continues (35–42) with the names of some of the villains in his retinue:

> Blanditiae comites tibi erunt Errorque Furorque
>> assidue partes turba secuta tuas.
> his tu militibus superas hominesque deosque;
>> haec tibi si demas commoda, nudus eris.

> laeta triumphanti de summo mater Olympo
>   plaudet, et appositas sparget in ora rosas.
> tu pinnas gemma, gemma uariante capillos,
>   ibis in auratis aureus ipse rotis.

> Flattery, Delusion, and Madness will be your retinue,
>   always following along behind you.
> With that army you conquer both men and gods.
>   Strip away those supports and you'll be naked.
> From the top of Olympus your mother will applaud your triumph
>   and shower roses in your face.
> Wings glittering with gems and gems glittering in your hair,
>   you yourself all gold will ride on your gilded chariot.

In this military context to be *nudus* (38) is be unarmed, defenceless, but Ovid is smiling again. Cupid is always naked. *Et puer est et nudus Amor* (1.10.15).

Venus is on the peak of Mount Olympus and her son is flying along below her on his dove-driven chariot through the showers of petals she is scattering into his face. '*Appositas*, "placed beside her" seems rather flat . . . Possibly Ovid is alluding to a specific pictorial representation of a triumph by Cupid'.[4] Possibly, but there is another way to visualize the scene. If rose petals are being scattered into the face of a charioteer they are not tossed up, but are fluttering down. In a triumphal procession through the streets of Rome they would be thrown down from viewing platforms along the streets, or from high windows and the tops of houses. In any case they would have to be prepared, and kept at the ready, *appositas*, perhaps in baskets, until the procession arrived. Romans climbed up 'to towers and windows' and strewed flowers in the triumphator's way in the first scene of Shakespeare's *Julius Caesar*. Shakespeare may well be drawing on the description of Curio's reception in North's Plutarch, 'there were some that cast flowers and nosegays upon him when he went his way, as they commonly use to do unto any man, when he hath obtained victory, and won any games' (*Caesar* ch. 30).

> talis erat domita Bacchus Gangetide terra:
>   tu grauis alitibus, tigribus ille fuit.
> ergo cum possim sacri pars esse triumphi,
>   parce tuas in me perdere victor opes.
> aspice cognati felicia Caesaris arma:
>   qua uicit, uictos protegit ille manu.

> Such was Bacchus after he had conquered Gangetic India –
>   he weighed down tigers, you weigh down birds.
> Therefore, since I might be a part of your sacred triumph,
>   do not waste your victorious powers on me.

---

[4] McKeown (1987–), ad loc.

> Look at the victorious powers of your kinsman Caesar:
>   the hand that defeats protects the defeated.

The golden-type line 51 rises towards the sublime, but contains the ridiculous. A central plank of the Augustan settlement was the need for moral reform, particularly in the sexual sphere, and Augustus took this seriously. His Julian Laws on matrimony, *Leges Iuliae de maritandis ordinibus* and *de adulteriis coercendis*, imposed strict rules for compulsory marriage and strict punishments for adultery. They were passed in 18 BC perhaps a couple of years before this edition of the *Amores*. The Julian family valued its descent from Iulus, son of Aeneas, and Augustus was doubly a Julian, Caesar's adopted son and the grandson of Caesar's sister Julia. Aeneas and Cupid were therefore sons of Venus by different fathers (see above on 1.29), and Ovid is here making play with that relationship at the beginning of this collection of cheerful poems about non-matrimonial love. He was brilliantly intelligent, sensitive, and experienced in the law. How on earth can he have been so foolish? Part of the explanation of this misjudgement may lie in his youth. At this time he was the bright new star in Roman poetry, a dazzlingly successful performer who loved performing, so much in love with his own intelligence that he may have thought himself above all danger. He knew that Horace was valued by Augustus, and was an intimate friend of Maecenas. He also knew that Horace and Maecenas teased each other boisterously and sometimes obscenely in verse and in letters. Augustus admired Horace and wrote to him affectionately, even trying gamely to join in the badinage in fragments of his own letters preserved in the Suetonian life of Horace. With this example before him young Ovid may have hoped to enjoy a similar relationship with the most powerful man in the world. He did not have Horace's *savoir faire*.

AMORES 1. 3

Ovid has capitulated, admitting defeat. He is now the spoil, the booty of the victor, *tua sum noua praeda, Cupido* (1.2.19), and continuity is established by *praedata* in the first line of 1.3:

> iusta precor: quae me nuper praedata puella est
>   aut amet aut faciat cur ego semper amem,
> a, nimium volui: tantum patiatur amari,
>   audierit nostras tot Cythera preces.
> accipe per longas tibi qui deseruiat annos.
>   accipe qui pura norit amare fide.

I appeal for justice: let the girl who has captured me
　　either love me or give me reason to love her for ever.
Alas! I have asked too much. Let her just allow herself to be loved,
　　and Venus of Cythera will have heard all my prayers.
Accept one who will be your slave throughout the long years,
　　one who would know how to love purely and chastely.

Lines 3–4 form a dramatic conditional sentence. 'Laugh and the world laughs
with you' is a vigorous version of 'If you laugh the world laughs with you'. The
same 'conditional by imperative' occurs in lines 19–20. If Venus answers
Ovid's prayer in the *Amores*, this can mean only one thing, and it is something
less than what he prayed for in line 2. There he wanted the girl to love him, or
else give him reason to love her for ever, and the crucial difference is the loss of
the word *semper*. When he now says that Venus will have answered his prayers
if the girl allows him to love her, he is lowering his sights. His only hope now
is to make love to her.

　　To achieve this, he tells her that he comes from a good equestrian family
and frugal parents who brought him up to know the value of money (*parcus
uterque parens* is a kind word for his mother). And he has allies, Apollo, the
Muses, Bacchus inventor of the vine, and Amor (13–16),

　　et nulli cessura fides, sine crimine mores,
　　　　nudaque simplicitas purpureusque pudor.
　　non mihi mille placent, non sum desultor amoris;
　　　　tu mihi, si qua fides, cura perennis eris.

　　and a loyalty which yields to none, a blameless character,
　　　　naked truth, and blushing modesty.
　　I am no philanderer. I don't love thousands.
　　　　If there is any truth in the world, you will be my love for ever.

But in lines 3–4 he gave up the hope that she would be his *cura perennis*. There
is a clear discrepancy. Ovid's persona in the *Amores* is that of the philanderer.
(*Desultores* were stunt riders who leapt from one galloping horse to another.)
His whole object in the *Amores* is to make love to Corinna or her hairdresser
or some other woman. The poems are a demonstration of the techniques of
seduction. Lines 13–16 are a sample of the required rhetoric. This interpretation of 1.3 is supported by the scheming which fills the whole of the next
poem and in particular the juxtaposition of this pious chicanery at the end of
1.3 before the first disgraceful couplet of 1.4. Guy Lee sees it in translating
3.13–14 with tongue in cheek:

　　　　fidelity, integrity,
　　　　sincerity, sensitivity.

The three mythological *exempla* (19–26) need to be looked at closely:

> te mihi materiem felicem in carmina praebe,
>> prouenient causa carmina digna sua.
> carmine nomen habet exterrita cornibus Io,
>> et quam fluminea lusit adulter aue,
> quaeque super pontum simulato uecta iuuenco
>> uirginea tenuit cornua uara manu.
> nos quoque per totum pariter cantabimur orbem
>> iunctaque semper erunt nomina nostra tuis.

> Give yourself to me as a rich subject for my songs,
>> and there will be harvests worthy of their inspiration.
> Io, terrified by horns, has her name in song,
>> as does the maid deceived by the river-bird adulterer,
> and the maid borne over the sea by a bull that was no bull,
>> gripping his crooked horns in her virgin hand.
> We too shall be sung the whole world over,
>> and my name shall ever be linked to yours.

Ovid will be as Jupiter, king of gods and men, and the tone is lofty with its golden-type lines 20 and 24, and antonomasia for Leda and Europa, that figure of speech so dear to the high style whereby a description is given instead of a name. On the face of it such love might be an alluring prospect for a mortal woman, but take Io, terrified by horns, and they were her own, which sprouted when Jupiter's avenging wife turned her into a cow; or Leda, *quam... lusit adulter* by strange means; or Europa, whose voyage was frightening and hard on the hands. *Virginea* and *uara* are an expressive pair. And these maidens were not loved by a model of fidelity like the Ovid who pleaded in 13–18, but were all three victims of a serial adulterer.

Ovid published this first book of the *Amores* in about 16 BC, a couple of years after the appearance of Propertius' first book of love elegies, which, like those of his predecessor Gallus, followed their Greek model Callimachus in deploying abstruse mythological learning. Not to be outdone, Ovid also plied learned mythological references, but with a difference. The *exempla* in 1.3.21–4 are made to sound learned and problematical, but are so presented that they would have been easily understood by his Roman audience. Io's horns, the adulterous river bird, and the maiden gripping the horns of the false bull, pose general knowledge questions, nicely graded to give an audience the pleasure of solving them.

This poem is the third in the series which forms an introduction to the *Amores*. It is not to be read as a serious declaration of love, but as a cheerful exposé of the deviousness of lovers, an *ars amatoria* in action, a demonstration of what is to come in the poems that follow.

AMORES 1.4

Vir tuus est epulas nobis aditurus easdem;
   ultima cena tuo sit, precor, illa uiro.

Your husband? Going to the same dinner as us?
   I hope it chokes him.

Guy Lee's version here catches the essence of this opening so deftly that it can be forgiven for losing the venomous repetition of *Vir tuus* in *tuo... uiro*. These poems were written with recitation in mind. The accomplished performer (I write with envy) can begin with a joke, and the audience is in the palm of his hand. In his student days Ovid was a promising declaimer, and he clearly knew how to begin. His first poem opens with a parody of the *Aeneid* and an epiphany, the second with a lover sleepless in his bed, the third with a passionate appeal, 'I beg for justice', the fourth now with the information that Ovid's *puella* has a husband and that Ovid wishes him dead, the fifth with an atmospheric siesta scene again parodying the *Aeneid*. Each of the next two poems sets its scene vividly and economically, each containing an emotive parenthesis, (*indignum!*), (*meruere catenas*), but the wittiest *captatio beneuolentiae* begins *Amores* 1.8:

Est quaedam (quicumque uolet cognoscere lenam
   audiat), est quaedam nomine Dipsas anus.

There's a woman I know (anybody who might need a Madam
   should listen), there's a woman called Mrs Thirst.

The barb in the brackets is typical of Ovid's technique, as is the run-on of *audiat*, and it's a fair guess that the reciter had to pause for laughter after it, repeating his opening to resume the thread of his discourse.

Amores 1.4.7–10 presents another example of the 'pseudo-abstruse' seen above in 3.21–4. Ovid is imagining himself watching his beloved, while her husband touches her, takes her in his arms, and puts his hand on her neck whenever he wants to:

desine mirari, posito quod candida uino
   Atracis ambiguos traxit in arma uiros.
nec mihi silua domus, nec equo mea membra cohaerent.
   uix a te uideor posse tenere manus.

Don't be surprised that when the wine was on the table
   fair Atracis drove the ambiguous men to arms.
My home is not the forest, and my limbs are not attached to a horse,
   and I can hardly keep my hands off you.

Few of Ovid's readers and even fewer members of his audience would have known the family details of Atrax, a Thessalian king, river, and city, but they would soon have deduced that the fair Atracis who drove the drunken centaurs to brawl was Pirithous' bride Hippodamia whose beauty provoked the battle between the Lapiths and drunken Centaurs at her wedding. The audience would have enjoyed their success in solving the mythological problem. They would also have enjoyed *ambiguos uiros*, and Ovid's confusion. If he had been a Centaur it is not his limbs that would have been attached to a horse, but his head. Then there is the verb *traxit*. Hippodamia dragged centaurs into arms. Surely if there was to be any dragging, the quadrupeds would have dragged the bride. And there is the assonance, *Átracis ámbiguos tráxit in árma uiros!*

Amores 1.4 is a stream of conspiratorial instructions to the lady he desires, to enable her to communicate silently with him throughout a dinner party, and to engineer an opportunity for some snatched moments with her after it. Ovid the *recitator* was not only master of the art of beginning (see on 1.4.1–2 above) but he also wielded a devastating *fulmen in clausula*. After sixty lines of scheming he realizes that his schemes must fail, and accepts that his *inamorata* will spend the night with her husband (3.69–70) (Guy Lee is responsible for 'and stick to that story'):

> sed quaecumque tamen noctem fortuna sequetur,
>   cras mihi constanti uoce dedisse nega.

> But whatever may be the fortune of the night, tomorrow
>   tell me you gave him nothing, and stick to that story.

AMORES 1.5

This is a masterpiece in miniature, an anecdote in three phases each of eight lines, and a delicious envoi in two (1–8):

> Aestus erat mediamque dies exegerat horam.
>   apposui medio membra leuanda toro.
> pars adaperta fuit, pars altera clausa fenestrae,
>   quale fere siluae lumen habere solent,
> qualia sublucent fugiente crepuscula Phoebo
>   aut ubi nox abiit nec tamen orta dies.

ilia uerecundis lux est praebenda puellis
    qua timidus latebras speret habere pudor.

The heat was great. The day had passed its middle hour,
    and I had laid my limbs to rest in the middle of my bed.
One shutter was open, the other closed the
    light often seen in woods,
like the dimness of dusk as Phoebus flees away,
    or when night has gone but day has not arisen.
That is the light bashful girls should have,
    so their anxious modesty can hope for concealment.

Nox erat et placidum carpebant fessa soporem | corpora per terras (*Aen.* 4.522). It was night, the last night of Dido's life, 'and weary bodies were quietly taking their sleep upon the earth', and Ovid's tale of love begins in similar tones. The epic hint is strengthened in line 4, which recalls the light through which Aeneas and the Sibyl descended to the Underworld in *Aeneid* 6.270–1, *quale per incertam lunam sub luce maligna | est iter in siluis*. McKeown hears 'the luxuriant -1- and -u- sounds' in both texts. Similes which offer alternatives with *aut* or *uel* are an epic feature, as in *Aeneid* 10.135, 273, 603, 725, 806. The adverb *fere* occurs four times in Virgil, and Ovid may here be glancing at *Aeneid* 5.835–6, *iamque fere mediam caeli Nox umida metam | contigerat*, 'And now dank Night had touched the middle turning point of the sky'. Having found his *puella* after eighty-two lines, after 178 he has still not made love to her, and now 'I laid my limbs to rest in the middle of the bed'—clearly he did not expect company. In lines 4–6 the lofty epic tone of the triple simile with the golden-type line 5 is all a feint. Lines 7–8 suggest what is to come. The atmosphere is brought sharply back from epic to erotic in the half-light which should be provided for bashful maidens so that their timid coyness might have hope of concealment. Lines 7–8 may seem to be a sensitive and sympathetic description of young girls' nervousness, but on Ovid's lips they are a knowing and useful observation for seducers. This is love elegy, not epic.

ecce Corinna uenit, tunica uelata recincta,
    candida diuidua colla tegente coma,
qualiter in thalamos formosa Semiramis isse
    dicitur, et multis Lais amata uiris.
deripui tunicam: nec multum rara nocebat,
    pugnabat tunica sed tamen illa tegi.
cumque ita pugnaret tamquam qui uincere nollet
    uicta est non aegre proditione sua.

(lines 9–16)

In comes Corinna, wearing an unbelted gown,
  her hair parted to fall round her white neck,
like the fair Semiramis coming into the bedchamber,
  so they say, or like Lais loved by many men.
I pulled down the gown. Being diaphanous it was not doing any harm,
  but for all that she fought to keep it on,
and since she fought as though she did not want to conquer,
  she was conquered without difficulty by her own betrayal.

Ecce Corinna uenit at last. This is the fifth phase of Ovid's approach to love, his first experience of it, and the first time that Corinna is named. She is wearing a *tunica*, a long-sleeved gown reaching to the feet (*OLD*, 1b), but it is *recincta*, ungirt, loose, not the dress of one who is *uerecunda*, *timida*, or *pudica* like those in lines 7–8. In a lofty-sounding double simile she is compared to Semiramis and Lais. Semiramis was the Queen of Babylon who murdered her lovers in her bedchamber (Euphorion, *SH* 415 col. 1.9ff.), and even, if Pliny *Natural History* 8.155 is to be believed, made love to a horse *usque in coitum*. Lais was the name of two famous Greek courtesans. Although *thalamus* was often used as a plural with a singular sense, in view of the statement that Lais was loved by many men, *thalamos* may hint that Semiramis made a habit of entering bedrooms with her gown unbelted.

In 14 the postponed *sed tamen* is emphatic. The negligée was not doing any harm from Ovid's point of view, *but for all that* she was fighting to remain covered by it, but not fighting very hard.

  ut stetit ante oculos posito uelamine nostros,
    in toto nusquam corpore menda fuit.
  quos umeros, quales uidi tetigique lacertos!
    forma papillarum quam fuit apta premi!
  quam castigato planus sub pectore uenter!
    quantum et quale latus! quam iuuenale femur!
  singula quid referam? nil non laudabile uidi
    et nudam pressi corpus ad usque meum.

                                        (lines 17–24)

When she stood there unclad before my eyes,
  there was not a blemish on her whole body.
What shoulders, what arms I saw and touched!
  The curve of her breasts how made to be pressed!
How flat the belly under the trim bosom!
  What a flank! O! the length of it! And the girlish thigh!
Why make a list? Everything I saw was perfect
  and I pressed her naked body hard against my own.

The pace of this scene is set by the rhythms of the pentameters: *in tóto núsquam córpore ménda luit*, a measured scrutiny; then *fórma pápillárum quam fúit ápta prémi*, where only the first syllable and *ápta* carry both metrical stress and word accent, and *apta premi* almost echoes the alliteration of *papillarum*: then *quántum et quále látus, quám iuuenále femur*, where the triple alliteration of -*qu*- and the quintuple assonance of -*a*- leave Ovid open-mouthed; then *et núdam préssi córpus ad úsque méum* with the urgency of its five dissyllables.

Apart from some few lapses into obscenity, Ovid is elegant and refined in his poetic love play. In line 20 *quos umeros* waits for the verb that will govern the accusative, and there are two of them, 'What shoulders (I saw and touched), what arms I saw and touched.' This suggests his wonderment at the sight of this perfection, as he touches her shoulders and then draws his hands down her arms. His eyes and the pentameter come to the shape of the breasts but there is no touching, only the thought of it. In 21–2 *castigato, plano, quantum*, and *iuuenale* describe a tall slender youthful body, but *latus* gives pause. As often as not in the *Amores* it is used in various senses in contexts of sexual intercourse, as in 1.8.48, but here it seems to be purely anatomical, without any such overtone. This has been a hymn to female beauty in seven lines. The only touch of Ovidian mischief is the eloquent reprise of *apta premi* (20) in *pressi* (24).

The elevation in the hymn comes partly from the rhetoric. At the banquet which Dido provided for Aeneas and his shipwrecked comrades, Dido pro-longed the night with all manner of talk, drinking long draughts of love, asking question after question about Priam and Hector, and in 1.751–2 *what* armour Memnon was wearing when he came, *what kind* of horses Diomede had, *how tall* was Achilles, and her infatuation is audible in *nunc quibus, nunc quales, nunc quantus*:

> nunc quibus Aurorae venisset filius armis,
> nunc quales Diomedis equi, nunc quantus Achilles.

Anaphora is the repetition of a word at the beginning of several clauses, and this is anaphora with a difference. The clause begins with similar words— quasi-anaphora? Ovid's infatuation is even more acute, a septuple quasi-anaphora followed naughtily by *singula quid referam*, and then *quis* leading to the fervent hope which ends the poem (25–6):

> cetera quis nescit? lassi requiescimus ambo.
> proueniant medii sic mihi saepe dies.
>
> Everybody knows the rest. Exhausted, we slept.
> May many a midday yield me such a harvest!

9

Rome and Persia 357–9: The Role of Tamsapor

Robin Seager

I. TAMSAPOR AND MUSONIANUS

In 357 hostilities between Rome and Persia on Rome's eastern frontier were for the moment muted.[1] Sapor was occupied on his northern borders in campaigns against the Chionitae (16.9.4), and so the Persians were restricting themselves to raids in quest of plunder (15.13.4), with only limited success (16.9.1). However, these raids were facilitated by the behaviour of the praetorian prefect Musonianus and Prosper, deputy for the absent Ursicinus (cf. 14.11.5). Acting in concert, they devoted themselves to extorting money from their subjects instead of protecting them from Persian incursions (15.13.1–3).

But despite this dereliction of duty Musonianus now, in consultation with the *dux Mesopotamiae* Cassianus, devised a scheme to establish a peace (16.9.2). He sent out *speculatores* to enquire into the *consilia* of the Persians (16.9.2). In fact their report seems to have constituted an account of what Sapor was doing rather than of his *consilia*, except perhaps in the negative sense that he appeared to be too heavily committed in the north to have any immediate plans for serious campaigning against the Romans (16.9.3).

The news of Sapor's difficulties led Musonianus to hope that the king might be prepared to turn the current lull in hostilities into a formal and possibly durable agreement. He therefore entered into negotiations, probably early in 357, with the satrap Tamsapor, suggesting that he advise the king by letter to make a peace with Constantius that would leave Sapor free to concentrate on

The views adumbrated in this paper had their origin in discussions with my former pupil Julian Chater. I am grateful to members of the Liverpool Classics and Ancient History Seminar for some helpful suggestions and to Bruce Gibson for valuable comments on a subsequent draft. All references in the text are to Ammianus.

[1] For the general situation on the eastern frontier at this time, cf. e.g. Barceló (1981), 88–91; Blockley (1989), 479–82; Seager (1997), 254–7.

his northern borders without worrying that the Romans would try to take advantage of his absence (16.9.3).[2]

Tamsapor agreed to write to his master. But the content of his letter was not at all what Musonianus would have wanted or perhaps expected. Musonianus had implied that the initiative should come from Sapor. His attitude is easily comprehensible. Roman self-respect might demand it; moreover, Musonianus could not say that Constantius was offering peace, since he was acting without the emperor's knowledge. There is no reason to doubt Ammianus' accuracy in this matter. It is theoretically possible, but extremely far-fetched, to claim that Constantius had in fact authorized Musonianus' initiative, only to disown it later when it failed to bear fruit.[3] Ammianus clearly knew nothing of such a possibility; if he had heard of it, he would hardly have passed up the chance to discredit Constantius for such treatment of a loyal subordinate.[4]

Ammianus claims that Tamsapor acted *his fretus*. The exact sense of this phrase is not at all clear.[5] In fact Tamsapor told the king that Constantius was pleading for peace because he was enmeshed in difficult wars (16.9.4, cf. 17.5.1). Why did Tamsapor write as he did? To answer this question it is necessary to consider the options open to him and their likely consequences. He could have rejected Musonianus' suggestion out of hand. In that case the situation might have remained as it was or more probably war would eventually have been renewed after Sapor's return from the north, whenever the king felt that the time was ripe to try to rectify the injustice, as Persia saw it, of the status quo. Or he might have written to Sapor along the lines adumbrated by Musonianus, urging the king to make the first move in opening negotiations with Constantius. It is a reasonable conjecture that on receipt of such a letter Sapor would have flown into a rage with both the Romans, for their arrogance, and Tamsapor, for daring to recommend such an unworthy course of

---

[2] Despite corruption in the text of 16.9.3 the general sense is clear.

[3] Though the picture of Constantius and Musonianus as prototypes of George I and April Glaspey has, it must be confessed, a certain macabre charm.

[4] It is, however, rash to assume with Pighi (1936), 146–9, that Musonianus and Cassianus were 'indirect' sources of Ammianus, mediated through Libanius. This presupposes a relationship between Ammianus and Libanius that is as implausible as it is unattested. Cf. the cautionary remarks of Sabbah (1978), 119–20, 169.

[5] Translators are divided between impersonal and personal interpretations: thus Rolfe ('this information'); Galletier ('fort de ces informations'); Hamilton ('their good faith'); Seyfarth ('im Vertrauen auf die beiden Genannten'); Blockley (1992), 19 ('based upon the approach from the Romans'). Grammatically the personal interpretation seems more plausible, with the meaning no more than that Tamsapor judged the Roman initiative to be sincere and so decided that he would be able to exploit it for his own ends. Translations that mention Roman good faith are dangerous, as they may imply that Tamsapor too sincerely wanted peace.

action. A renewal of the war would be virtually certain, but Tamsapor might well have lost his command, if not his head.

What then did Tamsapor hope to achieve by the letter he actually sent? It is just conceivable that he too wanted to secure what Musonianus hoped for, a peace that in essence reaffirmed the status quo, but felt that the only chance of securing Sapor's agreement was by making it appear that Constantius was begging for peace. To respond to such an abject appeal would involve no loss of face for the king and might satisfy the demands of his boundless ego. But such an interpretation has little to commend it. It is hard to see why Tamsapor should have wanted such an outcome, even harder to reconcile such a pacific turn of mind with his subsequent eagerness to make use of Antoninus (see below, section II).

Moreover, such a manoeuvre on the satrap's part would be almost certain to misfire. Sapor's likely reaction to Tamsapor's letter would be to return as soon as possible, either to invade without prior negotiation while Constantius was allegedly weak and distracted, or at least to offer terms so demanding, backed by the threat of war if they were not met, that Constantius was bound to reject them. The latter is of course what in fact happened. The natural conclusion is that this is what Tamsapor wanted and expected to happen, in other words that he saw in Musonianus' attempt to secure a lasting peace the chance to bring about instead an escalation of the war, with no risk to his own position and a strong possibility of increasing his credit with his master.

The prudent Musonianus must have informed Constantius at once of what he had done. After his state visit to Rome in spring 357 the emperor summoned Ursicinus to Sirmium. There lengthy deliberations took place about Musonianus' report of a possible peace with Persia (16.10.21). The question arises: what exactly did Musonianus report?[6] Primarily that he had made an approach to Tamsapor, suggesting that peace would be in Persia's best interests, and that the satrap had agreed to write to his master. He may have emphasized the point that such a peace might keep Sapor well away from his border with Rome. But he cannot have revealed the content of Tamsapor's letter, of which he knew nothing. It is difficult to gauge Constantius' reaction to the news. But once the discussions were over he sent Ursicinus back to the East as commander-in-chief, a move that might suggest he had no great hopes of peace.

It was not until 358 that the king received Tamsapor's letter. By this time he had made a treaty with the Chionitae and Gelani and was on the point of returning home (17.5.1, cf. 16.9.4). Again Ammianus highlights the emphasis

---

[6] That Musonianus' report was Ammianus' principal source is rightly maintained by Sabbah (1978), 169.

placed by the satrap on Constantius' supposedly suppliant posture. Sapor reacted exactly as might have been expected. Believing that Constantius was in serious difficulties, he saw the chance to impose harsh terms (17.5.2). His letter to the emperor was pitched at the height of his not inconsiderable arrogance. He complimented Constantius on learning at last the disastrous results of coveting the territory of others (17.5.3). This is no more than an offensive way of presenting the standard Persian view of the treaty of 299. He then assumed a pose of moderation. By ancestral right he could and should legitimately claim all the lands as far as the Strymon and the boundaries of Macedonia. But he would rest content with the restoration of the balance upset by the peace of 299 and demand only Armenia and Mesopotamia (17.5.5–6). This minor concession would suffice to win Constantius security for the future (17.5.7). The letter ended with an unequivocal threat of war in the spring of 359 should the emperor fail to comply (17.5.8).

Before considering Constantius' reply it may be as well to reflect briefly on what Sapor might have expected it to be. Even if he had been led by Tamsapor's letter to an exaggerated estimate of Constantius' difficulties, the king can hardly have hoped that Rome would meekly surrender the gains made in 299. Sapor's terms were such that Constantius was in honour bound to refuse them, even if he had been in as weak a position as Tamsapor had disingenuously suggested. The king must have been aware that the likely outcome of his letter would be a war in the next campaigning season and must therefore have been ready to accept that outcome. So Tamsapor had achieved precisely what he had set out to do: to bring his master home in bellicose mood, ready for a full-scale invasion of Roman territory.

Constantius made the only possible answer. He stressed (without deigning to name either of them) that Musonianus' approach to Tamsapor, though well intentioned, had been undertaken on the prefect's own initiative and without his prior knowledge. The implied point is clear: Constantius had not approached Sapor, cap in hand or not. Nevertheless he declared himself amenable to peace, provided only that the terms were honourable and compatible with his dignity—as Sapor's terms were manifestly not. He went on to refute by implication the king's assumption that he was currently in a weak position, stressing that his mastery of the entire Roman world was now unchallenged (17.5.13). It should not, however, be assumed that Constantius was aware of the nature of Tamsapor's letter. A desire to underline the absurdity of Sapor's behaviour and to warn him against rash aggression is enough to explain the emperor's turn of phrase. In conclusion (17.5.14) he claimed only to defend what was rightfully his—but that again is no more than the standard Roman version of the status quo since 299.

Constantius followed up this reply with an embassy bearing gifts and a further letter, demanding peace on the terms of the status quo, and with instructions to delay Sapor's preparations for as long as possible (17.5.15).[7] He must have realized that war was inevitable as a result of his rejection of Sapor's demands and that all he could do was to try to buy time in which to complete his work on the Danube and prepare to meet the Persian threat. The envoys found, predictably enough, that Sapor was determined to recover Armenia and Mesopotamia, and so returned empty-handed. They did, however, achieve their principal objective, spending a great deal of time in accomplishing nothing (17.14.1–2). Constantius even sent a further embassy with the same remit, which can only be seen as yet another delaying tactic (17.14.3).

II. TAMSAPOR AND ANTONINUS

The next report is of Sapor's preparations for the threatened campaign in 359 (18.4.1). There then intervenes the tale of the renegade Antoninus, which also brings Tamsapor back into the story (18.5.1–3). In Ammianus' account the initiative in Antoninus' treason comes solely from Antoninus himself, albeit in response, as the historian concedes, to considerable provocation from unjust officials (18.5.1–2, cf. 8.6). Antoninus compiled a vast dossier of military resources, troop movements, planned expeditions and so forth, then carefully plotted his desertion, buying and moving to an estate in Iaspis, near the bank of the Tigris. Once there, he established contact with Tamsapor. Again the initiative comes from Antoninus.

The result of their negotiations was that Tamsapor gave active support to ensure the safe evacuation of Antoninus and all his household across the Tigris into Persian territory (18.5.3). He must have been impressed by the information on offer, since Antoninus' person was of no value in itself. What is more, Antoninus was promptly conducted to the king's winter quarters, received with open arms and made a member of the royal council (18.5.6). This welcome can only have been due to the enthusiastic support of Tamsapor, who must have commended his protégé to the king very warmly indeed.

From the first Antoninus advised the king to change his strategy, advocating the abandonment of time-consuming sieges and set-piece battles in

---

[7] In the last sentence Bentley's *dum* should be read.

favour of a blitzkrieg that would secure control of the whole of Roman Asia (18.5.6–7). After some debate this strategy was approved (18.6.3–4, cf. 5.8), as was eventually reported to Ursicinus at Amida by a messenger from Constantius' second embassy (18.6.17–19).

At this point two questions arise, to which any answers can unfortunately be only speculative. (1) When did Antoninus first make contact with Tamsapor, and in particular was it before or after the satrap's letter to Sapor? (2) Whenever that first contact was made, did Tamsapor obtain from Antoninus at that time information valuable enough to persuade him to abet Antoninus' desertion? The first of these questions demands the evaluation of an extremely interesting aside in Ammianus' account of the negotiations that took place after Antoninus' move to Iaspis: that Tamsapor was already known to Antoninus (18.5.3: *et antea cognitus*, presumably to be taken with *qui*, sc. Tamsapor).

The first point to be determined, if possible, is what *cognitus* means in this context. Of the various senses of the word, two are prima facie possible: (a) 'personally acquainted' (b) 'known by reputation'. In either case *cognitus* will have a causal connotation: it was because of his previous knowledge of Tamsapor, whatever its precise nature, that the satrap now seemed to Antoninus a suitable person to approach.[8] The standard translations and commentaries all agree that the first sense is intended here.[9] But the matter deserves further consideration.

In the usage of Ammianus, whenever *cognitus* means 'known by reputation', the specific actions or qualities for which the subject is famous are usually specified.[10] There are, however, two passages where *cognitus* means 'known by reputation' without specifying the precise grounds. At 21.12.16 Agilo is described as *probe cognitum*, either to Julian or to the world at large or both; the precise meaning is debatable, but the reference is clearly to Agilo's reputation.[11] Antioch is praised at 14.8.8 as *mundo cognita ciuitas*: no doubt in Ammianus' view its merits were too many, various, and manifest to need listing.

Two further passages merit closer attention. At 22.9.13 Julian warmly greets Celsus, *iam inde a studiis cognitum Atticis*. This is universally and probably

---

[8] Cf. De Jonge (1980) ad loc.

[9] Thus Rolfe ('whom he already knew'); Hamilton ('who was already known to him'); Sabbah ('qu'il connaissait avant ces événements'); Seyfarth ('schon seit langem bekannt').

[10] Thus 14.11.3 of Ursicinus' sons, 22.8.38, 25.9.7 of Jovian, 26.8.7 of Cyzicus, 26.9.5 of Arbitio, 27.8.3 of Theodosius, 27.11.1 of Probus; cf. 31.14.1 of the qualities of Valens.

[11] Translators and commentators differ as to whether the description of Agilo is positive (thus Hamilton: 'had a great reputation'; Fontaine: 'honorablement connu'; den Boeft et al. (1991), ad loc.) or neutral (thus Rolfe: 'well known'; Seyfarth: 'wohlbekannt').

correctly understood as 'personally known to him from their student days in Athens', rather than 'known to him for his studies in Greek', though no other source specifically states that Celsus and Julian knew each other as students. At 26.5.14 Valentinian chooses Gaudentius for an important mission, *olim sibi cognitum et fidelem*. Again commentators and translators agree that *cognitum* means 'personally known', but the phrase might be a hendiadys for 'knowing his reputation for loyalty' without necessarily implying personal acquaintance.

The standard view of 18.5.3 raises questions which its proponents do not ask, much less attempt to answer: exactly how, when and where did Tamsapor become personally known to Antoninus? It is not in fact easy to imagine the circumstances in which a meeting might have occurred. It is true that Antoninus had once been a merchant, in which role Ammianus describes him as *per omnes illas notissimus terras*, which, despite De Jonge's doubts ad loc., probably means 'very well known throughout the whole of Mesopotamia'. His commercial activities may well have taken him to Persia by way of the permitted crossing point of Nisibis.[12] But it is hardly likely that his commercial activities would have brought him into contact with Tamsapor unless he had made a conscious effort to gain an audience, and during his time as a merchant he had no motive to do so. It is only after Antoninus had decided to put together his dossier of military intelligence that Tamsapor would have entered into his calculations as a potentially suitable recipient of the information he would eventually have to offer. Even after he moved close to the border his negotiations with the satrap were carried out through intermediaries.

It could be argued that, even if they had not met, Antoninus might have written to Tamsapor and received an encouraging reply. Whether *cognitus* could bear this meaning is uncertain: Ammianus offers no parallel. But even if it could, the contingency seems implausible. To send even the most cursory missive would be a tremendous risk, since its interception would undoubtedly have cost Antoninus his life. He appears in Ammianus as a careful and patient planner, for whom such a perilous gamble would have had no attraction.

In the light of these difficulties the alternative interpretation of *cognitus* has much to commend it. In that case Ammianus is saying only that Tamsapor was known to Antoninus by reputation as a hawk, who might therefore be expected to be interested in any information or strategic advice that Antoninus had to offer. It would follow that Antoninus had no opportunity to give Tamsapor information or advice before the negotiations between them that

---

[12] As assumed e.g. by Sabbah (1996), 196 n. 165.

took place after Antoninus' move to Iaspis, as is indeed the natural inference from the run of Ammianus' narrative. Therefore in composing his letter to the king Tamsapor could not have been influenced by anything learned from Antoninus.[13]

On the other hand it is clear that when Tamsapor brought Antoninus to the king he regarded his protégé as a very special acquisition. It is tempting to suppose that Antoninus' exalted standing depended on something more than mere information, even if his information was much more detailed and reliable than that supplied by other sources. He may therefore by that time have already put before the satrap his plan for a new strategy, a plan that might well have appealed to the aggressive Tamsapor and encouraged him to recommend Antoninus to the king.

Tamsapor's letter can hardly be said to have changed the course of history. It is true that it succeeded in bringing Sapor home intent on invading Mesopotamia. But Sapor would have done that anyway sooner rather than later. As for Antoninus' strategy of blitzkrieg, it was never given a fair trial, but was aborted before the walls of Amida thanks to Sapor's fit of pique at being shot at (19.1.5–6) and (far more importantly) Grumbates' insistence on vengeance for the death of his son (19.2.1). But even if it had been pursued as planned it would have been unlikely to have brought any permanent gain. Eventually Sapor would have been forced to withdraw, like Hannibal before him—a pleasing irony, given that Ammianus sees fit to cast Antoninus as Maharbal (18.5.6).

Why then does Ammianus show so much interest in the episode? Various reasons suggest themselves. Two of his major characters, Constantius and Sapor, played prominent roles. He casts Antoninus as a man whose actions were unjustified but who behaved as he did only under extreme pressure and with some extenuating circumstances, and such cases seem to have intrigued him, witness his very elaborate account of the attempted usurpation of Procopius, who similarly found himself in an impossible situation (cf. esp. 26.2.3–4). He had been present at the confrontation between the renegade and his hero Ursicinus (18.8.5–6). Moreover, by a chapter of accidents, Antoninus' invasion strategy had led (in)directly to the first great traumatic event in Ammianus' military career, the siege of Amida.

---

[13] Both Barceló (1981), 89 with n. 416, and Blockley (1989), 480 and (1992), 19, assert as fact that Antoninus and Tamsapor had been in regular contact before Musonianus made his approach. This goes well beyond what might legitimately be assumed from Ammianus, even if *cognitus* did connote personal acquaintance. Neither considers how the contact posited might have been made.

Part III

Poetry and Politics

10

Munera uestra cano: The Poet, the Gods, and the Thematic Unity of Georgics 1

Damien Nelis

Virgil's *Georgics* is considered by many to be the most difficult poem in Latin literature. Certainly, it continues to attract intense scholarly investigation. The last twenty years have seen the publication of three major commentaries,[1] a number of important monographs,[2] and a series of surveys in handbooks and companions.[3] In an attempt to contribute to ongoing debates about certain features of this extraordinarily complex text, taking as a starting point advances in our understanding of the poem and its generic background, I intend to offer some thoughts about the structure of the first book and its thematic coherence by looking at the ways in which Virgil relates his description of the life and work of the farmer to the movement of the solar year, to Roman history, and to contemporary politics. And I hope that this study of a didactic text will be of some interest to a scholar who has taught me so much and who has always shown the way.

The poem's authorial voice immediately establishes control over its exquisitely outlined subject matter by revealing the contents of its four books in precisely four lines and by emphasizing its power over the choice of a precise beginning point: *hinc canere incipiam* ('from this point I will begin to sing', 1.5).[4] The unobtrusive adverb, often overlooked, can be interpreted on a

I would like to thank the editors for their invitation to contribute, their most useful comments on my initial draft, and their patience.

[1] Thomas (1988), Mynors (1990), Erren (2003).

[2] e.g. Farrell (1991), Morgan (1999), Gale (2000), Nappa (2005).

[3] e.g. Horsfall (1995), Martindale (1997), Hardie (1998), La Penna (2005), Holzberg (2006), von Albrecht (2006).

[4] The opening sentence reveals the four main subjects to be ploughing, viticulture, herding, and bee-keeping and establishes some key words for the four books to follow: *segetes*, cf. 1.47, 54, 77, 112, 152, 212, 226, 270, 319; *sidere*, cf. 1.32, 73, 204, 311, 335; *terram uertere*, cf. 1.147; *ulmis*, cf. 2.18, 70, 72, 83, 221, 361, 367, 446, 530; *uitis*, cf. 2.63, 70, 97, 191, 221, 233, 273, 289, 299, 397, 407, 410, 416; *boum*, cf. 3.52, 211, 369, 419, 532; *pecori*, cf. 3.6, 72, 75, 125, 155, 159,

number of levels.[5] Most obviously, *hinc* has a straightforward temporal force, meaning simply 'from this point in time'. But by drawing the reader's attention to his ability to select this particular starting point for his poem, the poet underlines his control over its subject matter and provides it with a sense of a trajectory. The effect is to draw attention to the very act of 'singing' or, to put it another way, to the initiation of a didactic message and the direction or form it will take subsequently. In addition, an impression is created of dramatic immediacy, that the 'song' is actually being delivered or performed and that the information it conveys, imagined as a pre-existing body of knowledge, is being transmitted at the very moment in which it is being read.[6] In generic terms, the effect is similar to that created by the beginning of the *Theogony* of Hesiod, 'Let us begin to sing *from* the Heliconian Muses', introducing a hymn to Zeus. Closely comparable too is the opening of the *Phaenomena* of Aratus, 'Let us begin *from* Zeus'. But Virgil distances himself from his didactic predecessors by delaying the naming of a deity. Initially at least, he assumes sole responsibility for his didactic lesson and the direction it will take. In doing so, the variation on his Latin predecessor and close model, Lucretius, is particularly noteworthy.[7] The *De Rerum Natura* begins with Venus (1–49), presented as the creator of the natural world and, as a Muse-like figure, of the poem itself. Subsequently, Epicurus is revealed as the quasi-divine authority figure for the philosophical truths Lucretius is going to reveal (62–79).[8]

299, 326, 342, 419, 445, 554; *apibus*, cf. 4.8, 37, 139, 149, 177, 197, 220, 251, 285, 318, 534, 556. Unless stated otherwise, all references are to the *Georgics* and all translations are from Wilkinson (1982), sometimes slightly modified.

[5] Nappa (2005), 24 has a sense of its importance and offers insightful analysis, pointing out that the word brings up the the whole question of the poem's thematic unity, especially in inviting the reader to follow the logic of the work's structure as it unfolds from this precise point.

[6] See Volk (2002), 13–24, 124–5 on this effect of 'poetic simultaneity'. Obviously, the introduction of a named addressee in line two, Maecenas, reinforces the impression of a specific performance context for this particular poetic utterance and relates it to a very particular sociopolitical milieu (on which see Du Quesnay (1984)), even if his role as addressee is partially effaced by subsequent concentration on an audience of farmers. On addressees in didactic poetry see Schiesaro et al. (1993), esp. 129–47 on the *Georgics*.

[7] See Gale (2000), 25–31.

[8] On Lucretius' imitation of Empedocles' prologue and its hymn to Love see Sedley (1998), 1–34, Trépanier (2004), 31–107, Garani (2007), 37–43. If Empedocles fr. 112 DK, in which Empedocles actually describes himself as a god, belongs somewhere in the prologue of his *On Nature*, Virgil's opening *uariatio* on didactic's traditional expression of a close relationship with the divine is even more visible. On Empedocles and the *Georgics* see Hardie (2002), Nelis (2004).

In his opening sentence, therefore, Virgil avoids claiming for himself any external source of divine origin or authority for the body of knowledge he is about to share. But he gives his poem a strong sense of a trajectory as he articulates its precise starting point and opening movements with great precision and clarity. Each of these aspects requires more detailed analysis if we wish to answer an obvious question: given that the declared aim of the first book is to explain how to grow crops successfully, how exactly is the poet going to present the relevant information? If the work is to avoid becoming a list of dry precepts, what order or structure will he impose on his material? It is perhaps simplistic to state that Virgil gave this question a lot of thought, but the difficulties involved must not be underestimated. The experience of reading the *Georgics* is very different from that involved in perusing Cato and Varro and the poem is certainly not a practical handbook. But the information it contains is in general detailed and accurate, and the poet evidently went to great pains to get such matters right.[9]

The contents of the first book can be summarized broadly as follows:

1–42:   Prologue
43–203:   The farmer's work
204–350:   The farmer's calendar
351–514:   Weather signs

It is clear that Virgil has used Hesiod's *Works and Days* and Aratus' *Phaenomena* as key elements in working out his overall structure.[10] As a result, the information provided, while on one level quite practical and detailed, is also selective and literary, one further result of which is that the farmer's world evoked in the poem is in some ways local and realistic, but in others also anachronistic and idealistic.[11] This effect paradoxically helps to clarify the ways in which Virgil weaves religious and philosophical ideas together with historical and political concerns. The end result for the reader is an impression of a perfectly coherent and ordered progress through the book, as one section leads smoothly into another, allowing the authorial voice to shift from passages of detailed advice about ploughing and sowing to passages involving religious or political material. Much has of course been written about the relationship between what are often termed the didactic portions of the work and its frequent digressions, but there exists no full and detailed modern study of the exact ways in which Virgil constructs his poem, even if there is

[9] See Spurr (1986) = Volk (2008), 14–42 and Mynors (1990), *passim* on the accuracy of much of the poem's technical detail.
[10] See Farrell (1991), 131–68.
[11] See Perkell (1989), 28–9.

now general agreement that imposing strong division between dry didactic tuition and digressive purple passages is unhelpful.[12]

On the one hand, therefore, the authorial voice introduced by the first-person *incipiam* of line 5 launches the poem on its way from a particular point (*hinc*) and then establishes gradually its authority and relevance and a sense of control over its material through the precision and truth of its utterances. But it is also a poetic, artistic voice, which changes in interesting ways throughout the book, and of course the whole work, in constant dialogue with other literary texts. If the poem's narrating voice is at pains to establish both its didactic value and its generic identity, it is only by paying attention to sophisticated patterns of allusion and to such basic linguistic phenomena as the use of imperatives, iussive subjunctives, the expression of personal experience in the first-person singular and plural, direct address couched in the second person, direct and indirect questions, gerundives, and conjunctions that its readers can appreciate key features of the poet's modulating voice and of the poem's evolving structure and themat-ic unity.[13]

As if to inculcate from the very begining the importance of following closely the work's unfolding narrative or plot, the initial <u>canere</u> incipiam (5) is picked up almost immediately in line 12 by the words *munera uestra* <u>cano</u> ('yours are the gifts I sing'), addressed to the Fauns and Dryads. The emphasis on the first-person is strengthened, but this time it is associated with the gods. Here, as throughout the whole invocation of the deities concerned with farming (*studium quibus arua tueri*, 21; 'who love to guard the country'), the poet gives great prominence to the idea of divine help (the nymphs are described as *agrestum praesentia numina*, 10, 'the present help of farmers'), underlining all that the various gods have done for the farmer (cf. *munere*, 7, *inuentrix*, 19, *monstrator*, 19; note also the verbs, strongly evocative of divine intervention and assistance: *ducitis*, 6, *fudit*, 13, *fauens*, 18, *ferens*, 20, *alitis*, 22, *demittitis*, 23).[14] In emphasizing this aspect, Virgil establishes one of the poem's central themes, the close relationship between man and the divine and, more precisely, between himself as poet, his role highlighted by the two

---

[12] Cf. Horsfall (1995), 66–7.

[13] See Horsfall (1995), 66–7, Rutherford (1995) = Volk (2008), 81–93, Volk (2002), 123–4. Burck (1929) remains required reading. The discussion of the Book's structure by Otis (1964), 148–90 has not been superseded. Putnam (1979), 17–81 and Miles (1980), 64–110 offer extremely insightful readings of the book as a whole.

[14] His model is of course Varro, *RR* 1.4, who invokes the *deos Consentis . . . qui maxime agricolarum duces sunt*, 'the twelve councillor-gods . . . who are the special patrons of husband-men' (trans. Hooper and Ash (1935)).

first-person verbs *incipiam* and *cano*, and the gods.[15] This is a crucial element
in the unity of the first book. The nature of this relationship is immediately
refined when, following the poem's second sentence of 18.5 lines devoted to
the initial list of twelve deities, is added an equally long third sentence of 19
lines which brings the reader up to line 42 and the end of the prologue.

The figure invoked in the second half of the prologue is named 'Caesar', a
kind of god-in-waiting (*quem mox quae sint habitura deorum | concilia
incertum est*, 24 f., 'it is uncertain which council of the gods will soon receive
you') who, it is hoped, will also be seen as actively beneficent to farmers
(*auctorem frugum tempestatumque potentem*, 27, 'Author of fruits and poten-
tate of seasons'). At issue also is the way in which the world will receive and
consider him (*te maximus orbis... accipiat*, 26–8), and it is to him that the
final lines of the proem are addressed (40–2):

> da facilem cursum atque audacibus adnue coeptis,
> ignarosque uiae mecum miseratus agrestis
> ingredere et uotis iam nunc adsuesce uocari.

> But smooth my path, smile on my enterprise,
> Pity with me the steps of farmers ignorant of the way,
> Come forward, and learn already to answer prayer.

The poet and the new god are here put on the same level, linked together in a
highly original manner.[16] And this Caesar is a highly complex figure. On the
one hand, he is the traditional figure of a thirteenth deity added to a pantheon
of twelve, as Virgil adopts a standard topos of Hellenistic panegyric and the
practices of Alexandrian 'court' poetry.[17] He can also be seen as a kind of
replacement for Jupiter, whose omission from the whole proem is striking,
particularly given Hesiodic and Aratean precedent.[18] Furthermore, the reference to his mother's myrtle in line 28 (*cingens materna tempora myrto*, your
brow | Bound with a wreath ancestral, Venus' myrtle') probably hints at
Lucretius' Venus. And also in Lucretian terms, he can be seen as replacing
Epicurus.[19] But for the purposes of this paper, two points stand out. By
creating a close connexion with the quasi-divine Caesar, the poet shows
astonishing confidence and accords great authority to himself and to his

---

[15] Cf. Gale (2000), 31. On the relationship between knowledge, teaching, and the gods in the
work as a whole see the important paper by Schiesaro (1997).

[16] See Buchheit (1972), 18–26 on the parallelism between Virgil and Octavian throughout
the poem. On various aspects of this *uia*, including its relationship to didactic plots of initiation
and instruction see Fowler (2000), Hardie (2002), Nelis (2008).

[17] See the survey of the prologue at Mynors (1990), 1–3.

[18] See Thomas (1988), ad 1.1–42.

[19] See Gale (2000), 25.

poem. The authorial voice now asks for help (*da facilem cursum*), but it also states the ambitious nature of his own initiatives and intentions (*audacibus . . . coeptis*). When he goes on to invite Caesar to join with him in pitying the countryfolk (*mecum,* construed with *miseratus*), he creates the impression that they share both a sense of compassion and useful and important knowledge. The countryfolk, who are the centre of attention (with *agrestis* compare *agrestum* in line 10), are 'ignorant of the way' (*ignaros uiae*), and so together, the poet and Caesar are setting out on a journey, or to be more accurate, journeys, which will help to show them the right way.[20] In fact, these lines create three trajectories, inextricably linked but necessarily identifiable as separate paths: the *cursus* begun by the poet and his poem, the *uia* of which the farmers are ignorant, and the suggestion that Caesar too must 'set out' (*ingredere*) on a journey of some kind. Each of these three strands requires some comment.

CURSUS

On one level, the *cursus* is the particular course the poem itself will take as it unfolds in the act of reading it through from beginning to end. It involves therefore both writer and reader in a specifically didactic tradition which can be traced back to Parmenides' famous 'way'. At the same time, when he asks Caesar to oversee its launch and facilitate its progress, Virgil relates his poem to the contemporary political scene.[21] In doing so, he has in mind specifically the imagery of the Roman circus. His opening invocation of the gods must be seen in terms of the *pompa circensis,* the grand procession of deities which opened the races in the Circus Maximus, a combination of religious ritual and sporting contest which was reorganized by Octavian and Agrippa as a massive spectacle in the late 30s and early 20s BC.[22] At key moments, and most strikingly at the end of Book 1, in the simile of the chariot out of control (1.512–14), and in the prologue to Book 3, where he announces plans for the celebration of triumphal games (3.17–20), Virgil will use descriptions of chariots and the *ludi circenses* to extend this pattern of imagery throughout the poem in a coherent manner. Within this overall thematic pattern, one

[20] This point is further supported by the frequently noticed allusion to *uiam . . . quaerere* at Lucr. 2.10; see Hardie (1986), 158.

[21] See Horsfall (1995), 93 for a useful and enlightening list of the references to contemporary history in the poem.

[22] See Nelis (2008) for a full presentation of this argument.

aspect is of essential importance here. By invoking Caesar as he does and demanding that his poem be read in the light of contemporary history, Virgil is in fact relating the *cursus* of his poem to the course of both world and Roman history.[23] This link becomes obvious in the simile which ends Book 1, where the chariot can be linked to the image of the chariot of state. In recent scholarship, this point has been made again and again.[24] But it is worth looking carefully at the way in which Virgil creates the necessary setting for this connexion. As we shall see, the final simile must be seen in the light of the thematic coherence of the whole book, and that coherence is grounded in the opening section, to which we must now return.

VIA

As well as being asked to grant a favourable start to the course this poem seeks to follow, Caesar is also asked, as we have already seen, to join the poet in pity of the countryfolk who are 'ignorant of the way' (1.41):

> ignarosque uiae mecum miseratus agrestis

The phrase *ignarosque uiae . . . agrestis* implies the ellipse of something akin to 'of agriculture'.[25] More generally, there may be a hint at the idea of the 'path of life'. But there is definitely a connexion between this 'way' and the poem itself. By paying attention to the poem's didactic message, the farmers, like any reader of the poem, can learn the right way. We will soon learn, however, that this way is not easy (1.121–4):

> Pater ipse colendi
> haud facilem esse uiam uoluit, primusque per artem
> mouit agros, curis acuens mortalia corda
> nec torpere graui passus sua regna ueterno.
>
> The Father himself
> Willed that the path of tillage be not smooth,
> And first ordained that skill should cultivate
> The land, by care sharpening the wits of mortals,
> Nor let his kingdom laze in torpid sloth.

---

[23] See Hardie (2005), 23–6.
[24] Cf. Jenkyns (1998), 299, 'a world out of control'.
[25] See Page (1898), ad loc.

Jupiter's dispensation has made life difficult in order to force mankind to work hard. And we soon learn that his world is one in which there is a need for teaching (*prima Ceres ferro mortalis uertere terram | instituit*, 147f., 'First Ceres taught men how to turn the earth | With iron') and learning (*ut uarias usus meditando extunderet artis | paulatim*, 133 f., 'that step by step practice and taking thought | Should hammer out the crafts'). Ceres here prefigures the poet, since she it was, under the new dispensation imposed by Jupiter, who first taught mankind to plough, teaching to which man responded well, in an image of the ideal reception of a didactic message.[26] The same developmental process must be imagined in line 41. There the *uia* reflects content of the poem as a whole, since it is the text which, with Caesar's help, will show the way to the ignorant. It is vital, therefore, to appreciate the connexion between the use of *uia* and that of the *cursus* mentioned in the preceding line. As the poem follows its trajectory (*cursus*), it will guide its intended audience of countryfolk, who are ignorant of the way (*uia*). The prologue thus constructs a model of its ideal readership and its ideal reception in a perfect example of didactic communication between teacher and pupil. And it is Caesar who is asked to grant the poem its safe course and, having pitied the countryfolk, to begin: *ingredere* (42).[27]

INGREDERE

Many commentators and translators take this verb, which has no complement, to have the sense of 'enter into a sphere of activity', and there can be no doubt that the poet is here putting an end to the issue of which divine sphere Caesar will occupy, by suggesting that he accept his divine status (*uotis iam nunc adsuesce uocari*) and assume responsibility for the earth and so for farmers. But given the presence of *uia* and *cursus* there is also a hint of another meaning: 'begin your own course or way'. The verb *ingredior* is often used with *uia* and one of the most frequent senses of the verb is 'take the first steps on a path or journey'.[28] Caesar is here being invited to set out on

---

[26] *uertere terram* in line 146 recalls *terram | uertere* of the poem's opening and facilitates the parallel between the instruction of Ceres to that offered by the poet. Cf. Hardie (2004), 89

[27] On Caesar, the poet, and patterns of knowledge and instruction in the poem see Schiesaro (1997), *passim*, and esp. 80 on this passage.

[28] See *OLD*, s.v. 2. Gale (2000), 25 n. 15, 26 n. 24, compares Lucr. 1.80–2: *Illud in his rebus uereor, ne forte rearis | impia te rationis inire elementa uiamque | indugredi sceleris.* 'One thing I fear in this matter, that in this your apprenticeship to philosophy you may perhaps see impiety, and the entering on a path of crime' (trans. M. F. Smith (1992)).

a path or journey of his own, one which parallels that of the poet. Their activities are thus inextricably linked from the very beginning, and will remain so until the poem's end.[29]

This reading of lines 40–2 suggests that Virgil brings his prologue to a close by presenting the poem which is about to begin in terms of interconnected ways or paths involving the poet, Caesar, and the countryfolk. Ultimately, of course, the reader is also involved, since the act of reading the text implies the working-out of the poem's didactic course. It is instructive, therefore, to appreciate just how Virgil operates in the opening didactic sequence. Following the *mecum* of line 41, the *mihi* of line 45 (*depresso incipiat iam tum mihi taurus aratro | ingemere*, 'Then it's high time for my bull at the deep-driven plough | To groan') links the poet closely to the ploughman. Furthermore, the *incipiat* picks up the *incipiam* of line 5, suggesting a possible parallel between composing and ploughing. On the one hand, this idea looks back to the very first line, *Quid faciat laetas segetes, quo sidere terram | uertere*, where the enjambed *uertere* surely plays on *uersus*, equating turning the earth and turning from one verse to the next.[30] On the other, it looks forward immediately to the use of *scindimus* in line 50, which is remarkable on two counts. Not only does this word create an image of poet and farmer ploughing together ('we cleave the earth'), it has also been suggested that it may also permit a metapoetic reading, with *ferro* as the stylus and *aequor* the flat surface about to be written on.[31] Then, suddenly moving away from the assimilation of poet and farmer, the poet addresses each individual farmer directly in the second person with *nonne uides* (56) and *ergo age* (63). Subtle shifts of this kind are in operation consistently throughout the work, providing vital transitions and bringing variety to the expository mode. But beyond such formal requirements imposed by the poet's chosen didactic form,[32] Virgil creates overarching structures providing thematic coherence. In order to try to see how Virgil's use of the imagery of the way or path plays out in practice as the work unfolds, we will attempt to follow three of the plots or narratives running through Book 1, and all ultimately interconnected: the movement of the solar year, the course of Roman history, and the journey of Caesar towards apotheosis.[33]

---

[29] It is very tempting to take *mecum* with *ingredior* as well as with *miseratus*, as does for example Volk (2002), 133 n. 22.

[30] For the etymological link between *uertere* and *uersus* see Maltby (1991), 638 s.v. *uersus* (1).

[31] See Harrison (2007b).

[32] On which see Volk (2002), 34–43.

[33] Cf. Gale (2004) for a narratological approach to Lucretius; Trépanier (2007) outlines Lucretius' debt to Empedoclean precedent in terms of didactic plot.

VERE NOVO

At the end of the prologue, as we have seen, the poem continues with the words *Vere nouo*. This opening picks up the words *quo sidere* of line 1 in the first line by suggesting that the movement of the year will be a central structuring element in the book. By line 68 we have already encountered summer (*aestas*, 66) and looked forward to September (*sub ipsum Arcturum*, 67f.). In line 100 we find both summer and winter (*umida solstitia atque hiemes orate serenas*). In the famous passage at lines 231–58 describing the earth's five zones, one temperate and two each of fierce cold and heat, we also find the four seasons. There is a clear physical, scientific connexion between the former (*certis dimensum partibus orbem*, 'The fixed measures of the orbit-course', the first line of this section) and the latter (*temporibus parem diuersis quattuor annum*, 'The fourfold seasons of the balanced year', the section's closing line).[34] Subsequently, the reader encounters winter (*hiems ignaua*, 299) and autumn (*tempestates autumni*, 311) and once again spring (*imbri-ferum uer*, 313). In the whole closing movement of the book (starting from line 351), as Virgil provides his own Hesiodic 'works and days' and engages also in detailed *imitatio* of Aratus, the issue of weather signs dominates and the advice to the farmer to study the information and warnings provided by the sun and moon keeps the turning year in the reader's mind. When we find the sun and the moon together at line 424, the poet is preparing the brilliant transition which will enable him to switch from weather signs to prodigies announcing civil war after the assassination of Julius Caesar (*ex-stincto . . . Caesare*, 466), as we move from the endlessly repeating farmer's working year which has dominated the poem so far to one particular day in a very important year, the Ides of March 44 BC.

In order to appreciate what Virgil achieves here, it is necessary to recall that the first deities invoked in his prologue were the sun and the moon (5–6): *uos, o clarissima mundi | lumina, labentem caelo qui ducitis annum*, 'You brightest lamps | That lead the year's procession across the sky'. The cosmic year and a key event in Roman history unite in the figure of the sun, when in mid-verse, the poet moves from signs about rain the sun will (always) provide (*sol tibi signa dabit*, 463) to signs it has (already) given to Romans (*signa dabant*, 471). This sudden shift from the eternally recurring year to a specific year leads

---

[34] Cf. Putnam (1979), 44.

into the closing section with both its ghastly vision of civil war and Philippi (489–97) and a prayer for help (500-1):[35]

> hunc saltem euerso <u>iuuenem</u> succurrere saeclo
> ne prohibete.
>
> Do not at least prevent this <u>youthful prince</u>
> From saving a world in ruins:

That this *iuuenis* is indeed Octavian is confirmed almost immediately in line 503:

> iam pridem nobis caeli te regia, <u>Caesar</u>,
> inuidet . . .
>
> The courts of heaven,
> <u>Caesar</u>, have long begrudged your presence here.

Here too the passing of time is a key theme, because only thirty-seven lines earlier, as we have just seen, the same name had been used to refer to Julius Caesar. And the relationship between 'Caesar' and the farmer's year of the rest of Book 1 becomes even more complex when we appreciate the further levels on which the Book's close is related to its opening.

CAESAR

The name 'Caesar' appears three times in *Georgics* 1, in lines 25, 466, and 503. On the first and last occasion it refers to Octavian, in the second to Julius Caesar. As we have just seen, the close proximity of the final two occurrences locates the book's closing sequence in a precise period in Roman history. It also suggests that the poet wishes to draw attention to the essential continuity between the two men. Modern usage of course easily makes the distinction between Julius Caesar and Octavian, but it is vital to appreciate that in the late 30s and early 20s BC the latter's full official name was 'Imperator Caesar Diui filius'.[36] Recollection of this point helps to bring into focus a further aspect of the relationship between the Book's opening and its close: it is as the son of a god that the Caesar of line 25 is assured divine status. Virgil alludes to the

---

[35] On the interpretation of the prayer and its relation to the closing lines of the book see the important contribution of Kaster (2002).

[36] On the importance of this name and its evolution see the pertinent remarks of Millar (2000). For discussion of the handling by Octavian/Augustus of the figure of Julius Caesar see Kienast (2001). On the ambiguity surrounding the identity of the Caesar described at *Aen.* 1.286–90, see O'Hara (1994).

family connexion in line 28 in the words *materna tempora myrto.* As Mynors notes, 'Octavian, as Julius Caesar's adopted son, was *diui filius,* and inherited the descent from Venus or Dione..., to whom the myrtle was sacred'.[37] Further details are also relevant. At 1.41 the word *miseratus* is used of the pity Caesar and the poet share for the farmers. At 1.466 the same word reappears, this time to refer to the sun's pity for Rome at Caesar's death: *ille etiam exstincto miseratus Caesare Romam,* 'He too, when Caesar fell, showed pity for Rome'. Neither the repetition of the verb nor its collocation with Caesar is otiose. It is worth quoting here Oliver Lyne, in a paper first published in a landmark collection of essays edited by Tony Woodman and David West, in 1974:[38]

This Sun and Caesar are so to speak of the same stature—a feeling which emerges from the balance and phrasing of 466. There, while the Sun displays human emotion (*miseratus*), Caesar's dying (*exstincto*), given the context, manifestly magnifies in significance to suggest the extinction of a cosmic body... The world, it seems, had in Caesar a 'Sun' capable of preventing the covert darkness of civil war. At his eclipse, the heavenly Sun correspondingly reacts, removing his light.

Appreciation of the connexion between Caesar and Sol gives added force to the simile which brings the book to a close (509–14):

> hinc mouet Euphrates, illinc Germania bellum;
> uicinae ruptis inter se legibus urbes
> arma ferunt; saeuit toto Mars impius orbe,
> ut cum carceribus sese effudere quadrigae,
> addunt in spatia, et frustra retinacula tendens
> fertur equis auriga neque audit currus habenas.

> Euphrates here,
> There Germany is in arms, and neighbour cities
> Break covenants and fight; throughout the world
> Impious War is raging. As on a racecourse,
> The barriers down, out pour the chariots,
> Gathering speed from lap to lap, and a driver
> Tugging in vain at the reins is swept along
> By his horses and heedless uncontrollable car.

Here, in the figure of the charioteer, we see the son takes over the reins of the chariot. In doing so, we glimpse a hint of Phaethon: the son of the Sun is in a chariot running out of control.[39] The book ends in stark contrast to the

---

[37] Mynors (1990), on 1.28.
[38] Lyne (1974), 51–2 = Hardie (1999), 166 = Lyne (2007), 43.
[39] See Gale (2000), 36–7.

regular movement of the sun described earlier (231–2), where its fixed course was a symbol of the divinely structured cosmos and therefore a source of reliable signs for mankind:[40]

> Idcirco certis dimensum partibus orbem
> per duodena regit mundi sol aureus astra.

> This is the reason why the golden Sun
> Marks through the twelve Signs of the Zodiac
> Fixed measure of the orbit-course he steers.

There is also a further parallel between the two occurrences of *miseratus*, as has been well explained by Alessandro Schiesaro:[41]

The sun 'takes pity' on Rome not just by hiding the shameful sight she offers, but by sending a clear, if unheeded, sign of the impending catastrophe of civil war. Virgil and Octavian will 'take pity' on their Roman readers by a similar act of instruction.

This parallel between the sun and Caesar/Octavian is implicated in part in the thematic link between Caesar/Julius and the solar year,[42] but it also introduces another element, that of the poet and the act of instruction. When we put together the insights of Lyne and Schiesaro, the crucial point is this: at this dangerous time of civil war, when one Caesar is eclipsed and the regular motions of the solar year are disturbed, both the poet and a new Caesar have important lessons to communicate concerning the possibility of a return to order and peace. Furthermore, their knowledge and its power are inextricably associated with the issue of the divine, i.e. of Caesar's divinity and Virgil's relationship with this new god. And this brings us on to a third plot in Book 1: the history of Rome.

---

[40] For the chariot of the sun see line 250 in the same passage, *nosque ubi primus equis Oriens adflavit anhelis*, 'And when the Orient sun with panting horses'.

[41] Schiesaro (1997), 80.

[42] Feeney (2007), 207 is right to note that Virgil works with a calendar which is based on meteorological patterns and lunar parapegmata, and that despite the fact that the *Georgics* is published some fifteen years after the Julian reform of the calendar his days 'are not Caesar's solar days, but Greek lunar days'. But at the close of Book 1, following assimilation of Caesar and Sol, when the assassination of Caesar leads to bizarre solar phenomena which announce civil war and the destruction of the georgic world as depicted thus far, we can see that Virgil does parallel the farmer's year and the ordered movement of the solar year at the very point at which both collapse into chaos. Not only is there not a single date in the poem, as Feeney notes, at the close of Book 1 we are threatened with the elision of all temporal distinctions in eternal night (*impiaque aeternam timuerunt saecula noctem*, 468, 'a guilty age feared everlasting night'). For a slightly different interpretation see Nappa (2005), 54–5.

SCILICET ET RERUM FACTA EST
PULCHERRIMA ROMA (2.534)

We have seen that the initially independent first-person voice which opened the poem without any kind of request for or declaration of divine authority or assistance subsequently aligned itself with Caesar, an authority figure of exemplary status. One available 'way' established in the prologue, therefore, is a path of successful instruction strongly associated with someone who is soon to become a god (23–42). By the end of this poem, Maecenas, the farmers, and all readers should have acquired a body of knowledge which is expounded in close relation to a narrative trajectory related to the preservation of the Roman state at a time of crisis. For the reader, following this particular trajectory involves the process of reading the text, and this is a text which will end with Caesar.[43] His journey in the poem, beginning from the injunction to 'set out' at 1.42 (*ingredere*), culminates in his path towards Olympus (4.559–62):

> Haec super aruorum cultu pecorumque canebam
> et super arboribus, Caesar dum magnus ad altum
> fulminat Euphraten bello uictorque uolentes
> per populos dat iura **uiamque adfectat Olympo**.

> This song of the husbandry of crops and beasts
> And fruit-trees I was singing while great Caesar
> Was thundering beside the great Euphrates
> In war, victoriously for grateful peoples
> Appointing laws and setting his course for Heaven.

At the beginning of the poem we are told that he will soon become a god; at the end, military victories pave his way to immortality. The *Georgics* thus comes to an end with Caesarian triumph and immortality, and the poem's historical 'plot' here finds satisfying closure. And Virgil explicitly relates the composition of the poem to this historical situation, *illo Vergilium me tempore dulcis alebat | Parthenope...*, 4.563, 'I, Virgil, <u>at that time</u> lay in the lap | Of sweet Parthenopê...'. But within this overarching thematic structure embracing the work as a whole, it is important also to appreciate the slow

---

[43] It is not by accident that so much criticism of the *Georgics* has been based on a linear book-by-book approach, e.g. the monographs of Putnam, Miles, Ross, Farrell, Cramer, and Nappa. Many readers have obviously felt the need to follow faithfully the *cursus* the poem lays out for them in an effort to get some kind of grip on the poem's complexities and apparent contradictions.

unfolding of the narrative dynamic which is played out on a book-by-book basis.

Looking back from the poem's final lines, the actual victories of Caesar are outlined in the prologue to Book 3 (especially lines 26–33), where again his achievements are inextricably related to the ambition of the poet to celebrate them. Looking further back, however, Book 1 ends not with Caesar flying towards Olympus in a triumphal chariot but instead with the image of a charioteer who is unable to control a chariot which seems to be heading for imminent destruction amidst worldwide strife. The striking difference between the end of Book 1 and both the opening of Book 3 and the end of Book 4 suggests that as readers we must be prepared to think carefully about the historical dynamic which underpins the unfolding of the poem's didactic message. To read the *Georgics* is to experience the unfolding history of Rome as one moves through the poem. The reading of the work creates a strong sense of historical process and of the place of Rome and Italy in world affairs, both historically and geographically. As if to inculcate this approach, right from the beginning Virgil helps his readers to appreciate the importance of time itself as a central element in the poem.[44] As we have seen, the poem begins with the year's annual turn from winter to spring: as soon as the thaw comes, the farmer must set to the hard work of ploughing the earth. But almost immediately, we find ourselves going back in time (50–2):

> ac prius ignotum ferro quam scindimus aequor
> uentos et uarium caeli praediscere morem
> cura sit . . .

> But with untried land, before we cleave it with iron,
> We must con its varying moods of wind and sky
> With care . . .

And then at once we are taken right back to the beginning of human life on earth (60–3):

> continuo has leges aeternaque foedera certis
> imposuit natura locis, quo tempore primum
> Deucalion uacuum lapides iactauit in orbem,
> unde homines nati, durum genus.

> Nature imposed these everlasting covenants
> From the first on certain regions, right from the time
> When Deucalion over the empty spaces of the earth
> Cast those stones that produced the race of men –
> A hard race.

---

[44] What follows owes much to Hardie (2005).

The image of this 'hard race' is picked up soon after in lines 145–9, where, given the harsh nature of human life, the poet emphasizes the necessity of both hard work and instruction:

> labor omnia uicit
> improbus et duris urgens in rebus egestas.
> prima Ceres ferro mortalis uertere terram
> instituit, cum iam glandes atque arbuta sacrae
> deficerent siluae et uictum Dodona negaret.

> Toil mastered everything, relentless toil
> And the pressure of pinching poverty.
> First Ceres taught men how to turn the earth
> With iron, when acorns now and arbute-berries
> In the sacred wood were failing and Dodona
> Scanted her sustenance.

Here, as we have already seen, the poet relegates his own instruction to a secondary position, after that achieved by the goddess Ceres. In order to underline this idea, lines 147–8 recall closely the prologue, with (as already noted) *uertere terram* echoing *terram | uertere*.[45] The very act of instruction is inextricably linked to the divine throughout the poem, with the poet acting as a kind of demiurge, his teaching being secondary to divine authority and his ability to pass on knowledge being dependent on his insight into the structures underpinning the divinely ordered cosmos in which humans must live their lives.[46] And in these lines, the poem also traces an evolution from one dispensation to another, from the Golden Age of Saturn to the Iron Age of Jupiter. But as well as working itself out on the cosmic level, this theme unfolds on a specifically historical and political level. It is not difficult to see the connexion with the Book's close, when one world ends with Caesar's death and a new and terrible age of civil war begins. But in the midst of chaos, eventually, a glimpse of hope appears. As Philip Hardie has written:[47]

At the end of *Georgics* 1 the chariot of history is out of control, but the image allows, at least, for the possibility of reaching the finishing line, the end of the poem, of instruction, of history.

Another end is indeed foreseen within the poem, when the victories of Octavian as outlined in the prologue to Book 3 (*uictorisque arma Quirini*, 3.27) will put an end to civil strife and bring closure to the chaotic wars described at the end of Book 1 (*saeuit toto Mars impius orbe*, 1.511)

---

[45] Cf. also *Chaoniam . . . glandem* (8) and *glandes . . . Dodona* (148–9).
[46] Again, see Schiesaro (1997).
[47] Hardie (2005), 27.

and hinted at indirectly at the close of Book 2 (*necdum etiam audierant inflari classica* . . . , 2.539). Little wonder that this poem has inspired so much debate about whether it offers an optimistic or a pessimistic vision.[48] In fact, the poem offers visions of Roman history from both pre- and post-Actium perspectives, the former necessarily pessimistic, the latter inevitably more optimistic, even if not totally sanguine. The reader who follows carefully the complex ways in which Virgil works with time throughout the poem is in a position to appreciate this crucial point. The *Georgics* is a profoundly historical work. Its viewpoint embraces both all world history and within it the history of Rome. The latter is envisaged in terms of its past, present, and future as the act of reading the work draws the reader into following the actual processes of Rome's unfolding history. When at the close of Book 1 we see the city caught up in civil war, presented as a crucial turning point in the implicit image of the *meta* the charioteer must negotiate, the reader comes to appreciate the absolute central importance of Caesar for both the coherence of the book and the future of the Roman state.

Virgil's seamless combination of the literary and the historical may perhaps be best illustrated by drawing on a quotation from a recent study of the relationship between two of his key models, Empedocles and Lucretius. Simon Trépanier has summed up thus the deep underlying parallels between the two *On Natures*:[49]

In both epics (assuming again the single-work hypothesis for Empedocles), the overall rhetorical structure was the same: attention-grabbing criticism of traditional religion, made in the opening sections, which then required, as the vindication and explanation for right religion, a true account of the nature of the universe. In both cases, the approach presents an analogous solution to the same problem, that of having to invoke a divinity at the opening of a didactic epic (more conventionally so in the case of Lucretius) for the sake of generic convention, even as the ultimate aim of the epic is to undermine belief in such divinities as traditionally understood. Both also generate dramatic interest through a vivid example of wrong religion, although the Lucretian example of the sacrifice of Iphigeneia is rather forced, perhaps so for the sake of alluding to the model. Lastly, the proem is also the obvious place to establish the authority for the doctrines to come, and here as well there are similarities. In Empedocles' own case, if I am right, the authority was himself, as a god; in Lucretius, the poem's authority is the *Graius homo*, Greek man, who first broke the bonds of

---

[48] See the fine survey of the issues by Cramer (1998); unfortunately, his proposed solution to the question is flawed because of his bizarre attitude to the state of the text, which he considers to be heavily interpolated. Morgan (1999), against the trend established by Putnam (1979), Ross (1987), and Thomas (1988), offers an optimistic reading.

[49] Trépanier (2007), 280.

superstition and explored by superhuman flight of the mind the boundaries of the universe.

It is fascinating to imagine Virgil reading his predecessors along similar lines. Like his predecessors, Virgil's didactic text directs its focus towards religion, the gods, and the issue of knowledge and divine authority. But it is obvious that he disagrees with his models even as their presence provides the context within which the reader is able to appreciate the power of a new vision. Virgil's aim is to explore the appearance of a new deity, one who offers hope of peace and the return of established religious norms and practices to a people caught up in an apparently endless series of disasters. The presence of Caesar is presented as capable of ushering in a new cosmic dispensation, of producing a new natural as well as political order in a new Roman cosmos. It is Caesar who is the divine figure who offers a vision of hope at a crucial moment in Rome's history and indeed of the history of the whole world. As a god, he is like Empedocles and Epicurus, a new saviour. And it was in the study of his didactic models that Virgil found a way of reflecting on the state of contemporary Rome and Italy and their relationship with the wider world. As Virgil writes himself into the didactic tradition, Caesar is integrated into the structure of the cosmic order. Study of the poem's intertextuality helps to demonstrate Virgil's engagement with the ways in which Romans thought about contemporary strife, moral decline, and their idealized past in an ideological nexus involving farming; to write about agriculture in the late 30s and early 20s BC meant inevitably to write about Roman history and identity, just as it inevitably led to reflection on the human condition and man's place and function in the natural order. It also involved, inevitably, writing about the divine Caesar and the Roman revolution.

11

Eros and Empire: Virgil and the Historians on Civil War

John Marincola

That there was a close connexion for the Romans between history and poetry can hardly be denied. Historical epic in particular was dear to the Roman heart: beginning with Naevius and Ennius at the dawn of Roman literature, historical epic never lost its appeal so long as the Romans wrote poetry.[1] It had, moreover, a close, perhaps at times symbiotic, relationship with prose history, and the techniques of one could often influence those of the other.[2] In this paper I explore some connexions with historical texts that I believe have not been sufficiently emphasized, and that can illuminate important aspects of Virgil's engagement with Roman history. The *Aeneid* is clearly much focused on Roman history, whether it be Jupiter's prophecies of future Roman greatness, the presentiments of Roman–Carthaginian conflict that permeate the affair of Aeneas and Dido, the parade of future Roman heroes in the underworld, or the scenes of Roman history on Aeneas' shield. Despite

It would be impossible to acknowledge adequately all that I owe Tony Woodman. It must suffice to say that he has given encouragement and support at critical moments; in some sense, I can hardly imagine my career without him. His scholarship and friendship have meant more that he could ever know or I could ever express. I hope that he, as one interested in the interplay between poetry and history, may find this contribution a not completely worthless *antidosis* for all he has given me.

Earlier versions of this paper were delivered at Oxford (St Anne's College Classical Society), Cambridge, and Princeton, and I thank the audiences there for helpful criticism and discussion. Franco Basso, Ed Bispham, Denis Feeney, Harriet Flower, Peta Fowler, Miriam Griffin, Philip Hardie, Matthew Leigh, Nino Luraghi, and Stephen Oakley offered help with individual points. Laurel Fulkerson, Christina Kraus, James O'Hara, and Christopher Pelling read an earlier version of this chapter and offered many helpful corrections, comments, and elucidations. I owe very special thanks to Alessandro Barchiesi for his encouragement, his criticism of an earlier draft, and his sharing of (then) unpublished work with me. Naturally, these readers do not necessarily share my point(s) of view.

[1] On Roman historical epic before Virgil see Hussler (1976-8), I.92–238; Goldberg (1995); on the connexions between epic and historiography, Leigh (2007).

[2] See references in n. 3, below.

his divergences from the arrangement and subject matter of earlier historical epic, Virgil nonetheless left no doubt that he meant his work as a meditation on Roman destiny and Roman history.

I shall not, however, be arguing (as much of recent scholarship has)[3] for the similar formal methods of both historians and epic poets, nor will I analyse particular reminiscences or particular intertexts; nor is individual character my interest here. Rather, I want to suggest that the second half of the *Aeneid*, specifically its focus on the 'civil' war of Trojans and Latins, shares important points of contact with some of the major issues discussed and debated by both Greek and Roman historians of the late Republic. I shall work outward from the final scene of the *Aeneid*, to examine three themes that I see as closely interconnected: civil war itself; the conflict between punishment and mercy; and the spoils of empire.

The final scene is as follows:[4]

> incidit ictus
> ingens ad terram duplicato poplite Turnus.
> consurgunt gemitu Rutuli totusque remugit
> mons circum et uocem late nemora alta remittunt.
> ille humilis supplex oculos dextramque precantem
> protendens 'equidem merui nec deprecor' inquit;
> utere sorte tua. miseri te si qua parentis
> tangere cura potest, oro (fuit et tibi talis
> Anchises genitor) Dauni miserere senectae
> et me, seu corpus spoliatum lumine mauis,
> redde meis. uicisti et uictum tendere palmas
> Ausonii uidere; tua est Lauinia coniunx,
> ulterius ne tende odiis.' stetit acer in armis
> Aeneas uoluens oculos dextramque repressit;
> et iam iamque magis cunctanctem flectere sermo
> coeperat, infelix umero cum apparuit alto
> balteus et notis fulserunt cingula bullis
> Pallantis pueri, uictum quem uulnere Turnus
> strauerat atque umeris inimicum insigne gerebat.
> ille, oculis postquam saeui monimenta doloris
> exuuiasque hausit furiis accensus et ira
> terribilis: 'tune hinc spoliis indute meorum
> eripiare mihi? Pallas te hoc uulnere, Pallas

---

[3] See. esp. the essays of Cairns, Pagán, Damon, Wheeler, Hardie, Kyriakidis, Rossi, Ash, Vasaly, and Wiseman in Levene and Nelis (2002) with the editors' helpful overview, pp. ix–xv; Woodman (1989), (2003); Rossi (2004a).

[4] *Aen.* 12.926–52; translations of the *Aeneid* are my own.

immolat et poenam scelerato ex sanguine sumit.'
hoc dicens ferrum aduerso sub pectore condit
feruidus. ast illi soluuntur frigore membra
uitaque cum gemitu fugit indignata sub umbras.

Enormous Turnus, struck, falls to earth on bended knee. The Rutulians rise up with a groan, the whole mountain around re-echoes, and the deep forests return the voice. That one humble, suppliant, stretching forth his eyes and right hand, says, 'I have indeed deserved this, and I ask for nothing. Use your chance. But if any care for a wretched parent can touch you, I pray (and Anchises your sire was once such to you), pity the old age of Daunus, and return me, or if you prefer my dead body, to my own. You have conquered, and the Ausonians have seen me, defeated, stretch forward my hands. Lavinia is yours as wife; go no further in hatred.' Aeneas stood fierce in arms, shifting his gaze, and he held back his right hand; and more and more the speech began to move him as he hesitated, when high on Turnus' shoulder the ill-starred belt appeared, and the baldric with its well-known studs shone out, of the boy Pallas whom Turnus had stretched out defeated, and he was wearing the hostile sign on his shoulders. Aeneas, when he drank in with his eyes these reminders of savage grief and the spoils, aflame with fury and formidable in anger, said, 'Are you, clad in the spoils of my people, to be snatched from me? Pallas sacrifices you by this wound, Pallas takes the penalty from your wicked blood.' Seething he says this and buries the sword in the breast set against him. But the limbs of the other are loosened in cold, and his life, with a moan, flees, resentful, down to the shades.

As is well known, the scene has been a vicious battleground for scholars, many of whom centre on the individual characters of Aeneas and Turnus and the roles that they have played in the epic to this point.[5] Some scholars see in Aeneas' final act a failure of the hero to master his emotions and transcend the narrowly parochial Homeric world of private vengeance, while others emphasize the appropriateness of the execution of Turnus, who is the *real* Homeric figure, so to speak, motivated by a fanaticism, a desire for individual glory, and a lust for battle that can have no place in a new civic-minded and well-ordered community. At its crudest, we often hear of an 'optimistic' and a 'pessimistic' school. Both sides in the debate can marshal impressive arguments to support their positions, so I wish to focus instead on a consideration of the larger context: for Aeneas is not simply Aeneas but also the representative of Roman history, Roman character, and Roman destiny, while Turnus is not just Turnus but also the first in a long line of opponents of Rome, and he

[5] The bibliography is immense and listing it here would have little point; see Suerbaum (1980), 256–8 for works to 1975; more recent discussions that I have found helpful include Stahl (1981), Renger (1985), Burnell (1987), Galinsky (1988), Hardie (1997), Galinsky (1994), Traina (1994), Thomas (1998), Putnam (1999), Edgeworth (2005), and Fulkerson (2007).

embodies many of the characteristics that the Romans attributed to those who tried to stand in the way of their rise to empire.

It should not be necessary, I trust, to demonstrate the importance of this final scene: as a whole generation of narratological studies has shown, the ending of a work is essential in establishing the larger meaning of that work, and it fundamentally influences the way in which we 'read' and interpret a work of literature; this is especially so in narrative genres, with their carefully chosen points of beginning and conclusion.[6] And perhaps not the least reason that we return to the end of the *Aeneid* so often is that Virgil here has parted ways with his major models, the *Iliad* and *Odyssey*, and his jarringly different conclusion merits study for that reason alone.[7]

I. CIVIL WAR AND THE SOCIAL WAR

Discussions of the war that pervades the second half of the *Aeneid* often note that its character is that of a civil war: Aeneas is 'descended' from Dardanus, who had set out from Italy to Troy (*Aen.* 7.206–7), and the two people, Trojans and Latins, will eventually unite to form the ancestors of the Romans (12.834–8).[8] Certainly different historical events are in play here: the civil wars of the great men of the late Republic are on Virgil's mind, as are the wars fought between Rome and the Latin League in the fourth century;[9] not of the least significance is the Marsic or Social War of 91–88 BC, where a number of Rome's allies banded together in a short but bloody and destructive conflict.

The Social War has not received nearly as much treatment as the civil wars of the great men of the late Republic,[10] and there are perhaps several reasons

---

[6] See esp. D. Fowler (1989), and the collection of essays in Roberts, Dunn, and Fowler (1997); on historiographical endings see Marincola (2005).

[7] I leave aside here Lucretius' poem which has a similar 'open' ending and will have certainly influenced Virgil; but as the *de Rerum Natura* is a different genre, the narratological effect is somewhat different. See P. Fowler (1997) who well relates the ending of the poem to didactic conventions.

[8] On the war of the second half as a civil war see Camps (1964), 96–7; Buchheit (1963), 151–72; Horsfall (1995), 155; cf. Liv. 1.23.1, *ciuili simillimum bello, prope inter parentes natosque.*

[9] For the latter see Sordi (1964).

[10] Ando (2002) is excellent on Virgil's contribution to the late-Republic debate about Italy, but he concentrates on the *Georgics* rather than the *Aeneid*; see now Barchiesi (2008) for a penetrating exploration of the theme. My own observations in this section are meant to build on both of these scholars' works.

for this. First, there are clear 'markers' in the text that we are meant to be thinking of Pompey, Caesar, Antony, and Octavian.[11] Second, the ancient commentators have nothing to say about the Social War but plenty to say about the great figures of the late Republic. Third, the Social War does not loom particularly large in modern histories of Rome (our sources for the war are fragmentary and late). Fourth, scholars sometimes envision the effects of the Social War as long settled by Virgil's time, with Italy integrated and unproblematically on Octavian's side.

Each of these points can be taken in turn. The first is, of course, obvious, but the presence of such markers does not preclude interest on Virgil's part in other conflicts from the past.[12] As to the second point, the interests of Servius and his brethren were elsewhere, and they lacked the tools to see Italian issues contemporary with Virgil.[13] The third and fourth points have had more of an influence than might be thought, since it is all too easy to pass over the great struggles of 91–88. What, after all, was the Social War compared with Pharsalus or Mutina, Philippi or Actium? The answer, it turns out, was quite a lot, at least as some of the ancient historians saw it. Posidonius treated the war in his universal history; Lucullus apparently wrote a separate treatise on the war;[14] and Sisenna began his *Histories* with the war's outbreak.[15] Closer to Virgil's own time, Livy devoted the majority of his history's eighth decade (Books 71–7) to the war, the first Book treating a mere three-quarters of the year 91, and including the Italians' 'gatherings and conspiracies, and the speeches in conferences of their leading men'.[16] Some sense of the magnitude

---

[11] Anchises in the underworld exhorts both Pompey and Caesar to throw down their arms and spare their country (6.830–5); Dido is clearly a Cleopatra figure (see Pease (1935), 24–8), under whose influence Aeneas, temporarily at least, becomes Caesar or Antony; the battle of Actium with its defeat of Antony and Cleopatra occupies the central scene on the shield of Aeneas (8.675); and this is preceded by the correlation of Aeneas with Hercules, the bringer of peace and order to Evander's kingdom, and so through to Augustus, the destroyer of civil war and the guarantor of peace in the Roman state (8.362–9, with Galinsky (1972), 142–5; I. Morgan (1999)).

[12] Quinn (1968), 55: 'even on the most fundamental points more than one correlation is possible. Though one thinks first of the civil war, it is often the problems and situations of the social war that are illuminated in Aeneas' war.'

[13] Mouritsen (1998), 173 points out that because most of the diversity of Italy was wiped out in the 1st cent. BC, the result was a 'tradition which had no experience of Italy as anything but a direct extension of Rome herself'. Cf. Ando (2003), 139–41, esp. 140: 'Servius could not understand Virgil's intent because the fate of Italy as a political ideal had been decided four centuries before.'

[14] Plut. *Luc.* 1.7.

[15] *HRR* F 6 (= *FRH* 16 F 6), cited from Book I, concerns the year 91.

[16] Liv. *per.* 71.2–3: *eorum coetus (Duker: coitus mss) coniurationesque et orationes in consiliis principum referuntur;* on Livy's account of the war see Haug (1947).

of the war can be found in Diodorus who was writing in the 60s, and had actually lived through the war, and who introduces it thus (37.1.1):

In all the time that men's deeds have been handed down by history to the memory of posterity the greatest war known to us is the Marsic, so named from the Marsi. This war surpassed all previous wars both in the bravery of its generals and in the greatness of the deeds (ταῖς τῶν στρατηγῶν ἀνδραγαθίαις καὶ τῷ μεγέθει τῶν πράξεων).[17]

He follows with the standard historiographical trope of the inferiority of previous wars to this one,[18] and concludes (37.1.6):

Because, from the actual results, first place in manly valour in war was awarded to the Romans and to the peoples who inhabit Italy, Fortune as if deliberately put these two at variance and set ablaze the war that surpassed all in magnitude. Indeed when the nations of Italy revolted against Rome's domination, and those who from time immemorial had been accounted the bravest of men fell into discord and contention, the war that ensued reached the very summit of magnitude.

Diodorus' account of the Social War is thought to go back to Posidonius, although the magnification here is generally considered Diodorus' own.[19] Yet there is another passage in Diodorus, considered genuinely Posidonian, that emphasizes the pathos of the war (37.2.3):

In this war all sorts and manner of sufferings, including the storming of cities, befell the two parties in the war, since Victory, as if deliberately, tipped the scales now this way, now that, and remained securely in the possession of neither; nevertheless, after innumerable casualties on either side it was belatedly and with difficulty (ὀψὲ καὶ μόλις) that Rome's power was firmly established.

What makes the Social War an apt analogue for the wars of *Aeneid* 7–12 are its causes and its course.[20] The main cause, as nearly all our sources tell us, was the desire of the Italian allies, who had served Rome in so many campaigns, to share in Rome's empire.[21] The Italians had been the victims of neglect and sometimes severe mistreatment by the Romans in the years

---

[17] Translations of Diodorus are modified from Walton's Loeb. For Diodorus and the Social War see Mouritsen (1998), 5–7 with reff. to earlier scholarship; cf. Yarrow (2006a), 215–19.

[18] Diod. 37.1.2–5. Jacoby thinks this is Posidonian, but it is difficult to tell: the magnitude of one's war is a staple of historiographical prefaces going back to Herodotus: see Marincola (1997), 34–43.

[19] Malitz (1983), 34–42, 385, with references.

[20] Sources for the Marsic War in Greenidge–Clay (1960), 138–41; modern treatments include Kiene (1845); Marcks (1884); Gabba (1954); Brunt (1965); De Sanctis (1976); Sherwin-White (1973), 134–50; Gabba (1994); Mouritsen (1998).

[21] See esp. Vell. 2.15.2; App. *BC* 1.38; Cic. *Off.* 2.75; Gell. 10.3.3, and Diod. 37.2 (cited below, §III). Moderns appraise the goals of the rebels differently: see, e.g., Brunt (1965); Sherwin-White (1973), 134–49 (with summary of some other opinions); Mouritsen (1998), esp. 129–71, who

leading up to the Marsic War.[22] In 133, the allies apparently were to be deprived of their lands by the legislation of Ti. Gracchus, but were not to be recipients or beneficiaries of its redistribution. Fulvius Flaccus in 125 proposed the extension of citizenship to the Italians, but was sent off to fight in Gaul before he could do anything to bring this about. Angered at this rebuff, the town of Fregellae revolted from Rome, and the Romans promptly despatched L. Opimius who razed the city and emptied it of its inhabitants. During the German invasions of 113–101 the Italians rendered yeoman service, but received no rewards; and in 95 the consuls promulgated a law that penalized anyone pretending to be a Roman citizen, and they expelled from Rome all Italians who were not Roman citizens. Such treatment caused growing resentment amongst the Italians, and the breaking point came in 91, when M. Livius Drusus the younger, as tribune of the plebs, brought forward an ambitious legislative programme, including a *lex de sociis* that extended citizenship to the Italians. The bill was not passed and some time towards the end of his year in office Drusus was murdered by an unknown assassin; with his death, it seems, went the last hope of the Italians to be enfranchised.

Though not long in duration, the Social War had disproportionately large casualties. The slaughter of all the Roman citizens inside the town of Asculum,[23] the event that precipitated the hostilities, was only the beginning, and by the end of the war, hardly any part of Italy had not seen some action; the number of men under arms was enormous,[24] and the economic consequences were perhaps even greater than those of the Hannibalic War.[25] Moreover, if any Roman war had a right to be seen as wasteful and senseless, it was the Social War, since the Romans ended up by giving the Italians the very citizenship that they had demanded at the outset. Three years of bloodshed and destruction could have been avoided simply by allowing some form of partnership in empire at the very beginning. This circumstance alone gives particular pathos to Virgil's apostrophe of Jupiter before the final battles of *Aeneid* 12 (503–4):

> tanton placuit concurrere motu,
> Iuppiter, aeterna gentis in pace futuras?

argues that the allies wanted independence from Rome, not partnership in empire; Pobjoy (2000) steers a middle course.

[22] C. Gracchus had collected instances of abuse against the allies: see Aul. Gell. 10.3.1–5; Sherwin-White (1973), 134.

[23] Liv. *per.* 72; App. *BC* 1.38.

[24] Brunt (1971), 439 estimates *c.* 300,000 men total on both sides.

[25] Brunt (1971), 103.

Was it your will, O Jupiter, that people who were to live in eternal peace should clash with such turmoil?

If we accept that Italy and the Social War are on Virgil's mind in the second half of the *Aeneid*, certain matters become clearer. When, for example, Virgil introduces the second half of the *Aeneid* with the words *maius opus moueo* (7.45), scholars see (rightly) a reference to the *Iliad*, which was traditionally considered greater than the *Odyssey*. But lurking behind those words as well was the narrator's recognition that he was now to portray the struggle for empire, the beginnings of what was to become the enormously powerful state of his own day. And although the actual locus of Aeneas' conflict with the natives is located in Latium, Virgil lays emphasis throughout these latter books again and again on Italy. The Trojans' opponents are 'Ausonia', 'Italy', or the 'Italians', as can be seen especially in Book 7: the theme is now 'horrid wars . . . and all Hesperia driven to arms'; when the conflict begins, 'Ausonia' is aflame, although at peace and without alarm before the Trojan arrival; in his catalogue of Italian forces, Virgil speaks of the kings, armies, and heroes who flourished at that time 'in the land of Italy'. Nor is the focus on Italy lost in the later books: in Book 10, Jupiter, angry at the gods' interference with his plan, says that he had 'forbidden Italy to clash with the Trojans'; and in the final book Aeneas and Latinus swear oaths on behalf of Italy and Italians, and Juno implores Jupiter on behalf of Italy (see below); Turnus says to Aeneas at the end that 'the Ausonians' have seen him stretch out his hands in defeat.[26] It may be tempting to see such references as Virgilian hyperbole, with 'Italian' simply a synonym for 'Latin'.[27] Yet Virgil is hardly likely to have been so free with his language. On the contrary, there can be little doubt that we are in fact meant to think of Italy throughout the latter books.[28] As we can see from the historiographical passages above, Virgil's insistence on the greatness of the struggle has good antecedents in writers of his own time and slightly earlier.

---

[26] *Aen.* 7.41–44: *dicam horrida bella, . . . totamque sub arma coactam Hesperiam;* 7.623: *ardet inexcita Ausonia atque immobilis ante;* 7.641–4: *bello exciti reges, quae quemque secutae | complerint campos acies, quibus Itala iam tum | floruerit terra alma uiris* (for the historical perspective inherent in *iam tum*, see Fraenkel (1964) II.16); 10.8: *abnueram bello Italiam concurrere Teucris;* 12.187–93, 200–4, and 820–8 (the last three quoted below); 12.937 (quoted above). This is, of course, only a small sample.

[27] The notion already in Servius ad 7.43: 'totam [sc. Hesperiam] autem ὑπερβολικῶς dixit.'

[28] Note especially the catalogue of Italians at the end of Book 7, where the heroes do not come only from Latium, and include the Aequi, Rutuli, the Volsci, and (perhaps significantly) the Marsi. On this catalogue see Warde Fowler (1918); Horsfall (2000), 414–530; on Virgil and Italy generally, see Saunders (1930); Toll (1991) and (1997); Ando (2002); Barchiesi (2008); on the contradictions in Virgil's portrait of the Italians see O'Hara (2007), 96–103; cf. Barchiesi (2008), 248–55.

But this is only part of the story. It would be all too easy to see the issues that had arisen from the Social War as being dead by Virgil's time, and thus his interest in Italy as merely 'antiquarian': after all the integration of Italy had been underway for half a century, and more immediate conflicts had over-shadowed the war for Italy: and had not *tota Italia* sworn allegiance to Octavian in his conflict with Antony?[29] The assumption that these issues were dead or settled, however, underestimates, on the one hand, the reluc-tance with which the Romans integrated the Italians and, on the other hand, the persistence of local patriotism and local memory amongst the peoples of Italy. The process of the Romanization of the peninsula was hardly straight-forward, and the Roman ruling class showed great reluctance to integrate even the elites of Italy: the process was hardly complete in Virgil's own lifetime.[30] Simultaneously, local memory and local loyalty can still be seen in late Republican and early imperial writers, not least in the poetry of Propertius and Ovid,[31] and such memories would have been kept alive not least by the continued contemporary disruptions in Italy. There is thus both immediate relevance and deep irony[32] in a number of individual incidents from the later books, such as Aeneas' disavowal, before his final duel with Turnus, of any desire for rule over the 'Italians' (12.187–93):

> sin nostrum adnuerit nobis uictoria Martem
> (ut potius reor et potius di numine firment)
> non ego nec Teucris Italos parere iubebo
> nec mihi regna peto: paribus se legibus ambae
> inuictae gentes aeterna in foedera mittant.
> sacra deosque dabo; socer arma Latinus habeto,
> imperium sollemne socer.

But if Victory should give our prowess the nod (as I rather believe, and may the gods confirm it with their will), I shall not order Italians to obey Trojans, nor do I seek kingdoms for myself. Both nations, unconquered, shall move forward, with equal laws, into an everlasting treaty. I shall give the rites and the gods. Latinus, as my father-in-law, is to have his arms, and, as my father-in-law, the solemn authority.

---

[29] Aug. *RG* 25.2: *iurauit in mea uerba tota Italia sponte sua*; cf. Syme (1939), 276–93 on the more likely historical reality.

[30] On the slow integration of Italy see Syme (1939), 88–96; Mouritsen (1998); Lomas (2000); Dench (2005), 152–221; Bispham (2007), 161–204; Farney (2007).

[31] Prop. 1.22; Ov. *Amores* 3.15.8–9: *Paelignae dicar gloria gentis ego,* | *quam sua libertas ad honesta coegerat arma,* | *cum timuit socias anxia Roma manus*; see further Farney (2007), 222–3; Barchiesi (2008), 251–2. Cornell (1976), 423, notes that the *elogia Tarquiniensia* show 'that at Tarquinia feelings of local patriotism were still strong even at the time of the early Roman Empire'.

[32] Barchiesi (2008), 245 formulates it beautifully: 'gli attori della storia si trovino presi in un meccanismo di anticipazione ironica'.

The juxtaposition *Teucris Italos* can hardly be accidental, and part of the dramatic irony here is that what awaits in the future is just such a war. The Marsic War was fought precisely *because* the Italians saw themselves as a subject people, contributing to the empire of Rome but not receiving its rewards, subject to the whims of the Roman Senate, but with no means to redress those grievances. Thus, with equal irony, Latinus prays (12.200–3):

> audiat haec genitor qui foedera flumine sancit.
> tango aras, medios ignis et numina testor:
> nulla dies pacem hanc Italis nec foedera rumpet,
> quo res cumque cadent.

And let the Father himself, who sanctions treaties with his lightning, hear these things. I touch his altars and call to witness the gods and the fires between us. Let no day break this peace for the Italians, nor violate the treaties, however things may fall out.

In the epic, the treaty is about to be broken almost immediately, and will of course be broken again in the future.

It is not necessary here to enter into the question of where Virgil's sympathies lie. Whether he thought the Italian cause 'iustissima', as did Velleius (2.15.2), we cannot say; it will suffice for now to note his interest in Italy throughout, and his recognition that at the base of the Roman empire lay Italian manpower. Juno's plea at 12.822–7:

> cum iam leges et foedera iungent,
> ne uetus indigenas nomen mutare Latinos
> neu Troas fieri iubeas Teucrosque uocari
> aut uocem mutare uiros aut uertere uestem.
> sit Latium, sint Albani per saecula reges,
> sit Romana potens Itala uirtute propago

When they join laws and treaties, do not order that the native Latins change their ancient name, become Trojans or be called 'Teucrians'; or that they, men as they are, change their language or alter their dress. Let Latium continue, let there be Alban kings through the ages; let Roman offspring be powerful with Italian *uirtus*

is answered by Jupiter's promise (834–9):

> sermonem Ausonii patrium moresque tenebunt,
> utque est nomen erit; commixti corpore tantum
> subsident Teucri. morem ritusque sacrorum
> adiciam faciamque omnis uno ore Latinos.
> hinc genus Ausonio mixtum quod sanguine surget,
> supra homines, supra ire deos pietate uidebis.

The Ausonians will keep their native speech and customs; their name will be as it now is; the Teucrians, joined in blood only, will fade away. I shall add custom and religious rites, and I shall make them all Latins with one voice. Hence a race will arise which, mixed with Ausonian blood, you will see exceed men, exceed gods in piety.

To sum up my first point, then, the recognition that the pervasiveness of Italy in the epic's second half alludes, at least partially, to the Social War provides a helpful context for understanding the delicate position of Aeneas and the Trojans vis-à-vis the native Italians, and it indicates the continued importance of these issues to Virgil and his contemporary audience.

II. PUNISHMENT AND MERCY

Let us move on to a second aspect of the *Aeneid*'s final scene, Aeneas' decision whether or not to spare Turnus. If we consider the characters themselves, it is not hard to see the motivation of Aeneas for taking the action that he does, but neither is it difficult to understand why many have found this a troubling conclusion. The choice takes on additional resonance, however, when we recall that the second half of the *Aeneid* is pervaded by the sense of civil war, and the final conflict is therefore about not only Caesar and Pompey or Octavian and Antony, but also Rome and Italy. I want to suggest that the 'open-endedness' of the *Aeneid* is the direct result of just this aspect, and for this interpretation, Sallust's *Catiline* has some important contributions to make.

The *Catiline* was probably published shortly after the death of Cicero.[33] It thus pre-dates by about a decade the traditional date for Virgil's commencement of work on the *Aeneid*. The *Catiline*, as is well known, has an extensive preface in which Sallust expostulates on ancient *uirtus* and on the progressive decline of Roman standards and morality.[34] Indeed, the *Catiline* is positively leisurely in getting about the business of its actual topic, not really settling into the narrative of events until about one-fifth of the way through the work. By contrast, however, the ending of the *Catiline* is strikingly abrupt: the conclusion focuses on the final battle in which Catiline is killed. Significantly, Sallust, although he claimed his topic was the *war* with Catiline, chose not to treat the mopping-up operations in central and southern Italy a few months after Catiline's death, nor does he tell of Catiline's head brought to Rome to

---

[33] Certainty is impossible: see Syme (1964), 121–37 for the evidence, such as it is.

[34] *Cat.* 1–4 + 6–13; but for the argument that this is a single preface, see McGushin (1977), 291–2. As with the *Aeneid*'s final scene there is a vast bibliography on the preface, but there is no purpose in citing it here.

establish the proof of his death.[35] Instead, Sallust chose as his final incident the battle in which Catiline himself was killed. At the end of his narrative there is no comment by the narrator, no intrusive interpretation, but rather a focalization on those viewing the battlefield:[36]

neque tamen exercitus populi Romani laetam aut incruentam uictoriam adeptus erat; nam strenuissumus quisque aut occiderat in proelio aut grauiter uolneratus discesserat. multi autem qui e castris uisundi aut spoliandi gratia processerant, uoluentes hostilia cadauera amicum alii, pars hospitem aut cognatum reperiebant; fuere item qui inimicos suos cognoscerent. ita uarie per omnem exercitum laetitia, maeror, luctus atque gaudia agitabantur.

Yet neither had the army of the Roman people achieved a delightful or bloodless victory: all the most committed had either fallen in the battle or retired seriously wounded. As for the many who had emerged from the camp for the purposes of viewing or plundering and were turning over the enemy corpses, some discovered a friend, others a guest or relative; likewise there were those who recognized their own personal antagonists. Thus, throughout the entire army, delight, sorrow, grief and joy were variously experienced.

The work does not end on a calm or even 'concluding' note, and its powerful effect, with grief and joy indistinguishably mixed, results largely from the *subversion* of two common closural devices, death and victory: the result is that they produce not resolution, their usual effect, but disquiet and disturbance. This is a powerful scene, full of emotional ambiguity and uncertainty, and in that sense perfectly embodying some of the reactions towards civil war that many contemporaries must have felt. For Catiline's conspiracy *was* a civil war, in as much as citizens (including those from several prominent families) plotted against citizens, and Romans fought Romans in battle. Sallust's open-ended narrative is perhaps the result of his own situation, since, writing in the 40s under renewed threat of civil war, he did not really know whether there was yet an end to that conflict between nobles and people that had found expression in Catiline's conspiracy. The same is certainly true of Virgil: he could not have known, when he was writing the *Aeneid* in the 20s, that there truly had been an end to the wars of the late Republic: there had been peace, of course, for some time, but we know of conspiracies against Augustus. His reign was not universally applauded, particularly in the early years, and a successful coup would have plunged the country back into war.[37]

---

[35] See Oros. 6.6.7; Suet. *Aug.* 3.1; Dio 37.40.2 (Catiline's head), 37.41.1; Syme (1964), 137.

[36] *Cat.* 61.7–9; translations of Sallust are those of Woodman (2007).

[37] See Vell. 2.91.2, Dio 54.3.4 ff. (Murena and Caepio in 24); Syme (1939), 414, 420 (possible conspiracy of Cn. Cornelius Cinna).

The relevance of such a final scene for the *Aeneid* should be clear: first, the *Catiline*, like the *Aeneid*, ends on the battlefield itself, not with burial or triumph or any number of other common closural motifs available to the authors: it ends as it had begun, so to speak, *in mediis rebus*. Second, both works end on an emotional high point. Third, each narrator portrays mixed emotions, both those of the victor and those of the vanquished.[38] Finally, in both cases, the reader is left wanting more, or perhaps to put it differently, the reader is directed to look elsewhere for the work's ultimate meaning.[39]

It is possible, of course, to interpret Aeneas' decision as a 'personal' one, and the epic certainly allows this. But again, Aeneas is not just Aeneas nor is Turnus just Turnus, and their actions have important consequences for their descendants. Aeneas standing over the defeated Turnus will have suggested to any Roman a recurrent scene in Rome's rise to empire: the conqueror after his victory deciding how to treat the conquered—although the issue here is somewhat more complicated since Turnus is not quite a 'foreigner', as we know. Now we have in the *Catiline* the extensive and famous debate between Caesar and Cato, in which they discuss the appropriate punishment to be meted out to Catiline and his followers: it is a debate on what to do with enemies in your own house. Caesar argues against death, Cato in favour.

There is a fundamental difference in the way that Cato and Caesar approach the issues. Cato's speech, not surprisingly, is critical of the love of excess, and of the moral corruption of the state, and it concentrates on individual control: it is an inward-looking speech, urging each Senator to take care of his own house and show a discipline, austerity, and authority worthy of a true *paterfamilias*. Caesar's approach, by contrast, is more suited to a man who had seen the world and conquered a good portion of it. It is outward-looking and concerned above all with how the Romans, and the Senate in particular, will appear to others, and why they should care about these appearances; it especially concentrates on how the Romans act towards their subjects. Caesar's speech is much focused on the future, Cato's on the present. The difference between the two men in the way they invoke Roman history is instructive: both men use *exempla* to bolster their points, but Cato uses one only, that of Manlius Torquatus killing his own son because the

[38] In Sallust, this is explicit, as we see from the final sentence, while in Virgil this is conveyed in more subtle ways: there is the groaning of the Rutulians (*gemitu*, 928), Turnus is laid low and imploring (*supplex... precantem*, 930), and he appeals to pity (*miserere*, 934); he characterizes Aeneas' actions in terms of 'hatreds' (*odiis*, 938), and then Aeneas himself is characterized when he sees the baldric of Paris as *furiis accensus et ira terribilis* (946–7), and *feruidus* (951); while in the same line Turnus is cold in death (*frigore*), and his own life ends with a groaning (*gemitu*, 952) that echoes that of the Rutulians before.

[39] Hardie (1997), 142–51; (1998), 71–4.

young man had fought against the enemy contrary to orders (*Cat.* 52.30); Caesar, on the other hand, gives a series of *exempla* designed to show the traditional clemency of the Roman people against their enemies when they had conquered them—he mentions the Rhodians, the Carthaginians, and the Macedonians (we must leave aside, of course, whether these really were examples of Roman clemency)—noting as well the open Roman approach to adopting the ways of foreigners (51.4–6, 27–34, 37–9).

Caesar begins by warning that all who debate *de rebus dubiis* should be free from 'hatred, friendship, anger and pity', for these emotions stand in the way of making a judgement that is advantageous.[40] Later he says that those who live in humble circumstances need not be as careful in their decisions and actions, since few will know if they have made bad judgements through anger. Those, however, possessed of great empire, who live their lives in full public view, will perform deeds that are known by all: and so paradoxically the greater the empire, the more circumscribed the field of action. And in this *public* arena, Caesar continues, it is fitting neither to show favour nor to act from hatred, and least of all to show anger (51.12–13, 15). The reason for this, again, is the public perception of Roman behaviour: 'that which in others would be considered anger is, for those with an empire, marked out as arrogance and cruelty' (51.14: *quae apud alios iracundia dicitur, ea in imperio superbia atque crudelitas appellatur*).

In a very important sense, the final scene of the *Aeneid* is a dramatization on the battlefield of the Cato/Caesar debate. Just as Sallust does not choose sides,[41] so Virgil does not provide a tidy solution to Turnus' fate. And indeed how could he? Aeneas' decision would have to be remade a thousand times by later Romans, by every victorious general in the field, by every group of Senators gathered to receive embassies from defeated peoples. That Turnus was Italian or Catiline Roman only added to the complexities: if anything, it meant that more issues were in play, not fewer.

This was civil war at its most difficult: not the actual winning of the battles, but what to do with the defeated, those people who are very often bound to the victors by innumerable relationships. Indeed, it is the very confusion of civil war that makes moral evaluation so problematic. This more than anything else, I think, accounts for Virgil's decision to depart from his Homeric models. His war was not like that of the *Iliad*, nor was his community like that of Ithaca; Virgil's 'suitors' are, in a fundamental sense, kinsmen, as are also his 'enemy'. This is assuredly not to say that Virgil did not take sides: as we know

---

[40] *Cat.* 51.1–2; the same phrase used of the Council of Latins at *Aen.* 11.445–6 (*illi haec inter se dubiis de rebus agebant | certantes*); for the phrase see Norden (1957), 190–1.

[41] Both speakers are praised for their *uirtus*: *Cat.* 53.2–54.6, with Levene (2000), esp. 191.

from the shield of Aeneas and the depiction of the underworld, Virgil could certainly tell a Catiline from a Cato (*Aen.* 8.668–9). Nor is there any doubt that Catiline in Sallust is a 'bad guy', one who must be eliminated; yet one cannot avoid the sense that there are aspects of Catiline's cause—his view of the depredations of the nobility, especially[42]—that merit our attention and perhaps even our sympathy, even if the means he took to redress those wrongs cannot be approved. Something similar is at work with Turnus: although he is historically on the 'wrong' side, there is force, and even justice, in some of the things he says (even if, or perhaps because, he has only a limited perspective). This balancing act, this equilibrium of perspective had been accomplished by Virgil before, of course, perhaps most notably in the first *Eclogue*, where the very different experiences of Tityrus and Meliboeus are juxtaposed; there too there is no resolution, and although Meliboeus, like Turnus, is on the wrong side of history, his voice is not silenced.[43] Because these were *civil* wars, it was far more difficult, if not impossible, to separate out the emotional register, to feel *only* happiness or sadness, grief or joy: and that difficulty is mirrored in the conclusions of both *Catiline* and *Aeneid*.

III. SPOILS

The immediate reason that Aeneas kills Turnus is that he catches sight of the baldric of Pallas on Turnus' shoulder. The language here is powerful and emotional, both in the metamorphosis that Aeneas undergoes and in his last speech to Turnus. Quite apart from the 'personal' motivation, the issue of the spoils of war was of paramount importance in late Republican discussions of Roman imperialism.

When Turnus in Book 10 took the spoils from the dead Pallas, his action was highlighted in two ways: first, implicitly, by the later contrast with Aeneas, who refuses to despoil Lausus' body, even to the point of picking it up and conveying it to his comrades;[44] second, explicitly, by the narrator's apostrophe at the moment that Turnus dons the spoils (*Aen.* 10.501–5):

---

[42] *Cat.* 20.11 ~ 12.3, 13.1; on Catiline's rhetoric, see Innes (1977).

[43] I agree with Klingner (1965), 302, who remarks (in a different context): 'so ist das Wesentliche von Virgils Ansicht der Geschichte schon in den Bucolica vorgezeichnet'; cf. in a rather different vein Powell (2008). For the connexion between *Eclogue* 1 and the end of the *Aeneid* see Putnam (1999), 228–30.

[44] *Aen.* 10.490–500 (Turnus); 821–32 (Aeneas), with discussion and references in Harrison (1991), 196, 267.

nescia mens hominum fati sortisque futurae
et seruare modum rebus sublata secundis.
Turno tempus erit magno cum optauerit emptum
intactum Pallanta, et cum spolia ista diemque
oderit.

The mind of human beings is ignorant of fate and future chance, and, when raised up
by prosperity, of how to observe moderation. A time will come to Turnus when he will
wish to pay, and pay greatly, for an unharmed Pallas, and he will hate those spoils and
that day.

The apostrophe has good Homeric precedent, Zeus looking upon Hector as
he puts on the armour of Patroclus:[45]

Ah, poor wretch, there is no thought of death in your mind now, and yet death stands
close beside you as you put on the immortal armour of a surpassing man. There are
others who tremble before him. Now you have killed this man's dear friend, who was
strong and gentle, and taken the armour, as you should not have done, from his
shoulders and head.

Virgil's words, as always, are similar and different.[46] The Homeric passage
clearly lacks the universality of the Virgilian passage. Zeus looks down in pity
for *this* particular warrior, a favourite of his. Virgil, by contrast, begins with a
universal observation before narrowing the focus to Turnus himself, and it is
that universal observation on which I want to concentrate. The commentators
tell us—and they are not wrong, of course—that much of what Virgil says is
commonplace: nothing in excess, *nemesis* follows *hybris*, and so on.[47] The
precedents are thus not particularly epic, and some have tried to align them
with tragedy, where pride goeth before a fall, and change of circumstances
brings disaster with sudden fury. Yet Virgil's apostrophe comes in a particular
context that is best understood, I believe, through the role that such musings
play neither in epic nor in tragedy but rather in historiography. First, however,
the spoils themselves.

For the Romans of the late Republic, it was extremely difficult to explain
what had happened to their state, and how it had come about that a city that
conquered the world then turned its weapons against itself. In place of
harmony and unity in the face of external danger, the Roman state was now
filled with dissension, lawlessness, and violence. We can see any number of

---

[45] *Il.* 17.201–6 (Lattimore, tr.).

[46] There has been much discussion of whether Turnus' individual action is wrong or morally
blameworthy—see e.g. Hornsby (1966); Harrison (1991), 199; id. (1998)—but the issue, while
important, is not my concern here.

[47] Harrison (1991), 200.

thinkers grappling with this problem, and it is not surprising, of course, that their explanations were not in terms of political structures or economic factors, but rather in terms of what they believed was the moral change that had come about when Rome had its greatest success. Sallust in the *Catiline* provides one very common view (10.1–4, 6):

sed ubi labore atque iustitia res publica creuit, reges magni bello domiti, nationes ferae et populi ingentes ui subacti, Carthago aemula imperi Romani ab stirpe interiit, cuncta maria terraeque patebant, saeuire fortuna ac miscere omnia coepit. (2) Qui labores pericula, dubias atque asperas res facile tolerauerant, iis otium diuitiae, optanda alias, oneri miseriaeque fuere. (3) Igitur primo pecuniae, deinde imperi cupido creuit: ea quasi materies omnium malorum fuere. (4) Namque auaritia fidem probitatem ceterasque artis bonas subuortit; pro his superbiam, crudelitatem, deos neglegere, omnia uenalia habere edocuit. . . . (6) Haec primo paulatim crescere, interdum uindicari; post ubi contagio quasi pestilentia inuasit, ciuitas inmutata, imperium ex iustissumo atque optumo crudele intolerandum factum.

But when the commonwealth had grown through hard work and justice, and great kings had been tamed in war, and wild nations and mighty peoples subdued by force, and Carthage—the rival of Roman for command of an empire—had been eradicated, and all seas and lands became accessible, then Fortune began to turn savage and to confound everything. (2) Those who had easily tolerated hard work, danger, and uncertain and rough conditions, regarded leisure and riches (things to be craved under other circumstances) as a burden and a source of misery. (3) Hence it was the desire for money first of all, and then for empire, which grew; and those factors were the kindling (so to speak) of every wickedness. (4) For avarice undermined trust, probity, and all other good qualities; instead, it taught men haughtiness, cruelty, to neglect the gods, to regard everything as for sale. . . . (6) At first these things grew gradually; sometimes they were punished; but after, when the contamination had attacked like a plague, the community changed and the exercise of command, from being the best and most just, became cruel and intolerable.

Not all writers agreed when moral decline began: Livy, for example, notes that Marcellus' settlement of Syracuse after his conquest in 212 was done with integrity, but although the spoils were legitimate, they were 'the origin of our admiration of Greek art, and started the universal and reckless spoliation of all buildings sacred and profane which prevails today'.[48] Another turning point was L. Mummius' conquest of Corinth, which brought a vast supply of luxury goods from Greece into Rome.[49] Or it might be the point where Sulla's army was in Asia, an event referred to by Sallust as introducing luxury

---

[48] Livy 25.40.2: *ceterum inde primum initium mirandi Graecarum artium opera licentiaeque hinc sacra profanaque omnia uulgo spoliandi factum est.*

[49] Vell. 1.13.4–5, with Elefante (1997), 187–8; Yarrow (2006b).

and corruption to the Roman soldiers: 'that was the first time an army of the Roman people became accustomed to love affairs and drink; to admire statues, paintings, and engraved goblets; to seize them regardless of whether privately or publicly owned; to despoil shrines and to pollute everything sacred and profane alike', leaving nothing to the vanquished.[50] Now although authors might focus on different dates, the destruction of Carthage, Rome's great rival, in 146 is most often the single most important event, and the notion that *metus hostilis*, fear of the enemy, preserved Rome before that date is strongly ingrained in the tradition.[51] Closely allied to this, as we can see from Sallust, is the belief that the corruption brought about by the loss of Rome's enemy led to cupidity, spoliation, and the movement from *iustum* to *iniustum imperium*, marked by a failure to respect the conquered and use them instead for one's private gratification.

Sallust here hints at the perspective of the victims of Roman imperialism, and it was a viewpoint that he was to take up later in the *Histories*, where the letter that he writes for Mithridates is a valuable document of Roman self-criticism.[52] Addressed to the Parthian king Arsaces, it urges him to take thought for the 'real' character of the Romans:[53]

Namque Romanis cum nationibus populis regibus cunctis una et ea uetus causa bellandi est, cupido profunda imperi et diuitiarum. (. . .) (17) An ignoras Romanos, postquam ad occidentem pergentibus finem Oceanus fecit, arma huc conuortisse, neque quicquam a principio nisi raptum habere, domum coniuges agros imperium? Conuenas olim sine patria parentibus, peste conditos orbis terrarum, quibus non humana ulla neque diuina obstant quin socios amicos, procul iuxta sitos, inopes potentisque trahant excindant, omniaque non serua, et maxume regna, hostilia ducant?

The Romans have only a single reason—and that too a long-standing one—for making war on all nations, peoples, and kings: a profound desire for empire and for riches. . . . Or are you unaware that the Romans turned their arms in this direction only after the Ocean had put an end to their progress westwards, and that from their very inception they have possessed nothing except what they have seized—home, spouses, land, empire? That they were formerly migrants without fatherland or parents, founded to be a plague upon the globe, who are prevented by nothing human or divine from looting and destroying allies and friends, peoples distant and

---

[50] *Cat.* 11.6: *ibi primum insueuit exercitus populi Romani amare potare, signa tabulas pictas uasa caelata mirari, ea priuatim et publice rapere, delubra spoliare, sacra profanaque omnia polluere.* Cf. Plut. *Sulla* 12.9–14.

[51] See Lintott (1972); further bibliography at Hackl (1980), 151 n. 1, to which add Purcell (1995).

[52] For recent discussion see Adler (2005–6), esp. 386–96; cf. Levene, ch. 17 in this volume.

[53] Sall. *Hist.* 4.69[= 4.67 McG.].5, 17.

nearby, needy or powerful, and from regarding everything which is not subservient—especially monarchies—as their enemy?

The nature of Roman imperialism is here closely connected with the Roman desire (*cupido*) to have everything: and, as in the *Catiline*, it is this desire for wealth and indeed spoils that, for Roman writers, has brought Rome to the brink.

To return to the *Aeneid*: such observations in other genres and in the context of the late Republican discussion of Roman imperialism help to give point to the references by the Italians to Aeneas and the Trojans as 'plunderers' or 'thieves': Amata calls Aeneas a 'lying brigand' (*perfidus praedo*), and Mezentius vows the 'brigand's body' (*praedonis corpore*) for his son Lausus; the Italian matrons similarly pray to Pallas to break the spear of the 'Phrygian brigand' (*Phrygii praedonis*); and Juno, in the council of gods in Book 10, claims that the Trojans 'put other men's lands under their yoke and carry off plunder' (*arua aliena iugo premere atque auertere praedas*).[54] Similarly, the emphasis on the harshness or virility of the Italians and the references to the 'soft' invaders from the East suggest not only the luxury-laden Romans of the late first century but also hint at Roman reliance on others for their victories.[55] Although these words are placed in the mouths of Rome's enemies, they should not therefore be immediately dismissed. On the contrary, they reflect, on the one hand, an act of literary allusion, since we know that in some earlier versions of the Aeneas story, Aeneas was the aggressor;[56] and they constitute, on the other hand, Virgil's own contribution to the debate about Roman imperialism, alluding to the reputation that the Romans believed that some—perhaps all—of their subjects had of them.[57] The inclusion of these viewpoints is a reminder of their reality to the subjects, the victims of the empire—or, if we move the focus back to Italy, to the claims made by the Italians in their war against Rome. Again, this is why Virgil is so careful to have Aeneas present himself *not* as a conqueror and *not* as someone who will deprive the Latins of their lands and rule.

[54] *Aen.* 7.360–2; 10.774–6; 11.484–5; 10.74–78, respectively; cf. 12.236–7: *nos patria amissa dominis parere superbis | cogemur.*

[55] I cannot help but wonder whether the summary description of Aeneas' shield—*illic res Italas Romanorumque triumphos*, 8.626—mirrors, by its juxtaposition, Roman dependence on Italian resources.

[56] The early tradition is problematic and, at times it seems, contradictory: see e.g. Cato, *FRH* 3 FF 8–10 (= *HRR* FF 8–10), which seem to suggest both peaceful integration and violent strife between the Trojans and the Italian natives.

[57] And Virgil could do this despite the fact that he portrays his own Mantua as an ally of the Trojans: *Aen.* 10.198–202.

We can now return to the narrator's apostrophe of Turnus in Book 10: it cannot be coincidence, I think, that it is at the very point where Turnus puts on the spoils that we find remarks about keeping one's head in prosperity, inasmuch as humans are ignorant of fate and future chance. This allusion to the theme of the mutability of human fortune, first found in *Iliad* and *Odyssey*[58] and a commonplace of ancient literature, is taken up by the early historians,[59] and becomes in Hellenistic historiography almost a leitmotif: Polybius says that the reading of history is the only sure education in how to bear changes of fortune nobly,[60] and he often focuses on moments of triumph, praising those who know how to maintain the proper perspective. In a striking scene Hannibal and Scipio Africanus confer before Zama, and Hannibal uses himself as an *exemplum* of the mutability of fortune, noting that he had once not so long before been master of Italy (15.6.4–7.9); just as important are the reflections by Aemilius Paullus after his conquest of Perseus, using Perseus himself as an example of the truth of his observations, where the conqueror notes: (29.20.1–2):

It is chiefly at those moments when we ourselves or our country are most successful that we should reflect on the opposite extremity of fortune; for only thus, and then with difficulty, will we prove moderate in the season of prosperity.

Paullus makes good on his words by showing moderation in his success and exhibiting self-control in the face of the overwhelming temptations of Macedonian wealth. And his son, Scipio Aemilianus, at the fall of Carthage shows his ability to keep his head in success when he recognizes the possibility that such a fate may one day befall his own city.[61]

All this is to say that Turnus putting on the spoils of Pallas is anything but a 'personal' action. For a Roman of the late Republic, schooled in the notion that wealth and empire had ruined the Roman state, the action of Turnus at the height of his good fortune—his fate begins to turn thereafter—could not help but call to mind the plundering that the Roman state itself had engaged in. Nor can it be coincidence that Pallas' baldric, now to be taken up by Turnus, is a beautiful work of *Greek* art, the love for which had influenced Marcellus, Mummius, Sulla, and had come to serve as a key marker of Roman decline.

---

[58] e.g. *Il.* 24.525–51; *Od.* 17.419–26.
[59] e.g. Hdt. 1.5.4; Thuc. 4.18.3.
[60] Pol. 1.1.2, a sentiment that he says has been enunciated by many.
[61] Pol. 38.21–2. Cf. Evander's memorable words to Aeneas, 'my guest, dare to despise riches' (8.364: *aude, hospes, contemnere opes*): this is not simply a personal injunction not to be greedy, but a political warning of the dangers brought about by empire.

And here I come back finally to the Marsic War and Posidonius. Diodorus preserves an explanation of the causes of the Social War that is thought to be Posidonian, and although we cannot be certain, we have sufficient evidence that Posidonius did indeed have a critical view of the Romans' empire and of the role that wealth and luxury played in the strength of a state.[62] Here is Diodorus (37.2.1–2):

The primary cause of the war was the fact that the Romans, from the disciplined, frugal, and stern manner of life through which they had grown great, fell into a destructive zeal for luxury and licence. (2) The plebs and the Senate being at odds as a result of this deterioration, the latter called on the Italians to support them, promising to admit them to the much-desired Roman citizenship, and to confirm the grant by law; but when none of the promises made to the Italians was realized, war flared up between them and the Romans.

Whatever we think of this as historical causation (and Diodorus may have misunderstood Posidonius), it is noteworthy that a luxurious manner of living leads to *civil* dissension.[63]

And what of the *exuuiae* themselves? They are described as a *monimentum saeui doloris*, a 'reminder of savage grief' at which Aeneas becomes enraged, caught up in fury and anger, and he is described, as he deals the death blow to Turnus, as *feruidus*, 'boiling'. We may well ask what this reaction in Aeneas is: is it the flame of that individual *cupido* that had driven Nisus, Euryalus, and Camilla towards a fatal love of spoils that resulted in their deaths?[64] Is it perhaps the collective *cupido* for empire and riches that Mithridates had said animated the Roman state, here directed against its first victim? Or is Aeneas here trying to pre-emptively wipe out this emblem of what will become for his people both their glory and their destruction?[65] For there is a noteworthy ambiguity in Aeneas' address to Turnus as *spoliis indute meorum*. The words in their immediate context refer to Pallas as one of Aeneas' men, but such a possessive can carry a greater meaning as we see when Anchises refers to the younger Marcellus' tragic fate as the *ingens luctus tuorum*, 'the enormous grief of your people' (6.868): he clearly means future Romans. Similarly, here at the conclusion, 'my people' refers not only to Aeneas' contemporary allies but to the entire future race of Romans. Furthermore, the word *monimentum* is an

---

[62] See Strasburger (1965), 47–9; further references in Sacks (1990), 46 n. 94; Posidonius' varied attitude towards Rome is treated by Malitz (1983), 359–408, 424–7.

[63] M. Griffin (2009) shows the interconnectedness of domestic politics and foreign policy in Cicero's thought.

[64] *Aen.* 9.184–5 with Hardie (1994), 26, 109, 130; 11.768–77, esp. 782 (*femineo praedae et spoliorum ardebat amore*) with Horsfall (2003), 218.

[65] I owe this last interpretation (which I think the most likely) to Laurel Fulkerson.

important word in historiography, where it retains both meanings of something that reminds and something that warns (these two functions being closely connected in historiography):[66] these spoils are at one level a reminder to Aeneas of what he has lost, and on the other hand they are a warning of what is in store for the future Roman race.

Nor can it be accidental that these spoils both show strife amongst families[67] and are described as beautiful works of *Greek* art: they are Greek spoils showing a Greek myth, beautifully engraved. They, of course, provide the immediate justification for Aeneas' anger and Turnus' death, but they link both men—for both men, after all, are affected by them—into the long pattern of Roman imperialism, closely connected in the minds of many Greek and Roman historians with luxury, decline, and the fraternal strife of the last century of the Republic.

Scholars have long admired Virgil's manipulation of time in the *Aeneid*, as past, present, and future often bleed one into the other. In this sense, of course, the end of the *Aeneid* is not really the end. Indeed, in many important ways, Turnus is only the beginning: he is the first, essential step towards empire. And so all the issues are there, including, but not limited to, recent history: Caesar and Pompey, Antony and Octavian, of course, but also the whole sorry century going back to the period of civil disturbance ushered in by the Gracchi, where, we are told, the issue of Italian citizenship first arose. I have tried to examine here how Virgil has been influenced by historiographical discussions in the late Republic concerning how the Roman state had come to that point which Livy so memorably marked (*praef.* 9) as one in which the Romans could endure neither their vices nor the remedies for them. A consideration of these few points of contact between the historians and Virgil—and there is, of course, much more to be said—helps us put the issues into a larger historical and political context, and allows us to see how late Republican writers tried to portray Rome's wars in their deep emotionalism and their full complexity. It also provides a corrective to the oft-expressed view that the Romans portrayed their history only in a favourable or jingoistic light.[68] Sallust's histories and Virgil's *Aeneid* show that the Romans—or, at least, their great writers—were aware of the competing and conflicting demands of empire made no less on the conquerors than on the conquered.

---

[66] Kraus–Woodman (1997), 57–8; cf. Meadows–Williams (2001), esp. 33, 37, 42 ff. on the cult of Juno Moneta and the connexion between memory and advising.

[67] There has been much discussion of Pallas' armour: see Conte (1970); Spence (1991); Putnam (1994); Harrison (1998).

[68] Cf. the papers of Levene (ch. 17) and Rutherford (ch. 18) in this volume.

12

Fathers and Sons: The Manlii Torquati and Family Continuity in Catullus and Horace

Denis Feeney

I

The *gens Manlia* was a patrician house of great lustre.[1] Along with the Aemilii, Claudii, Cornelii, Fabii, and Valerii, they were one of the six patrician *gentes maiores*, comprising an inner circle of the inner circle. Almost two centuries after the last time a Manlius had held the consulate, Tacitus would still fall back on their name as emblematic of the glorious families of the old Republican aristocracy.[2] The family, indeed, fetishized their glorious past.[3] It was from a lofty peak of patrician self-regard that L. Manlius Torquatus (*RE* 80, pr. 49) could describe Cicero, because of his origins in a *municipium*, as the third foreign-born king after Tarquin and Numa, just as the patrician L. Sergius Catilina had called him an 'immigrant citizen of the City of Rome'.[4]

---

[1] On the *gens Manlia* in general, see Münzer (1928); I must state how greatly indebted I am to Münzer's articles on the *gens*, which are not only packed with all the pertinent information but studded with fine moments of interpretation of the poems I shall be considering here. My thanks to Andrew Feldherr for commenting on a draft, and to the editors for their valuable assistance. It is a privilege to contribute to a volume honouring a scholar such as Tony Woodman, whom I am lucky to have had as a friend for twenty-five years. Since he has done so much to elucidate both Roman history and Latin poetry, I hope he will not find too much to object to in this study of how two of his favourite Latin poets incorporate Roman history into their work.

[2] As Harriet Flower points out to me, in AD 22 there were *imagines* from twenty highly distinguished families carried at the funeral of Junia, widow of Cassius and sister of Brutus, and the Manlii head Tacitus' list: *uiginti clarissimarum familiarum imagines antelatae sunt, Manlii, Quinctii aliaque eiusdem nobilitatis nomina* (*Ann.* 3.76.2). As noted by Woodman–Martin (1996), 497, 'T. perhaps selected each name for its resonances of *prisca uirtus*'.

[3] Münzer (1928), 1150.58–67.

[4] Cic. *Sull.* 22, *tertium peregrinum regem*; Sall. *Cat.* 31.7 *inquilinus ciuis urbis Romae*, with the translation of Woodman (2007); unless otherwise stated, all other translations are my own.

The true glory days of the Manlii were in the first two-thirds of the fourth century, especially during the Gallic and Latin wars.[5] M. Manlius Capitolinus (*RE* 51, cos. 392) saved the besieged Capitol from the Gauls in 390 (Liv. 5.47), although he was hurled from the same Capitol six years later after being convicted of aspiring to *regnum* (Liv. 6.20.12): thereafter, the *gens* never again used the *praenomen* Marcus (Liv. 6.20.14). T. Manlius (*RE* 57, cos. 347, 344, 340) inherited the *cognomen* 'Imperiosus' from his father, and acquired another, 'Torquatus', as a young man in 361, when he performed the heroic deed of defeating a giant Gaul in a David-and-Goliath encounter, stripping him of his torque (Liv. 7.10).[6] He gained a further degree of fame, or notoriety, as consul in 340, commanding the army against the Latins near Capua, when he executed his son for leaving the ranks to fight an opponent in single combat in attempted emulation of his own heroic duel just over twenty years earlier—crucially, the father had carefully asked his commander for permission whereas the son violated a direct command against fighting out of the ranks (Liv. 8.7). This episode is the most famous in the family's long history, and we shall return to consider it in more detail shortly. Here we need note only that the rigidly strict discipline meted out by T. Manlius Imperiosus Torquatus gave the Manlii Torquati a name for old-fashioned harsh severity, so much so that the episode is demonstrably responsible for projections forward and backward in time, as Manlian anecdotes were crafted to make other members of the family fit in with the template of rigidly enforced strict discipline.[7]

Following their dazzling and formidable prominence in the fourth century, the Manlii Torquati produced few outstanding figures. After the first Torquatus, they had to wait more than a hundred years for another truly prominent member of the family to appear, T. Manlius Torquatus (*RE* 82, cos. 235, 224). In the historical tradition he satisfyingly embodies all the familial characteristics of harshness and toughness, especially in his opposition to the ransoming of Hannibal's Roman prisoners after Cannae.[8] After his second consulate in 224, there is a gap of fifty-nine years before the name of Manlius Torquatus returns to the Fasti, and then there are two in a row, his grandsons— T. Manlius Torquatus (*RE* 83, cos. 165), who contributes, as we shall see, the family's most repellent example of paternal severity, followed immediately

---

[5] Münzer (1928), 1150.38–52. All dates are BC unless otherwise stated.

[6] See Oakley, *Comm.* II.124 for the parallels with 1 Samuel 17.

[7] Oakley, *Comm.* II.86–7; on this process in general, citing the Manlii Torquati among others, see Wiseman (1979), 25; on Livy's use of such familial patterns see Vasaly (1987), esp. on the Appii Claudii, and (1998–9) on the Quinctii. See Önnerfors (1974), 14–23 for T. Manlius Imperiosus Torquatus as exemplary of paternal *seueritas*.

[8] Münzer (1928), 1152.6–9; we return to this episode below.

by his brother A. Manlius Torquatus (*RE* 73, cos. 164). Then another gap, of almost precisely a century, until the year 65, when L. Manlius Torquatus (*RE* 79) gives his name to the year of Horace's birth by holding the office (*O nata mecum consule Manlio*, *Carm.* 3.21.1; *Torquato . . . consule . . . meo*, *Epod.* 13.6).

This man was the last Manlius Torquatus to hold the consular fasces. His son L. Manlius Torquatus (*RE* 80) attained the praetorship in 49 and might have hoped for the consulship in due course if he had not been swept away, with so many others, by the tidal wave of Julius Caesar's war: taking Pompeius' side, he maintained the Republican cause until the battle of Thapsus in 46, and was killed in its aftermath, attempting to sail to Spain.[9] A certain Manlius Torquatus is attested without *praenomen* as *quaestor* under Pansa in 43;[10] so far as we know, he is the last of the family ever to hold office, and the family itself must have disappeared after the next generation, dying out with the Republic it had served so mightily: 'So ist das Geschlecht mit dem Ende der Republik erloschen'.[11]

The last prominent member of the family, then, is L. Manlius Torquatus, the praetor of 49 and son of the consul of 65. He is the addressee of two poems by Catullus, 61, an epithalamium celebrating his marriage, and 68.[12] Some thirty-five to forty years later a member of the family from its last generation, probably the son of Catullus' friend, the very son whose birth is prayed for in Catullus' epithalamium, is the addressee of two poems by Horace, *Epist.* 1.5 and *Carm.* 4.7.[13] Each poet draws on the rich historical tradition surrounding the family as he composes, and in each case a knowledge of the fate of the Manlii Torquati can inform our understanding of the poems.[14]

The crucial episode in moulding the exemplary value of the family is, as noted above, T. Manlius' execution of his son in 340. To put the execution in context we need to go back to Manlius' youth, which he passed in rustic

---

[9] For a clear synopsis of his life, see Berry (1996), 17–20; useful discussion in Neudling (1955), 116–25; we return to him below. It is not certain that he was praetor in 49 (Berry (1996), 19 n. 116), although that is the date conventionally assumed on the basis of Caesar's reference to 'the praetor L. Manlius' in the year 49 (*BC* 1.24.3). It is regularly said that he committed suicide when caught after Thapsus (e.g., Münzer (1928), 1207.18–20), but the only explicit evidence we have states that he was killed (*occisus est*, Orosius 6.16.5; cf. Berry (1996), 20 n. 128). The date of his death is 46, not 48 as often stated (e.g. Citti (1994), 233), presumably following the wrong date given in Mitchell (1966), 28, 31.

[10] App. *BC* 3.69, 76. Mitchell (1966), 27 misleadingly gives the impression that we know this individual's praenomen; I return below (n. 65) to her (I think mistaken) identification of this person as Horace's addressee in *Epistles* 1.5 and *Carm.* 4.7.

[11] Münzer (1928), 1153.14–15.

[12] Of 68a at the very least, and perhaps of 68b also, as we shall see below.

[13] I argue the case for the identification below.

[14] As has already been excellently demonstrated in the case of Hor. *Epist.* 1.5 by Nisbet (1959) and Eidinow (1995).

deprivation, barred from the city by his stern father on account of his supposed slowness of utterance (*quia infacundior sit et lingua impromptus*, Liv. 7.4.6). His father, L. Manlius (*RE* 54, dict. 363), already boasted the *cognomen* Imperiosus, 'the Boss'. According to Livy, 'he had adopted the nickname himself to show off his harsh nature, which he exercised just as much on his nearest connexions and blood relations as on people outside the family' (*cognomen . . . ab ostentatione saeuitiae adscitum, quam non magis in alienis quam in proximis ac sanguine ipse suo exerceret*, 7.4.3). When a tribune attempted to prosecute the father for abusing the citizens in a harsh levy, he also cited the maltreatment of the son, charging unnatural cruelty. The son came in from the country and entered the tribune's house with a hidden knife; alone with the tribune, he threatened him with the knife and extracted a promise to drop the prosecution (7.5). The act became a paradigmatic example of filial *pietas*,[15] and it was thrown into harsh relief twenty-two years later when this same man, now consul in joint command of the Roman army fighting the Latins, had his own son executed for accepting a challenge to single combat against orders.[16] The paradox is at first arresting— as Cicero put it, 'the same man who was very indulgent towards his father was harshly severe towards his son' (*qui perindulgens in patrem, idem acerbe seuerus in filium, Off.* 3.112)—but it is not a true paradox. Bettini has finely elucidated the structuralist significance of Torquatus' double role as *pius* son and *seuerus* father: 'By defending the uncompromising sternness of his imperious father, he defended the possibility of becoming imperious in his turn toward his son: he defended, in short, the existence and the prestige of the *pater*.'[17] The consul had inherited the *cognomen* Imperiosus from his father, so that he is already called *Imperiosus* when he issues the orders for his son's execution and creates the new catchphrase of *imperia Manliana*, 'Manlian orders', forever paradigmatic as a sombre *exemplum*.[18] Not just the name of the father, but the natural characteristic it embodies, has been transmitted to the son, and the name has been given extra meaning by his terrible act,

---

[15] Liv. 7.5.2, 7; Cic. *Off.* 3.112; Val. Max. 5.4.3, 6.9.1; Sen. *Ben.* 3.37.4.

[16] His Latin opponent has a name that is too good to be true: *Geminus* Maecius (Liv. 8.7.2: 'otherwise unknown', comments Oakley, *Comm.* ad loc.): the reason that the consuls had forbidden the Romans to fight on their own initiative is that they wished to avoid confusion with an enemy who so much resembled them (8.6.15–16).

[17] Bettini (1991), 8; cf. 8–9 on the merely apparent paradox of Cic. *Off.* 3.112.

[18] Liv. 8.7.21–2, *ut . . . Manliana . . . imperia non in praesentia modo horrenda sed exempli etiam tristis in posterum essent*. The catchphrase is so closely tied to the execution of the son that Livy, earlier in his history, speaks of the *cognomen* Imperiosus as if it accrued to Torquatus for the execution of his son rather than being inherited from his father (4.29.6).

becoming an emblem not just of a certain kind of person but of a certain kind of command.[19]

This story is part of a web of connexions in Livy's narrative, all focusing on the relationship between the individual as member of a family and as member of the *res publica*: these cannot detain us in detail here.[20] One parallel story is crucially important, however, for our understanding of the vital themes of continuity and similarity within the family of the Manlii Torquati, and that is the story of the other consul of 340, P. Decius Mus, joint commander of the Roman army fighting the Latins. His fate is a complementary foil to that of his colleague Torquatus, not only in Livy but in other sources as well.[21] While Manlius Torquatus kills his son to preserve Roman discipline, Decius Mus shortly afterwards kills himself in *deuotio* to ensure victory for the army at the battle of the Veseris (Liv. 8.9). Both consuls sacrifice themselves, one meta-phorically, one literally, in order to demonstrate not only that a Roman's 'bond to Rome must transcend the ties of mere kinship' but also that Roman identity can be channelled only through the authority structures of the state.[22] Further, and crucially, both of their actions are exemplary within their families.[23] Decius' son and grandson will follow in the footsteps of the consul of 340 and perform *deuotio* when they become consuls in their turn;[24] the Torquati are looking back to prototypes in the family when they accept their

---

[19] Litchfield (1914), 39 draws too strong a contrast between the 'universal commendation' accorded Torquatus' execution of his son by 'pre-Christian casuists', and the 'silence or censure' of Christian writers. Livy's own presentation is by no means so straightforward ('Torquatus was a highly ambiguous figure, of whose actions the author does not wholly approve', Oakley, *Comm.* II.706); and Virgil achieves a similar effect with his placement of the single Torquatus in *Aen.* 6.824–5, 'savage with his axe', right after the morally complex presentation of Brutus' similar choice (817–23; cf. Feeney (1986), 12).

[20] On the theme in general, Feldherr (1998), 116–21. See Lipovsky (1981), 112–30, Oakley, *Comm.* II.705–7, and Chaplin (2000), 108–12 for the way the story of the Manlii is used as a foil for the story of the more indulgent father of Q. Fabius Maximus Rullianus later in Book 8 (30.1–37.2). The first consul, L. Junius Brutus, is a parallel, with his youthful inarticulateness and his execution of his sons while consul (Liv. 1.56.8; 2.5.5–10; Litchfield (1914), 38–9; Münzer (1928), 1180.13–20); another connected story of a son-killer is that of A. Postumius Tubertus (Liv. 4.29.5–6; Oakley, *Comm.* II.439). Torquatus' youthful duel has a doublet later in Book 7 in the duel of M. Valerius Corvus with a Gaul: the duels are carefully connected by Livy (7.26.2: see Feldherr (1998), 92–105, Chaplin (2000), 20; on the links in general between Manlius and Corvus, see Nisbet (2002), 84–5).

[21] They are linked in Cic. *Fin.* 2.61, and Virg. *Aen.* 6.824–5, where we see Torquatus in the singular after the two father/son pairs of Decii and Drusi (Feeney (1986), 12). On the pairing of the father/son figures in the Manlii and Decii, see Kraus (1998), 269–72.

[22] See Feldherr (1998), ch. 3 for a full discussion of the complementary narratives (quotation from p. 84).

[23] Feldherr (1998), 85, 100.

[24] See Oakley, *Comm.* II.477–80 for a full discussion of these three (or, probably, two) *deuotiones*.

challenges to single combat,[25] and the father's execution of his son also becomes exemplary, since the family will witness another example of a father causing his son's death almost two centuries later, as we shall see shortly.

In the case of both families we see a strange kind of pressure being put on the concept of continuity by these acts of emulation. Every Roman aristocrat is meant to live up to the model provided by his father,[26] but this ideal becomes intensely charged when living up to the father's model means killing yourself (if you are a Decius Mus) or killing your son (if you are a Manlius Torquatus).[27] Decius and Manlius both perform deliberately self-sacrificial acts which guarantee the continuity of the *res publica* while imperilling the continuity of the family; at the same time, these are acts which become exemplary within the family, so that the same family keeps repeating them even though they thereby risk running out of people to keep up the pattern. For the Manlii Torquati, it could be hard to perpetuate a family tradition if the tradition dictates that you have to be prepared to kill your inheritor.

In Livy's account of Torquatus executing his son, as part of these larger themes of continuity and emulation, the issue of similarity comes to be of crucial importance. The son thinks that his success in the duel makes him resemble his father and proves that he really is his father's son (*ut me omnes, inquit, pater, tuo sanguine ortum uere ferrent...*, 8.7.13); the father thinks that his son will show he really is his son by putting up with his punishment for the sake of restoring military discipline (*ne te quidem si quid in te nostri sanguinis est recusare censeam, quin disciplinam militarem culpa tua prolapsam restituas*, Liv. 8.7.19).[28] The hunt for exemplarity goes awry here. The son thought he was emulating his father's heroism, but he failed to perform it properly and ended up following another of his father's templates: he emulated his father's peculiar *pietas* instead—indeed, he exceeded it, by being killed instead of merely mistreated.[29] It was left to his father to emulate—and exceed—*his* father's toughness, by killing instead of merely mistreating his son.

---

[25] 'Torquatus's son accepts the Latin's challenge because the consul himself, when young, had earned his *cognomen* by defeating a Gaul in single combat', Feldherr (1998), 85; and, as Oakley, *Comm.* II.132, points out, the father was himself already trying to emulate an ancestor in taking on the Gaul: 'Manlius...desires to fight a Gaul, so as to rival the exploit of his kinsman Capitolinus'; cf. Kraus (1998), 269–70.

[26] Bettini (1991), 182; Oakley, *Comm.* II.132.

[27] Cic. *Rab.* 2 spells out the general moral of family exemplarity and cites the Decii as an example of son imitating father.

[28] See the fine analyses of Bettini (1991), 8 and Miles (1995), 71–2.

[29] Frontinus (*Str.* 4.1.41) makes the point all too explicit by having the son beg the angry army to allow his father to punish him, whereas Livy leaves it up to us to decide what the son's attitude might have been, and whether he went along with his father's interpretation.

The exemplary tradition of the Manlii's paternal severity is so strong in Livy that it can impose itself even on family members who precede Torquatus' paradigmatic action. The first consul of the *gens Manlia*, Cn. Manlius (*RE* 19, cos. 480), issues orders exactly like those which his great-great-great-great-grandson will give to such tragic effect 140 years later. He and his colleague, M. Fabius, trying to restore the spirits of a demoralized army, temporize and refuse to allow the army to respond to the jeers and taunts of their Etruscan opponents; to make sure that everyone abstains from combat, they pro-nounce that 'if anyone fights without orders, they will punish him as if he were an enemy' (*si quis iniussu pugnauerit, ut in hostem animaduersuros,* 2.45.8). Our expectation is deflected, however: no son of Manlius steps forth to bring down upon his head the axes of his father's lictors, and we must wait another six books to have our anticipation of the devastating results of this Manlian order fulfilled.[30]

A revealing moment in Livy shows how the archetype of paternal severity must remain associated with this family above all. In Book 4 Livy engages in discussion of a tradition that A. Postumius Tubertus (*RE* 63, dict. 431) executed his son for leaving his post without orders during the victory over the Aequi and Volsci at the Algidus. Livy expresses scepticism about the tradition, arguing that the catchphrase for draconian discipline was *Manli-ana,* not *Postumiana imperia,* and that the first person to have been the source of such a savage example would have given his name to the distinguishing label of cruelty (*et argumento est quod imperia Manliana, non Postumiana appellata sunt, cum qui prior auctor tam saeui exempli foret, occupaturus insignem titulum crudelitatis fuerit*); besides, he continues, it was Manlius who got the nickname 'Imperiosus', while Postumius was not marked out by any grim branding (*Imperioso quoque Manlio cognomen inditum; Postumius nulla tristi nota est insignitus,* 4.29.6).[31] The claims of Postumius are brought forward only to be firmly denied: this story must remain in the family of the Manlii Torquati, and other contenders to be the archetype of parental severity cannot oust the Manlii Torquati as the prototypes of this compellingly horrific pattern.

Once the Manlii Torquati are fixed in this harsh mould, the tradition relishes displaying their adherence to the family's characteristics—by a certain stage, we may be confident, so must the individuals themselves, who are the

---

[30] But the first consul from the *gens* does come closer to enacting another part of the Manlian paradigm, with the issue of continuity: he is killed in the ensuing battle (Liv. 2.47.7), and thus becomes the first consul after Brutus to die in office (Münzer (1928), 1157.6–10).

[31] As we have already remarked, Livy here writes as if the *cognomen* Imperiosus came to Torquatus for the execution of his son, rather then being inherited from his father.

inheritors of a crushing burden of expectation, heavy even by the regular standards of the Roman aristocracy.[32] The family's grim adherence to harsh exactitude is played up in the behaviour of T. Manlius Torquatus (*RE* 82, cos. 235, 224). When he stands up in the Senate to fight the proposal to ransom the Romans captured by Hannibal after Cannae, he is introduced by Livy as 'a man of antique and—so it seemed to most—excessively harsh severity' (*priscae ac nimis durae, ut plerisque uidebatur, seueritatis*, 22.60.5): the case he makes to the Senate is based on the grounds that the prisoners have not lived up to the standards of Roman military tradition (22.60.6–27).[33] He is made to play upon his family's association with *imperia* when he declines to be elected consul for the third time for the year 210, although the *iuniores* of the *centuria praerogatiua* have already cast their vote for him; he asks to be excused because of his bad eyesight, and when the young men of the century doggedly say that they will vote for him anyway, he replies, 'I will not be able to put up with your behaviour if I am consul and you will not be able to put up with my *command*' (*neque ego uestros . . . mores consul ferre potero neque uos imperium meum*, 26.22.9).[34] The *iuniores* thereupon consult with the *seniores* of their tribe, and follow their advice to select from a different slate. In both of these interventions Torquatus is acting like a kind of super-father to the youth of Rome: in refusing the ransom deal he punishes his 'sons' for not living up to Roman traditions, and in chastising the young men in the voting pens he reinforces the power of the father, since his reprimand makes them consult with their seniors before rethinking their first decision.

This man's grandson, T. Manlius Torquatus (*RE* 83), was consul in 165, and his treatment of his son represents the most loathsome entry in the family's dossier of *seueritas*. In 140 he privately held an inquiry into allegations against his son of bribery in the province of Macedonia, pronounced that he considered the case proved, and barred him from his sight; the young man hanged himself, but on the day of the funeral the unbending father remained at home without even changing into mourning, giving legal advice to his clients and friends in his *atrium*, where hung the *imago* of his ancestor Imperiosus

---

[32] See Flower (1996), 220–1 for the pressure created by the expectations embodied in the ancestral *imagines* ('the ancestors served as an inspiration or as a daunting standard to live up to', 221, with reference in n. 160 to T. Manlius Torquatus (cos. 165), whom we consider in the next paragraph).

[33] 'In ihm war offenbar die Heftigkeit, Leidenschaftlichkeit und Härte, die in der Tradition seinen Vorfahren beigelegt wird, am stärksten verkörpert', Münzer (1928), 1152.5–8; cf. Chaplin (2000), 59.

[34] See Oakley, *Comm.* II.86 for the diverting mobility of this trenchant putdown, which some authorities put in the mouth of the first Torquatus instead.

Torquatus, clearly visible for its severity (*in quo Imperiosi illius Torquati seueritate conspicua imago posita erat,* Val. Max. 5.8.3).[35]

II

Catullus addresses an epithalamium to a member of the Manlii Torquati ('Mallius' or 'Manlius', 61.16, 215; 'Torquatus', 61.209). The groom of this poem is now generally recognized to be L. Manlius Torquatus (*RE* 80, pr. 49), the son of the consul of 65.[36] The epithalamium celebrates his marriage to Vibia Aurunculeia, whose Oscan *praenomen* shows that she is, like Torquatus' own mother, not from the elite of the city of Rome but from a central Italian town.[37] Since Torquatus was praetor in 49 and an *adulescens* when prosecuting P. Sulla in 62, he will have been born around 90 or 89, and his marriage could have taken place at any time from the late 60s to the early or middle 50s: even if he had got married in 55, he would still have been only 34 or 35 years old at the time. The frequent spelling of 'Manlius' as 'Mallius' in the manuscripts of 61 reflects the common pronunciation of 'Manlius' as far back as Republican times,[38] and 'Mallius' is also the name behind the tangle of manuscript attestations for the addressee of 68a.[39] 68a, then, will be addressed to the same man.[40] The pronunciation of his name as 'Mallius' is needed to effect the trick whereby the 'Mallius/Manlius' of 68a becomes the 'Allius' of 68b: in the first line of 68b, *non possum reticere, deae, qua me Allius in re* | *iuuerit* (68.41–2), the elision of *me* and *Allius* produces, precisely, *Mallius.*[41]

---

[35] Cf. Cic. *Fin.* 1.24, Liv. *Per.* 54.

[36] For the identification, the original suggestion of Schwabe (1862), 339–41, see Münzer (1928), 1204.63–1205.39; Neudling (1955), 119, 124; Wiseman (1974), 103.

[37] 'Vibia' is the palmary suggestion of Syme, to replace the 'Vinia' or 'Iunia' of the MSS, reported by Neudling (1955), 185, and accepted by Wiseman (1995), 112, n. 70. See Cic. *Sull.* 25 for the origin of the mother.

[38] Münzer (1928), 1149.11–49.

[39] See the discussion of the manuscript evidence for the name in both 61 and 68 in Wiseman (1974), 88–9.

[40] Wiseman (1974), 102–3.

[41] As first suggested by Frank (1914), 69, developing the initial suggestion by Palmer (1879), 348, that 'Allius' in 68b was a 'disguise' for the 'Mallius' of 68a, who could not be openly implicated in conniving at the adultery of Catullus and Lesbia. Mallius, then, becomes 'someone else', as 'Allius' hints at *alius/ἄλλος* (Kennedy (1999), 42–3; Skinner (2003), 143, 158). As Chris Kraus suggests to me, *non possum reticere* ('I cannot keep silent') signals that there is a riddle coming up to decipher: Catullus must keep quiet about the name, but he will contrive not to keep it silent.

This individual is comparatively well known to us from Cicero. Although Cicero was his mentor, he found himself on the opposite side of the court in the year 62, defending P. Sulla against Torquatus' prosecution. Cicero plays upon the compelling exemplary power of the young man's family history at two points in the speech. Responding to Torquatus' accusations of *regnum*, he alludes to Manlius Capitolinus in his jibe that if Torquatus wants to find examples of people who have aimed at *regnum* he can find them in his ancestor masks at home (*ex domesticis imaginibus inuenies, Sull.* 27);[42] he responds to charges of executing the conspirators by saying that 'no one finds fault with the very famous man of your stock and name who deprived his own son of life so that he could firm up his command over the others' (*an uero clarissimum uirum generis uestri ac nominis nemo reprehendit, qui filium suum uita priuauit ut in ceteros firmaret imperium*, 32).[43] It was during this trial that a sneer of Torquatus' backfired on him, producing a memorable bon mot: after he made fun of Q. Hortensius, who was defending Sulla along with Cicero, for his effeminate gestures, calling him 'Dionysia' after a famous dancing-girl, Hortensius softly and gently replied (*uoce molli atque demissa*) that he would rather be a Dionysia 'than what you are, Torquatus—a stranger to the Muses, to Aphrodite and to Dionysus' (ἄμουσος, ἀναφρόδιτος, ἀπροσδιόνυσος, Gell. 1.5.3).[44]

After being killed by Caesar's troops following the defeat at Thapsus in 46, Torquatus receives a tribute in Cicero's *Brutus*, more for his character than for his oratorical skill (265). In particular, he appears posthumously as the spokesman for Epicureanism in *De Finibus* 1 and 2, written in the summer of 45:[45] Cicero actually refers to the first book of the *De Finibus* as the *Torquatus*.[46] Cicero parades the ancestral stories of paternal severity before the character of Torquatus in order to shame him out of his Epicurean pose, citing the first Torquatus' execution of his son together with the action of the consul of 165 in banning his son from his sight (*Fin.* 1.23–4); Torquatus replies as best he can, arguing that his ancestors were not acting without thought for their own advantage when they were so cruel towards their

---

[42] Cf. Berry (1996), 195.

[43] See Berry (1996), 201–2 for the play on *imperia Manliana* in the last word of the sentence, *imperium*. One might also see a play on the first Torquatus' despoiling of his Gallic opponent in Cicero's reference to Torquatus being 'adorned with spoils' (*ornatus exuuiis*, 50), as a result of being entitled to wear the *toga praetexta* after his first, successful, prosecution of the senatorial Sulla in 65.

[44] With the translation of Wiseman (1974), 103.

[45] Cicero says that he has given the various roles in *De Finibus* to dead people to avoid arousing envy (*Att.* 13.19.4).

[46] Cic. *Att.* 13.5.1; 13.32.3.

children (1.34–5). Cicero returns to the first Torquatus in the next book, this time citing his youthful duel against the Gaul as an example of someone performing heroically through motivations not of pleasure but of bravery and virtue for their own sake (2.72–3). All of this pointed reference to the family history must be read under the sign of Torquatus' heroic defence of the Republic and his death at the hands of Caesar's troops. The dramatic date of the *Torquatus* is the year before Torquatus' praetorship in 49, the first year of the civil war, and Cicero generates a measure of moving irony from the fact that his protreptic 'worked', since Torquatus is in retrospect now known to have lived up to his family's traditions in the end despite his dogged defence of Epicureanism in times of peace.

Catullus knows this man.[47] In the epithalamium he may be playing on knowledge of Torquatus' vicissitudes in court when he proclaims that 'Venus does not neglect you' (*neque te Venus* | *neglegit*, 61.191–2): the favour of the goddess of love is a motif of epithalamium,[48] but Catullus' words could be a riposte to Hortensius' devastating put-down in the Sulla case in 62.[49] However that may be, Torquatus' family traditions certainly resonate behind the stanzas on the propagation of the family line, beginning with the address to the bride and groom (61.204–18):

> ludite ut lubet, et breui
> liberos date. non decet
> tam uetus sine liberis
> nomen esse, sed indidem
> semper ingenerari.
>
> Torquatus uolo paruulus
> matris e gremio suae
> porrigens teneras manus
> dulce rideat ad patrem
> semihiante labello.
>
> sit suo similis patri
> Manlio ut facie omnibus
> noscitetur ab insciis,
> et pudicitiam suae
> matris indicet ore.

---

[47] Perhaps even as a fellow poet: see Plin. *Ep.* 5.3.5 for 'Torquatus (in fact the Torquati)' in a list of men of status who had written poetry: cf. Neudling (1955), 124.

[48] Cf. Sappho, fr. 112.5 L–P, cited by Kroll (1923), ad loc.; Fedeli (1983), 124.

[49] So Münzer (1928), 1205.21–39. Note the suggestion of Nisbet (1978), 92 n. 36, citing 61.191–2, that Hortensius' jibe may itself 'be the rebuttal of some claim of [Torquatus'] own to be a protégé of Venus and the Muses'.

Play as you please, and in a short time produce children. It is not appropriate that so old a name be without children, but it should always be reproduced from the same source. I wish a little Torquatus to reach out his tender hands from the lap of his mother and smile sweetly at his father with half-parted lip. May he be similar to his father Manlius, so that he may be recognized by his appearance by everyone who doesn't know him, and declare the chastity of his mother with his face.

The stress on the need to keep the family name alive by breeding from the same source, without adoption, might be addressed to any *nobilis*, but it acquires extra edge in the case of a Manlius Torquatus—especially if the groom is the only son of his father.[50] It is an epithalamium topos to hope that the child will resemble the parents;[51] but *sit suo similis patri Manlio* is an eerie thing to say to a Manlius Torquatus, whose family tradition enforces a grim exemplary pattern of imitation of the father.[52] As Panoussi points out, building on an observation of Newman: 'Continuity is particularly crucial in the case of the Torquati, a family famous for . . . putting a son to death . . . The image of the young child reaching over to his father has therefore particular resonance. Without children this noble family, as well as any other family, is bound to face extinction'.[53] There is nothing snide or undercutting in Catullus' image; rather, he gives us a vivid actualization of the awareness that any family's fond dreams of continuity into the future are subject to contingent shock, and the fate of the Manlii provides him with an economically drastic way of catching this apprehension.

The little Torquatus, smiling and holding out his hands, is a kind of reverse image of the reaction of Hector's child to the grim sight of his armoured father, who then laughs at his child's response before going on to pray that his son will become just like himself (*Il.* 6.467–77). Syndikus remarks on the rarity before Catullus of images of a happily smiling child reaching out to his parent, and refers only to Medea's children smiling at her at the end of the play, describing it as an unelaborated case.[54] But his reference to Medea is closer to the mark than he recognizes, and Virgil certainly picks up on the

---

[50] As observed by Neudling (1955), 119, 124, referring to the stemma of Münzer (1928), 1181–2. Mitchell (1966), 28–9 correctly points out that it is not certain that our Torquatus was an only son, but it is not proven that he had a brother, as in her stemma (31).

[51] Pease (1935), on Virg. *Aen.* 4.329; Fedeli (1983), 138–40; Woodman (1983), 281.

[52] As Chris Kraus points out to me, the postponed and enjambed *Manlio* adds to the effect.

[53] Panoussi (2007), 289; cf. Newman (1990), 206–7.

[54] Syndikus (1990), 46 n. 223, referring to Eur. *Med.* 1041, τί προσγελᾶτε τὸν πανύστατον γέλων; ('Why do you smile your last smile at me?'). Chris Pelling reminds me of the horrific related moment in Aeschylus' *Agamemnon*, where Clytemnestra fantasizes that Iphigenia will embrace and kiss her father in the underworld (1555–9).

frisson engendered in these Catullan lines in his often-noted imitation of Catullus in Dido's first speech to Aeneas in *Aeneid* 4 (327–30):

> saltem si qua mihi de te suscepta fuisset
> ante fugam suboles, si quis mihi paruulus aula
> luderet Aeneas, qui te tamen ore referret,
> non equidem omnino capta ac deserta uiderer.

At least if I had had from you some acknowledged child before your flight, if some little Aeneas were playing in my hall, who would nevertheless recall you with his face, I would not seem completely taken and abandoned.

Not only the unique diminutive *paruulus*, but also the topos of the similarity between son and father, send us back to Catullus' Torquatus.[55] Schiesaro has well demonstrated that Dido is a potential Medea figure at this point in Virgil, and that her language here 'alerts us to a fault line in her feelings, and to a conflict between contrasting emotions', with her 'suggestive, if unconscious, play with the language of infanticide'.[56] Although he refers to the Catullan prototype of *Torquatus . . . paruulus* as 'an image of future conjugal bliss',[57] his comment on the 'further voice' in Dido's language can equally well be applied to the Catullan model as well: 'The "further voice" . . . turns the cheerful resemblance of son to father into a potentially ominous feature.'[58] There is, then, already an ominous flash of Medea in Catullus, used to activate a memory of a tradition within the groom's family which is potentially at odds with the hoped-for continuation of the family line.[59]

III

A generation after Catullus, Horace addresses two poems, *Epist.* 1.5 and *Carm.* 4.7, to a member of this same family. Our understanding of the resonance of the *Epistle*, a dinner invitation to a Torquatus, was greatly

---

[55] 'This is the only occurrence of a diminutive adjective in the whole *Aeneid*', Austin (1955), ad loc., with ref. to the Catullus lines. Note also the way that Virgil's *luderet* (4.329) picks up Catullus' *ludite* (61.204).

[56] Schiesaro (2005), 91, with reference to his discussion (89) of Dido's later speech in which she describes how she could have murdered Ascanius (4.601–2).

[57] Schiesaro (2005), 89.

[58] Schiesaro (2005), 95.

[59] It is worth noting in closing that the final simile in a poem drenched in simile compares the hoped-for child to Telemachus (61.221–3): here is a child who managed to evade the fate of being killed by his father (see *RE* V A, 326.60–8 for references to the story of Palamedes placing the infant Telemachus in front of Odysseus' plough as he pretended to be mad).

advanced by Nisbet, who built on the penetrating observations of Münzer to demonstrate that the poem is laced throughout with hinting references to the famous family traditions. When Horace says he has some wine to offer his guest that was produced between marshy Minturnae and Petrinum near Sinuessa (1.5.4–5), he is alluding to the location of the first Torquatus' famous victory over the Latins in his consulate of 340;[60] when he says that Torquatus can bring something better if he has it, but otherwise will have to put up with Horace's 'command' (*uel imperium fer*, 6), he is playing on the proverbial *imperia Manliana*.[61]

Nisbet's arguments have now been comprehensively developed by Eidinow, who has incisively demonstrated how much of Horace's wit in the *Epistle* depends on our precise knowledge of Cicero's *De Finibus* and the role that Catullus' friend L. Manlius Torquatus plays there as spokesman for Epicureanism.[62] To his databank of parallels I can add only Horace's promise of 'friendly conversation' (*sermone benigno*, 11), which picks up the way Cicero quotes Lucilius to prove to Torquatus that what makes for good dining is 'good conversation' (*sermone bono*, *Fin*. 2.25 = Lucil. fr. 207 Warmington). If we follow Eidinow, we see that Horace is not just playing off the general knowledge of the family traditions that would have been shared by his reading public, but off a particular Ciceronian text in which these traditions played an important part in an argument about public service and private philosophical allegiance. Horace is playfully reversing Cicero's appeals, urging Torquatus to ignore the 'leitmotiv of Torquatian history—that abandonment of duty is as good as, and deserving of, death—' and instead 'to relax into a (quasi-Epicurean) pursuit of his own pleasures, with Horace as his companion'.[63]

It matters a great deal, then, that Horace's addressee in the *Epistle* should be seen in the light of his family history, as a member of the family of the Manlii Torquati. But which member? Although it has been recently reasserted that we

---

[60] Nisbet (1959), 2, resurrecting a suggestion of Estré (1846), 497.

[61] Nisbet (1959), 1–2, referring to Münzer (1928), 1193.10–12; they both draw attention also to the odd use of *imperor* in line 21, which best makes sense in this light.

[62] See Eidinow (1995), esp. 194 for the connexion between the idiom of line 2 and Cicero's use of the phrase *edere de patella* in addressing L. Manlius Torquatus in *Fin*. 2.22; 196–7 for Horace responding to Cicero's marshalling of exemplary Manlian *seueritas* in *Fin*. 1.24 by telling Torquatus 'not to be too *seuerus* with himself *ob heredis curam*' (line 13).

[63] Eidinow (1995), 193, 194. One may reflect that *De Finibus* came out in summer 45, when Horace was 19 years old and will already have been studying in Athens; it was there, very possibly, that he read the book for the first time. The brilliant evocation of student life in Athens which Cicero gives at the beginning of the fifth book, with the friends meeting in the Academy for a walk, must have made a powerful impression on the young student who was studying there at the time, and who later wrote that he learnt 'to seek the truth among the groves of the Academy' (*inter siluas Academi quaerere uerum*, *Epist*. 2.2.45).

cannot know precisely who Horace's addressee was, Nisbet and Eidinow themselves allude to the possibility that Horace's man was the grandson of the consul of 65, the son of Catullus' and Cicero's friend L. Manlius Torquatus. It is worth considering what the implications are if we follow up this identification.[64] A man born around 55 would be in his early to mid-thirties when the *Epistles* were published in 20 or 19, and this is an age that would not be out of place amongst the addressees of that book in general.[65] There is certainly a link through Epicureanism, as we have already seen. Horace's addressee is given a strong Epicurean tinge: this would provide a connexion with his 'father', the dogmatic Epicurean spokesman in *De Finibus*, and with his 'grandfather', the consul of 65, since an anecdote recounted by Cicero's character Torquatus in *De Finibus* 1.39 is evidence that his father was an Epicurean.[66] Eidinow's demonstration of how pervasively Horace's *Epistle* alludes to Cicero's *De Finibus* gains considerable extra power if Horace is addressing the son of the man in Cicero's work; indeed, it is difficult to see quite why Horace would so meticulously and pointedly allude to Cicero's text if his Torquatus were not at the least a close relative of Cicero's.[67] Again, as Eidinow shows, in Horace's poem we are not seeing just incidental family colour, but a systematic rewriting of the thrust of Cicero's protreptic,

[64] Citti (1994), 231–6 surveys previous views and comes up with a verdict of *non liquet*; for Horace's friend as 'presumably' the grandson of the consul of 65, see Nisbet (2002), 83; as 'possibly' the son of the praetor of 49, see Eidinow (1995), 193; see Harrison (1996), 287 for the case, made independently of Eidinow, that 'it would be apt if Horace's orator Torquatus were the son of the bridegroom celebrated by Catullus and presented as a great orator by Cicero'. Syme (1986), 396 hints at the possibility when he says that 'Horace's friend may have been a poet', referring to Pliny's list of poets, which includes 'Torquatus (in fact the Torquati)' (*Ep.* 5.3.5): Pliny's reference is usually taken to be to the consul of 65 and to his son, the friend of Cicero and Catullus, the praetor of 49 (Neudling (1955), 124); but it could just as well refer to the praetor and his son, Horace's putative addressee.

[65] See Mayer (1994), 8–11 on the date of publication and on the comparative youth of the addressees apart from Maecenas. The age range of the people honoured in *Odes* 4 is more diverse, outside the cluster of young nobles: Nisbet (2007), 16–17. For the appropriateness of 'a son of the praetor Torquatus' in the context of both collections, see Harrison (1996), 286. The candidate of Mitchell (1966) for Horace's addressee, Manlius Torquatus (*RE* 72, quaest. 43), who has not figured in our discussion, would be anomalously old both in the *Epistles*, when he would be around 50, and in *Odes* 4, when he would be in his late fifties (note that Mitchell, on p. 27 and in her stemma on p. 31, misdates the publication of *Odes* 4 to 19, rather than 13). For scepticism about Mitchell's identification of the quaestor of 43 with the A. Manlius Torquatus sheltered by Atticus after Philippi (26–7), see Horsfall (1989), 81–2.

[66] On the family's Epicurean connexion, see Syme (1986), 396. For the Epicureanism of the consul of 65, see Nisbet (1961), 107 (needlessly doubted by Castner (1988), 41–2); on the Epicureanism of Horace's addressee, see Eidinow (1995); Moles (2002b), 151 with n. 44.

[67] Note Eidinow's fine description of Cicero's *De Finibus* as being '(as it were) one of the documents of Torquatus's family history' (Eidinow (1995), 194).

encouraging the son to close his ears to Cicero, to relax his severity and indulge in quasi-Epicurean *uoluptates.*

Nothing in my argument hangs directly on whether Horace's addressee is the son of Catullus' and Cicero's friend, the hoped-for child of Catullus 61. Catullus and Horace could well be independently keying in to the notorious *fata* of the Manlii Torquati and using them for their own different ends. But Eidinow's establishment of such a close connexion between the *Epistle* and Cicero's *De Finibus* makes the identification attractive, coming so close, as it does, to making the intertextuality seem oddly redundant if there is not a very close connexion between Horace's and Cicero's Torquatus. If we take the family connexion seriously, we may detect more edge to Horace's use of Cicero. Torquatus' mighty ancestors are still an unavoidable point of reference, just as they had been for Cicero, and the jokes about *imperium* activate the family's illustriously ghastly history. But there has been a change since Cicero brought in the family's ancestors as a model to the father and as a spur to self-sacrificing behaviour, since Cicero's readers know in retrospect that Torquatus actually lived up to Cicero's urgings, dying for the Republic four years after the dramatic date of the dialogue. His son is now a model for decorous behaviour on the occasion of the birthday of Caesar's heir (*nato Caesare festus* | ... *dies*, 9–10), having his leg gently pulled about how he ought to bend from severity, indulge in mild *uoluptates*, and adopt the pose that Cicero had attempted to jolt his father out of. 'No surprise, therefore,' as Syme remarks, 'if Torquatus in fact renounced the career of honours, disdaining ambition, intrigue, or subsidy from Caesar. Thus ended the Manlii.'[68]

The end of the Manlii is alluded to with some directness in Horace's *Epistle*, and also in the other poem addressed to Torquatus, *Carm.* 4.7, for both poems talk about Torquatus' heir. Although the two poems share an addressee, they have few direct verbal overlaps, and the fact that both address the question of Torquatus' heir therefore makes the issue of his succession stand out all the more clearly.[69] In the *Epistle*, Horace tells Torquatus that 'he who is overly thrifty and severe because he's too concerned about his heir is next to insane' (*parcus ob heredis curam nimiumque seuerus* | *adsidet insano, Epist.* 1.5.13–14). Here Horace is playing on the family stories of filicide, as Eidinow points out: 'The two lines (especially with the use of *seuerus*) suggest an oblique reference to the way in which the Torquati famously treated those who might have expected to be their heirs.'[70] In the *Ode*, Horace tells

---

[68] Syme (1986), 396, on the Epicureanism of the family in its late stages.
[69] Putnam (2006), 407–8 on the shared references to the heir.
[70] Eidinow (1995), 196. For *seuerus/seueritas* as the *mot juste* to describe the Torquati's treatment of their sons, see Cic. *Fin.* 1.24, Liv. 8.8.1, Val. Max. 5.8.3 (*bis*).

Torquatus that whatever he gives to himself 'will escape the greedy hands of the heir' (*manus auidas fugient heredis, Carm.* 4.7.19). In both cases, the pointed reference to an alien heir draws attention to the fact that Torquatus has no son to inherit his name and estate:[71] he is represented as the last of his line.[72]

In the *Ode*, the Manlian associations give an extra bite to Horace's overall construction of a contrast between continuity in the world of nature and rupture in the life of the individual human.[73] This broad theme is starkly enforced when the addressee is the last of his line, a line which had always been under threat of self-imposed rupture anyway thanks to the grim family tradition of filicide.[74] If the addressee is indeed the child whose birth was prayed for in Catullus 61, then the atmosphere is more poignant yet, as we see the anxieties about precarious continuity which had been adumbrated by the earlier poet being now fully realized in the next generation.

A more specifically Manlian resonance of Torquatus' fate is activated at the moment when he is finally named (*Carm.* 4.7.21–8):

> cum semel occideris et de te splendida Minos
>   fecerit arbitria,
> non, Torquate, genus, non te facundia, non te
>   restituet pietas;
> infernis neque enim tenebris Diana pudicum
>   liberat Hippolytum,
> nec Lethaea ualet Theseus abrumpere caro
>   uincula Perithoo.

When once you have fallen and Minos has delivered his splendid judgements on you, neither your family, Torquatus, nor your eloquence, nor your loyalty will restore you; neither indeed does Diana let loose chaste Hippolytus from the darkness below, nor does Theseus have the power to break the chains of Lethe off his dear Perithous.

It is a commonplace to say that high birth will not save you from death.[75] A great deal more is at work than commonplace, however, when a Manlius Torquatus is told, as he is here, that once the judge has passed sentence his

---

[71] Eidinow (1995), 197; Kiessling–Heinze (1968), 427.

[72] Kiessling–Heinze (1968), 427: 'Einen Sohn hat Torquatus nach v. 19 nicht gehabt, wie wir denn auch von dem altadligen Geschlecht . . . der Manlii Torquati später nichts mehr gehören'; cf. Nisbet–Hubbard (1978), 238, for these two references to the heir addressed to 'Manlius Torquatus, the last of his line'.

[73] Commager (1962), 278–80; Putnam (1986), 136.

[74] Newman (1990), 206–7, leading into quotation of *Carm.* 4.7.19–24, acutely remarks that 'the family tradition had come full circle over the centuries. Those who could once afford to kill their own children were now faced with the extinction of their line.'

[75] Nisbet–Hubbard (1970) on *Carm.* 1.28.4.

family will not save him (21–4).[76] The family references continue: the immediately following *facundia* is a personal touch, referring to this man's eminence as a lawyer, so stressed in the *Epistle*,[77] but it also looks like a reference
to the way he is 'following his father in oratory';[78] his *pietas* is certainly a
familial, rather than just personal trait, referring to the way the Torquati show
unflinching loyalty to their fathers and to the state.[79] The ode strives to
remove any apparent exceptions to the universal law of death, correcting
Virgil's versions of Aeneas' apotheosis and of Diana's rescue of Hippolytus,
together with Euripides' version of Theseus' rescue of Perithous.[80] The appearance of Torquatus powerfully reinforces the message that one law applies
to all, with no exceptions: Torquatus will stand before Minos, and the judge of
the underworld will become an inexorable father figure himself, with the
young man unable to plead his case, despite his family claims.

There is another father–son pair at the close of the *Ode*, this time from
Greek myth rather than Roman history, but the Greek father and son follow
the same structural function as the Roman Manlii. Horace tells us that
Hippolytus could not be saved from death or resurrected by Diana, for all
his chastity (25–6):[81] in the next line we meet Hippolytus' father, Theseus, as
the helpless friend of Perithous. It is strange that no one, so far as I discover,
spells out the fact that Theseus pronounced sentence on his son Hippolytus,
thereby causing his death.[82] The names of Theseus and Hippolytus should
prompt the reader to remember this myth, so as to corroborate the intuition

---

[76] Münzer (1928), 1193.10 sees *genus* here as a specific reference to the high birth of the
addressee. Woodman (1972a), 765 sees the importance of *genus*, but refers it to the relationship
with the offspring, rather than with the father. If Tony Woodman still feels the same way about
Carm. 4.7 as he did in 1972, I hope my paper may cause him to feel more charitably disposed
towards the poem.

[77] Eidinow (1995), 192.

[78] So, convincingly, Harrison (1996), 287.

[79] On the *pietas* of the first Torquatus towards his grim father, see Liv. 7.5.2, 7; for a
chart showing the Torquati under the heading of *pietas erga patriam/parentes*, see Litchfield
(1914), 32.

[80] Line 15 corrects the story of Aeneas' apotheosis in Virg. *Aen.* 12.794–5 (Lyne (1995), 207);
lines 25–6 correct *Aen.* 7.765–9; the last couplet corrects Euripides' *Peirithous*, in which the
Lapith escaped from Hades (*RE* 19.1.125.30–47). One may compare *Carm.* 1.24.13–15, where
Horace 'seems to be hinting at, and implicitly contradicting, the story of the recovery of
Eurydice, which Virgil had told in the *Georgics*' (Nisbet–Hubbard (1970), 287).

[81] As Chris Pelling points out to me, the carefully chosen verb *liberat* allows allusion both to
Euripides' play, where Artemis explains that she cannot save Hippolytus from death (*Hipp.*
1327–34), and to Virgil's story of how Diana brought Hippolytus back to life (*Aen.* 7.765–9).

[82] In a valuable note, Kelly (1982) points out the importance of the connexion between
Theseus and Hippolytus, as well as between Theseus and Perithous, but he refrains from
explicitly mentioning that Theseus was responsible for the death of his son (nor does he
make the link with the Torquati).

that the name of Torquatus is not picked at random, but is meant to trigger an association with a particular family and its perilously harsh traditions.[83] The Greek myth is, of course, very different in its treatment from the Roman: the Greek father kills the son through thoughtlessness and impetuosity (as he had already killed his father), and bitterly repents when he realizes his mistake, crying out 'If only I could become, child, a corpse instead of you' (Εἰ γὰρ γενοίμην, τέκνον, ἀντὶ σοῦ νεκρός, Eur. *Hipp.* 1410).[84] The contrast throws into yet sterner relief the rigid severity of the Manlian model.

Horace's addressee is the last member of the family of whom we know.[85] The tenacity of the great Roman noble families over time is an astounding phenomenon, and the Manlii have a role in Roman collective tradition as a vehicle for thinking about the costs and perils of maintaining such a continuity. One of Rome's great poets was present to express the hope that they might continue, against the odds; another was present to record the fact that, in the end, they could not.

---

[83] Since the *Epistle* to Torquatus is so dense with allusions to Cicero's *De Finibus*, it would be agreeable to find one in the *Ode*; it may be worth noting that when Cicero's Torquatus discusses Epicurean friendship he comments on how rare true friendship is in myth, claiming that 'you will hardly find three pairs of friends, starting from Theseus and ending with Orestes' (*Fin.* 1.65).

[84] Cited by Kelly (1982), 015.

[85] Münzer (1928), 1153.6–11; Eidinow (1995), 192.

13

Juvenal and the *Delatores*

J. G. F. Powell

Who are the targets of Juvenal's second satire—and specifically the beginning of it? Some of their characteristics, at any rate, have been accurately identified by the recent commentators. They pontificate on moral matters (Braund (1996), 121; Ferguson (1979), 127): 'aliquid de moribus audent' (2: 'they venture something about morals'), 'de uirtute locuti' (20: 'after speaking about virtue'). They are hypocritical (Braund 1996): 'Curios simulant et Bacchanalia uiuunt' (3: 'they act the part of Curius and live the life of the Bacchanalia'), 'frontis nulla fides' (8: 'you can't trust their appearance'), 'de uirtute locuti clunem agitant' (20–1: 'after speaking about virtue they wiggle their buttocks'). And they are professed Stoics (Courtney (1980), 120–1): 'Stoicidae' (65), owners of busts of Chrysippus and Cleanthes (5, 7) though their collection of portraits extends also to other philosophers (6) and, because of one particular set of associations connected with Plato and Socrates, they can be jeered at as 'Socratici cinaedi' (10).

From these undoubted characteristics, commentators have extrapolated others. Courtney (1980), 120 says that at any rate those attacked in the first part of satire (for he postulates a shifting set of targets)[1] are, presumably in a straightforward sense, 'philosophers'. But they can hardly be professional philosophers, teaching for a living; in that case they would have to be, culturally speaking, Greeks or at least *semigraeci*. What Courtney cites as 'the best parallel' is, indeed, a Greek one (from Athenaeus 13.563d–565f).[2] But in line 3 we are told that Juvenal's hypocrites 'Curios simulant', and in line 35 we are to see them as 'fictos . . . Scauros', 'pretended Scauri'. Manius Curius

---

It is a pleasure to include this paper in a volume presented to Tony Woodman; I trust that he will approve of the method, whether or not the conclusions carry conviction. Earlier versions of the paper were delivered at the University of Vienna and at the Institute of Classical Studies, London. I am grateful to Lene Rubinstein and to the editors for their comments.

[1] Courtney (1980), 120 'the train of thought is not organized on a systematic and logical plan'.

[2] Courtney (1980), 120–1, referring also to parallels in Lucian.

Dentatus is one of the archetypes of old Roman *uirtus*: the consul and war hero who still lived the life of a peasant farmer. The Aemilii Scauri, a long-lasting Republican family who survived into the early Empire, were of fabled aristocratic lineage and deportment. Any reader of Cicero, for example, will recognize both of these families as Roman cultural icons.[3] This does not suit an attack on Greeks: those who pretend to uphold the standards of the Curii or the Scauri must surely be, in cultural terms, Romans—as is correctly pointed out by Braund in her essay on the satire ((1996), 168).

Further considerations point in the same direction. The outward signs of austerity of morals exhibited by Juvenal's victims are, one would think, more likely to be culturally Roman than Greek: 'hispida membra quidem et durae per bracchia saetae | promittunt atrocem animum' (11–12: 'certainly their shaggy limbs and the stiff bristles on their arms give promise of a stern character') and 'rarus sermo . . . et magna libido tacendi | atque supercilio breuior coma' (14–15: 'sparing conversation and great delight in silence, and hair shorter than their eyebrows'). The eyebrows in particular recall Cicero's portrait of the stern consul and philosophical amateur Piso (*Pis.* 1 with Nisbet's note, *Sest.* 19, etc.), and compare also Seneca the Elder on Labienus (*Contr.* 10 pr. 4) 'Adfectabat enim censorium supercilium, cum alius animo esset' ('He aspired to the censor's stern eyebrow, though inwardly he was quite a different kind of person'). In lines 21–2 Juvenal conjures up a man called Varillus to attack the hypocrites: he addresses one of them with the Roman *praenomen* 'Sextus'.[4]

In lines 24–35 no fewer than seven examples are invoked as comparisons to highlight the theme of hypocrisy—and they are all Roman and historical. First there are the 'Gracchi protesting about sedition' (Juvenal here exemplifies the conventional, and Ciceronian, view of both Gracchi as archetypal trouble-makers). Then a set of four Ciceronian examples: Verres representing theft, Milo representing murder, Clodius representing adultery, and the Catilinar-ians representing conspiracy: would we not complain 'si fur displiceat Verri, homicida Miloni, | Clodius accuset moechos, Catilina Cethegum'[5] (26–7: 'if a

---

[3] It is interesting to note in passing that a Scaurus of Tiberius' reign is described by Tacitus at *Ann.* 6.29.2 as 'insignis nobilitate et orandis causis, vita probrosus'. But the edge of Juvenal's satire might be blunted by awareness of the irony that the historical Scauri had not always been all they were cracked up to be. The family was extinct by Juvenal's own time.

[4] If I was right (Powell (1984), 238–9) about the use of the *praenomen* alone as a sign of Greek atmosphere, and if the usage persisted into Juvenal's time, the address 'Sexte' may here be used to mock a Roman with Greek philosophical pretensions; but this would not alter the fact that 'Sextus' is a Roman. Dickey (2002), 64 (with n. 21) classifies this passage as a contemptuous use of the *praenomen* alone, citing several passages from Cicero and elsewhere.

[5] 'Catilina Cethegum' adds the extra twist of an arch-conspirator accusing his own associate (not just one suspected of a similar crime).

thief were displeasing to Verres, or a murderer to Milo, if Clodius were to accuse adulterers or Catiline Cethegus')? The remaining two examples are the Second[6] Triumvirate (28 'in tabulam Sullae si dicant discipuli tres', 'if Sulla's three pupils were to speak against his proscription notice') and the late unlamented emperor Domitian, who enforced the adultery laws but was himself alleged to have combined adultery with incest (29–33). Such Roman examples would surely be off target if used to attack Greeks. The outward allegiance of the hypocrites is evidently to Roman values. They are Socratics and Stoics only in the special sense that they are elite Romans with an avowed enthusiasm for those kinds of philosophy—a very familiar type from the later Republic onwards; this is *philosophia togata* in so far as it is philosophy at all. In fact, Juvenal's first complaint ('primum', 4) is that these people are not proper philosophers; they are 'indocti' (ibid.) and their sole concrete claim to philosophical status is the fact that they have filled their houses with philosophical statuary (4–7). What is more, the statuary is of a rather miscellaneous kind. Courtney (1980), 124 remarks that the appearance of Pittacus among the philosophers is 'somewhat incongruous', quite correctly; the incongruity is surely deliberate, to suggest that they do not in reality know one Greek sage from another.[7]

But if the targets of this satire are elite Romans, the question then arises of the context in which they are supposed to have flaunted their Stoically coloured moral views. Braund (1996), 121 calls them 'hypocritical moralists', without specifying the context of their moralizing. Ferguson (1979), 127 had previously gone further and called them 'preachers', but at the risk of anachronism. The term 'preacher' conjures up familiar images in modern times, from the pulpit to the popular press. But in early imperial Rome we are dealing with a religious culture without sermons and a world more or less without mass media.[8] What then were the means whereby a moralist in those

[6] It must be the second, as Sulla's first set of three disciples did not imitate his proscription.

[7] There is more philosophical and artistic wit in this passage than has usually been seen. 'Omnia plena' recalls the philosophical tag πάντα πλήρη θεῶν, 'everything is full of gods' (Thales ap. Arist. *Anim.* 1, 411a8, cf. Virg. *Ecl.* 3.60); in the house of the patron of philosophy, everything is full of busts of Chrysippus (or perhaps, considering the singular 'gypso', just one enormous one). Is it an accident, against the background of Aristotle's reasonably well-known theories about *mimesis*, that the bust of that philosopher is called 'Aristotelen similem'? The 'archetypos Cleanthas' of line 7 are seen by commentators to be expensive originals and not cheap copies, pointing to the wealth and ostentation of the owner. But the point of the next, admittedly grammatically ambiguous, line 'et iubet archetypos pluteum seruare Cleanthas', is usually not seen: it is presumably that the collector orders these busts of Cleanthes to occupy the *pluteus* as though they were slaves on sentry-duty. A *pluteus* in classical usage is a screen, barrier, or balustrade dividing one part of a building from another (*OLD*).

[8] I say 'more or less' because there did undoubtedly exist laborious ways of reaching a mass audience, e.g. through duplicated inscriptions like the *Res Gestae* of Augustus.

days, hypocritical or otherwise, might seek to reach an impressionable public? If we were following up Ferguson's suggestion we might perhaps be led in the direction of the popular philosophical lecture or 'diatribe',[9] whose well-known representatives are Bion of Borysthenes, Teles the supposed Cynic, and (to come nearer to Juvenal's time) Epictetus. But these are all Greek, and, as I have argued, we should be looking for elite Romans. Street-corner Cynics or other exponents of popular philosophy may indeed have been a feature of early imperial life, but in this context it is to be suspected that they are a red herring.

There was, of course, Roman philosophical literature. One thinks immediately of figures like Seneca or Musonius Rufus. It is, as it happens, difficult to find Domitianic or Trajanic examples of Romans of similar stature who wrote moral philosophy, but this is not necessarily a problem; the texts we have are doubtless the tip of an iceberg. However, genial literary exhortations to virtue, of the kind produced by a Seneca or a Musonius, do not seem likely targets for Juvenal's venom; and indeed the satire itself contains no specific reference to literary activity of the kind found at, say, 1.1–14 or 6.434–56. Juvenal regularly laughs at literary people as mere chatterboxes and wasters of paper, but the atmosphere of this satire is quite different. The moralists we are dealing with here seem to be more dangerous. At the very least they must be shapers of public opinion of some kind. Varillus (line 21) asks rhetorically whether he should be afraid of them. if he has to defend himself in this way, there must (one would have thought) have been something to be afraid of.

There is another possibility as regards the nature of Juvenal's hypocrites which, as far as I know, has not been canvassed. If it is accepted that they are Romans of the upper classes, we should surely consider the possibility that they are being satirized for precisely those activities which filled much of the life of upper-class Romans (in the early Principate as much as at any other period), and which embodied their main medium of communication with a wider public. The activities were politics and the law; the medium was oratory.

In this context, discussion of moral issues might take place in two different arenas.[10] One of these was the Senate, where there were debates on moral legislation (such as those narrated in some detail by Tacitus e.g. at *Annals*

---

[9] On popular philosophical sermonizing in the imperial period see now most conveniently Trapp (2007), 189–203, esp. 195–8 on 'diatribe' as the expression of 'non-denominational Socratic moral philosophy' rather than specifically of Cynicism, as often thought in the past.

[10] We may for the moment discount the censorship, as its functions had been taken over entirely by the emperors; but see also below, p. 234.

3.25). In this context, discussion would be on a general level and while it might often involve strictures on the morals of the community, it would not directly endanger individuals. The other arena was the law courts, where the legislation was applied to individual cases. Specifically, we may think of prosecution oratory, because this was the type that was likely to take a severe line on moral questions and to set out to expose particular instances of immorality. It attacked specific individuals and could result in their being fined, deprived of citizen rights, banished, or executed: hence, unlike the moralizings of philosophers, it had concrete practical effects, sometimes highly unwelcome. What is more, accomplished prosecutors were assumed to use their oratorical skills to gain verdicts against the innocent as well as against the guilty: most often, no doubt, by defendants or their advocates (as e.g. in Sen. *Contr.* 7.4.6, where Vatinius asks whether he should be condemned just because of the prosecutor's eloquence), but also, one suspects, more generally.

Hostility to prosecutors was already established in the Greek tradition, where the derogatory term 'sycophant' was applied to those who prosecuted for personal gain, especially if they made a habit of it. A prosecutor who attempted to seize the moral high ground, as did Aeschines in his prosecution of Timarchus, was open to allegations of hypocrisy (see Demosthenes 19 *De Falsa Legatione* esp. sect. 241). In the Roman Republic, too, a similar situation obtained: apart from Cicero's routine attacks on prosecutors in his capacity as defence advocate, one may point particularly to *De Officiis* 2.49–51 where the moral ambivalence surrounding the prosecutor's role is highlighted; to be known as a prosecutor is 'sordidum' (mean, disreputable, or ungentlemanly). Thus by the early Empire there was a ready-made tradition of infamy attaching to the activities of habitual prosecutors; and we shall see how this was reinforced by the ill repute attaching to certain prosecutors of the early imperial period who possibly approached still more closely the role of a 'professional' prosecution advocate.

Is it, then, possible that the targets of *Satire* 2 are in fact prosecutors?

At this point it is appropriate to refer to two near-contemporary Roman parallels to Juvenal's attack on hypocrisy, which are well enough known in themselves (because they are regularly quoted as background to the satire); their implications have not, however, as a rule been drawn out. Particularly relevant is Quintilian *Inst. Or.* 12.3.12, which criticizes two groups of people who fail to measure up to Quintilian's conception of the ideal orator. One of these consists of those who specialize in the technicalities of the law and neglect wider considerations. Here is his description of the other kind:

subito fronte conficta immissaque barba, ueluti despexissent oratoria praecepta, paulum aliquid sederunt in scholis philosophorum, ut deinde in publico tristes, domi dissoluti, captarent auctoritatem contemptu ceterorum.

Others...suddenly put on a solemn face and let their beards grow. As though disdainful of the precepts of rhetoric, they took their seats for a time in the philosophers' lecture rooms, so that later on, dour in public and dissolute at home, they could claim authority by despising everybody else. (tr. D. A. Russell)

Now an unwary reader might suppose that this referred to persons who had given up proper oratory or rhetoric and had turned to philosophy as a full-time pursuit; but the context makes it clear that this is not the case. In fact they are practising Roman advocates, who affect a philosophical manner in order to give an impression of superior moral authority; and the reason why they want to claim that authority must be the same as the reason why other orators want it (though they may use different means to achieve it): i.e. to win cases. Quintilian does not, indeed, say whether they were prosecutors or defenders or advocates in civil suits; but perhaps, without outraging probability, we may suspect the first of these.

An even closer parallel is to be found in an epigram of Martial, 1.24:

> Aspicis incomptis illum, Deciane, capillis,
>   cuius et ipse limes triste supercilium,
> qui loquitur Curios adsertoresque Camillos?
>   Nolito fronti credere: nupsit heri.

> Decianus, do you see that man with the shaggy hair,
> of whose grim eyebrow you too are afraid,
> who talks of the Curii and the Camilli to support his case?
> You are not to believe his appearance: yesterday he was a bride.

The verbal similarities to Juvenal are extremely striking here. Admittedly the hairstyle is different ('incomptis capillis' in Martial, a close crop in Juvenal), but otherwise the two authors could be talking about the same person:

Martial line 2: 'times'	cf. Juvenal line 21 'verebor'
Martial line 2: 'supercilium'	cf. Juvenal line 15 'supercilio'
Martial line 2: 'triste'	cf. Juvenal line 9 'tristibus'
Martial line 3: 'Curios'	cf. Juvenal line 3 'Curios'
Martial line 4: 'nolito fronti credere'	cf. Juvenal line 8 'frontis nulla fides'
Martial line 4: 'nupsit heri'	cf. Juvenal line 10 'cinaedos', 21 'clunem agitant' and 'ceuentem'; and esp. the extended passage on homosexual marriage at lines 117–42.

The literary parallel has long been noticed. But the important thing about this Martial epigram is that its scene must be a law court. The key is the legal word in line 3 'adsertores': the Curii and Camilli are brought in as rhetorical examples to vindicate a legal claim. The speaker, then, must be an advocate. Martial is pointing out the speaker to Decianus as they both watch the case. Again, we are not told explicitly on which side or in what kind of court the advocate is speaking, but 'adsertores' suggests that he is pursuing a claim. And again there is the reference to the frightening severity of his expression ('times triste supercilium'), which sits less well with the notion of an advocate for the defence. This too, then, may be an accuser.[11]

To return now to the text of Juvenal. It has always been clear that by line 67 of the satire he is talking about a man called Creticus who prosecutes adulteresses (67–8 'perores | in Proculas et Pollittas; est moecha Fabulla ...'): more detailed consideration of that passage will follow later. Let us work backwards from this point. The preceding paragraph consists of a speech by a woman called Laronia, which results in the rout of the 'Stoicidae' (64–5). Most of the speech is taken up with accusations of effeminate practices. It is the context of these complaints that is revealing.

Laronia speaks in response to 'one of them' who is looking fierce (36 'toruum'), a standard epithet of prosecutors,[12] and specifically invoking the Julian law: 37 'ubi nunc, lex Iulia, dormis?'[13] Now of course laws may be invoked in several different types of context,[14] but one of the commonest must have been the context in which a prosecutor complains that the law has been flouted, and apostrophizes the statute itself to call it into action. So Cicero, at one of the climactic moments of his prosecution, accuses Verres of having violated the rights of a Roman citizen and in doing so calls upon the laws that protected those rights: 'o lex Porcia legesque Semproniae!' (*Verr. II* 5.163).

Moving to the end of Laronia's speech, we find the rhetorical question (62) 'de nobis post haec tristis sententia fertur?' Now, as Braund correctly points out on this line, 'tristis sententia' is a standard phrase for an adverse verdict in a court of law (*OLD*, s.v. 'tristis' 5c) and 'sententiam ferre' means to cast one's

---

[11] There is a subtlety to be noticed in the use of 'et': even the uninvolved spectator is afraid of the man's stern expression.

[12] It is applied e.g. by Tacitus in *Ann.* 16.29 to describe the threatening gaze of the prosecutor Eprius Marcellus.

[13] Housman (1931), ad loc. took care to explain that 'ubi' was meant rhetorically to signify that the law was nowhere to be seen. Perhaps he half suspected that readers of a less reverent cast might see a subsidiary meaning: that the *lex Iulia* itself had been sleeping around. The joke, if it was so intended, seems entirely in Juvenal's manner.

[14] For example, the deliberative context of Cic. *Phil.* 5.8.

vote as a judge or juror in such contexts (*OLD*, s.v. 'fero' 27a). Laronia therefore speaks for women who risk an adverse verdict in court (whether or not she is herself one such),[15] and it is not altogether unreasonable to put this together with the invocation of the *Lex Iulia* at the beginning and suppose that these women are on trial for adultery.

If this is right, Laronia's opponent is a prosecutor under the adultery law, exactly as Creticus is in 67–8. And since the phrase 'ex illis quendam' (36), which introduces her speech, clearly refers back to the class of men described in the first section of the satire (1–35), it must follow that they, too, are precisely that—prosecutors who bring charges under the statutes dealing with immoral behaviour and especially with adultery. If this interpretation is accepted, it follows further that the group of people attacked is consistently the same from the very beginning of the satire up to line 78. This makes much more coherent sense of the satire as a whole.

A more detailed examination of the text of the satire will reveal further pointers in the same direction. In the first twenty-one lines the references to the activities of the hypocrites remain on a general level: 2 'aliquid de moribus audent', 9 'castigas turpia', 19–20 'talia uerbis | Herculis inuadunt, et de uirtute locuti'. The 'Herculean words' however certainly suggest oratorical denunciation. At the very beginning, Juvenal expresses a desire to flee 'beyond the Sarmatians and the icy Ocean' whenever they open their mouths: here one may perhaps catch an allusion to the penalties of exile and relegation (as imposed, for example, on Ovid). The first more specific indication comes at line 22 with the introduction of Varillus, who is described as 'infamis'. This could mean just that he had a bad reputation in general, but the word is also used more specifically in legal contexts to mean 'under suspicion' of having committed a crime (*OLD*, 2c).[16] This makes good sense if it is assumed that Varillus is **under suspicion of a sexual offence, *stuprum* or *adulterium*,** and is defending himself in court by alleging hypocrisy in the prosecutor.[17]

---

[15] Courtney (1980), on line 36 says that this is 'generally assumed' and expresses scepticism. Certainly, Laronia's attitude is not clearly that of a defendant in person, unless she is to be thought of as remarkably self-possessed (note esp. 38 'subridens' and her feline enquiry as to the source of the man's perfume). More likely, she is to be imagined as an impromptu speaker from the sidelines: 37 'non tulit' suggests that she was expected to listen in silence but could not bear it any longer, like the satirist himself at the recitation at the beginning of *Satire* 1. In that case 'nobis' would merely suggest her own identification with the class of women who were at risk.

[16] It is less likely, in this context, to mean that he had already undergone the penalty of *infamia*, loss of civil rights.

[17] There is also another possibility. It is tempting to wonder whether the choice of the name 'Varillus' has any connexion with one of the earliest causes célèbres involving the Julian law of adultery: the case of Appuleia Varilla of AD 17, reported in Tac. *Ann.* 2.50 (Tacitus is however less interested in the adultery than in the charge of *maiestas* which followed). Even before Tacitus

Editors usually assign only lines 21–2 to Varillus, implying that the authorial voice resumes at 23. But an alternative and, to my mind, preferable
punctuation would give Varillus a substantial speech, precisely half the length
of Laronia's, extending to line 33 '... effunderet offas'. It would then be
Varillus who brought out the historical and Ciceronian examples in lines
24–8: the mention of Verres, Milo, and Clodius would be especially apt in a
courtroom context. In particular, line 27 'Clodius accuset moechos' would
strike home if the setting were actually a court in which an adulterer was being
prosecuted: 'accuso' is the mot juste for 'prosecute' (*OLD*, 2). And the
reference to Domitian would be absolutely to the point: the law now being
invoked, which nobody liked (30–1 'amaras omnibus'), was in fact revived,
after long desuetude, by an emperor who (according to popular belief, at
least) himself committed adultery, and with a member of his own family to
boot—in fact a Julia, who bore the same name as the adultery law itself. Thus
Varillus (if it is Varillus) impugns not only the prosecutor, who is just as bad
as those he attacks, but also, if not the author of the law, at least the authority
for its current use. I would read lines 34–5 'nonne igitur iure ac merito ...' as
an authorial comment on the justice of Varillus' comments. 'Castigata re-
mordent' (35) is especially appropriate in this light: on the present interpretation Varillus is actually being 'castigatus' (i.e. in this context, prosecuted in
court) and is 'biting back' at the pretended representatives of Roman aristocratic morals, the 'ficti Scauri'.

Next, Laronia's speech contains several points which make better sense in a
legal context. Against the invocation of the Julian law, Laronia cites another
law, the *Scantinia* against sodomy, another statute enforced by Domitian.
'Respice', she says: 'look behind you' (i.e. to the prosecutor's benches)[18] and
examine the morals of the men who sit there. Then there is the name 'Hispo'
in line 50. Some discussion is needed to establish who is referred to here.
Pliny's letters (4.9) reveal a contemporary bearer of this name who was
prominent in the Senate at precisely the time Juvenal was writing:[19] Tiberius[20]

wrote, Juvenal and his contemporaries might have known this as a 'leading case'. If that were
true, 'Varillus' here would be a type-name heavy with historical resonance: compare on 'Hispo'
just below. The original Varillus would not have been a defendant but a member of Varilla's
family who appeared in her defence; he would be 'infamis' because suspected of aiding
and abetting the adultery. Did some record of his speech survive? But this must remain a
speculation.

[18] For the risks attached to the use of 'respicere' in a forensic context cf. Cic. *Cluent.* 58–9.
[19] Pliny's letter refers to events of *c.* AD 101; the latest datable event referred to in Book I of
Juvenal's satires is the condemnation of Marius Priscus in AD 100 (cf. Plin. *Ep.* 2.11) and this
very satire apparently refers to Tacitus' *Histories* (lines 102–3, cf. Plin. *Ep.* 7.33).
[20] The *praenomen* is not mentioned by Pliny but is supplied from inscriptional evidence. Cf.
Highet (1954), 291–2.

Caepio Hispo. But this man, it seems, was popular at least with his fellow senators: he was applauded as soon as he got up to speak, and his proposal regarding the governor Julius Bassus was exceptionally lenient. Of course, Juvenal might have had his own reasons for attacking him, of which no evidence happens to have survived. But even so it is a little puzzling to find Juvenal being quite so outspoken against a contemporary senator, in view of his caution at 1.150–71. There is a further reason for scepticism, in that after the first mention, Pliny refers to this man only as 'Caepio', not as 'Hispo'.

But there was a more famous bearer of the name Hispo, not to be found in the contemporary Senate but in the annals of the Roman law courts. This was Romanus Hispo,[21] who is best known to modern scholars from a passage of Tacitus (*Ann.* 1.74.1–5), not yet written when Juvenal composed this satire; but Tacitus' account presupposes a pre-existing tradition, and Hispo is mentioned many times in Seneca the Elder.[22] This Hispo was, in fact, a notorious prosecutor, with, according to Seneca, a terrifying style of oratory. He was associated with Caepio Crispinus in one of the first *maiestas* trials under Tiberius, the trial of Granius Marcellus. Tacitus uses this as a peg on which to hang a succinct characterization of the type of prosecutor who, rising from obscure origins, made a career out of prosecuting prominent men, and gained the favour of the emperor in the process. The Tacitean passage is at first sight ambiguous as to whether the description is supposed to apply to Caepio Crispinus or to Romanus Hispo.[23] But in any case the two men belonged to the same type, and it is not too much to suppose that 'Hispo' was well enough known as an archetypal prosecutor to make it possible to use

---

[21] On him see most conveniently Rutledge (2001), 10–11, 262–3, and on Caepio Crispinus 206–7. It has naturally enough been hypothesized that the Caepio Hispo in Pliny's letters was a descendant of both Caepio Crispinus and Romanus Hispo.

[22] Once also in Quintilian (6.3.100), as 'Hispo' *tout court*, but unfortunately the passage is so corrupt that not much can be made of it. One may guess that what is missing from our texts is some kind of slur on his character, perhaps not unrelated to Juvenal's; but that would remain only a guess.

[23] My own view is that the whole description applies to Hispo. Syme's argument ((1958), 693), that 'egens ignotus' could not apply to the senator Crispinus, is fairly conclusive. 'Addidit Hispo' towards the end of the paragraph does not necessarily mark a change of subject; it could simply be resuming the summary of the accusations after Tacitus' authorial intervention 'nam . . . credebantur'. It may be asked, in that case, why there is so much more detail about Hispo as *subscriptor* than is provided about his principal Caepio Crispinus. I would hazard the answer that Hispo may well have been, with historical hindsight, the better known of the two, and Tacitus takes care to notice his first appearance, which would necessarily have been in a subordinate capacity: note the phrase 'uitam iniit' ('he entered on a course of life').

his name to refer to any member of the genus: Juvenal's use of 'type-names' is well enough established.[24]

Laronia continues by asking rhetorically whether women usurp men's roles. But the first examples she gives of characteristically masculine activities are precisely those of the law court: 51–2 'numquid nos agimus causas, ciuilia iura | nouimus, aut ullo strepitu fora uestra mouemus?'. If one is not attuned to Juvenalian irony one will see a contradiction in my interpretation here: I have claimed that Laronia is imagined as interrupting a prosecutor's speech at a trial, yet she now claims to have nothing to do with law courts. But that is, perhaps, precisely the joke. The passage in fact gains in point from being spoken against the background of a law court, and referring to the daily occupation of her opponent. 'Look here: do we women ever plead cases? Are we experts in civil law? Do we make any kind of noise to disturb your law courts?' The implication is that this occasion is the one exception to the rule, born of utter desperation.

In line 62 we have the explicit reference to 'tristis sententia', discussed above. In the last line of the speech the word 'censura' may give us pause: but it was precisely in the context of Domitian's censorship that the adultery law was revived.[25] Legal terminology continues with 'uera ac manifesta' at line 64: a proven case is 'uera causa' (examples at OLD, 8), a criminal caught red-handed is 'manifestus' (OLD, 1 and 2).

The next section attacks the prosecutor Creticus (the name is well attested, but it seems that there is not enough evidence to identify him with a historical individual; the scholia name a lawyer called Julius Creticus but this is hardly more than a guess). Clearly again we are in the adultery court. Juvenal attacks Creticus' taste in togas: he is wearing one made of *multicia*, a fine cloth more often associated with women's dresses.[26] Even if the defendant Carfinia were convicted, and had to wear the toga as a sign of disgrace, she would not wear one of that kind (69–70). Such a garment does not suit the champion of 'leges ac iura' (72, cf. 43): how will it appear to the returned soldiers and mountain

---

[24] e.g. 1.61 'Automedon' for a charioteer; 155 'Tigellinus' for an imperial favourite. The clearest examples are those drawn from literature or history which *cannot* be taken to refer to the original bearer of the name, because of anachronism or some other feature. Sometimes a type-name is qualified by an adjective to make its status clear, e.g. 1.71 'melior Lucusta', 2.40 'tertius . . . Cato', 4.38 'calvo . . . Neroni'; but this is not always the case. Cf. also 3.53–4 'carus erit Verri qui Verrem tempore quo uult | accusare potest'.

[25] There are other reminiscences of the censorship in the satire, such as the reference to Cato at line 4, or the use of the word 'castigare' (a characteristically censorial word) at 9 and 35. Evidently there was a continuing relationship in the Roman mind between the censorship and political or legal control of morals.

[26] This is a reasonably conventional type of insult to an opponent's masculinity: compare Aeschines' ridicule of Demosthenes' attire in Aesch. 1.131.

farmers who make up the crowd of spectators (72–4)? What would Creticus himself say if he saw a juryman wearing one (75–6)? Or a witness (76)? Line 76 contains one of the best legal jokes in the satire: the question 'does it suit a witness?' is introduced by the word 'quaero' which is the actual word used when interrogating a witness (Cic. *Vat.* 40, 41). We might therefore translate: 'Answer yes or no: does chiffon suit a witness?' And the climax comes at line 78 'Cretice, perluces'. 'Perluceo' in rhetoricians' talk was a compliment, referring to the clarity of an orator's speech or the way in which his character shines through it (Quintilian, *Inst.* 6.2.13). But the satirist can 'see through' Creticus in another way: his toga is too transparent. So much for what was doubtless, after all, nothing more than the latest fashion in menswear. No single insinuation is produced to reflect on Creticus' character, other than the delicacy of his dress; but according to the satirist (82–3), this is just the first step towards transvestism.

I pass now to some more general observations on the ethics of prosecution, which were among the most controversial aspects of ancient legal systems. Few ancient states had anything resembling an official state prosecution service of the kind which most developed countries have nowadays. In Rome as in Athens and many other Greek states,[27] the burden of prosecution in public cases was taken on by individual volunteers. The only early Roman criminal statute of whose text a considerable portion survives the inscribed *repetundae* law—specifies volunteer prosecution in the succinct phrase 'eius rei qui uolet petitio nominisque delatio esto', and it appears very likely that other statutes did likewise, since volunteer prosecutors are a continuing feature of the legal system in the late Republic and into the early Empire. Because the official procedure for entering a charge against an individual was called *nominis delatio*, prosecutors came to be called, without further qualification, *delatores*. More specifically, the *delator* was the principal prosecutor as contrasted with the subsidiary members of the prosecution team, who were called *subscriptores*; the common name for both was *accusator*. The terminology is precisely illustrated by a passage of the *Lex Coloniae Genetiuae Ursonensis* (sect. 102) 'isque IIvir in singulos accusatores, qui eorum delator erit, ei horas IIII, qui subscriptor erit, horas II accusandi potestatem facito'. This also illustrates the fact that to be called a *delator* in the technical sense one did not have to prosecute regularly, although some, of course, did so.

    These simple facts are often obscured by imprecise translation and interpretation. There is an English convention that the word *delator* is rendered as 'informer', partly because the Latin verb *deferre* does have a wider meaning 'to

---

[27] See Rubinstein (2003), 87–113.

report', and partly because under the early Principate we do sometimes see *delatores*, i.e. practising prosecutors, also acting as collectors of information against political suspects and passing it on to the emperors. This dual role, as expert prosecutor on the one hand and imperial agent on the other, would render a man particularly dangerous. But I would venture to suggest that in the texts we have (certainly in Tacitus, Pliny, and Juvenal), the word *delator* itself (when not further qualified) always makes better sense if taken with its precise legal meaning of '(leading) prosecutor'. If a man is said to be a *delator*, it does not necessarily imply that he collected or passed on information for any purposes other than the particular trial in hand; and a person who passes on information does not qualify as a *delator* unless he also sees the prosecution through. (Latin has a perfectly good word for an informer, which is *index*.) Of course, expertise in the collection of incriminating evidence had always been part of the prosecutor's job, and this would explain why some of them slipped easily into the role of imperial agents and even in some cases into that of agents provocateurs. But this is not inherent in the meaning of the word *delator*.[28]

A *delator*'s business, then, was to assemble a case for the prosecution, and for that purpose, evidence was necessary in the form of documents, witnesses, and so on.[29] The *delator* had to get a prosecution team together (few important cases were conducted by just one prosecutor), organize the order of presentation, prepare and deliver his own speech, produce and interrogate witnesses, and so on. Because of the convention that a prosecutor should be a volunteer acting on his own initiative in the interests of the community, Roman legal culture tended at first to discourage situations in which the information was collected by one person and then handed over to another who would actually conduct the case; the latter would then be virtually offering his services for hire and would incur criticism on that ground, as Cicero criticized Erucius as a hired prosecutor in the *Pro Roscio Amerino*. The same ethos appears to have persisted into the Principate: in Tac. *Ann.* 3.10, Vitellius and Veranius claim the right to prosecute Piso in preference to the

---

[28] Rutledge (2001) is to be recommended as a study of these matters in general, with particularly useful prosopographical studies of individual *delatores*; see also Fanizza (1988). Neither book entirely succeeds in clarifying the basic terminological confusion as to what a *delator* was. Rutledge (in the summary of his views at Rutledge (2007), 113) maintains that the meaning of the term *delator* was 'fluid'. I argue that its meaning was quite precise and, indeed, technical (at least from the end of the Republic onwards), but that the range of activities undertaken by *delatores* was wider than would usually be associated with prosecution advocates in modern times: a *delator*'s household could combine the functions of lawyer's chambers and detective agency.

[29] The assertion by Ferguson (1979), 259, on 10.70, that 'the *delator* denounces, sometimes anonymously, and without evidence' is thus completely wrong.

seasoned accuser Fulcinius Trio, on the ground that they have personal knowledge of the case and he does not; they claim to be *rerum indices* rather than simply *accusatores* and therefore more credible.

However, to prepare and present a prosecution case demanded considerable expertise, experience, and application, and it is not surprising that a class of orators grew up in early imperial Rome who specialized in prosecutions. The Ciceronian and Quintilianic ideal of the orator as a specialist in defence, who undertook prosecutions only occasionally, was evidently not universally shared. In fact if one thinks about the practicalities of it, one will see that such an ideal cannot possibly have been applied universally in practice, since if there had been nobody to conduct prosecutions there would have been no cases for the great defenders to defend: in fact without volunteer prosecutors the whole legal system would have been rendered ineffective. This fact was seldom mentioned, though it was pointed out on one occasion by the emperor Tiberius (Tac. *Ann.* 4.30). Tactless the *princeps* may have been, but he was quite right. The issue on that occasion was whether the accusers should have the reward normally due on conviction, if the defendant evaded condemnation by committing suicide first. As Tiberius implied, it was the rewards offered to successful prosecutors that drew people to this branch of what may loosely be called the oratorical profession. Although habitual prosecutors incurred odium (and despite the risks of failure), the financial rewards to be gained from successful prosecution and, in due course, the prospect of imperial favour for the more successful of what one may anachronistically call 'Treasury counsel', were too great to be resisted.

It follows from what has been said that *delatores*, i.e. prosecutors, were an inevitable and constant feature of the Roman legal system. There was no part of the classical period, Republican or Imperial, at which they did not operate in some form: the system could not have functioned at all without them. Yet there can have been no period at which they were generally popular. Already in Cicero's time, as suggested above, there is a repertoire of general topoi that can be used against prosecutors. They are customarily suspected of bringing false or malicious charges (*calumnia*) and reaping rewards from the misfortunes of others (as in *Rosc. Am.* 56–7 and esp. 83 'qui ascendit per alterius incommodum et calamitatem'), or alternatively of colluding with the defendants to secure an acquittal (*praeuaricatio*), as in the *Diuinatio in Caecilium*.

Later on, under the Principate, particular issues arose with respect to certain statutes, which, as was regularly the case, relied on *delatores* for their enforcement. One of these was the *maiestas* law, the effects of which are famously chronicled in Tacitus: this was the context in which *delatores* spied on their victims, recorded conversations that could be construed as politically suspect, or made secret reports to the emperor, who was judged by the

historians in proportion to his willingness or unwillingness to take account of
such information. Another set of laws that invited *delatio* were those
concerning inheritance, which among other things imposed disabilities on
the childless and the unmarried: they could not receive inheritances outside
the family and anything left to them was forfeit to the *aerarium* (regardless of
what was written in the will: hence complaints that wills were constantly
overturned). Evidently numerous cases of this kind came to court. Both
Tacitus[30] and Pliny the Younger[31] mention the dangers posed by *delatores*
who specialized in cases of this kind. According to Pliny, a number of these
delatores had themselves been sent into exile by Trajan, presumably for
bringing false charges.[32] But whether the charges they brought were true or
false, such *delatores* would be bound to be unpopular with the moneyed
classes; and they could have gathered their information only by an unseason-
able prying into other people's financial affairs.

Once Domitian decided to reopen the door to adultery prosecutions, there
was room for *delatores* with a yet more uncomfortable specialism. The sources
for the *Lex Iulia*[33] indicate that, as might be expected, the injured husband
had first refusal of the right to prosecute ('ius mariti'): he was first required to
divorce his wife, and exceptionally was not liable for *calumnia* if the accusation failed. But if the husband failed to prosecute within two months, or
formally renounced the right of prosecution, it was then open to any person
(in accordance with the usual rules of public prosecution) to proceed against
the divorced wife and co-respondent within six months from the divorce.
There was also provision for an accusation of adultery to be brought against a
woman still married, provided that the husband was first accused and convicted of *lenocinium* ('pimping').[34] Thus the adultery court provided ample

[30] Already under Tiberius: *Ann.* 3.25 'multitudo periclitantium gliscebat, cum omnis domus
delatorum interpretationibus subuerteretur.' Again it is a mistake to translate *delatores* here as
'informers' (as Grant does): it refers to prosecutors who argue in court for a wide interpretation
of the law. But the interpretations of the *delatores* would have done no harm before a court that
was not predisposed in their favour.

[31] *Paneg.* 34–6; see Giovannini (1987). Despite the impression given by Pliny in his flattering
speech to Trajan, it is a misapprehension to suppose that Domitian had particularly encouraged
delatores of this kind: according to Suet. *Dom.* 9.2, he decreed that simple failure to prove their
case would make them liable to an automatic penalty of exile. It may simply be that Trajan
enforced the same ruling more efficiently.

[32] This passage led Courtney (1980), 82, to suppose that there were no more *delatores* of any
kind in Rome after this, hence Juvenal in attacking *delatores* (e.g. in 1.33–5) was living in the
past; the same argument is found in Gérard (1976), 31–2. But even if one particular group of
prosecutors had been banished, others must have remained—or the whole system of criminal
trials would have come to a stop.

[33] See Corbett (1930), 133–46. For a list of adultery prosecutions under the Julio-Claudians
see Treggiari (1991), 509–10.

[34] Compare the occurrence of 'leno' in the sense of 'husband who condones adultery' at Juv.
1.55.

scope for the *delator*. One may hazard a guess, also, that not all injured husbands would choose to conduct their cases alone, and the services of a seasoned prosecutor might thus be in demand also in the capacity of *subscriptor*.

It is always difficult to demonstrate the fact of adultery to any reputable legal standard of proof, as a glance at the civil divorce courts in relatively modern times will show: the Roman political decision to criminalize adultery will have thrown the problem into still sharper relief. The *delatores* in these cases (who, as pointed out above, were responsible for assembling their own information) must often have used evidence obtained surreptitiously or treacherously, and in court they must often have relied on circumstantial arguments and general rhetorical denunciations of the character of the accused. The assumption of a high moral tone, perhaps with an injection of Stoicism, will have been an obvious tactic to use—perhaps a higher moral tone than the private character of the prosecution advocate would naturally warrant, but the boundary between pleading a case on the one hand and hypocrisy on the other is always a fine one. In sum, these prosecutors must have been intensely unpopular, perhaps still more so than in other types of case. They were also perhaps more difficult to attack without appearing to condone adultery itself.[35]

However, Juvenal saw the obvious way to attack them satirically: by counter-accusation through the mouths of their victims. The alleged adulterers whom they prosecuted may have been no better than they should be, but at least they were red-blooded men and women. The allegations of effeminacy against the *delatores* may have had little basis in fact; but as a way of turning the tables on those who prosecuted under the adultery law, few strategies could have been more effective. In a system where prosecutors were volunteers and undertook cases on their own initiative and responsibility, the moral character of the prosecutor mattered more than it does in a system like the modern one, where prosecuting counsel are virtually anonymous hired professionals;[36] yet even nowadays, a lawyer who (for example) made a living from prosecuting on drugs charges, but was believed to take cocaine in secret, might raise a few eyebrows. In imputing effeminate practices to the *delatores* Juvenal took his cue from Martial, as so often, but improved on the conventional topos of hypocrisy by dramatizing the scene in court and making the defendants themselves 'bite back'.

---

[35] It is interesting that Pliny, in his denunciations of *delatores* in the *Panegyricus*, says not a word against those who prosecuted for adultery. In *Ep.* 6.31.4–6 he records an adultery case heard by Trajan as a *cognitio*, but this did not involve a prosecutor.

[36] For this contrast see also Rubinstein (2000), 195–7.

I cannot claim that the case I have made is established beyond reasonable doubt; there are few matters of interpretation of literary texts of which that can be said. But I hope at least to have indicated that there is a balance of probability in its favour. This satire was for a long time neglected because its subject matter was thought unmentionable, while in recent times the focus of attention has been on the gender issues it raises to the exclusion of other considerations. Such discussions tend to presuppose that the insinuations made by Juvenal against the 'hypocrites' are broadly true exposures of a homosexual counter-culture,[37] but otherwise have difficulty in pinning the satire down to a particular context in the Rome of the 100s AD; there is a problem in deciding whether Juvenal's self-consciously 'normal' authorial pose is meant straight or as self-parody.[38] In the present interpretation, the satire is restored to a clearly recognizable historical and social context and the truth or otherwise of its allegations does not matter: it is primarily a prize example of facetious literary insult, with the high satirical purpose of libelling a group of Roman aristocrats (prosecutors under the *Lex Iulia*) who were potentially, or had recently been, a real menace. In turn, they are revealed as part of a wider group (*delatores* in general) which attracted considerable opprobrium from Juvenal's contemporaries Tacitus and Pliny the Younger; indeed, without the help of these prose texts we would never have been in a position to know who or what Juvenal was really talking about. This volume is about historiography and its contexts: I hope that this chapter will have given an example of the way in which a reading of (among other things) historiography can cast light on texts in other literary genres.

To round off the discussion, I shall briefly survey four other passages in Juvenal which mention prosecutors. In three of the four we shall see further aspects of the anti-*delator* topos, which complement the above discussion in different ways.

1.33–5

First, 1.33–5 'magni delator amici | et cito rapturus de nobilitate comesa | quod superest, quem Massa timet, quem munere palpat | Carus...'. This character comes as one of a list of unwelcome sights of the city of Rome. The commentators generally translate *delator* here as 'informer', but this is

---

[37] Ferguson (1979), 127: 'Its subject is homosexuality...Juvenal's attack is directed... against...the particular perversion which leads a man to play a woman's role'. One might as well say that the journalists who called Mr Blair 'Bush's poodle' were attacking poodles.
[38] Braund (1996), 168–72.

not just an informer: it is a man who has launched a prosecution against a noble friend, and has obviously done this successfully, as he is about to proceed to further exploits of the same kind against other members of the nobility. This realization makes Juvenal's train of thought easier to grasp: the last example given was a portly *causidicus* named Matho, i.e. a defence advocate; after him, what could be more natural to appear than a prosecutor? Here, then, the *delator* is represented as preying on the rich, and there is an additional point in 'amici': *delatores* in Tacitus are often alleged to have gathered evidence against their victims under the guise of friendship.

This passage also makes the point that *delatores* fear one another. Baebius Massa and Mettius Carus were themselves *delatores*; again, not 'informers', as the commentators all say, but prosecutors. Tacitus (*Hist.* 4.50) calls Massa 'optimo cuique exitiosus', already suggesting the role of *delator* (cf. his remarks on Hispo quoted above), and promises to mention him often thereafter; if we had the rest of Tacitus' *Histories*, we might know more of Massa's exploits (though historians do not always keep their promises). As things are, our evidence yields only one prosecution by him: a tit-for-tat charge of *impietas* launched against Pliny the Younger and Herennius Senecio when they had prosecuted him (Plin. *Ep.* 7.33). As for Carus, he famously prosecuted Senecio for *maiestas* on the ground that he had written a life of Helvidius Priscus. Tacitus remarks (*Agr.* 45) that at the time of Agricola's death in AD 93 Carus had only one victory to his credit, but to judge from Martial 12.25.5 'ecce reum Carus te detulit', he seems to have become proverbial as a prosecutor. Here in Juvenal, the obviously formidable Massa and Carus are represented as anxiously trying to keep on the right side of the anonymous *delator*.[39]

3.116–20

At *Satire* 3.116–20, Juvenal's character Umbricius, in the middle of his tirade against the Greeks, is made to mention the prosecution of Barea Soranus, a celebrated case from Juvenal's own childhood in the reign of Nero (AD 66):

[39] I accept, as Courtney does, Heinrich's correction of mss. *et* to *ut*: Carus soothes the anonymous *delator* with gifts as the actor Latinus, playing the lover in the 'adultery mime', sends Thymele to calm her jealous husband (Heinrich (1839), II.44–5). The scholia say that Latinus too was a *delator* and some modern commentaries repeat this, but for a mime actor to be also a regular prosecutor in the courts would be unusual. These scholia contain a vast amount of nonsense (e.g. that Massa was a clown and Carus a dwarf, both favourites of Nero) and one should be very careful before accepting any statement of theirs unless it is supported by other evidence.

> et quoniam coepit Graecorum mentio, transi
> gymnasia, atque audi facinus maioris abollae:
> Stoicus occidit Baream, delator amicum,
> discipulumque senex, ripa nutritus in illa
> ad quam Gorgonei delapsa est pinna caballi.

The reference, as commentators agree, is to P. Egnatius Celer, a Graeco-Oriental by origin (born at Beirut according to Dio, though this passage of Juvenal seems to link him with Tarsus). According to Tacitus' account of the trial (*Ann.* 16.23 and 30–3) the prosecutor was in fact one Ostorius Sabinus and Egnatius merely gave evidence for the prosecution. But Dio too attributes *sykophantia* to Egnatius. It may be that popular tradition made him one of the accusers, or that he had gained a reputation as an accuser in other contexts which was sufficient to brand him as one here, though that may not have been his role in this particular trial. Certainly we do not need to suppose that *delator* can also mean 'prosecution witness', or to attribute to Juvenal an unusual use of the word. At most, Juvenal may have combined inaccurate recall of who the actual prosecutors were with a desire for rhetorical point: 'delator amicum' makes the same point as 'delator amici' in *Satire* 1, and is reinforced by 'discipulumque senex'. The main emphasis, however, goes on 'Stoicus'. One can imagine several reasons why a Stoic *delator* is a particularly intolerable variety[40] (e.g. cultivated insensitivity to human qualities such as pity; dialectical invincibility; moral arrogance) and this provides a further parallel to the pretended Stoics of *Satire* 2.

4.48

Delatores appear next in *Satire* 4 (46–56):

> ... quis enim proponere talem
> aut emere auderet, cum plena et litora multo
> delatore forent, dispersi protinus algae
> inquisitores agerent cum remige nudo,
> non dubitaturi fugitiuum dicere piscem
> depastumque diu uiuaria Caesaris, inde
> elapsum ueterem ad dominum debere reuerti?[41]
> Si quid Palfurio, si credimus Armillato,

---

[40] The type evidently survived despite Cicero's strictures on Cato as Stoic prosecutor in the *Pro Murena*.

[41] I have improved the punctuation of this passage slightly: 'agerent' continues the construction of 'cum ... forent'.

> quidquid conspicuum pulchrumque est aequore toto
> res fisci est, ubicumque natat. donabitur ergo,
> ne pereat.

The commentators again talk of informers, but do not explain why catching or selling a large fish was a crime that would attract the notice of informers. Courtney has trouble with the passage, observing ((1980), 210) that 'the point of *delatio*... was to get a share in the victim's property... and a *remex nudus* would not make anyone rich'. But Juvenal's point seems quite clear once one has grasped the true function of the *delator*. A monstrous turbot has been caught; the *delatores* are waiting in readiness to bring an action to claim it as Imperial property.[42] These *delatores* are voluntary advocates for the *fiscus*, as those who dispute illegal inheritances are for the *aerarium*. Just as the latter, if successful, received a substantial proportion of the sum at issue as a reward, so no doubt also the former would receive a proportion of the value of the disputed property (in this case, the fish: the market value of a large fish could be high, as we have already learned earlier in the satire). It is the *delatores* themselves who send their own 'inquisitores' to search for evidence to support their case and to serve notice of prosecution on the fisherman.[43] We know Palfurius Sura as an orator from Suetonius *Domitian* 13: the argument attributed to him by Juvenal is of course a parody of the kind of arguments that advocates in such cases might use. The final remark 'donabitur ergo | ne pereat' also gains in point on this interpretation. The fish has to be presented to the emperor the same day, because if it is put up for sale, it will immediately become the object of a protracted legal wrangle—and will have rotted away long before the issue is resolved. A wasting asset indeed.

10.69–72

The picture of the *delator* in the passages just discussed is uniformly negative, and it may be thought that Juvenal, like other writers of his time, has nothing

[42] There is a parallel here, as Lene Rubinstein points out to me, with the Athenian procedure of *phasis* (see MacDowell (1991), 187–98) which was used to effect the confiscation of enemy property or contraband goods found in private Athenian hands. The volunteer prosecutor was rewarded with half of the value of the goods at issue. Such rewards naturally encouraged *sykophantai*.

[43] Braund (1996), 246 says that '*inquisitor* is here transferred from its technical usage, denoting the person appointed to collect evidence in a prosecution (*OLD*, 2b)' but there is no reason to assume transference; the usage is precisely the technical one. Note also the legal or official term 'agerent cum', 'were raising the matter with'. (One might imagine a scene like that between Trachalio and Gripus in Plautus, *Rudens* 938–1044.)

good to say of the professional prosecutor. But there is one passage in which the *delator* appears in an entirely different light. This is the passage on the fall of Sejanus in *Satire* 10.69–72:

> 'Sed quo cecidit sub crimine? quisnam
> delator quibus indicibus, quo teste probauit?'
> 'Nil horum; uerbosa et grandis epistula uenit
> a Capreis.'

'But under what charge did he meet his downfall? Tell me who the prosecutor was: with what information or witnesses did he prove the case?' 'None of these: a long verbose letter came from Capri.'

So far from appearing in a sinister light, the *delator*, who proves a case by means of the evidence provided by his informants and witnesses, is here a sign of proper legal procedure. The tyranny of Tiberius' later years is illustrated by the fact that no formal prosecution is necessary to secure a man's downfall. The tenth satire belongs to the same period as the *Annals* of Tacitus (and may have been partly inspired by that work). While Tacitus chronicled the excesses of the *delatores* of past generations, Juvenal allowed himself to admit that the alternative to a system of *delatores* could be something worse: odious as prosecutors could be, they could also be seen as an integral part of the Roman system of justice. Only the rediscovery of Tacitus' lost account of the fall of Sejanus could tell us whether Tacitus also made this point, or whether it was peculiar to the satirist.

14

Roma and Her Tutelary Deity: Names and Ancient Evidence

Francis Cairns

For over a century the 'secret name of Rome' and the identity of the supposed secret protector deity of Rome have excited scholarly curiosity.[1] Enquiries into other distinct but easily confusable topics (the etymon of *Roma*, and the date when the city was first named *Roma*) have also been made,[2] and commentators on the combination *Roma/amor* in Latin poetry have begun to speculate anew about the secret name, sometimes without full reference to its background.[3] Hence it may be opportune to revisit the secret name and protector deity of Rome, and to ask what the texts mentioning them actually say, and whether they are credible. This paper therefore subjects the ancient evidence to critical scrutiny. Its conclusions are mainly sceptical.

An earlier version of this paper formed part of a presentation given at the University of St Andrews Classics Research Seminar in 1997 at the invitation of Prof. Stephen Halliwell. I am grateful to that audience for their comments. My thanks also go to Prof. W. Jeffrey Tatum, Prof. Christina Kraus, and Prof. Christopher Pelling, who advised on subsequent drafts. Errors, opinions, and inadequacies are my own responsibility.

Translations of Greek and Latin texts were added at the request of the editors. To avoid biasing them towards my own approach I have wherever possible used versions in print, mainly in the Loeb Classical Library, with minimal essential alterations indicated typographically. Their linguistic unevenness (and at times inelegance) will, I hope, be compensated for by their impartiality. Where others' translations were unavailable, I have attempted my own literal renderings.

[1] Cf. esp. Basanoff (1947), 25–30, ch. 4; Brelich (1949); De Angelis (1947), 7–33; Stanley (1963); Köves-Zulauf (1972), 64–108, esp. 90–108 (a painstaking examination of all the evidence leading mainly to non-sceptical conclusions); Skulsky (1985); and (most recently) Murphy (2004b). Horstmann (1979) is not a work of scholarship.

[2] For earlier bibliography etc., cf. Rochette (1997a), (1997b), (1998).

[3] e.g. Ahl (1985), 265; Poulle (1994); McKeown (1987–), III.178–9 on Ov. *Am.* 2.9.17–18: *Roma*; Grewing (1998), 339–40.

I. THE TEXTS

Most of the principal relevant texts are grouped here for convenience in advance of discussion (Plut. *Pomp.* 10 will be quoted at a later point); they will subsequently be referred to by their number in square brackets. In the translations places where my adaptation has significantly altered the sense of the original translator are indicated by emboldening.

[1] ... superque Roma ipsa, cuius nomen alterum dicere arcanis caerimoniarum nefas habetur optimaque et salutari fide abolitum enuntiauit Valerius Soranus luitque mox poenas. non alienum uidetur inserere hoc loco exemplum religionis antiquae ob hoc maxime silentium institutae. namque diua Angerona, cui sacrificatur a. d. XII kal. Ian., ore obligato obsignatoque simulacrum habet. (Plin. *NH* 3.65, ed. Zehnacker)[4]

dicere arcanis *codd.* 'nisi' inter 'dicere' et 'arcanis' inseruit Mommsen *CIL* I, p. 409

and besides all these Rome herself, whose other name, **because of the secrecy surrounding rituals, it is regarded as a sacrilege to speak**, and when Valerius Soranus divulged the secret religiously kept for the weal of the state, he soon paid the penalty. It seems pertinent to add at this point an instance of old religion established especially to inculcate this silence: the goddess Angerona, to whom sacrifice is offered on December 21, is represented in her statue with a sealed bandage over her mouth. (tr. H. Rackham, Loeb Classical Text, modified)

[2] Verrius Flaccus auctores ponit, quibus credat in oppugnationibus ante omnia solitum a Romanis sacerdotibus euocari deum cuius in tutela id oppidum esset promittique illi eundem aut ampliorem apud Romanos cultum. et durat in pontificum disciplina id sacrum, constatque ideo occultatum in cuius dei tutela Roma esset, ne qui hostium simili modo agerent. (Plin. *NH* 28.18, ed. Ernout)

Verrius Flaccus cites authorities **on whom he relies** to show that it was the custom, at the very beginning of a siege, for the Roman priests to call forth the divinity under whose protection the besieged town was, and to promise him the same or even more splendid worship among the Roman people. Down to the present day this ritual has remained part of the doctrine of the Pontiffs, and it is certain that the reason why the

---

[4] Zehnacker (2004), 40, 160 rejects Mommsen's *nisi* and interprets *arcanis* etc. as ablative of cause: 'en raison de rites mystérieux' (40); 'en raison du secret qui entoure ces cérémonies' (160). Zehnacker expresses interest in the possibility of 'Voluptia' being the secret name of Rome since, as he notes citing Macrob. *Saturn.* 1.10.8, Solin. 1.6 and *Fast. Praenest. a.d. XII Kal. Ian.* (Degrassi), her *sacellum* held the image of Angerona. Murphy (2004b), 129 prints and translates Mommsen's emended text with no indication that it is emended, and incorrectly translates *uel in sacris* in Servius [6]'s *urbis enim illius uerum nomen nemo uel in sacris enuntiat* as 'except in worship' so as to eliminate the contradiction between Servius [6] and Mommsen's emended text of Pliny [1].

tutelary deity of Rome has been kept a secret is to prevent any enemy from acting in a similar way. (tr. W. H. S. Jones, Loeb Classical Text, modified)

[3] "Διὰ τί τὸν θεὸν ἐκεῖνον, ᾧ μάλιστα τὴν Ῥώμην σῴζειν προσήκει καὶ φυλάττειν, εἴτ᾽ ἐστὶν ἄρρην εἴτε θήλεια, καὶ λέγειν ἀπείρηται καὶ ζητεῖν καὶ ὀνομάζειν· ταύτην δὲ τὴν ἀπόρρησιν ἐξάπτουσι δεισιδαιμονίας, ἱστοροῦντες Οὐαλέριον Σωρανὸν ἀπολέσθαι κακῶς διὰ τὸ ἐξειπεῖν;" πότερον, ὡς τῶν Ῥωμαϊκῶν τινες ἱστορήκασιν, ἐκκλήσεις εἰσὶ καὶ γοητεῖαι θεῶν, αἷς νομίζοντες καὶ αὐτοὶ θεούς τινας ἐκκεκλῆσθαι παρὰ τῶν πολεμίων καὶ μετῳκηκέναι πρὸς αὐτοὺς ἐφοβοῦντο τὸ αὐτὸ παθεῖν ὑφ᾽ ἑτέρων; ὥσπερ οὖν Τύριοι δεσμοὺς ἀγάλμασι λέγονται περιβαλεῖν, ἕτεροι δ᾽ αἰτεῖν ἐγγυητὰς ἐπὶ λουτρὸν ἢ καθαρμόν τινα προπέμποντες οὕτως ᾤοντο Ῥωμαῖοι τὸ ἔρρητον καὶ τὸ ἄγνωστον ἀσφαλεστάτην εἶναι θεοῦ καὶ βεβαιοτάτην φρουράν. (Plutarch, *Roman Questions* 278f–279a, ed. Nachstädt–Sieveking–Titchener)

'Why is it forbidden to mention or to inquire after or call by name that deity, whether it be male or female, whose especial province it is to preserve and watch over Rome, a prohibition they connect with a superstition and relate that Valerius Soranus came to an evil end because he revealed the name?' Is it because, as certain Roman writers have recorded, there are certain evocations and enchantments affecting the gods, by which the Romans also believed that certain gods had been called forth from their enemies, and had come to dwell among themselves, and they were afraid of having the same thing done to them by others? Accordingly, as the Tyrians are said to have put chains upon their images, and certain other peoples are said to demand sureties when they send forth their images for bathing or for some other rite of purification, so the Romans believed that not to mention and not to know the name of the god was the safest and surest way of shielding him. (tr. F. C. Babbitt, Loeb Classical Text)

[4] traditur etiam proprium Romae nomen, uerum tamen uetitum publicari, quoniam quidem quo minus enuntiaretur caerimoniarum arcana sanxerunt ut hoc pacto notitiam eius aboleret fides placitae taciturnitatis, Valerium denique Soranum, quod contra interdictum eloqui id ausus foret, ob meritum profanae uocis neci datum. inter antiquissimas sane religiones sacellum colitur Angeronae, cui sacrificatur ante diem XII K. Ian.: quae diua praesul silenti ipsius praenexo obsignatoque ore simulacrum habet. (Solinus 1.4–6, ed. Mommsen)

It is recorded that there is a true name of Rome, but that it is forbidden to make it known since the secrecy of rituals has decreed that it should not be uttered, so that in this way adherence to prescribed silence might eliminate knowledge of it, and finally that Valerius Soranus, because he dared to pronounce it contrary to the prohibition, was deservedly executed for his sacrilegious utterance. Indeed among the oldest objects of veneration is the shrine of Angerona, to whom sacrifice is made on December 21; this divine patroness of silence itself has a statue whose mouth is tied up and sealed.

[5] constat enim omnes urbes in alicuius dei esse tutela, moremque Romanorum arcanum et multis ignotum fuisse ut, cum obsiderent urbem hostium eamque iam capi posse confiderent, certo carmine euocarent tutelares deos; quod aut aliter urbem capi posse non crederent, aut etiam si posset, nefas aestimarent deos habere captiuos. nam propterea ipsi Romani et deum in cuius tutela urbs Roma est et ipsius urbis Latinum nomen ignotum esse uoluerunt. sed dei quidem nomen non nullis antiquorum, licet inter se dissidentium, libris insitum et ideo uetusta persequentibus quicquid de hoc putatur innotuit. alii enim Iouem crediderunt, alii Lunam, sunt qui Angeronam, quae digito ad os admoto silentium denuntiat, alii autem quorum fides mihi uidetur firmior, Opem Consiuiam esse dixerunt. ipsius uero urbis nomen etiam doctissimis ignoratum est, cauentibus Romanis ne quod saepe aduersus urbes hostium fecisse se nouerant, idem ipsi quoque hostili euocatione paterentur, si tutelae suae nomen diuulgaretur. (Macrobius, *Saturnalia* 3.9.2–5, ed. Willis)

For it is well known that every city is under the protection of some deity, and it is an established fact that it was the custom of the Romans (a secret custom and one that is unknown to many) by means of a prescribed formula to call forth the tutelary deities of an enemy city which they were besieging and now felt confident of being able to take; either because they believed that unless they did so the city could not be taken after all or rather because, were the capture possible, they held it to be an offence against the divine law to make prisoners of gods. That is why the Romans, for their part, were careful to see to it that the tutelary god of the city of Rome and the Latin name of the city should not be known. However, the name of the tutelary god of Rome is given in a number of books by old writers (although these writers do not agree among themselves what the name is), and so students of antiquity are acquainted with all the theories about it. For some have believed the tutelary deity to be Jupiter, others the moon; some have said that it is Angerona (who is represented with a finger to her lips as though enjoining silence); others again—and it seems to me that there are stronger grounds for believing them—that it is Ops Consivia. But even the most learned of men do not know the name of the city, for the Romans took care that an enemy should not do to them what, as they well knew, they had often done to enemy cities and call forth the divine protector of Rome, if the name were revealed. (tr. P. V. Davies, *Macrobius: The Saturnalia* (New York and London, 1969), 217)

[6] ROMANOSQUE SUO DE NOMINE DICET perite non ait Romam, sed Romanos. urbis enim illius uerum nomen nemo uel in sacris enuntiat. denique tribunus plebei quidam *Valerius Soranus*, ut ait Varro *et multi alii*, hoc nomen ausus enuntiare, *ut quidam dicunt raptus a senatu et* in crucem leuatus est, *ut alii, metu supplicii fugit et in Sicilia comprehensus a praetore praecepto senatus occisus est.* hoc autem urbis nomen ne Hyginus quidem cum de situ urbis loqueretur expressit. (Servius on *Aeneid* 1.277, ed. Thilo–Hagen)[5]

---

[5] The typographical distinction in Servius [6], [7], and [8] is between Servius (Roman) and Servius auctus (Italic).

AND HE WILL CALL THEM ROMANS AFTER HIS OWN NAME He <Virgil> shows his knowledge when he does not say 'Rome' but 'Romans'. For no one pronounces the true name of that city, even in sacred rituals. And in fact a certain tribune of the plebs, *Valerius Soranus*, as Varro says *and many others*, having dared to utter this name, was, *as some say, arrested by the Senate and* crucified, *as others say, fled in fear of punishment and was seized in Sicily by the governor and executed on the order of the Senate.* Not even Hyginus, when he spoke of the location of the city, gave this name of the city.

[7] EXCESSERE quia ante expugnationem euocabantur ab hostibus numina propter uitanda sacrilegia. *inde est, quod Romani celatum esse uoluerunt, in cuius dei tutela urbs Roma sit. et iure pontificum cautum est, ne suis nominibus dii Romani appellarentur, ne exaugurari possint. et in Capitolio fuit clipeus consecratus, cui inscriptum erat 'genio urbis Romae, siue mas siue femina'. et pontifices ita precabantur 'Iuppiter optime maxime, siue quo alio nomine te appellari uolueris': nam et ipse ait <IV 576> sequimur te, sancte deorum, quisquis es.* (Servius on Aeneid 2.351, ed. Thilo–Hagen)

THEY WENT OUT since before a city was stormed the gods were called forth by the enemy in order to avoid sacrilege. *That is why the Romans wanted kept secret the identity of the deity under whose protection the city of Rome is, and it is forbidden by pontifical law to call the Roman gods by their own names, so that they cannot be summoned forth. And in the Capitol there was a shield dedicated upon which it was written 'To the spirit of the city of Rome, whether it be male or female'. And the Pontiffs prayed as follows: 'Jupiter best and greatest, or by whatever other name that you have decided to be called'. For he himself says 'We follow you, holy one among the gods, whoever you are'.*

[8] DII PATRII patri dii sunt, qui praesunt singulis ciuitatibus, ut Minerua Athenis, Iuno Karthagini. INDIGETES indigetes proprie sunt dii ex hominibus facti, quasi in diis agentes, abusiue omnes generaliter, quasi nullius rei egentes. VESTAQUE MATER QUAE TUSCUM TIBERIM ET ROMANA P.S. poetice: nam uerum nomen eius numinis, quod urbi Romae praeest, sciri sacrorum lege prohibetur: quod ausus quidam tribunus plebis enuntiare in crucem leuatus est. (Servius on *Georgics* 1.498, ed. Thilo–Hagen)

THE GODS OF THE FATHERLAND The gods of the fatherland are those in charge of individual cities, as Minerva is in Athens and Juno in Carthage. INDIGETES. The *indigetes* are properly speaking gods made from men, i.e. acting among the gods. It is improperly applied to all gods as needing nothing. AND MOTHER VESTA WHO PRESERVES THE ETRUSCAN TIBER AND THE ROMAN PALATINE: <said> with poetic licence, for the true name of the power in charge of the city of Rome is forbidden by sacred law to be known. A certain tribune of the plebs, having dared to pronounce it, was crucified.

[9] *Τῇ πρὸ δεκαμιᾶς Καλενδῶν Μαΐων ὁ Ῥωμύλος τὴν Ῥώμην ἐπόλισε, πάντας τοὺς πλησιοχώρους συγκαλεσάμενος ἐντειλάμενός τε αὐτοῖς ἐκ τῆς ἑαυτῶν χώρας βῶλον ἐπικομίσασθαι, ταύτῃ πάσης χώρας δεσπόσαι τὴν Ῥώμην οἰωνιζόμενος· αὐτός τε ἱερατικὴν σάλπιγγα ἀναλαβών—λίτουον δ' αὐτὴν πατρίως Ῥωμαίοις ἔθος καλεῖν ἀπὸ τῆς λιτῆς—ἐξεφώνησε τὸ τῆς πόλεως ὄνομα, πάσης ἱερατικῆς τελετῆς ἡγησάμενος. ὀνόματα δὲ τῇ πόλει τρία, τελεστικὸν ἱερατικὸν πολιτικόν· τελεστικὸν μὲν οἱονεὶ Ἔρως, ὥστε πάντας ἔρωτι θείῳ περὶ τὴν πόλιν κατέχεσθαι, διὸ καὶ Ἀμαρυλλίδα τὴν πόλιν ὁ ποιητὴς αἰνιγματωδῶς βουκολιάζων καλεῖ· ἱερατικὸν δὲ Φλῶρα οἱονεὶ ἄνθουσα, ὅθεν κατὰ ταύτην ἡ τῶν Ἀνθεστηρίων ἑορτή· πολιτικὸν δὲ Ῥώμα. καὶ τὸ μὲν ἱερατικὸν πᾶσιν ἦν δῆλον καὶ ἀδεῶς ἐξεφέρετο, τὸ δὲ τελεστικὸν μόνοις τοῖς ἀρχιερεῦσιν ἐξάγειν ἐπὶ τῶν ἱερῶν ἐπετέτραπτο· καὶ λόγος, ποινὰς ὑποσχεῖν τινα τῶν ἐν τέλει ποτέ, ἀνθ' ὧν ἐπὶ τοῦ πλήθους τὸ τελεστικὸν ὄνομα τῆς πόλεως ἀναφανδὸν ἐθάρρησεν ἐξειπεῖν.* (Johannes Lydus, *De Mensibus* 4.73, ed. Wuensch)

On 21 April Romulus founded the city of Rome, after calling together all the people dwelling about and telling them each to bring a clod of earth from his own land, thus portending Rome's rule over every land. He himself taking his sacred trumpet, which the Romans were traditionally accustomed to call a *lituus* from λιτή ('prayer'), pronounced the name of the city as he presided over the entire sacred ritual. The city has three names, its mystic name, its sacred name, and its civil name. Its mystic name is 'Amor' (i.e. 'Love'), so all men are bound by divine love of the city, and that is why the poet (i.e. Virgil) riddlingly calls the city 'Amaryllis' in his *Eclogues*. Its sacred name is 'Flora', i.e. 'flowering', from which is derived the feast of the Anthesteria. Its civil name is 'Roma'. The sacred name was known to all and was spoken without fear. The mystic name was permitted to be uttered only by the high priests in the sacred rituals. And there is a story that once a magistrate paid the penalty because he dared to pronounce the mystic name of the city openly in an assembly.

II. A CRITIQUE OF SOME OF THE TEXTS

Some of the texts confuse or appear to conflate the secret name and the protector deity. Pliny [1] and Solinus [4], who concentrate on the secret name, also mention the goddess of silence, Angerona, attested earlier by Varro (*LL* 6.23) and identified by some as the protector deity (cf. [5]). Contrariwise Servius [6] and Johannes Lydus [9] concentrate exclusively on the name of Rome, while Pliny [2], Servius [7], and Servius [8] restrict themselves to the name of the tutelary deity. Plutarch [3] is muddled: whereas [1], [4], and [6] allege that the secret name of the city was improperly publicized by Valerius Soranus (cf. also [9]), Plutarch [3] claims that he revealed the secret name of the protector deity (cf. also Servius [8]). Macrobius [5] does not confuse the two topics, but juxtaposes them, speculating about the identity of the deity before declaring that the secret Latin name of the city is unknown even to the most learned. These combinations and confusions may imply that some ancient scholars believed the two names to be identical or related, but no surviving text explicitly asserts this.

Johannes Lydus [9] differs from all the others: far from regarding the secret name of Rome as unknown, he offers not one but two names additional to 'Rome'! This confidence has been shared by some modern enquirers: Basanoff (1947), ch. 4 believed he had discovered the secret name of Rome in '*Palatium*' (and indeed the secret tutelary deity in *Pales*), while Stanley (1963), following De Angelis (1947), 7–33, held that the secret name of Rome was *Amor*. The *Amor* theory was also embraced by Skulsky (1985).[6] Curiously in view of what Macrobius says about the comparative state of knowledge of the two issues in his day, scholarship has been less consensual about the name of Rome's protective deity: diverse answers have been proposed ranging from Pales to Angerona; and Brelich (1949) lumped all possible known deities together as protective 'Gottheiten der Stadt'.[7]

One misleading line of interpretation can be rejected straightaway: it has sometimes been claimed that the secret name of Rome was used legitimately only in sacred rites. But in fact all three texts which discuss the use of the secret name—([1], [4], and [6])—report nothing of the sort: they all agree that the secret name was not permitted to be pronounced even during sacred rites. However, these texts have not been allowed to tell their story. The oldest (Pliny [1]) was emended by Theodor Mommsen; he inserted *nisi* before *dicere* to alter the sense and to make the passage say what he wanted it to say, namely that legitimate utterance of the secret name of Rome was confined to sacred rites. Mommsen and his followers then privileged their emended text of [1] over Solinus [4] and Servius [6].

This procedure is patently illicit. Mommsen's emendation could be accepted only if the transmitted text was demonstrably corrupt, and if the emended text could be reconciled with Solinus [4] and Servius [6], or alternatively if it could be shown that Solinus and Servius were deceived by a corrupt, i.e. the pre-Mommsen, text of Pliny [1].[8] None of these conditions can be met. Pliny's language is admittedly compressed, possibly because his presumed source, Varro (see below), was either quoting an archaic phrase, or expressed himself clumsily, or was unsure of the meaning of the source which he in turn had used. Nevertheless Pliny's transmitted text cannot be impugned on

---

[6] However, O'Hara (1995), 156 reacted with scepticism to the notion that Virgil was alluding to *Amor* as the secret name of Rome at *Aen*. 4.347.

[7] On Brelich (1949) see esp. Weinstock (1949).

[8] As is suggested by Linderski (1986), 2255 n. 424 in the case of Solinus.

grounds of latinity. The clause *cuius nomen alterum dicere arcanis caerimo-niarum nefas habetur* means: 'whose other name, because of the secrecy surrounding rituals, it is regarded as a sacrilege to speak'. The subsequent words (*optimaque et salutari fide abolitum*) then confirm that Pliny was writing about a complete ban on uttering the name. Even if much modern scholarship finds it hard to grasp the meaning of *arcanis caerimoniarum*, Solinus [4] did not find difficulty in the phrase. He tells the same story as Pliny, paraphrasing Pliny to make Pliny's point more lucid.[9] Solinus' second clause (*ut hoc pacto . . . taciturnitatis*) represents Pliny's *optimaque et salutari fide abolitum*, while his first clause (*[proprium Romae nomen] quo minus enuntiaretur caerimoniarum arcana sanxerunt*) interprets Pliny's *cuius nomen alterum dicere arcanis caerimoniarum nefas habetur*. Solinus thus explicitly states that the 'rules of ritual secrecy' prohibit publicizing the name. It strains credulity to imagine that, if Pliny's text is as obviously corrupt as Mommsen thought it was, an educated native speaker of Latin like Solinus could have accepted its latinity and paraphrased its content without a qualm.

That Varro is the source of Servius [6] is implied by Servius' citation of Varro for his next piece of information, and this makes Varro also Pliny's likely source. Servius unequivocally denies that the name of Rome was ever used in sacred rites: *urbis enim illius verum nomen nemo vel in sacris enuntiat*—'for no one pronounces the true name of that city even in sacred rites'. Servius' *in sacris* and Pliny's *arcanis caerimoniarum* probably render different elements of Varro's account; in the other Servian texts the phrases *iure pontificum* [7] and *sacrorum lege* [8] resemble *arcanis caerimoniarum* more than *in sacris*. All three writers, then, make negative statements about the utterance of the secret name of Rome, and Servius definitely rules out its use in sacred rites.[10]

This verdict might seem obvious; but an eminent specialist in Roman religion, Prof. Jerzy Linderski, was convinced of the opposite: he accepted Mommsen's emendation and its consequences, and extrapolated from Pliny's *arcanis caerimoniarum* certain *arcanae caerimoniae* at which the secret name was permitted to be pronounced.[11] One of Linderski's arguments remains to be countered, namely that secrecy was endemic in Roman religion. Were this true, it might be thought that Mommsen's emendation is defensible not on

---

[9] This is not to say that Solinus' only source at this point was Pliny [1]: since Solinus' *ausus* is absent from Pliny but crops up in Servius [6], derived from Varro, and Servius [8], it is possible that Solinus was using Varro as well. If so, Solinus' testimony is doubly valuable.

[10] Compare too *ipsius uero urbis nomen etiam doctissimis ignoratum est* (Macrobius [5]). Köves-Zulauf (1972), 95–6 also rejected Mommsen's <*nisi*>, but went on to offer a different explanation.

[11] Cf. Linderski (1975), 285–6, amplified at Linderski (1986), 2254–5 and n. 424.

linguistic but on historical grounds because the proposition produced by Mommsen's emended text 'Rome, whose other name it is *nefas* to utter except at the *arcanae caerimoniae*'[12] was typical of Roman religious practice. In support of his conviction Linderski cited Savage (1945), who claimed that secrecy was an integral part of Roman religion. But what her paper actually identified was not endemic secrecy but two groups of Roman religious practices, the first tangential to the matter in hand and neither demonstrating a culture of secrecy in Roman religion. Savage's material is really only germane to the present discussion because her second group (along with the texts assembled above) exemplify the concepts which led to widespread ancient belief in the secret name and the secret divine protector of Rome, despite their probable chimerical nature.

Savage's first (tangential) category of practices[13] consists of:

a) Cicero's proclamation of his ignorance of pontifical law:

dixi a principio nihil me de scientia uestra, nihil de sacris, nihil de abscondito iure pontificum dicturum. quae sunt adhuc a me de iure dedicandi disputata, non sunt quaesita ex occulto aliquo genere litterarum, sed sumpta de medio, ex rebus palam per magistratus actis ad conlegiumque delatis, ex senatus consulto, ex lege. illa interiora iam uestra sunt, quid dici, quid praeiri, quid tangi, quid teneri ius fuerit. (*De Domo* 138)

I said at the outset that I should base no assertion upon my own knowledge, upon religious observance, or upon the secret regulations of the pontiffs. The arguments dealing with the rules of dedication which I have hitherto adduced have been culled from no esoteric treatise; they are drawn from a common stock, from open proceedings of magistrates in which they have deferred to the College, from senatorial decrees, and from the statutes. As to the questions that remain, the correct words to be uttered, responses to be dictated, and objects to be touched or held, these are your own intimate concern. (tr. N. H. Watts, Loeb Classical Text)

Savage also referred to two other passages of *De Domo* which are worth quoting because their similar content provides a context for *De Domo* 138. They are:

nihil loquor de pontificio iure, nihil de ipsius uerbis dedicationis, nihil de religione, cacrimoniis; non dissimulo me nescire ea quae, etiam si scirem, dissimularem, ne aliis molestus, uobis etiam curiosus uiderer; etsi effluunt multa ex uestra disciplina quae etiam ad nostras auris saepe permanent. (*De Domo* 121)

---

[12] The translation is that of Linderski (1986), 2254–5.
[13] Savage (1945), 157–62.

I say nothing about the prerogatives of pontiffs, or the forms of the actual ceremony of dedication, or of sanctity, and all the ritual attached to it. I will not attempt to hide my ignorance of all this; indeed even were I not ignorant, I would conceal my knowledge, lest I should seem to others inquisitive and to you even interfering; though it is true that there are many details of your lore that often leak out, and even penetrate to our ears. (tr. N. H. Watts, Loeb Classical Text, modified)

quid est enim aut tam adrogans quam de religione, de rebus diuinis, caerimoniis, sacris pontificum conlegium docere conari, aut tam stultum quam, si quis quid in uestris libris inuenerit, id narrare uobis, aut tam curiosum quam ea scire uelle de quibus maiores nostri uos solos et consuli et scire uoluerunt? (*De Domo* 33)

For what act could be so presumptious as to endeavour to instruct the Pontifical College in religion, in our relation to the divine powers, in ritual, or in sacrifice; or so foolish as to recount to you discoveries that have been made in your own books; or so officious, as to wish to know matters whereon our ancestors desired that you should be the sole referees and the sole experts? (tr. N. H. Watts, Loeb Classical Text)

A final relevant parallel passage about the *augures* may be added:

uenio ad augures, quorum ego libros, si qui sunt reconditi, non scrutor; non sum in exquirendo iure augurum curiosus; haec quae una cum populo didici, quae saepe in contionibus responsa sunt, noui. (*De Domo* 39)

I proceed now to the augurs, into whose books, such of them at least as are secret, I forbear to pry. I am not curious to inquire into augural regulations. There are some, however, of which I share the knowledge with the populace, which have often been revealed, in answer to inquiry, in mass meetings, and with these I am familiar. (tr. N. H. Watts, Loeb Classical Text)

b) The restriction of access to the *penus Vestae* and its contents to the Vestals, and of access to the *sacrarium* of Opiconsiva in the *Regia* to them and the *sacerdos publicus*.

c) The limited audience at the rites of the Argei on the Tiber bridge.

d) The *libri reconditi* of the augurs, their oath of secrecy, and the details of their ceremony on the *arx* which was not recorded in writing but was passed down by memory.

e) The prohibition upon the *quindecemuiri* of revealing the contents of the Sibylline Books.

f) The exclusion of men from some Roman ceremonies and of women at others.

Neither individually nor as a group do these practices demonstrate a culture of secrecy in Roman religion. The *De Domo* passages are extracts from a highly tendentious speech to the *pontifices*.[14] Moreover their author, who was

---

[14] For further discussion of these passages and of the '*libri reconditi*' cf. Linderski (1985).

at that time neither *pontifex* nor *augur* (he obtained the augurate later), is manifestly salivating in deferential mode for either priesthood. When Cicero's tendentiousness and flattery are set aside, the residue of what he says accords with the implications of the other items in Savage's first category. Privileged ongoing priestly colleges with a limited and elite membership such as the *pontifices* and *augures* naturally wanted to keep their sacred records and ritual practices confidential to themselves; and they were sometimes successful, as for example with the unwritten rites of the augurs on the *arx* or the locking up of the Sibylline Books except when the *XVuiri* were instructed by the Senate to consult them. But the fact that a great deal of information about the activities of the priesthoods leaked and/or was published shows that secrecy was not much observed: Cicero admits this in the first three *De Domo* passages quoted above, most explicitly in *De Domo* 121. As for the remaining items in Savage's first category, the rituals and ritual locations with a restricted entry or limited participation, these again do not argue for a general culture of secrecy in Roman religion but rather for a belief in the appropriateness of particular cults/cult locations to particular subsections of society.

Savage's second category[15]—religious formulae in which some uncertainty about the identity of deities is manifested—is no more indicative of a cult of secrecy than the first. Rather it illustrates a recurrent dilemma of Roman[16] worshippers, namely that they were sometimes unsure not just about gods' names but about their gender. The *numina* worshipped by Romans might be nameless and/or of unknown gender, and collective *numina* in particular (e.g. the Lares, Penates, and Di Indigetes) lacked individual names and identities. Roman religion combined this haziness about the divine with a scrupulous fear that, if a god was not addressed by his/her correct or preferred name, or if the right deity was not invoked, then prayers might be inefficacious. 'Catch-all' formulae were therefore used in prayers to evade these difficulties.[17] These sought to remedy a lack of information about the deity's gender (e.g. *sei deus sei dea*), or identity (e.g. *quisquis es*), or name (e.g. *quoquo nomine / siue quo alio nomine fas est te nominare / te appellari uolueris*). These formulae do not demonstrate Roman gods' possession of secret names; indeed they are often combined with mention of a god's name! Rather the formulae reveal the factors which some ancient commentators failed to understand and which led

---

[15] Savage (1945), 162–3.

[16] What is said here about Roman religion applies also to Greek religion, but to a significantly lesser extent.

[17] For these and further examples and for discussion cf. Appel (1909), 75–82; Norden (1913), 143–6.

them to advance unhistorical conjectures about secret names to resolve uncertainties about the names and identities of certain *numina*.

This process of false explanation, and its motivations, can be charted in texts cited by Savage (1945) to support the notion of gods' secret names. Festus 94L *s.v. indigites: dii quorum nomina uulgari non licet* ('*indigites*: gods whose names it is not permitted to make public') shows how the namelessness of multiple deities could be misunderstood. Servius auctus on *Aen.* 3.12, discussing the Penates of Rome—*quod eorum nomina nemo sciat*—is parallel. Other texts concerning *euocatio/exauguratio* derive from an incorrect interpretation of formulae like *si deus, si dea est* and *quoquo nomine fas est te nominare*. Among these the statement of Servius (auctus) [7] *et iure pontificum cautum est, ne suis nominibus dii Romani appellarentur, ne exaugurari possint* looks at first sight impressive because of its reference to pontifical law, but it is unreliable for at least two reasons. First it is unique in its claim that (presumably all) Roman gods had names other than their usual names; this is clearly a generalization based on, although unsupported by, the supposed secret protector deity of Rome and the catch-all formulae of the type which Servius then goes on to cite. Then again, Servius adds a second claim, linking the secret name with fear of *evocatio*. He probably derived this notion from Pliny [2]. Servius' *in cuius dei tutela urbs Roma sit* is very close to Pliny's *in cuius dei tutela Roma esset*, while his *et iure pontificum cautum est* looks like a paraphrase of Pliny's *durat in pontificum disciplina id sacrum*. Hence Servius' linking of the secret name with *euocatio* is also likely to be Pliny's.[18]

In fact this link is highly suspect: the Romans conducted *evocationes* of gods from other cities without imagining that they knew all the names of the deity being evoked.[19] Macrobius, *Saturnalia* 3.9.7–8 preserves the evocation used at Carthage; it starts with a catch-all formula and it does not even attempt to name the protector deity of Carthage:

Si deus, si dea est, cui populus ciuitasque Carthaginiensis est in tutela, teque maxime, ille qui urbis huius populique tutelam recepisti, precor uenerorque ueniamque a uobis peto ut uos populum ciuitatemque Carthaginiensem deseratis, loca templa sacra urbemque eorum relinquatis, absque his abeatis eique populo ciuitati metum formidinem obliuionem iniciatis, proditique Romam ad me meosque ueniatis, nostraque uobis loca templa sacra urbs acceptior probatiorque sit, mihique populoque

---

[18] Verrius Flaccus or/and his sources may also have linked the two concepts, but this is not quite clear since Pliny seems prone to add his own link or conclusion to information obtained from a source (cf. also Pliny [1]).

[19] For *euocatio* and the bibliography thereon cf. Beard, North, and Price (1998), I.34–5, 62, 82, 111, 132–4.

Romano militibusque meis praepositi sitis ut sciamus intellegamusque. si ita feceritis, uoueo uobis templa ludosque facturum.

To any god, to any goddess, under whose protection are the people and state of Carthage, and chiefly to thee who art charged with the protection of this city and people, I make prayer and do reverence and ask grace of you all, that ye abandon the people and state of Carthage, forsake their places, temples, shrines, and city, and depart therefrom; and that upon that people and state ye bring fear and terror and oblivion; that once put forth ye come to Rome, to me and to mine; and that our places, temples, shrines, and city may be more acceptable and pleasing to you; and that ye take me and the Roman people and my soldiers under your charge; that we may know and understand the same. If ye shall so have done, I vow to you temples and solemn games. (tr. P. V. Davies, *Macrobius: The Saturnalia* (New York and London, 1969), 218)

Livy 5.21.3 attributes to Camillus a briefer formula of *euocatio* of Juno from Veii, although a complete reproduction of what Camillus said may not be intended:

te simul, Iuno regina, quae nunc Veios colis, precor, ut nos uictores in nostram tuamque mox futuram urbem sequare, ubi te dignum amplitudine tua templum accipiat.

At the same time I entreat you, Queen Iuno, who now dwell in Veii, to follow us as victors to the city which is ours and which will soon be yours, that a temple worthy of your greatness may receive you there.

The 'information' offered by Servius [7] / Pliny [2],[20] is, then, untrustworthy since it does not accord with the historical record about *euocatio*; and its repetition by Plutarch [3] and Macrobius [5] gives it no more credibility. Indeed Plutarch [3] may, like Pliny [2], derive from Verrius Flaccus: Plutarch's ὡς τῶν Ῥωμαϊκῶν τινες ἱστορήκασιν is reminiscent of the *auctores* invoked, according to Pliny, by Verrius Flaccus. Some of Macrobius' phraseology also recalls that of Pliny. It might, of course, be conjectured that *euocationes* went ahead whether or not the secret name of the god being invoked was known, but that it was believed that the chances of success were greater if the name was known. In that case we would expect a Roman historian to mention somewhere the employment of a god's secret name in an *euocatio*, but there is no such mention. Moreover we might expect to hear of failed *euocationes* when a god's secret name was unknown, but again (although perhaps less surprisingly!) we do not.

One reason why errors about secret names have persisted so long is that supposed evidence for them is usually presented in the form of extracts. But

---

[20] On a straightforward reading of Pliny the error was not shared by Verrius Flaccus.

these extracts immediately reveal themselves as unreliable if they are seen in their contexts, where they may rub shoulders with alternative and obviously specious speculations. Servius [8] is typical. It hints at the standard error about *euocatio*, and contains other patent nonsense based on ancient pseudo-etymology: the *di indigetes* were not in fact so described because they were men become gods, let alone because they 'want for nothing'. Similarly, as has been shown, Servius [7] usefully highlights the problems which bothered ancient antiquarians and led them to speculate without foundation that gods had names which were deliberately kept secret. Others of the texts quoted above are similar hotch-potches, i.e. Plutarch [3], Macrobius [5], and Johannes Lydus [9]. Lydus' account is even more fanciful than the others.[21] His is the only (Greek) text to assert that the secret name of Rome was used in sacred rites (τὸ δὲ τελεστικὸν μόνοις τοῖς ἀρχιερεῦσιν ἐξάγειν ἐπὶ τῶν ἱερῶν ἐπετέτραπτο), a statement contradicted by all three (earlier) Latin writers; Lydus then claims in all seriousness that Virgil called Rome 'Amaryllis'! His unreliability is amply confirmed by further errors on his part which will emerge below (p. 263).

In conclusion, the ancient sources so far examined do not offer proof of a culture of secrecy at Rome, or of the existence of a secret name or secret protector deity of Rome, and they provide no support for Mommsen's emendation of Pliny. Rather they document the circumstances in which, and the processes whereby, these chimeras were invented.[22]

III. 'VALERIUS SORANUS'

Despite the conclusions reached above, it is undeniable that the secret name of Rome was a subject of speculation by the first century BC, and that Rome's secret protector deity was a talking point by the first century AD, if not earlier. The history of these notions therefore merits investigation. A focal point is the enigmatic 'Valerius Soranus': his identity, the historicity of his story, and its relevance to ancient knowledge of the secret name of Rome. The relevant texts are [1], [3], [4], [6], [8], and [9]. Pliny [1] says that someone called Valerius Soranus divulged the secret name of Rome and 'soon paid the penalty'. Plutarch [3] and Solinus [4] add nothing new. Servius [6] offers more details, some supplied by Servius auctus: he cites Varro 'and many others' for the

---

[21] *Pace* Linderski (1986), 2255 n. 424.

[22] Savage (1945), 163 cites a Greek text about Consus (Dion. Hal. *A.R.* 2.31.2–3) whose name 'might not be spoken'. But even Dionysius expresses scepticism about his own report.

information that 'a certain tribune of the plebs' called Valerius Soranus
revealed the name and, 'as some say', was 'seized by the Senate' and crucified,
or, 'as others say', fled in fear of punishment to Sicily, was captured by the
governor (or by a *praetor*), and was executed on the orders of the Senate.
Servius [8] and Johannes Lydus [9] present cut-down versions of the story.

At first sight these texts tell a simple, if embroidered, tale. But the historically attested Valerii Sorani do not fit easily into it. Cicero (*Brutus* 169)
mentions two brothers, D. and Q. Valerius Soranus, as his friends and
neighbours before describing them as *docti et Graecis litteris et Latinis*. Cicero
also names Q. Valerius Soranus as *literatissimum togatorum omnium* (*De
Orat.* 3.43). Again, Pliny, *N.H.* pr. 33 identifies a Valerius Soranus as the
author of *Epoptides*, while a Soranus crops up at Varro, *Logistorici* fr. 38 as the
author of a philosophical work in verse and a Valerius Soranus at Varro, *De
Lingua Latina* 7.31 as the author of a literary work. Finally a Q. Valerius
Soranus appears at Gellius, *Noctes Atticae* 2.10.3 pronouncing on a linguistic
matter. It is not unreasonable to suppose (although not certain) that Cicero's
Q. Valerius Soranus is the subject of all these passages, especially since the last
two both concern points of Greek/Latin usage. But once we move from
literature to history difficulties appear. A text greatly relied on by those
identifying the scholar Q. Valerius Soranus with the alleged divulger of the
secret name of Rome is Plutarch, *Pompey* 10. It recounts, on the authority of
the Caesarian C. Oppius, that a learned Q. Valerius was cruelly killed by
Pompey in Sicily (in 82 BC), before going on to question the veracity of
Oppius' account:

Γάϊος δὲ ᾿Όππιος ὁ Καίσαρος ἑταῖρος ἀπανθρώπως φησὶ καὶ Κοίντῳ Οὐαλλερίῳ
χρήσασθαι τόν Πομπήϊον. ἐπιστάμενον γὰρ ὡς ἔστι φιλόλογος ἀνὴρ καὶ φιλομαθὴς
ἐν ὀλίγοις ὁ Οὐαλλέριος, ὡς ἤχθη πρὸς αὐτόν, ἐπισπασάμενον καὶ συμπεριπατήσαντα
καὶ πυθόμενον ὧν ἔχρῃζε καὶ μαθόντα, προστάξαι τοῖς ὑπηρέταις εὐθὺς ἀνελεῖν
ἀπαγαγόντας. ἀλλ᾿ ᾿Οππίῳ μέν, ὅταν περὶ τῶν Καίσαρος πολεμίων ἢ φίλων διαλέγηται,
σφόδρα δεῖ πιστεύειν μετὰ εὐλαβείας. (ed. K. Ziegler)

Furthermore Caius Oppius, the friend of Caesar, says that Pompey treated Quintus
Valerius also with unnatural cruelty. For, understanding that Valerius was a man of
rare scholarship and learning, when he was brought to him, Oppius says, Pompey
took him aside, walked up and down with him, asked and learned what he wished
from him, and then ordered his attendants to lead him away and put him to death at
once. But when Oppius discourses about the enemies or friends of Caesar, one must
be very cautious about believing him. (tr. B. Perrin, Loeb Classical Text)

Pompey's victim has his *praenomen, nomen*, and learning in common with
the scholarly friend of Cicero, and he shares his *nomen* and ethnic with the
alleged divulger of the secret name ([1], [3], [4], [6]) and his *nomen* and

execution in Sicily with the *tribunus plebis* of [6] who allegedly divulged the secret name (for whom cf. also [8]). Moreover Florus, *Epitome* 2.9, when discussing some political victims of this period, writes of *fata Sorani*, presumably referring to the execution of this 'Q. Valerius' in Sicily. Hence Rudolf Helm at *RE* VIII.A.1 (1955) *s.v.* Valerius No. 345, following the lead of Cichorius (1906), identified the scholar friend of Cicero with the victim of Pompey and the divulger. Other authorities adopt similar approaches.[23]

In contrast Sumner (1973), 101 declined to identify Cicero's friend either with the man executed in Sicily or with the alleged divulger. Sumner stressed 'Cicero's two gentle references to Q. Valerius of Sora' and noted that 'Sora may well have produced more than one Q. Valerius' before reaching the conclusion that 'there may be an ancient confusion of identities involved in this puzzle'. There are good reasons for Sumner's scepticism: Valerius is indeed an extremely common *nomen*;[24] 'Soranus' is not a *cognomen* but an ethnic;[25] and Plutarch does not tell us that the Q. Valerius of *Pompey* 10 was 'of Sora'. Finally Florus' testimony could easily be dismissed as the product of later confusion. Nevertheless, although nothing is certain, it is not impossible that the scholar Q. Valerius Soranus was a victim of Pompey. We need only suppose that, having obtained the tribunate and being a Marian, he somehow found himself in Sicily, was captured, and was then executed by Pompey.

But the further identification of the scholar or/and learned victim with the alleged divulger is even harder to sustain. Plutarch does not link the death of his 'Q. Valerius' in *Pompey* with a religious indiscretion, even though he (cf. [3]) believed in *Roman Questions* that a 'Valerius Soranus' had revealed the name of the protector deity of Rome and had come to a bad end because of it—and *Pompey* is probably later than *Roman Questions*.[26] On the other hand in *Pompey* Plutarch was seeking to blacken his subject, so he could have suppressed the offence of 'Q. Valerius' in case it might have been thought to justify his execution.[27] But other considerations also weaken the identification. To press Sumner's point, would Cicero have referred to Q. Valerius Soranus twice with such approbation if Quintus had betrayed the secret name

---

[23] Cf. e.g. Anon. (1983), Index onomastique *s.v.* Q. Valerius (de Sora); Solin (1993), 5, referring to his fuller treatment in Anon. (1982), I.424–5; J.-M. David in Anon. (1982), I.40. Wiseman (1971), 269 (no. 457) notes Cichorius's (1906) views and records Della Corte's (1935) identification of Q. Valerius Soranus with the poet Valerius Aedituus.

[24] The argument advanced by Cichorius (1906), 63 to support his identifications, i.e. that the *praenomen* Quintus was extraordinarily rare among Republican Valerii, is unimpressive: there were very many Valerii, most of whom have left no epigraphic or other trace.

[25] Cf. Solin (1993), 5 (but hedging his bets).

[26] Cf. Jones (1966), esp. 106–14, 120, 122.

[27] For parallel differences between Plutarch's *Lives* which are mainly explicable by narrative needs and emphases cf. Pelling (1979), 271–7.

of Rome? And surely Cicero would have known this if it really happened? So is the divulgation story a fiction? It certainly contains unreliable and conflicting elements: the assertion of Servius [8] (and of Servius/Servius auctus [6] where he is named as Valerius Soranus) that a *tribunus plebis* was seized by the Senate and crucified not only conflicts with Plutarch's information that his Q. Valerius died in Sicily and with Servius auctus' [6] similar alternative information about the divulger, but in itself it is manifestly fictitious: crucifixion is intrinsically unlikely, no texts except [6] and [8] mention it, and [6] does so only as an alternative, and by implication less credible, version. The story more generally in circulation was presumably that Soranus 'soon paid the penalty' (cf. Pliny [1]), i.e. what happened to him later for different reasons was regarded by third parties as punishment for his impious indiscretion.

But there are also difficulties over the divulgation itself. To begin with, no ancient source offers an occasion or motive or context for it. The best attempt to hypothesize one is Alfonsi (1948), based on the reconstruction of Cichorius (1906) of the life of Q. Valerius Soranus from all available sources. Alfonsi (1948), 88 suggested that Soranus, as a Latin and a Marian, revealed the secret name of Rome in order to impede Sulla's campaign of 82 BC. The fact that Soranus' native town, Sora, had been on the Roman side during the Social War might be thought to weaken this hypothesis. A more serious objection is that to construct his hypothesis Alfonsi needed to assume that the divulger, the scholar, and Pompey's victim were one and the same individual. There remains too the more troublesome conundrum about how the secret name was divulged, i.e. was it in writing or orally, and how and why knowledge of it spread (or failed to spread) from that point on. If in writing—as might be presumed, particularly if the guilty Valerius Soranus was the scholar—then surely Soranus' text would have circulated sufficiently for someone before late antiquity to profess to know the secret name? And if the indiscreet text was the *Epoptides*,[28] Pliny, who cites that work's index as a precedent for his own (*NH praef.* 33), would certainly have known that the *Epoptides* was the guilty source, and he would also have known the secret name. This difficulty persuaded Alfonsi (1948), 85–6 that the revelation must have been oral only—which may in any case be implied by Pliny's *enuntiauit* ([1]) and

---

[28] It is not immediately clear what the title *Epoptides* means. Murphy (2004b), 133 notes various scholarly attempts to interpret it along the lines of 'watchers', or 'initiates', or 'guardians'. He himself adopts the view of Köves-Zulauf (1970), esp. 324–6 that the *Epoptides* are 'Tutelary Goddesses'. If this theory, which Köves-Zulauf supports with a dense array of evidence and argumentation, is correct, it would certainly make the *Epoptides* a suitable locus for Soranus' supposed revelation—if it had ever taken place. However, I nurture a lingering hesitation over whether supervision/oversight, rather than protection, may be the key concept behind ἐποπτεύω and its cognates (cf. *LSJ*, s. vv.).

Solinus' *eloqui* ([4]). But in this case how did the act of revelation, but apparently not its circumstances or the name itself, come to the attention of Varro or Varro's sources? Again there is no mention of such a revelation anywhere in Cicero's voluminous surviving writings; and surely Cicero would have mentioned it somewhere, particularly if the indiscreet Valerius Soranus was one of his two friends from neighbouring Sora? One might, of course, try to sidestep all the arguments so far advanced about the divulgation by hypothesizing that the name was actually known to Varro, Cicero, Pliny, and others from Soranus' revelation, and that all those who knew it were either too superstitious or too patriotic to pass on the information. But that is surely incredible, given human nature and the evidence of active speculation about the name.

In view of these difficulties an alternative reconstruction is perhaps needed which would account both for the surviving evidence and for the gaps in it. It might run as follows: Varro is the earliest named source for the story of Valerius Soranus; this shows that by the early first century BC at the latest a belief had gained ground that Rome had a secret name;[29] a parallel belief in a secret tutelary deity may or may not also have been current. Misunderstandings of, or extrapolations from, the *Libri Pontificales*, and/or incorrect reasonings about the catch-all clauses of prayers lay behind such beliefs, which, once they were in circulation, would inevitably have triggered speculation about the identity of the secret name/deity. It may even be that Ennius' account of the foundation of Rome in his *Annales* already referred to such speculations; and it certainly must have stimulated them. At some point a rumour arose that someone had divulged the secret name of Rome. This rumour cannot have implied a written revelation; otherwise it could easily have been confirmed or refuted; and, if confirmed, the secret name would have become current knowledge. The rumour must, then, have been of an oral divulgation; and the name allegedly divulged was probably not part of the rumour, for otherwise it would not have disappeared as completely as it seems to have done. As for the alleged divulger, even if he was identified from the beginning as a 'Valerius of Sora', he may not have been Cicero's Q. Valerius Soranus. Later, if the Q. Valerius executed by Pompey in Sicily was, or was thought to be, Cicero's scholar, this could then have helped to underpin the story by providing as a candidate for the divulger a learned man of unorthodox religious opinions[30] who was thought subsequently to have met an unpleasant end. Varro or his sources were the vector for the story of how a 'Valerius Soranus' revealed the secret name. But seemingly neither Varro nor his

---

[29] This is also the (unsupported) verdict of Weinstock (1950), 149.
[30] Cf. esp. Varro, *Logistorici* fr. 38.

sources mentioned what name Soranus revealed, since no one subsequently appears to have known it. It is unclear what further details Varro offered. His account must have fuelled further speculation, but there was obviously again no agreed result, since Hyginus in his *De Situ Urbis* was just as ignorant as Varro about the name (cf. Servius [6]).

A different question involving texts [1], [4], and [5] can be answered quickly: has *diva Angerona* any relevance to either of the two alleged secret names? Pliny [1] does not imply that she is the secret protector deity of Rome: she is mentioned simply to underline the high value accorded to silence in older Roman religion; in this Soranus [4] follows Pliny. Angerona is present in Macrobius [5] because he, like Brelich 1947, was rounding up all the possibilities for the protector deity, and in fact Macrobius expresses a preference for *Ops Consiuia*. Angerona, then, has no relevance.

IV. ANCIENT GUESSES AT THE SECRET NAMES?

Johannes Lydus [9] starts impressively with Romulus founding Rome as *pontifex* and *augur*. But this Ennian scenario loses credibility when Lydus goes on to claim that Romulus gave Rome not two, but three, names, distinguished as τελεστικόν, ἱερατικόν, and πολιτικόν. The political name *Roma* and the 'hieratic' but not secret name *Flora* are, so Lydus says, known to and used by all; the secret 'telestic' name is the palindromic *Amor* (οἱονεὶ Ἔρως). Now Flora had an old cult at Rome, her name is a part-anagram of *Roma*, and from the fourth century AD on Flora was iconically important for Rome.[31] She may even have been identified with the *Fortuna/Tyche* of Rome (cf. below), and she was certainly closely associated with Venus, mother of the Roman race and an important Roman divinity from the first century BC. Specific fourth-century AD events like the alleged naming by Constantine of the *Tyche* of Constantinople as Ἄνθουσα (= *Flora*), Constantine's transportation to his new capital of the statue of the Τύχη of Rome, and the later countering of this at Rome in 393–4 by the restoration of the temple of Flora during a pagan revival—all these factors suggest that the notion of Flora as a protector deity of Rome (or even as the main protector deity of Rome) had become current in late antiquity. Lydus' assertion that *Roma*'s ἱερατικὸν ὄνομα was '*Flora*' probably reflects this development; and his claim may even imply that in his time the names of the city and of its protector deity were thought to

---

[31] For what follows cf. Stanley (1963), 242–3.

be identical. But there is no evidence that the *Roma–Flora* link antedates late antiquity: Stanley's assertion that it appears in Aelius Aristides' Εἰς Ῥώμην 99, delivered in AD 143, is incorrect.[32] Moreover, if *Flora* had for any reason been closely connected with *Roma* in the minds of earlier generations— whether in substance, or through pseudo-etymology, or as an alternative name of Rome—then we would expect to find *Roma* and *Flora* and/or their cognates juxtaposed in republican and early imperial Roman poetry. But there is not a single collocation of the two terms before the fourth century AD, when they start to appear.[33] On this basis I conclude that '*Flora*' was unknown before later antiquity as any sort of name of Rome.

Lydus' secret name of Rome, *Amor*, is not just an anagram of *Roma* but also a palindrome. There is ample evidence that in later antiquity *Roma* and *Amor* were publicly linked;[34] and the quadrate ROMAMOR graffito from Pompei, which antedates the eruption of Vesuvius in AD 79, demonstrates, independently of literary evidence, that the anagram was well known before then. Earlier, first-century BC, familiarity with the anagram is confirmed by the not infrequent and manifestly intentional collocations of *Roma* and *Amor* in classical Latin poetry.[35] A parallel Greek link between the part-anagrammatic ῥώμη and ἔρως was already present in a much anthologized passage of Plato,[36] so the *Roma/Amor* link could have been known at Rome before the classical period, although its absence from Plautus and Terence enjoins caution. The close association between *Roma* and *Amor* in the minds of many Romans from at least around 30 BC could imply that some of them believed that *Amor* was the secret name of Rome. But, if so, their belief was without foundation. To begin with, the *Roma/Amor* link appears to have been anything but secret. One might counter this argument by maintaining that this was because Valerius Soranus had revealed it! But if Soranus had revealed *Amor* (or anything else) as the secret name of Rome, surely some source before Lydus would have told us this explicitly. On the contrary our earlier sources' remarks

---

[32] Stanley (1963), 243 n. 25 refers to Oliver (1953), 885, who concluded, on the analogy of Aristides' many references to *Roma/Amor* (on which see below), that in ch. 99 Aristides was alluding to *Roma/Flora*. But nothing in ch. 99 compels this conclusion: Aristides is simply exploiting there the standard epideictic topos that the bounty and fruitfulness of the earth are brought about by the virtues of the ruler, in this case Rome.

[33] Ausonius ((?) *Cento* 7–8; *Epist.* 9.89) and Claudian (*Carm. Maior.* 1.19; 17.84; 24.125) seem to be the first poets to feature this collocation.

[34] Cf. esp. Stanley (1963).

[35] Cf. Skulsky (1985); O'Hara (1996), 156; McKeown (1987–), III.178–9 on Ov. *Am.* 2.9.17–18: *Roma*.

[36] i.e. Plat. *Phaedr.* 238b–c. For various quotations/echoes cf. Isocr. *Hel.* 55; Diod. 8.9.1; Dion. Hal. *De Demosth. dict.* 7; Philostr. *Heroic.* p.182.27–8 Kayser; Liban. *Epist.* 1021.4; Proclus, *In Plat. Crat.* 16.38; *In Parmenid.* p. 852.15–16; Stob. *Anth.* 4.20b.77.

about the secret name—*optimaque et salutari fide abolitum* ([1]), *ut hoc pacto notitiam eius aboleret fides placitae taciturnitatis* ([4]) and *ipsius uero urbis nomen etiam doctissimis ignoratum est* ([5])—show that no secret name of Rome was common property. So, since the *Roma/Amor* link was well known, *Amor* cannot have been the secret name of Rome, however many incorrectly shared Lydus' theory that it was.

If Lydus' claim can be rejected easily, Macrobius' information about names given to the tutelary deity of Rome ([5]) in 'old books' is less easy to evaluate. He mentions Jupiter, Luna, and Angerona as possible candidates before expressing his own preference for *Ops Consiuia*. The same methodology which confirmed the early reality of the *Amor/Roma* link and revealed an early *Roma/Flora* association as a mirage can be applied to these new candidates. In brief the connexions *Roma/Luna* and *Roma/Angerona* are unsubstantiated in Latin poetry, while *Roma/Iuppiter* naturally occurs to some extent, but not so frequently as to reinforce Macrobius' guess. The most interesting results, although their import is not clear, come from *Roma/Ops* and their cognates and 'etymologically' related terms. *Opes* and *opus* are fairly general concepts and *Roma* and its cognates are named frequently in Latin poetry, so the chances of spontaneous collocations are high. On the other hand the documented pseudo-etymological links between *opes, opus,* and *oppidum,* in which *Ops* plays a key role (cf. Maltby (1991), *s.vv.*), mean that *Roma/Ops* collocations are likely to be 'etymological' and hence deliberate. Some of these additionally introduce the most popular pseudo-etymology of *Roma* (*vires* from Greek Ῥώμη or Latin *Valentia*), or they add the related *urbs/ orbis* 'etymology', and some are also concerned directly or indirectly with the foundation of Rome, spoken of as an *opus* or the result of *operae*. So, while there is no proof that *Ops* was ever historically the secret tutelary deity of Rome, these collocations suggest that others before Macrobius had come to this conclusion. Catullus 34.21–4 (*sis quocumque tibi placet | sancta* **nomine, Romulique,** | *antique ut solita's, bona | sospites* **ope** *gentem*) is tempting although inconclusive. Its combination of *nomen* (an etymological marker,[37] as well as a pointer to the 'name' of Rome), of the founder Romulus, and of the *ops* of Diana in a context where she is the protector of the Roman race hint that Catullus is identifying *Ops* with Diana and thus characterizing Diana as the protectress of Rome; but he might simply be referring to Diana's role as Lucina.

---

[37] On 'etymological markers' cf. Maltby (1993); Cairns (1996), 29–51; O'Hara (1996), 75–9 and n. 331; Grewing (1998), 327–40.

V. CONCLUSIONS

This paper's verdict contradicts that of most modern scholarship, which has been content to reconcile and synthesize the ancient texts, with some scholars even believing that they have identified the names in question and with only a few sceptical voices being raised.[38] Contrariwise this paper concludes that certain of the relevant ancient texts contain manifest errors, that others are reconstructions with no more validity than modern attempts, that there are inconsistencies in the narratives offered which undermine their credibility, and that at the end of the day there is no sound evidence that the secret name of Rome and the secret protector deity of Rome ever existed in the ways in which optimistic modern reconstructions have assumed. It is, of course, ultimately possible that, despite the defective and flawed nature of the ancient testimonies, these names were kept secret, and that this is the reason why the evidence is in the state it is. But such a view would be based on faith alone. For all this, the indications of attempts by Roman poets to conjecture or to refer allusively to candidates for these names, some of which this paper has adumbrated, are of considerable interest, and they will merit future treatment.[39]

[38] Esp. Weinstock (1950), 149, cited with approbation by Latte (1967), 125 n. 2.

[39] I hope to pursue this enquiry in a subsequent paper provisionally entitled '*Roma* and her Tutelary Deity: Ancient Poetic Speculations about their Names?'.

Part IV

Tacitus Reviewed

15

Seven Passages of the *Annals* (and One of Manilius)

Edward Courtney

After the publication of a paper by me on Catullus in 1985, I received a letter from one A. J. Woodman asking for an offprint and stating that my contentions in one area were exactly what he had been teaching his students (Tony, if you have changed your mind since then, don't tell anyone). We kept up an intermittent correspondence, and it was a great joy to me when he became my successor as Gildersleeve Professor at the University of Virginia. A no longer intermittent exchange of ideas and queries has ensued, of which the following paper in an earlier version was one item; not that Tony knew what its destination was to be. I look forward to the continuance of our converse, a word which will reverberate in the following.

I. *ANN.* 11.14.3

(The Claudian letters of the alphabet): aspiciuntur etiam nunc in aere publico †dis plebiscitis† per fora ac templa fixo.

Nothing here seems suspicious beyond the obelized words; for *aere publico* cf. 12.53.3 *fixum est <aere> publico senatus consultum*, where there is a gap in the manuscript but the marginal supplement by a late hand, which probably should rather be *<in aere>* as proposed by Andresen, seems certain. *plebiscitis* could conceivably be right, but is open to such grave suspicion that it is prudent to alter it into *plebi s(enatus) c(onsul)tis* with Grotius. For the former word *<diuulgan>dis* would provide palaeographical cause for corruption.

II. *ANN.* 11.23.2

(The leading men of Gallia Comata requested the right of acquiring honours, such as the *latus clauus*, at Rome. Opponents argued that Italy was not so feeble that it could not supply a senate for its own city; they claimed that) suffecisse olim indigenas consanguineis populis.

This last phrase is usually taken to mean 'natives had sufficed for kindred peoples', as it is translated by Woodman, who explains 'in the distant past neighbouring peoples such as Latins or Sabines had been content that only natives of the City of Rome were members of the Senate'. There are two problems with this: first, *suffecisse* is divorced from any link in sense with *suppeditare* ('supply' in the above paraphrase), whereas it looks as if the present-day alleged inability of Italy to supply senators is being contrasted with former ability to do so. Second, the point is a contrast between Rome + Italy and Gallia, and the Gauls were not likely to be impressed by being referred to a set-up, obsolete now for centuries, in which Italians acquiesced in Roman domination, as if that could be referred to in the first century AD as an ideal. Therefore I propose *indigenas <et e> consanguineis populis* (meaning Romans and Italians), and take *olim* to mean not 'in days of old' but 'since long ago' (*OLD* 2a). For the ellipse '<men> from kindred peoples' see Hofmann–Szantyr (1965), 411 and Goodyear (1981), 382.

III. *ANN.* 12.5.1

(Claudius' decision to marry Agrippina was unprecedented); quin et incestum ac, si sperneretur, ne in malum publicum erumperet metuebatur.

It is far from clear what subject we are to assume for *sperneretur*, and editorial explanations of the phrase presuppose an unacceptable degree of authorial confusion of thought and expression (which is not the same thing as 'Tacitean brevity'). I propose to provide one by *<mos> sperneretur*. What is referred to is the convention of refraining from marrying a niece; Vitellius in ch. 6.3 defends the proposed marriage by claiming *morem accommodari prout conducat*, and Paulus, *Digest* 23.2.39 states *siquis ex his quas moribus prohibemur uxores ducere duxerit incestum dicitur committere.* Now the subject of *erumperet* will be *mos spretus*.

IV. *ANN.* 12.65.2

(Narcissus argues against the intrigues of Britannicus' stepmother Agrippina that) nouercae insidiis domum omnem conuelli. maiore flagitio quam si impudicitiam prioris coniugis reticuisset.

To say that Agrippina's intrigues were a greater outrage than the possibility that Narcissus could have kept silent about Messalina's adultery seems to constitute an illogical association of two items on very different footings. Therefore I propose *flagitio <transmissis silentio>*, words which could easily have been omitted because of homoeoteleuton. Now Narcissus says that staying silent about Agrippina's intrigues is worse than it would have been to suppress Messalina's adultery. As the honorand points out to me, Tacitus elsewhere says *silentio transmittere* in that order, but here he would have wanted to avoid *flagiTIO silenTIO*.

V. *ANN.* 14.61.3

(Poppaea, frightened by popular support for Octavia, argues) arma illa aduersus principem sumpta; ducem tantum defuisse, qui motis rebus facile reperiretur, omitteret modo Campaniam.

Since the leader intended is Octavia herself, now banished to Campania and the subject of *omitteret, qui* should surely be *quae;* mutatis mutandis one may compare *Agricola* 31.3, *femina duce* (Boadicea).

VI. *ANN.* 15.63.3

(On the point of committing suicide Seneca) aduocatis scriptoribus pleraque tradidit, quae in uulgus edita eius uerbis inuertere supersedeo.

This sentence shows two problems. The honorand in his translation of the *Annals* renders 'which, issued to the public in his version, I forbear to convert', and notes 'How else could Seneca's final utterances have been issued to the public except "in his version" (lit. "in his words", *eius uerbis*)? As transmitted, T.'s statement . . . is extremely odd. Hartman proposed *meis* for *eius* ("which, issued to the public, I forbear to convert in my own version/words")' (Woodman (2004), 335 n. 89). Hartman (1905), 259 argues that if *eius* were meant to

contrast with *inuertere supersedeo*, it should have been *ipsius*, and compares
67.3, where in reporting the retort of Subrius Flavus to Nero, Tacitus says *ipsa
rettuli uerba, quia non, ut Senecae, uulgata erant*. All this is acute, but perhaps
pushes a bit too hard. However, the other problem, namely the use of
inuertere, seems greater to me. The only parallel generally quoted for this
sense is Manilius 2.898, where Manilius is talking about one of the temples of
the dodecatropos and Housman emends the text to read thus:

> Daemonien memorant Grai, Romana per ora
> quaeritur inuersus titulus

(*inuersu* or *in uersu* codd.), 'a rendering of the name in Roman speech is
wanting' (Goold). Housman notes:

uertere et *conuertere* sic uulgo ponebant...; *inuertere* non plane dissimili modo
usurpauit Tacitus ann. xv 63 7 *scriptoribus...supersedeo*, id est paraphrasi uertere.

There are three comments to be made on this. First, as Housman admits,
the parallel is not exact. Second, one cannot but be uneasy if a 'parallel' is used
to buttress a conjecture, and then the conjecture turns out to be the only
support for the 'parallel'. Thirdly, one must raise the question whether the
conjecture is correct. It would seem to me much preferable to emend in
accordance with attested usage by reading *hinc uersus*, 'a name translated
from this' (i.e. from Daemonie); on the difficulty of translating into Latin see
Housman on 887. Just to anticipate a possible objection I should perhaps
mention the manuscript reading at Varro, *De Lingua Latina* 7.82. There Varro
reports that Euripides (in a passage no longer extant) gave the obvious
etymology for the name Andromache, but

> Hoc Ennii quis potest intellegere inuersum significare
> 'Andromachae nomen qui indidit recte dedit'?

(This is Tragedies fr. 99 Jocelyn.) Though Goetz-Schoell and Jocelyn maintain
the transmitted text, clearly one has to emend with L. Spengel to *Ennium*, but
all editors also adopt Turnebus' emendation *in uersu* ('who can understand
that this is what Ennius means in the verse "Andromachae..."', R. G. Kent in
the Loeb edition), comparing ibid. 88, where Varro quotes a line of Pacuvius,
alcyonis ritu litus peruolgans feror, and comments *quod est in uersu 'alcyonis
ritu', id est eius instituto* ('as for the expression *alcyonis ritu* "in halcyon
fashion" in the verse, this means "according to the habit of that bird"', Kent).

Apart from these problems the verb in the Tacitean context is singularly
unhappy because *inuertere uerba* means, as it should, to turn words upside
down, 'to cause words to convey (by irony, etc.) the opposite sense' (so *OLD*,

s.v. *inuerto* 2c, where Apul. *Apol.* 72 may be added; cf. ibid. *inuersio* 2 'the use of words to convey something other than their overt meaning'). The sense 'paraphrase' desired in Tacitus is conveyed by *uertere* at Quint. 1.9.2, 10.5.5, who also uses *conuersio* in a similar sense (10.5.4). It is true that we do not here have the exact combination *inuertere uerba* because Tacitus is distinguishing between oral and written record, but the notion of verbalization is still strong enough to cause severe discomfort.

It remains for consideration whether *inuertere* could be used simply in the sense 'change, alter (into something else)', as *OLD*, 3a has it (cf. Woodman's 'CONvert'). Between them *OLD* and *TLL* quote the following alleged classical instances:

(1) Val. Flac. 7.547–48:   uos mihi nunc primum in flammas inuertite, tauri,
                            acquora, nunc totas aperite et uoluite flammas.

Here, in an unusual display of unanimity, all modern editors (Courtney, Ehlers, Liberman, Taliercio, Stadler, Perutelli, Spaltenstein, Caviglia; Soubiran leaves the word in the text but expresses grave doubts in his note) agree that the first *flammas* is corrupt, and, however the text is to be emended, it looks as if *inuertite* means literally 'turn upside down' (Virg. *Georg.* 1.64: *solum . . .* | *fortes inuertant tauri*).

(2) Celsus 2.8.34:   si tormina . . . inuersa sunt uel in aquam intercutem uel intesti-
                     norum leuitatem.

The variant *uersa* of manuscript J, noted in *TLL*, has lost stemmatic weight since the discovery of its congener, the Toledo manuscript, which G. Serbat in the Budé edition reports to read *inuersa*. Nevertheless *uersa* is right; it is Celsus' normal way of talking about a shift of one malady into another (nine times, according to the word index of Richardson (1982)), whereas he nowhere else uses *inuertere* in any sense.

(3) *Laus Pisonis* 146:   ipsa uices natura subit uariataque cursus
                          ordinat, inuersis et frondibus explicat annum.

The one source of the text here, the edition of Sichardus (1572), based on a now lost Lorsch manuscript, reads as above, but many editors have found this difficult to explain; the best, but inadequate, defence rests on Hor. *Sat.* 1.1.36: *inuersum contristat Aquarius annum* and Manil. 3.479: *annique inuertitur orbis*. Other editors, rightly in my judgement, have accepted the emendation of J. A. Martyni-Laguna *frontibus*, put forward in Wernsdorf's *Poetae Latini Minores*, vol. 3 p. 252 in Lemaire's 1824 reprint, but not, I think, rightly understood by its own author; it is a metaphor from the faces of reversible theatrical scenery (see Virg. *Geo.* 3.24 *scaena ut uersis discedat frontibus,*

Vitruv. 5.6.8). The backdrop of one season is replaced by that of another. I had written the above before I saw the edition of Di Brazzano (2004), who in a footnote on p. 289 refers to the passage of Virgil, but without connecting it with the interpretation of the passage.

(4) Sil. It. *Pun.* 16.568:   serna albentis inuertere lanas | murice Gaetulo docta.

F. Spaltenstein in his commentary (1986–90) here remarks 'D'après le TLL, le changement que note "inuertere" va en general "in peius". Or, la teinture des étoffes est parfois décrite comme une operation repréhensible, parce qu'elle va contre l'ordre des choses; Silius peut y faire allusion avec ce verbe'. My discussions have, I hope, established that generalization is out of place, but Spaltenstein's observation perceptively catches a nuance in Silius.

This last passage then is an ineffective defence of *inuertere* in Tacitus, for one can hardly envisage that Tacitus would choose a word implying that his version would be inferior to Seneca's original words. So enough suspicion remains on the transmitted text to justify testing other options; as such an option I propose *edita eius uerbis in <mea> uertere*. Now we do have an antithesis which gives point to *eius*, and the similarity between *me-* and *ue-* could easily have caused an omission due to what Postgate called parablepsy.

VII. *ANN.* 15.65

(It is alleged that some of the Pisonian conspirators had decided that after Nero's assassination Piso too would be assassinated and power would be handed over to Seneca), quasi insontibus claritudine uirtutum ad summum fastigium delecto.

Insontibus is usually taken to mean 'by innocent men', as they would appear to be after assassinating Piso, which would suggest that they had not been part of his conspiracy to assassinate Nero. Many scholars have felt this to be beyond bounds difficult and demanding too much from the reader, but, at least palaeographically, better than their emendations would seem to be *insontibus <artibus>*. Seneca would be a good candidate for emperor because of his 'innocent pursuits and the brilliancy of his achievements', with an asyndeton; this is only a rough translation because both *artes* and *uirtutes* permit a wide semantic range. The honorand remarks to me that outside verse *insons* is applied only to persons, which does not seem to be a great problem in Tacitus.

16

The Great Escape: Tacitus on the Mutiny of the Usipi (*Agricola* 28)

Rhiannon Ash

One of the most peculiar and memorable passages from Tacitus' *Agricola* is his excursus on the mutinous adventures of a disaffected auxiliary cohort, consisting of men conscripted from the tribe of the Usipi. After murdering their centurions and hijacking three *liburnicae*, they successfully (but unintentionally) circumnavigate Britain, only to be reduced to cannibalism and for the survivors then to be captured and sold as slaves (*Agr.* 28). Clarke calls this extraordinary sequence 'the least civilized to find a place in the work'.[1] It certainly forms a lively hiatus between Agricola's sixth season of campaigning (*Agr.* 25–7) and the climactic campaign of Mons Graupius (*Agr.* 29–38), but while it is undeniably gripping, it also raises many questions. What is such a peculiar episode doing in the narrative at all? It does not, after all, trigger any consequences of tremendous strategic importance, and none of the protagonists is named or fleshed out in terms of characterization. Should we see it primarily as an intriguing diversion, or is something more at stake historiographically in Tacitus' inclusion of this sequence? And what is its relationship with the surrounding narrative, in which it seems to sit rather precariously, anchored by a loose chronological marker (*eadem aestate*) at the opening of the account?

These are central questions which can and should be asked about any digression in a continuous narrative. Yet this label 'digression' may not be

An earlier version of this paper was delivered to the research seminar at the University of Manchester, where the audience made many helpful suggestions for which I am most grateful. I would also like to thank the editors of this volume, both for the invitation to contribute and for their constructive comments. My most heartfelt thanks are reserved for Tony Woodman himself. This current paper cannot possibly do justice to his extraordinary kindness, patience, and generosity towards me and many others over the years, but I hope that he will enjoy it nonetheless.

[1] Clarke (2001), 110.

quite right for the mutiny of the Usipi. After all, Tacitus does not apologetically or formally signal, either at the beginning or end of the chapter, that he is departing from or returning to the main narrative. As various scholars have observed, digressions in ancient historiography are often signalled by certain set formulae. So Sallust declares *nunc ad inceptum redeo* (Sall. *BJ* 4.9), 'Now I am returning to the topic with which I started', when he closes his survey of moral decline in Rome, or *de Africa... satis dictum* (Sall. *BJ* 19.8), 'Enough has been said about Africa', concluding his geographical and ethnographical survey of Africa.[2] Yet no such device is associated with the material at *Agricola* 28, which suggests that Tacitus wants us to consider the episode as an integrated part of the main narrative. There is another possibility to consider in assessing the potentially digressive status of the Usipi sequence. Emmett notes that the commonest way among Greek and Roman historians to denote a digression is not the introductory or concluding formula, but a 'syntactic device', either a back-reference to an earlier point in the narrative (e.g. Tac. *Hist.* 5.11.1, *uti diximus*) or a connecting word such as *itaque, sed,* or *at* (e.g. Tac. *Ann.* 4.67.3, where *sed* follows the digression on Capri).[3] Again, there is no such syntactic device in or near *Agr.* 28, so it seems misleading to call it a 'digression'.

In addition, we can quickly see some intriguing points of verbal and thematic contact with the broader narrative, suggesting that the placement and details of the episode are not arbitrary. So, Agricola follows his victory at Mons Graupius by pointedly ordering the captain of his fleet to circumnavigate Britain (*Agr.* 38.3):[4]

ibi acceptis obsidibus praefecto classis <u>circumuehi Britanniam praecipit</u>. datae ad id uires, et praecesserat terror. ipse peditem atque equites lento itinere, quo nouarum gentium animi ipsa transitus mora terrerentur, in hibernis locauit. et simul classis secunda tempestate ac fama Trucculensem portum tenuit, unde proximo Britanniae latere praelecto omnis redierat.

[2] On Sall. *BJ* 4.9, see Wiedemann (1979) and cf. Tac. *Ann.* 4.33.4. See too *nunc ad rem redeo* (Sall. *BJ* 79.10, closing the digression about the Philaeni brothers), and *haud fuerit absurdum tradere* (Tac. *Ann.* 4.65.1, opening a digression about the Caelian hill). Martin–Woodman (1989), 238–9 gather other instances of such formulae in Tacitus and discuss their significance. See too Woodman (1983), 162 on Vell. 2.68.5 and Hahn (1933).

[3] Emmett (1981), 28.

[4] Whether or not this celebratory circumnavigation really happened has prompted much debate about Tacitus' geography. So, Hind (1974) proposes *Tunocelensem portum* (i.e. the port at *Tunocelum*, possibly near Moresby in Cumbria) instead of *Trucculensem portum* (otherwise unknown) at *Agr.* 38.4, concluding as a result that Agricola's circumnavigation did take place. The precise location of *Trucculensis portus* is impossible to pin down, but Agricola's instructions clearly demand our attention. See further Birley (2005), 90 and Wolfson (2008), 35–46.

There [i.e. the territory of the Boresti],[5] after hostages were taken, Agricola instructed the captain of the fleet to sail around the north of Britain. Forces were assigned for that purpose, and panic had preceded them. Agricola himself led his infantry and cavalry by a slow march, in order that the feelings of the newly conquered tribes might be terrified by the very leisureliness of his progress, and settled them in winter-quarters. At the same time the fleet, accompanied by favourable weather and reputation, reached the harbour of Trucculum, from where [it had started and] after sailing along the adjacent coast of Britain [to where] it had returned intact.

This ostentatious move seems to express a sense of rivalry and one-upmanship with the more haphazard circumnavigation achieved by the mutinous Usipi. However, the very fact that the rebellious auxiliaries manage the feat first seems to diminish Agricola's own glory. Indeed, this muting effect becomes even more conspicuous because before this point Tacitus regularly includes a eulogizing theme whereby Agricola does things first, in the manner of an ideal general.[6] The circumnavigation of Britain at least is one area where Agricola was beaten to it.[7]

There are signs too that Tacitus intended us to make precisely this sort of comparison. So, Tacitus' phrase *circumuehi Britanniam* (*Agr.* 38.4) in relation to Agricola's instructions must surely echo the closural expression *circumuecti Britanniam* (*Agr.* 28.3) in the earlier narrative of the mutiny of the Usipi. The close intratextual relationship of these two passages is further suggested because *Britannia* and *circumuehor* are juxtaposed only twice in the *Agricola*. It is also pointed that Tacitus early on triggers the 'dialogue' by the controversial claim (*Agr.* 10.4): *hanc oram nouissimi maris tunc primum Romana classis circumuecta insulam esse Britanniam affirmauit*, 'It was then for the first

---

[5] The ontological status of these people is contentious: Ogilvie and Richmond (1967), 282 say that they are 'wholly unknown'. Birley (2005), 90 rejects their existence. See further Wolfson (2008), 65–73.

[6] Cf. four instances of Agricola doing things first: *tum primum perdomita est* (*Agr.* 10.1), *hanc oram... tunc primum Romana classis circumuecta* (*Agr.* 10.5), *naue prima transgressus* (*Agr.* 24.1), and *quae ab Agricola primum adsumpta* (*Agr.* 25.1). Also, Julius Caesar entered Britain with an army, *primus omnium Romanorum* (*Agr.* 13.1). Cf. a similar motif in Curtius Rufus' portrayal of Alexander the Great (5.6.14, 5.7.5, 7.9.5, 8.11.8, 8.11.11, 9.2.29). Plin. *NH* 7.191–215 (with Beagon (2005), 416–72) offers a wide-ranging catalogue of discoverers in various spheres. It is also an agonistic motif amongst writers in a variety of genres (Volk (2002), 114 n. 119).

[7] One relevant passage is Quintilian's example of Julius Caesar deliberating whether to attack Britain, which also involves considering whether the country is an island: *an Britannia insula (nam tum ignorabatur)* (7.4.2). The implication is that by the time Quintilian produced the *Institutio Oratoria* (written and published probably before Domitian's death in AD 96), Britain's status as an island was secure, although even before Agricola's activities, people had certainly suspected that it was an island (Ogilvie and Richmond (1967), 171). Dio 39.50.3 credits Agricola as the first to prove clearly that Britain was an island.

time that a Roman fleet sailed around this coast of the remotest sea and
confirmed that Britain was an island'. A trio of verbal echoes, then, prompts
Tacitus' readers to evaluate Agricola's achievement in being the first successfully to circumnavigate the island in the context of the strange events associated with the Usipi.[8]

Another point of contact with the subsequent narrative suggests that the
story's inclusion has been carefully considered. Even before the battle of Mons
Graupius, the exploits of the Usipi feature as an important and emotive
reference point. So Calgacus uses the Usipi as an *exemplum* in his rousing
pre-battle harangue, telling his men that *tam deserent illos ceteri Germani,
quam nuper Usipi reliquerunt* (*Agr.* 32.3), 'The other Germans will abandon
them, just as the Usipi recently deserted them'.[9] Naturally, Calgacus is selective
in his colouring of the episode: the whole *raison d'être* for the *exemplum* is to
show the capacity of auxiliaries to desert Rome, not to demonstrate the
extraordinary human instinct for survival, apparently the keynote of the
episode related by Tacitus at *Agricola* 28. Perhaps Calgacus' succinct retroac-
tive reference might even make us suspicious that Tacitus has strategically
incorporated the whole story of the Usipi shortly before this speech just to
prepare the ground for the *exemplum*.[10] That is certainly one purpose of the
episode, but as we will see, it is only one of many roles it plays in the *Agricola*.

TEXT: TACITUS *AGRICOLA* 28

Let us turn now to the dramatic narrative itself:

[1] eadem aestate cohors Usiporum per Germanias conscripta et in Britanniam
transmissa magnum ac memorabile facinus ausa est. occiso centurione ac militibus,
qui ad tradendam disciplinam immixti manipulis exemplum et rectores habebantur,
tres liburnicas adactis per uim gubernatoribus ascendere; et uno †remigante† suspec-
tis duobus eoque interfectis, nondum uulgato rumore ut miraculum praeuehebantur.

---

[8] Clarke (2001), 110 highlights the interconnectedness of these three passages.

[9] In narrating Boudicca's revolt, Tacitus similarly constructs a catalogue of grievances
discussed amongst the Britons, who again look to the precedent of German rebellions as an
incentive to take action (*sic Germanias excussisse iugum, Agr.* 15.3, an allusion to Arminius'
defeat of Varus).

[10] Provided that we accept a publication date for the *Agricola* of AD 98, we can at least say that
Tacitus did not concoct the entire story. There were at least three other accounts of this famous
mutiny. Before Tacitus, one account (not extant and author unknown) was drawn on by the
poet Pompullus (Martial 6.61). We also have Cassius Dio's later version (66.20), with intriguing
differences from Tacitus' account.

[2] mox <ubi> ad aquam atque ut<ensi>ilia rapt<um ex>isse<nt>, cum plerisque Britannorum sua defensantium proelio congressi ac saepe uictores, aliquando pulsi, eo ad extremum inopiae uenere, ut infirmissimos suorum, mox sorte ductos uescerentur. [3] atque ita circumuecti Britanniam, amissis per inscitiam regendi nauibus, pro praedonibus habiti, primum a Suebis, mox a Frisiis intercepti sunt. ac fuere quos per commercia uenumdatos et in nostram usque ripam mutatione ementium adductos indicium tanti casus illustrauit.[11]

During the same summer a cohort of Usipi, having been conscripted in Germany and sent across into Britain, dared to carry out a great and memorable deed. After killing their centurion and those soldiers who, in order to instil a sense of discipline, had been joined to their units and were serving as models and guides, the Usipi boarded three galleys, having violently coerced the helmsmen. They had only one †helmsman steering†, since they had become suspicious of the other two and killed them, and since the rumour of what had happened had not yet been bandied about, they sailed along causing surprise. Soon, when they disembarked to get water and supplies, they fought at close quarters with various Britons who were defending their own possessions, and they often won, even if they suffered some defeats, but eventually they reached such an extreme point of deprivation that first, the weakest of their group, then those selected by lot were what they were eating. In this way, they sailed around Britain, but after losing their ships from lack of skill in controlling them, they were regarded as pirates and captured, first by the Suebi, then by the Frisii. There were some who were sold as slaves, and after passing into the hands of one buyer after another, they reached our bank of the river Rhine. Their disclosure of such a momentous adventure brought them into the limelight.

This is indeed a curious tale, a skeletal version of something one might expect to find narrated much more lavishly in a different genre, say, the ancient novel.[12] Judging from Tacitus' later historical narratives about military rebellion, we might have assumed that this account would unambiguously manifest stern authorial condemnation of an auxiliary cohort which killed its

---

[11] The Latin text is from Delz (1983). Burn (1968), 315 offers the engaging (but unprovable) observation that several passages in the *Agricola* (including the mutiny of the Usipi) showing signs of textual corruption come at the most interesting point in the story, 'as if the archetype of all our manuscripts had been much "thumbed" and worn exactly there'.

[12] For another sequence from ancient historiography which likewise seems to recall the world of the ancient novel, see Livy 39.9–14 (with Scafuro (1989)), the story of Publius Aebutius and the prostitute Hispala. One particularly intriguing area of cross-fertilization in a later context involves the *boukoloi*, outlaw herdsmen from the Egyptian Delta in AD 171, who disguise themselves as women, murder a centurion, eat his entrails, and trigger a revolt (Cassius Dio 72.4). Similar semi-barbarous *boukoloi* also feature in Achilles Tatius *Cleitophon and Leucippe* 3.9–22, Xenophon of Ephesus *Ephesiaka* 3.12, and Heliodorus *Aithiopika* 2.17–20. See Rutherford (2000), with further bibliography. I owe these parallels involving the *boukoloi* to Tim Cornell. Given the prevalence of shipwreck scenes in the ancient novel (Whitehouse (1985)), there may be scope for detecting cross-fertilization of genres in Tacitus' version of the spectacular 'collapsing ship' sequence in the run-up to Agrippina's death (*Ann.* 14.1–7).

commanding officers and stole three *liburnicae*. That expectation seems even more plausible given that the supreme commander undermined by the mutiny was Agricola himself, whose biography Tacitus characterizes as a *professio pietatis* (*Agr.* 3.3) for that man.[13] We can compare the start of the Batavian revolt, when the rebels switch sides during a naval battle and kill their helmsmen and centurions. Tacitus robustly denounces conduct explicitly labelled *improuisa proditio* and *perfidia* (*Hist.* 4.16.3):

nec diu certato Tungrorum cohors signa ad Ciuilem transtulit, perculsique milites improuisa proditione a sociis hostibusque caedebantur. eadem etiam in nauibus perfidia.

Soon after the battle began, a Tungrian cohort deserted to Civilis, and the Romans were so startled by this unexpected treachery that they were being cut to pieces by a combined force of their allies and their enemies. There was the same treachery as well on the ships.

Yet such vocabulary of treachery is conspicuously absent[14] from his version of the Usipian mutiny, despite what we might expect. While it is true that Tacitus initially dubs the episode a *facinus*, which could be taken pejoratively, this is a word which he can and does use in its earlier neutral sense of 'deed' (*OLD* 1), rather than 'misdeed' (*OLD* 2).[15] In such cases, the precise shade of meaning for *facinus* (positive or negative) is usually determined by modifying adjectives, but here the addition of *magnum ac memorabile*[16] is hardly conclusive, since 'great and memorable' could allow the moral pendulum to swing in

---

[13] However, on the pitfalls of extrapolating Tacitus' general opinions from his narratives, see Luce (1986), who argues that the impact of individual historical circumstances at a particular time and place should caution against the practice of extracting timeless, all-purpose Tacitean opinions from the text.

[14] A phrase formulated by Lord John Russell in 1859 and inspired by Tac. *Ann.* 3.76.2 (Mellor (1993), 133, 186 n. 98).

[15] See Gerber and Greef (1904), 439.

[16] There are examples of this alliterative combination of adjectives in other authors (Ter. *Heaut.* 314, Livy 39.51.10, Livy fr. 60 = Sen. *Suas.* 6.22, Virg. *Aen.* 4.94, Ov. *Met.* 10.608, Vell. 2.33, and Luc. 4.496). Perhaps the most provocative association is with Sallust's *egregium atque memorabile facinus* (*BJ* 79.1), opening the digression on the heroic self-sacrifice of the Carthaginian Philaeni brothers, another episode which runs counter to readers' expectations, as representatives of a society which was the traditional enemy of Rome engage in exemplary and altruistic conduct. For *facinus* + *memorabile* see Sall. *Cat.* 4.4, Tac. *Hist.* 1.44.2, Livy 23.7.6, 24.22.16, 40.40.9, and Apuleius *Met.* 8.22. As John Briscoe points out to me, what is striking is that Tacitus uses *memorabilis* very selectively (again only at *Hist.* 1.44.2), while Livy uses it no fewer than 63 times, largely with *agere*, *facere*, and *gerere* to indicate that a magistrate achieved nothing of importance in his province. I am also grateful to John Briscoe for drawing my attention to *facinus memorabile* at the opening of Livy 38.24.2–11 (Plut. *Mor.* 258d–f), another 'novelistic' sequence involving the dramatic story of Chiomara, the wife of the Gallic chieftain Ortiago (also separating two sets of battle narratives). See further Briscoe (2008), 94–5.

either direction to give a good or a bad sense to *facinus*. Similar ambiguity applies to the verb *ausa est*, since an act of daring can involve outrageous transgression or commendable bravery.[17] At the very least, we can see that Tacitus introduces the episode in ambiguous language and leaves open the possibility that his audience could take *magnum ac memorabile facinus* positively, or at least suspend judgement until the end of the episode.[18] However, even if a reader takes the phrase pejoratively, we will see that as the episode unfolds, it is not endorsed subsequently by decisive condemnation of the Usipi; quite the opposite.[19]

Furthermore, although no explicitly laudable motives are assigned to the auxiliaries to explain their actions, the opening assertion that they had first been conscripted in Germany and then transferred to serve in Britain is still suggestive. In another context, enforced conscription already features as a grievance before the revolt of Boudicca (*abstrahi liberos, iniungi dilectus, Agr.* 15.3), and it will appear again in the rebel Civilis' rousing speech before his revolt: there, a process which is already *suapte natura grauis* becomes unbearable as the old and weak are forced to purchase exemptions and the young and beautiful are dragged off to satisfy the soldiers' lusts (*Hist.* 4.14.2).[20] Without wishing to read too creatively between the lines, it seems that our unfortunate Usipi have been press-ganged to serve in the Roman army before promptly being taken overseas. Indeed, this conclusion is endorsed by the nature of their mutiny: they commandeer three *liburnicae*, presumably aiming to leave Britain by sea and get home,[21] rather than to trigger any further rebellion on British soil.[22] In this respect, Tacitus leaves it open for the reader to feel that

---

[17] e.g. *Saturninus . . . pessimum facinus audet* (Tac. *Hist.* 2.85.2, negative) and *ex quibus* (sc. *captiuis) unus egregius facinus ausus* (Tac. *Hist.* 4.34.2, positive).

[18] It may also be phrasing which helps to justify the presence of the sensational episode (dubbed *memorabile*) in the grand genre of historiography (*memoria rerum gestarum*).

[19] It is also unclear how far the frame of reference for *facinus* extends, whether to the story as a whole, or to a selected part of it. Does it point to the killing of Roman military personnel? Or to their act of cannibalism, transgressive, but handled in a way to earn our respect?

[20] See too *Agr.* 13.1, where Britons are said to tolerate conscription, but only *si iniuriae absint*, and Calgacus' speech, where children and kin *per dilectus alibi seruituri auferuntur* (*Agr.* 31.1).

[21] Where was home? The sources imply that the Usipi had undergone some localized migration. Caesar *BG* 4.1.1 says that he defeated them at the confluence of the Rhine and the Mosa, after they had been driven from their territory by the Suebi. By AD 14, they were apparently living east of the Rhine between the rivers Lippe and Issel near the Batavians (*Ann.* 1.51; cf. Dio 54.33.1, 54.32.2). They then headed south across the Lippe, and during Civilis' revolt, they assisted in attacking Mogontiacum in AD 70 (*Hist.* 4.37) and apparently lived east of the Rhine around the river Lahn. See Rives (1999), 252–4.

[22] It is noticeable that—despite the title of my paper—Tacitus avoids the pejorative language of Dio who describes the soldiers as στασιάζοντες (66.20). Nor does the fact that they hug the coast on their journey suggest that home was not their final destination: sailors in antiquity lacking sophisticated navigational aids probably liked to stay close to the coast, and anyway,

these men deserve some sympathy after experiencing the heavy-handed side of Roman imperialism. Elsewhere, we can see that Tacitus understands and respects passion for the homeland, whether Roman or non-Roman. So, when he argues that Germans must be an indigenous people, he offers as conclusive proof the fact that surely nobody else would tolerate such an unlovely landscape and harsh climate, *nisi si patria sit* (*Germ.* 2.2). The emotional pull of the homeland is taken for granted, even when that *patria* is cold, miserable, and pointedly inferior to temperate Italy.[23]

Another aspect of Tacitus' account supports this sympathetic reading, namely the fact that a number of Roman legionaries were posted to this unit to inculcate *disciplina* in the Usipi. Clearly, the military authorities, anticipating trouble because of the circumstances in which this auxiliary cohort had been created, had decided that the new recruits needed the presence of legionaries to serve either as role models or disciplinarians, depending on how events unfolded.[24] This is the context of Tacitus' reference to *disciplina*, which indicates that what the Usipi lacked was proper Roman military training and the capacity to obey military authority.[25] It does not mean that these men were fundamentally unruly or excessively ferocious by nature (as the stereotype of German barbarians might suggest).[26] Instead, it

these Usipi were not experienced mariners (cf. *amissis per inscitiam regendi nauibus, Agr.* 28.3). Besides, as Tacitus has already made clear, in Britain *nusquam latius dominari mare* (*Agr.* 10.6), so caution is sensible. On the peculiar nature of northern seas, see Murphy (2004a), 179–83.

[23] Tacitus is more sympathetic than Pliny the Elder, who after documenting the miserable lifestyle of the Chauci on the tidal mudflats, adds a sarcastic comment: *et hae gentes, si uincantur hodie a populo Romano, seruire se dicunt!* (*NH* 16.4). See further Sallman (1987), who suggests (120) that Pliny's exasperation is because the Chauci refused to embrace Roman culture.

[24] There is a curious reversal at *Hist.* 2.66, where legionaries of the XIV Gemina Martia Victrix, ardent supporters of the dead and defeated Otho, have foisted upon them some pro-Vitellian Batavian auxiliary cohorts to keep them in line.

[25] Phang (2008), 246 observes: 'The Roman authors did not believe that Gauls and Germans were by nature *incapable* of learning Roman ways. In fact, the most rapid path of assimilation for these groups was through service in the imperial army'. Yet that process of assimilation brought with it dangers, as former auxiliaries such as Arminius exploited their Roman military training to attack Romans. Phang (2008), 77–81 also discusses recruitment, *disciplina militaris*, and ethnic identity.

[26] Rives (1999) speculates from the Celtic origin of the name, the ties with tribes west of the Rhine, and the retreat under pressure from the Suebi that the Usipi were either Celtic in origin or Celticized. Such nuances were unlikely to undermine expectations raised by the German stereotype, particularly since Tacitus says that the cohort was conscripted *per Germanias* (*Agr.* 28.1). The Celtic aspect of the Usipi is preserved in the termination of their alternative name, Usipetes, the earlier form consistently used by Caesar in the *BG* (5 times) and once by Tacitus (*Ann.* 1.51.2). Other suggestive passages include Polybius 2.7.6–11 about some treacherous Gallic mercenaries who pillage Agrigentum during the First Punic War and plunder the temple of Venus at Eryx, which leads the Romans to put them on a ship and forbid them to return to Italy, and Pausanias 1.7.2 and Callimachus *Hymn to Delos* 171–90 about some treacherous Gallic

implies that they had not yet been sufficiently downtrodden to accept the ways of the Romans who had seized them against their will and forced them into military service. It is interesting too that although Dio 66.20 refers to the killing of centurions and a tribune, he gives no details about their function as watchdogs over these unwilling conscripts.

Indeed, some details of the subsequent adventure suggest that the Usipi were really quite enterprising, rational, and coordinated. So, it must have taken careful planning first to kill the centurion and the soldiers specifically assigned to keep order and then to dove-tail this move with the seizure of the three *liburnicae*. Whatever the solution to the textual crux *remigante*[27] (usually taken as a participle referring to one of the hijacked helmsmen), the Usipi clearly conducted their operations with sufficient speed and efficiency for their coastal journey to cause surprise (*nondum uulgato rumore ut miraculum praeuehebantur, Agr.* 28.1).[28] Rather a deft reflection of their competence is Tacitus' reversal of a familiar topos: elsewhere, the usual trope is for rumour or gossip to outstrip events on the ground, as for example in his formulation *pernicibus, ut assolet, nuntiis et tarda mole ciuilis belli* (*Hist.* 2.6.1), 'News travelled quickly, as it usually does, but the civil war moved slowly and laboriously'. Earlier instances of this motif can be seen in Caesar's assertion that *plerumque in nouitate rem fama antecedit* (*BC* 3.36.1), 'For the most part, in the case of something novel, rumour outstrips the event', or in the opening of one of Cicero's letters to his brother: *etsi non dubitabam, quin hanc epistulam multi nuntii, fama denique esset ipsa sua celeritate superatura . . .* (*Q.F.* 1.1.1), 'Although I have no doubt that many messengers, and indeed rumour itself with its usual rapidity, is likely to outstrip this letter . . .'.[29]

---

mercenaries banished by Ptolemy Philadelphus to an island in the Nile who resort to starvation and ritual suicide. I owe these references to Bryan Sitch.

[27] Ogilvie and Richmond (1967), 246 remind us that this word 'has been more emended than any other in the *Agricola* and may be corrupt'. The basic concern is that the verb *remigo* is not appropriate for the helmsman of a boat. Paton (1902) supports *remigante*; Illfe (1927) proposes *uno rem agente*; Spilman (1929) suggests *uno remigantium gubernante*; Lynch (1944) opts for *re negante*; and Baldwin (1970) comes full circle to reinstate *remigante* (and as a coda, makes the imaginative but fanciful suggestion (323) that the Usipi lost their ships because they had eaten the one surviving hapless helmsman).

[28] One could compare here the wonder stirred in Catullus' Nereids *monstrum . . . admirantes* (64.15), as they gaze at the Argo, the first ship to sail on the sea. Feeney (2007), 123 sees this as an important 'moment of rupture when the technology and ingenuity of human civilization first definitively smash the boundaries of nature ordained by God'.

[29] Writers regularly attribute speed to *fama* (Virg. *Aen.* 4.174 with Pease (1935), 211–14, Luc. 1.471, Curt. 4.1.24, Val. Flac. 2.124–5, Stat. *Theb.* 3.425–30).

Yet here the auxiliaries themselves travel more quickly than the *rumor* of their mutiny, which is left lagging behind.[30]

Two other factors powerfully suggest Usipian efficiency and coordination. First, as they progress along the coast, they disembark explicitly in order to acquire water and supplies (*ad aquam atque ut<ensi>ilia rapt<um>*, *Agr.* 28.2). This is a surprisingly utilitarian and modest objective, given that German barbarians are so often pejoratively cast as unable to resist the opportunity to plunder. Although *raptum* momentarily evokes that familiar stereotype, the practical focus of their raid (water and supplies) simultaneously pulls against that negative image.[31] Secondly, there is the response of the Usipi to the ultimate crisis, when lack of food finally drives them to cannibalism. Both Tacitus' details and language are striking: *eo ad extremum inopiae uenere, ut infirmissimos suorum, mox sorte ductos uescerentur* (*Agr.* 28.2), 'they reached such an extreme point of deprivation that first, the weakest of their group, then those selected by lot were what they were eating'. This translation is a little awkward, but tries to reflect the shock value established by the word order, whereby the impact of *uescerentur* is intensified by its postponement until the end of the sentence.[32] Moreover, the ordered response of the Usipi to their desperate situation is conveyed by their process of selecting food (first the very weakest members of their group and then those unlucky enough to be chosen randomly by lot). It seems that in a tight spot, the practical Usipi have learned something of Roman *disciplina* after all. Tacitus' language is succinct and restrained, but still expressive: in ancient literature, cannibalism understandably often serves as a metaphor for inhumanity and as an indisputable marker of the 'other'.[33] There are many examples, but Homer offers a particularly memorable one, when Achilles forcefully rejects Hector's appeal in the face of death to be spared being eaten by dogs. Instead, after addressing Hector as a dog, Achilles says (*Il.* 22.346–7):

αἰ γάρ πως αὐτόν με μένος καὶ θυμὸς ἀνείη
ὤμ' ἀποταμνόμενον κρέα ἔδμεναι, οἷά μ' ἔοργας

I wish I could eat you myself, that the fury in my heart would drive me to cut you in pieces and eat your flesh raw, for all that you have done to me.

---

[30] This is also a motif associated with the ideal general: see Woodman (1977), 269–70 on the related topos of 'winning before they knew they were at war'.

[31] See Woodman–Martin (1996), 202–3, Oakley, *Comm.* I.634.

[32] Tacitus subsequently uses the verb selectively and only in the *Annals* (*Ann.* 1.49.1, 4.59.1, 13.16.1).

[33] For cannibalism indicating inhumanity, see Tacitus *Hist.* 4.42.2, Amm. Marc. 31.2.15, with Wiedemann (1983); and for cannibalism marking the 'other', see Hdt. 3.38, 4.26, and 4.106. It was a charge often directed against the early Christians and associated with human sacrifice: see McGowan (1994) and Rives (1995).

Here, Achilles' shocking wish expressively marks the inhumanity to which war has reduced him.[34] Yet Tacitus seems to depict a different type of cannibalism which does not straightforwardly reflect the inhumanity of the Usipi or accentuate their identity as 'other': so, his superlative *infirmissimos*[35] hints at horrified acceptance that, if they must indulge in anthropophagy to survive, then at least they can try to restrict the scale of transgression by choosing people who are near death in any case.[36] Then, after circumstances fail to improve, their decision to draw lots suggests a further effort to depersonalize their enforced participation in breaking the ultimate taboo. Whether the individual Usipi have to eat, or be eaten, drawing lots means that the roles are assigned by fate.[37] Although Stewart suggests that transgressive eating habits are often associated with the British Isles,[38] this case of reluctant cannibalism amongst the Usipi is unusual: they eat human flesh only because they have no other choice. Their conduct can be read in a similar way to depictions of cannibalism during the deprivations of a siege. In this context, we can recall Rankin's arguments that defending cannibalism perhaps constituted a challenging rhetorical exercise for budding orators: 'particularly persuasive to Romans as a justification for anthropophagy would be the stress of siege'.[39] Of course, the Usipi are not under siege, but their *inopia* could be thought of as some kind of an equivalent.

[34] The motif also features in various similes and in connexion with Hera (*Il.* 4.34–6) and (memorably) Hecuba, who echoes Achilles' wish in her express desire to eat her son's killer raw (*Il.* 24.213–14). See further O'Brien (1990-1), 106: 'The lust for raw-eating or *omophagia* . . . is the epic's primary image of moral degeneration'.

[35] Tacitus uses this superlative form selectively, only appearing once more in his extant work (*Germ.* 15.1).

[36] Cf. Critognatus' suggestion at the siege of Alesia that they should eat the bodies of the elderly, *qui aetate ad bellum inutiles uidebantur* (Caes. *BG* 7.77.12).

[37] Cf. Lord Byron's unfinished poem, *Don Juan* (1819–23), where Don Juan's ship sinks and he and the crew are cast adrift in a small boat. The second canto vividly describes how eventually the desperate men draw lots to select one of their number to be eaten. Joseph Conrad presents a different scenario in his short novel *Falk: A Reminiscence* (1903), where those cast adrift on a broken-down ship reject the drawing of lots, but eventually engage in a warped Darwinian game of 'survival of the fittest' which culminates in a particularly disturbing kind of cannibalism.

[38] Stewart (1995), 2. See too Str. 4.5.4 on Ireland.

[39] Rankin (1969), 384. See Thuc. 2.70.1, Sall. *Hist.* 3.87, Caes. *BG* 7.77, Livy 23.29.13, Val. Max. 7.6 ext. 1–2, ext. 3, Josephus *BJ* 6.3.4, [Quintilian] *Decl.* 12, App. *Ib.* 96.416, *Bell. Mith.* 38, Juvenal 15.93–126, Florus 1.34.14, 2.10.9, Orosius 5.23.14, and Garnsey (1988), 28–9. Elsewhere, Tacitus depicts Roman soldiers undergoing the rigours of a siege at Vetera and forced to eat *iumenta, equi, uirgulta, stirpes,* and *herbae,* although they resist eating one another (*Hist.* 4.60); and Germanicus' shipwrecked soldiers are reduced to eating the *corpora equorum* (*Ann.* 2.24.2). Cf. Alexander's starving Macedonian soldiers in Cedrosia, who resort to eating *radices palmarum, iumenta,* and *equi* (Curt. 9.10.11–12). Memorable later examples of the besieged resorting to cannibalism include the Siege of Maarat in 1098 (Asbridge 2004) and the Siege of Leningrad (9 Sept. 1941 to 18 Jan. 1943). Kirschenbaum (2006), 238–44 discusses the accusations

Other aspects of the narrative may be designed to elicit our sympathy for these men. So, Tacitus offers an intriguing point of contrast with the Usipi in his later portrait of Germanicus' army after the disastrous storm which wrecked the fleet in AD 15. Some soldiers were swept all the way to Britain, and returned with miraculous tales of fantastic things they had seen there: *uim turbinum et inauditas uolucres, monstra maris, ambiguas hominum et beluarum formas* (*Ann.* 2.24.4), 'the violence of whirlwinds, unheard-of birds, monsters of the sea, shapes halfway between men and beasts'. In comparison with these credulous Roman soldiers and their extraordinary stories, those Usipi who live to tell their tale retain dignity by showing relative restraint in narrating their experiences. They pointedly do not indulge in stories of fantastic birds or sea-monsters (at least in Tacitus' version), and there is no equivalent to his wary coda to the episode about Germanicus' soldiers: *uisa siue ex metu credita*, 'perhaps they had actually seen such things, or else their fear made them believe they had done so' (*Ann.* 2.24.4). We can also compare here the level-headed self-censorship of Tacitus at the end of the *Germania* when he reaches the Hellusii and Oxiones, who apparently have human faces and features, but the bodies and limbs of beasts. Such things he deems *fabulosa* (*Germ.* 46.6) and therefore outside the bounds of his own investigation.[40] There is certainly some common ground between Tacitus' rational persona as narrator at the end of the *Germania* and the measured self-control exercised by the Usipi in disclosing their story. In this context, Tacitus' language at the end of the passage is also striking: *fuere quos... indicium tanti casus illustrauit* (*Agr.* 28.3), 'There were those whom disclosure of such a momentous adventure brought into the limelight'. The choice of *indicium* (*OLD* 1), 'disclosure', which perhaps retains some hint of its association with the law courts, is a more grounded and unsensational way to describe their account than many alternatives would have been: think about the tone if Tacitus had used an alternative such as *fabula*, for instance.[41] And where Germanicus' soldiers are said to describe *miracula* (*Ann.* 2.24.4), the

---

of cannibalism surrounding this siege. Threatened or realized cannibalism amongst those adrift on the sea also recurs memorably, for instance during the wreck of the *Dumaru* during the First World War (Thomas 1931).

[40] There is a similar tone when Tacitus disapproves of earlier writers on Britain who embellished unestablished facts with undue eloquence in a bid to enhance his own *rerum fide* (*Agr.* 10.1). Tacitus is always sensitive to such boundaries between truth and fiction and often treats them in a nuanced way. See Woodman (1992), 186 = (1998), 185 on Tacitus' pointed adoption of the narrative persona of a paradoxographer at *Ann.* 15.37 as an apt move in describing the worst aspects of Nero's transformation of Rome into an alien capital.

[41] Petronius has Trimalchio in his miniaturized autobiography draw attention to the rich potential of shipwrecks to provide material for embellished or even fictionalized narratives: *omnes naues naufragarunt, factum, non fabula* (*Sat.* 76.4).

Usipi themselves appear *ut miraculum* (*Agr.* 28.1), rather than such language being applied to their story. In addition, the metaphor of light contained in the verb *illustro* is another way in which dignity is added to these particular storytellers. As Lendon notes, it is striking how many 'honour' words in Latin (e.g. *claritas, claritudo, splendor, illustris*) deploy the metaphor of shining.[42] Finally, the narrative self-control of the Usipi seems more impressive, given Tacitus' emphasis elsewhere on the intensely oral nature of Germanic culture (*Germ.* 2.3).

By telling their story in a dignified way, then, these surviving Usipi emerge from Tacitus' narrative with some prestige. This much seems clear from a close reading of the passage. Yet the unusually positive portrait of the Usipi may have been further accentuated for readers aware of their story from pre-existing pejorative sources, against which Tacitus seems to pull. So, Martial preserves some sense of the perceived capriciousness of the Usipi in one epigram, published perhaps in December AD 91 (seven years before the *Agricola*).[43] Broadly speaking, this epigram is about poetics, and shows Martial responding to the recently published work of his fellow poet Pompullus (otherwise unknown): although he deems the poems *ingeniosa* and *docta*, they lack the necessary genius to secure immortality. The epigram (6.61) takes the form of a conversation between Martial (apparently adopting rather a gauchely enthusiastic persona for the occasion), and his wealthy friend and patron Faustinus, himself a poet, and here characterized as a stern interlocutor:

> rem factam Pompullus habet, Faustine: legetur
>   et nomen toto sparget in orbe suum.
> 'sic leue flauorum ualeat genus Usiporum,
>   quisquis et Ausonium non amat imperium.'
> ingeniosa tamen Pompulli scripta feruntur.
>   'sed famae non est hoc, mihi crede, satis:
> quam multi tineas pascunt blattasque diserti,
>   et redimunt soli carmina docta coci!
> nescio quid plus est, quod donat saecula chartis:
>   uicturus genium debet habere liber.'

[M] Pompullus has made it, Faustinus. He will be read and scatter his name all over the world.

---

[42] Lendon (1997), 274. The verb *illustro* appears only here in the *Agr.*, but the adjective *illustris* is twice associated with Agricola himself, *uetere et illustri colonia . . . ortus* (*Agr.* 4.1) and awarded the *illustris statuae honorem* (*Agr.* 40.1).

[43] On this epigram more generally, see Spisak (1994). Sullivan (1991), 37 dates Book 6 to December AD 91.

[F] 'So may the fickle race of the yellow-haired Usipi prosper and whoever does not love Ausonia's empire!'

[M] And yet Pompullus' work is said to have talent.

[F] 'But believe me, that is not enough to make him famous. How many good poets are food for moths and bookworms, and only cooks buy their accomplished verses! There is something more that gives centuries to paper. A book that is to live must have genius.'

After Martial's breezy opening expression of confidence that Pompullus has now secured immortality through his excellent poetry, Faustinus forcefully suggests that he is wrong. His formulation, rather tricky and elusive, involves the wish that 'the fickle race of the yellow-haired Usipi . . . and whoever does not love Ausonia's empire' should prosper in exactly the same way as Pompullus' poetry. The obviously negative protagonists introduced and the ironizing analogy drawn with Pompullus' poetry show that Faustinus confidently predicts the exact opposite of Martial, namely that Pompullus' poetry will *not* survive. Whether the 'fickle Usipi' had any special relevance to Pompullus' poetry is impossible to say, although it is tempting to speculate that they may even have featured as subject matter.[44] Yet it does seem that they must have been instantly recognizable to Martial's audience, since the 'shorthand' reference to the *leue . . . genus*, 'fickle . . . race' of the Usipi presupposes a people of some notoriety. Martial's formulation, apparently a succinct allusion to the treacherous desertion of Agricola's army in AD 83, suggests that the Usipi had become something of a byword for disloyalty.[45] If this reading is at all persuasive, it sheds an interesting light on Tacitus' version which, in comparison, is much more sympathetic to the Usipi and may actively play on his audience's expectations of a negative portrait of these mutineers.[46]

[44]   After a seminar presentation of this paper in Manchester, Tim Parkin raised the interesting possibility that the eating theme suggested by *pascunt* and *coci* may make us think of the cannibalistic eating of the Usipi.

[45]   The date of the mutiny is significant for determining the date of Domitian's war against the Chatti, since some scholars have suggested that it was during this conflict that the Usipi were annexed and enrolled as auxiliaries. Jones (1973) argues that the war was in fact undertaken in AD 82 and was virtually completed by the summer of AD 83 when Domitian adopted the title Germanicus. Evans (1975) questions this chronology in favour of AD 83 as the date for the war. Jones (1992), 128–31 reasserts his own alternative chronology, although it does not seem to have won many supporters. For a comprehensive survey of the war, see Strobel (1987).

[46]   It seems relevant that Tacitus draws a veil over what ultimately happened to the survivors. Ogilvie and Richmond (1967), 322 speculate that they met with a grim end: 'whether recognized or self-declared, they were presumably thoroughly interrogated and sentenced to death. The complete version of the facts must certainly have emerged at the official inquiry following recognition of the slaves as ex-recruits'. Tacitus' adventure story avoids the bathos of allowing harsh reality to intrude.

CONTEXT AND INTERPRETATION

If we accept this reading of *Agricola* 28 that Tacitus casts the Usipian mutineers in a relatively positive light, then we must also ask, why did Tacitus tell
the story in this way? What follows are four possible strategies for responding
to the episode: one is character-based, suggesting that the shape of the mutiny
narrative has a direct bearing on the portrayal of Agricola (although this
approach is not unproblematic); the second is a politicized reading, which
links the portrayal of the Usipi at *Agricola* 28 with Tacitus' hostile analysis of
Domitian more generally; the third develops Clarke's line of inquiry, which
reads the Usipi as manifesting the beneficial effects of the island environment
of Britain, particularly in the north; and the fourth returns to a factor raised
earlier in the paper about the entertainment value of the episode.

Ogilvie and Richmond offer an important critical response to the episode.
For them, it 'serves also to high-light the difficulties against which Agricola
had to contend'.[47] This may well be broadly true, but the narrative itself gives
no indication of Agricola's response, direct or indirect, or even that it unset-
tled him at all. In fact, the closest point of contact in the immediate narrative
is not with Agricola but with his over-confident army, described in the
previous chapter as *prompti post euentum ac magniloqui* (*Agr.* 27.1). As a
cautionary tale, the mutiny of the Usipi may problematize the bullish stance
of the soldiers, but it apparently has little bearing on Agricola himself. In
addition, the strategic consequences for the Romans of losing this auxiliary
cohort are apparently relatively insignificant, particularly when one considers
that a cohort usually contained about 480 men. This was a drop in the ocean,
given that Agricola had at his disposal the resources of four legions (normally
5,000–6,000 men each, plus auxiliary troops) and that at the battle of Mons
Graupius, the legionaries were kept entirely in reserve (*Agr.* 35.2).[48] In
addition, the emphasis in Tacitus' version is placed on the running battles
between the Britons and the Usipi along the coast—and however accidental

---

[47] Ogilvie and Richmond (1967), 245.

[48] A *liburnica* was usually manned by 60 rowers and carried 30 troops: as Ogilvie and
Richmond (1967), 246 point out, the Usipi presumably acted as their own rowers 'but even
so these three vessels could hardly have carried more than 400–450 men in all'. That speculative
figure suggests seriously overladen boats, with each vessel carrying an extra 45–60 men. Perhaps
the cohort of the Usipi was under strength. Even if Domitian had weakened the army in Britain
by diverting some men to participate in campaigns against the Chatti in AD 83, Agricola still had
at his disposal the resources of the *II Augusta*, *II Adiutrix*, *IX Hispana*, and *XX Valeria*. So, the
absence of one restive auxiliary cohort was hardly likely to have rocked the boat. See Ogilvie and
Richmond (1967), 76–9 and Birley (2005), 227–30 on the composition of Agricola's army.

and unplanned this eventuality might have been, surely it would only have *helped* the Roman cause to have the resources of the Britons stretched by such troublesome skirmishes. We can compare here *Histories* 2.14, where in AD 69 Otho's fleet supports his land campaign by threatening Gallia Narbonensis and successfully making several diversionary coastal raids.[49] In any case, if Tacitus had wanted to accentuate Agricola's difficulties, then he could have done a much better job, either by narrating the murders more emotively (perhaps by naming the centurion),[50] or by commenting directly on the inconvenience to the fleet of losing these three *liburnicae* just before embarking on their diversionary terror raids (*Agr.* 29.1), or indeed by relating Agricola's response to the incident. Yet Tacitus avoids such approaches, so the idea that the episode straightforwardly enhances Agricola's profile remains rather unsatisfactory, however overtly eulogistic the biography is as a whole.

More productive perhaps is to view the episode more broadly as one component of Tacitus' pervasive strategic assault on the martial achievements and legacy of Domitian. So, Tacitus acerbically claims the emperor's campaigns in Germany against the Chatti involve peoples *triumphati magis quam uicti* (*Germ.* 37.6), and he talks stridently in the same chapter about the enduring *Germanorum libertas* (*Germ.* 37.3).[51] This theme is certainly anticipated in the *Agricola*, where Tacitus highlights what he sees as the embarrassingly shallow posturing of Domitian's *falsum . . . triumphum* (*Agr.* 39.1) over the Germans and relays the notorious incident of the desperate emperor buying slaves resembling Germans for use in his triumph.[52] Whatever the truth of this damning story—almost identical to one told about Caligula (Suet. *Calig.* 47)—it was enthusiastically taken up by Tacitus' friend Pliny (*Paneg.* 16.3) and is certainly expressive of the intensity of Tacitus' own hostility to Domitian. Against this backdrop, the intractability of these short-lived Usipian auxiliaries is another eloquent reminder of the potential

---

[49] See Ash (2007a), 114: 'An intimidating Roman fleet can inspire fear (*Agr.* 25.2) or, at times, defiance, as in Calgacus' speech to the Britons (*imminente nobis classe Romana, Agr.* 30.1)'.

[50] Cf. Aulus Atticus, the prefect killed at Mons Graupius and named when Tacitus records the dead on both sides (*Agr.* 37.6). Naming the centurion would also have adhered to Caesar's practice in the *BG* of naming dead centurions: since Tacitus in the *Agricola* is heavily influenced by this work, it seems pointed that the centurion killed here remains nameless.

[51] Sallmann (1987), 123 even says that the purpose of the *Germania* 'is to disguise and to satirize Domitian's policy (the *Germania* thus being a parallel pamphlet to the *Agricola*)'. Rives (1999), 52–3 acknowledges that Tacitus in the *Germania* belittles Domitian's achievements, but resists seeing this as the main purpose of the work, particularly since his portrayal of the Chatti (the object of Domitian's campaigns) as the most formidable of Germanic tribes would better suit praise of Domitian. It is a paradox that interpretative readings of the *Germania* so often keep returning to Domitian, who is not even named once in the whole work.

[52] See further Strobel (1987), 433.

gulf between the mere appearance of conquest and the much more elusive reality of converting defeated enemies into a cooperative force within the empire.[53]

For some critics, Tacitus' rehabilitation of the Usipi is part of a broader dynamic in the *Agricola*, whereby liminal Britain, located as far away as possible from the corrupting influence of Rome at the centre, invigorates all those who find themselves on her shores and allows scope for acts of *uirtus* which the contemporary imperial system now regards with suspicion and hostility.[54] So, Clarke suggests that for the Usipi, the wholesome environment of Britain allows 'the recapturing of a *libertas* which had now been lost in their native Germany'.[55] This is true up to a point; but if we believe Tacitus' subsequent assertion about the formidable *Germanorum libertas* (*Germ.* 37.3), that sense of freedom is apparently alive and well, despite all Domitian's efforts. What also seems relevant as an interpretative strategy here is the fundamental alignment of Germans and Caledonians, whose physical characteristics (red hair and large limbs) imply a *Germanica origo* (*Agr.* 11.2). Tacitus places this observation prominently in the memorable ethnographical and geographical excursus, and even though he actually rejects Germanic origin for the Britons as a whole, he never closes down this implicit parallelism between the Germans and the Caledonians. So far, the Caledonians have maintained a surprisingly low profile in the narrative,[56] but just as Tacitus is about to narrate the climactic battle of Mons Graupius, he incorporates a revealing episode about the Germanic Usipi, with whom the Caledonians share roots. A story about enterprising and resilient men, who are even ready to resort to cannibalism to stay alive, serves as a timely reminder of the robustness typifying the Germans and (probably) the Caledonians, since the two peoples have shared origins. The hint of bestiality in the cannibalism incident (whatever the extenuating circumstances) is also a well-judged dramatizing touch.

---

[53] Is it just a coincidence that *per commercia*, used first of the Usipi (*per commercia uenumdatos, Agr.* 28.3), recurs again in Domitian's sham triumph in reference to slaves *emptis per commercia* (*Agr.* 39.2)? This is not to imply that the enslaved Usipi are the same men who feature in Domitian's display, but rather to suggest that Tacitus establishes a conceptual link between two episodes, which together cast Domitian in a dim light. Domitian may claim the conquest of Germany, but here we see the Usipi (part of the fruits of that supposed victory and duly enlisted in the Roman army) ably demonstrating a lively sense of their own independence and refusing to cooperate with their conquerors.

[54] Cf. Pomeroy (2003), 361: 'Geography often turns out to be a state of mind rather than a collection of empirically verifiable facts'.

[55] Clarke (2001), 110.

[56] Caledonia and her inhabitants feature at *Agr.* 10.4, 11.2, 25.3, 27.1, and 31.5. See further Wolfson (2008).

Last but not least, there is the issue of the entertainment value of the story. Although the *Agricola* itself should not be categorized formally as a piece of historiography, it arguably contains many elements which allow us to see it as a kind of 'dry run' for Tacitus' later endeavours within that grand genre. Historiography traditionally had as its cornerstones the twin considerations of material which was *utile* (fulfilling the moralizing agenda of the genre) and material which was *dulce* (entertaining the audience and often serving as a means of making the *utile* more palatable). Tacitus' account of the mutiny of the Usipi is a gripping episode in a narrative which admittedly does not have many such moments of lightness. As if to bring this home, the chapter which immediately follows (*Agr.* 29) opens sombrely with the focus on a *domesticum uulnus* suffered by Agricola when his young son dies.[57] It may seem odd to characterize an episode of cannibalism as having entertainment value, but it must hold a ghoulish fascination for an audience, adding *uariatio* and capturing our imaginations, as well as underscoring the hazardous nature of this strange, liminal country which serves as Agricola's centre of operations.

It also engages us in another way. Clarke rightly says that 'the *Agricola* is full of paradox and ambiguity'[58] and the bizarre adventure story of the hapless Usipi is a good illustration of the way in which these paradoxes and ambiguities extend even to a single chapter of this intriguing work. Its apparent oddness and difference from the surrounding narrative should nevertheless challenge Tacitus' readers to analyse it in the wider context of the biography. If we do so, there are some suggestive comparisons in play between this incident of cannibalism on the margins and the violent, self-destructive activities taking place in Rome under the bloodthirsty Domitian. His conduct, after all, was not forced on him, but even so *uelut uno ictu rem publicam exhausit* (*Agr.* 44.6), 'he drained off the state's lifeblood as though by a single wound'; and Tacitus expresses relief that Agricola did not live to see *eadem strage tot consularium caedes* (*Agr.* 45.1), 'the slaughtering of so many consular men in the same bloodbath'. So too Tacitus characterizes this as a time when *nos innocenti sanguine Senecio perfudit* (*Agr.* 45.1), 'Senecio drenched us in his innocent blood'. Such climactic and relentless piling up of startlingly bloody imagery around Domitian is certainly far more extreme than anything we find in the episode of cannibalistic Usipi (where we might justifiably have expected to find some explicit goriness). On the margins, these one-time auxiliaries are driven to cannibalism, but even so they manage to retain some degree of integrity in Tacitus' narrative. Yet the Roman *princeps* at the centre seems to relish the taste of aristocratic blood (even if this will soon become a prelude to

---

[57] Agricola has already lost one young son (*Agr.* 6.2).
[58] Clarke (2001), 109.

his own assassination). Tacitus' creative use of such cannibalistic imagery in the epilogue of the *Agricola*, pointed up through the contrast with the Usipi, will reach new levels of subtlety during the closing stages of Tiberius' principate in *Annals* 6.[59] Perhaps here again we have another element where the *Agricola* serves as a dry run for the mordant historical voice which Tacitus will subsequently develop. In one sense, the mutiny narrative certainly offers us material which is *dulce*, but in the wider context of the *Agricola*, we are surely faced with *misera laetitia*. The final irony may be that whereas the Usipi successfully manage to engineer their great escape, we as readers are relentlessly dragged back to the dark world of Domitian.[60]

[59] See Woodman (2006) for a subtle reading of this sustained imagery in the last book of the Tiberian hexad.

[60] Cf. Rubrius Fabatus, arrested for attempting to flee from Rome to the mercy of the Parthians and promptly brought back to the capital (*Ann.* 6.14.2).

17

Pompeius Trogus in Tacitus' *Annals*

David Levene

Perhaps the most famous line in all of Tacitus is the opening sentence of the *Annals*: *urbem Romam a principio reges habuere* (*Ann.* 1.1.1: 'from the beginning kings controlled the city of Rome'). The sentiment of course is unexceptional—the traditional story of the growth of Rome had kings ruling the city as soon as it was a city and continuing to do so for several generations—but it is made more striking by its position, placed at the very start of the work, introducing a summary narrative of Roman history before the *Annals*' subject matter has been established, and indeed before Tacitus has introduced any of the familiar tropes of historical prefaces to justify either his choice of topic or the methodology that he will employ.

Given that this sentence in the *Annals* gains its primary force from its position, there might appear to be one natural point of comparison: the opening sentence of Justin's abridgement of Pompeius Trogus' *Philippic History*: *principio rerum gentium nationumque imperium penes reges erat* (1.1.1: 'At the beginning of history the rule over peoples and nations was in the power of kings'). The sentiment is obviously close, so too the language is similar (not only the key words *principio* and *reges*, but the emphatic position of the latter in both sentences), and above all the prominence given to both by standing at the start of their respective works. But in fact Justin is rarely cited in this context.[1] Among the standard commentaries on Tacitus, he is mentioned by neither Furneaux nor Koestermann, nor (most markedly, given his strong interest elsewhere in Trogus and Justin) by Goodyear.[2] All three refer instead to another passage, Sallust, *Cat.* 6.1: *urbem Romam, sicut ego accepi, condidere atque habuere initio Troiani* ('The city of Rome, as far

My thanks to Chris Kraus and Chris Pelling for their useful comments on an earlier draft.

[1] The similarity of the phrases was noted by Cornelius (1888), 16; he however assumed without comment that it reflects Justin's imitation of Tacitus rather than Tacitus' of Trogus, which seems less likely for reasons I shall discuss below. The link is also briefly mentioned by Yardley and Heckel (1997), 7 n. 20.

[2] Furneaux (1896), 179; Koestermann (1963), 56; Goodyear (1972), 89.

as I understand, was founded and initially controlled by Trojans'). This is not in itself unreasonable: *urbem Romam . . . habuere* is itself a sufficiently distinctive phrase to encourage a Sallustian reminiscence, as is the placement at the beginning of Sallust's 'Archaeology', his back-narrative of earlier Roman history. But Sallust's content is rather different from Tacitus', nor is the position of the sentence within the work as a whole as emphatic. This is not to suggest that an allusion to Trogus should be highlighted to the detriment of Sallust: it is not impossible—indeed, quite plausible—that Tacitus in the same sentence should have combined allusions to both historians. But most modern critics appear to have regarded the allusion to Sallust as the only significant one, and ignored the other.

There appear to be two related reasons for this neglect. The first is the uncomfortable state of our knowledge of Pompeius Trogus; the second is the consequence of a broader difficulty with the identification of allusions in historiography and understanding their significance.

To begin with the first problem, there is a long-standing and probably insoluble controversy over how closely most of Justin's text represents Trogus. On his own account, Justin was not writing an epitome (in the sense of a work which summarizes its predecessor's content without any particular regard to the manner of expression) but something much closer to an anthology: at *Praef.* 4 he describes himself as having 'excerpted whatever was most worthy of consideration' (*cognitione quaeque dignissima excerpsi*) and says that he 'made a little collection—so to speak—of flowers' (*breve ueluti florum corpusculum feci*). This would appear to imply that the words are all Trogus', and Justin's own input was in the selection alone. But this is demonstrably not the case.[3] There are a number of passages where the wording can only be Justin's, where he refers to Trogus in the third person while discussing Trogus' account of his own writings (38.3.11, 43.1.1–2, 43.5.11–12). There is also one passage which assumes a historical situation which makes no sense for Trogus writing under Augustus, but only for Justin writing (probably) in the high Empire, namely 41.5.8, where he compares the naming of all Parthian kings 'Arsaces' with the Romans' calling their own rulers 'Caesares' and 'Augusti'.[4] And even apart from that, the continuity of Justin's narrative shows that he must be

---

[3] Cf. Jal (1987). Though he barely mentions Justin and Trogus, Brunt (1980) is especially revealing on the ways in which the activities of excerpting and epitomizing historians regularly shaded into one another.

[4] Seel (1972), 178–80 argues that the phrase derives from Trogus and points to his writing after Tiberius had succeeded to the throne with the titles of Caesar and Augustus; but it seems unlikely that Trogus could have made so bold a generalization after a mere two rulers, the second of whom had a family connexion to justify his using a similar titulature to his predecessor.

doing some degree of rewording in order to make a coherent story—he cannot literally be merely excerpting Trogus' phrases and sentences and stringing them together. The question then is precisely how much authentically Trogan material is present and (more importantly) whether it is possible to identify it reliably. The depressing answer to the latter is that in most cases we probably cannot. Critics have varied in their assessment of the degree of Justin's rewording: Goodyear regarded it as relatively minimal,[5] Yardley has more recently collected extensive data to suggest that much—though certainly not all—of the language of Justin belongs to the high imperial period rather than the reign of Augustus.[6] But even on Goodyear's account, it is hard to find clear criteria for demonstrating that *specific* passages are Trogan rather than Justinian,[7] with the single exception of the speech of Mithridates at 38.4–7, which Justin claims to have inserted in full (38.3.11). In which case, the thing that is usually our chief criterion for identifying literary allusion—namely linguistic similarity—becomes problematic to use in the case of Justin and Tacitus, since other things being equal it might appear no less probable that Justin is drawing on Tacitus than that Tacitus drew on Trogus, unless we can show that some particular aspect of the similarity marks one of the two passages as prior.

This provides one reason why scholars might be cautious about claiming that Tacitus drew on Trogus. But there is a second reason too, one which has a wider bearing on the whole treatment of allusion in historiography.[8]

In all genres, one primary way in which allusions are identified is, as I said, simply through linguistic similarity. However, this is not an absolute requirement. All that is needed for allusions to be identifiable is some aspect of the alluding text which focuses a reader's attention on part or whole of the text alluded to.[9] This can be a marked linguistic resemblance, but it does not have to be. So, for example, even though Virgil does make various specific linguistic allusions to the 'Harpies' scene in Apollonius, *Argonautica* 2 in the 'Harpies' scene in *Aeneid* 3.210–67, we do not need to find such linguistic echoes to recognize that Virgil is alluding to Apollonius here. We can spot the

---

[5] Goodyear (1982).

[6] Yardley (2003), esp. 113–80; he had anticipated most of the argument more briefly in Yardley (1994).

[7] As one possible criterion, Goodyear (1984) suggests that Virgilian imitations are likely to be Trogan, since (on his account) Justin is unlikely to have paid sufficient care to his rewritings to introduce such sophistication into them; but note the strong counterarguments of Yardley (1994), 67–70.

[8] The following discussion is a brief summary of a much more complicated question: I explore these and other issues relating to allusion in historiography in more detail in the second chapter of my forthcoming book *Livy on the Hannibalic War*.

[9] For the underlying theory see Wills (1996), 15–41.

connexion through the subject matter alone: and indeed it is the very fact that
we have been alerted to the salience of Apollonius through the similarity of
subject matter that encourages us to observe various closer echoes of language.[10]

This might be thought to provide an alternative method of identifying
historiographical allusions, via thematic similarity rather than verbal reminiscence. But there are substantial complications about finding allusions in
historiography purely via such means. Historiography, unlike poetry, pur-
ports to represent an external reality. In practice real-life events can resemble
other real-life events with or without the intervention of a historian to draw
attention to that resemblance, and indeed historical figures can deliberately
act in ways that recall historical predecessors whether or not a historian is at
hand to describe them doing so. And that is to leave aside the further
question—which one finds also in poetry—of the topos: the construction
of events according to a familiar literary pattern which may or may not
recall specific earlier literary accounts which apply the same pattern.[11] For
these reasons, scholars have—not unreasonably—tended to be cautious about
identifying allusions based solely on a resemblance between narrative sequences in two different historians.

But although not unreasonable, such caution may be taken too far. As is
well known, ancient historians did not regard themselves in all respects as
constrained by the historical traditions that they inherited, but allowed
themselves considerably more licence to rewrite than their modern counterparts do (though the precise amount of licence is controversial).[12] If a later
historian transforms a sequence of events to produce a narrative which echoes
the sequence of events in a particular predecessor who was himself narrating
events in a distinctive fashion, that can alert the reader to an allusion just as a
linguistic similarity would. Tacitus sometimes sets out a narrative sequence
that is distinctive to him—in other words is not narrated by him in a
particular fashion merely because the events actually occurred that way or
because he is applying a standard narrative pattern. If that distinctive narrative sequence in Tacitus recalls a similarly distinctive narrative sequence in
Justin—who can be assumed to reflect Trogus' account of events, even if not

[10] On Virgil's allusions to Apollonius in this scene see Nelis (2001), 32–8.

[11] On the way in which the apparently inert use of familiar topoi may blend into active
allusions to particular earlier uses of those same topoi, see Hinds (1998), 34–47.

[12] A proper analysis with full bibliography is not possible here, but I cannot pass up the
opportunity to observe that the single scholar most central to the discussion is this volume's
honorand, whose transformative work has, among other things, set the entire debate on a new
footing by offering a powerful justification for the historians' practice in terms of ancient
historical theory. See in particular Woodman (1979), (1983), and above all (1988).

always his language—it would not be unreasonable to identify it as an allusion to Trogus.

There is a further point that may be made here, one related, but worth highlighting in its own right. Historians do not only offer distinctive narratives in individual scenes; their entire history can be constructed and arranged so as to foreground particular interpretations of history. At various points in Justin there are generalizing comments suggesting a particular significance to historical events or offering certain historical patterns; and it is reasonable to assume that the sentiment, if not necessarily the wording, went back to Trogus, especially if the events of his history appear to be constructed so as to reflect them. If similar ideas appear in Tacitus, then here too an allusion to Trogus is plausible.

The opening of the *Annals* discussed at the start of the chapter is one example. I noted the parallels with Justin in both language and position in the work, but in fact the significance of the resemblance extends considerably further than this. Tacitus is using his opening paragraph not merely to offer a summary of Roman history, but one specifically focused around the dialectic across Roman history between monarchy—or despotism—and freedom (*Ann.* 1.1.1):[13]

urbem Romam a principio reges habuere; libertatem et consulatum L. Brutus instituit. dictaturae ad tempus sumebantur; neque decemviralis potestas ultra biennium, neque tribunorum militum consulare ius diu valuit. non Cinnae, non Sullae longa dominatio; et Pompei Crassique potentia cito in Caesarem, Lepidi atque Antonii arma in Augustum cessere, qui cuncta discordiis civilibus fessa nomine principis sub imperium accepit.

From the beginning kings controlled the city of Rome; Lucius Brutus instituted liberty and the consulship. Dictatorships were taken up for short periods, nor did the power of the decemvirs last more than a year, nor the consular authority exercised by military tribunes for long. Neither Cinna's domination nor Sulla's was lengthy; and the power of Pompey and Crassus quickly gave way to Caesar, the arms of Lepidus and Antony to Augustus, who, since the whole state was exhausted by civil discord accepted its rule under the name of *princeps*.

For Tacitus Roman history began with the city ruled by kings, and power ultimately returned to those who were kings in all but name. In the interim was 'liberty and the consulship', which was itself repeatedly but temporarily punctuated by periods of domination by individuals, whether or not constitutional. One effect of this is to flatten all non-republican varieties of political rule into the single issue of domination: there is implicitly little substantial

---

[13] See Leeman (1975), 192–9.

difference between Romulus and (e.g.) Cincinnatus or Sulla except the shorter
time that the latter held control; there is implicitly no substantial difference at
all between Romulus and Augustus.

Trogus' perspective is broader, but in some respects similar.[14] For him,
according to the opening sentence of Justin (quoted above, p. 294), beginning
with kings is not something unique to Rome, but is the universal condition of
human anthropology. This is not of course an idea original to him,[15] but it is
far from uniformly held in ancient political thought;[16] and in any case Trogus
in his history insists on the point to an unusual degree and, as we shall see
shortly, interprets it in unusual ways. So, for example, the Athenians were a
monarchy from the time of Cecrops to that of Codrus (2.6.7–7.1); the
Macedonians began as a unified kingdom under kings (7.1); even the primitive and nomadic Scythians appear to be a monarchy from the beginning
(1.1.6). On Trogus' reading of Jewish history the earliest Jewish patriarchs,
including Abraham and Israel, were kings (36.2.3–5), as were the priestly
descendants of Moses (36.2.16). It is easy enough for us nowadays to note this
as a misreading of traditional Jewish history, but it has less often been
remarked that it is a misreading that is distinctive to Trogus:[17] in Tacitus'
more famous though usually no less inaccurate account of the Jews in
Histories 5 monarchy is not mentioned until the (correct) notice that the
Hasmonean rulers after obtaining independence from the Seleucids were the
first to take the kingship and high priesthood together (*Hist.* 5.8.3). For
Trogus the idea of monarchy as the original state of mankind is present
throughout.

But one can take this further. For Trogus, monarchy is not only the original
political state: it is in some sense the basic condition out of which all
human political interactions grow. He is naturally well aware of states which
had non-monarchic constitutions, but he treats those as deviations from the

---

[14] On Trogus' political thought as set out in this passage, see Lühr (1980).

[15] Most obviously it is found in Aristotle, *Pol.* 1252b19 in language quite close to Trogus'.
Aristotle's reasoning is that kingship appeared in the earliest communities out of the quasi-
kingly rule of the master in each individual household.

[16] For example, Cicero, *Rep.* 1.41–2 appears to suggest that primitive communities formed all
different constitutional types. In Plato, *Leg.* 679D–681D, and Lucretius 5.1105–12, monarchy is
the basis of the earliest human political communities, but such communities themselves arrive
gradually and relatively late in human development. A closer parallel to Trogus is Polybius 6.5–7:
Polybius, like Plato and Lucretius, sees kingship arising gradually, but one key stage in the
development towards it is μοναρχία, which is distinguished from kingship proper by being one-
man control within a loosely defined community. (On the nature of Polybius' 'monarchy' and
its development into true kingship see Hahm (1995), 15–24; cf. Walbank (1972), 130–3.) Trogus
shares the same basic pattern, but the character of his primitive kingship is different from
Polybius', being both more formalized and more idealized: see further below, pp. 301–2.

[17] See Bloch (2002), 61.

fundamental norm that monarchy represents. So for example, the Athenians introduce elected magistracies only out of respect to Codrus (2.7.1), the Carthaginians slide seamlessly from the queenship of Elissa (18.4–6) to the domination of a family of generals who are said to hold 'dictatorships' (19.1.7) and described as 'ruling' the state (19.2.3), requiring the invention of a senate in order to keep them in check and prevent them from undermining a 'free state' (19.2.5–6). While it is possible that some of the vocabulary here is Justin's rather than Trogus', the implicit assimilation to monarchic rule even in a non-monarchic constitution is entirely of a tenor with the whole narrative.

But even more importantly, Trogus repeatedly centres his explanations for historical events on the existence of monarchies and people's attitudes to them. In Syracuse after the assassination of Dionysius I, the soldiers support his eldest son for the throne 'both following the law of nature and because the kingdom would be more secure if it remained under one man's control' (21.1.2 *et naturae ius secuti, et quod firmius futurum esse regnum, si penes unum remansisset*); similarly the Cappadocians, offered freedom by the Roman senate, refuse it, saying that a nation cannot live without a king (38.2.8 *negant uiuere gentem sine rege posse*). At 29.1.1 Trogus observes that 'around the same time the empires of almost the entire world changed with a new succession of kings' (*isdem ferme temporibus prope uniuersi orbis imperia noua regum successione mutata sunt*), the 'kings' in question including not only the accession of Philip V in Macedon and new Seleucid, Ptolemaic, Cappadocian, and Spartan rulers, but also the acquisition by Hannibal of the command in Spain (29.1.7); and it is the personal qualities of these 'boy kings' (29.1.8 *regibus pueris*), along with their desire to emulate their predecessors, which generate the events that follow.[18] Immediately after this Demetrius of Illyria provokes Philip's hostility to Rome by alleging that the Romans were attacking their neighbours out of a desire to have no kings on their borders—his main example of such a 'king' once again being Hannibal

---

[18] Polybius 4.2.4–11 likewise identifies this simultaneous succession as a key turning point in history, and does so in such similar terms that it is likely that Trogus was drawing on him directly. He lists the same six figures in precisely the same order (though with the addition of Achaeus' usurpation of Seleucid territories in Asia Minor, which Justin does not mention: conceivably that reflects Justin's omission rather than Trogus', since *Prologue* 30 shows that Trogus later recounted the Seleucids' recapture of the territory, which does not appear in Justin's abridgement). Polybius also explains (4.2.4) that at this time 'Fortune had made everything in the world new': cf. Justin 29.1.1 quoted above. He however avoids the vocabulary of kingship, and does not centre his explanation on the personalities of these 'monarchs' as Trogus does, but says more vaguely that 'with such innovations in every dominion (*dynasteias*) there was going to be the beginning of new events—for this is what is natural and tends to happen by nature' (4.2.10).

(29.2.4). And above all, Mithridates spends a good deal of his speech (38.6) denouncing the Romans' purported hostility to kings,[19] claiming that it was based not on dislike of their crimes, but on objections to their superiority and on jealousy over their superiority to the Romans' own past monarchs. Clearly we are not expected to take either Mithridates' or Demetrius' interpretation of Roman policy at face value,[20] but they both attest to the centrality of monarchy in Trogus' political thought.

When Tacitus not only begins his work with a comment on Roman kings that resembles Justin's first sentence about kings in general, but also continues with a summary of Roman Republican history that surprisingly places monarchy at its centre, it thus is likely to attest to his engagement with Trogus' distinctively monarchic focus. But we would regard it as unlikely a priori that Tacitus would appropriate Trogus' thought inertly, and indeed his account of Rome's various monarchic tendencies demonstrates something more sharply challenging.

Trogus, as I said, regards monarchy as the fundamental state from which all political institutions diverge; but at the same time the primitive Trogan monarchy is in certain crucial ways different from those which succeeded it.[21] Those early kings, according to Trogus, obtained their position through their merits alone (1.1.1) and ruled without the formalities of law: 'the decisions of the leaders were a substitute for law' (1.1.2 *arbitria principum pro legibus erant*). And they eschewed aggression against their neighbours: 'the custom was more to guard their empire's borders than to extend them: each one's kingdom was confined within its own heartland' (1.1.3: *fines imperii tueri magis quam proferre mos erat; intra suam cuique patriam regna finiebantur*). These themes are familiar ones in ancient literature, of course—they are both standard elements of the 'Golden Age' from which modern human society has supposedly declined.[22] Trogus, however, presents that law-free age of primitive peacefulness not, as in most writers, as a period prior to that of the kingly rule, but as itself a characteristic of primitive kingship.[23]

---

[19] The idea, like much else in this speech, is derived from the letter of Mithridates in Sallust, *Hist.* 4.69.15M ('their habit of overturning all kingdoms'), where it is however only a passing thought: Trogus takes that and develops it into a major thesis of Mithridates' analysis of Rome.

[20] On the weaknesses of Mithridates' arguments see Adler (2005-06), 396–401; though note also below, pp. 308–11.

[21] Cf. García Moreno (1993).

[22] See e.g. Pl. *Leg.* 680A–B, Dicaearchus F49 Wehrli, Lucr. 5.958–9, 999–1000, Virg. *Geo.* 2.536–40, Ov. *Met.* 1.89–100.

[23] This image of human development is not Trogus' own creation, but derives from Posidonius (F 284.5 Edelstein-Kidd = Sen. *Ep.* 90.5), who identified the Golden Age as a period of monarchy under the rule of philosophers. Posidonius then influenced various other writers, including not only Trogus and Seneca, but also (e.g.) Cic. *Leg.* 3.4, Sall. *Cat.* 2.1–2.

Only with Ninus of Assyria did this change as a result of his 'new eagerness for empire' (1.1.4 *noua imperii cupidine*). It is true that he had predecessors in Egypt and Scythia, but the difference with Ninus is that he expanded his empire by conquering neighbouring kingdoms rather than simply fighting wars abroad (1.1.4–8). Ninus' model then becomes the norm for the later empires whose histories the bulk of Trogus' work narrates. Only rarely, as with the effeminate Ninias at 1.2.11, do later rulers exhibit this primitive lack of ambition and greed. Elsewhere king after king comes into conflict with and seeks to win territory at the expense of his neighbours. Admittedly Trogus is ambivalent towards such aggression. On the one hand he frequently associates it with kings whose moral position is dubious, such as Dionysius I of Syracuse (20.1.1), the Seleucid king Demetrius I (35.1.1), and Rome's deadly enemy Mithridates of Pontus (37.3.1). But at other times Trogus is more willing to celebrate those aspiring to conquest. A clear example is his treatment of Pyrrhus in 25.3–5, where he comments—apparently critically—on his constant dissatisfaction with his current possessions, and on his desire for conquest which outweighed his ability to hold onto the territory that he gained (25.4.1–3), but ends with an obituary which celebrates him unreservedly as the greatest king who had ever lived up to that time, in morality as well as military exploits (25.5.3–6). This more positive appraisal of conquerors culminates in the very last lines of Justin's summary with Augustus' completion of the conquest of Spain and use of laws to reduce the Spaniards to civilization (44.5.8).[24]

Tacitus' Augustus is obviously rather different. In the description of him that immediately follows the opening section, law is identified as one of the things that he has taken into his own hands, with support from the provinces at least, since it had proved an inadequate defence against the depredations they had suffered in the Republic (*Ann.* 1.2.1; cf. 1.9.3 *nullus tunc legibus locus*). But 'law' now is simply reducible to Augustus' arbitrary fiat: in practice 'everyone, having divested themselves of equality, looked to the orders of the *princeps*' (1.4.1 *omnes exuta aequalitate iussa principis aspectare*), and 'the most important things happened through the decision of the leader' (1.15.1: *potissima arbitrio principis . . . fiebant*), a noticeably similar phrase to that in Justin 1.1.2.[25] And even more pertinently, Augustus is not represented as a

---

[24] On Trogus' attitude towards Roman imperialism cf. Yarrow (2006a), 242–3, though she does not examine his often (but not invariably) positive account of Roman conquest in the context of his ambivalent treatment of imperial aggression on the part of other figures in the work.

[25] Tacitus later presented a different—and more complex—account of the development of Roman law and of Augustus' place in that development at *Ann.* 3.25.2–28.4. There the primitive lawlessness of the Golden Age is succeeded by kingship, and that kingship may either be lawless

conqueror, even in the positive account of his achievements put into the mouths of his supporters at 1.9, who celebrate his stabilizing the empire within secure borders rather than his conquests (1.9.5). His only victories are over his fellow citizens; the only foreign wars mentioned are those against the Germans, and those were not undertaken *cupidine proferendi imperii* (1.3.6). This too is a phrase with a clear resemblance to those in Justin 1.1.3–4 quoted above, and which is also recalled later, when Tacitus famously laments the absence of the traditional subject matter for his history with the words 'an emperor uninterested in extending the empire' (4.32.2 *princeps proferendi imperii incuriosus*)—for Tiberius has followed Augustus' 'plan of containing the empire within its boundaries' (*Ann.* 1.11.4: *consilium coercendi intra terminos imperii*).

In other words, Tacitus' account of Augustus subverts that of Trogus by turning him into something that is not an idealized conqueror but a perverted recreation of Trogus' primitive monarchs.[26] Like them Augustus has substituted his personal will for settled law; like them he appears to have eschewed war and conquest for himself and his successors; but unlike them this is not the consequence of 'conspicuous moderation' (1.1.1 *spectata moderatio*),[27] but rather of 'fear or else envy' (1.11.4 *incertum metu an per inuidiam*).

In these passages we do not merely see verbal echoes (though these are certainly present), but echoes that appear in a context which is best explained if we understand Tacitus to be reworking Trogus' account of the development of world history through monarchy. This is as strong an argument as we are likely to find that these verbal echoes are the result of Tacitus imitating Trogus rather than Justin imitating Tacitus—for the broad narrative slant that Tacitus is reworking is certainly Trogus' creation, not Justin's, and it is thus far more likely than not that these linguistic echoes, which reflect and reinforce that

itself or may involve law. (The precise picture of constitutional development that Tacitus is offering here is however controversial: see the accounts in Woodman–Martin (1996), 242–5.) Laws subsequently developed through the Roman kings and then the Republic, but became excessive in number, until under the civil wars the state collapsed into lawlessness; Augustus offered new laws for his new constitutional arrangements, but those laws themselves turned into oppression (3.25.1). See also Heilmann (2000), esp. 411–12 on the relationship between this and the Posidonian/Trogan conception.

[26] This sense of Augustus as a twisted reviver of a primeval past might be accentuated if Trogus too, like some other Augustan writers, had presented him as the recreator of a Golden Age. Seel (1972), 304–5 suggests that we are to see Justin's final statement of Augustus as ruler of the world in that light; while García Moreno (1993), 202 claims that Trogus has constructed his primitive kings on the model of Augustus as he represented himself in the *Res Gestae*. Against this, however, the description of Augustus conquering Spain does not fit the image of the peaceful Golden Age monarch.

[27] This phrase in Justin appears in the context of the kings' acquisition of the throne rather than their subsequent actions, but it is of a piece with their conduct throughout.

reworked narrative slant, similarly are the result of Tacitean imitation and reworking of Trogus' original. And the linguistic echoes likewise strongly imply that Tacitus is deriving his picture from Trogus directly, rather than both authors independently drawing on Posidonius or some other original source.

We can see linguistic echoes coinciding with a distinctive narrative approach elsewhere also. Goodyear offers the following as a possible—but not conclusive—instance of Tacitus drawing on Trogus' language.[28] Justin 12.16.12 *uictus denique... est non uirtute hostili, sed insidiis suorum et fraude ciuili* ('finally he was conquered... not by enemy courage, but by the plots of his own people and his citizens' deceit'), has a certain similarity to Tacitus, *Ann*. 2.73.2 *utrumque... suorum insidiis externas inter gentes occidisse* ('Both perished through the plots of their own people among foreign nations'). Goodyear himself is characteristically cautious about the possible link: 'This would be insignificant, were it not for the contexts, in Tacitus a comparison between Alexander and Germanicus, in T/J concluding remarks on Alexander. The closeness of the contexts makes a link the more probable, but there is no way to determine priority.'

However, Goodyear may have understated his own case. The claim that Alexander perished 'through the plots of his own people' is not uniform throughout the Alexander tradition: it appears to be, though not original to Trogus, at least a vastly more significant aspect of his account than it was in most other sources. He does not offer a natural death even as a possibility, but elaborates at some length on the manner of his poisoning (Justin 12.14).[29] It is not merely that Tacitus is using the language of Trogus in the context of Alexander, but he is doing so while drawing on a version of Alexander's history which has a strongly Trogan colouring.

A slightly different issue arises with another of Goodyear's examples.[30] His single best case for Trogan influence on Tacitus comes with another passage in *Annals* 2, Tacitus' obituary for Arminius: 2.88.2 *qui non primordia populi Romani... sed florentissimum imperium lacessierit, proeliis ambiguus, bello non uictus* ('who did not challenge the earliest moments of the Roman people, but the most flourishing empire, and while equivocal in battles was undefeated in

---

[28] Goodyear (1982), 24 = Goodyear (1992), 232–3.

[29] All of the other Alexander historians report the poisoning story; none but Trogus presents it as the unquestioned account of his death. Diodorus 17.118.1–2 offers it as a competing version; Curtius 10.10.14–17 reports it as an account believed at the time. Arrian, *Anab.* 7.27.1–2 mentions the story but directly indicates that he gives it little credence (7.27.3); most importantly Plutarch, *Alex.* 77.1–5 not only challenges it himself, but says that most other writers agree with him in rejecting it.

[30] Goodyear (1982), 23–4 = Goodyear (1992), 231–2.

war'). This bears a strong resemblance in both phrasing and thought to Justin's account of the Parthians at 41.1.7: *a Romanis . . . florentissimis temporibus lacessiti soli ex omnibus non pares solum, uerum etiam uictores fuere* ('They alone of all, challenged by the Romans at times they were most flourishing, were not only equal, but even victorious'). Goodyear notes the similar basic outline of the events compared, as well as the similarity of the language; he further concludes that it fits Trogus' positive attitude towards Parthia so well that it is likely to originate with him.

All of these points are true and compelling, but there is one further issue that Goodyear fails to remark. Directly after making these positive comments about Arminius, Tacitus continues—and concludes his book—with a comment upon his historical predecessors (2.88.3):

canitur adhuc barbaras apud gentes, Graecorum annalibus ignotus, qui sua tantum mirantur, Romanis haud perinde celebris, dum uetera extollimus recentium incuriosi.

He is still sung of among barbarian peoples, but is unknown to the annals of the Greeks, who admire only their own things, and not celebrated as he deserves by the Romans, since we extol the old and are uninterested in the recent.

Whom is Tacitus criticizing here? The Greek historians are hard to identify,[31] and the Romans barely easier. In the former case it may simply be that he is relaying a stereotype of the self-regarding Greeks;[32] but the latter is in some ways even stranger, since the one Roman historian of Arminius' time whose works survive, namely Velleius, does in fact celebrate him, if only briefly (2.118.2–4).[33] But in the light of the (likely) imitation of Trogus in the previous sentence, Tacitus' comment here comes across as far more pointed. For Trogus' world history, at least to judge by the surviving account of him not only in Justin but also in the Prologues, hardly touched on Germany at all, let alone Arminius in particular.[34] The only mentions of Germany in the

---

[31] As noted by Syme (1958), 513.

[32] For parallels see Goodyear (1981), 448–9.

[33] See Woodman (1977), 193. Note however Sinclair (1995), 17–18 on the limitations of Velleius' praise for Arminius by comparison with Tacitus', though he implies, less plausibly, that Velleius might have therefore been one of Tacitus' targets here (Sinclair (1995), 21–2).

[34] This is of course assuming that Trogus wrote at least part of his history after AD 9, so that he could in principle have discussed Arminius' defeat of Quinctilius Varus had he been minded to do so. This is a reasonable though not certain conclusion (*contra* Alonso-Núñez (1987), 61, who insists that the work must pre-date Varus' defeat, which (he says) Trogus would certainly have mentioned—a questionable claim, given the absence of a wider treatment of Germany into which it might naturally have been inserted). The latest securely datable event in the surviving history is the arrival of Parthian royal hostages in Rome (42.5.12), which according to Strabo 16.1.28 was negotiated through M. Titius, governor of Syria in 10–9 BC. But there are also indications of a somewhat later date. The general description of kings of Parthia as 'parricides' (42.4.16) suggests that Trogus is thinking not only of the king directly under discussion,

whole surviving work are a couple of passing references in Justin (32.3.11, 38.3.6, 38.4.15): it is unlikely that any attention was paid to Arminius. While it would not be entirely fair to characterize Trogus as interested only in the distant past, since he certainly covers in some detail material which is at least as close to his own time as the reigns of the Julio-Claudians and Flavians were to Tacitus, the chronological structure of his work, in which a broad forward movement in time is constantly interrupted by long loops back into the past in order to set out the background of each new race that enters his history, militates against any sustained engagement with the events of his own day.[35] The further irony, however, is that the passage which Tacitus appears to be imitating here comes from one of the few exceptions, since the successes which Trogus attributes to the Parthians against Rome had occurred within recent memory at the time he was writing. But Trogus' failure to appreciate the present is visible even here, since he not only ignores the Germans in regarding the Parthians as unique in their defeat of Rome, but does not even give the Parthians their due, regarding their ability to overcome the Romans as less glorious than their original establishment of their power and subsequent maintenance of it against pressure from neighbouring countries (41.1.8–9). So even though the passage which Tacitus imitates might appear on the face of things to give the lie to his claim that Roman historians were

Phraates IV, who killed his father Orodes II, but Phraates' own son Phraates V, who murdered him in 2 BC. Most intriguing of all, however, is *Prologue* 42, which refers to 'the Asian kings of the Tochari and the fall of the Saraucae'. The 'Saraucae' are generally accepted to be the Indo-Scythian kings otherwise known as the 'Sacaraucae'; the Tochari—also known in China as the Yueh-Chih—took over their territory some time in the early to mid-1st century AD, founding the Kushan empire. Unfortunately the precise date and nature of these events are unclear, since yet another dynasty is known to have ruled the area in the interim: there may well not have been a neat succession. But an inscription on a Buddhist reliquary known as the 'Indravarman casket' appears to have been written while the Indo-Scythians were still in power, and uses a dating formula that probably—though not certainly—corresponds to AD 5/6: see Salomon (1982). So *if* that date is correct and the inscription does indeed indicate that the Indo-Scythian dynasty still had control then, and *if* (as it appears) 'the fall of the Saraucae' shows that Trogus recounted its fall from power, then it implies that he was writing Book 42 later than AD 5, and presumably some years later, since enough time has to be allowed both for the Indo-Scythians to fall and for enough information about it to reach Trogus for him to incorporate it into his history. (My thanks to Kevin van Bladel for his assistance with this note.)

[35] Cf. Clarke (1999), 271–4. As Clarke also observes, a key part of what generated not only Trogus' work, but other 'universalizing' works around this time like Diodorus and Strabo, was the unification of the Mediterranean world under the Romans, and in that sense the events of Trogus' own day are central to his entire historical conception, even when he was dealing with the distant past. But it is hardly surprising that Tacitus in his critique of his predecessor would pay more regard to the actual events being narrated than to the underlying historical concept that generated the narrative.

uninterested in contemporary glory, Trogus' own gloss on the Parthians' achievements bears out Tacitus' cynical comment.

In the cases above, Trogus' version of history is not always unique to him, but his slant is sufficiently marked that Tacitus can recognizably allude to him, especially when he combines a reference to a Trogan version with specifically Trogan language. The final issue I want to consider, however, is whether there might be cases where we can detect an allusion to or reworking of Trogus even in the absence of linguistic markers, much as I suggested that certain of Virgil's allusions to Apollonius can be detected through the narrative alone. Certain conditions would of course have to be met before such an allusion could be identifiable. One is that the narrative or theme in question would have to be genuinely distinctive to Trogus; a second, that Trogus would have to be a sufficiently strong presence elsewhere in Tacitus that the possibility of an allusion to him would be foregrounded in the reader's mind. Given how hard it is to be certain of the precise nature of Trogus' text, the second condition cannot be demonstrated conclusively; nevertheless I hope that this paper has already demonstrated that the hypothesis that Trogus was important to Tacitus is worth taking seriously.

The first condition is harder still to meet, since it is always possible to argue that even if a Trogan idea appears to us unique, he shared it with other writers now lost. Nevertheless, on the available evidence there are certain themes which Trogus handles in a quite distinctive way, so distinctive that Tacitus' employment of similar themes might be suggested to owe a debt to Trogus even in the absence of direct linguistic similarities—and of course we should remember that it is always possible that Tacitus was making linguistic allusions to the vast majority of Trogus' work that Justin failed either to anthologize faithfully or to anthologize at all. Various examples could be given: I have chosen one which develops one of Tony Woodman's most persuasive and important readings.

Woodman has argued that one striking feature of Tacitus' account of Tiberius in *Ann.* 4 and 6 is that he is treated as, in effect, an invader of his own country.[36] Tacitus famously complains that his subject matter gives him little scope for the traditional historiographical material of great international and domestic themes (4.32.1–2), since Rome was largely at peace. However, as the behaviour of Tiberius and his successors shows, this external security is an illusion, since the true danger to Rome comes from the attack that the emperor himself makes against the heart of the empire, Italy and Rome herself. Woodman provides a number of examples of Tiberius being

---

[36] Woodman (1988), 186–90 = (1998), 136–41.

metaphorically treated as, effectively, an enemy besieging his own city (notably 4.58.2–3, 4.62–3, 6.1.1–2).

Woodman sees Tacitus here as drawing on the common motif of civil war, since Tiberius is explicitly described as absent from his *patria*, and hence assumed to be a Roman; and the account certainly has elements which recall the civil wars of his own lifetime and those described in earlier historians and other writers. But on the other hand, as Woodman also observes, the place from which Tiberius is operating, namely Capri, is described in terms appropriate to a foreign city (4.67.1–3), 'emphasizing further the alienation of the emperor who inhabited it'.[37] And in this context the qualities ascribed to Tiberius take on connotations of actual foreignness: his Greek companions (4.58.1), his bizarre physical appearance (4.57.2 *praegracilis et incurua proceritas, nudus capillo uertex, ulcerosa facies*—'his skinny and bent height, his head bare of hair, his pockmarked face').[38] Tiberius is in some sense a Roman exile attacking his own city, but he is also treated metaphorically as a foreigner assaulting the empire from within.

This image of Tiberius needs to be read in conjunction with the scene that closes the book, following a Roman defeat in Germany (4.74.1):

clarum inde inter Germanos Frisium nomen, dissimulante Tiberio damna ne cui bellum permitteret. neque senatus in eo cura an imperii extrema dehonestarentur: pauor internus occupauerat animos cui remedium adulatione quaerebatur.

Hence the name of the Frisians became celebrated in Germany. Tiberius concealed the loss in order not to entrust anyone with the war. Nor was the Senate concerned in this matter whether the edges of the empire were humiliated: domestic fear had taken over their minds, and the cure was sought in flattery.

Tiberius, as I have already mentioned, followed Augustus' plan of rejecting foreign conquest; here neither he nor the Senate is even interested in responding to a foreign defeat. The Senate is instead preoccupied with the threat posed at the heart of the empire by Tiberius himself—the metaphorically foreign but also domestic enemy attacking Rome at its centre. That is where the true danger to Rome lies, not in border skirmishes whose losses lead to dishonour but do not seriously undermine Roman hegemony.

It is here that it is worth noting parallels with Pompeius Trogus. For Trogus is unusually insistent that the key vulnerability of the Roman empire lay not on its borders but closer to home. This is a central theme in the speech of

---

[37] Woodman (1988), 188 = (1998), 138.

[38] While bizarre physique could simply mark Romans as outsiders within their own community (on which see e.g. Corbeill (1996), 14–56), it also often carried overtones of foreignness: see Garland (1995), 159–70.

Mithridates, who lists the many occasions when Rome had come close to destruction as a result of an attack on their homeland within Italy, and describes the threat that the Italians themselves had repeatedly posed to Roman hegemony (38.4.5–16). The idea is not found in Trogus' primary model, the letter of Mithridates in Sallust, *Hist.* 4.69M, nor is it directly pertinent to Mithridates' situation, since he himself has no reasonable chance of assaulting Rome from within (though he hopes to profit from their current preoccupation with wars at home: 38.4.15–5.2).[39] It appears rather to reflect a particular preoccupation of Trogus' own: the greatness of the Roman empire belies its vulnerability, because of the possibility that an enemy might bypass the provinces and attack Rome at her heart, exploiting the hostility of the Italians to Roman rule.

The exemplary employer of such a strategy is of course Hannibal. As far as we can judge, Trogus' history included no systematic account of the Second Punic War, though it plays an ancillary part in other episodes that he recounts, notably the First Macedonian War (29.3.6–4.5) and the Roman conquest of Spain (44.5.6–7). But Hannibal himself has a major role in Books 31 and 32 as an adviser to Antiochus III and Prusias; and from the very start he advises Antiochus that his strategy should be to attack the Romans directly in Italy. His first advice to Antiochus comes when he 'said that the Romans could not be crushed except in Italy' (31.3.7 *negabat opprimi Romanos nisi in Italia posse*), and to demand forces to conduct an invasion (31.3.8–9). When he is forced to defend his strategy more extensively after being cut out of Antiochus' inner circle, he explains it as follows (31.5.3–9):

neque sedem belli Graeciam sibi placere, cum Italia uberior materia sit; quippe Romanos uinci non nisi armis suis posse nec Italiam aliter quam Italicis uiribus subigi; siquidem diuersum ceteris mortalibus esse illud et hominum et belli genus. aliis bellis plurimum momenti habere priorem aliquam cepisse occasionem loci temporisque, agros rapuisse, urbes aliquas expugnasse; cum Romano, seu occupaueris prior aliqua seu uiceris, tamen etiam cum uicto et iacente luctandum esse. quam ob rem siquis eos in Italia lacessat, suis eos opibus, suis uiribus, suis armis posse uincere, sicut ipse fecerit. sin uero quis illis Italia uelut fonte uirium cesserit, proinde falli ac si quis amnes non ab ipsis fontium primordiis deriuare, sed concretis iam aquarum molibus auertere uel exsiccare uelit. haec et secreto se censuisse ultroque ministerium consilii sui obtulisse, et nunc praesentibus amicis ideo repetisse, ut scirent omnes rationem gerendi cum Romanis belli, eosque foris inuictos, domi fragiles esse. nam prius illos urbe quam imperio, prius Italia quam prouinciis exui posse.

---

[39] Adler (2005–6), 399–400 notes the lack of pertinence of Mithridates' historical examples to his current circumstances, but regards this as merely a sign of his arguments' weaknesses: he does not consider the broader political point that emerges from them.

Nor (he said) did he want the war to be based in Greece, when Italy provided richer material; for the Romans could not be defeated except by their own weapons nor could Italy be subdued except by Italian forces; for it was a different class of men and a different class of war from other mortals. In other wars the most important thing was to have been the first to have taken some advantage in space or time, to have grabbed territory, to have stormed some cities. With the Romans, when you are the first to take hold of something or have beaten them, nevertheless one still has to struggle with them lying defeated. So if one attacks them in Italy, one can win by using their own resources, their own strength, their own weapons, just as Hannibal himself did. But if indeed one leaves them Italy as (so to speak) the source of their strength, one would be making the same mistake as someone who wanted to divert rivers not starting from the original springs, but to turn aside and dry up the water when they had already massed. He had both advised this privately and had offered directly to carry out the plan, and now he had repeated it in the presence of friends, so that everyone would know the method of waging war with the Romans, and that they were invincible abroad, but vulnerable at home. For they could be divested of the city before the empire, and of Italy before the provinces.

Naturally Antiochus fails to take Hannibal's advice, but the Seleucid empire's war against Italy under his command is left as a tantalizingly unfulfilled possibility, since it is only fear of Hannibal gaining credit for the plan which leads to its being scuppered (31.6.1–3).

  This interpretation of Hannibal's planning and of the ideal Seleucid strategy has few parallels in other sources. It is indeed generally recorded that Hannibal's original advice to Antiochus was to carry the war to the Romans in Italy: so at Livy 34.60.3–6 he briefly suggests that 'Italy would provide both supplies and soldiers for a foreign enemy' (34.60.3 *Italiam et commeatus et militem praebituram externo hosti*) and that it would undermine the Romans' ability to fight elsewhere; there are similar accounts in Appian, *Syr.* 7 and Nepos, *Hann.* 2.1 and 8.1. But this later speech is constructed by other authors in an entirely different way.[40] The long account of it at Livy 36.7 is focused largely on persuading Antiochus to recruit Philip into an alliance against Rome, and the proposed invasion of Italy is alluded to only as a subsidiary point (36.7.16, 36.7.20); Appian, *Syr.* 14 places a little more emphasis on the latter idea, but is in general sufficiently similar to Livy to suggest that they depended on a common source, presumably Polybius.[41] For these other authors, reflecting the Polybian tradition, Hannibal's proposed attack on Italy is merely one part of a two-pronged strategy that has Antiochus threatening them in Greece while Hannibal undermines them at home. In Trogus

[40] See the discussion in Passerini (1933), arguing for the greater historical plausibility of the version in Livy and Appian.
[41] See Briscoe (1981), 229–31.

the attack on Italy is the sole proposed strategy, to be pursued as an end in itself. More significantly still, neither Livy nor Appian has anything close to the systematic account of Roman vulnerability in Italy that is the centre of Hannibal's arguments in Trogus. One might wonder if those derived from an alternative source, but given their congruence with the theme of Roman weakness as it is set out in the speech of Mithridates, it is more likely to reflect Trogus' idiosyncratic interests. The size and strength of the Roman empire, for him, are misleading, because Rome's true weakness is where it has always been, in her homeland, and in particular in the possibility that a foreign enemy could gain the upper hand by using her own people against her.

The distinctiveness of this analysis rests not only in its account of a Roman empire whose weakness lies at its heart, but also in the idea that that weakness is best exploited by a combination of foreign and domestic enemies: the former invade from without, with the support of those within. Tacitus' treatment of Tiberius takes that point and metaphorically transforms it. Events on the empire's borders are not where the true danger to Rome lies. Tiberius is a Hannibal or Mithridates, but he is also the internal enemy by whose strength alone Rome can be undermined. He combines within himself the qualities of a foreign invader and a native rebel.

The possibility that Tacitus was deliberately reworking Trogus here can in our present state of knowledge only be offered as a suggestion: it certainly cannot be proved. For a conclusive demonstration we would need to have a considerably closer and more comprehensive knowledge of Trogus' text, such as would allow us to determine whether the account of Tiberius in *Annals* 4 and 6 (and perhaps also in Book 5, had that book survived) drew on Trogus in other ways, whether close linguistic reworkings of the sort discussed above or other thematic reminiscences that would alert the reader that Trogus was particularly salient. None are obviously detectable, and without them the idea of an active allusion to Trogus here cannot be regarded as more than speculative; we cannot exclude the possibility that in this case at least, Tacitus was drawing more directly on another author who was himself dependent on Trogus. But in the thematic similarity outlined here we can at least demonstrate that certain lines of thought linked Trogus and Tacitus, even if we cannot tell how directly the link was forged, or even indeed how conscious Tacitus himself was of the ancestry of the concepts that he deployed.

18

Voices of Resistance

Richard Rutherford

It is cheap and easy to malign great empires. And all too conventional.[1]

I

In this paper I examine some of the anti-imperialist rhetoric placed by Tacitus in the mouths of Rome's antagonists, and the responses made by a few Roman spokesmen. The main focus will be on the two speeches by Calgacus and Agricola in the *Agricola* and on the more complex series of speeches which figure in the fourth book of the *Histories*, especially those by Julius Civilis and Petilius Cerealis.[2] Much of what I say will involve comparison and contrast of the ways in which this kind of oratory is deployed in the early monograph and on the ampler canvas of the *Histories*. Clearly the treatment of the themes in the *Histories* is much more complex—more speeches and speakers, fuller background, more intricate political and military context; but as we shall see, the handling of the speeches in the *Agricola* is far from simple.

There are a number of questions we may ask in pursuing a comparison of this kind. First, it is necessary to see these passages as part of a historiographical tradition. Already in the Greek world historians were ready to treat themes of empire and conquest in agonistic debates shaped by sophisticated rhetorical theory. Thucydides can present forceful criticisms of Athenian

I am very grateful to Rhiannon Ash, Anna Clark, and Kathleen Coleman for reading and commenting on a draft of this essay.

[1] Syme (1958), 530. The comment presumably echoes Tacitus' formulation in commenting on Valentinus' anti-Roman rhetoric ('cuncta magnis imperiis obiectari solita', 'all the charges that are conventionally brought up against mighty empires', *Hist.* 4.68.5), of which more below.

[2] The *Annals* cannot be treated in any detail here, and in any case offer rather less material, but the exchanges between Arminius and Flavus in Book 2 are relevant, as is the obituary of the former at 2.88; see also Appendix, below, on Caratacus and Boudicca.

imperialism (e.g. 1.69–71, 6.76–80),[3] Polybius allows equal eloquence to the opponents of Rome's expansion.[4] More immediately relevant is the Roman tradition. Caesar in the *de bello Gallico* permits *oratio recta* to one speaker only, the Gallic chieftain Critognatus, who utters a violent attack on Roman rapacity, and urges his followers to resort to cannibalism rather than surrender (7.77). Sallust gives anti-Roman arguments to Mithridates, and some of his phrasing is clearly imitated by Tacitus (*Hist.* 4.69 [= 67 McG.).[5] Thus there is a vertical tradition well established in historiography:[6] when enemies meet, we may expect an *agōn*; when conquest is in question, we may anticipate an attack on the conqueror's actions. Genre, however, cannot explain everything. Indeed, as has often been observed, the use of speeches well suited to historical writing is an anomaly in the *Agricola*, ostensibly a biography.[7] Also, we may still consider how this traditional element is handled: are some arguments less conventional than others, or expressed in more effective ways? And how far are the arguments met?

We thus move on to a second issue, the creative adaptation of the tradition by Tacitus. This can be examined in terms of form (e.g. how many speeches, whether in *recta* or *obliqua*, and so forth), arguments (conventional or otherwise), and style (the rhetorical structure or texture). Comparison between these episodes illuminates the development of Tacitus' rhetorical and argumentative techniques.[8] It is naturally tempting to take the word 'development' seriously, and detect a linear pattern, an advance in sophistica-

---

[3] Cf. e.g. de Romilly (1963), 54–7. In contrast with the highly specific complaints in Roman texts (n. 14), it is striking how abstract and bloodless are the accusations in Thucydides, which focus above all on the Athenians' desire to extend their *power*.

[4] Polyb. 5.104, 11.5, 31.29; cf. Gruen (1984), 322–6, 342–51.

[5] e.g. Tac. *Agr.* 30.4 'raptores orbis' ('looters of the earth') ~ Sall. F 69.22 'latrones gentium' ('raiders of nations'). Similarly Horace's Hannibal speaks of the Romans as 'ravaging wolves' ('luporum rapacium', *Carm.* 4.4.50).

[6] See also Sall. *BJ* 10, 14; Livy 9.1 (the Samnite Pontius), with Oakley's note; Justin 4.1–7.10 (Mithridates to his forces, influenced by Sallust). For more general discussion see Schnayder (1928), Fuchs (1938); Balsdon (1979), ch. 12, esp. pp. 162–70, 182–91 (more examples of anti-Roman passages in Justin at his p. 288 n. 127); and Levene, Ch. 17 in this volume.

[7] See Ogilvie–Richmond (1967), 11–20; Marincola (1999), 316–21, esp. his intriguing comparison of the generic mixture with the use of elegy in Virgil's tenth *Eclogue*.

[8] Ogilvie–Richmond (1967), 233 call the speech of Calgacus a *declamatio*, and refer to the 'traditional Roman criticisms of imperialism such as were voiced in the schools'. But Prof. M. Winterbottom informs me that in his view declamation tended to avoid such political topics: certainly there is no exact parallel in declamatory texts. There are however connexions, esp. at 30.4, with the common denunciation of avarice, whether that of an individual or a class of rich men (Winterbottom (1974), index, s.v. 'rich'), and on another front with the geographical ambitions of those who seek to reach the ends of the earth (30.1, 3, 33.6, cf. Sen. *Suas.* 1, a motif going back to Alexander-panegyric (Norden on Virg. *Aen.* 6.788ff.)).

tion of thought or sharpness of epigram from the earlier works to the later; but again we should avoid writing the *Agricola* off as a work of juvenilia. If different techniques are used, they may be chosen with regard to the demands of the particular scene in question, or the larger strategies of the text. One area of obvious importance is the identity and the geographical origins of the critic of Rome: Calgacus the unconquered Briton might be expected to speak in different terms from the Batavo-Roman Civilis: but is this so? How far are Tacitus' versions shaped by a familiar template, and how far are different peoples differently characterized?[9]

With the last point we reach a higher level of interpretation: what do speeches of this type, and the specific episodes we shall consider, contribute to the work as a whole? Why has Tacitus included them, and how important are they in their context and within his oeuvre more generally? This does not represent an attempt to determine 'Tacitus' attitude to the Roman empire'.[10] Penetrating the mind of Tacitus, an author so rich in ambiguities and enigmas, can never be an easy objective (quite apart from any doubts one may have about authorial intentionalism more generally), and criticism has rightly adopted a more cautious approach in recent years. We read less about 'Tacitean opinions'. Biographically rooted criticism is not dead, but in the case of this author it is widely acknowledged that we have very little to go on.[11] Hence our focus will be on the text, and on the impact that these speeches make upon it—how they characterize speakers both individually and in terms of their relation to one another, how they relate to the narrative or analytical passages, how they fit in to the thematic structure of the work as a whole.[12]

Not all of these topics can be dealt with as they deserve in a paper of this compass, but I hope that what is said here will be of some interest to Tony Woodman, who has himself been so effective a voice of resistance to prevailing orthodoxies through his work over thirty years and more.

---

[9] Sherwin-White (1967), 29 notes that in Caesar the Germans are more 'wild' (*feri*) than Gauls. Balsdon (1979) includes some rather impressionistic collections of material on Roman views of different nationalities (e.g. chs. 4 and 14); more methodologically alert accounts in Williams (2001), ch. 2, and esp. Dench (2005). Important parallel work in Greek studies includes Hartog (1980; Eng. tr. 1988), Hall (1989), Pelling (1997).

[10] Benario (1991).

[11] For an admirable example of what can be done by a careful and judicious reader see Griffin (1999).

[12] For relevant recent essays see Clarke (2001) and Keitel (1993).

II

Within the short span of the *Agricola* Tacitus permits himself only two speeches in *oratio recta*: one by the chieftain Calgacus addressing his gathered forces, one by Agricola addressing his men. The form of exhortation before battle is traditional, as is the device of 'pairing' speeches of this kind. A duel of words precedes the actual military conflict. In the present instance, Agricola speaks second and thus stands in an advantageous position to gain the upper hand in argument; and there can be no doubt of the conclusiveness of his victory on the battlefield. But things are not quite so simple. Part of the convention is for one speaker to 'answer' or refute the other, in the manner of an *agōn*, despite the fact that they do not overhear each other's words. Point-by-point refutation is a common technique in Livy, and may indeed ultimately derive from epic.[13] The arguments of Calgacus on morale and tactics are conventional, and are either refuted or disproved in the event. The complaints about particular hardships endured by the subjects of Rome's dominion are recurrent in speeches of this type (though somewhat out of place in the mouth of an unconquered Caledonian).[14] But the most challenging parts of his speech, the denunciation of Roman empire-building as motivated by greed and disastrous for their subjects, receive no response. The omission is all the more striking since the formal model for Agricola's oration, the elder Scipio's speech in Livy 21.40 f., does relate to his opponent's speech point by point.[15] That Agricola does not address the larger issues of Roman expansion is hardly surprising in realistic terms: his soldiers presumably have no need to consider these matters, and would have little interest in hearing high-minded Panaetian doctrine. But in terms of the balance of arguments within Tacitus' text, the silence on this theme is striking. Agricola makes no use of the crucial terms *libertas* ('freedom') and *servitus* ('slavery').[16] The mismatch of the

---

[13] e.g. 33.39–40, 37.53–4; Walsh (1964), 231 ff. The technique goes back at least to Thucydides (e.g. 2.87–9, 7.61–8).

[14] For standard complaints see Balsdon (1979), 167–76: they include the burden of taxation and its abuse, conscription, billeting of troops, looting and wanton destruction, corruption of governors and officials, *libido* and arbitrary cruelty. Needless to say, their frequency does not imply that they are conventional in the sense of being unhistorical: 'a cliché need not be a lie' (Ogilvie (1965), 23).

[15] The opponent in this case is Hannibal, and the imitation obviously has a panegyrical aspect, magnifying the roles of Agricola and Calgacus to the heroic stature of the leaders of the Punic War. There is variation in that Scipio speaks first in Livy's pairing, and in that the engagement which follows represents only an early stage in the war, and is indecisive.

[16] There is however an interesting correspondence between Calgacus' words in 30.2 and Agricola's comment on Ireland paraphrased at 24.3. Agricola had asserted that it would be better

speeches resembles cases in Greek authors, especially the tragedians, in which
one speaker fails to meet the most forceful points of the other side: thus
Phoenix in the *Iliad* responds to Achilles' great speech with a strongly
emotional appeal, but one which does not address (perhaps can find no
way to address) the account given by the young hero of his dual destiny;
and Theseus in Euripides' *Suppliants* sings the praises of democracy but does
not engage with the herald's penetrating criticisms.[17] It is often possible to
speak of the interlocutors as 'talking past' each other.[18]

The effect is reinforced on the stylistic level. In the *Agricola* debate,
the devil gets the best epigrams. Calgacus' speech is sharper and more
memorable for its *sententiae*, its forceful, aggressive language, and its bold
turns of phrase, which seem notably lacking in Agricola's 'response'. Perhaps
only 33.3 'inventa Britannia et subacta' ('Britain, once discovered, was subdued'), and 34.3 'non restiterunt, sed deprehensi sunt' ('they have not taken
a stand, they have been caught out'), have the popular epigrammatic pointedness which we think characteristic of the period and which Aper demands
of the orators of his day (*Dial.* 20.4). The tone is judicious, measured, factual,
the sentiments almost conventional, the concluding exhortation builds to an
admirable tricolon climax, but with no unexpected variations or sting in
the tail.

It would be ludicrous to suggest that Tacitus was on Calgacus' side rather
than Agricola's. But the very fact that an exchange of speeches is introduced
increases the complexity of the work. There are three 'voices' in play, that of
the historian and those of Calgacus and Agricola. We are already clear, not
least from the ethnographic digression and the account of earlier conquests of
Britain, that the *Agricola* is more than a rhetorical encomium of a dead
relative. Praise and commemoration are of central importance, but other
elements enter into the text—not least, the political dimension which is

---

if Ireland too were subjugated, so that the Britons would have no free territory left on the
horizon ('et uelut e conspectu libertas tolleretur', 'and freedom would be, as it were, banished
from view'). Calgacus described himself and his followers as located in the innermost recesses
('shrines', *penetralibus*, is the word he uses) and thus seeing no shores of slavery: 'nec ulla
seruientium litora aspicientes, oculos quoque a contactu dominationis inuiolatos' ('out of sight
of the shores of those who have been subjugated, we could keep our eyes untainted by the
contagion of tyranny'). Agricola thus glances at the *libertas* theme, but very much in passing,
and from the point of view of the convenience of the conqueror; Calgacus' version of the motif
carries much more emotive weight (the religious metaphor, reinforced by the hint of pollution,
contrasts with the moderation of Agricola's formulation, in which a qualifying 'uelut' softens a
less bold metaphor).

[17] A mismatch of another kind is found in the dialogue between Meliboeus and Tityrus in the
first of Virgil's *Eclogues*.

[18] A formulation suggested to me by Robert Cioffi.

strongly emphasized in the prologue, occasionally hinted at in earlier parts of the work (e.g. 5.3, 6.3 ('quibus inertia pro sapientia fuit', 'a time when indolence counted as wisdom'), 7.1), and thrust into the foreground in the last quarter. One obvious difference between Tacitus and the opposing leaders is that the historian has outlived them both, a point highlighted in the text as regards Agricola. The latter was spared the full horrors of Domitian's reign of terror, although the grudging treatment he received from the emperor is made symptomatic of things to come. Both the preface and the conclusion of the biography emphasize the traumatic impact of this experience. But despite the horrors of the times, Tacitus surely expects the reader to assume that living through these years has made him a more alert and more perceptive historian— that his powers of analysis are now deepened by having witnessed the worst of which men and rulers are capable. Tacitus, in other words, may see more deeply than Agricola. The warm affection and evident admiration and gratitude with which he pays appropriate tribute to a beloved father-in-law do not preclude the historian from subjecting Agricola's career and achievements, and the process of Roman expansion of which they form a part, to a more sophisticated judgement. Calgacus' speech is one important element in that more complex narrative.

Part of the writer's persona involves a shrewd, even cynical scrutiny of human motives, including those underlying Roman imperialism. The note is first struck in the ethnography: the Britons 'exhibit more spirit, being a people whose strength has not yet been sapped by a lengthy peace' ('plus tamen ferociae Britanni praeferunt, ut quos nondum longa pax emollierit', 11.4). To suppose that the pearls of Britain are of high quality but inaccessible is to deny human avarice its due: 'ego facilius crediderim naturam margaritis deesse quam nobis auaritiam' ('I would more readily suppose the pearls to be lacking in quality than ourselves in avarice', 12.6). The Britons resent unjust treatment: 'has [iniurias] aegre tolerant, iam domiti ut pareant, nondum ut seruiant' ('such insults they are bear with resentment, for they have by now been so far conquered as to play the role of subject, but not yet that of slave', 13.1). Chapter 15 develops the last theme in *oratio obliqua*, with the account of the complaints of the subjects prior to rebellion. Most striking is the gloss which Tacitus gives to the measures Agricola takes to ensure a more Romanized way of life in the province (19–21). For the most part these are described without comment, but a darker note enters the concluding sentences: gradually the Britons were allured 'ad delenimenta vitiorum' ('into seductive vices'); 'idque apud imperitos humanitas uocabatur, cum pars seruitutis esset' ('In their inexperience they called this culture, though in fact it played a part in their enslavement', 21.2).[19] It is unlikely that these comments are meant to reflect the views of the governor himself; they indicate the longer perspective and more acute historical judgement of the historian.[20]

Indications of a gap between the narrator's outlook and evaluations and those of Agricola are also detectable in some of the biographical comments. Although 9.2 partly dismisses the conventional slights on military minds, we are still left with the impression that Agricola's *naturalis prudentia* ('natural common sense') is something on a lower level than *subtilitas* ('subtlety'). The much-quoted passage on Agricola's aspirations to philosophy being reined in by his mother also cuts both ways: on the one hand, such studies are ill-suited to a Roman and a senator; on the other, the constraint limits his 'sublime et erectum ingenium' ('lofty and ambitious talent'), which was naturally drawn to higher things (4.3); and Tacitus has already indicated disapproval of the expulsion of philosophers from Rome at a later date (2.2).

Agricola is praised throughout as an excellent general and a just governor. Calgacus' criticisms need not affect his reputation. But the anticipation of some of these complaints in the context of the earlier revolt, and the narrative of earlier governorships, has made clear that Roman government is not beyond criticism. That greed is a dominating motive and enslavement the eventual objective is confirmed by the narrator's own voice (above). The importance of *libertas* (the noun occurs four times in Calgacus' speech) is not confined to provincial subjects. The term is prominent in the prologue, where 'our age' has seen the ultimate in servitude, just as older times saw the acme of liberty; now after Domitian's oppression, Nerva has achieved the seemingly impossible union of *principatus* and *libertas*, principate and freedom (2.3, 3.1).[21] *Libertas* in its varying senses is central to the *Agricola*, as to all of Tacitus' work. That Agricola has nothing to say about it is at least worthy of comment.

There can (to repeat) be no question of turning the biography on its head and seeing it as an indictment of Agricola. The length and eloquence of the concluding encomium resists any kind of ironic reading. The last six chapters of the work do however enable us to see Agricola against the background of his times, as a figure in some ways ill-suited to those times. His admirable qualities as governor and general would be more at home in the (idealized) republic where merit and ambition received their due. In this light the fact

---

[19] Discussions of *Agr.* 21 include Woolf (1998), ch. 3 (esp. pp. 68–71); Dench (2005), 80–7. I hope that my discussion may help clarify the problem posed by Dench at 83 n. 148.

[20] Hutchinson (1995) has many fine observations on how Tacitus projects his own persona as a subtle and penetrating critic of historical events: see esp. 50–62.

[21] Yet *libertas* can also be misguided extravagance and meaningless gesture: 42.5, hinting at the Stoic martyrs.

that his oration echoes one of Livy's heroes is significant.[22] Just as the *Agricola* moves beyond the generic bounds of encomiastic biography, so its narrator shares with readers a deeper and darker historical perspective than its subject possesses.

III

In Book 4 of the *Histories* Tacitus treats a more extended conflict in consider-able detail (4.12–37, 54–79, 85–6; 5.14–26); its importance was already 'trailered' at 3.46.1.[23] Rebellion on the Rhine coincides with and arises out of civil war within the Roman empire. The military and the political (includ-ing the issue of the succession) are intertwined.[24] The *Agricola* dramatized the climactic campaign of a series of seasons, in which a decisive battle put an end to resistance: Agricola, as governor of the province of Britain, was the focus of attention throughout. In the relevant parts of the *Histories* there is diversity and ambiguity on all sides: disloyalty, secret motivations, shifting allegiances, changing political background, and the deaths and replacement of leaders, all ensure that no single figure remains the centre of interest, far less of sympathy, for long. One clear analogy with the *Agricola* is the way in which the theme of *libertas* is shared between events at the heart of the empire and on the frontiers: senate and provincials both seek to find some acceptable level of independence in a turbulent time. Even in the *Agricola* it appeared that the contrast between the Roman Agricola and the Caledonian Calgacus was not a simple one. Still less can such an easy opposition be found in the narrative concerning Civilis.[25]

Julius Civilis, of royal descent among the Batavi, is presented as the ringleader of the revolt, though other significant leaders are associated with him at different stages of the narrative (especially Tutor and Classicus, both leaders of the Treveri, and Sabinus: 55). It is Civilis who most vocally conveys the complaints of the provincial subjects (14, 17), laying particular stress on

[22] I am arguing a somewhat similar case to the one made regarding Germanicus by Pelling (1993), though Agricola is evidently a less flawed figure than the Germanicus of the Annals.
[23] Modern discussions: Griffin, *CAH*² XI.36–8; Levick (1999), 107–12. Brunt (1960)= (1990), 33–52 remains a fundamental treatment.
[24] Besides the obvious conflicts between the adherents of Vitellius and Vespasian, there are the abortive moves to acclaim other generals as emperor (even Cerealis is offered the *imperium Galliarum* at 4.75.1).
[25] For a fresh and suggestive account of Civilis and his historical legacy see Ash (2006), 99–116.

the burden of the levy and the abuses which accompany it (cf. *Agr.* 13.1, 31.1).[26] The language of *libertas/seruitus* is freely used (17 *bis*, 25, 32, etc.).[27] The position of the Batavi is ambiguous, however, as although liable to the levy, they are not subject to tribute (14; *Germ.* 29). In the early stages the emphasis is on the abuses; by the end, frustrated in the field and disappointed by Civilis, the common soldiers revert to their immunity to tribute, considering this 'a second best to liberty' (5.25 'id proximum libertati')! The mirroring of the introduction to the revolt in its final fizzling-out is an eloquent expression of its futility.

There are other ways in which the Batavi and their leader can be seen as ambiguous in status. Originally German and part of the Chatti, they have been transplanted and now occupy an island in the Rhine, a 'liminal' space: do they belong more to Gaul or to Germany, or to neither? The point gains in importance with Civilis' efforts to foment Gallic revolution. In the narrative and the rhetoric of these events Gauls and Germans are sometimes paired, sometimes dissociated (14, 17, 18.1; 25.3 [after initially supporting the Roman cause, Gauls are fired with aspirations to empire by German successes], 76, 78.1 'Gallos pro libertate, Batauos pro gloria, Germanos ad praedam' ('the Gauls they urged to fight for liberty, the Batavi for glory, the Germans with the hope of plunder')).[28] In his initial appeal to the Batavians, Civilis speaks of 'our kinsmen the Germans' (*consanguineos*, 14.4); but later he describes himself to the Treveri as 'prefect of a single cohort, with the Canninefates and Batavi, a trifling part of all the Gauls' ('exigua Galliarum portio', 32.3). As enthusiasm for an *imperium Galliarum* grows (55, 59),[29] Civilis seems at certain points almost to present himself and his followers as honorary Gauls; but he restrains his Batavians from subscribing to an oath of loyalty to the proposed empire (61), and at 76.1, addressing Germans, he is dismissive: 'Gallos quid aliud quam praedam uictoribus?' ('As for the Gauls, what are they but the prey of the conqueror?') Although Civilis' praenomen shows him to be a Roman citizen, the narrator takes pains to bring out attributes and behaviour which mark him or his followers as foreign or exotic:

[26] The Tencteri at 64 also refer to prohibitions against freedom of movement in arms: 'inermes ac prope nudi sub custode et pretio coiremus' ('we come together unarmed and virtually naked, under observation and taxed for the privilege').

[27] Woodman–Martin (1996), on *Ann.* 3.46.1 document the frequency of this opposition in *hortationes*.

[28] Levick (1999), 110: 'Civilis held his Batavians aloof, an elite distinct from Gauls and Germans.'

[29] 4.54 even suggests that in the aftermath of the burning of the Capitol extravagant hopes for the overthrow of Rome were entertained and exploited in propaganda for a new domination by Gaul. Tacitus paraphrases these and dismisses them with a concluding phrase: 'superstitione uana Druidae canebant' ('the Druids uttered prophecies of empty superstition').

quite apart from his one-eyedness, which associates him with Hannibal (13), we may note the celebration of the Batavian compact with savage rituals ('barbaro ritu', 15.1), the male chanting and female howling ('ululatu') which accompany entry into battle (18, cf. *Germ.* 7.3), the addition of fearsome *imagines* to the line of military standards (22), his dyeing of his hair red and his vow to wear it long ('barbaro uoto', 'a savage's oath', 61), and his devotion to the matriarch Veleda (61). As he reveals his true colours, he is given a more sinister character. Civilis' actual motives are doubtless irrecoverable, but the account of Tacitus brands him a hypocrite from the beginning: both Flavian partisanship and commitment to a war for freedom are represented as pre-texts, with personal ambition and long-standing grudges underlying both (13, 14, 18, 63). This type of account naturally suits the dark world of the *Histories*; there may have been another side.

Our main focus is again on the speeches, but here too there is no simple structure or opposition. Indeed, at one point the historian seems to give a clear indication that he is *not* concerned to give a straightforward *agōn* between an opponent of Roman rule and a defender. At 4.68 an assembly of Gallic states is addressed by a delegation from the Treveri, led by Julius Valentinus, 'acerrimo instinctore belli' ('the fiercest instigator of war'). His speech is not quoted but summarized: he brought up all the conventional charges against empires, and heaped insults and invective upon the Roman people; he is further characterized as a violent demagogue, somewhat remi-niscent of Thucydides' Cleon. In reply Julius Auspex of the Remi expounded the strength of Rome and the attractions of peace ('uim Romanam pacisque bona dissertans', 69.1) We are told that the audience admired the spirit of Valentinus but followed the counsel of Auspex. It would seem that Tacitus is drawing our attention to the possibility of a regular *agōn* along conventional lines, but proceeds to avoid so obvious a debating-structure.

Speeches play an important part in the narrative of the revolt. The follow-ing passages are relevant.

4.14   (Civilis to his fellow Batavian leaders: partially *recta*)
17   (Civilis in discussions with Gallic leaders: *obliqua*)
32   (Montanus, paraphrased, and Civilis, *recta*)
56   (Vocula, *obliqua*)
58   (Vocula, *recta*)
64–5   (speech by the most violent ['ferocissimus'] of the Tencteri, answered by the Agrippinenses, both *recta*)
68–9   (Valentinus and Auspex, summary only, both *obliqua*)
73–4   (Cerealis, *recta*)
5.17   (Civilis to his soldiers, *recta*)

5.25   (exchanges among the Batavians, divided between the *uulgus* and the
       proceres; both *obliqua*)
5.26   (Civilis' speech of surrender and self-defence, *recta*; unfinished when
       our text breaks off)

As we have already seen, the historian avoids presenting a single agonistic
debate; the closest we come to this is 64–5, which involves dialogue between
representatives of two provincial cities, the one group urging active rebellion,
the other prudence. The speeches are embedded in a developing situation;
individuals and citizen bodies need to consider at each point where their
interests lie (as a result, responses cannot always be completely frank or
explicit: 65.1).

The dramatization of a debate self-evidently allows scope to the viewpoint
of both sides, however well or ill-balanced the weight of argument. We might
expect the incidence of single speeches, especially those in *oratio recta*, to
indicate where the initiative lies.[30] That seems to be only part of the truth:
speeches are sometimes included although the speech achieves nothing, and
even when the speaker knows his task to be hopeless. In the early stages
Civilis' persuasive rhetoric goes unresisted: his speech in 14 wins enthusiastic
applause and support (15.1), and detecting a kindred spirit, he cunningly
prevails on the Flavian Montanus to fall in with his schemes (32). Roman
leadership by contrast is at first inept: Hordeonius Flaccus proves ineffectual
and unpopular (18–19, 24, and *passim*); it is appropriate that he is given no
speech, since its reception could only expose his complete lack of authority.[31]
He eventually hands over command to the more dynamic Vocula (25 fin.),
and is subsequently murdered by his own soldiers (36). Vocula is presented
more sympathetically, and is given two speeches in swift succession, one in
indirect speech protesting at the actions of Classicus and Tutor in opting for
the rebellious cause, the other in direct speech addressing his own troops (57,
58). The first of these, described as spoken in a fit of anger ('ferociter'), may
not have struck the ideal note: warning of retribution and recalling precedents, Vocula sternly declared that the Gauls were enemies now, because their
enslavement was too kind ('quia molle seruitium'); once despoiled and
stripped of their possessions, they would become friends perforce.[32] The
speech which follows, addressed to his men, is a splendidly patriotic and
impassioned performance, but one which from the start presupposes his own
failure: Vocula declares that he knows that the mutineers have already decided

---

[30] Cf. Laird (1999), 121–52, on historians' use of *recta* vs *obliqua*.
[31] The same is true of Tacitus' Vitellius, for similar reasons. See further Scott (1998).
[32] Somewhat confirmed by 4.71 ('proniores ad officia quod spernebantur', 'finding themselves despised, they were more ready to submit to orders').

on his own death (it follows in the next chapter, 59). Here then we have an example of futile rhetoric,[33] a speech which achieves nothing within the narrative (the troops' reactions 'varied between hope, fear and shame', 'inter spem metumque ac pudorem'). Why then is the speech included, and at some length? Perhaps partly as a vehicle for older Roman values, as the concluding prayer to Jupiter and Quirinus suggests—values which seem to have lost their force in the era of civil war.[34] The speech also allows the author to include a nightmare vision of what might have been, had the empire of the Gauls gained a firmer power base and a military reality: Roman soldiers marching in the train of Civilis and Classicus to invade Italy, Germans and Gauls leading Italians against the walls of Rome. It needs a defeated general to evoke these horrors: they would be less appropriate in the mouth of one who held the upper hand.

The third representative of Rome in this episode, and the most effective, is Petilius Cerealis, who despite a number of rash or ill-prepared moves succeeds in dampening the rebels' enthusiasm. By the end of the surviving text he is offering peace to the Batavians and negotiating a settlement which may involve pardon for Civilis (5.24). The narrator's comments are not wholly laudatory (71.1 'contemnendis quam cauendis hostibus melior' ('he was more adept at scorning than taking precautions against the enemy'), 77 'felici temeritate' ('a rash but successful move'); 78 fin; 5.21, 22.3).[35] Nevertheless, the comparison between him and Flaccus and Vocula (which he makes himself in one angry tirade at 72) is clearly favourable to him. For our purposes he is especially interesting as the only spokesman for Roman imperialism, in his speech to the assembly of Treveri and Lingones recalling them to their allegiance (4.73–4). This speech has been discussed in a valuable paper by Keitel, but there are perhaps some points still to be added.[36]

First, its placement in the narrative is striking. Cerealis evidently considers that the war is virtually concluded (73.1 'profligato bello'), one of a number of indications of his overconfidence. The audience he addresses, however, evidently share this view: at the end of 74 Tacitus remarks that his speech was successful in calming and reassuring his Gallic listeners, because they had feared much worse ('grauiora metuentis').[37] We have an indication that the speech itself is not the important factor; what matters more is superiority in

---

[33] Woodman (1998), 221 thinks that Tacitus is playing on the etymology of Vocula.

[34] Again the reminiscences of Livy may evoke an earlier 'heroic' age: cf. 4.58 fin. with Livy 9.8.8f.

[35] Cerealis' behaviour in Britain in AD 61 is also characterized by *temeritas* ('rashness', *Ann.* 14.33). Cf. Griffin, *CAH*[2] XI.37: Tacitus clearly thought he had 'more dash than common sense'.

[36] See Keitel (1993), 51–7; also important is Bastomsky (1988).

[37] Cf. Levick (1999), 111: 'Cerealis mercifully let the Gauls off with a stock lecture.'

force (the status of words is highlighted at the opening of the oration, though in a rather different way: see below). But the fact that the conflict will continue also diminishes the sense of finality which this defence of Roman authority might otherwise have possessed.

Second, there is the question of the merits of the defence. This is hardly the strongest case one might make for the Roman empire. Exaggerations and half-truths have long been observed: that the Gauls originally 'invited' Roman intervention is at best a one-sided view of Caesar's activities (cf. *BG* 1.31 ff.); and the claim that Gauls themselves are at the head of legions and provinces, so that they participate fully in government, is a gross overstatement (even for Tacitus' time). Cerealis does not deny that there are abuses and injustice; indeed, he comes close to declaring these inevitable, though one may hope for interludes. This stands in contrast with most justifications of empire in Greek and Roman literature, which tend to lay heavy emphasis on the justice of the ruler and the benefits or protection given to the oppressed.[38] An idealistic picture is discernible in the fragments of Cicero's *de re publica*: it is wrong to assume that existence or expansion of empire can only be achieved unjustly, for empire is not unjust if subjection is in the interest of the conquered. Rule by 'the best' is in the interest of the weak, just as when God rules man, soul rules body, reason dominates desire (3.21–2 Powell).[39] Tacitus gives this argument a sourer emphasis. The core of Cerealis' argument is that Roman government of the Gauls began in order to protect them from oppression by Germany, and that this remains the only alternative: independence is not an option, so that they must simply choose between two masters. It is a bleak argument, remote from idealizing images of the civilizing power welcomed by willing subject peoples.[40]

A third point takes us to the level of detail, and back to the relation between different speeches in this episode. Inevitably in history and historiography, facts often refute words or render them redundant. However, although

---

[38] Brunt (1993), 168–9, citing Thuc. 2.40.4, Isoc. 4.100–19. See further Brunt (1990), 290–1, 316 ff., esp. n. 101; Gruen (1984), 160–1, 274 ff. Note esp. Cic. *de imperio Cn. Pomp.* 36–42, *Q.F.* 1.1.34, *de off.* 1.41, 2.26 f., 75, 3.88 (contrast 85); Str. 16.2.20; Dio Chr. 32.69–71; Plin. *Pan.* 31 f.

[39] Syme (1958), 528 mentions Cicero's views, but his ironic presentation implies that they are unimportant. That they represent an intellectual's fantasy and in any case serve Roman self-interest is obvious, but (as Syme of course realized) they form part of the background against which Tacitus' presentation of Cerealis' thesis can be understood.

[40] Virg. *Geo.* 4.561 'uictorque uolentis | per populos dat iura' ('and victorious distributes laws among nations who welcome them'). Syme (1958), 529 n. 12 refers dismissively to Aelius Aristides' panegyric: 'One could perhaps manage without the panegyric of Aelius Aristides, εἰς Ῥώμην'. Yet however banal its rhetoric, it is relevant in that it shows what some provincials thought ought to be said, in that kind of oration. See Oliver (1953), 892–4, for a broad-brush comparison between Aristides and Tacitus.

Cerealis, seeing himself in a position of strength, might well make this point, what he actually says is more complicated.

neque ego umquam facundiam exercui, et populi Romani uirtutem armis adfirmaui: sed quoniam apud uos uerba plurimum ualent bonaque ac mala non sua natura, sed uocibus seditiosorum aestimantur, statui pauca disserere quae profligato bello utilius sit uobis audisse quam nobis dixisse. (4.73.1)

I have never practised oratory; rather, I have asserted the merits of the Roman people by force of arms. But since words have the greatest weight with you and you do not reckon good and evil according to their own nature, but estimate them by the talk of seditious men, I have decided to say a few things which now that the war is over are more useful for you to have heard than for me to have said.

Words have prevailed among the rebels, but words not controlled by clear understanding of their relation to reality. Now Cerealis considers that his own words can provide the antidote to the delusional thinking promoted by words misused. Among the words which have had most impact on the events narrated are the two opposing terms *libertas* and *seruitus*.[41] Civilis' early speech to the Gallic leaders had made play with the misnomers associated with Roman rule: 'admonebat malorum, quae tot annis perpessi miseram seruitutem falso pacem uocarent' ('he reminded them of the hardships which they had endured for so many years, while giving their miserable enslavement the misnomer of peace', 4.17.2). The point is similar to Calgacus' famous epigram, 'ubi solitudinem faciunt, pacem appellant' ('where they bring about desolation, they call it peace', *Agr.* 30.5).[42] (Later the council at Rheims is summoned to consider whether the Gauls prefer *pax* or *libertas* (67.2); Auspex voices praises of 'bona pacis', 69.1.) But the motif of false naming recurs in Cerealis' speech, in a harsher form. After declaring that German intrusions into Gaul always have the same motives, *libido* and *auaritia* ('desire' and 'greed', motives highlighted by the enemies of Rome in criticizing their territorial encroachments!),[43] he goes on to insist that their acquisitive goals are masked by fine words, words exploited by all such invaders.

---

[41] It is piquant to turn from Tacitus' virtual obsession with *libertas* to the speech of Mithridates in Sallust: there, the Pontic monarch is made to comment that 'pauci libertatem, pars magna iustos dominos volunt' ('Few men desire freedom; the great majority desire just rulers', F 69.18). There the emphasis falls on Rome's hostility to kings, as rival rulers.

[42] For the idea of language perverted for power-related ends, see esp. Thuc. 3.82–3; in Roman historians, esp. Sall. *Cat.* 52.11, *Hist.* 1.12; Tac. *Germ.* 19.1 ('nec corrumpere...'), 36.1, *Hist.* 1.30, 1.37, 1.52, 1.55.7, 1.77, 2.20.2, 2.101, 3.58, *Ann.* 4.19 etc. See Plass (1988), 144–5, 147, Mellor (1993), 92–7.

[43] Note already 4.14.1 'auaritia ac luxu'; cf. *Agr.* 15.5 'auaritiam et luxuriam', 15.3, 31.1.

ceterum libertas et speciosa nomina praetexuntur; nec quisquam alienum seruitium et dominationem sibi concupiuit ut non eadem ista uocabula usurparet.

freedom, however, and specious names are their pretexts; but no man has ever been ambitious to enslave another or to win dominion for himself without using those very same terms.

The formulation again reminds us of Calgacus: according to him, the Roman policy of devastation was masked by talk of peace; according to Cerealis, German imperialism is disguised as freedom. Freedom from Rome will only be a prelude to subjection to Germany. Peace is also mentioned (74.1) but it can be achieved only on Rome's terms; indeed, at the climax of his speech it is boldly united with Rome as an object of devoted loyalty: 'proinde, pacem et urbem, quam uicti uictoresque eodem iure obtinemus, amate colite' ('You should therefore give your love and devotion to the cause of peace, and to that city which we, victors and vanquished alike, possess on equal terms', 74.4).[44] The speech, then, serves partly to show that Romans can turn the tricks of anti-imperialist rhetoric to serve their own ends; also, Cerealis' bold over-statements indicate how little he is concerned to deal fairly with his audience. Both the main argument and the framing narrative make clear how limited the freedom of action of the Gallic peoples actually is. Once dissension at the centre of the empire is at an end, the imperial power reasserts its authority on the frontiers.

IV

This examination of two works by the leading historian of the early Roman empire prompts a number of concluding observations, which may be grouped under two headings, form (which embraces genre) and ideology.

In the *Agricola* the focus is more restricted and the cast of characters small. Both the encomiastic context and the limited information available to Tacitus regarding Caledonian tribes and politics encouraged a presentation in terms of two opposed champions, one representing barbarian defiance and the other a model of Roman generalship. No complexity or tribal rivalries are visible and probably none were known to Tacitus. Nevertheless, he allows Calgacus to seem a formidable opponent, partly by giving him a powerful

---

[44] Patriotism as a lover's devotion recalls Pericles' most impassioned oratory in the Funeral Speech (Thuc. 2.43.1). But Pericles was addressing fellow citizens, not provincial subjects, and men who were fighting in the same cause, not a defeated and disheartened people.

speech. Agricola's prestige is enhanced by his facing a suitably aggressive antagonist: the technique is familiar from epic (and cf. Caratacus' remarks in *Ann.* 12.36–7). At the same time the remoteness of Britain, long proverbial, gives the encounter something of the aura of an expedition to the 'ends of the earth' (again a motif of panegyric, at least since Alexander). A boldly romantic vision of ferocious but single-minded resistance at the brink of Ocean becomes possible. By contrast the setting of the Civilis episode within the larger context of the *Histories* excludes any sense of a self-contained adventure: civil and foreign wars are intertwined, and the mood of the work is pessimistic, with an emphasis on ambition and hypocrisy. The complex political situation is reflected in the diversity of locales, the variety of speakers, the shifting focalization. Civilis is not as effective a spokesman for the downtrodden subject peoples as Calgacus, and is increasingly eclipsed as the episode advances; neither, however, does Cerealis say much to repudiate the slurs on Roman government: in effect, he tells the Gauls they should be grateful things are not worse. There is a clear parallel with speeches in earlier episodes set in Rome, where speakers emphasize the necessity of accepting a less than satisfactory state (Galba in 1.15–16, Marcellus in 4.8 ('ulteriora mirari, praesentia sequi; bonos imperatores uoto expetere, qualiscumque tolerare': 'one must regard with admiration those more distant times, but accept the present day; pray and hope for good emperors, but accept those we have, whatever their character')).[45]

The motifs present in the Civilis episode, of factional antagonism, uncertain motives, fluctuating loyalties, excessive optimism frustrated by inadequate preparation or support and followed by disillusionment and resignation, are the same themes that dominate the civil war sections of the work. *Externa bella* offer a different kind of narrative, but thematically consistent, as the interweaving of the narratives helps demonstrate. This is visible above all in the handling of the triad of abstracts, *libertas, seruitium*, and *pax*. For both the Roman senators and the Batavians and Gauls, *libertas* is a will-of-the-wisp which seems potentially attainable but always out of reach. The argument of Cerealis, that *libertas* from one ruling power will come only at the cost of submission to another, may be cynical and opportunistic, but it is strongly supported by the narrative, and recalls the main thrust of the account of civil war. In the end *pax* seems more important in both spheres than freedom. It would not follow that this was Tacitus' own final view: indeed, it is hard to know what a 'final view' means with such complex

[45] Syme (1958), 192–3 already grouped these three speeches together, in an exemplary discussion of the role of speeches in the *Histories*. Later discussions are synthesized by Keitel (1991), cf. (1993).

arguments and with a historian who tends to avoid sustained passages of abstract argument.[46] In this paper I have assumed that interpreting Tacitus must be a matter of relating different passages to one another; but the different passages, not least the speeches, are situated in a particular context and the arguments arise from that context and are designed to respond to those circumstances; where speeches are concerned, characterization and historical evaluation must also play a part. The text remains polyphonic, not easily malleable into summary and generalization. In this sense too the work of Tacitus contains and engenders voices of resistance.

APPENDIX: THE BRITISH REVOLTS IN THE *ANNALS* (12.31–40, 14.29–39)

The *Annals* have much more to say about dynastic politics and the conflicts of the imperial family than the *Histories* (at least as far as the extant portions allow us to see), but provincial discontent is not neglected. The short account of Caratacus includes some points which can be invoked as comparisons. In 12.33 we read that Caratacus is reinforced by those Britons 'qui pacem nostram metuebant' ('who feared our peace'), a telling oxymoron. Here *pax* is presumably euphemistic for 'subjugation'. The next chapter includes a further version of the topos of fanning the flame of revolt: the tribal leaders encourage their men 'minuendo metu, accendenda spe aliisque belli incitamentis' ('making light of their fears, kindling their hopes, and the other forms of incitement to war'), while Caratacus, like Calgacus, declares that this day will mean the difference between freedom and slavery, and recalls the previous failure of Julius Caesar (cf. *Agr.* 15.4). After the failure of the revolt, Caratacus is the only one of Tacitus' opposing leaders who is brought to Rome in triumph, and although the historian insinuates that Claudius was endeavouring to boost his own status by parading this captive, the defeated leader is permitted both courage and a dignified speech. Although he might have sought alliance and friendship, he had preferred to fight for what was his: 'nam si uos omnibus imperitare uultis, sequitur ut omnes seruitutem accipiant?' ('If you [the Romans] wish to dominate all mankind, does it follow that all mankind must accept slavery?', 37). Again we have the implication that it is a matter of rule or be ruled; neutral independence is not an option, and

---

[46] Martin (1981), 99 is rightly cautious in assessing Cerealis' speech: earlier scholars had sometimes seen it as Tacitus' own defence of empire: e.g. Richmond (1944), 43: 'That Tacitus whole-heartedly shares these views is clear from the force with which he expresses them'.

the 'alliance' which Caratacus might have obtained would have been no more than a cloak for subjection to Rome's rule. But the triumph of the general and the standing of the emperor are qualified in what follows (38.1), through the slighting reference to the eminence of Agrippina (an unprecedented breach of tradition) and the suggestion of bombastic overstatement in the summary of senatorial speech-making on this occasion ('multa et magnifica', 'much full-blown oratory', 38.1)—the claim that the capture of Caratacus is as distinguished an achievement as the victories of Scipio or Paulus is clearly an abuse of history. The innovation is suspect, the appeal to tradition sycophantic; and finally we are told that the British campaign subsequently ran into difficulties.

The chief novelty introduced by the Boudicca episode is the leadership of a revolt by a woman. This point is emphasized wherever the revolt is mentioned (besides this episode, esp. 14.35, cf. *Agr.* 16.1; also 31.4, if 'Trinobantes' is rightly read there). Both narrator and character stress the insults to her person and the violation of her daughters by Roman oppressors (*Ann.* 14.31, 35). The stress on sexuality, even if historical, may perhaps have been thought suited to the complaints of a woman.[47] Prior to the final battle two speeches in *oratio obliqua* are included, by Boudicca and by the Roman general Suetonius Paulinus. Boudicca insists on her offended honour, even declaring herself to be taking revenge as a single individual rather than a queen: it is her own lost freedom, not her tribe's, that she is deploring, as the combination with the subsequent clauses suggests. But the second half of the speech rises to a more heroic note (conquer or die on the field), before stressing her sex once more but in terms of her superiority to those males who might contemplate submission: 'such (she declared) was the resolution of a woman; as for the men, they might live on and be slaves' ('id mulieri destinatum: uiuerent uiri et seruirent'). Paulinus' responding speech is less notable, but tries to use the feminine theme as a source of confidence (more women than youthful warriors to be seen on the opposing side). Unlike Caratacus, Boudicca ends her life on the field, by poison like Cleopatra, and receives no further mention. In all this the *libertas*-theme is less prominent than in the other texts,[48] but the tailpiece in ch. 39 offers a final twist. Nero's freedman Polyclitus is sent to inspect the situation in Britain, in the hope that his presence may reconcile dissenting factions among the Romans and subdue the Britons' spirit. Polyclitus did indeed overawe the Romans ('militibus nostris

---

[47] The female element is stressed elsewhere in the episode too: see 32.1, 34 ad fin. *Hist.* 3.45 on Cartimandua is equally interesting. For discussion of Tacitus' presentation of women see e.g. Syme (1981), Marshall (1984), Wallace (1991), but all of these focus on the women of the imperial court.

[48] Though note 31.2 'et qui alii nondum seruitio fracti' ('and those others so far not broken by slavery'), a close parallel to the comment on the Britons at *Agr.* 11.4.

terribilis')—but because of the immense burden of entertaining his entou-
rage. The Britons, by contrast, found him laughable and were astounded at
the submissiveness of the Roman forces to his authority; 'sed hostibus inrisui
fuit, apud quos flagrante etiam tum libertate nondum cognita libertinorum
potentia erat' ('to the enemy he was a laughing-stock, for at that time they
retained some of the fire of freedom, and had not yet come to know the power
of a freed slave', 14.39.2). Because they are a people who still enjoy *libertas*, the
Britons take a more critical view of the *libertinus* than the Romans who have
surrendered their own freedom and must respect Polyclitus' authority. Wordplay of this kind is frequent in Tacitus, and is often used to make devastating
rhetorical and analytical points.[49] The freedom of the governing power is a
frail thing indeed, if a general who has triumphed over a woman must kowtow
to an ex-slave.

---

[49] Woodman (1998), ch. 12, esp. pp. 218–29.

19

The Art of Losing: Tacitus and the Disaster Narrative

Elizabeth Keitel

'The art of losing isn't hard to master'. So begins Elizabeth Bishop's well-known poem 'One Art'. In this paper, I will examine a topic explored some years ago by Tony Woodman, the disaster narrative as written by Tacitus.[1] Woodman and others have established that most of Tacitus' accounts of disasters are linked somehow to his major thematic concerns.[2] No one, however, has looked closely at all the disasters in the major works nor has anyone examined closely how the historian depicts the experience of the victims in all of these episodes.[3] While it is true that Tacitus takes great interest in imperial largesse and rehabilitation after disasters, this is only part of the story. In the second section of this chapter, I will examine Tacitus' narratives of the quintessential man-made disaster in antiquity, sacks of cities. Some disasters, such as the *Titanic* sinking, have astonishingly long afterlives and function as *exempla* and warnings in a variety of contexts.[4] For the ancients, Troy was the *urbs capta exemplum* par excellence. We shall see how that sack resonates through Tacitus.

A perusal of the *OLD* quickly shows what the Romans regarded as a disaster. So that workhorse *clades* can describe exile, a military defeat, slaughter, the destruction of war, and physical ruins. *Calamitas* can denote a

---

[1] Woodman (1972b) and (1988), 180–96.

[2] Garson (1974), Ginsburg (1981), 100, Newbold (1982), 33, and Waldherr (1997), 165–72.

[3] Newbold (1982), 34 observes 'a lack of emphasis on human injury and suffering' in his samples taken from Thucydides, Diodorus, Tacitus, and Dio.

[4] For the *Titanic* as an *exemplum* in a variety of contexts, see Biel (1996). The Triangle Shirtwaist Factory fire (1911), the collapse of the Equitable Building during a fire (1912), and the *Titanic* disaster (1912) produced a powerful warning that affected building codes in New York City until the 1960s, when the lessons had been forgotten. See Dwyer and Flynn (2005), 107–10. The chief building inspector in Manhattan declared in 1912: 'The Titanic was unsinkable—yet she went down; our skyscrapers are unburnable—yet we shall have a skyscraper disaster which will stagger humanity'. See Glanz and Lipton (2003), 126.

disastrous failure of crops, blight, disease, or a military disaster. *Casus* can describe a misfortune or disaster of the military or political sort, as well as violent death. *Pestis* is applied to physical destruction, plague, pestilence, and the overthrow of people or institutions.

Western literature begins with suffering and disaster in the *Iliad*, and with a rich if painful survivor narrative in the *Odyssey*. Thucydides first sets out the elements of a historical disaster narrative as part of his claim that the Peloponnesian War surpassed all before it. He stresses the unprecedented suffering the war brought Hellas. He begins the list of catastrophes brought by the war with the capture and destruction of cities. His list also includes unprecedented loss of life caused in part by stasis. He closes with a catalogue of natural disasters, earthquakes, drought and famine, culminating with the plague (1.23.1–3).[5] As we shall see, in the preface to the *Histories* Tacitus gives a similar list that combines man-made and natural disasters, and wars of various types, including civil strife.

Woodman has pointed to Cicero's letter to Lucceius (*Fam.* 5.12) as an explanation of how such accounts could give pleasure. Cicero is trying to persuade Lucceius to write a monograph on his consulship. He believes that his experiences will give plenty of variety to his friend's narrative. Cicero continues:

nihil est enim aptius ad delectationem lectoris quam temporum uarietates fortunae-que uicissitudines. quae etsi nobis optabiles in experiendo non fuerunt, in legendo tamen erunt iucundae. habet enim praeteriti doloris secura recordatio delectationem; ceteris uero nulla perfunctis propria molestia, casus autem alienos sine ullo dolore intuentibus, etiam ipsa misericordia est iucunda. quem enim nostrum ille moriens apud Mantineam Epaminondas non cum quadam miseratione delectat? . . . cuius studium in legendo non erectum Themistocli fuga †redituque† retinetur? etenim ordo ipse annalium mediocriter nos retinet quasi enumeratione fastorum; at uiri saepe excellentis ancipites uariique casus habent admirationem, exspectationem, laetitiam, molestiam, spem, timorem; si uero exitu notabili concluduntur, expletur animus iucundissima lectionis uoluptate.

For nothing tends more to the reader's enjoyment than varieties of circumstance and vicissitudes of fortune. For myself, though far from desirable in the living, they will be pleasurable in the reading. For others, who went through no personal distress and painlessly survey misfortunes not their own, even the emotion of pity is enjoyable. Which of us is not affected pleasurably, along with a sentiment of compassion, at the

---

[5] Hornblower, *Comm.* I.62 notes that Thucydides in fact devotes little space to natural disasters despite the promise in 1.23 of 'a sensational and rhetorical narrative with plenty of natural disasters, vividly described human suffering and portents in the manner of Livy'. For the subject of the *Iliad* and *Odyssey* as 'suffering on a grand scale', see Macleod (1983), 157.

story of Epaminondas on the field of Mantinea...? Whose sympathies are not aroused and held as he reads of Themistocles' flight and death? The actual chronological record of events exercises no very powerful fascination upon us; it is like the recital of an almanac. But in the doubtful and various fortunes of an outstanding individual we often find surprise and suspense, joy and distress, hope and fear; and if they are rounded off by a notable conclusion, our minds as we read are filled with the liveliest gratification (Cic. *Fam.* 5.12.4–5, tr. D. R. Shackleton Bailey).[6]

It is these very vicissitudes of fortune that Tacitus misses when he bemoans his dreary subject matter in the *Annals* (4.32). Writers on earlier Roman history could describe 'mighty wars, stormings of cities, routed and captured kings' or political discord on the home front (*Ann.* 4.32.1), while his is *in arto et inglorius labor*, 'a confined and inglorious work' (*Ann.* 4.32.2). Though his narrative may be useful, *ita minimum oblectationis adferunt. nam situs gentium, uarietates proeliorum, clari ducum exitus retinent ac redintegrant legentium animum*, 'they bring very little delight. It is the localities of peoples, the fluctuations of battles, and the memorable deaths of leaders which hold and refresh readers' minds' (*Ann.* 4.33.3). While the emphasis in the passages from Cicero and Tacitus falls largely on the vicissitudes of great men, Tacitus does mention wars and sacks of cities, that is, large-scale disasters, and Thucydides in his preface speaks only of suffering and disaster on the grand scale. Moreover, ancient rhetoricians point repeatedly to sacks of cities when discussing the arousal of pity.[7]

I. FIRES, EARTHQUAKES, FLOODS

Let us turn now to Tacitus' accounts of natural disasters, beginning with a review of their placement within the narrative of the year. Tacitus dates only one disaster, the great fire at Rome, which began on 19 July 64 (*Ann.* 15.41.2). Six reports of disasters occur in material placed at the end of a year, even if they are out of order chronologically; for example the Campanian earthquake

---

[6] For the pleasurable in ancient historiography, see Woodman (1988), 70–4 and Fornara (1983), 120–34.

[7] See Quint. *Inst.* 8.3.67 (quoted below, p. 337) shows how to achieve *enargeia* through a detailed description: *sic <et> urbium captarum miseratio crescit* ('this too is how the pathos of a captured city can be enhanced'). The author of *Rhet. Her.* 4.39.51 demonstrates how to arouse indignation or pity through vivid description of the *miseriae* (miseries) of a captured city; Dio Chrys. *Or.* 32.89 observes that the final stages of the capture of a city make the victims more deserving of pity than ridicule.

of 62 (*Ann.* 15.22.2) which occurred in February according to Seneca (*NQ* 6.6.1) or the flood at Rome in 15 (*Ann.* 1.76) which probably occurred in January or February.[8] Once Tacitus places disasters among the *prodigia* at the end of the *res internae* of a year (*Ann.* 12.43 earthquake, grain shortage, and famine are taken as divine warnings). He twice opens a year with a disaster, the collapse of the amphitheatre at Fidenae (*Ann.* 4.62–3) and a grain shortage at Rome (*Ann.* 15.18.2). We should note too how brief most of these accounts are, seldom more than a sentence or two, and how the focus is largely on imperial or senatorial response to losses suffered by the victims. Nor as Newbold notes, did the historian feel obliged to report all such items; Tacitus omits at least one earthquake (AD 15, cf. Dio 57.14.7), one fire (AD 16, cf. Dio 57.16.2), and one flood (in 36, cf. Dio. 58.26.5), which all occurred at Rome during Tiberius' reign.[9] Moreover, Tacitus, unlike Suetonius and Dio, never reports that members of the Julio-Claudian family rushed to fires to give assistance and urge on the firefighters. According to Suetonius (*Tib.* 50.3), after Tiberius learned that Livia had gone to a fire near the Temple of Vesta and had urged on the people and firefighters to greater efforts, he warned her to 'keep away from matters that are important and not suitable for a woman' although she had done such things while Augustus was alive.[10]

In the *Histories*, we encounter only one natural disaster, a flood in Rome during Otho's brief reign (*Hist.* 1.86). It is included among the *prodigia* that precede his departure. Tacitus places these items right after his account of the mutiny that nearly ended in the murder of senators who were dining with Otho. Tacitus makes a transition to the flood from the unquiet city, with soldiers of Otho and Vitellius allegedly spying on frightened civilians, and senators carefully crafting their looks and responses so as to offend neither contender. Chapter 1.86 begins: *prodigia insuper terrebant diuersis auctoribus uolgata*, 'prodigies which were reported from different sources caused more

---

[8] On date of the flood of AD 15, see Ginsburg (1981), 35 and Goodyear (1981), 170. For seasonal patterns of rainfall and discharge of the Tiber in Rome, see Aldrete (2007), 58–66. The other disasters placed at the end of the year are the fire of AD 36 (*Ann.* 6.45.1), earthquakes in Asia and Achaea (*Ann.* 4.13.1), a fire near Cologne (*Ann.* 13.57.3), and an earthquake at Laodicea (*Ann.* 14.13.1). Ginsburg (1981), 35 sees traces in the *Annals* of Livy's practice of placing natural disasters at the end of a year regardless of when they occurred.

[9] Yet the floods and fires in Tacitus are the most detailed accounts in the sample of Newbold (1982), 33. For the disasters omitted by Tacitus in Tiberius' reign, see Newbold (1982), 36 n. 5.

[10] Dio 57.14.10 mentions that Drusus, son of Tiberius, was forced to help the praetorians lend aid to some people whose house was on fire. Gaius also helped soldiers put out a fire and gave assistance to the victims (Dio 59.9.4). According to Suetonius (*Claud.* 18.1), Claudius remained at the scene of a fire in the Aemiliana for two nights, summoned the people to help, and paid each on the spot for his services. This may be the same fire to which Agrippina accompanied Claudius as he gave assistance (Dio 60.33.12). See Hurley (2001), 139–40.

terror'. An old-fashioned list of *prodigia* follows, complete with a talking ox in Etruria and some unnatural animal births, things Tacitus says 'which in primitive ages used to be noted even during peace, but which now are heard of only in perilous times'. He continues, *sed praecipuus et cum praesenti exitio etiam futuri pauor subita inundatione Tiberis*, 'but there was particular fear connected with both present disaster and future danger caused by a sudden overflow of the Tiber' (*Hist.* 1.86.2).

This is a detailed account by ancient standards, yet it is little over eight Teubner lines, less than half the chapter. In one sentence Tacitus gives us the flood itself, caused by a blockage created by the wreckage of the *Pons Sublicius*, and its unusual severity: it affected not only the low-lying parts of the city usually flooded, *sed secura eius modi casuum impleuit*, 'but also filled areas normally free of such disasters' (*Hist.* 1.86.2). In the second sentence, Tacitus gives no count of fatalities, but instead a brief but graphic picture of how people died: *rapti e publico plerique, plures in tabernis et cubilibus intercepti*, 'many were swept away in the open, more cut off in shops and in their beds' (*Hist.* 1.86.2). As Damon observes, the pairing of *cubilibus* with *tabernis* is surprising and injects a note of pathos 'as death takes its victims unaware'.[11] Tacitus then describes the general misery of *insulae* collapsing when their foundations were undermined and the famine from which the *uulgus* suffered as food supplies ran out and men lost work. In closing, the historian notes that as soon as people's minds were relieved from the danger of the flood, the fact that Otho's route was blocked twice, once through the Campus Martius, and later on the via Flaminia, *a fortuitis uel naturalibus causis in prodigium et omen imminentium cladium uertebatur*, 'was turned from chance or natural causes into a prodigy and an omen of impending disaster' (*Hist.* 1.86.3). Plutarch states that most people regarded this flood as 'a baleful sign'. And while he notes the severity of the flood and the dire scarcity of food for many days after the grain market was flooded, he says nothing about how people died (Plut. *Otho* 4.5).

The shocking suddenness with which disaster overtakes people at *Hist.* 1.86 is a constant in Tacitus' accounts. So because the earthquake in Asia (AD 17) happened at night, 'its destruction was the more unforeseen and the more devastating' (*quo inprouisior grauiorque pestis fuit*, *Ann.* 2.47.1). Nor could the victims find safety in the usual fashion by running out into open ground, since chasms opened in front of them and swallowed them up.[12] Sudden

---

[11] Damon (2003), 279. On *Hist.* 1.86, see also Scott (1968), 63–6.

[12] Pliny *NH* 2.200 calls this earthquake *maximus terrae memoria mortalium . . . motus* ('the greatest earthquake in human memory'). For earthquakes as portents, see Krauss (1930), 49–53. For Tacitus' treatments of earthquakes as prodigial, see Davies (2004), 163–4.

death also overtakes the victims of the collapse of the amphitheatre at Fidenae, the fire of 64, and the plague of 65.[13]

Tacitus shows a marked interest in details of physical destruction and the consequent imperial largesse and rebuilding after disasters.[14] Indeed, these accounts in the *Annals* often reflect Tiberius' generosity, one of the few virtues the historian allows him. Tacitus recounts in detail the aid the *princeps* gave to the twelve famous cities in Asia after the earthquake (*Ann.* 2.47) calling it a *magnificam largitionem*, splendid largesse (*Ann.* 2.48.1). He again notes Tiberius' liberality after fire largely destroys the Caelian hill (*Ann.* 4.64). The emperor wins praise from all classes of people: *quia sine ambitione aut proximorum precibus, ignotos etiam et ultro accitos munificentia iuuerat*, 'for without respect of persons, and without the lobbying of relatives, he had helped with his liberality even unknown people or those whom he himself had sought out' (*Ann.* 4.64.2). Earlier, men had called the year *feralem*, 'ill-omened' (*Ann.* 4.64.1) and claimed that Tiberius' decision to absent himself from Rome had been adopted under *om<i>nibus aduersis*, 'unfavourable omens' (*Ann.* 4.64.1).[15] Likewise, Tiberius converts the disastrous fire of AD 36 to his own glory by paying the full value of the *domus* and *insulae* that were destroyed (*Ann.* 6.45.1).[16] Nero offers shelter to the many victims of the great fire of 64 and has grain brought to the city and sold at a reduced price (*Ann.* 15.39.2). He also pays for porticos for the new *insulae*, clears building sites at his own expense, and offers bonuses to those who rebuild within a fixed term (*Ann.* 15.43.2–3).[17]

As is apparent even from those examples, Tacitus can achieve multiple objectives in one disaster narrative. Tiberius seldom moves out from under a cloud in the *Annals*, even when being generous. And while Tacitus does not state flatly that Nero ordered the fire of 64, he still covers that emperor in odium, as we shall see shortly. A smaller example occurs at *Ann.* 1.76, when Tacitus mentions a serious flood of the Tiber, which left a *strages*, 'wreckage', of buildings and men (*Ann.* 1.76.1). The rest of the chapter concerns a proposal by Asinius Gallus that the Sibylline Books be consulted. Tiberius

[13] Juv. 3.255–67 describes the sudden death of a poor man at Rome, crushed by a load of marble falling from a wagon after its axle breaks. His corpse is obliterated while his unknowing family prepares dinner at home.

[14] Newbold (1982), 33.

[15] According to Suet. *Tib.* 48.1, this was one of only two instances in which Tiberius was generous to the public.

[16] Davies (2004), 163–4 points out that by his generous relief efforts Tiberius defused situations (*Ann.* 4.64 and 6.45) that could have been interpreted adversely.

[17] While Tacitus is exceptional in reporting these improvements, he does not give the reader any idea of the long-term effects of the fire on the populace. See Newbold (1974).

objects, *perinde diuina humanaque obtegens,* 'concealing divine and human things alike' (*Ann.* 1.76.1). Judith Ginsburg has shown how Tacitus has structured the narrative of AD 15, moving events out of chronological order, to produce a sustained contrast between the characters of Germanicus and Tiberius.[18] Tacitus likewise takes advantage of the flood to reinforce his portrait of Tiberius as secretive, controlling, and suspicious.[19] We should note too, however, that Tacitus does describe the attempt of Ateius Capito and Lucius Arruntius, appointed by the emperor to find a way to coerce the river. Their efforts come to nought, after protests from communities upstream that themselves fear flooding if the rivers that feed the Tiber are diverted (*Ann.* 1.79).

II. *URBS CAPTA*

I turn now to the sacks of cities, literal and metaphorical. To the ancients, the capture and sack of the city must have seemed the ultimate disaster. In one cataclysmic moment an individual could lose his house and property, his family, his homeland, and his freedom. And he could be condemned to live on, to borrow a phrase from Tacitus, to survive himself (*Agr.* 3.2). Or in the words of a survivor of the sack of Jerusalem, 'he has cast me into a place of darkness, like those long dead' (*Lam.* 3:5–6). It is clear from Quintilian that the sack of a city still had emotive power even after hundreds of years of literary and visual portrayal. In discussing *enargeia,* he observes that sometimes we create our picture through a number of details:

Sic <et> urbium captarum crescit miseratio. Sine dubio enim qui dicit expugnatam esse ciuitatem complectitur omnia quaecumque talis fortuna recipit, sed in adfectus minus penetrat breuis hic uelut nuntius. At si aperias haec, quae uerbo uno inclusa erant, apparebunt effusae per domus ac templa flammae et ruentium tectorum fragor et ex diuersis clamoribus unus quidem sonus, aliorum fuga incerta, alii extremo complexu suorum cohaerentes et infantium feminarumque ploratus et male usque in illum diem seruati fato senes: tum illa profanorum sacrorumque direptio, efferentium praedas repetentiumque discursus, et acti ante suum quisque praedonem catenati, et conata retinere infantem suum mater, et sicubi maius lucrum est pugna inter uictores. Licet enim haec omnia, ut dixi, complectatur 'euersio', minus est tamen

---

[18] Ginsburg (1981), 70–1 and Syme (1958), 314 n. 5.
[19] For possible reasons why Tiberius may not have wanted the Sibylline Books consulted, see Goodyear (1981), 170–1.

totum dicere quam omnia. Consequemur autem ut manifesta sint si fuerint ueri similia, et licebit etiam falso adfingere quidquid fieri solet.

This too is how the pathos of a captured city can be enhanced. No doubt, simply to say 'the city was stormed' is to embrace everything implicit in such a disaster, but this brief communiqué, as it were, does not touch the emotions. If you expand everything which was implicit in the one word, there will come into view flames racing through houses and temples, the crash of falling roofs, the single sound made up of many cries, the blind flight of some, others clinging to their dear ones in a last embrace, shrieks of children and women, the old men whom an unkind fate has allowed to see this day; then will come the pillage of property secular and sacred, the frenzied activity of plunderers carrying off their booty and going back for more, the prisoners driven in chains before their captors, the mother who tries to keep her child with her, and the victors fighting one another wherever the spoils are richer. 'Sack of a city' does, as I said, comprise all these things; but to state the whole is less than to state all the parts. We shall succeed in making the facts evident if they are plausible; it will even be legitimate to invent things of the kind that usually occur. (Quint. *Inst.* 8.3.67–70, tr. D. A. Russell)

G. M. Paul attributes the diffusion of the *urbs capta* motif to the popularity of the theme of the destruction of Troy: 'Influenced by such descriptions [as Hellanicus' *Troica*] the general theme of the capture of cities was also early established in epic, tragedy, and historiography, and no doubt recurring patterns of events were to be observed in actual captures'.[20] He also notes the restraint with which Sallust, Livy, and Tacitus describe these scenes after the excesses of the Hellenistic historians.[21] In the debate between Caesar and Cato about putting to death the Catilinarian conspirators, Sallust makes clear how hackneyed a topos the *urbs capta* had become. Caesar mocks earlier speakers for using it and trots out a few of their tropes: how girls and boys are ravished, children torn from their parents' arms, wives subjected to the lusts of conquerors, and so forth (Sall. *Cat.* 51.9). Cato, in reply, points out that some crimes need to be punished *before* they are committed: *capta urbe nihil fit reliqui uictis,* 'When a city is captured, nothing is left for the defeated' (Sall. *Cat.* 52.4). For the Romans, sometimes a mere mention of the theme will suffice. So Livy describes the sack of Victumulae: *neque ulla, quae in tali re memorabilis scribentibus uideri solet, praetermissa clades est; adeo omne libidinis crudelitatisque et inhumanae superbiae editum in miseros exemplum est,* 'nor was any calamity omitted which historians usually think noteworthy in

---

[20] Paul (1982), 148.

[21] Polybius (2.56) attacks Phylarchus for his 'ignoble and womanish' treatment of the sack of Mantinea. Plutarch (*Per.* 28) chastises Duris of Samos for inventing atrocities that did not occur when Pericles took control of that island. See also Paul (1982), 145.

such situations: every type of lust, cruelty, and inhuman arrogance was inflicted on the wretched' (Liv. 21.57.14).[22]

Woodman has analysed the *urbs capta* elements in the collapse of the amphitheatre at Fidenae in AD 27. Indeed Tacitus begins his account with *ingentium bellorum cladem aequauit malum improuisum,* 'an unexpected disaster equalled the casualties of great wars' (*Ann.* 4.62.1). The historian blames this disaster mainly on shoddy construction, for which the sponsor of the games is exiled, and which prompts changes in minimum property requirements for anyone who wants to put on a gladiatorial show. But Tiberius is also blamed since he had deprived the Romans of such pleasures. As a result *adfluxere auidi talium ... uirile ac muliebre secus, omnis aetas, ob propinquitatem loci effus<i>us; unde grauior pestis fuit,* 'fans streamed in ... both men and women, every age, pouring out in greater numbers because the site was near; hence the death-toll was greater' (*Ann.* 4.62.2). As Woodman observes, Tacitus creates a sickening contrast between Tiberius, the *princeps* who has abandoned Rome and his duty, the lonely debauchee at Sperlonga saved from the collapse of a ceiling by Sejanus in the preceding chapters, and the citizens crushed in an instant at Fidenae because of his meanness (*eius initium simul et finis exstitit,* 'it was over as soon as it began', *Ann.* 4.62.1).[23] Among the *urbs capta* elements in this scene are the collapse of the building, the description of the crowd, male and female, old and young, and the cries of the women and children in the aftermath of the disaster. The battlefield is also recalled when the relatives turn over the mutilated bodies to try to identify them.[24] Finally, the generosity of the Roman nobles, who opened their houses and offered medical assistance to the victims, recalls Roman behaviour after great battles of old (*Ann.* 4.63.2), especially Livy 2.47.12, when the consul M. Fabius billeted wounded soldiers on the patricians, who cared for them (*saucios milites curandos diuidit patribus*).

And it is that final point, I believe, that explains Tacitus' expansive treatment of the sufferings of the victims and their families, unique in his disaster narratives. Here he notes the innocent bystanders killed, when the building buckled outward in its collapse; the pitiable lot of the severely injured (presumably pinned in the wreckage) who see their relatives by day and hear their cries at night; the laments of those who learn of their losses (of a

---

[22] Walsh (1961), 195 discusses this and other examples of Livy's 'purposeful restraint' in such narratives, in contrast to the sensationalism of other historians.

[23] Woodman (1972b), 157–8 notes a second contrast between Tiberius, who survives his accident, and the many at Fidenae who do not.

[24] Woodman (1972b), 156 n. 2.

brother, a relative, a parent); the more widespread dread caused by the uncertainty of those who were missing someone; the rapid convergence of relatives on the corpses to embrace and kiss them; the quarrels that broke out over bodies with badly mangled faces. Tacitus puts the total number of casualties at 50,000 (*Ann.* 4.63.1), Suetonius at 20,000 (Suet. *Tib.* 40). Tacitus can be savagely critical of all classes of society, especially the lower ones, but when it comes to disasters perpetrated on them by the *princeps*, he stresses instead their common humanity. He calls the victims at Fidenae an *immensam uim mortalium*, 'a huge mass of humanity' (*Ann.* 4.62.2).[25] When the *proceres* open their homes to the victims, Tacitus describes Rome as a city *quamquam maesta facie, ueterum instituti<s> similis*, 'though of sorrowful appearance, yet resembling the customs of old' (*Ann.* 4.63.2). This is Rome united as if against a foreign foe. If Tiberius is not yet that foe, he soon will be. Tacitus has already indicated such at *Ann.* 4.58.3, where he looks ahead to the years when Tiberius often sits beside/besieges the walls of Rome (*saepe moenia urbis adsidens*), and this will become crystal clear in Book 6.[26] Tacitus thus uses the disaster to rouse in the reader the emotions recommended by the rhetoricians for the *urbs capta*—*indignatio* at the cruelty displayed and *miseratio* for the victims.[27]

Tacitus shows a similar blend of compassion and indignation for the victims of a pestilence in 65. The last chapter of that year begins: *tot facinoribus foedum annum etiam dii tempestatibus et morbis insigniuere*, 'the gods also marked out a year fouled by so many crimes with storms and diseases' (*Ann.* 16.13.1). A whirlwind which lays waste crops and farms in Campania even comes near Rome, *in qua omne mortalium genus uis pestilentiae depopulabatur, nulla caeli intemperie, quae occur<er>et oculis*, 'in which the force of a disease was ravaging every class of mortal, though with no visible blight in the air' (*Ann.* 16.13.1).[28] But the houses were filled with corpses, the streets with funerals. Neither sex, nor age, nor class gave immunity from danger. Tacitus brilliantly captures the speed with which the disease overwhelmed its victims:

---

[25] Martin–Woodman (1989), 235 note the pathos and precariousness of life expressed in *immensam uim mortalium*.

[26] For Tiberius in full bloom in *Annals* 6 as a tyrant making war on his own city, see Keitel (1984), 307. On Tiberius and Nero as stock tyrants in the *Annals*, see Walker (1952), 204–14. For cruelty as proverbial in sacks of cities, see Woodman (1972b), 155 and n. 3.

[27] See Martin–Woodman (1989), 235 on *miserandi magis*: 'By actually referring to pity T. intensifies the emotional tone'. See also Garson (1974), 24 on how the style of *Ann.* 4.62.3 'admirably conveys the helplessness of the victims'.

[28] Tacitus links the two disasters of *Ann.* 6.13, the whirlwind and the plague, through their speed and indiscriminate destruction. See Koestermann (1968), 358 on the whirlwind and Garson (1974), 25 on the plague. Pliny *NH* 7.169 and 26.3–4 notes that some diseases attacked different social classes.

while wives and children sat by the bedside, while they mourned, they too were burnt on the same pyre: *qui dum adsunt, dum deflent, saepe eodem rogo cremabantur* (*Ann.* 16.13.2).[29] The deaths of *equites* and *nobiles*, although indiscriminate, were less lamentable, because they had, Tacitus says, through the common mortality, escaped the *saeuitiam principis*. Tacitus chooses to emphasize Nero's cruelty rather than connect the plague specifically to the overcrowded and substandard living conditions that many Romans must have endured after the fire.[30]

As usual, Tacitus achieves multiple effects here. First, simple compassion for the sufferings of the Romans at the end of a catastrophic year. Savage reprisals, the *saeuitia principis*, set off by the abortive Pisonian conspiracy, flow right into the next year, 66, when Nero decides to exterminate virtue itself, in the persons of Thrasea Paetus and Barea Soranus (*Ann.* 16.21.1). The very last item in 16.13 is Nero's gift to Lugdunum after a *clades*, presumably a fire, in thanks for their generosity to Rome after the fire of 64. Thus the year ends with a reminder of another catastrophe allegedly wrought by the ruler against his own people. The *saeuitiam principis* may recall the *saeuitiam unius* by which the unfortunate Christians perished as scapegoats for the fire of 64. Nero turned their punishment into a spectacle at which he presided dressed as a charioteer. The Christians were covered in animal skins and torn apart by dogs or used as torches to light his gardens (*Ann.* 15.44.4): *unde quamquam aduersus sontes et nouissima exempla meritos miseratio oriebatur, tamquam non utilitate publica, sed in saeuitiam unius absumerentur*, 'whence pity arose for those, because although guilty and deserving the severest punishment, they were destroyed not for the public good but to satisfy the cruelty of the *princeps*' (*Ann.* 15.44.5).[31]

Tacitus does *not* use the plague narrative or any other disaster episode in the *Annals* to depict a mass breakdown of *nomoi* among ordinary Romans, such as Thucydides described among the Athenians during the plague. The dead are mourned and cremated. Though relatives sometimes are forced to cremate two family members on the same pyre, Tacitus makes no criticism.[32]

---

[29] See Syme (1958), 347 on the style at *Ann.* 6.13.2.

[30] Newbold (1974), 868–9.

[31] While Tacitus spares the reader a description of people burning to death in the fire, he lays out in graphic detail the execution of the Christians. See Garson (1974), 24–5. As Murgatroyd (2005), 53 observes, the execution of the Christians 'provides a pointed final image of people being done away with/consumed (by fire) to gratify Nero's savagery'. For Tacitus' tendency to omit ugly details, see Syme (1958), 189.

[32] As part of deteriorating behaviour during the plague at Athens, Thucydides describes some Athenians placing corpses of their kin on other people's pyres (Thuc. 2.52.4). Tacitus aims at pathos, not criticism in *Ann.* 13.16; perhaps he also did not see multiple cremations by one family on the same pyre as an affront to *pietas*.

Relatives still sit by the bedside of the dying though they are themselves at risk. Only the henchmen of the *princeps* can prevent this. So at *Ann.* 6.19, friends and relatives of those executed for associating with Sejanus are forbidden from standing by or even mourning the corpses before they are dragged to the Tiber. No one even dared touch or cremate the bodies when they washed up later: *inciderat sortis humanae commercium ui metus, quantumque saeuitia glisceret, miseratio arcebatur,* 'the dealings of the human lot had fallen by the force of fear, and, as cruelty grew, pity was kept at a distance' (*Ann.* 6.19.3). Tacitus in the *Annals* reserves his analysis of the breakdown of *nomoi* for the principes themselves and their allies in the political sphere.[33]

The most extensive disaster narrative in the extant *Annals* is the fire at Rome in 64, nearly five Teubner pages. Tacitus places it right after the 'marriage' of Nero to a catamite (15.38.1):

Sequitur clades, forte an dolo principis incertum (nam utrumque auctores prodidere), sed omnibus, quae huic urbi per uiolentiam ignium acciderunt, grauior atque atrocior.

Disaster followed, it was uncertain whether by chance or by the *princeps'* cunning, (for authors have given each version), but one more grievous and terrible than all which have befallen this city through raging fire.

Unlike Suetonius and Dio, Tacitus does not blame Nero outright for starting the fire, though he states that Romans were prevented from putting it out, that they saw people feeding the blaze (*Ann.* 15.38.7), and that the fire began again mysteriously, from the Aemilian estates of Tigellinus, which earned Nero more infamy amidst rumours that he wanted to destroy Rome to build a new city (*Ann.* 15.40.2). Tacitus does make it clear, however, that the populace held Nero responsible (*Ann.* 15.44.1).[34]

A comparison of Tacitus' account of the fire itself with the epitome of Dio is illuminating (Dio 62.16–18).[35] Both use the same four *urbs capta* motifs familiar from Quintilian: flames racing through houses and temples; the cries of the old and young, male and female; confusion exemplified by some people moving and others stopping or standing still; and pillaging. Of course, this time Romans are taking the belongings of their fellows. Tacitus merely mentions the possibility of looters (*Ann.* 15.38.7), while the epitome of Dio twice describes their activities. But differing versions of how the fire started

---

[33] Keitel (1984), 317–25. The Roman *nobiles* can no longer afford to show compassion as they had after the Fidenae disaster since their own lives are now at risk.

[34] For Tacitus' technique here see Ryberg (1942), 398–400 and Murgatroyd (2005).

[35] For the common source(s) used by Dio, Suetonius, and Tacitus for the fire of 64, see Beaujeu (1960), 11–13. Daugherty (1992), 233 also points out the absence of fire-suppression in all three accounts.

colour the rest of their accounts. Tacitus asserts a single point of origin, with suspicious fires arising elsewhere later, whereas Dio describes multiple fires set at the outset. While both writers stress the victims' confusion and varied reactions, Tacitus emphasizes much more the speed of the fire, spread by the wind and the resulting helplessness of its victims.[36] And the narrow, winding streets and irregular blocks of old Rome did not help (*Ann.* 15.38.3). No matter where the Romans turn, there is the fire (*Ann.* 15.38.5). And Tacitus textually envelops the victims with references to Nero's alleged role in starting the conflagration.[37] Suetonius' much briefer account features Nero attacking the walls of Rome and destroying a stone building with *bellicis machinis*, siege engines, on property he wanted near his palace (*Ner.* 38.1).

The epitome of Dio reports that some, grieving over the public calamity and 'crazed', threw themselves in the flames (62.18.1). Tacitus simply states that some, having lost their livelihood or grieving for loved ones they could not save, died when they could have escaped (*Ann.* 15.38.6).[38] These are the only deaths Tacitus mentions, while the epitome of Dio recounts that many were suffocated and many were trampled underfoot (Dio 62.16.7) and 'countless persons perished' (Dio. 62.18.2). Indeed, in his disaster accounts, Tacitus focuses less on people dying than on the grief and despair of the living. Unlike the epitome of Dio, Tacitus does not provide much realistic detail, even omitting the smoke that must have caused fatalities or made escape even more difficult.[39] In both accounts, Romans recall the burning of the city by the Gauls (*Ann.* 15.41.2; Dio 62.17.3). Tacitus, the epitome of Dio, and Suetonius all agree that Nero sang the *excidium Troianum* (the fall of Troy) as the city burned (*Ann.* 15.39.3; Suet. *Ner.* 38.2; Dio 62.18.1). The epitome of Dio concludes with the obvious: 'to the eyes of the spectators it was the capture of Rome' (Dio 62.18.1).

Tacitus has already characterized Rome as a captive city under Nero in Book 13, when he brawls in disguise with citizens in the streets at night (*Ann.* 13.25.2). While Tacitus does allude to the *urbs capta* in his account of the fire itself, he amplifies the theme in the aftermath: the emperor's pillaging of Italy and the provinces to build the *domus aurea* (15.45.1):

[36] Garson (1974), 24.

[37] Miller (1973), 89 and Garson (1974), 24. See also Murgatroyd (2005), 50.

[38] For examples of suicide during a modern disaster, see Milton (2008), 339 and 365 on the sack of Smyrna.

[39] For Tacitus' omission of heat and smoke from his description of the fire, see Newbold (1982), 33. On Tacitus' avoidance at *Ann.* 15.38 of realistic detail in favour of creating 'an immediate perception of a psychological state', see Walker (1952), 190–1.

Interea conferendis pecuniis peruastata Italia, prouinciae euersae sociique populi et quae ciuitatium liberae uocantur. inque eam praedam etiam dii cessere, spoliatis in urbe templis, egestoque auro, quod triumphis, quod uotis omnis populi Romani aetas prospere aut in metu sacrauerat.

In the meantime, for contributions of money, Italy was ravaged, the provinces ransacked, and the allies and those communities which are called free. Even the gods formed part of that plunder, their temples in the city plundered and their gold carried off, which during triumphs and vows every generation of the Roman people had sanctified in prosperity or fear.

To Tacitus and Suetonius (*Ner.* 38.3), Nero is the looter par excellence.[40]

Tacitus certainly alludes to Book 5 of Livy in this narrative, especially, as Christina Kraus has noted, when describing the new urban plan instituted after the fire.[41] Broad straight streets replaced the jerry-built city that had sprung up after 390 BC (*Ann.* 15.43.1) While Tacitus has the Romans recall the capture and burning of Rome by the Senones, he does not lace his account with reminiscences from Livy. He may want to avoid giving a heroic patina to a catastrophe caused not by a foreign foe but perhaps by the ruler himself. Nor does the historian evoke the fall of Troy aside from Nero's musical performance. Baxter argues that the paucity of Virgilian reminiscences in *Annals* 15.38–44 arises not only from a shift in his style away from the poetic in the later books, but also because Tacitus had in *Histories* 3 and *Annals* 1 'developed his use of Virgilian reminiscences to their limit'.[42] This may be, but as Baxter himself showed, Tacitus has already applied the sack of Troy to the travails of Rome in the civil wars of 69. And to that I now turn.

In the preface to the *Histories* Tacitus announces a disaster narrative, in Woodman's words, 'of the most vivid and dramatic type': *Opus adgredior opimum casibus, atrox proeliis, discors seditionibus, ipsa etiam pace saeuom,* 'I begin a work abundant in incident, fierce with battles, discordant with civil strife, savage even in peace' (*Hist.* 1.2.1).[43] We meet the familiar theme of vicissitudes of fortune in various guises five times: Britain conquered and almost immediately lost; the towns of Campania buried by Vesuvius; the sea swarming with exiles and Romans being ruined by their friends or slaves; the wars both foreign and civil and natural disasters on a grand scale. Tacitus

---

[40] Tacitus begins his account of Nero's restoration efforts with *urbis quae domui supererant,* 'those parts of the city that survived his house', *Ann.* 15.43.1). As Murgatroyd (2005), 52 observes, Tacitus thus undercuts his account of Nero's restorative measures before he describes them. See also Edwards (1996), 52: 'Nero's appropriation of the city is like that of a foreign enemy'. For other instances of Nero making war on Rome, see Keitel (1984), 307–8.

[41] Kraus (1994b), 286–7.

[42] Baxter (1968), 168. On the Virgilian reminiscences in *Ann.* 15, see Baxter (1968), 149–56.

[43] Woodman (1988), 167.

concludes the preface with a reference to portents and other premonitions of good and evil: *nec enim umquam atrocioribus populi Romani cladibus magisue iustis indiciis adprobatum est non esse curae deis securitatem nostram, esse ultionem*, 'for never was it proven with more terrible disasters or with fuller portents that the gods are concerned not with our safety but with our punishment' (*Hist.* 1.3.2). Finally, the historian omits many positive features of this period which might have mitigated the air of gloom.[44]

In the preface Tacitus stresses elements of the *urbs capta* when discussing Rome: the city burned twice; temples destroyed; and the *delatores* (malicious prosecutors) who took priesthoods and consulships as their *spolia* (spoils) (*Hist.* 1.2.3).[45] And the *urbs capta*, literal and metaphorical, dominates the first three books of the *Histories*, with two emperors killed in Rome, the burning of the Temple of Jupiter, and the sack of Cremona. The structure and content of the preface suggest that Rome's disaster was ongoing. So Fuhrmann observed that Tacitus' epigram about the gods creates an atmosphere that is maintained throughout the whole work.[46] And long before her actual capture by the Flavians Rome exhibits the symptoms of a captured city. As we look at Rome under Galba and Vitellius, we also need to revisit how and why Tacitus uses Virgilian reminiscences in those narratives to keep the fall of Troy before the reader.

In the 'archaeology' (*Hist.* 1.4–11) as the year 69 opens, Tacitus surveys *qualis status urbis, quae mens exercituum, quis habitus prouinciarum*, 'the condition of the city, the mind of the armies, the attitude of the provinces' (*Hist.* 1.4.1) and stresses the same three motives, greed, hatred, and fear, at work everywhere.[47] The situation is volatile when individuals, armies, and communities, angered at having their self-interest threatened, or feeling guilty or frightened because of their half-hearted support of the new ruler, realize that further treachery may bring them rewards. The preface is a litany of such complaints and possible betrayals.[48] When discussing the causes of recurring Roman civil wars in Book 2, Tacitus notes that greed and the innate human desire for power are inextricably linked (*Hist.* 2.38.1). And Otho, trying to calm the mutinous praetorians, calls hatred and greed the usual causes of

---

[44] Damon (2003), 82–3.

[45] Woodman (1988), 166–7 discusses some of these. For the *delatores* see Powell, Ch. 13 in this volume.

[46] Fuhrmann (1960), 253.

[47] On the greed of the soldiers as a recurring theme in the *Histories*, see Sage (1990), 914–15.

[48] Greed: of the praetorians (*Hist.* 1.5.1); of Galba's courtiers (*Hist.* 1.7.3); of Galba himself (*Hist.* 1.5.2). Anger/resentment: Gallic communities closest to the Rhine angered by Galba's treatment of them (*Hist.* 1.8.1). Fear/resentment: armies of lower Germany (*Hist.* 1.8.2); Romans' hatred of Galba for inflicting punishments on Roman citizens without trial (*Hist.* 1.7.2).

sedition (*Hist.* 1.83.2). Tacitus underlines these basic points with allusions to the *urbs capta* and to Troy.

From the outset, Tacitus intimates that Rome is under siege from within and without. He calls Galba's entrance into the city, *infaustus omine,* 'ill omened' (*Hist.* 1.6.2), a reminiscence of *Aen.* 11.589, because he had massacred *tot milibus inermium militum,* 'so many thousands of unarmed soldiers' (Nero's marines) within sight of the city. The context of the Virgilian reminiscence is Diana's instructions to Opis to avenge the death of Camilla. N. P. Miller calls the reminiscence, 'a fitting comment on the first conflict on Latin soil of what was to be a long year of civil strife and slaughter'.[49] When Galba's advisers debate whether he should leave the palace and try to face down the revolt of Otho and the praetorians, Vinius urges Galba to hide out in the palace until the praetorians come to their senses. Miller notes the use of *firmandos aditus,* 'the doors should be blocked' (*Hist.* 1.32.2), an unusual phrase, a reminiscence of Turnus' orders to his troops to guard Latinus' city, *pars aditus urbis firmet,* 'part should secure the approaches to the city' (*Aen.* 11.466).[50] Others urge the princeps to go out by sarcastically picturing Galba with his cowardly friends ready to endure a siege (*obsidionem*) while Otho invades the forum (*Hist.* 1.33.1). Thus Galba, Priam-like, is besieged in his own palace. Such language is absent from the other ancient accounts. And Tacitus may well have also added the simile with which he describes the praetorians bursting into the forum as if they were about to drive a Vologaeses or Pacorus from the throne of the Arsacids, *ac non imperatorem suum inermem et senem trucidare pergerent* 'and were not hurrying to cut down, their own emperor—an unarmed old man' (*Hist.* 1.40.2).[51]

Herbert Benario suggested that Galba might well recall Priam in that both are old men, both don armour which proves useless, both are savagely slain at a sacred spot, and the corpses of both are mutilated and decapitated.[52] And Tacitus may evoke Priam's death when he says that the disloyal praetorians 'aware of their actions, were ready to pollute the city with the blood of their ruler' (*foedare principis sui sanguine sobrii parabant, Hist.* 1.26; cf. *Aen.* 2.501–2: *Priamumque per aras | sanguine foedantem quos ipse sacrauerat ignis,* 'Priam among the altars polluting with his blood the fires which he himself had consecrated'). Tacitus may also have Virgil in mind when he calls Galba an *inualidum senem,* 'a weak old man' (*Hist.* 1.6.1). Thus Virgil describes the old

---

[49] Miller (1986), 94.
[50] Miller (1986), 94–95.
[51] That Galba's own supporters break down the Palace doors and carry him off only to desert him later reflects one cause of the emperor's ruin—his faithless friends. See Keitel (2006), 230–2.
[52] Benario (1972).

men going to the walls and towers of Latinus' city to watch the duel between Aeneas and Turnus (*Aen.* 12.132). Miller suggests that Tacitus uses a Virgilian echo and Virgilian context to emphasize Galba's helplessness and a siege-like condition at Rome.[53] After Galba's murder, Otho is carried through the Forum which, in best *urbs capta* fashion, is still strewn with corpses (*cruento adhuc foro per stragem iacentium, Hist.* 1.47.2).[54]

Tacitus charges the armies of all three pretenders with cruelty and depradations against Italians and Romans worthy of a foreign foe. So the Othonian troops burn, devastate, and pillage northern Italy *tamquam externa litora et urbes hostium*, 'as if they were on foreign shores and the cities of an enemy' (*Hist.* 2.12.2). Tacitus' rhetoric escalates when recounting the excesses of the Vitellians: *ceterum Italia grauius atque atrocius quam bello adflictabatur. dispersi per municipia et colonias Vitelliani spoliare rapere, ui et stupris polluere*, 'But Italy was now afflicted more grievously and savagely than in war. The troops of Vitellius, scattered among the municipalities and colonies, pillaged, plundered, and raped' (*Hist.* 2.56.1). Vitellius has to be dissuaded from entering Rome *ut captam urbem*, 'as if it were a captured city' (*Hist.* 2.89.1), but the next day he addresses the Senate and people as if they were of a foreign state (*Hist.* 2.90.1). And success only brings out the Flavian commander Antonius' *auaritia* and *superbia*: he scours Italy as if it were captured territory (*Hist.* 3.49.1). Book 4 opens with the armed and victorious Flavians pursuing their defeated enemies through the city *implacabili odio*, 'with implacable hatred' (*Hist.* 4.1.1). Greed then follows this outburst of savagery: *quae saeuitia recentibus odiis sanguine explebatur, dein uerterat in auaritiam*, 'with fresh hatreds, savagery was sated by bloodshed, then later turned to greed' (*Hist.* 4.1.2). Rome exhibits the classic symptoms of a captive city: *ubique lamenta, conclamationes et fortuna captae urbis*, 'everywhere were laments, cries of grief, and the misfortune of a captured city' (*Hist.* 4.1.3).

Let us now look at the sack of Cremona, a lengthy narrative encompassing the siege and capture of the Vitellian camp outside the city, the surrender of the Vitellian troops, and the destruction of the city. Tacitus refuses to blame Antonius alone for the sack, as if to counter the Flavian 'line', but whether Hormus or Antonius was to blame, he calls it a *pessimum flagitium* (3.28) not

---

[53] Miller (1986), 92.

[54] Tacitus' account diverges from those of Suetonius (*Otho* 7.1) and Plutarch (*Otho* 1.1) in his apparent hyperbole about the bodies, since he only relates the deaths of Galba, Piso, Vinius, and the centurion Sempronius Densus, and in having Otho make his sacrifice on the Capitoline on the evening of the coup, not the morning after. See Damon (2003), 196. Courbaud (1918), 88 believes Tacitus made the change for dramatic effect, to have Otho pass by the corpses in the Forum. Chilver (1979), 106 defends the version of Tacitus.

unworthy of the life of either.[55] The troops have sufficient motivation themselves: *exercitus praeter insitam praedandi cupidinem uetere odio ad excidium Cremonensium incubuit*, 'the army aside from their ingrained desire for plunder, because of their old hatred, pressed on to the destruction of Cremona' (*Hist*. 3.32.1). The Cremonese had been pro-Vitellian, and Tacitus details aggravating incidents (*Hist*. 3.32.2). The Flavian troops when they reach Cremona are inclined to press on and attack the camp, despite their exhaustion: *omnisque caedes et uolnera et sanguis auiditate praedae pensabantur*, 'all slaughter and wounds and blood were outweighed by their greed for booty' (*Hist*. 3.26.2). When they falter during the siege, their leaders point to Cremona (*Hist*. 3.27.3). The wealthy town was also full of visitors for the market days (*Hist*. 3.32.2). The sack itself contains the familiar topoi of the *urbs capta*, but Tacitus stresses the self-destruction of the looters as they fight over captives or property. We see the victims here as the victors did, merely as loot. There are no cries of lamentation or anguish, no pathetic scenes of families torn apart, though Tacitus reports in the next chapter that some Cremonese had been taken captive. In Tacitus' account, all is silence until four days later, *cum omnia sacra profanaque in igne considerent*, 'when everything sacred and profane sank into the flames' (*Hist*. 3.33.2), a reminiscence of the death of Troy (*Aen*. 2.624–5: *tum uero omne mihi uisum considere in ignis | Ilium*).

When the Flavians approach Rome, Antonius tries to calm them and delay their entrance to the city, for he fears 'that the troops, enraged by battle, might take no thought for the people, the senate, or even for the temples and shrines of the gods' (*ne asperatus proelio miles non populo, non senatui, ne templis quidem ac delubris deorum consuleret, Hist*. 3.82.1). But when battle is joined in the city, Tacitus describes instead the grotesque behaviour of the civilians who stand by and applaud as if at some entertainment. They give away those who had hidden and demand that they be killed, *parte maiore praedae potiebantur: nam milite ad sanguinem et caedes obuerso spolia in uolgus cedebant*, 'for so they gained a greater share of the booty, since the troops were bent on blood and slaughter, the spoils fell to the people' (*Hist*. 3.83.1). The appearance of the city was cruel and disfigured (*saeua ac deformis urbe tota facies, Hist*. 3.83.2) since it combined the debauchery and passion of peace (and the party of the Saturnalia) with whatever crime was committed in the bitterest conquest of a city (*quidquid in acerbissima captiuitate scelerum*). Tacitus underscores the horror by comparing the Romans' behaviour unfavourably even with that in previous civil wars: there had been no less

---

[55] For the attempts of pro-Flavian writers to make Antonius the scapegoat for excesses at Cremona and Rome, see Briessman (1955), 48–9.

cruelty when Sulla and Cinna had fought in the city, but now people were wholly indifferent to either side and found pleasure in public misfortune (*Hist.* 3.83.3).

Baxter has shown that Tacitus clusters reminiscences from the *Aeneid*, especially from Book 2, in three major episodes of *Histories* 3: the storming of the camp and sack of Cremona, the siege of the Flavians on the Capitoline, and the fight for the praetorian camp and the death of Vitellius. Baxter believed Tacitus used the reminiscences in part to give 'an epic grandeur to the major episodes'.[56] There is some truth in this. But Baxter overlooks the ambiguous resonances of Tacitus' technique. Would the historian want to impart an air of grandeur to what he regards as criminal acts? He twice calls the sack of Cremona a *flagitium*, 'a shameful act' (*Hist.* 3.28; 3.34.2), and the burning of the Temple of Jupiter was the most calamitous and shameful crime the Roman state had suffered since its foundation (*facinus post conditam urbem luctuosissimum foedissimumque rei publicae populi Romani accidit, Hist.* 3.72.1). Civil war is a *rabies* (madness) that drives men to self-destruction (*Hist.* 2.38.2). So perhaps, as Miller argues, Tacitus uses Virgil to evoke pathos and horror for the victims rather than the conventionally heroic in human behaviour, but what else is he up to?[57]

The Virgilian reminiscences noted by Baxter and others in the *Histories* create a sort of portable, endlessly repeatable last night of Troy.[58] Galba may well recall Priam to the reader, but that is only the beginning. The Vitellian camp outside Cremona, that city itself, the Capitoline, and the praetorian camp all become Troy. Through most of *Histories* 3, the Vitellians are cast in the role of the Trojans as their camp outside of Cremona is stormed, the pro-Vitellian Cremona is sacked, and they fight to the death at the praetorian camp in Rome.[59] But on one significant occasion, the two forces exchange

---

[56] Baxter (1972), 107.

[57] Miller (1986), 100. She grants that Virgilian reminiscences also give 'an epic tone and overtone to an epic theme'.

[58] Kraus (1994b), 282 sees the *urbs capta* topos as 'the ideal medium in which to represent the particular combination of repetition and progress that Livy creates in Book V'. See also Rossi (2004a), 29–30, who reads Virgil's version of the fall of Troy as a topos that 'calls attention to its inherent reusability and thus to the potential for its endless repetition'.

[59] The following reminiscences from *Aeneid* 2 in the key scenes of *Hist.* 3 are not discussed in this chapter: battle for the Flavian camp: *Hist.* 3.28, *uaria pereuntium forma et omni imagine mortium* ~ *Aen.* 2.369 *plurima mortis imago*, cf. Baxter (1972), 96, Austin (1964), 158, and Heubner (1972), 80; the siege on the Capitoline hill: *Hist.* 3.71.2 *decora maiorum* ~ *Aen.* 2.447 *uetera decora . . . parentum*, cf. Baxter (1972), 102, Wellesley (1972), 172, and Heubner (1972), 169; the battle in the streets of Rome: *Hist.* 3.82.3 *per angusta et lubrica uiarum* ~ *Aen.* 2.332 *obsedere alii telis angusta uiarum*, cf. Baxter (1972), 104 and Heubner (1972), 193; the battle for the praetorian camp: *Hist.* 3.84.2 *domos arasque cruore foedare* ~ *Aen.* 2.501–502 *uidi Hecubam centumque nurus Priamumque per aras* | *sanguine foedantem quos ipse sacrauerat ignis*, cf. Baxter

roles, when the Flavians are besieged on the Capitol by the Vitellians. Here Tacitus, unlike the other ancient sources, blames the Flavians, now in the role of the Greeks, for the fire that destroys the Capitolium.[60]

By linking Rome with Troy from the outset, Tacitus underlines the gravity of the situation and the sufferings of this horrible year. Rome and Italy labour under lawlessness, looting, and murder which do not end in one night, but arise again as each new contender comes on the scene. The city itself is profaned, in the words of Agnès Rouveret, by the murders of Galba, Vinius, and Piso at sacred sites, and profaned again by the burning of the Capitoline temple and accompanying bloodshed in the streets.[61] Furthermore, by casting Galba as Priam and then having the Vitellians and Flavians exchange roles, Tacitus underlines the vicissitudes and ambiguities of civil war, just as he does through repetition and variation of topoi and *sententiae* in the speeches of the commanders and principes.[62] Finally, one could try to be more positive: Rome appears down repeatedly, but she is not out. She is not Troy, in the sense of being totally destroyed; she survives.

One can only speculate as to the source for Tacitus' portrayal of Rome, the Vitellian camp, Cremona, and the praetorian camp as Troy and the shifting identities of the soldiers. Did he borrow from *Aeneid* 9–12, where both the Trojan camp and Latinus' city are assimilated to Troy and each side is cast as Trojans?[63] Did he recall Livy 5, where both Veii and Rome become Troy, and Romans play both the Greeks and the Trojans? Have the Romans in the *Histories* set aside civil strife and refounded Rome for good, as the Romans do in the Livian narrative?[64] Tacitus' description of the refounding of the Capitoline temple (4.53) is certainly an antidote to the profanation of

---

(1972), 105 and Wellesley (1972), 185; *Hist.* 3.84.2 *suprema uictis solacia amplectebantur* ~ *Aen.* 2.354 *una salus uictis nullam sperare salutem,* cf. Baxter (1972), 105 and Wellesley (1972), 185.

While Baxter (1972), 105–6 argues that Tacitus means the reader to associate Vitellius with Priam at *Hist.* 3.84.4 by juxtaposing his name with the phrase *capta urbe* (cf. *Aen.* 2.507), he does not satisfactorily explain the three Virgilian reminiscences applied to him later in that section which seem to link the feckless emperor to Aeneas. For a different interpretation, see Keitel (2008).

[60] Tacitus again distances himself from the Flavian version, according to which the Vitellians plundered the Capitoline temple and then burned it (Jos. *BJ* 4.649; Dio 65.17.3). See Briessman (1955), 73–5. Other anti-Vitellian versions include Suetonius (*Vit.* 15.3), who states that Vitellius ordered the Temple burned, and Pliny *NH* 34.38, who asserts that the Vitellian troops burned it.

[61] Rouveret (1992), 3071–2.

[62] Keitel (1987) and (1991).

[63] Rossi (2004a), 171–8.

[64] Kraus (1994b), 282.

monuments in Rome and the reversal of foundation that civil war represents.[65] Moreover, in the extant text, Tacitus is positive, on the whole, about the reign of Vespasian.[66] Although Rome survived the exceedingly dangerous year 69, almost her last (*Hist.* 1.11.3), Tacitus' analysis of what drives men to civil strife focuses on an innate and therefore recurring quality, man's greed for power (*potentiae cupido, Hist.* 2.38.1), and he notes a continuity of motives between those who fought at Pharsalia and Philippi and those who fought in 69 (*Hist.* 2.38.2). Moreover, the historian reminds the reader that the battle in Rome in December 69 did not merely echo the mythic or distant past, but also recalled earlier Roman civil wars. So he evokes, through Sallustian reminiscences, Catiline's alleged plot in 66 BC (*Hist.* 3.72.1, *id facinus post conditam urbem... foedissimumque*; Sall. *Cat.* 18.8), the plot of 63 (*Hist.* 3.83.2, *saeua ac deformis*; Sall. *Cat.* 31.1), the proscriptions of Sulla (*Hist.* 3.84.2, *cruore foedare*; Sall. *Hist.* 1.47), and the deaths of Catiline and his men on the battlefield at Pistoia (*Hist.* 3.84.3, *cecidere omnes contrariis uolneribus, uersi in hostem*; Sall. *Cat.* 61.3). And of course Tacitus had lived through the civil war of 69 and had seen dangerous military unrest under Nerva.

In conclusion, I want to touch briefly on how Tacitus helps preserve what was destroyed. Disaster, obviously, threatens to eradicate the past, by destroying monuments, cities, cultures, and the people who can remember them. Tacitus does fix in memory some of what was lost. So he accords an obituary to both Cremona and the Capitoline temple. (Cremona's begins with the formulaic *hic exitus Cremonae*, which may recall the death of Priam, *Aen.* 2.554–6.)[67] After fire destroys the Caelian hill and it may be renamed the Augustan, Tacitus gives us the history of the hill's name. No more is heard about the sycophantic proposal. The digression, by preserving memory, effaces attempts to erase it (*Ann.* 4.65).[68] After the fire of 64, Tacitus lists the temples and shrines destroyed (*Ann.* 15.41.1). Though the new city was strikingly beautiful, the *seniores* remembered much that could not be replaced

---

[65] For civil war as the reverse of foundation, see Rouveret (1992), 3070–1. Edwards (1996), 82 takes a pessimistic view of the burning of the temple and its reconstruction: 'the scars of civil war can never be healed'. Ash (2007b), 236 sees 'muted optimism' in Tacitus' 'pointed evocation' of the Gallic siege of the Capitol narrated by Livy. As there is a fresh start at Rome in Livy 6, so there may be a similar new beginning at Rome under the Flavians.

[66] Tacitus praises Vespasian as the only *princeps* of all those before him who changed for the better (*Hist.* 1.50.4). Absent his *auaritia*, Vespasian was *antiquis ducibus pars*, 'equal to the rulers of old' (*Hist.* 2.5.1).

[67] On the obituaries of cities, see Pomeroy (1991), 255–7.

[68] According to Suetonius (*Tib.* 48.1) Tiberius had the Senate pass this measure, but there is no evidence that the name change was ever instituted.

(15.41.1).[69] I close with a fire at Augusta Taurinorum started carelessly by Vitellian troops, who left fires burning as they departed the town in 69. Part of the colony was destroyed, *quod damnum, ut pleraque belli mala, maioribus aliarum urbium cladibus obliteratum,* 'but this loss, like most of the misfortunes of the war, was effaced by the greater disasters of other cities' (*Hist.* 2.66.3).[70] Not forgotten by the locals, and Tacitus makes sure that we do not forget it either. This is the art of losing. As Elizabeth Bishop puts it in a crucial parenthesis in 'One Art': 'Write it!'

---

[69] Rouveret (1992), 3067 observes that Tacitus wants to show Nero as a worse scourge to Rome than the Gauls had been, since he succeeded in destroying monuments that bore witness to the city's origins. She also notes that Tacitus (*Ann.* 15.41.1) gives more detail about monuments associated with Rome's foundation than those that evoked the glory of the Republic.

[70] Ash (2007a), 261: 'Tacitus simultaneously rescues the disaster from oblivion and deplores that it was outstripped by even greater catastrophes'.

20

The Historian's Presence, or, There and Back Again

Cynthia Damon

INTRODUCTION

In the sixth book of the *Annals* Tacitus presents a vignette that illustrates well the effect of vivid narrative. The scene is a meeting of the senate, the subject the death of Germanicus' second son, Drusus, who was starved to death as a prisoner in the imperial palace. Tiberius attempted to justify his cruelty by showing what Drusus had done to deserve it: he ordered the 'intelligence file', so to speak, on Drusus read out (6.24.1 *recitari . . . factorum dictorumque eius descripta per dies iussit*). Senators were shocked to learn that Drusus had been under surveillance for years, and could hardly believe their ears when Tiberius made the day-to-day reports public, reports that revealed, towards the end, the physical and mental abuse inflicted on Drusus by his jailers, and Drusus' dying curse on Tiberius (6.24.1–2). This openness was especially remarkable coming from Tiberius, past master of concealment, and the effect was as if Tiberius had removed the walls of Drusus' cell to show what was taking place within (6.24.3): *tamquam dimotis parietibus ostenderet nepotem sub uerbere centurionis, inter seruorum ictus, extrema uitae alimenta frustra orantem. Dimotis parietibus*, 'with the walls removed', the senators were in effect present at Drusus' agony, a terrifying experience (6.24.3 *penetrabat pauor*); their immediate response was to restore the façade (*species*): *obturbant quidem patres specie detestandi* (6.24.3).

The governing simile in this passage is one of physical presence, of being there in the room with the dying man and his torturers.[1] Tacitus ascribes this vividness-effect not to stylistic excellence—there is no historical narrative, just entries in the jailers' log—but rather to the credibility of the evidence provided (6.24.2 *uix fides, nisi quod Attii centurionis et Didymi liberti epistulae*

---

[1] As Martin (2001) notes ad loc., the simile, an unusual one, depends on the idea that 'house walls are spoken of as concealing crimes, misconduct, etc.'.

seruorum nomina praeferebant ut quis egredientem cubiculo Drusum pul-
sauerat, exterruerat, etc.).[2] The 'author', insofar as one can speak of an author
here, is Tiberius, who was acting from Capri. But physical separation did not
prevent him from using evidence to make the past very present indeed,
tamquam dimotis parietibus. In this paper, written in honour of a scholar
who has done so much to remove the barriers to a proper understanding of
Tacitean historiography, I look for other traces of this concept of historical
vividness in Tacitus' works, and connect it with his demonstration of the
historian's power over the future.

I. *PRAESENS PRAETERITO*

Enargeia has been admired and analysed since antiquity, and its governing
metaphors and the literary techniques that support them are well known. The
essential idea is that an 'audience' (listeners or readers) should see what
participants saw and feel what they felt. The dominant metaphors are
drawn from the visual arts and from drama. But as a historian who distrusts
species and despises all but the absolutely necessary forms of play-acting, and
who regularly associates fondness for spectacle with civic irresponsibility and
worse,[3] Tacitus needs a new metaphor. This is not to say that Tacitus shuns
tried-and-true *enargeia* techniques. One can certainly find in his *Histories* and
Annals the conventional syntactic features such as historical presents and
infinitives, primary sequence tenses, *oratio recta*, generalizing second-person
verbs (*spectares, discerneres*, even *putares*), and first-person references to
participants (e.g., *nostri* for Roman soldiers), as well as familiar structural
features such as *agones* and internal audiences. But he also develops a new
metaphor that puts the emphasis not on the audience seeing or watching but
on the historian being present.

Since the time of Herodotus, autopsy and, failing that, access to eyewitness
evidence have been both important markers of authority and sources of
authenticating detail.[4] In none of the surviving books of the *Histories*
or *Annals* is actual autopsy explicitly claimed by Tacitus. He seems likely,

---

[2] For an equally grim visualization based on proximity cf. *Ann.* 6.39.2, where Tiberius is
waiting in the vicinity of Rome for news of two deaths: *haec Tiberius non mari, ut olim, diuisus
neque per longinquos nuntios accipiebat, sed urbem iuxta . . . quasi aspiciens undantem per domos
sanguinem aut manus carnificum.*
[3] Well illustrated, of course, in Woodman (1993), an analysis of the extended theatrical
metaphor used by Tacitus to display and explain the failure of the Pisonian conspiracy.
[4] For an overview in both Greek and Roman historians see Marincola (1997), 63–86.

however, to have claimed it at least once in the *Histories'* Domitianic books, in connexion with the Secular Games of AD 88, at which, as Tacitus tells us in his account of Claudius' games, he was present (*Ann.* 11.11.1 *iis... adfui*) and about which he wrote (ibid. *utriusque principis rationes praetermitto, satis narratas libris, quibus res imperatoris Domitiani composui*). He must have had many such opportunities in these books, which covered the period of his own political successes (*Hist.* 1.1.4 *dignitatem nostram... longius prouectam a Domitiano*). For the *Annals*, no autopsy, or practically none.[5] Eyewitness accounts are mentioned occasionally in both works and frequently inferred.[6] But the reader's sense of Tacitus' access to the events he narrates is due above all to literary techniques, including a set of metaphors for physical presence.[7]

Metaphors of movement through space, as applied to the historian's narrative, cover a spectrum from the possibly trivial to the certainly significant. Possibly trivial are the verbs of motion applied to the author's progress through his narrative. In Tacitus this metaphor, familiar from, among other things, didactic poetry, commonly appears in connexion with his digressions. Thus at *Ann.* 4.4.3 *quod mihi exsequendum reor* the notion of pursuit intrinsic to the verb (and still felt in its application to funerals) is vestigial at best: Woodman (2004) translates 'which I deem should be recounted by me', but the motion verb may resonate with the immediately preceding *percensuit cursim* used in reference to Tiberius' review of Rome's military dispositions, which is what prompts Tacitus' own account (it is the antecedent of *quod* in our sentence), and the expression *persequi incertum fuit* (4.5.4) which concludes the review. In this passage and at *Ann.* 3.65.1 *exsequi sententias*, however, the verbs' objects, by their nature, fight against the notion of movement. Similarly at *Ann.* 2.83.2 *haud facile quis numerum inierit*. More clearly relevant to the present category (but possibly still trivial) are expressions such as *Hist.* 2.38.2 *me... longius tulit, nunc ad rerum ordinem uenio*, or *Ann.* 4.33.4 *sed <ad> inceptum redeo*, or *Ann.* 6.22.4 *ne nunc incepto longius abierim*, by means of which Tacitus signals the end of a digression and the return to the narrative proper, or *Ann.* 16.16.2 *transire licet*, which refers to a historian's decision to 'pass over' some events in silence.[8]

---

[5] On Tacitean autopsy see Devillers (2003), 71; Syme (1982), esp. 68–71.

[6] e.g, *Hist.* 3.65.2, 4.81.3, *Ann.* 4.53.2 As Syme (1958), 176 says apropos of the *Histories* in particular, 'there survived eyewitnesses in abundance'. On eyewitness sources, both oral and written, in the *Annals* see, in Devillers's inventory (2003), ##2, 3, 5, 14, 20–8, 65, and his pp. 69–71.

[7] For an overview see Hommel (1936), esp. 120–9.

[8] In effect, with expressions like these Tacitus 'realizes' the metaphor built into the rhetorical terms (*digressio, digressus*) used for the sort of narrative detour (see *OLD*, s.vv.) in which Tacitus' narratives are rich; as is his wont, he avoids the technical terms.

Less banal, indeed quite original, is the use of *ant(e)ire* at *Ann.* 4.71.1 *auebat animus antire*, where ardent language, abstraction, and alliteration combine to produce a striking expression of Tacitus' eagerness to race ahead in his narrative to the deaths of the villains whose villainy he has just described; the *TLL* lists no parallels for this usage.[9] Sometimes events come to him instead of the other way around: thus at *Ann.* 6.7.5 *nobis pleraque digna cognitu obuenere.*[10]

The movement metaphor in the phrase *opus aggredior* at *Hist.* 1.2.1 is more complicated. At first it looks like an instantiation of the author qua 'voyager' idea familiar from poetry, picking up on *cessere* in the preceding paragraph, which referred to the post-Actium 'withdrawal' of great talents from the enterprise of writing history (1.1.1 *postquam bellatum apud Actium . . . magna illa ingenia cessere*). The initial modifier of *opus* (*opimum casibus*) suits the idea of *opus* as a literary work perfectly well.[11] But as the description continues the modifiers are increasingly odd for 'work' and appropriate, instead, for the period described: *atrox proeliis, discors seditionibus, ipsa etiam pace saeuom.* And the following sentence is wholly concerned with the events, not the work: *quattuor principes ferro interempti*, etc. It is as if Tacitus approached the task of writing his *Histories* and found himself amongst the events themselves.[12]

This movement/presence metaphor is most fully and originally developed in Tacitus' *Annals* 4 digression on historiography, where historians both republican and imperial take up metaphorical residence in their chosen periods.

Historians of the *ueteres populi Romani res*, Tacitus says, put their period on record *libero egressu* (*Ann.* 4.32.1). The force of this modal ablative is not immediately clear, for, as Martin–Woodman note, 'the precise metaphorical use of *egressus* is most unusual'. The translation they offer ad loc., 'with unrestricted elaboration', does not really capture the spatial component of *egressus*; Woodman's 2004 translation 'with freedom to explore' comes closer. The first (and largest) section of the word's *TLL* entry falls under the heading 'actio egrediendi'; the word usually denotes either a 'setting out', often of an

---

[9] Chris Kraus aptly compares Livy's *legentium plerisque . . . festinantibus ad haec noua* (*praef.* 4), where, however, the idea of motion through space is less prominent.

[10] For a passage that moves to this kind of 'encounter' with the past from a mental replay of the evidence see *Ann.* 3.18.4 *mihi, quanto plura recentium seu ueterum reuoluo, tanto magis ludibria rerum mortalium cunctis in negotiis obversantur.*

[11] See my note ad loc. In a recent paper Baldwin (2005) compares the metaphorical *fetura* at Plin. *NH praef.* 1.

[12] With both *magna illa ingenia cessere* and *opus aggredior* it is perhaps useful to contrast *Ann.* 1.1.2 *temporibusque Augusti dicendis non defuere decora ingenia*, where historians are kept firmly in their own present both by *dicendis*, with its reference to the act of composition, and by the following temporal clause, *donec gliscente adulatione deterrerentur*, in which the deterrent *adulatio* is contemporary with the desire to write, not a feature of the past.

important person for an important task (e.g., a governor's departure for his
province) or 'emergence from one's house into the public sphere', again
generally with reference to notables. The 'subjects' of *egressus* in Tacitus are
an elite bunch—sought-after orators (*Dial.* 6.4), a governor and his lady
(*Ann.* 3.33.4), the emperor's wife (11.12.3, 13.45.3), and the emperor himself
(15.53.1, 16.10.4)—amongst whom it is no surprise to find historians, at least
not in a digression on historiography. Since our passage concerns itself with
choice of subject matter rather than freedom to publish, the first of these two
basic meanings given above seems the more appropriate as the source of the
metaphor here: as a modifier for *ingentia illi bella, expugnationes urbium, fusos
captosque reges . . . memorabant, libero egressu* ought to mean something like
'having set forth [*sc.* onto their task] without hindrance'; Syme (1958), 320
appropriately evokes 'themes of . . . wide horizon'. There is a tension here
between the verb *memorabant*, with its emphasis on (the creation or evocation of) memory, and its modifier *libero egressu*, with its emphasis on
movement through space.[13]

Apropos of Tacitus' own work—*nobis in arto . . . labor* (4.32.2)—the picture
is more harmonious, however painful the situation thus described may be for
our author. With *in arto*, which stands in antithesis to *libero egressu*, we lose
the 'wide horizon' but retain a consciousness of physical surroundings.
Tacitus in fact adds a spatial dimension to its model here, Virgil's *in tenui
labor* (*Geo.* 4.3), whence he also gets the *labor* that emphasizes the struggle
involved in writing rather than the mode of production, thereby avoiding the
tension produced by *memorabant*.

The notion of the author's physical proximity to his subject matter is
reinforced by *introspicere* in the following sentence—*non tamen sine usu fuerit
introspicere illa primo aspectu leuia*—where *leuia* is a shorthand reference to
the material that sent Tacitus into this digression on historiography in the first
place (cf. 4.32.1 *pleraque eorum quae rettuli quaeque referam parua forsitan et
leuia memoratu uideri non nescius sum*). As Martin–Woodman note, '*introspicere* is commonly used of investigating behaviour, etc.'; it is a much more
'hands-on' metaphor for the historian's work than *memorabant*, and, more
importantly, it is consistent with Tacitus' distrust of *species* and dislike of
spectacle: *introspicere*, not *spectare*.[14] The exhilarating freedom of movement

[13] The same peculiar combination is found at *Ann.* 1.1.1 *temporibus . . . dicendis . . . cessere*
(on which see n. 12 above), where a movement verb is coupled with a memory-producing task.
[14] Elsewhere Tacitus uses *introspicere* for important investigations (*Ann.* 1.7.7, on Tiberius'
covert investigation of senatorial attitudes to his accession; 3.60.3, on the senate's investigation
of asylum rights) and accurate insights (*Ann.* 1.10.7 and 5.4.1, on insight into Tiberius'
character and plans; 6.21.2 and 11.38.1, on consciousness of impending events).

enjoyed by historians of the Republic thus finds a satisfying counterpart in in-depth scrutiny of the imperial period: useful, if not thrilling.

The physical presence metaphor crops up again in the next sentence, since, when Tacitus does 'investigate' these at first glance trivial matters, he comes face to face with a depressing sameness of material, *obuia . . . similitudine* (4.33.3), an expression that anticipates the idea encountered above in *pleraque . . . obuenere* (6.7.5). And in Tacitus' view even readers will feel a spatial continuity with the past, worrying that the faults of others, *nimis ex propinquo*, are being imputed to themselves (4.33.4).

The metaphorical underpinnings of this famous passage on the historian's task are thus coherent both amongst themselves and with Tacitus' larger historiographical programme.[15] They also prepare the way for the equally famous, and adjacent, account of the trial of the historian Cremutius Cordus (*Ann.* 4.34–5), whose presence in the text takes the form of a long speech. Brought before a senatorial court, with Tiberius looking on, he offers a defence against what Tacitus calls a 'novel charge, heard then for the first time' (4.34.1 *nouo ac tunc primum audito crimine*): *quod editis annalibus laudatoque M. Bruto C. Cassium Romanorum ultimum dixisset.* The novelty lies in the fact that *uerba*, not *facta*, constitute the crime.[16] Thus Cordus' defence culminates in a question about *facta—num . . . populum . . . incendo?* (4.35.2)—that presses for the answer 'No': Cordus is not currently inciting the populace. He is, as he says, *factorum innocens* (4.34.2). Even on the more subtle reading of this passage offered by Woodman (see Martin–Woodman ad loc.), a 'no' is required in the trial context, where Cordus stresses his temporal distance from the tyrannicides (*illi quidem septuagesimum ante annum per-empti*). As Woodman paraphrases: 'For surely it is not the case that, just because C. and B. hold the field in full armour at Philippi [*sc.* in my history], I am inflaming the people, etc.' Once again, Cordus is not currently inciting the populace, but on this reading the incitement, had there been incitement, would have been due to the *enargeia* of Cordus' account of Philippi: 'By omitting all reference to his role as an author, . . . Cordus represents as *actually* taking place that which in his history is merely described. He thus uses the same technique to refer to the immediacy (*enargeia*) of his historical narrative as Horace had used to praise that of Pollio's (*Odes* 2.1.17–19, with

---

[15] Another possible occurrence of this metaphor suffers from a corrupt text. At *Ann.* 3.24.3 M reads *in que tendi*, which Woodman–Martin emend to the well-paralleled *quae intendi* (see their note ad loc.), but which Ernesti emended to the less banal *in quae tetendi*, 'towards which I directed my course'.

[16] Or part of the novelty. The trial also expanded the purview of *maiestas* to cover victims outside the imperial family and to punish praise as well as libel.

Nisbet–Hubbard ad loc.)'.[17] On Woodman's reading, the historian in the text—the only historian who makes an appearance qua historian in Tacitus' works—attributes to the history he has written an effect similar to that of the various metaphors of presence we have seen in Tacitus' historical works.[18]

However, there is also a way to answer Cordus with a 'Yes'. As Martin–Woodman put it at the end of their long note on 4.35.2 *num... incendo*, 'It would not have been difficult to interpret Cordus' narrative as criticism of the principate and a call to arms'. Indeed this is surely how his accusers presented it. Such a reading reinstates the gap between event and historian: in narrating the past, particularly in narrating the past without truckling to authority, the historian produces an effect on his present; historiographical vividness is less relevant than authorial attitude. And this effect continues into the future, as is shown by the example of Cordus himself, whose prediction *nec derunt, si damnatio ingruit, qui... mei meminerint* (4.35.3) came true.[19]

II. *PRAESENS FUTURO*

What of Tacitus? Does he ever say something comparable to Cordus' *num... incendo*? Not explicitly, no. That is, there are no passages where the metaphor of the historian's presence is used by Tacitus with reference to his own present or future. However, there *are* passages where one can see him relishing his effect, particularly his effect in the future.[20]

For example, one can see him deliberately frustrating what he deems to be Tiberius' *ambitio in posteros* (6.46.3), that is, deliberately challenging the emperor in the court of the future.

Tiberius' *ambitio* becomes the subject of discussion at a senate meeting about a proposal to erect a temple to Tiberius and his mother (*Ann.* 4.37–8), a passage located in significant proximity to the digression on historiography

---

[17] The actuality-effect in this reading comes from the combination of present participle *obtinentibus* and present tense *incendo*—the full version of Cordus' question is *num enim armatis Cassio et Bruto ac Philippenses campos obtinentibus belli ciuilis causa populum per contiones incendo*—the former referring to Cassius and Brutus, the latter to Cordus: the combination cancels the 70-year gap.

[18] Woodman himself notes (in the words elided in the quotation above) that Cordus is using here 'a device T. had adopted in his own person at 33.4 (n. *gloria*)', though the passage at 4.33.4 is not one I discuss in this paper.

[19] For Cordus' survival as an *exemplum* see e.g. Sen. *Cons. ad Marc.* 1.3–4, 22.4–7; Dio 57.24.2–3. On Cordus, see also Pelling in this volume, pp. 366–8, 376–7.

[20] The passages mentioned below are offered *exemplorum gratia*, not as an exhaustive list.

and the Cordus trial.[21] Tacitus gives his Tiberius a long *oratio recta* speech on that occasion, in which 'Tiberius' describes how he would like to be remembered by posterity (4.38.1): *qui* (sc. *posteri*) *satis superque memoriae meae tribuent, ut maioribus meis dignum, rerum uestrarum prouidum, constantem in periculis, offensionum pro utilitate publica non pauidum credant.* Tiberius also alludes to the 'court of the future' in making the point that temples are no better than tombs if one's memory is abhorrent (4.38.3): *quae saxo struuntur, si iudicium posterorum in odium uertit, pro sepulchris spernuntur.* Tacitus makes no immediate comment on the speech itself, though he does offer some fairly acid reactions to Tiberius' refusal of divine cult (4.38.4–5), but practical interventions elsewhere in the narrative show that he was alert to the possibilities suggested by Tiberius' *si iudicium posterorum in odium uertit.*

To see Tacitus frustrating Tiberius' aspirations with respect to posterity we can consider the execution of Sempronius Gracchus, who had spent fourteen years in exile on an island off the coast of Africa after his conviction for adultery with Julia (*Ann.* 1.53.3–6). Upon Julia's death in AD 14 soldiers were sent to kill Gracchus (*Ann.* 1.53.3 *milites ad caedem missi*). After the *exitus*-scene Tacitus appends a remark on a variant in the historical tradition (1.53.6): *quidam non Roma eos milites, sed ab L. Asprenate pro consule Africae missos tradidere auctore Tiberio, qui famam caedis posse in Asprenatem uerti frustra sperauerat.* There are several things to note here. First, although Tacitus does not specify who dispatched the soldiers or whence, the whole episode is motivated by Tiberius' *saeuitia in Sempronium Gracchum* (1.53.3). Next, even the variant version makes Tiberius responsible, but it also implicates the governor of Africa. Third, the indicative *sperauerat* shows that Tacitus himself vouches for the discreditable explanation underlying the involvement of Asprenas; that is, even though he himself did not include Asprenas in his narrative, he explains why others did.[22] And finally, *frustra*. This is a little Tacitean victory celebration: by not mentioning Asprenas in his own narrative of events, he frustrated Tiberius' hopes, if such they were, about *fama*.[23] If Tiberius did in fact attempt this ruse (Tacitus offers no warrant), the *posteri* he aimed to dupe are protected by their historian as they read his narrative.[24]

---

[21] For some of the significance see Martin–Woodman (1989) introductory note ad loc.

[22] For discussion, and rejection, of Freinsheim's emendation *sperauerit*, see Goodyear's note (1972) ad loc.

[23] The same could be said about the death of Julia herself (*Ann.* 1.53.1–3), of which the narrative ends *obscuram fore necem longinquitate exilii ratus* (sc. *Tiberius*). In Tacitus' *Annals*, at any rate, her death is not *obscura*. For another passage where Tacitus attributes a purpose to Tiberius and then himself frustrates it, see n. 26 below.

[24] For a passage where Tacitus makes sure that posterity is informed about something that Tiberius wanted erased consider *Ann.* 4.42.3, where Apidius Merula is removed from the

In another set of passages where Tacitus seems particularly conscious of his impact in the future his protection is extended beyond readers to society itself: he aims to do what statutory penalities had never been unable to accomplish, namely, to check *delatores*, described by Tacitus as a *genus hominum publico exitio repertum et <ne> poenis quidem umquam satis coercitum* (*Ann.* 4.30.3).

His narrative of the *maiestas* trial of Vibius Serenus *père*, for example, is meant to point a moral (*Ann.* 4.28.1): *miseriarum ac saeuitiae exemplum atrox*. Given that Serenus' accuser was his own son (*reus pater accusator filius*), this trial offered a vivid demonstration of how delation destroyed the social fabric (particularly the elite social fabric), and it is narrated at length (4.28–30). To open, Tacitus brings in the defendant pitiably filthy and shackled: *inluuie... ac squalore obsitus et tum catena uinctus*. As Martin–Woodman note, this was 'standard practice for orators, if they wished to rouse the pity of their audience', but Serenus seems to have had no orator defending him—no *patronus* is mentioned, anyway—and the most important member of the audience in this trial was implacable (4.28.2 *non occultante Tiberio uetus odium aduersum exulem Serenum*). It is therefore in the *iudicium posterorum* that this instantiation of 'standard practice' will have its pity-arousing effect. And not only pity. To quote Martin–Woodman again, such details 'evoke the reader's indignation against the prosecutor'. With his narrative Tacitus ensures that Serenus *fils* earns considerable readerly indignation, in effect inflicting on him the punishment (or at least a punishment) for *calumnia* that ought to have ensued after his failure to prove his case (4.29.1 *quaestio aduersa accusatori fuit*, cf. 4.29.3 *tormenta peruicacia seruorum contra euenissent*).[25]

But Tacitus' case here against Tiberius is even more damning: he was responsible for a guilty verdict that ignored the (lack of) evidence, and his intervention in the trial's aftermath exacerbated the problem of delation.[26] Troubled by the fact that a senator, having been mentioned as an associate of Serenus *père*, and *quia periculum pro exitio habebatur*, committed suicide, the senate drafted legislation depriving *delatores* of their reward money if an

---

senatorial roll because he did not swear *in diui Augusti acta*, but Tacitus, by mentioning his removal, makes sure that posterity knows that Merula was once a senator.

[25] For two other passages where Tacitus attacks a *delator* in the court of the future see *Ann.* 4.69.3 (on accusers who hid in a coffered ceiling to gather evidence) *suumque ipsi dedecus narrauere*, and, less viciously, *Ann.* 4.52.4 (on a talented but morally problematic speaker) *capessendis accusationibus aut reos tutando prosperiore eloquentiae quam morum fama fuit*. For more on *delatores* see Powell, Ch. 13 in this volume.

[26] Tacitus also takes the opportunity here to attribute to Tiberius a purpose (4.33.1 *quo molliret inuidiam*) that is frustrated by his invidious account of Tiberius' role in the trial. Foiled again, Tiberius!

accused killed himself before trial (4.30.2). Tiberius, however, argued publicly on behalf of *delatores* (*palam pro accusatoribus Caesar*), among other things calling them 'the laws' guardians' (*subuerterent potius iura quam custodes eorum amouerent*). Which Tacitus counters immediately with the description of *delatores* quoted above, *genus hominum publico exitio repertum et <ne> poenis quidem umquam satis coercitum* (*Ann.* 4.30.3), the language of which Martin–Woodman appropriately characterize as 'apocalyptic'. Such vehemence suits the accusation with which Tacitus concludes this long episode: on the evidence of the Vibius Serenus trial, he charges Tiberius not with failure to check *delatores*, but rather with encouraging them: *per praemia eliciebantur* (4.30.3).

Given that deterring, indeed punishing, *delatores* was official policy under Nerva and Trajan (see e.g. Dio 68.1.2, Plin. *Pan.* 34–5, 42, esp. 34 *uidimus delatorum iudicium, quasi grassatorum quasi latronum*), if not universally applied (see, e.g., Plin. *Ep.* 4.22.4–6), Tacitus, like his contemporary Juvenal at *Sat.* 1.33–6, may be beating something of a dead horse here (while of course creating an evil foil for the virtues of the present *princeps*). But a *delator*-friendly Tiberius or Domitian could be just around the corner, and Tacitus' narrative will be there as implicit threat and perhaps even deterrent (cf. *Ann.* 3.65.1 *ut ... ex posteritate et infamia metus sit*) when he arrives.

CONCLUSION

A model for the connexion between the contrafactual evocation of physical presence in the past (section I), and the insistence on the historian's impact in the future (section II), can perhaps be found in a peculiar little incident in *Annals* 4 that shows Tiberius once again doing work comparable to that of the historian. One of the cases referred to the senate in AD 24 concerned the death by defenestration of one Apronia, wife to the praetor Plautius Silvanus (4.22). Tacitus tells us right off that the husband did it (4.22.1 *coniugem in praeceps iecit*). He can do so because Tiberius investigated the matter personally after Silvanus asserted that his wife had killed herself (4.22.2): *non cunctanter Tiberius pergit in domum, uisit cubiculum, in quo reluctantis et impulsae uestigia cernebantur. refert ad senatum* ... He goes, he looks, he perceives, he reports. As Martin–Woodman note ad loc., 'Tiberius' role as personal inquisitor seems odd'. However, his investigation does clarify who did it, if not why (*incertis causis ... coniugem in praeceps iecit*); as Tacitus knows all too well, the why sometimes eludes even the best historian. Tiberius' investigation also resulted in a punishment, severe if somewhat indirect (Silvanus' grandmother, Urgulania, Livia's friend, sent him a dagger with which he duly committed suicide, 4.22.2–3). As eagerly as Tiberius, even if only via a metaphor, Tacitus betakes himself to the historical scene of the crime, so to speak, and, again like Tiberius, he makes do with the prospect of extrajudicial punishment. Circumscribed his subject matter may have been, but in terms of temporal range his *labor* was anything but *in arto*.

21

The Spur of Fame: *Annals* 4.37–8

Christopher Pelling

[37] Per idem tempus Hispania ulterior missis ad senatum legatis orauit ut exemplo Asiae delubrum Tiberio matrique eius extrueret. qua occasione Caesar, ualidus alioqui spernendis honoribus et respondendum ratus iis quorum rumore arguebatur in ambitionem flexisse, huiusce modi orationem coepit:

(2) 'scio, patres conscripti, constantiam meam a plerisque desideratam, quod Asiae ciuitatibus nuper idem istud petentibus non sim aduersatus. ergo et prioris silentii defensionem, et quid in futurum statuerim, simul aperiam. (3) 'Cum diuus Augustus sibi atque urbi Romae templum apud Pergamum sisti non prohibuisset, qui omnia facta dictaque eius uice legis obseruem, placitum iam exemplum promptius secutus sum quia cultui meo ueneratio senatus adiungebatur. ceterum ut semel recepisse ueniam habuerit, ita per omnis prouincias effigie numinum sacrari ambitiosum, superbum; et uanescet Augusti honor, si promiscis adulationibus uulgatur.

[38] 'Ego me, patres conscripti, mortalem esse et hominum officia fungi satisque habere, si locum principem impleam, et uos testor et meminisse posteros uolo; qui satis superque memoriae meae tribuent, ut maioribus meis dignum, rerum uestrarum prouidum, constantem in periculis, offensionum pro utilitate publica non pauidum credant. (2) haec mihi in animis uestris templa, hae pulcherrimae effigies et mansurae: nam quae saxo struuntur, si iudicium posterorum in odium uertit, pro sepulchris spernuntur. (3) proinde socios ciuis et deos et deas ipsas precor, hos ut mihi ad finem usque uitae quietam et intellegentem humani diuinique iuris mentem duint, illos ut, quandoque concessero, cum laude et bonis recordationibus facta atque famam nominis mei prosequantur.'

(4) Perstititque posthac secretis etiam sermonibus aspernari talem sui cultum. quod alii modestiam, multi, quia diffideret, quidam ut degeneris animi interpretabantur: (5) optimos quippe mortalium altissima cupere: sic Herculem et Liberum apud Graecos, Quirinum apud nos deum numero additos; melius Augustum, qui sperauerit; cetera principibus statim adesse; unum insatiabiliter parandum, prosperam sui memoriam: nam contemptu famae contemni uirtutes.

My thanks to Christina Kraus, Rhiannon Ash, and Ellen O'Gorman for very valuable comments and suggestions.

[37] During the same period Farther Spain sent legates to the senate pleading that on the example of Asia it might set up a shrine to Tiberius and his mother. On this occasion Caesar, who was generally firm in spurning honours and deemed that he should reply to the rumours in which he was criticized for deviating towards self-aggrandizement, began a speech of this kind:

(2) 'I know, conscript fathers, that consistency has been demanded of me by many people, because I did not oppose the communities of Asia when recently they sought the very same thing which is under discussion. Therefore I shall expound simultaneously both a defence of my previous silence and what I have decided for the future. (3) 'Since Divine Augustus had not prevented a temple to himself and to the City of Rome from being placed at Pergamum, and given that I observe all his actions and words as if law, I followed an already agreeable example more readily because the cult of myself was being joined by veneration of the senate. Yet, though a single acceptance may prove pardonable, to be consecrated throughout all the provinces by the likeness of divinities would be aggrandizing, haughty; and honour for Augustus will vanish if it is vulgarized by indiscriminate sycophancies.

[38] 'That I am mortal, conscript fathers, and perform the duties of men, and consider it satisfying if I fill the place of princeps—these things I both call on you to witness and wish posterity to remember. The latter will make a satisfying contribution and more to my memory, should they believe me worthy of my ancestors, provident of your affairs, in dangers steadfast, and not panicked by affronts for the public good. (2) These are the temples in your hearts, these the likenesses which are finest and destined to survive: those which are set up in stone are spurned like sepulchres if the judgement of posterity turns to hatred. (3) Accordingly I pray to allies, citizens, and to the gods and goddesses themselves—to the latter that till the end of my life they may bestow a mind which is peaceful and understanding of human and divine law, to the former that, whenever I depart, they may attend my actions and the reputation of my name with praise and benign recollections.'

(4) And he persevered thereafter even in his private conversations in spurning such cult of himself. Some interpreted this as modesty, many that he was diffident, others as the sign of a degenerate spirit: (5) it was the best of mortals, they said, who had the highest desires: thus it was Hercules and Liber among the Greeks, and Quirinus among ourselves, who had been added to the number of the gods; better was the reaction of Augustus, who had hoped. Principes enjoyed immediate access to everything else; they should prepare insatiably for one thing alone—a favourable memory of themselves. Contempt for fame meant contempt for virtues.

(Tacitus, *Annals* 4.37–8, tr. Woodman)[1]

---

[1] All further translations from the *Annals* are also taken from Woodman (2004), adapted to British spelling. A tacit tribute to that translation is the frequency with which we shall see Woodman's consistent choices of vocabulary capturing suggestive echoes in the original. It will also be clear how much I owe to Martin–Woodman's commentary on *Annals* 4; it will be scarcely

I

At this point of the *Annals*, memory is in the air. The memories that posterity will cherish are the main point of the Cremutius Cordus episode (4.34–5)— the memory of Cassius and Brutus that Cremutius has revered in his history and pays for with his life; the memory of Cremutius himself that he predicts will survive if he is condemned (35.3); the memory ('the memory of a subsequent age', *sequentis aeui memoriam*, 35.5) that the burners of Cremutius' books vainly hope might be extinguished. There is a comparison too between the memories reflected in physical representations and those preserved by historical writing (4.35.2):

Is it not rather the case that, slain as they [Cassius and Brutus] were seventy years ago, they for their part not only come to be known by their images—which not even the victor abolished—but retain some part of their memory among writers in exactly the same way?

That 'which not even the victor abolished' insinuates a further point, for even if the victor (Augustus, presumably—memories of Augustus recur repeatedly through these chapters—though a fairer verdict here might have pointed to both Augustus and Antony) did not destroy the images, he might well have chosen to do so: and that is even sharper in view of the memorable end of the previous book, where the funeral is described of Junia, the wife of Cassius and the sister of Brutus. The *imagines* of many glorious forebears were borne in that funeral parade,

but outshining all were Cassius and Brutus, for the very reason that likenesses of them were not on view. (3.76.2)

So even if the victor Augustus did not suppress the men's images, the atmosphere of Tiberius' reign had done so. Cremutius' claim that 'they come to be known by their images' already requires qualification.[2] Perhaps, then, history is not merely parallel to artistic representation, it outdoes it: if

---

less clear how much I, like all students of ancient historiography, owe to the constant stimulation of Tony Woodman's work in the last generation and a half. A more personal debt is owed to Tony's friendship, and to all those e-mails where discussion has veered alarmingly between questions of Latin historiography and mutual condolences on the footballing fortunes of Sunderland and Cardiff City.

[2] Similarly Martin–Woodman (1989), 184: 'the fact that it was still too dangerous to allow their *imagines* to be displayed publicly undermines the validity of the analogy on which his present argument is based'. Or perhaps the analogy is sound, but it suggests that literature not merely matches but also surpasses visual art?

that suggestion is caught, Tacitus' narrative juxtapositions are intimating a claim that other authors make explicit, that literature spreads further or lasts better or inspires more forcefully than any image or statue.[3] Nor is it difficult to catch an implied claim for Tacitus' own writing here, the more so because the Cremutius episode abuts so closely on to the reflections on Tacitus' themes and his readers' response at 4.32–3. It is, after all, Tacitus' account that ensures that everyone who reads that proud claim of Cremutius—'there will be no lack of those who remember not merely Cassius and Brutus but also myself'—also knows that it is true. Future memory is what the historian has to offer, try though others may to destroy it.

Destroying memory is difficult; distorting it is easier—and that is what makes memory so difficult to control. That is what Cremutius' book-burners found, failing to heed what they might have remembered, that others who had done the same had achieved nothing except their own disgrace and their enemies' glory (35.5). But historians find it difficult too. That was how the historiographical excursus had concluded, dwelling on the way that some (not all) of Tacitus' own audience may read against his grain:

Even glory and courage receive a ferocious response, as being critical of their opposites from too close at hand. (4.33.4)

In one way that cross-grained response may seem at odds with the Cremutius sequence, implying that even the 'glory' that Cremutius won may have its detractors;[4] but in a much stronger sense Cremutius' fate verifies the insight, showing that the glory of Cassius and Brutus, and the reflected glory that Cremutius won by presenting it, did indeed provoke a hostile response among the distempered and powerful. One moral, doubtless an unsurprising one, is that the way memories work upon an audience will be directed by the moral make-up that this audience brings to it; and perverse morality produces perverse reactions.

One chapter intervenes between the Cremutius sequence and the Spanish story, again one rich in suggestion. One of those suggestions concerns imperial cult, and the difficulty of getting it right. The people of Cyzicus suffered

---

[3] It is as old as Pind., *Nem.* 5.1–5: cf. also Isocr. *Evag.* 73–5; Cic. *Arch.* 30 and *Fam.* 5.12.7; Sall. *BJ* 4.5–6; Hor. *Odes* 3.30.1 (with Nisbet–Rudd ad loc.), 4.8.13–22, and *Epist.* 2.1.248–50; Ov. *Met.* 15.871–2; Plut. *Per.* 2.1–4 and *A Philosopher should particularly converse with Princes* 776c–d with Mossman (1991), 101. The idea is also implicit at *Agr.* 46.3–4 (cf. n. 25 below), where the transience of statues is contrasted with the eternal memory which Tacitus' work will secure: Harrison (2007a), esp. 311 and 317.

[4] O'Gorman (2000), 102, making the further good point that Tacitus' insistence on contemporary relevance 'forecloses on Cremutius' claim that praise of the tyrannicides has *only* to do with the past'.

for, among other things, their neglect of the cult of Augustus; the result was the loss of the liberty they had earned a century earlier in the war against Mithridates (36.2). So easily can memories of good service be wiped out by a false move; and so difficult it is to judge matters of imperial cult aright.

II

The transition into the Spanish episode is a gradual one. After the Cyzicene item the focus stays on Asia, but there is a narrative bridge back to Rome: Fonteius Capito is acquitted of charges concerning his governorship of Asia, because it emerges that the accusations were trumped up by the hated Vibius Serenus (36.3). Not that Vibius suffers for it, powerful *accusator* as he is— so the grimy atmosphere of Rome, intimidating and vindictive, is also summoned up, even in a case where justice prevails.

Asia is in other minds too. It is 'on the example of Asia' that Farther Spain bases its request: this was the case two years earlier recorded at 4.15.3, when 'the cities of Asia decreed a temple to Tiberius and his mother and the senate'. In his speech Tiberius notes that 'the senate' has been dropped from the Spanish request.[5] If one adds the further time-dimension of the Augustan precedent that Tiberius cites, one notes the development whereby 'Augustus and the city of Rome' becomes 'Tiberius and his mother and the senate' and then just 'Tiberius and his mother', as Rome itself is progressively redefined in royal terms.

Nor is it just in Spain that this Asian case had been noted. When Tiberius 'deemed that he should reply to the rumours in which he was criticized for deviating towards self-aggrandizement', we infer that these were Roman rumours, circulating among those whose opinions matter most. It conjures up an atmosphere where Romans and Spanish alike have all been talking about Tiberius, all trying to gauge what he wanted. In Rome, at least, those opinions have clearly been negative ones: *arguebatur, ambitionem*, and *flexisse* all insinuate, without any of them quite requiring, a pejorative air, and Woodman's translation—'criticized', 'self-aggrandizement', 'deviating'— rightly emphasizes that tone. Once the speech begins, the implication is similar: when Tiberius says 'a single acceptance might prove pardonable', the 'pardon', *uenia*, of which he speaks might be pardon from the gods, but just as readily suggests pardon from human observers; the same goes for the words they might use—'aggrandizing' (*ambitiosum*, which as Martin–

---

[5] This is especially striking, as Ellen O'Gorman points out to me, as Baetica was a senatorial province.

Woodman observe picks up the earlier 'self-aggrandizement'), 'haughty' (*superbum*)—if Tiberius were to accept the Spanish proposal now. So ambition for divine honours is as unwelcome to these commentators as it had been to those critics of the dead Augustus who commented that 'nothing was left with which to honour the gods, since he wished himself to be worshipped with temples and with the likenesses of a divinity by flamines and priests' (1.10.6)—even though those criticisms had immediately been followed in Tacitus' narrative by the Senate's decision to decree 'a temple and heavenly rituals' (1.10.8). Hypocrisy is not a preserve of the emperor alone; nor is inconsistency. And sure enough, once Tiberius has spoken here the criticisms take a different tack, and now Tiberius is derided for *not* wanting divine cult: Augustus' aspirations are now given a positive twist, 'better was the reaction of Augustus, who had hoped'. A world of constant talk and rumour is evoked, and a world where such criticisms cannot be ignored. It is a world, too, where, as far as his critics are concerned, Tiberius cannot do anything right.[6]

Those hostile criticisms will be the main concern of this chapter, but first some points about the style of Tiberius' speech itself. Scholars have sensed a close following of Tiberius' own language, for instance in the solemn archaisms—*duint, fungi* with the accusative—and other points of vocabulary (*desideratam*) and linguistic mannerism (*et deos et deas*):[7] they are probably right.[8] Other features too seem to breathe the authentic Tiberius. One is the withering conclusion[9] of ch. 37: 'and honour for Augustus will vanish if it is vulgarized by indiscriminate sycophancies'. Tiberius knows the ways of the empire all too well, and knows both that 'sycophancy', *adulatio*, is what such honours really amount to, and that giving them to Tiberius is no mark of real respect (*promiscis*, 'indiscriminate'). That is the true voice of the man who is so scornful of the *adulatio* which others pour upon him (3.47.4, 3.65.3, etc.).

What, then, of the epigrammatic phrase about tombs, 'those which are set up in stone are spurned like sepulchres if the judgement of posterity turns to hatred'? Commentators play down the word *spernuntur*, 'spurned': 'Tiberius has in mind neglect rather than desecration'.[10] True, *spernere* can carry

---

[6] Cf. Davies (2004), 179: 'the "you-can't-win" factor in Roman "celebrity gossip"'.

[7] Syme (1958), 284, 319, 702; Miller (1968), esp. 12.

[8] Though notice the caution of Adams (1973), esp. 137–8, Goodyear (1981), 304, and Wharton (1997). On balance Woodman–Martin (1996), 104 (cf. Martin–Woodman (1989), 118) accept that Tiberius' speeches are likely to 'include mannerisms which reflect, or are intended to suggest, the emperor's style'.

[9] 'Der Sarkasmus des Kaisers', Koestermann ad loc.

[10] Shotter (1989), 168. Koestermann has 'gemieden' ('avoid', 'shun') and 'vernachlässigt' ('neglected'); Wuilleumier's Budé has the stronger 'méprisés'. Martin–Woodman also speak of 'neglect', and so does Grant's Penguin translation. So already Furneaux: '[t]he temple of an unpopular prince has no more sanctity than a tomb: it is not desecrated, but neglected and

so weak a meaning (*OLD* s.v. 2c), but that does not seem likely in a context where 'spurning' figures so prominently: Tiberius is 'generally firm in spurning honours', *ualidus alioqui spernendis honoribus*; 'he persevered thereafter even in his private conversations in spurning such cult of himself', *aspernari talem sui cultum*; 'contempt for fame meant contempt for virtue', *contemni famae contemni uirtutem*. Tombs characteristically and proverbially risked more than neglect, and spurners would often find the most direct and vulgar way of leaving a physical mark of their contempt.[11] Statues were vulnerable in a similar way—*cuius ad effigiem non tantum meiere fas est*, 'on whose statue pissing is not enough' (Juvenal 1.131).[12] Such explicit crudity does not fit elevated prose, least of all a speech expressing such noble sentiments; but it lurks not far beneath the surface, and one again senses the emperor who knew how to make his words count (*Ann.* 13.3.2). We might compare the phrases used by Syme to characterize Tiberius' diction in other speeches: 'harsh and brutal' (2.38), 'strong, but colloquial' (3.17.2), 'unbridled' (4.71.3).[13] This is not a man for empty politenesses, either to be won by them or to produce them.

A further point tells the same way. Tiberius is contrasting non-material fame with the vulnerability of physical memorials. As we have seen, the context has developed a further comparison of the historian's role with such physical memorials; it does not take much readerly effort to put the two points together. If one does, then it is clear that the historian can contribute not merely to a person's neglect among posterity, but also to besmirching.[14] The historian—this historian—writes 'to prevent virtues from being silenced and so that crooked words and deeds should be attended by the dread of posterity and infamy' (3.65.1):[15] infamy, not just neglect. Tiberius has exactly that awareness of posterity which the historian thinks appropriate, and that

unvisited by the public.' He notes, though, that '[t]he comparison modifies the sense of "spernuntur".' Modifies it too much, surely.

[11] Cf. esp. Petr. 71.8, where Trimalchio takes thought for his own death: 'And I will take care to make provision in my will that I should not suffer injury after death. I will appoint one of my freedmen to keep watch over my grave, to stop people running to my monument to crap on it'. Smith ad loc. quotes parallels: 'this danger is frequently mentioned in inscriptions and in literature, presumably because the tombs lining the roads just outside towns proved too convenient for passers-by'.

[12] Compare esp. Hor. *Sat.* 1.8.38–9, where *sepulchra* also have just figured. Braund (1996), 104 quotes further parallels in her note on the Juvenal passage.

[13] Syme (1958), 701.

[14] A point that, as Rhiannon Ash points out to me, Pliny *Ep.* 9.27 illustrates particularly well.

[15] Luce (1991) brings out that in this passage Tacitus—unusually for Roman historians—dwells on the moral impact of a history on those active in the present, who may be deterred from bad behaviour by the fear of future memory, rather than on its inspiring effect on audiences drawing *exempla* from the past. I avoid here the difficult question of how the clause syntactically

'dread' of what that memory may be: here at least he is speaking as the historian might wish. So there is that hint that the future memory of Tiberius may be one, not of the glory he seeks, nor even of neglect, but of spurning contempt; and Tacitus' writing may be able to affect that, one way or the other.

But which way will it be?

III

Spurning contempt is certainly what it gets from those critics in the text. Once again, the comparison with the scene after Augustus' funeral is telling (1.9–10). In that scene there were some positive as well as negative critics; true, their remarks may be excuses as much as defences, but their words were not to be lightly discarded.[16] No such friendly voices here: all the comments now are negative ones. And do they represent Tacitus' view too? In old-fashioned intentionalist terms, is that what he 'wants us to think'? That is the traditional way of viewing Tacitus' use of *rumores*, 'what people think' passages, as one of 'the resources employed by Tacitus the artist to produce an impression for which Tacitus the historian is not willing to take the responsibility'[17]—in other words, what Tacitus' contemporary Plutarch termed 'shooting his barbs from under cover' and listed as one of the diagnostic symptoms of a historian's 'bad character' (*On Herodotus' Malice* 856c). Such use of *rumores* is certainly part of the traditional art of the orator, who develops his skill in exploiting them in whichever direction 'brings advantage to his case' (Cic. *De Inv.* 2.46, cf. *ad Her.* 2.12, 4.53, Quint. 5.1.2, 5.3, etc).[18] Does that approach work here?

Some scholars have thought that it does. Thus, for instance, Paratore, arguing that Tacitus wants to point Tiberius' two-facedness, even though he also thinks that Tiberius comes out in a good light 'without Tacitus' realizing it'.[19] Thus also, apparently, Walker, who includes these chapters among instances of 'the practice of inferring motives which make an action appear

relates to the preceding *quod praecipuum munus annalium reor,* 'which I deem to be a principal responsibility of annals': the issue is discussed by Woodman (1995) and Woodman–Martin ad loc.

[16] 'The favourable tribute of Tacitus (some will object) is unduly brief. Yet it is not perfidious or grudging. It is monumental.' (Syme (1958), 432, on 1.9.)

[17] Ryberg (1942), 384.

[18] There were also clearly commonplace arguments ready to be used along the lines that rumours ought *not* to be believed: Cic. *De Inv.* 2.50, *Brut.* 124 with Douglas' note, *ad Her.* 2.5, 9, 12. Splendid examples of both sorts of argument can be found in ps.-Quint. *Decl. min.*, e.g. 252.17, 259.11, 325.14 and 18.

[19] Paratore (1962), 494 n. 126 and (1967), 132–3.

hypocritical or at least give it a meaning unlike the obvious one,' and finds it significant that the negative interpretations are given so much more space than the positive suggestion of *modestia*;[20] then *contemptu famae contemni uirtutes* figures in her list of cases where '[c]omment on a particular event strikes directly at the decadence and pettiness of society in general', one of those paragraph-endings that 'drive home most forcefully Tacitus' view of the nature of tyranny'.[21] Thus also, it seems (though the argument is more nuanced), Sinclair, who observes that the critics' insistence on the value of *fama* is in line with traditional Roman values, and indeed coincides closely with what Tacitus says in his own person elsewhere.[22] For Sinclair, Tiberius' words 'display a raw negativity that rejects what the Romans traditionally viewed as the legitimate purpose of all political activity, namely, posthumous fame. According to Tacitus, Tiberius now exhibits a cynicism that is thoroughly destructive to the body politic'.[23]

Tacitus has certainly framed the criticisms with literary sharpness. *Quidam ut degeneris animi interpretabantur*, 'others [interpreted it] as the sign of a degenerate spirit', recalls *Aeneid* 4.13, *degeneres animos timor arguit*: 'it is fear that exposes the degenerate spirit'.[24] The Virgilian line expands and explains the one that precedes, when Dido is weighing up the impressive Aeneas: *credo equidem, nec uana fides, genus esse deorum*, 'I believe, and my belief is well based, that his blood is divine': so divinity as well as degeneracy is in point. And Dido is indeed right: Aeneas is of divine blood. So now, the suggestion may be, Tiberius is no Aeneas, *degener* indeed not merely from Augustus but also from the legendary progenitor of the Julian race. It is *timor* that shows it, too, Tiberius' diffident fear of presuming to rival his forebears. So Tacitus has given the criticisms point; does that mean, though, that they are felt to be well aimed?

The obvious difficulty with that interpretation is that they are so transparently unfair. 'Contempt for fame meant contempt for virtue'—yet fame is precisely what Tiberius is *not* spurning; fame is his concern, and fame of the highest kind. He is thoroughly in line with Roman tradition. 'Tiberius' wish

[20] Walker (1952), 49, in the long n. 4 to p. 47.

[21] Walker (1952), 57 n. 1. Rather similar is Develin (1983), who at 91–2 includes 4.38 among examples of Tacitus' technique of 'insidious suggestions': in other cases he is explicit that these are ways in which we can tell what Tacitus 'wanted his readers to believe' (94).

[22] Sinclair (1995), 111, quoting Earl (1967), 81–3. In 1991 Sinclair had given a different emphasis: 'Tacitus himself seems to admire the *princeps*' moderate and rather old-fashioned ways. But he attests that Tiberius' detractors received his refusal of divine honours with sarcasm that was all the more ferocious for its being unjustified' ((1991), 334). 'All the more ferocious for its being unjustified' seems to be Sinclair's own gloss: at least, it goes beyond anything that Tacitus explicitly 'attests'.

[23] Sinclair (1995), 112.

[24] Martin–Woodman (1989), 192.

might be the prayer of Agricola himself.'[25] And nobody here doubts that he means it,[26] not even the most unfriendly of these critics:[27] they can tell that, for once, this master of *dissimulatio* is saying what he means.

There is also the problem of the critics' own inconsistency, at this time when it is the emperor's consistency that is under attack.[28] We have already seen that these criticisms sit uncomfortably with those which Tiberius was answering, when it was his *ambitio* for divine honours that was presumed and attacked (above, pp. 368–9); now it would have been better for him to emulate Augustus, and 'hope'. That phrasing may also recall those criticisms made of Augustus himself at 1.10.6 (above, p. 369), which had centred on those hopes. True, these critics need not be identical with those critics; and eleven years have passed, and memories of Augustus may be growing warmer. But the impression persists that in these jaundiced eyes an emperor cannot win.

Intertextuality tells against the critics as much as in their favour. As Martin–Woodman observe, that *altissima cupere*, 'had the highest desires', has an off-key sound: Tacitus 'undermines its validity by echoing Sall. *Cat.* 5.5, "nimis alta semper cupiebat" ["always had over-high desires"], where the revolutionary Catiline is described'.[29] Then the striking word *insatiabiliter* recalls a remarkable line of Lucretius, 'but it was we who wept insatiably for you as you were turned to ashes on the shudder-inducing pyre' (3.907), where once again the whole context is in point: Lucretius is mocking the genuine though excessive grief of those who mourn one they have loved. 'It was difficult to use the word seriously.'[30] Martin–Woodman are right to follow Syme in suggesting that 'his opponents are thus made to choose a word whose tone again undermines their contention'.[31]

[25] Walker (1952), 237 n. 2. The reference is to the very similar words in praise of Agricola in Tacitus' peroration, *Agr.* 46.3: see Ogilvie–Richmond ad loc. for further parallels, and also above, n. 3, for cases where this future fame is couched in terms of *literary* memory.

[26] One point in the Latin might be taken as suggesting that Tiberius did find the idea of cult attractive: at 37.3 he refers to the example set by Augustus as *placitum iam*, and Martin–Woodman take that as '"already pleasing" to Tiberius' (his reason being that it had already been adopted by Augustus). Better, I think, to take the *placitum* as referring to *Augustus'* approval: it was an *exemplum* that therefore had 'already been approved' before Tiberius considered it.

[27] Contrast Seager (2005), 123, 'It is striking too that his hearers had grown so accustomed to assuming that Tiberius was never telling the truth that even this lucid and noble declaration was greeted with distrust'. Yet in Tacitus' text the hearers do believe Tiberius, and 'distrust' is not the right word. It is left to a modern critic to suspect insincerity: Paratore (1962), 494 n. 126 and (1967), 135–6.

[28] Cf. Davies (2004), 178.

[29] Martin–Woodman (1989), 192.

[30] Syme (1958), 727 n. 3.

[31] Martin–Woodman (1989), 193.

So it is hard to think that the critics are right, or at least straightforwardly right. It is notable too that Tacitus emphasizes that point that the emperor meant what he said: 'he persevered thereafter even in his private conversations in spurning such cult of himself'. The historian might have preferred, for instance, to note times when the emperor was more indulgent to divine cult: that might have supported the criticisms of inconsistency.[32] But the Tiberius that we have in the text is as solid now in rejecting such distinctions as— again, the historian goes out of his way to note—he has always been in the past ('generally firm in spurning honours', *ualidus alioqui spernendis honor-ibus*).

Once again there is a parallel with 1.9–10, and those comments on the dead Augustus. Perhaps the critics there had the better of the argument; that is what most readers have thought. Yet the text hardly encouraged readers to accept without further reflection what those critics said. In one point in particular—the culminating one, which occupies nearly a quarter of the speech—the critics' point had been undermined in advance. They claimed that 'not even Tiberius had been adopted as successor through any affection or concern for the state, but, because he [Augustus] had had insight into the man's arrogance and savagery, by the basest of comparisons he had sought glory for himself' (1.10.7). Yet Tacitus had already tellingly shown that Tiberius was, almost literally, the last person that Augustus had wanted (1.3.1–3): he had made every previous choice he reasonably could to avoid it. Whatever Tacitus' reasons for including that passage in 1.10, it was not to make his readers think that the critics were right. What those reasons were is another question: doubtless something more to do with preparation for Tiberius' reign, including the circumstances when he in his turn would pick his successor (cf. esp. *Ann.* 6.46), than with a fair interpretation of Augustus.

IV

So the view of Martin–Woodman on 4.37–8 is surely the better one. They see Tacitus as critical of the critics rather than of the emperor himself: Tacitus

---

[32] Price (1984), 58 notes that Tiberius, with priests in eleven cities, was the emperor who came closest to Augustus in the number of his civic cults in the Greek east. But it does seem that Tiberius' 'personal pronouncements . . . are always consistent' (Seager (2005), 122) in resisting cult unless there were special reasons or a clear precedent, from his response to Gytheum in AD 15 (EJ 102) onwards. 'Where private individuals and even communities acted on their own initiative, there was little Tiberius could do' (Seager, ibid.).

attributes to public opinion a point-by-point rejection of Tib.'s words which manifestly fails to hit its target and from which Tib. emerges with his reputation enhanced.
Such manipulation of his reader's sympathies, first in one direction and then in
another, is typical of T., and especially of his treatment of an emperor for whom he
cannot conceal his reluctant admiration.[33]

That was also the view of Syme, who speaks of Tacitus as 'satirizing'[34] the
critics; if some of their language echoes the commonplaces of Augustan
literature (talk of Hercules, Dionysus, and Romulus), or if their talk of *uirtus*
reflects commonplace Roman values, then that shows pointedly how such
language can be used as readily to disparage as to acclaim:[35] so, one might
add, the resonance of the language itself continues Tiberius' own point, how
delicate is the line between retrospective glory and retrospective 'spurning'.

Another advantage of this approach is that it seems truer to the breadth of
Tacitus' interpretative interests. It will not be the only occasion where Tacitus
is ungenerous to an emperor's critics: in analysing Tacitus' version of Claudius' citizenship speech, Griffin brought out how the emperor's critics 'are
generally presented as more narrow-minded and reactionary than the opposition the real Claudius seems to expect' (as we can see from the version
preserved on the Lyons tablet).[36] Here, Tacitus has just been emphasizing that
'many who during Tiberius' rule suffered punishment or infamy have descendants remaining', including moral descendants as well as physical ones
(4.33.4): 'many', we notice, not just the emperor or his closest acolytes, and
Tacitus' gaze takes in many who are open to criticism. These anonymous
snipers at Tiberius would doubtless not rank among the topmost candidates
for 'infamy', but that does not mean they are immune from that critical gaze.
They need not be just a filter for adjusting the light cast on the emperor
himself or for evaluating his actions.

Yet of course they can be that as well, even if the evaluation is done in a
more nuanced way than simply by our joining in with their malice. Depiction
of atmosphere is historically important,[37] here as at 1.9–10, in helping us to
grasp the hostility that Tiberius has to face, and to understand why he has to

---

[33] Martin–Woodman (1989), 186–7.

[34] Syme (1958), 514 n. 2. Others who take Tacitus as criticizing the critics include Koestermann
(1965), 133 (who finds it surprising that Tacitus did not include a barb against the emperor, but
reflects that he did not always write with 'ice-cold logic' and may have been torn between
contradictory reactions).

[35] Syme (1958), 315 n. 6.

[36] Griffin (1982), 406, cf. 414.

[37] Cf. Ries (1969), esp. 8–10, 95–132, and 172–3 ('ein Machtfaktor ersten Ranges'), and
Gibson (1998), both emphasizing the large consequences that often follow from rumours or
public comments, however inaccurate they may be.

tread so carefully.[38] We surely feel some sympathy for him too, just as we might at earlier times in the reign: when he had to cope with public pressure for activity during the Sacrovir rebellion, for instance, when his policy was resoundingly vindicated by events and his reply to his critics was devastating (3.47); or even—admittedly, a more complicated narrative case—when Germanicus' crowd-pleasing heroics were at odds with Tiberius' own insight into the right way to treat Germany (2.26, cf. 1.62.2).[39]

Germanicus might also be suggestive in a different way, for in his case one comes not merely to note the popular reaction but also, at least to some extent, to understand it: and it is relevant here to recall the frequency with which readers and critics of Tacitus' narrative have shared that popular enthusiasm for the glamorous Germanicus and his old-fashioned ways.[40] There is a level of reading which is aware how easy it would be to take a simple, black-or-white moral view of the events described, at the same time as knowing that there is a lot more to it and that in different moods or mindsets one might judge things differently. That is as familiar from high culture as from low, from appreciating Brutus' high principles in *Julius Caesar* or feeling the *joie de vivre* of Don Giovanni as from immersion in James Bond's latest round of casual brutality; and it is not unusual for the same work to invite and exploit both levels of reaction, as in those cases of *Julius Caesar* or *Don Giovanni*. (I am not so sure about James Bond.)

So it is here—though this may be a case of understanding how readily others might react in a particular way rather than thinking one could react in different ways oneself. Even as one senses the extremity of the critics' comments, it is not difficult to understand why they should feel so malicious: one can empathize with their hostility without sympathizing with the points they make. Part of that understanding comes from the preceding narrative. We have seen how that context has conveyed an imperial world much less noble and less nurturing of future memory than Tiberius' speech would suggest. True, Tiberius does not bear total responsibility for that world; there were those others who 'during Tiberius' reign suffered punishment and infamy' (33.4, above p. 375); it was Satrius Secundus and Pinarius Natta, Sejanus' men, who accused Cremutius (34.1); Tiberius did not condemn Cremutius (nor did anybody else), and it was the Senate, not Tiberius, who ordered the burning of the books. But Tiberius does bear some of that responsibility. The

---

[38] In other words, to invite the response which Seager (2005), 123 makes explicit: 'In the face of such a total lack of understanding it is hardly surprising that Tiberius, naturally uncommunicative, became even more taciturn and withdrawn with the years.'

[39] I have discussed this elsewhere (Pelling (1993), esp. 74–8); see also now O'Gorman (2000), 46–77.

[40] Once again, cf. Pelling (1993), and bibliography cited there.

'callous look with which Caesar received his defence' (34.2) did Cremutius no good; and the 'savage orders, constant accusations, deceitful friendships, the ruin of innocents and always the same reasons for their extermination' (33.3) that typify the age combine the 'orders' that are largely the emperor's doing, the 'accusations' that are others', and the 'deceitful friendships' which are both, together with the disastrous results, the 'ruin' and the 'extermination', that follow from that lethal mix.

Some of these uncomfortable features are even there in Tiberius' speech, lurking just beneath the surface. Take that sequence 'worthy of my ancestors, provident of your affairs, in dangers steadfast, and not panicked by affronts for the public good'. Good phrases; it is indeed as if Tiberius is 'issuing his own epitaph' (Martin–Woodman (1989), 188); but the ordering of the list is not coincidental. Tiberius looks back to his ancestors and forward—*proui-dum*—for the good of others; but what might these 'dangers' be? The virtue of 'steadfastness' (*constantia*) is a traditional one, but for the elderly and non-belligerent Tiberius these will not be the traditional heroisms of battle:[41] 'peace was immovable or only modestly challenged, affairs in the City were sorrowful, and the princeps indifferent to extending the empire', 32.2. The dangers that threaten now will be those within this sorrowful city, and the 'steadfastness' that Tiberius shows will be against his fellow citizens. So it leads on naturally to the *offensiones* which are only to be expected, 'affronts' which the emperor is not afraid to cause as well as to suffer.[42] *Offensio* is a distinctively Tiberian word[43] for a distinctively Tiberian thing. We have already noted, too, the pointedness of 'likenesses which are finest *and destined*

---

[41] Cf. Martin–Woodman (1989), 189 ad loc., who also bring out that *constantia* may not have been one of the virtues paraded by the historical Tiberius: it appears on the coinage of Claudius.

[42] I here depart from Martin–Woodman, who take *offensiones* as passive, 'not afraid of being attacked'. They cite as a parallel 3.54.6, where Tiberius says *graues et plerumque iniquas* [sc. *offensiones*] *pro re publica suscipiam*. Yet, in context, the parallel may suggest the giving as well as the taking of offence. There Tiberius has just been objecting to the readiness of magistrates to carp at public vices and cause the emperor *simultates*, then leave it to him to deal with them: he is assuring them that he is no more eager for *offensiones* than they are. A *simultas*—'a state of animosity, quarrel, feud', OLD—characteristically involves combative actions, not just passivity (*pace* Woodman's translation of that passage, 'I too am not greedy for affronts to be levelled at me'). 6.15.2, cited by Woodman–Martin in their note on 3.54.6, points the same way: Tiberius there refers to the *offensiones ob rem publicam coeptas*, affronts which he has initiated (again *pace* Woodman's translation, 'incurred') on behalf of the state. OLD is however too simple in classifying the present instance just under 6a, 'giving offence', rather than 6b, 'taking it': it is rather the case that, for an emperor, the taking of offence readily leads to actions that cause further offence, and Tiberius is not 'afraid' to behave as he must.

[43] Miller (1968), 13: 'of twenty-nine examples, about twenty appear in Tiberian contexts'; cf. Woodman–Martin on 3.54.6.

to survive', et mansurae.[44] In a world where not merely others—Cremutius'
book-burners among them—but also Tiberius himself have tried to annihi-
late memory, in particular by the destruction of images involved in *damnatio
memoriae*,[45] this can suggest not merely what Tiberius is trying to avoid for
himself but what he has done or sanctioned in the case of others.

Nor does what follows make Tiberius any more likeable, nor any easier for
public or reader to interpret in a straightforward way. Immediately after the
Spanish sequence the focus switches to Sejanus. He begins his appeal for
Livia's hand carefully (39.2):

Through the benevolence of his father Augustus, and later through the very many
tokens of Tiberius' esteem, he had become accustomed to take his hopes and prayers
not primarily to the gods but to the ears of principes.

In one way that echoes Tiberius' sentiment: the *princeps* is not a god. But the
suggestion now is that the *princeps* is a sort of divine equivalent, the new and more
efficacious recipient for 'prayers', *uota*. Such language recurs in the very next
words: 'And he had never pleaded for the glittering of honours'. 'Pleaded' renders
the Latin *precatum*, once again literally 'prayed for'. Even the shape of Sejanus' plea
has something of the prayer-form about it: you have often helped me in the past,
help me again now.[46] Tiberius had dwelt on what he shared with ordinary mortals,
princeps though he was; Sejanus implies the gulf that separates the two. The very
fact that it has become customary to approach the emperor by letter (even 'though
present', *praesens*, another word often used of divinities)[47] tells a tale, 39.1.[48] This is
not the normal communication of mortals.

[44] Rhiannon Ash points out to me the similarity to Tacitus' comment on Otho's tomb,
modicum et mansurum ('modest and destined to survive', *Hist.* 2.49.4), where again there is an
implied contrast with the pretentious and vulnerable memorials favoured by others.

[45] On *damnatio memoriae* see Flower (2006), esp. her remarks on 'the years under Tiberius,
when sanctions against the memory of prominent individuals were regularly put into effect and
enforced' (131) and on the case of Cn. Calpurnius Piso (132–8). Martin–Woodman also note
the echo of this passage at 6.2.1, of the hatred aimed at the younger Livia after her death: *atroces
sententiae dicebantur, in effigies quoque ac memoriam eius* ('frightening proposals were voiced
also against her likenesses and memory'): evidently the proposals concerned the removal of her
effigies, as later with Messalina, 11.38.3. Cf. Flower, 169–82 (Livia), 182–9 (Messalina). Juv.
10.62–4 gives an especially gripping picture of the realities of statue-destruction.

[46] Pulleyn (1997), 65–6, Furley–Bremer (2001) I.57–8. Classic instances are Homer *Il.* 1.451–6
and 5.115–17, Sappho fr. 1.5, Pind. *Isth.* 6.42–6, Soph. *OT* 165–7, Arist. *Thesm.* 1156–9, Cat.
34.22–4, Hor. *Odes* 1.32.1–4 with Nisbet–Hubbard ad loc.

[47] e.g. Virg. *Ecl.* 1.41, Hor. *Odes* 1.35.2 with Nisbet–Hubbard ad loc., 3.5.2, 4.14.43, *Epist.*
2.1.15 with Brink ad loc.

[48] A tale, though, that is misleading: Martin–Woodman (1989), 194 pertinently ask 'why
does T. comment on a practice which had begun with Caesar, continued thereafter, and
remained absolutely normal in his own day?' Perhaps, as they suggest, to prepare for the
emperor's later absence from Rome, and all the further letters that this made necessary; and
perhaps to accentuate this impression that an emperor does not communicate in the same way
as other human beings. On Tiberius' letters, see Morello (2006), arguing convincingly that they

'And he had never pleaded for the glittering of honours': one already senses the parallelism of tone, too, with what Tiberius has said,[49] echoing a theme that runs through this book and would doubtless have persisted to the end of Book 5, the mirroring styles of emperor and minister. Here it is almost parodic. Tiberius had wanted only to be a mortal, Sejanus only to behave 'like one of the soldiers'. Tiberius wished to be remembered as 'provident of your affairs', Sejanus had 'preferred lookouts and toils . . . for his commander's preservation': once again the emperor is coming, in the language of adulation, to take the place of Rome and its citizens, just as it does when Sejanus stresses the need for 'the family' to be 'strengthened against the unfair affronts (*offensiones*) of Agrippina'. The word picks up the *offensiones* which Tiberius has proudly declared his readiness to confront, 38.1, but there it was the 'affronts' which threatened more widely (p. 377): again Sejanus' focus is narrowing to the house alone. The point recurs with Sejanus' pride in being 'believed worthy of a connexion with Caesar': 'believed', evidently, by the emperor himself, whereas Tiberius aspired to the good opinion of Rome as a whole. Tiberius spoke of being 'worthy of my ancestors'; now Sejanus is conscious of his humbler status, even as he aspires to that new and greater family. Tiberius proclaimed it as *satis*—'satisfying'—to fill the place of *princeps*; it would be *satis* for Sejanus—'he would be satisfied'— to think that his marriage would strengthen the royal house. People would give *satis superque*—'a satisfying contribution and more'—to Tiberius' memory if they remembered his service to the state; Sejanus would have *multum superque uitae*—'any portion of his life would be full and more'—if he spent it with a *princeps* like this.

Sejanus' adulation is transparent; the aping of the imperial style is itself a commentary on the fawning techniques now thought appropriate—perhaps again *mistakenly* thought appropriate for this *princeps* who hates *adulatio* (after all, it does not work here), but still telling for the shabby expectations that surrounded the court. And no reader of this letter is likely to think that its humble phrasing adequately reflects Sejanus' true aspirations, especially as we already know from the book's proem that Sejanus was to set his eye on the principate itself (*quo facinore dominationem raptum ierit*, 'the act by which he moved to seize mastery', 4.1.1). So the servant can mimic the characteristic

---

'abandon or invert many of what we regard as the normal functions of letters', and that the generic inversions are made expressive of the emperor's character (349). In particular, '[t]he Sejanus letters are . . . associated in Tacitus's text with secrecy and control more than they are with the traditions of friendship' that the genre conventionally embodied (ibid.).

[49] Some of these echoes are noted by Sinclair (1995), 112–13, stressing the 'cynicism' which he thinks the sequence reveals in both minister and emperor. Cf. also Martin–Woodman (1989), 195 on 39.4: 'Sejanus addresses the emperor "in his own language" '.

Tiberian *dissimulatio* too, even in this case where the emperor himself meant what he said. Once again the flavour of the reign is clear; and also why it was so easy to be malicious about it.

The minister mimics the master; but it is a pale imitation. Another aspect that the reader knows from this book's proem is that Sejanus' 'artfulness' (*sollertia*) was no match for that of Tiberius: *quippe isdem artibus uictus est*, 'indeed it was by the same means that he was vanquished' (4.1.2). Tiberius' response to Sejanus' letter (40) begins to show us how. If we had Book 5 as well, we might see even more clearly how this marks the beginning of the change in Sejanus' fortunes, with (as Martin–Woodman observe)[50] this circumlocutory exchange of letters eventually mirrored by that other letter, the 'wordy and long letter from Capri' (*uerbosa et grandis epistula uenit | a Capreis*, Juv. 10.71–2): that fatal letter, after some initial obliquity, eventually made its meaning very clear indeed. The bemused Sejanus was arrested and killed; Sejanus' estranged wife Apicata—estranged because of his affair with Livia, 4.3.5—took her own life; their children were executed too, most horribly (5.9). Dio 58.10–11 gives a memorable narrative of the reading of that letter; Tacitus' version, doubtless, would have been no less chilling. The path to it starts here.

If the letter exchange itself marks a distortion of normality (p. 378), Tiberius' response puts normal communication under even more strain. It is not so much that what Tiberius says is hypocritical or false: a great deal is clearly true, most particularly the way he exposes the inappositeness of Sejanus' Augustan 'precedent' and the unreality of the suggestion that he could remain in the same station (40.4–6). It is rather that, after giving all these decisive reasons why the marriage cannot take place, he adds 'but I shall not oppose either your designs or Livia's' (40.7). No? Even Tiberius himself does not sound as if he expects Sejanus to take that seriously: at least, he goes on (most obscurely) to mention some 'further relationships I am preparing to make you and me inseparable'. More menacingly, Tiberius ends

This only will I disclose, that there is nothing so lofty as not to be deserved by those virtues of yours and by your intentions toward me, and given the right time, either in the senate or at a public meeting, I shall not keep silent. (40.7)

As Martin–Woodman comment, it is hard to avoid, once again, the suggestion of that final lethal senate meeting that looms for Sejanus a few years later;[51] and, even if the audience do not catch that roistering anticipation, the language itself—especially from the menacing and sinister Tiberius—can as easily suggest 'when the time comes to speak out in your defence' as 'when the

---

[50] Martin–Woodman (1989), 193–4; cf. Morello (2006), 343.
[51] Martin–Woodman (1989), 199.

time for your promotion comes'. No wonder that 'in response Sejanus no longer talked about marriage,' but nursed 'a deeper dread' (*altius metuens*, 41.1, echoing and reversing those 'highest desires' appropriate for the best of mortals, 38.5 (above p. 373)). He may have misjudged his moment to seek the marriage, but he can read Tiberius correctly now.

That final 'either in the senate or at a public meeting' carries a further point. Sejanus, we saw, stressed the divergence of a *princeps'* lot from that of an ordinary mortal; Tiberius now agrees.

The counsels of all other mortals depended on what they thought advantageous to themselves; but the lot of principes was different, since they had to regulate paramount affairs with regard to their own reputation. (40.1)

Even if the emphasis is different, this is not inconsistent with what he said at 37–8—here too it is 'other' mortals, and there too, as earlier at 3.54.5, he had been alert to 'the place of princeps' and the way he hoped he would be remembered as filling it; and the concern for 'reputation', *fama*, is a constant feature. But now that 'reputation' that guides his conduct is in the here and now, among the living, not that of future generations; and his remarks progress in a way that corrects, with an eye to this 'reputation', that implication of Sejanus' letter that the royal house has come to be all that matters. Tiberius starts there, certainly, with those 'antagonisms of Agrippina' (*offensiones*, 40.2–3) which had figured in Sejanus' own argument (39.4), and which we will see soon enough again in the narrative, when Agrippina faces Tiberius with her own, much more combative brand of 'prayers' (*preces*, 53.1)—and, just before that, some pointed echoes of this Spanish sequence (52.2).[52] But Tiberius' argument here moves on. Whatever Tiberius himself may think, others would not allow a husband of Livia to remain a mere *eques* when they remembered the commands held by her brother and father and 'our ancestors' (40.4)—those ancestors again that figured in Tiberius' thinking at 38.1, and again the point is what others, not just Tiberius or his own family, think of them. 'You, of course, wish to stay within that position of yours,' he goes

[52] Agrippina there comes upon Tiberius sacrificing to Augustus, and chides him for reverencing the dead man while persecuting his descendants: 'his divine spirit had not been transfused into mute likenesses: *she* was his real image, the offspring of his heavenly blood' (4.52.2). So: if Tiberius has at 37–8 shown such respect to Augustus and concern for a fame that transcends mere 'likenesses', *effigies*, is this not at odds with current realities? That is then further recalled at 67.4, where she and her son are (maliciously) advised to flee to the German armies or 'to embrace the likeness of Divine Augustus in the throng of the forum and to call upon people and senate for aid'. Agrippina too, like Tiberius, is wise enough to 'spurn' such advice (*spreta*); but in her case too it made little difference to the hostility she faced.

on, not without a certain knowing edge as he addresses the point where
Sejanus' *dissimulatio* might most readily be sensed:

but those magistrates and leaders who burst in on you against your will and consult
you about every affair make no secret of maintaining that you have passed long ago
the pinnacle of an equestrian and have far outstripped my father's friendships; and in
their resentment of you they censure me too. (40.5)

So 'magistrates and leaders' do matter too, and Tiberius cannot ignore them.
That 'in the senate or at a public meeting' has more point against this background. It will not be an audience brimming with goodwill; and it will be an
audience whose opinions count. The non-royal aspects of Rome are not, after
all, politically dead, and that royalistic trajectory is nowhere near complete.

'And in their resentment of you they censure me too.' The movement of
Tiberius' words has emphasized hostility; the indirectness of his language, with
its baffling 'I shall not oppose either your designs or Livia's', has again pointed
to one of the less genial aspects of his reign; the position of Sejanus himself is a
further sore. So many features of the surrounding narrative, then, help us to
understand why those malicious critics in ch. 38 felt as they did, and the more
off-beam and unreasonable their criticisms seem, the more historically telling
they are. The concern of Tacitus' narrative is not just to score points off those
malcontents; it is to illuminate the audience that the *princeps* had to impress,
this man who knew that emperors 'had to regulate paramount affairs with
regard to their own reputation' (40.1), and to show how hopeless was the task;
and to help us to understand how, even if the critics were wrong, they were
wrong through a hostility whose reasons we can fathom.

V

Ellen O'Gorman has highlighted 'misreading' as a constant ingredient in Tacitean
interpretation, particularly in the case of the Tiberian narrative where so many
people find the emperor riddling and elusive: 'Tiberius represents the Tacitean
narrative, in that the difficulties of reading the princeps are a dramatization of the
difficulties of reading the *Annals*.'[53] One can also put it the other way round, and
emphasize how the reading process replicates the difficulties that contemporaries
found in grasping Tiberius.[54] Reading Tacitus—even (one might unfashionably

---

[53] O'Gorman (2000), 78.
[54] This too is of course implied in O'Gorman's discussion, e.g. 87, 'Tacitus'
reader . . . becomes once more implicated in the power struggle of princeps and senator', even

suggest) reading Tacitus' authorial intentions—can replicate reading Tiberius and *his* intentions, and the riddling quality can promote reflection on the events in the narrative, not just on the reading process. In its simplest form, this can be seen as high-level *mimesis*, as the dramatic immediacy of a narrative draws us in to feel the responses or ask the questions that contemporaries would have felt and asked: that is the sort of *enargeia* that makes us feel as if we were onlookers, and an external audience—including 'us'—becomes as close as it ever can to the internal audience of observers at the time.[55]

As close as it ever can . . . —but that is not that close. For one thing, external audiences almost always have some extratextual knowledge, even as first-time readers, of how it will all progress. Most of Tacitus' contemporary readers would have known of Sejanus' looming demise. Indeed, this combination of empathy and detached foreknowledge is typically essential to narrative explanation, drawing a reader in to understand the emotions that drive events at the same time as knowing where those events are heading. There is also a detachment in the reading experience, just as in the theatre the pity and fear that even the most involved viewer feels can never be an exact replica of the pity and fear generated in real-life parallel experiences. If that gap is not there, there is the danger that, like Nero's guard who leapt on stage to free his master when he was in chains, one blurs reality and pretence (never a danger far away in Tacitean Rome: witness Woodman's analysis of 'amateur dramatics at the court of Nero').[56] That distance leaves one able to survey and evaluate those responses of contemporary onlookers, as at the same time the quality of the narrative makes it possible for us to understand them. I discuss this elsewhere, arguing that often the response of a Tacitean reader to events is a close, but not exact, counterpart of the responses of observers in the text, precisely through that process of imaginative involvement coupled with detached monitoring of that involvement.[57] David Levene has similarly suggested that readers of *Histories* 3 become a 'meta-audience', engaged with but also judging popular reactions to Vitellius' fall.[58]

That is close to what I have been suggesting here, as we pass our own, more detached verdict on the criticisms of those malicious commentators. They may not be 'misreading' in the most normal way for the *Annals*, as no one doubts that Tiberius is being sincere. It is more *misevaluation*, and one that, if

---

if her emphasis falls on the reading process ('the unattainability of certain knowledge through a process of reading', ibid.).

[55] See esp. Walker (1993).

[56] Woodman (1993); cf. Bartsch (1994), esp. 47–9 on the story of the soldier leaping on to stage (Suet. *Nero* 21.3 and Dio 63.10.2).

[57] Pelling (forthcoming, a), in particular p. 160.

[58] Levene (1997).

this analysis has been on the right lines, the reader should not be tempted to share. But even without sharing, the reader may be able to understand; and the understanding of the critics' mentality can in its turn promote understanding of the dilemmas confronting Tiberius, and of the ways in which his own actions, however 'understandable' in their turn, would have made them worse.

There is a further implication too. Judging whether such criticisms are 'right' or 'wrong', just like judging whether an emperor is 'good' or 'bad', is always likely to be too simple if it is made to serve as a final verdict. Tacitus deals in understanding and interpretation as well as in praise and blame. Yet it is essential too to see how such over-simple questions were basic to people's responses at the time. As we replicate our own version of those responses, good-and-bad judgements may therefore form part of the *process* of response that may eventually elicit a more complicated verdict, just as much of this chapter has catalogued features that could easily elicit unpopularity—basically, were 'bad'. That is part of understanding too, especially in a case like this, where judging the divine aspects of this reign in Spain was always going to be anything but plain.

Bibliography

Adams, J. N. (1973) 'The Vocabulary of the Speeches in Tacitus' Historical Works', *BICS* 20: 124–44.

—— (1980) 'Review of R. Pitkäranta, *Studien zum Latein des Victor Vitensis* (Helsinki 1978)', *CR* 30: 282–3.

Adcock, F. E. (1956) *Caesar as Man of Letters* (Cambridge).

Adler, E. (2005–6) 'Who's Anti-Roman? Sallust and Pompeius Trogus on Mithridates', *CJ* 101: 383–407.

Ahl, F. (1985) *Metaformations: Soundplay and Wordplay in Ovid and Other Classical Poets* (Ithaca, NY and London).

Aldrete, G. S. (2007) *Floods of the Tiber in Ancient Rome* (Baltimore and London).

Alfonsi, L. (1948) 'L'importanza politico-religiosa della «*Enunciazione*» di Valerio Sorano (à proposito di CIL, I, I², p.337)', *Epigraphica* 10: 81–9.

Allison, J. W. (1997) *Word and Concept in Thucydides* (APA American Classical Studies, 41; Atlanta, Ga.).

Alonso-Núñez, J. M. (1987) 'An Augustan World History: The "Historiae Philippicae" of Pompeius Trogus', *G&R* 34: 56–72.

Ando, C. (2002) 'Vergil's Italy: Ethnography and Politics in First-Century Rome', in Levene and Nelis (2002), 123–42.

Andrewes, A. (1959) 'Thucydides on the Causes of the War', *CQ* 9: 223–39.

—— (1961) 'Thucydides and the Persians', *Historia* 10: 1–18.

Anon. (1982) *Atti del Colloquio internazionale AIEGL su epigrafia e ordine senatorio, Roma, 14–20 maggio 1981*, 2 vols. (Tituli 4–5; Rome).

Anon. (1983) *Les "Bourgeoisies" municipales italiennes aux IIe et Ier siècles av. J.-C.* (Colloques internationaux du centre national de la recherche scientifique N. 609 sciences humaines; Paris and Naples).

Anon. (1988) *Die Welt der Etrusker: Archäologische Denkmäler aus Museen der sozialistischen Länder* (Exhibition catalogue; Berlin).

Anon. (1994) *La presenza etrusca nella Campania meridionale* (Biblioteca di *Studi Etruschi* 28; Florence).

Appel, G. (1909) *De Romanorum precationibus* (Religionsgeschichtliche Versuche und Vorarbeiten VII.2; Giessen).

Asbridge, T. (2004) *The First Crusade: A New History* (London).

Ash, R. (2006) *Tacitus* (Bristol).

—— (2007a) *Tacitus: Histories Book II* (Cambridge).

—— (2007b) 'Victim and Voyeur: Rome as a Character in Tacitus' *Histories* 3', in D. J. H. Larmour and D. Spencer, edd., *Sites of Rome* (Oxford), 211–37.

Astin, A. E. (1967) *Scipio Aemilianus* (Oxford).

Austin, R. G. (1955) *P. Vergili Maronis Aeneidos Liber Quartus* (Oxford).

—— (1960) *M. Tulli Ciceronis Pro M. Caelio Oratio*, 3rd edn. (Oxford)

Austin, R. G. (1964) *P. Vergili Maronis Aeneidos Liber Secundus* (Oxford).

Avenarius, W. (1957) 'Die griechischen Vorbilder des Sallust', *SO* 33: 48–86.

Badian, E. (1966) 'The Early Historians', in T. A. Dorey, ed., *Latin Historians* (London and New York), 1–38.

—— (1990) 'Thucydides and the Outbreak of the Peloponnesian War: A Historian's Brief', in J. W. Allison, ed., *Conflict, Antithesis and the Ancient Historian* (Columbus, Ohio), 46–91; rev. version in Badian (1993), 125–62.

—— (1993) *From Plataea to Potidaea: Studies in the History and Archaeology of the Pentecontaetia* (Baltimore and London).

Bakker, E. J. (2006) 'Contract and Design: Thucydides' Writing', in Rengakos and Tsakmakis (2006), 109–29.

Bakker, E. J., I. J. F. de Jong, and H. van Wees (2002) *Brill's Comparion to Herodotus* (Leiden and Boston).

Baldwin, B. (1970) 'The Hapless Helmsman', *CJ* 65: 322–3.

—— (2005) 'Stylistic Notes on the Elder Pliny's Preface', *Latomus* 64: 91–95.

Balsdon, J. P. V. D. (1972) 'L. Cornelius Scipio: A Salvage Operation', *Historia* 21: 224–34.

—— (1979) *Romans and Aliens* (London and Chapel Hill, NC).

Baragwanath, E. (2008) *Motivation and Narrative in Herodotus* (Oxford).

Barbieri, A. (1987) '*Praeco-poeta, sal e urbanitas*', *RCCM* 29: 111–50.

Barceló, P. A. (1981) *Roms auswärtige Beziehungen unter der constantinischen Dynastie (306–363)* (Regensburg).

Barchiesi, A. (2008) '*Bellum Italicum*: L'unificazione dell'Italia nell'Eneide', in G. Urso, ed., *Patria diversis gentibus una? Unità politica e identità etniche nell'Italia antica: Atti del convegno internazionale, Cividale del Friuli, 20–22 settembre 2007* (Pisa), 243–60.

Barsby, J. (1973) *Ovid's* Amores: *Book One* (Oxford).

Bartsch, S. (1994) *Actors in the Audience: Theatricality and Doublespeak from Nero to Hadrian* (Cambridge, Mass. and London).

Basanoff, V. (1947) *Evocatio: Étude d'un rituel militaire romain* (Bibliothèque de l'École des Hautes-Études, sciences religieuses 61; Paris).

Bastomsky, S. J. (1988) 'Tacitus, Histories IV, 73–74: A Unique View of Roman Rule?', *Latomus* 47: 413–16.

Batstone, W. W. (1990) '*Etsi*: A Tendentious Hypotaxis in Caesar's Plain Style', *AJPh* 111: 348–60.

Batstone, W. W. and C. Damon (2006) *Caesar's Civil War* (New York and Oxford).

Baxter, R. T. S. (1968) *Virgil's Influence on Tacitus* (diss. Stanford).

—— (1971) 'Virgil's Influence on Tacitus in Book 3 of the Histories', *CPh* 66: 93–107.

Beagon, M. (2005) *The Elder Pliny on the Human Animal: Natural History Book Seven* (Oxford).

Beard, M., J. North and S. Price (1998) *Religions of Rome*, 2 vols. (Cambridge).

Beaujeu, J. (1960) *L'Incendie di Rome en 64 et les chrétiens* (Brussels).

Bechtle, G. (1995) 'The Adultery-tales in the Ninth Book of Apuleius' *Metamorphoses*', *Hermes* 123: 106–16.

Bedon, R. (1994) 'L'Emploi du mot *urbs* dans le *Bellum Gallicum* de César, à propos d'Alésia, d'Avaricum et de Gergovia', in C. M. Ternes, ed., *Présence des idées romaines dans le monde d'aujourd'hui: Mélanges offertes à R. Chevallier*, vol. 1 (Caesarodunum 28 bis; Luxembourg), 65–79.

Benario, H. (1972) 'Galba and Priam', *CW* 66: 146–7.

—— (1991) 'Tacitus' Attitude to the Roman Empire', *ANRW* II.33.5: 3332–53.

Berry, D. H. (1996) *Cicero: Pro P. Sulla Oratio* (Cambridge).

Bettini, M. (1991) *Anthropology and Roman Culture: Kinship, Time, Images of the Soul*, trans. J. van Sickle (Baltimore and London).

Biel, S. (1996) *Down with the Old Canoe: A Cultural History of the Titanic Disaster* (New York).

Birley, A. R. (2005) *The Roman Government of Britain* (Oxford).

Bispham, E. (2007) *From Asculum to Actium: The Municipalization of Italy from the Social War to Augustus* (Oxford).

Bloch, R. (2002) *Antike Vorstellungen vom Judentum: der Judenexcurs des Tacitus im Rahmen der griechisch-römischen Ethnographie* (Stuttgart).

Blockley, R. C. (1989) 'Constantius II and Persia', in C. Deroux, ed., *Studies in Latin Literature and Roman History V* (Brussels), 468–89.

—— (1992) *East Roman Foreign Policy: Formation and Conduct from Diocletian to Anastasius* (Leeds).

Boedeker, D. (2002) 'Epic Heritage and Mythical Patterns in Herodotus', in Bakker, de Jong, and van Wees (2002), 97–116.

Bond, J. and A. S. Walpole (1901) *Gai Juli Caesaris de Bello Gallico Commentariorum VII* (London).

Bowie, A. M. (1993) 'Homer, Herodotus and the "Beginnings" of Thucydides' History', in H. D. Jocelyn, ed., *Tria Lustra: Essays and Notes presented to John Pinsent* (Liverpool), 141–7.

Braund, D. (1996) *Ruling Roman Britain: Kings, Queens, Governors and Emperors from Julius Caesar to Agricola* (London).

Braund, S. M. (1996) *Juvenal: Satires, Book I* (Cambridge).

Brelich, A. (1949) *Die geheime Schutzgottheit von Rom* (Albae Vigiliae n.f. 6; Zurich).

Briessman, A. (1955) *Tacitus und das flavische Geschichtsbild* (Wiesbaden).

Brink, C. O. (1982) *Horace on Poetry: Epistles Book II. The Letters to Augustus and Florus* (Cambridge).

Briscoe, J. (1981) *A Commentary on Livy Books XXXIV–XXXVII* (Oxford).

—— (2008) *A Commentary on Livy Books 38–40* (Oxford).

Brown, R. D. (2004) '*Virtus consili expers*: An Interpretation of the Centurions' Contest in Caesar, *De Bello Gallico* 5, 44', *Hermes* 132: 292–308.

Brunt, P. A. (1960) 'Tacitus on the Batavian Revolt', *Latomus* 19: 494–517; repr. in Brunt (1990), 33–52.

—— (1965) 'Italian Aims at the Time of the Social War', *JRS* 55: 90–109.

—— (1971) *Italian Manpower 225 B.C.–A.D. 14* (Oxford).

—— (1980) 'On Historical Fragments and Epitomes', *CQ* 30: 477–94.

—— (1990) *Roman Imperial Themes* (Oxford).

Brunt, P. A. (1993) *Studies in Greek History and Thought* (Oxford).

Buchheit, V. (1962) 'Ludicra latina', *Hermes* 90: 252–6.

—— (1963) *Vergil über die Sendung Roms* (Heidelberg).

—— (1972) *Der Anspruch des Dichters in Vergils Georgica* (Darmstadt).

Büchner, K. (1963) 'Das *verum* in der historischen Darstellung von Sallust', *Gymnasium* 70: 231–52.

—— (1982) *Sallust*, 2nd edn. (Heidelberg).

Burck, E. (1929) 'Die Komposition von Vergils Georgika', *Hermes* 64: 279–321.

—— (1964) *Die Erzählungskunst des T. Livius*, 2nd edn. (Berlin and Zurich).

Burn, A. R. (1968) 'Review of Ogilvie and Richmond (1967)', *CR* 18: 314–16.

Burnell, P. (1987) 'The Death of Turnus and Roman Morality', *G&R* 34: 186–200.

Cairns, F. (1982) 'Cleon and Pericles: A Suggestion', *JHS* 102: 203–4.

—— (1996) 'Ancient "Etymology" and Tibullus: on the Classification of "Etymologies" and on "Etymological Markers" ', *PCPhS* 42: 24–59.

Canfora, L. (2006a) 'Biographical Obscurities and Problems of Composition', in Rengakos and Tsakmakis (2006), 3–32.

—— (2006b) 'Thucydides in Rome and Late Antiquity', in Rengakos and Tsakmakis (2006), 721–53.

Canter, H. V. (1936) 'Irony in the Orations of Cicero', *AJPh* 57: 457–64.

Carawan, E. (1989) 'Stesimbrotus and Thucydides on the Exile of Themistocles', *Historia* 38: 144–61.

Carolsfeld, H. S. von (1888) *Über die Reden und Briefe bei Sallust* (Leipzig).

Castner, C. J. (1988) *Prosopography of Roman Epicureans from the Second Century B.C. to the Second Century A.D.* (Frankfurt).

Cawkwell, G. L. (1997) *Thucydides and the Peloponnesian War* (London and New York).

Cerchiai, L. (1995) *I Campani* (Milan).

Chahoud, A. (2007) 'Alterità linguistica, *latinitas* e ideologia tra Lucilio e Cicerone', in R. Oniga, ed., *Plurilinguismo letterario* (Udine), 39–56.

Chaplin, J. D. (2000). *Livy's Exemplary History* (Oxford).

Chausserie-Laprée, J. P. (1969) *L'Expression narrative chez les historiens latins* (Paris).

Chilver, G. E. F. (1979) *A Historical Commentary on Tacitus' Histories I and II* (Oxford).

Christ, K. (1974) 'Caesar und der Ariovist', *Chiron* 4: 251–92.

Cichorius, C. (1906) 'Zur Lebensgeschichte des Valerius Soranus', *Hermes* 41: 59–68.

Cipriani, G. (1986) *Cesare e la retorica dell'assedio* (Amsterdam).

Citti, F. (1994) *Orazio: L'invito a Torquato, Epist. 1,5. Introduzione, testo, traduzione e commento* (Bari).

Clarke, K. (1999) 'Universal Perspectives in Historiography', in Kraus (1999), 249–79.

—— (2001) 'An Island Nation: Re-Reading Tacitus' *Agricola*', *JRS* 91: 94–112.

Coleman, R. G. G. (1995) 'Complex Sentence Structure in Livy', in *De usu: Études de syntaxe latine offertes en hommage à Marius Lavency* (Bibliothèque des Cahiers de l'Institut de Linguistique de Louvain 70; Louvain-la-Neuve), 85–94.

Commager, S. (1962) *The Odes of Horace: A Critical Study* (Bloomington and London).

Conte, G. B. (1970) 'Il balteo di Pallante', *RFIC* 98: 292–300.

Corbeill, A. (1996) *Controlling Laughter: Political Humor in the Late Roman Republic* (Princeton).

Corbett, P. (1986) *The Scurra* (Edinburgh).

—— (1930) *The Roman Law of Marriage* (Oxford).

Corcella, A. (2006) 'The New Genre and Its Boundaries', in Rengakos and Tsakmakis (2006), 33–56.

Cornelius, E. (1888) *Quomodo Tacitus, historiarum scriptor, in hominum memoria versatus sit usque ad renascentes literas saeculis XIV. et XV.* (diss., Marburg).

Cornell, T. J. (1976) 'Etruscan Historiography', *ASNP*³ 6: 411–39.

Courbaud, E. (1918) *Les Procédés d'art de Tacite dans les Histoires* (Paris).

Courtney, E. (1980) *A Commentary on the Satires of Juvenal* (London).

—— (1999) *Archaic Latin Prose* (Atlanta).

—— (2003) *The Fragmentary Latin Poets*, 2nd edn. (Oxford).

Cramer, R. (1998) *Vergils Weltsicht: Optimismus und Pessimismus in Vergils Georgica* (Berlin and New York).

Crane, G. (1993) 'Politics of Consumption and Generosity in the Carpet Scene in the *Agamemnon*', *CPh* 88: 117–36.

Crawford, J. W. (1994) *M. Tullius Cicero, The Fragmentary Speeches: An Edition with Commentary* (Atlanta).

Crawford, M. H., ed. (2010) *Imagines Italicae*, *B1CS* Supplement (London).

Cristofani, M., ed. (1990) *La grande Roma dei Tarquini* (Rome).

Cugusi, P. and M. T. Sblendorio Cugusi (2001) *Opere di Marco Porcio Catone censore* (Turin).

D'Arms, J. H. (1967) 'Two Passages from Cicero's Correspondence', *AJPh* 88: 195–202.

—— (1970) *Romans on the Bay of Naples: A Social and Cultural Study of the Villas and their Owners from 150 B.C. to A.D. 400* (Cambridge, Mass.).

Damon, C. (1994) 'Caesar's Practical Prose', *CJ* 89: 183–95.

—— (2003) *Tacitus: Histories I* (Cambridge).

Daugherty, G. N. (1992) 'The *Cohortes Vigilum* and the Great Fire of 64', *CJ* 87: 229–40.

Davidson, J. (1991) 'The Gaze in Polybius' *Histories*', *JRS* 81:10–24.

Davies, J. P. (2004) *Rome's Religious History: Livy, Tacitus, and Ammianus on their Gods* (Cambridge).

De Angelis, P. (1947) *Roma: Il nome arcano* (Rome and Milan).

De Jonge, P. (1980) *Philological and Historical Commentary on Ammianus Marcellinus XVIII* (Groningen).

de Romilly, J. (1963) *Thucydides and Athenian Imperialism*, trans. P. Thody (Oxford and New York).

—— (1988) 'Le Conquérant et la belle captive', *BAGA* 43: 3–15.

De Sanctis, G. (1976) *La guerra sociale*, ed. L. Polverini (Florence).

de Ste Croix, G. E. M. (1972) *The Origins of the Peloponnesian War* (London and Ithaca, NY).

Dehn, W. (1960) 'Einige Bemerkungen zum "Murus gallicus"', *Germania* 38: 43–55.

Della Corte, F. (1935) 'Per l'identità di Valerio Edituo con Valerio Sorano', *RFIC* 13: 68–70.

Delz, J. (1983) *P. Cornelii Taciti Libri Qui Supersunt*, II (Stuttgart).

den Boeft, J., D. den Hengst and H. C. Teitler, edd. (1991) *Philological and Historical Commentary on Ammianus Marcellinus XXI* (Groningen).

Dench, E. (2005) *Romulus' Asylum: Roman Identities from the Age of Alexander to the Age of Hadrian* (Oxford).

Detienne, M. and J.-P. Vernant (1978) *Cunning Intelligence in Greek Culture and Society* (Hassocks).

Develin, R. (1983) 'Tacitus and the Techniques of Insidious Suggestion', *Antichthon* 17: 64–95.

Devillers, O. (2003) *Tacite et les sources des Annales: Enquêtes sur la méthode historique* (Louvain).

Dewald, C. J. (2005) *Thucydides' War Narrative: A Structural Study* (Berkeley and Los Angeles).

Di Brazzano, S. (2004) *Laus Pisonis: Introduzione, edizione critica e commento* (Pisa).

Di Niro, A. (1977) *Il culto di Ercole tra i Sanniti, Pentri e Frentani* (Campobasso).

Dickey, E. (2002) *Latin Forms of Address from Plautus to Apuleius* (Oxford).

Dietler, M. (1998) 'A Tale of Three Sites: The Monumentalization of Celtic Oppida and the Politics of Collective Memory and Identity', *World Archaeology* 30: 72–89.

Diggle, J. (1983) '*Facta dictis aequare*: Sallust, *Hist.* II fr. 98', *PACA* 17: 59–60.

Dodington, P. (1980) *The Function of the References to Engineering in Caesar's 'Commentaries'* (diss., Iowa).

Dominik, W. and J. Hall, edd. (2007) *A Companion to Roman Rhetoric* (Malden, Mass. and Oxford).

Douglas, A. E. (1966) *M. Tulli Ciceronis Brutus* (Oxford).

Dover, K. J. (1965) *Thucydides: Book VII* (Oxford).

Du Quesnay, I. M. LeM. (1973) 'The *Amores*', in T. W. Binns, ed., *Ovid* (London and Boston), 1–48.

—— (1984) 'Horace and Maecenas: The Propaganda Value of *Sermones* 1', in Woodman and West (1984), 19–58.

Dutoit, E. (1948) 'Silences dans l'œuvre de Tite-Live', in *Mélanges de philologie, de littérature et d'histoire anciennes offerts à J. Marouzeau* (Paris), 141–51.

Dwyer, J. and K. Flynn (2005) *102 Minutes: The Untold Story of the Fight to Survive: Inside the Twin Towers* (New York).

Dyck, A. R. (1996) *A Commentary on Cicero* De Officiis (Ann Arbor).

Dyson, S. L. (1971) 'Native Revolts in the Roman Empire', *Historia* 20: 239–74.

Earl, D. C. (1966) *The Political Thought of Sallust* (Cambridge).

—— (1967) *The Moral and Political Tradition of Rome* (London and Ithaca, NY).

Eckert, K. (1970) '*Ferocia*—Untersuchung eines ambivalenten Begriffs', *Der Altsprachliche Unterricht* 13.5: 90–106.

Eckstein, A. (1995) *Moral Vision in the Histories of Polybius* (Berkeley and Los Angeles).

Eden, P. T. (1962) 'Caesar's Style: Inheritance Versus Intelligence', *Glotta* 40: 74–117.

Edgeworth, R. J. (2005) 'The Silence of Virgil and the End of the *Aeneid*', *Vergilius* 51: 3–11.

Edwards, C. (1996) *Writing Rome: Approaches to the City* (Cambridge).

Eidinow, J. S. C. (1995) 'Horace's Epistle to Torquatus (Ep. 1.5)', *CQ* 45: 191–9.

Ek, S. (1942) *Herodotismen in der Archäologie des Dionys von Halikarnass* (Lund).

Elefante, M. (1997) *Velleius Paterculus Ad M. Vinicium consulem libri duo* (Hildesheim, Zurich, and New York).

Emmett, A (1981) 'Introductions and Conclusions to Digressions in Ammianus Marcellinus', *Museum Philologum Londiniense* 5: 15–33.

Erb, N. (1963) *Kriegsursachen und Kriegsschuld in der ersten Pentade des T. Livius* (Winterthur).

Ernout, A. (1954) *Aspects du vocabulaire latin* (Paris).

——— (1957) 'Le Vocabulaire poétique', in id., *Philologica* II (Paris) 66–86; originally published as review of B. Axelson, *Unpoetische Wörter* (Lund 1945) in *RPh* 21 (1947), 55–70.

Erren, M. (2003) *P. Vergilius Maro: Georgica* (Heidelberg).

Estré, I. G. F. (1846) *Horatiana Prosopographeia* (Amsterdam).

Evans, J. K. (1975) 'The Dating of Domitian's War against the Chatti Again', *Historia* 24: 121–4.

Fairweather, J. (1981) *Seneca the Elder* (Cambridge).

Fanizza, L. (1988) *Delatori e accusatori: L'iniziativa nei processi di età imperiale* (*Studia Juridica* 84; Rome).

Fantasia, U. (2004) 'ἀκριβής', *LHGL* 1.36–66.

Fantham, E. (2004) *The Roman World of Cicero's De Oratore* (Oxford).

——— (2009) 'Caesar as an Intellectual', in Griffin (2009), 141–56.

Farney, G. (2007) *Ethnic Identity and Aristocratic Competition in Republican Rome* (New York and Cambridge).

Farrell, J. (1991) *Virgil's Georgics and the Traditions of Ancient Epic* (New York and Oxford).

Fedeli, P. (1983) *Catullus' Carmen 61* (Amsterdam).

Feeney, D. C. (1986) 'History and Revelation in Vergil's Underworld', *PCPhS* 32: 1–24.

——— (2007) *Caesar's Calendar: Ancient Time and the Beginnings of History* (Berkeley and Los Angeles).

Feldherr, A. (1998) *Spectacle and Society in Livy's* History (Berkeley and Los Angeles).

Ferguson, J. (1979) *Juvenal: The Satires* (London).

Fleckinger, R. C. (1921) 'Livy i.25.9', *CJ* 16: 369–70.

Flower, H. I. (1996) *Ancestor Masks and Aristocratic Power in Roman Culture* (Oxford).

——— (2006) *The Art of Forgetting: Disgrace and Oblivion in Roman Political Culture* (Chapel Hill, NC and London).

Fornara, C. W. (1983) *The Nature of History in Ancient Greece and Rome* (Berkeley and Los Angeles).

Fowler, D. P. (1989) 'First Thoughts on Closure: Problems and Prospects', *MD* 22: 75–122, repr. in id., *Roman Constructions: Readings in Postmodern Latin* (Oxford, 2000), 239–83.

Fowler, D. P. (1995) 'From Epos to Cosmos: Lucretius, Ovid, and the Poetics of Segmentation', in Innes–Hine–Pelling (1995), 1–18.

—— (2000) 'The Didactic Plot', in M. Depew and D. Obbink, edd., *Matrices of Genre: Authors, Canons, and Society* (Cambridge, Mass.), 205–19.

Fowler, P. 'Lucretian Conclusions', in Roberts–Dunn–Fowler (1997), 112–38.

Fox, M. (1996) *Roman Historical Myths: The Regal Period in Augustan Literature* (Oxford).

Fraenkel, E. (1964) *Kleine Beiträge zur klassischen Philologie*, 2 vols. (Rome).

Frank, T. (1914), 'A Rejected Poem and a Substitute: Catullus LXVIII A and B', *AJPh* 35: 67–73.

Fries, J. (1985) *Der Zweikampf: Historische und literarische Aspekte seiner Darstellung bei T. Livius* (Meisenheim am Glan).

Fuchs, H. (1938) *Der geistige Widerstand gegen Rom in der antiken Welt* (Berlin).

Fuhrmann, M. (1960) 'Das Vierkaiserjahr bei Tacitus: Über den Aufbau der Historien Buch I–III', *Philologus* 104: 250–78.

Fulkerson, L. (2008) 'Patterns of Death in the *Aeneid*', *SCI* 27: 17–33.

Funari, R. (1996) *C. Sallusti Crispi Historiarum Fragmenta*, 2 vols. (Amsterdam).

Furley, D. and J. Bremer (2001) *Greek Hymns*, 2 vols. (Tübingen).

Furneaux, H. (1896) *The Annals of Tacitus, Volume I: Books 1–6*, 2nd edn. (Oxford).

Gabba, E. (1954) *Le origini della Guerra Sociale e la vita politica romana dopo l'89 a.C.* (Pavia).

—— (1991) *Dionysius and the History of Archaic Rome* (Berkeley and Los Angeles).

—— (1994) 'Rome and Italy, the Social War', *CAH* IX^2: 104–28.

Gale, M. (2000) *Virgil on the Nature of Things: The Georgics, Lucretius and the Didactic Tradition* (Cambridge).

—— (2004) 'The Story of Us: A Narratological Analysis of Lucretius' *De Rerum Natura*, in ead., ed., *Latin Epic and Didactic Poetry: Genre, Tradition, and Individuality* (Swansea), 49–71.

Galinsky, G. K. (1972) *The Herakles Theme: the Adaptations of the Hero in Literature from Homer to the Twentieth Century* (Oxford).

—— (1988) 'The Anger of Aeneas', *AJPh* 109: 321–48.

—— (1994) 'How to be Philosophical about the End of the *Aeneid*', *ICS* 19: 191–201.

Garani, M. (2007) *Empedocles Redivivus: Poetry and Analogy in Lucretius* (New York and London).

García Moreno, L. A. (1993) 'Hellenistic Ethnography and the Reign of Augustus in Pompeius Trogus', *AncW* 24: 199–212.

Garland, R. (1995) *The Eye of the Beholder: Deformity and Disability in the Greco-Roman World* (Ithaca, NY and London).

Garnsey, P. (1988) *Famine and Food Supply in the Graeco-Roman World* (Cambridge).

Garson, R. W. (1974) 'Observations on the Death Scenes in Tacitus' Annals', *Prudentia* 6: 23–31.

Genette, G. (1980) *Narrative Discourse: An Essay in Method*, trans. J. Lewin (Ithaca, NY and London).

Gérard, J. (1976) *Juvénal et la realité contemporaine* (Paris).

Gerber, A., and A. Greef (1903) *Lexicon Taciteum* (Leipzig; repr. Hildesheim 1964).

Gibson, B. J. (1998) 'Rumours as Causes of Events in Tacitus', *MD* 40: 111–29.

Ginsburg, J. (1981) *Tradition and Theme in the Annals of Tacitus* (New York).

Giovannini, A. (1987) 'Pline et les délateurs de Domitien', in *Opposition et résistance à l'Empire d'Auguste à Trajan* (Fondation Hardt, Entretiens 33; Vandœuvres-Geneva), 219–48.

Glanz, J. and E. Lipton (2003) *City in the Sky: The Rise and Fall of the World Trade Center* (New York).

Goldberg, S. M. (1995) *Epic in Republican Rome* (New York and Oxford).

—— (2005) *Constructing Literature in the Roman Republic: Poetry and Its Reception* (Cambridge).

Goodyear, F. R. D. (1972) *The Annals of Tacitus Books 1–6: Volume 1 (Annals 1.1–54)* (Cambridge).

—— (1981) *The Annals of Tacitus Books 1–6: Volume II (Annals 1.55–81 and Annals 2)* (Cambridge).

—— (1982) 'On the Character and Text of Justin's Compilation of Trogus', *PACA* 16: 1–24 = Goodyear 1992: 210–33.

—— (1984) 'Virgil and Pompeius Trogus', in *Atti del Convegno mondiale scientifico di studi su Virgili, Mantova, Roma, Napoli 19–24 settembre 1981*, vol. II (Milan) 167–79 = Goodyear (1992), 234–44.

—— (1992) *Papers on Latin Literature* (London).

Gotoff, H. C. (1981) 'Cicero's Style for Relating Memorable Sayings', *ICS* 6: 294–317.

Grant, M. (1971) *Tacitus: the Annals of Imperial Rome*, rev. edn. (Harmondsworth).

Gray, V. (1997) 'Reading the Rise of Pisistratus: Herodotus 1.56–68', *Histos* 1 (electronic publication: <www.dur.ac.uk/Classics/histos/1997/gray.html>).

Greenhalgh, P. (1981) *Pompey: The Roman Alexander* (Columbia, MO).

Greenidge, A. H. J. and A. M. Clay (1960) *Sources for Roman History 133–70 B.C.*, 2nd edn. rev. E. W. Gray (Oxford).

Greenwood, E. (2006) *Thucydides and the Shaping of History* (London).

Grethlein, J. (2005) 'Gefahren des λόγος: Thukydides' "Historien" und die Grabrede des Perikles', *Klio* 87: 41–71.

—— (2006) 'The Unthucydidean Voice of Sallust', *TAPhA* 136: 299–327.

Grewing, F. (1998) 'Etymologie und etymologische Wortspiele in den Epigrammen Martials', in id., ed., *Tota notus in orbe: Perspektiven der Martial-Interpretation* (Palingenesia 65; Stuttgart), 315–56.

Gribble, D. (1998) 'Narrator Interventions in Thucydides', *JHS* 118: 41–67.

—— (1999) *Alcibiades and Athens: A Study in Literary Presentation* (Oxford).

Griffin, J. (1980) *Homer on Life and Death* (Oxford).

—— (1985) *Latin Poets and Roman Life* (London and Chapel Hill, NC).

Griffin, M. T. (1982) 'The Lyons Tablet and Tacitean Hindsight', *CQ* 32: 404–18.

—— (1999) 'Pliny and Tacitus', *SCI* 48: 139–58.

—— (2009) 'Iure plectimur: The Roman Critique of Roman Imperialism', in T. C. Brennan and H. I. Flower, edd., *East and West: Papers in Ancient History presented to Glen W. Bowersock* (Cambridge, MA) 85–111.

Griffin, M. T. ed. (2009) *A Companion to Julius Caesar* (Malden, Mass. and Oxford).

Gruen, E. S. (1984) *The Hellenistic World and the Coming of Rome*, 2 vols. (Berkeley and Los Angeles).

——— (1994) 'The "Fall" of the Scipios', in I. Malkin and Z. W. Rubinsohn, edd., *Leaders and Masses in the Roman World: Studies in Honor of Zvi Yavetz* (*Mnemosyne* suppl. 139; Leiden and New York), 59–90.

Guillaumin, J.-Y. (1987) 'Les *flumina* chez César', *Latomus* 46: 755–61.

Haberman, L. (1980) '*Nefas ab libidine ortum*: Sexual Morality and Politics in the Early Books of Livy', *CB* 57: 8–11.

Habinek, T. N. (2005) *Ancient Rhetoric and Oratory* (Oxford and Malden, Mass.).

Hackl, U. (1980) 'Poseidonios und das Jahr 146 v. Chr. als Epochendatum in der antiken Historiographie', *Gymnasium* 87: 151–66.

Hahm, D. E. (1995) 'Polybius' Applied Political Theory', in A. Laks and M. Schofield, edd., *Justice and Generosity* (Cambridge), 7–47.

Hahn, E. (1933) *Die Exkurse in den Annalen des Tacitus* (Leipzig).

Haley, S. P. (1989) 'Livy's Sophoniba', *C&M* 40: 171–81.

——— (1990) 'Livy, Passion, and Cultural Stereotypes', *Historia* 39: 375–81.

Hall, E. (1989) *Inventing the Barbarian: Greek Self-Definition through Tragedy* (Oxford).

Hammond, C. (1996) *Julius Caesar: Seven Commentaries on the Gallic War* (Oxford).

Hanssen, J. S. T. (1952) *Latin Diminutives: A Semantic Study* (Bergen).

Hardie, A. (2002) 'The *Georgics*, the Mysteries and the Muses at Rome', *BICS* 48: 175–206.

Hardie, P. (1986) *Virgil's* Aeneid: *Cosmos and Imperium* (Oxford).

——— (1994) *Virgil:* Aeneid *Book IX* (Cambridge).

——— (1997) 'Closure in Latin Epic', in Roberts–Dunn–Fowler (1997), 139–62.

——— (1998) *Virgil* (Greece & Rome New Surveys in the Classics no. 28; Oxford).

——— (1999) *Virgil: Critical Assessments of Classical Authors*, vol. 2 (London and New York).

——— (2004) 'Political Education in Virgil's Georgics', *SIFC*[4] 2: 83–111.

——— (2005) 'Time in Lucretius and the Augustan Poets: Freedom and Innovation', in J. P. Schwindt, ed., *La Représentation du temps dans la poésie augustéenne* (Heidelberg), 19–42.

Harrison, S. J. (1991) *Vergil: Aeneid 10* (Oxford).

——— (1992) 'Apuleius eroticus: Anth. Lat. 712 Riese', *Hermes* 120: 83–9.

——— (1996) 'Hereditary Eloquence among the Torquati: Catullus 61.209–18', *AJPh* 117: 285–7.

——— (1998) 'The Sword-Belt of Pallas: Moral Symbolism and Political Ideology', in Stahl (1998), 223–42.

——— (2007a) 'From Man to Book: The Close of Tacitus' *Agricola*', in S. J. Heyworth, ed., *Classical Constructions: Papers in Memory of Don Fowler, Classicist and Epicurean* (Oxford), 310–19.

——— (2007b) 'The Primal Voyage and the Ocean of Epos: Two Aspects of Metapoetic Imagery in Catullus, Virgil and Horace', *Dictynna* 4 (electronic publication: <http://dictynna.revue.univ-lille3.fr/1Articles/4Articlespdf/Harrison.pdf>).

Hartman, J. J. (1905) *Analecta Tacitea* (Leiden).

Hartog, F. 1988. *The Mirror of Herodotus: the Representation of the Other in the Writing of History*, trans. Janet Lloyd (Berkeley and Los Angeles).

Haug, I. (1947) 'Der römische Bundesgenossenkrieg 91–88 v. Chr. bei Titus Livius', *WJA* 2: 100–258.

Haury, A. (1955) *L'Ironie et l'humour chez Ciceron* (Leiden).

Häussler, R. (1976–8) *Das historische Epos der Griechen und Römer*, 2 vols. (Heidelberg).

Heath, M. (1986) 'Thucydides 1.23.5–6', *LCM* 11: 104–5.

—— (1997) 'Invention', in S. E. Porter, ed., *Handbook of Classical Rhetoric in the Hellenistic Period 330 B.C.–A.D. 400* (Leiden and Boston), 89–120.

Heilmann, W. (2000) 'Die Eigenart der taciteischen Vorstellung von der Urzeit in Ann. 3, 26', *Gymnasium* 107: 409–24.

Heinrich, C. F. (1839) *D. Iunii Iuvenalis Satirae cum commentariis*, 2 vols. (Bonn).

Hellegouarc'h, J. (1982) *Velleius Paterculus: Histoire romaine*, vol. 1 (Paris).

Herring, E. and K. Lomas (2000) *The Emergence of State Identities in Italy in the First Millenium B.C.* (London).

Heubner, H. (1972) *P. Cornelius Tacitus, Die Historien, Band III* (Heidelberg).

Highet, G. (1954) *Juvenal the Satirist* (Oxford).

Hijmans, Jr. B. L. et al. (1995) *Apuleius Madaurensis Metamorphoses Book IX* (Groningen).

Hillman, T. P. (1990) 'Pompeius and the Senate: 77–71', *Hermes* 118: 444–54.

Hind, J. G. F. (1974) 'Agricola's Fleet and Portus Trucculensis', *Britannia* 5: 285–8.

Hinds, S. (1998) *Allusion and Intertext: Dynamics of Appropriation in Roman Poetry* (Cambridge).

Hine, H. M. (1978) 'Livy's Judgement on Marius (Seneca, *Natural Questions* 5.18.4; Livy, *Periocha* 80)', *LCM* 3: 83–7.

Hofmann, J. B. (2003) *La lingua d'uso latina* (Bologna), 3rd (Italian) edn. by L. Ricotilli of *Lateinische Umgangssprache*, 2nd edn. (Heidelberg 1951).

Hofmann, J. B. and Szantyr, A. (1965) *Lateinische Syntax und Stilistik* (Munich).

—— (2002), *Stilistica latina*, Italian edn. of Hofmann and Szantyr (1965) by A. Traina et al. (Bologna).

Holford-Strevens, L. (2003) *Aulus Gellius: An Antonine Scholar and His Achievement*, 2nd edn. (Oxford).

Holzberg, N. (2006) *Vergil: Der Dichter und sein Werk* (Munich).

Hommel, H. (1936) 'Die Bildkunst des Tacitus', *WSA* 9: 116–48.

Hooper, W. D. and H. B. Ash (1935) *Cato and Varro on Agriculture* (Cambridge, Mass.).

Hornblower, S. (1994) 'Narratology and Narrative Techniques in Thucydides', in id., ed., *Greek Historiography* (Oxford), 131–66.

—— (1997) '*Odium Thucydideum*: Review of W. K. Pritchett, *Thucydides Pentekontaetia and Other Essays*', *CR* 47: 270–2.

Hornsby, R. A. (1966) 'The Armor of the Slain', *Philological Quarterly* 45: 347–59.

Horsfall, N. (1982) 'The Caudine Forks: Topography and Illusion', *PBSR* 50: 45–52.

—— (1987) 'Illusion and Reality in Latin Topographical Writing', *G&R* 32: 197–208.

—— (1989) *Cornelius Nepos: A Selection, including the Lives of Cato and Atticus* (Oxford).

—— (1995) *A Companion to the Study of Virgil* (Leiden, New York and Cologne).

—— (2000) *Virgil, Aeneid 7: A Commentary* (Leiden and Boston).

—— (2003) *Virgil, Aeneid 11: A Commentary* (Leiden and Boston).

—— (2006) *Virgil, Aeneid 3: A Commentary* (Leiden and Boston).

Horstmann, E. (1979) *Der Geheime Name der Stadt Rom* (Stuttgart).

Housman, A. E. (1931) *D. Iunii Iuvenalis Saturae, Editorum in usum edidit* (Cambridge).

Huelsenbeck, B. (2009) *Figures in the Shadows: Identities in Artistic Prose from the Anthology of the Elder Seneca* (diss. Duke).

Hurley, D. W. (2001) *Suetonius: Divus Claudius* (Cambridge).

Hutchinson, G. O. (1995) *Latin Literature from Seneca to Juvenal: A Critical Study* (Oxford).

Illfe, J. H. (1927) 'Tacitus, *Agricola* XXVIII', *CR* 5: 175–6.

Immerwahr, H. R. (1966) *Form and Thought in Herodotus* (Cleveland).

Innes, D. C. (1977) '*Quo usque tandem patiemini*', *CQ* 27: 468.

Innes, D. C., H. Hine, and C. Pelling, edd., (1995) *Ethics and Rhetoric: Classical Essays for Donald Russell on his Seventy-Fifth Birthday* (Oxford).

Irwin, E. and E. Greenwood, edd. (2007) *Reading Herodotus: A Study of the Logoi in Book 5 of Herodotus' Histories* (Cambridge).

Jacobs, J. (2009) Anne iterum capta repetentur Pergama Roma? *The fall of Rome in the Punica* (diss. Yale).

Jaeger, M. K. (1997) *Livy's Written Rome* (Ann Arbor).

Jal, P. (1987) 'A propos des *Histoires Philippiques*: Quelques remarques', *REL* 65: 194–209.

Jenkyns, R. (1998) *Virgil's Experience* (Oxford).

Jervis, A. (2001) *Gallia scripta: Images of Gauls and Romans in Caesar's* Bellum Gallicum (diss. University of Pennsylvania).

Jones, B. W. (1973) 'The Date of Domitian's War against the Chatti', *Historia* 22: 79–90.

—— (1992) *The Emperor Domitian* (London and New York).

Jones, C. P. (1966) 'Towards a Chronology of Plutarch's works', *JRS* 56: 61–74; repr. in and cited from Scardigli (1995), 95–123.

Jones, H. S. and J. E. Powell (1942) *Thucydidis Historiae*, 2 vols. (Oxford).

Jones, P. J. (2005) *Reading Rivers in Roman Literature and Culture* (Lanham, Md.).

Jong, I. J. F. de and R. Nünlist, edd. (2007) *Time in Ancient Greek Literature* (Leiden and Boston).

Jordan, H. (1860) *M. Catonis praeter librum De re rustica quae extant* (Leipzig).

Joshel, S. (1992) 'The Body Female and the Body Politic: Livy's Lucretia and Verginia' in A. Richlin, ed., *Pornography and Representation in Greece and Rome* (New York and Oxford), 112–30.

Jouanna, J. (2005) 'Cause and Crisis in Historians and Medical Writers', in P. J. van der Eijk, ed., *Hippocrates in Context* (Leiden and Boston), 3–27.

Kallet, L. (2006) 'Thucydides' Workshop of History and Utility outside the Text', in Rengakos and Tsakmakis (2006), 335–68.

Kaster, R. (2002) 'Invidia and the End of *Georgics* 1', *Phoenix* 56: 275–95.

—— (2006) *Cicero: Speech on Behalf of Publius Sestius* (Oxford).

Katz, B. (1982) 'Sallust and Pompey', *RSA* 12: 75–83.

Keitel, E. (1984) 'Principate and Civil War in the *Annals* of Tacitus', *AJPh* 105: 306–25.

—— (1987) 'Otho's Exhortations in Tacitus' *Histories*', *G&R* 34: 73–82.

—— (1991) 'The Structure and Function of Speeches in Tacitus' *Histories* I–III', *ANRW* II.33.4: 2772–94.

—— (1993) 'Speech and Narrative in *Histories* 4', in Luce and Woodman (1993), 39–58.

—— (2006) 'Sententia and Structure in Tacitus, *Histories* 1.1–39', *Arethusa* 39: 219–44.

—— (2008) 'The Virgilian Reminiscences at Tac. *Hist.* 3.84.4', *CQ* 58: 705–8.

Kelly, S. T. (1982) 'The Shackles of Forgetfulness: Horace, *C.*, 4, 7', *Latomus* 41: 815–16.

Kelsey, F. W. (1907) 'Cicero as a Wit', *CJ* 1: 3–10.

Kennedy, D. F. (1999) '"Cf.": Analogies, Relationships and Catullus 68', in S. M. Braund and R. Mayer, edd., *Amor: Roma. Love and Latin Literature* (Cambridge), 30–43.

Kenney, E. J. (1990) 'Introduction', in *Ovid: The Love Poems* (Oxford).

Kienast, D. (2001) 'Augustus und Caesar', *Chiron* 31: 1–26.

Kiene, A. (1845) *Der römische Bundesgenossenkrieg* (Leipzig).

Kierdorf, W. (1980) *Laudatio funebris: Interpretationen und Untersuchungen zur Entwicklung der römischen Leichenrede* (Meisenheim am Glan).

Kiessling, A. and R. Heinze (1968) *Q. Horatius Flaccus: Oden und Epoden*, 13th edn. (Dublin and Zurich).

Kirschenbaum, L. A. (2006) *The Legacy of the Siege of Leningrad* (Cambridge).

Klingner, F. (1965) *Römische Geisteswelt*, 4th edn. (Munich).

Knox, P. E. (1986) 'Adjectives in –*osus* and Latin Poetic Diction', *Glotta* 64: 90–101.

Koestermann, E. (1963) *Cornelius Tacitus Annalen: Band I: Buch 1–3* (Heidelberg).

—— (1965) *Cornelius Tacitus Annalen: Band II, Buch 4–6* (Heidelberg).

—— (1968) *Cornelius Tacitus Annalen: Band IV, Buch 14–16* (Heidelberg).

Konrad, C. (1995) 'A New Chronology of the Sertorian War', *Athenaeum* 83: 157–87.

Konstan, D. (1986) 'Narrative and Ideology in Livy: Book I', *ClAnt* 5: 198–215.

Köves-Zulauf, T. (1970) 'Die "Ἐπόπτιδες" des Valerius Soranus', *RhM* 113: 323–58.

—— (1972) *Reden und Schweigen: Römische Religion bei Plinius Maior* (Studia et Testimonia Antiqua 12; Munich).

Kowalewski, B. (2002) *Frauengestalten im Geschichtswerk des T. Livius* (Munich and Leipzig).

Kramer, E. A. (2005) 'Book One of Velleius' *History*: Scope, Levels of Treatment, and Non-Roman Elements', *Historia* 54: 144–61.

Kraus, C. S. (1991) '*Initium turbandi omnia a femina ortum est*: Fabia Minor and the Election of 367 B.C.', *Phoenix* 45: 314–25.

—— (1994a) *Livy: Ab Urbe Condita Book VI* (Cambridge).

—— (1994b) '"No second Troy": Topoi and Refoundation in Livy, Book V', *TAPhA* 124: 267–89.

—— (1998) 'Repetition and Empire in the Ab Urbe Condita', in P. Knox and C. Foss, edd., *Style and Tradition: Studies in Honor of Wendell Clausen* (Stuttgart and Leipzig), 264–83.

—— (2002) 'Reading Commentaries: Commentaries as Reading', in R. K. Gibson and C. S. Kraus, edd., *The Classical Commentary* (Leiden and Boston), 1–27.

—— (2007) 'Caesar's Account of the Battle of Massilia (*BC* 1.34–2.22): Some Historiographical and Narratological Approaches', in Marincola (2007), 371–8.

—— (2009) '*Bellum Gallicum*', in Griffin, ed. (2009), 159–74.

——, ed. (1999) *The Limits of Historiography: Genre and Narrative in Ancient Historical Texts* (Leiden and Boston).

Kraus, C. S. and A. J. Woodman (1997) *Latin Historians* (*Greece and Rome* New Surveys in the Classics, 27; Oxford).

Krauss, F. B. (1930) *An Interpretation of the Omens, Portents and Prodigies Recorded by Livy, Tacitus and Sallust* (diss. University of Pennsylvania).

Krebs, C. B. (2006) '"Imaginary Geography" in Caesar's *Bellum Gallicum*', *AJPh* 127: 111–36.

Kroll, W. (1923) *C. Valerius Catullus* (Leipzig and Berlin).

Krostenko, B. A. (2001) *Cicero, Catullus and the Language of Social Performance* (Chicago).

La Penna, A. (2005) *L'impossibile giustificazione della storia: Un'interpretazione di Virgilio* (Rome and Bari).

Laird, A. (1999) *Powers of Expression, Expressions of Power* (Oxford).

Latte, K. (1967) *Römische Religionsgeschichte*, 2nd edn. (Handbuch der Altertumswissenschaft 5.4; Munich).

Leeman, A. D. (1963) *Orationis Ratio: The Stylistic Theories and Practice of the Roman Orators Historians and Philosophers*, 2 vols. (Amsterdam).

—— (1975) 'Structure and Meaning in the Prologues of Tacitus', *YCS* 23: 169–208.

Leeman, A. D., H. Pinkster, and E. Rabbie, edd. (1989) *M. Tullius Cicero De Oratore Libri III: Komm. 3. Band: Buch II, 99–290* (Heidelberg).

Leigh, M. (2000) 'Founts of Identity: The Thirst of Hercules and the Greater Greek World', *Journal of Mediterranean Studies* 10: 125–38.

—— (2007) 'Epic and Historiography at Rome', in Marincola (2007), 483–92.

Lendon, J. E. (1997) *Empire of Honour* (Oxford).

Levene, D. S. (1997) 'Pity, Fear and the Historical Audience: Tacitus on the Fall of Vitellius', in S. Braund and C. Gill, edd., *The Passions in Roman Thought and Literature* (Cambridge), 128–49.

—— (2000) 'Sallust's *Catiline* and Cato the Censor', *CQ* 50: 170–91.

—— (2006) 'History, Metahistory, and Audience Response in Livy 45', *ClAnt* 25: 73–108.

—— (2007) 'Roman Historiography in the Late Republic', in Marincola (2007), 275–89.

Levene, D. S. and D. Nelis, edd. (2002) *Clio and the Poets* (Leiden and Boston).

Levick, B. M. (1999) *Vespasian* (London).

Linderski, J. (1975) 'Review of Köves-Zulauf (1972)', *CPh* 70: 284–9 = Linderski (1995), 584–9.

—— (1985) 'The *Libri Reconditi*', *HSCPh* 89: 207–34 = Linderski (1995), 496–523.

—— (1986) 'The Augural Law', *ANRW* II.16.3: 2146–312.

—— (1995) *Roman Questions: Selected Papers* (Stuttgart).

Lintott, A. W. (1972) 'Imperial Expansion and Moral Decline in the Roman Republic', *Historia* 21: 626–38.

Lipovsky, J. (1981) *A Historiographical Study of Livy, Books VI–X* (New York).

Litchfield, H. W. (1914), 'National *Exempla Virtutis* in Roman Literature', *HSCPh* 25: 1–71.

Lomas, K. (2000) 'Cities, States and Ethnic Identity in Southeast Italy', in Herring and Lomas (2000), 79–90.

Loraux, N. (1986) 'Thucydide a écrit la guerre du Péloponnèse', *Mètis* 1: 139–61.

Luce, T. J. (1986) 'Tacitus' Conception of Historical Change: The Problem of Discovering the Historian's Opinions', in Moxon–Smart–Woodman (1986), 143–57

—— (1991) 'Tacitus on "History's Highest Function": *Praecipuum munus annalium*' (*Ann.* 3.65)', *ANRW* II.33.4: 2904–27.

Luce, T. J. and A. J. Woodman, edd. (1993) *Tacitus and the Tacitean Tradition* (Princeton).

Lülu, E.-F. (1980) 'Nova imperii cupiditate: Zum ersten Kapitel der Weltgeschichte des Pompeius Trogus', *GB* 9: 133–54.

Lynch, C. A. (1944) '*Agricola* 28', *AJPh* 65: 246.

Lyne, R. O. A. M. (1974) 'Scilicet et tempus veniet . . . : Virgil, *Georgics* 1.463–514', in Woodman and West (1974), 47–66.

—— (2007) *Collected Papers on Latin Poetry* (Oxford).

MacDowell, D. M. (1991) 'The Athenian Procedure of Phasis', in M. Gagarin, ed., *Symposion 1990: Vorträge zur griechischen und hellenistischen Rechtsgeschichte* (Cologne and Vienna), 187–98.

Macleod, C. (1975) 'Rhetoric and History (Thucydides 6.16–18)', *QS* 2: 39–65; repr. in and cited from id., *Collected Essays* (Oxford), 68–87.

—— (1983) 'Thucydides and Tragedy', in id., *Collected Essays* (Oxford), 140–58.

Malitz, J. (1983) *Die Historien des Poseidonios* (Munich).

Maltby, R. (1979) 'Linguistic Characterization of Old Men in Terence' *CPh* 74: 136–47.

—— (1991) *A Lexicon of Ancient Latin Etymologies* (Leeds).

—— (1993) 'The Limits of Etymologising', *Aevum Antiquum* 6: 257–75.

Marcks, E. (1884) *Die Überlieferung des Bundesgenossenkrieges, 91–89 v.Chr.* (diss. Marburg).

Marincola, J. (1997) *Authority and Tradition in Ancient Historiography* (Cambridge).

Marincola, J. (1999) 'Genre, Convention and Innovation in Greco-Roman Historiography', in Kraus (1999), 281–334.

—— (2003) 'Beyond Pity and Fear: The Emotions of History', *AncSoc* 33: 285–315

—— (2005) 'Looking to the End: Structure and Meaning in Greco-Roman Historiography', *PLLS* 12: 285–320.

—— ed. (2007) *A Companion to Greek and Roman Historiography*, 2 vols. (Malden, Mass. and Oxford).

Marshall, A. J. (1984) 'Ladies in Waiting: The Role of Women in Tacitus' *Histories*', *AncSoc* 15–17: 167–84.

Martin, R. H. (1955) 'Tacitus and the Death of Augustus', *CQ* 5: 123–8.

—— (1981) *Tacitus* (London).

—— (2001) *Tacitus, Annals V & VI* (Warminster).

Martin, R. H., and A. J. Woodman (1989) *Tacitus: Annals Book IV* (Cambridge).

Martinelli, N. (1963) *La rappresentazione dello stile di Crasso e di Antonio nel De oratore* (Rome).

Marx, F. (1904–5) *C. Lucilii Carminum Reliquiae*, 2 vols. (Leipzig).

Masters, J. (1992) *Poetry and Civil War in Lucan* (Cambridge).

Mattern, S. P. (1999) *Rome and the Enemy* (Berkeley and Los Angeles).

Maurenbrecher, B. (1891–3) *C. Sallusti Crispi: Historiarum reliquiae*, 2 vols. (Leipzig; repr. Stuttgart, 1967).

May, J. M. and J. Wisse (2001) *Cicero: On the Ideal Orator* (New York and Oxford).

Mayer, R. (1994) *Horace: Epistles Book I* (Cambridge).

McDonald, A. H. (1938) 'Scipio Africanus and Roman Politics in the Second Century B.C.', *JRS* 28: 153–64.

—— (1957) 'The Style of Livy', *JRS* 47: 155–75.

McGowan, A., (1994) 'Eating People: Accusations of Cannibalism against the Christians in the Second Century', *JECS* 2: 413–42.

McGushin, P. (1977) *C. Sallustius Crispus: Bellum Catilinae: A Commentary* (Leiden).

—— (1992) *Sallust: The Histories Volume I: Books i–ii* (Oxford).

—— (1994) *Sallust: The Histories Volume II: Books iii–v* (Oxford).

McKeown, J. C. (1987–) *Ovid's Amores: Text, Prolegomena and Commentary*, 3 vols. to date (Liverpool).

McLaren, M. (1966) 'Wordplays involving *Bovillae* in Cicero's *Letters*', *AJPh* 2: 192–202.

Meadows, A. and J. Williams (2001) 'Moneta and the Monuments: Coinage and Politics in Republican Rome', *JRS* 91: 27–49.

Melchior, A. (forthcoming) 'Conjuring the Imperator and Other Uses of the *Cohortatio* in Caesar'.

Mellor, R. (1993) *Tacitus* (New York and London).

Mensching, E. (1966) 'Tullus Hostilius, Alba Longa, und Cluilius', *Philologus* 110: 102–18.

Meyer, E. A. (1997) 'The *Outbreak of the Peloponnesian War* after Twenty-Five Years', in C. D. Hamilton and P. Krentz, edd., Polis *and* Polemos: *Essays on Politics*,

War and History in Ancient Greece, in Honor of Donald Kagan (Claremont, Calif.), 23–54.

—— (2008) 'Thucydides on Harmodius and Aristogeiton, Tyranny, and History', *CQ* 58: 13–34.

Michel, J.-H. (1981) 'La Folie avant Foucault: *furor* et *ferocia*', *AC* 50: 517–25.

Miles, G. B. (1980) *Virgil's* Georgics: *A New Interpretation* (Berkeley and Los Angeles).

—— (1995) *Livy: Reconstructing Early Rome* (Ithaca, NY and London).

Millar, F. (2000) 'The First Revolution: Imperator Caesar, 36–28 BC', in A. Giovannini, ed., *La Révolution romaine après Ronald Syme: Bilan et perspectives* (Vandœuvres–Geneva), 1–30.

Miller, N. P. (1968) 'Tiberius Speaks: An Examination of the Utterances Ascribed to Him in the *Annals* of Tacitus', *AJPh* 89: 1–19.

—— (1973) *Corneli Taciti Annalium Liber XV* (London).

—— (1986) 'Virgil and Tacitus Again', *PVS* 18: 87–106.

Milton, G. (2008) *Paradise Lost: Smyrna 1922* (New York).

Miniconi, P. J. (1951) *Étude des thèmes "guerriers" de la poésie épique gréco-romaine* (Paris).

Mitchell, J. F. (1966) 'The Torquati', *Historia* 15: 23–31.

Mitchell. W. J. T. (1980) 'Spatial Form in Literature: Toward a General Theory', *Critical Inquiry* 6: 539–67.

Moatti, C. (1997) *La Raison de Rome* (Paris).

Moles, J. L. (1993) 'Truth and Untruth in Herodotus and Thucydides', in C. Gill und T. P. Wiseman, edd., *Lies und Fiction in the Ancient World* (Exeter and Austin, Tex. 1993), 88–121.

—— (1994) 'Xenophon and Callicratidas', *JHS* 116: 70–84.

—— (1995) 'Review of Badian (1993)', *JHS* 115: 213–15.

—— (1996) 'Herodotus Warns the Athenians', *PLLS* 9: 258–84.

—— (2001) 'A False Dilemma: Thucydides' History and Historicism', in S. J. Harrison, ed., *Texts, Ideas and the Classics: Scholarship, Theory and Classical Literature* (Oxford) 195–219.

—— (2002a) 'Herodotus and Athens', in Bakker–de Jong–van Wees (2002), 33–52.

—— (2002b) 'Poetry, Philosophy, Politics and Play: *Epistles* I', in Woodman and Feeney (2002), 141–57.

—— (2005) 'The Thirteenth Oration of Dio Chrysostom: Complexity and Simplicity, Rhetoric and Moralism, Literature and Life', *JHS* 125: 112–38.

—— (2007) '"Saving" Greece from the "Ignominy" of Tyranny? The "Famous" and "Wonderful" Speech of Socles (5.92)', in Irwin and Greenwood (2007), 245–68.

Monteil, P. (1964) *Beau et laid en latin: Étude de vocabulaire* (Paris).

Moore, T. J. (1993) 'Morality, History, and Livy's Wronged Women', *Eranos* 91: 38–46.

Morel, J.-P. (1976) 'Sur quelques aspects de la jeunesse à Rome', in *Mélanges offerts à Jacques Heurgon: L'Italie préromaine et la Rome républicaine* (Rome), ii. 663–83.

Morello, R. (2006) 'A Correspondence Course in Tyranny: The *cruentae litterae* of Tiberius', *Arethusa* 39: 331–54.

Morgan, Ll. (1999) *Patterns of Redemption in Virgil's* Georgics (Cambridge).

Morgan, Ll. (2005) 'A Yoke Connecting Baskets: *Odes* 3.14, Hercules, and Italian Unity', *CQ* 55: 190–203.

—— (2008) 'Assimilation and Civil War: Hercules and Cacus', in Stahl (1998), 175–98.

Morrison, J. V. (2006) 'Interaction of Speech and Narrative in Thucydides', in Rengakos and Tsakmakis (2006), 251–77.

Mosci Sassi, M. G. (1983) *Il sermo castrensis* (Bologna).

Moskalew, W. (1982) *Formular Language and Poetic Design in the* Aeneid (Leiden).

Mossman, J. M. (1991) 'Plutarch's Use of Statues', in M. A. Flower and M. Toher, edd., *Georgica: Greek Studies in Honour of George Cawkwell* (*BICS* suppl. 58; London), 98–119.

Mouritsen, H. (1998) *Italian Unification: A Study in Ancient and Modern Historiography* (London).

Moxon, I. S., J. D. Smart, and A. J. Woodman, edd. (1986) *Past Perspectives: Studies in Greek and Roman Historical Writing* (Cambridge).

Munson, R. V. (2001) *Telling Wonders: Ethnographic and Political Discourse in the Work of Herodotus* (Ann Arbor).

Münzer, F. (1928) 'Manlius', *RE* XIV.1: 1149–53.

Murgatroyd, P. (2005) 'Tacitus on the Great Fire at Rome', *Eranos* 103: 48–54.

Murphy, T. M. (2004a) *Pliny the Elder's Natural History: The Empire in the Encyclopedia* (Oxford).

—— (2004b) 'Privileged Knowledge: Valerius Soranus and the Secret Name of Rome', in A. Barchiesi, J. Rüpke, and S. Stephens, edd., *Rituals in Ink: A Conference on Religion and Literary Production in Ancient Rome held at Stanford University in February 2002* (Stuttgart), 127–37.

Mynors, R. (1990) *Virgil:* Georgics (Oxford).

Nappa, C. (2005) *Reading after Actium: Vergil's* Georgics, *Octavian and Rome* (Ann Arbor).

Nelis, D. (2001) *Vergil's* Aeneid *and the* Argonautica *of Apollonius Rhodius* (Leeds).

—— (2004) 'Georgics 2.458–542: Virgil, Aratus and Empedocles', *Dictynna* 1 (electronic publication: <http://dictynna.revue.univ-lille3.fr/1Articles/1Articlespdf/ nelis.pdf>).

—— (2008) 'Caesar, the Circus and the Charioteer in Vergil's *Georgics*', in J. Nelis-Clément and J.-M. Roddaz, edd., *Le Cirque romain et son image* (Bordeaux), 497–520.

Neudling, C. L. (1955) *A Prosopography to Catullus* (Oxford).

Newbold, R. F. (1974) 'Some Social and Economic Consequences of the A.D. 64 Fire at Rome', *Latomus* 33: 858–69.

—— (1982) 'The Reports of Earthquakes, Fires and Floods by Ancient Historians,' *PACA* 16: 28–36.

Newman, J. K. (1990) *Roman Catullus and the Modification of the Alexandrian Sensibility* (Hildesheim).

Nicolet, C. (1991) *Space, Geography, and Politics in the Early Roman Empire* (Ann Arbor).

Nicols, J. (1999) 'Sallust and the Greek Historical Tradition', in R. Mellor and L. Tritle, edd., *Text and Tradition: Studies in Greek History and Historiography in Honor of Mortimer Chambers* (Claremont, Calif.), 329–44.

Nisbet, R. G. M. (1959) 'Notes on Horace, *Epistles* I', *CQ* 9: 73–6, repr. in and cited from Nisbet (1995), 1–5.

—— (1961) *M. Tulli Ciceronis in L. Calpurnium Pisonem Oratio* (Oxford).

—— (1978) 'Notes on the Text of Catullus', *PCPhS* 24: 92–115, reprinted in and cited from Nisbet (1995), 76–100.

—— (1995) *Collected Papers on Latin Literature*, ed. S. J. Harrison (Oxford).

—— (2002) 'A Wine-jar for Messalla: *Carmina* 3.21', in Woodman and Feeney (2002), 80–92.

—— (2007) 'Horace: Life and Chronology', in S. J. Harrison, ed., *The Cambridge Companion to Horace* (Cambridge), 7–21.

Nisbet, R. G. M. and M. Hubbard (1970) *A Commentary on Horace: Odes Book I* (Oxford).

—— —— (1978) *A Commentary on Horace: Odes Book II* (Oxford).

Nisbet, R. G. M. and N. Rudd (2004) *A Commentary on Horace: Odes Book III* (Oxford).

Noché, A. (1974) *Gergovie: Vieux problèmes et solutions nouvelles* (Leiden).

Norden, E. (1913) *Agnostos Theos: Untersuchungen zur Formen-Geschichte religiöser Rede* (Leipzig and Berlin).

—— (1957) *P. Vergilius Maro Aeneis Liber Sextus*, 4th edn. (Stuttgart).

Nousek, D. L. (2004) *Narrative Style and Genre in Caesar's* Bellum Gallicum (diss. Rutgers).

O'Brien, J. (1990–91) 'Homer's Savage Hera', *CJ* 86: 105–25.

O'Gorman, E. (2000) *Irony and Misreading in the* Annals *of Tacitus* (Cambridge).

O'Hara, J. J. (1994) 'Temporal Distortions, 'Fatal' Ambiguity, and Julius Caesar at *Aeneid* 1.286–96', *SO* 69: 72–82.

—— (1996) *True Names: Vergil and the Alexandrian Tradition of Etymological Wordplay* (Ann Arbor).

—— (2007) *Inconsistency in Roman Epic: Studies in Catullus, Lucretius, Vergil, Ovid and Lucan* (Cambridge).

Ogilvie, R. M. (1965) *A Commentary on Livy, Books 1–5* (Oxford; repr. with addenda, 1970).

Ogilvie, R. M. and I. Richmond (1967) *Cornelii Taciti De Vita Agricolae* (Oxford).

Oliver, J. H. (1953) 'The Ruling Power: A Study of the Roman Empire in the Second Century after Christ through the Roman Oration of Aelius Aristides', *Transactions of the American Philosophical Society* 43: 871–1003.

Olmstead, A. T. E. (1948) *History of the Persian Empire* (Chicago).

Önnerfors, A. (1974) *Vaterporträts in der römischen Poesie unter besonderer Berücksichtung von Horaz, Statius und Ausonius* (Stockholm).

Otis, B. (1964) *Virgil: A Study in Civilized Poetry* (Oxford).

Page, T. E. (1898) *P. Vergilis Maronis Bucolica et Georgica* (London).

Palmer, A. (1879) 'On Ellis's Catullus', *Hermathena* 3: 293–363.

Panoussi, V. (2007) 'Sexuality and Ritual: Catullus' Wedding Poems', in M. B. Skinner, ed., *A Companion to Catullus* (Malden, Mass. and Oxford), 276–92.

Paratore, E. (1962) *Tacito*, 2nd edn. (Rome).

—— (1967) *De libro IV Annalium Taciti Praelectiones* (Rome).

Pasetti, L. (2007) *Plauto in Apuleio* (Bologna).

Pasoli, E. (1966) 'Pensiero storico ed espressione artistica nelle Historiae di Sallustio', *Bollettino del comitato per la preparazione dell'edizione nazionale del classici greci e latini*, NS 14: 23–50.

Passerini, A. (1933) 'Studi di storia ellenistico-romana, V: L'ultimo piano di Annibale e una testimonianza di Ennio', *Athenaeum* 11: 10–28.

Paton, W. R. (1902) 'On Tacitus *Agricola* 28', *CR* 16: 283.

Patzer, H. (1941) 'Sallust und Thukydides', *Neue Jahrbücher*, 4: 124–36; repr. in and cited from V. Pöschl (ed.), *Sallust: Wege der Forschung* (Darmstadt 1981), 102–20.

Paul, G. M. (1982) '*Urbs capta*: Sketch of an Ancient Literary Motif', *Phoenix* 36: 144–55.

Pease, A. S. (1935) *Publi Vergili Maronis Aeneidos Liber Quartus* (Cambridge, Mass.).

Pelling, C. B. R. (1979) 'Plutarch's Method of Work in the Roman Lives', *JRS* 99 (1979), 74–96; repr. with added postscript in, and cited from, Scardigli (1995), 265–318.

—— (1993) 'Tacitus and Germanicus', in Luce and Woodman (1993), 59–85.

—— (1997) 'East is East and West is West—or are they? National Stereotypes in Herodotus', *Histos* 1 (electronic publication: http://www.dur.ac.uk/Classics/histos).

—— (2000) *Literary Texts and the Greek Historian* (London and New York).

—— (2006) 'Educating Croesus: Talking and Learning in Herodotus' Lydian *logos*', *ClAnt* 25: 141–77.

—— (2007) 'The Greek Historians of Rome', in Marincola (2007), 244–58.

—— (forthcoming, a) 'Tacitus' personal voice', in A. J. Woodman, ed., *Cambridge Companion to Tacitus* (Cambridge), 147–67.

—— (forthcoming, b) ' "Learning from that Violent Schoolmaster . . .": Thucydidean Intertextuality and Some Greek Views of Roman Civil War', in C. Damon, A. Rossi, and B. Breed, edd., *Citizens of Discord: Rome and its Civil Wars* (Oxford).

Penella, R. J. (1990) '*Vires/Robur/Opes* and *Ferocia* in Livy's Account of Romulus and Tullus Hostilius', *CQ* 40: 207–13.

Perkell, C. (1989) *The Poet's Truth: A Study of the Poet in Virgil's Georgics* (Berkeley and Los Angeles).

Perrochat, P. (1949) *Les Modèles grecs de Salluste* (Paris).

Perruccio, A. (2002) 'Q. Granius in Lucilio e Cicerone: Integrazione culturale di un banditore d'asta?' *Mediterraneo Antico* 5: 677–90.

Petrone, G. (1971) *La battuta a sorpresa (ἀπροσδόκητον) negli oratori latini* (Palermo).

Phang, S. E. (2008) *Roman Military Service: Ideologies of Discipline in the Late Republic and Early Empire* (Cambridge).

Phillips, J. E. (1979) 'Livy and the Beginning of a New Society', *CB* 55: 87–92.

Pichon, R. (1902) *De sermone amatorio apud latinos elegiarum scriptores* (Paris).

Pighi, G. B. (1936) *Nuovi studi ammianei* (Milan).

Plass, P. (1988) *Wit and the Writing of History: The Rhetoric of Historiography in Imperial Rome* (Madison).

Pobjoy, M. (2000) 'The First *Italia*', in Herring and Lomas (2000), 187–211.

Pomeroy, A. J. (1988) 'Livy's Death Notices', *G&R* 35: 172–83.

—— (1991) *The Appropriate Comment: Death Notices in the Ancient Historians* (Frankfurt am Main).

—— (2003) 'Center and Periphery in Tacitus's *Histories*', *Arethusa* 36: 361–74.

Poulle, B. (1994) 'Les Jeux de mots sur le nom de Rome chez Ovide', in D. Conso, N. Fick, and B. Poulle, edd., *Mélanges François Kerlouégan* (Annales littéraires de l'Université de Besançon 515; Paris), 533–8.

Powell, A. (2008) *Virgil the Partisan* (London and Swansea).

Powell, J. G. F. (1984) 'A Note on the Use of the *praenomen*', *CQ* 34: 238–9.

Price, J. J. (2001) *Thucydides and Internal War* (Cambridge).

Price, S. R. F. (1984) *Rituals and Power: The Roman Imperial Cult in Asia Minor* (Cambridge).

Pritchett, W. K. (1995) *Thucydides' Pentekontaetia and Other Essays* (Amsterdam).

Pulleyn, S. J. (1997) *Prayer in Greek Religion* (Oxford).

Purcell, N. (1995) 'On the Sacking of Carthage and Corinth', in Innes–Hines–Pelling (1995), 133–48.

Putnam, M. C. J. (1979) *Virgil's Poem of the Earth: Studies in the* Georgics (Princeton).

—— (1986) *Artifices of Eternity: Horace's Fourth Book of Odes* (Ithaca, NY and London).

—— (1994) 'Virgil's Danaid Ekphrasis', *ICS* 19: 171–89; rev. version in Putnam (1998), 189–207.

—— (1998) *Virgil's Epic Design: Ekphrasis in the* Aeneid (New Haven and London).

—— (1999) 'Aeneid 12: Unity in Closure', in C. Perkell, ed., *Reading Vergil's* Aeneid: *An Interpretive Guide* (Norman, Okla.), 210–30.

—— (2006) 'Horace to Torquatus: Epistle 1.5 and Ode 4.7', *AJPh* 127: 387–413.

Quinn, K. (1968) *Virgil's Aeneid: A Critical Description* (London and Ann Arbor).

Rambaud, M. (1974) 'L' Espace dans le récit Césarien', in *Littérature gréco-romaine et géographie historique: Mélanges offerts à Roger Dion* (*Caesarodunum* IX bis; Paris), 111–29.

Rankin, H. D. (1969) '"Eating People is Right": Petronius 141 and a *ΤΟΠΟΣ*', *Hermes* 97: 381–4.

Rapsch, J. and D. Najock (1991) *Concordantia in Corpus Sallustianum*, 2 vols. (Hildesheim, Zurich, and New York).

Rauh, N. K. (1989) 'Auctioneers and the Roman Economy', *Historia* 38: 451–71.

Rawlings, H. R. (1981) *The Structure of Thucydides' History* (Princeton).

Rawson, E. (1991) *Roman Culture and Society: Collected Papers* (Oxford).

Reitzenstein, R. (1901) 'Scipio Aemilianus und die stoische Rhetorik', in *Strassburger Festschrift zur XLVI: Versammlung deutscher Philologen und Schulmänner* (Strasbourg), 143–69.

Renehan, R. F. (2000) 'Further Thoughts on a Sallustian Literary Device', *AncW* 31: 144–7.

Rengakos, A. and A. Tsakmakis, edd. (2006) *Brill's Companion to Thucydides* (Leiden and Boston).

Renger, C. (1985) *Aeneas und Turnus: Analyse einer Feindschaft* (Frankfurt).

Reynolds, L. D. (1991) *C. Sallusti Crispi: Catilina, Iugurtha, Historiarum Fragmenta Selecta, Appendix Sallustiana* (Oxford).

Rice Holmes, T. (1911) *Caesar's Conquest of Gaul*, 2nd edn. (Oxford).

Richardson, W. F. (1982) *A Word Index to Celsus, De Medicina* (Auckland).

Richlin, A. (1993) 'Not before Homosexuality: The Materiality of the *Cinaedus* and the Roman Law against Love between Men', *Journal of the History of Sexuality* 3: 523–73.

Richmond, I. A. (1944) 'Cn. Iulius Agricola', *JRS* 34: 34–45.

Richter, W. (1977) *Caesar als Darsteller seiner Taten* (Heidelberg).

Ries, W. (1969) *Gerücht, Gerede, öffentliche Meinung: Interpretationen zur Psychologie und Darstellungskunst des Tacitus* (Heidelberg).

Riggsby, A. M. (1995) 'Appropriation and Reversal as a Basis for Oratorical Proof', *CPh* 90: 245–56.

—— (2006) *Caesar in Gaul and Rome: War in Words* (Austin, Tex.).

Rives, J. B. (1995) 'Human Sacrifice among Pagans and Christians', *JRS* 85: 65–85.

—— (1999) *Tacitus: Germania* (Oxford).

Roberts, D. H., F. M. Dunn, and D. Fowler, edd. (1997) *Classical Closure: Reading the End in Greek and Roman Literature* (Princeton).

Rochette, B. (1997a) ''Ρώμη = ῥώμη', *Latomus* 56: 54–7.

—— (1997b) '*Ruma* ou *Roma*', *Maia* 49: 215–17.

—— (1998) ''ΡΩΜΑΙΑ', *Maia* 50: 253–6.

Rogkotis, Z. (2006) 'Thucydides and Herodotus: Aspects of Their Intertextual Relationship', in Rengakos and Tsakmakis (2006), 57–86.

Rood, T. (1998) *Thucydides: Narrative and Explanation* (Oxford).

—— (1999) 'Thucydides' Persian Wars', in Kraus (1999), 141–68.

Ross, D. O., Jr. (1987) *Virgil's Elements: Physics and Poetry in the* Georgics (Princeton).

Rossi, A. (2004a) *Contexts of War: Manipulation of Genre in Virgilian Battle Narrative* (Ann Arbor).

—— (2004b) 'Parallel Lives: Hannibal and Scipio in Livy's Third Decade', *TAPhA* 134: 359–81.

Rouveret, Agnès (1992) 'Tacite et les monuments', *ANRW* II.33.4: 3051–3099.

Rubinstein, L. (2000) *Litigation and Cooperation: Supporting Speakers in the Courts of Classical Athens* (Stuttgart)

—— (2003) 'Volunteer Prosecutors in the Greek World', *Dike* 6: 87–113.

Rüpke, J. (1992) 'Wer las Caesars *bella* als *commentarii*?', *Gymnasium* 99: 201–26.

Rutherford, I. (2000) 'The Genealogy of the *Boukoloi*: How Greek Literature Appropriated an Egyptian Narrative-Motif', *JHS* 120: 106–21.

Rutherford, R. B. (1995). 'Authorial Rhetoric in Virgil's *Georgics*', in Innes–Hine–Pelling (1995), 19–29.

—— (2007) 'Tragedy and History', in Marincola (2007), 504–14.

Rutledge, S. H. (2001) *Imperial Inquisitions: Prosecutors and Informants from Tiberius to Domitian* (London and New York).

—— (2007) 'Oratory and Politics in the Empire', in Dominik and Hall (2007), 109–21.

Ryberg, I. S. (1942) 'Tacitus' Art of Innuendo', *TAPhA* 73: 383–404.

Sabbah, G. (1978) *La Méthode d'Ammien Marcellin* (Paris).

—— (1996) *Ammien Marcellin: Histoire Tome II (Livres XVII–XIX)* (Paris).

Sacks, K. S. (1990) *Diodorus Siculus and the First Century* (Princeton).

Sage, M. M. (1990) 'Tacitus' Historical Works: A Survey and Appraisal', *ANRW* II.33.2: 853–1030.

Sallmann, K. (1987) 'Reserved for Eternal Punishment: The Elder Pliny's View of Free *Germania* (*HN* 16.1–6)', *AJPh* 108: 108–28.

Salomon, R. (1982) 'The "Avaca" Inscription and the Origin of the Vikrama Era', *JAOS* 102: 59–68.

Saunders, C. (1930) *Vergil's Primitive Italy* (New York and London).

Savage, S. (1945) 'Remotum a notitia vulgari', *TAPA* 76: 157–65.

Sblendorio Cugusi, M. T. (1982) *M. Porci Catonis Orationum reliquiae: Introduzione, testo critico e commento filologico* (Turin).

Scafuro, A. (1989) 'Comic Strategies in Livy's Bacchanalia', *Helios* 16: 19–42.

Scanlon, T. F. (1980) *The Influence of Thucydides on Sallust* (Heidelberg).

—— (1998) 'Reflexivity and Irony in the Proem of Sallust's *Historiae*', in C. Deroux, ed., *Studies in Latin Literature and Roman History*, ix (Brussels), 186–224.

—— (2002) '"The Clear Truth" in Thucydides 1.22.4', *Historia* 51: 131–48.

Scardigli, B., ed. (1995) *Essays on Plutarch's Lives* (Oxford).

Scarola, M. (1984–5) 'Alesia "accerchiata" (Cesare, B.G. 7, 72–74): Racconto e strategia', *AFLB* 27–8: 119–50.

—— (1997) 'Il muro di Avaricum: lettura di Cesare, B.G. 7,23', *MD* 18: 183–204.

Schiesaro A. (1997) 'The Boundaries of Knowledge in Virgil's *Georgics*', in T. Habinek and A. Schiesaro, edd., *The Roman Cultural Revolution* (Cambridge), 63–89.

—— (2005) 'Under the Sign of Saturn: Dido's Kulturkampf', in J. P. Schwindt, ed., *La Représentation du temps dans la poésie augustéenne* (Heidelberg), 85–110.

Schiesaro, A., P. Mitsis, and J. S. Clay, edd. (1993) *Mega nepios: Il destinatario nell'epos didascalico* (special issue of *MD*, vol. 31).

Schmal, S. (2001) *Sallust* (Hildesheim, Zurich, and New York).

Schmitzer, U. (2000) *Velleius Paterculus und das Interesse an der Geschichte im Zeitalter des Tiberius* (Heidelberg).

Schnayder, J. (1928) *Quibus conviciis alienigenae Romanos carpserint* (Cracow).

Schultze, C. (1986) 'Dionysius of Halicarnassus and his audience', in Moxon–Smart–Woodman (1986), 121–41.

Schwabe, L. (1862) *Quaestiones Catullianae* (Giessen).

Schwartz, E. (1929) *Das Geschichtswerk des Thukydides*, 2nd edn. (Bonn).

Scott, J. M. (1998) 'The Rhetoric of Suppressed Speech: Tacitus' Omission of Direct Discourse in his *Annals* as a Technique of Character Denigration', *AHB* 12: 8–18.

Scott, R. T. (1968) *Religion and Philosophy in the Annals of Tacitus* (Rome).

Scott, W. C. (1969) 'Catullus and Cato (c. 56)', *CPh* 64: 24–9.

Scullard, H. H. (1970) *Scipio Africanus: Soldier and Politician* (London and Ithaca, NY).

Seager, R. (1997) 'Perceptions of Eastern Frontier Policy in Ammianus, Libanius, and Julian (337–363)', *CQ* 91: 253–68.

—— (2005) *Tiberius*, 2nd edn. (Oxford and Malden, Mass.).

Seel, O. (1972) *Eine römische Weltgeschichte: Studien zum Text der Epitome des Iustinus und zur Historik des Pompeius Trogus* (Nuremberg).

Shackleton Bailey, D. R. (1977) *Cicero: Epistulae ad Familiares*, 2 vols. (Cambridge).

—— (1978) *Cicero's Letters to his Friends*, vol. 1 (Harmondsworth).

Sherwin-White, A. N. (1973) *The Roman Citizenship*, 2nd edn. (Oxford).

—— (1967) *Racial Prejudice in Imperial Rome* (Cambridge).

Shotter, D. C. A. (1989) *Tacitus: Annals IV* (Warminster).

Sinclair, P. (1991) '"These are my temples in your hearts" (Tac. *Ann.* 4.38.2)', *CPh* 86: 333–5.

—— (1995) *Tacitus the Sententious Historian: A Sociology of Rhetoric in* Annales *1–6* (University Park, Pa.).

Skinner, M. B. (1982) 'Pretty Lesbius', *TAPhA* 112: 197–208.

—— (2003) *Catullus in Verona: A Reading of the Elegiac Libellus, Poems 65–116* (Columbus, Ohio).

Skulsky, S. (1985) '"*Invitus, regina . . .*": Aeneas and the Love of Rome', *AJPh* 106: 447–55.

Skutsch, O. (1985) *The Annals of Quintus Ennius* (Oxford).

Smethurst, S. E. (1950) 'Women in Livy's History', *G&R* 19: 80–7.

Smith, M. F. (1992) *Lucretius: De Rerum Natura* (Cambridge, Mass.)

—— (1975) *Petronius: Cena Trimalchionis* (Oxford).

Solin, H. (1993) 'Zur Tragfähigkeit der Onomastik in der Prosopographie', in W. Eck, ed., *Prosopographie und Sozialgeschichte: Studien zur Methodik und Erkenntnismöglichkeit der kaiserzeitlichen Prosopographie* (Cologne, Vienna, and Weimar), 1–33.

Solodow, J. B. (1979) 'Livy and the Story of Horatius, 1.24–26', *TAPhA* 109: 251–68; repr. in J. D. Chaplin and C. S. Kraus, edd., *Livy* (Oxford, 2009), 297–320.

Sorabji, R. and R. Sharples, edd. (2007) *Greek and Roman Philosophy 100 BC–200 AD*, 2 vols. (*BICS* suppl. 94; London).

Sordi, M. (1964) 'Virgilio e la storia romana del IV secolo a.C.', *Athenaeum* 40: 80–100; repr. in ead., *Scritti di storia romana* (Milan, 2002), 85–105.

Spaltenstein, F. (1986–90) *Commentaire des Punica de Silius Italicus*, 2 vols. (Geneva).

Spence, S. (1991) 'Clinching the Text: The Danaids and the End of the *Aeneid*', *Vergilius* 37: 11–19.

Spilman, M. (1929) 'Some Notes on the *Agricola* of Tacitus', *CPh* 24: 376–93.

—— (1932) *Cumulative Sentence Building in Latin Historical Narrative* (Berkeley and Los Angeles).

Spisak, A. L. (1994) 'Martial 6.61: Callimachean Poetics Revalued', *TAPhA* 124: 291–308.

Spurr, M. S. (1986) 'Agriculture and the Georgics', *G&R* 33: 164–87.

Stadter, P. A. (1993) 'The Form and Content of Thucydides' Pentecontaetia (1.89–117)', *GRBS* 34: 35–72.

Stahl, H.-P. (1981) 'Aeneas—an "Unheroic" Hero?', *Arethusa* 14: 157–77.

—— (2006) 'Narrative Unity and Consistency of Thought: Composition of Event Sequences in Thucydides', in Rengakos and Tsakmakis (2006), 301–34.

—— ed. (1998) *Vergil's Aeneid: Augustan Epic and Political Context* (London and Swansea).

Stahl, J. M. and E. F. Poppo (1875) *Thucydidis de bello Peloponnesiaco libri octo,* vol. II.1 (Leipzig).

Stanley, K. (1963) 'Rome, Ἔρως, and the *Versus Romae*', *GRBS* 4: 237–49.

Starr, R. J. (1981) 'The Scope and Genre of Velleius' History', *CQ* 31: 162–74.

Stevens, C. E. (1952) 'The "Bellum Gallicum" as a Work of Propaganda', *Latomus* 11: 3–18.

Stewart, P. C. N. (1995) 'Inventing Britain: The Roman Creation and Adaptation of an Image', *Britannia* 26: 1–10.

Stramaglia, A. (2003) *Città che si cibò dei suoi cadaveri: Declamazioni maggiori, 12 Quintiliano* (Cassino).

Strasburger, H. (1965) 'Poseidonios on Problems of the Roman Empire', *JRS* 55: 40–53.

Strobel, K. (1987) 'Der Chattenkrieg Domitians: historische und politische Aspekte', *Germania* 65: 423–52.

Strodach, G. K. (1933) 'Latin Diminutives in *-ello/a* and *-illo/a*: A Study in Diminutive Formation', *Language* 9:1, Language Dissertation 14 (Philadephia).

Suerbaum, W. (1980) 'Hundert Jahre Vergil Forschung: Eine systematische Arbeitsbibliographie mit besonderer Berücksichtigung der Aeneis', *ANRW* II.31.1: 3–358.

—— ed. (2002) *Handbuch der lateinischen Literatur der Antike: Die archaische Literatur* (Handbuch der Altertumswissenschaft VIII.1.; Munich).

Sullivan, J. P. (1991) *Martial: The Unexpected Classic* (Cambridge).

Sumner, G. V. (1970) 'The Truth about Velleius Paterculus: Prolegomena', *HSCPh* 74: 259–97.

—— (1973) *The Orators in Cicero's* Brutus: *Prosopography and Chronology* (Toronto).

Syme, R. (1939) *The Roman Revolution* (Oxford).

—— (1958) *Tacitus,* 2 vols. (Oxford).

—— (1964) *Sallust* (Berkeley and Los Angeles).

—— (1982) 'Tacitus: Some Sources of His Information', *JRS* 72: 68–82.

—— (1981) 'Princesses and Others in Tacitus', *G&R* 28, 40–52; repr. in id., *Roman Papers,* iii (Oxford, 1984), 1364–75.

—— (1986) *The Augustan Aristocracy* (Oxford).

Syndikus, H. P. (1990) *Catull. Eine Interpretation. Zweiter Teil: Die grossen Gedichte (61–68)* (Darmstadt).

Thomas, L. (1931) *The Wreck of the Dumaru: A Story of Cannibalism in an Open Boat* (London).

Thomas, R. F. (1988) *Virgil: Georgics,* 2 vols. (Cambridge).

—— (1998) 'The Isolation of Turnus', in Stahl (1998) 271–302.

Thompson, L. A. (1981), 'Carthage and the Massylian Coup d'Etat of 206', *Historia* 30: 120–6.

Till, R. (1968) *La lingua di Catone*, Italian trans. of *Die Sprache Catos* (Leipzig, 1935), with suppl. by C. de Meo (Rome).

Toll, K. (1991) 'The *Aeneid* as an Epic of National Identity: *Italiam laeto socii clamore salutant*', *Helios* 18: 3–14.

—— (1997) 'Making Roman-ness and the *Aeneid*', *ClAnt* 16: 34–56.

Tompkins, D. P. (1972) 'Stylistic Characterization in Thucydides: Nicias and Alcibiades', *YClS* 22: 181–214.

Torigian, C. (1998) 'The Logos of Caesar's *Bellum Gallicum*, especially as revealed in its first five chapters', in Welch and Powell (1998), 45–60.

Traina, A. (1994) 'Il libro XII dell'Aeneide', *Atti e Memorie dell'Accademia Nazionale Virgiliana di Scienze Lettere ed Arti* 62: 19–36.

—— (1999) *Forma e suono: Da Plauto a Pascoli*, 2nd edn. (Bologna).

Trapp, M. (2007) 'Cynics', in Sorabji and Sharples (2007), i. 189–203.

Traub, H. W. (1953) 'Tacitus' Use of *Ferocia*', *TAPhA* 84: 250–61.

Treggiari, S. (1973) 'Cicero, Horace, and Mutual Friends: Lamiae and Varrones Murenae', *Phoenix* 27: 245–61.

—— (1991) *Roman Marriage: Iusti Coniuges from the time of Cicero to the time of Ulpian* (Oxford).

Trépanier, S. (2004) *Empedocles: An Interpretation* (London).

—— (2007) 'The Didactic Plot of Lucretius, *De Rerum Natura*, and its Empedoclean Model', in Sorabji and Sharples (2007), i. 243–82.

Trethewey, K. T. (2002) 'The Image of Scipio Africanus, 235–201 as a Resource for the Study of Roman Cultural Change during the Middle Republic' (diss. Princeton).

Tritle, L. A. (2006) 'Thucydides and Power Politics', in Rengakos and Tsakmakis (2006), 469–91.

van den Hout, M. P. J. (1988) *M. Cornelii Frontonis epistulae schedis tam editis quam ineditis* (Leipzig).

van Wonterghem, F. (1973) 'Le Culte d'Hercule chez les Paeligni', *Ant. Class.* 42: 36–48.

Vasaly, A. (1987) 'Personality and power: Livy's depiction of the Appii Claudii in the First Pentad', *TAPhA* 117: 203–26.

—— (1998–9) 'The Quinctii in Livy's First Pentad: The Rhetoric of Anti-Rhetoric', *CW* 92: 513–30.

—— (2002) 'The Structure of Livy's First Pentad and the Augustan Poetry Book', in Levene and Nelis (2002), 275–90.

Volk, K. (2002) *The Poetics of Latin Didactic: Lucretius, Vergil, Ovid, Manilius* (Oxford).

——, ed. (2008) *Oxford Readings in Classical Studies: Vergil's Georgics* (Oxford).

von Albrecht, M. (2006) *Vergil: Eine Einführung* (Heidelberg).

Walbank, F. W. (1938) '*ΦΙΛΙΠΠΟΣ ΤΡΑΓΩΙΔΟΥΜΕΝΟΣ*: A Polybian Experiment', *JHS* 58.55–68; repr. in Walbank (1985), 210–23.

—— (1960) 'History and Tragedy', *Historia* 9.216–34; repr. in Walbank (1985), 224–41.

—— (1965) 'Political Morality and the Friends of Scipio', *JRS* 55: 6–11.

—— (1972) *Polybius* (Berkeley and Los Angeles).

—— (1975) '*Symplokē*: Its role in Polybius' *Histories*', *YClS* 24: 197–212.

—— (1985) *Selected Papers: Studies in Greek and Roman History and Historiography* (Cambridge).

—— (2004) *Polybius, Rome and the Hellenistic World* (Cambridge).

Waldherr, G. H. (1997) *Erdbeben: das aussergewöhnliche Normale* (Stuttgart).

Walker, A. D. (1993) '*Enargeia* and the Spectator in Greek Historiography', *TAPhA* 123: 353–77.

Walker, B. (1952) *The Annals of Tacitus, a Study in the Writing of History* (Manchester).

Walker, P. K. (1957) 'The Purpose and Method of "the Pentekontaetia" in Thucydides, Book I', *CQ* 7: 27–37.

Wallace, K. G. (1991) 'Women in Tacitus, 1903–1986', *ANRW* II.33.5: 3556–74.

Walsh, P. G. (1961) *Livy: His Historical Aims and Methods* (Cambridge).

Warde Fowler, W. (1918) *Virgil's 'Gathering of the Clans', being Observations on Aeneid VII.601–817*, 2nd edn. (Oxford).

Warmington, E. H. (1967) *Remains of Old Latin*, iii (Cambridge, Mass. and London).

Weinstock, S. (1950) 'Review of Brelich (1949)', *JRS* 40: 149–50.

Weissenborn, W., and H. J. Müller (1909) *Livius*. Erster Band, Buch 1, 9th edn. (Berlin).

Welch, K. and A. Powell, edd. (1998) *Julius Caesar as Artful Reporter: The War Commentaries as Political Instruments* (London and Swansea).

Wellesley, K. (1972) *Cornelius Tacitus, The Histories, Book III* (Sydney).

Westlake, H. D. (1968) *Individuals in Thucydides* (Cambridge).

—— (1977) 'Thucydides on Pausanias and Themistocles: a Written Source?', *CQ* 27: 95–110; repr. in id., *Studies in Thucydides and Greek History* (Bristol, 1989), 1–18.

Wharton, D. B. (1997) 'Tacitus' Tiberius: The State of the Evidence for the Emperor's *ipsissima verba* in the *Annals*', *AJPh* 118: 119–25.

White, H. (1987) *The Content of the Form: Narrative Discourse and Historical Representation* (Baltimore and London).

Whitehouse, H. (1985) 'Shipwreck on the Nile: A Greek Novel on a "Lost" Roman Mosaic?', *AJA* 89: 129–34.

Wiedemann, T. E. J. (1979) '*Nunc ad inceptum redeo*: Sallust, *Jugurtha* 4.9 and Cato', *LCM* 4: 13–16.

—— (1983) 'Thucydides, Women, and the Limits of Rational Analysis', *G&R* 30: 163–70.

—— (1986) 'Between Men and Beasts: Barbarians in Ammianus Marcellinus', in Moxon–Smart–Woodman (1986), 189–201.

Wiedemann, T. E. J. (1993) 'Sallust's *Jugurtha*: Concord, Discord and the Digressions', *G&R* 40: 48–57.

Wiesehöfer, J. (2006) '" . . . Keeping the Two Sides Equal": Thucydides, the Persians and the Peloponnesian War', in Rengakos and Tsakmakis (2006), 657–67.

Wilkins, A. S. (1892) *M. Tulli Ciceronis De Oratore Libri Tres, with Introduction and Notes* (Oxford; repr. Amsterdam 1962).

Wilkinson, L. P. (1982) *Virgil: The Georgics* (Harmondsworth).

Williams, C. A. (1999) *Roman Homosexuality: Ideologies of Masculinity in Classical Antiquity* (New York and Oxford).

Williams, J. H. C. (2001) *Beyond the Rubicon: Romans and Gauls in Republican Italy* (Oxford).

Wills, J. (1996) *Repetition in Latin Poetry: Figures of Allusion* (Oxford).

Winbolt, S. E. (1910) *G. Iulii Caesaris de bello gallico liber septimus* (London).

Winterbottom, M. (1974) *The Elder Seneca: Declamations*, 2 vols. (Cambridge, Mass. and London).

Wiseman, T. P. (1971) *New Men in the Roman Senate 139 B.C.–A.D.14.* (Oxford).

—— (1974) *Cinna the Poet and Other Roman Essays* (Leicester).

—— (1979) *Clio's Cosmetics: Three Studies in Greco-Roman Literature* (Leicester and Totowa, NJ).

—— (1985) *Catullus and His World: A Reappraisal* (Cambridge).

—— (1992) 'Julius Caesar and the *mappa mundi*', in id., ed., *Talking to Virgil: A Miscellany* (Exeter), 22–42.

—— (1995) *Remus: a Roman Myth* (Cambridge).

—— (1998) 'The Publication of *De Bello Gallico*', in Welch and Powell (1998), 1–9.

Wisse, J., M. Winterbottom and E. Fantham (2008) *M. Tullius Cicero: De Oratore Libri III, volume 5: A Commentary on Book III, 96–230* (Heidelberg).

Witte, K. (1910) 'Über die Form der Darstellung in Livius' Geschichtswerk', *RhM* 65: 270–305, 359–419.

Wolfson, S. (2008) *Tacitus, Thule, and Caledonia: The Achievements of Agricola's Navy in Their True Perspective* (Oxford).

Woodman, A. J. (1969) 'Sallustian Influence on Velleius Paterculus', in J. Bibauw, ed., *Hommages à Marcel Renard*, 3 vols. (Brussels), i. 785–99.

—— (1972a) 'Horace's Odes *Diffugere niues* and *Soluitur acris hiems*', *Latomus* 31: 752–78.

—— (1972b) 'Remarks on the Structure and Content of Tacitus, *Annals* 4.57–57', *CQ* 22: 150–8; reprinted in Woodman (1998) 142–154.

—— (1977) *Velleius Paterculus: The Tiberian Narrative (2.94–131)* (Cambridge).

—— (1979) 'Self-Imitation and the Substance of History: *Annals* 1.61–5 and *Histories* 2.70, 5.14–15', in D. West and T. Woodman, edd., *Creative Imitation and Latin Literature* (Cambridge), 143–55; repr. in Woodman (1988), 70–85.

—— (1983) *Velleius Paterculus: The Caesarian and Augustan Narrative (2.41–93)* (Cambridge).

—— (1984) 'Horace's First Roman Ode', in Woodman and West (1984), 83–94.

—— (1985) *Tacitus and Tiberius: The Alternative Annals* (Inaugural Lecture, University of Durham).

—— (1988) *Rhetoric in Classical Historiography: Four Studies* (London, Sydney, and Portland).

—— (1989) 'Virgil the Historian: *Aeneid* 8.626–62 and Livy', in J. Diggle, J. B. Hall, and H. D. Jocelyn, edd., *Studies in Latin Literature and its Tradition in honour of C. O. Brink* (Cambridge) 132–45.

—— (1992) 'Nero's Alien Capital: Tacitus as Paradoxographer (*Annals* 15.36–7)', in T. Woodman and J. Powell, edd., *Author and Audience in Latin Literature* (Cambridge), 173–8, 251–5; repr. in Woodman (1998), 168–89.

—— (1993) 'Amateur Dramatics at the Court of Nero: *Annals* 15.48–74', in Luce and Woodman (1993), 104–28, repr. in Woodman (1998) 190–217.

—— (1995) '*Praecipuum munus annalium*: the Construction, Convention, and Context of Tacitus, *Annals* 3.65.1', *MH* 52: 111–26, repr. in Woodman (1998) 86–103.

—— (1998) *Tacitus Reviewed* (Oxford).

—— (2003) 'Poems to Historians: Catullus 1 and Horace, *Odes* 2.1', in D. Braund and C. Gill, edd., *Myth, History and Culture in Republican Rome: Studies in Honour of T. P. Wiseman* (Exeter), 191–216.

—— (2004) *Tacitus: The Annals*, trans. with introd. and notes (Indianapolis).

—— (2006) 'Tiberius and the Taste of Power: The Year 33 in Tacitus', *CQ* 56: 175–89.

—— (2007) *Sallust: Catiline's War, The Jugurthine War, Histories* (Harmondsworth).

—— (2008) 'Cicero on Historiography: *De Oratore* 2.51–64', *CJ* 104: 23–31.

Woodman, A. J. and D. Feeney, edd. (2002) *Traditions and Contexts in the Poetry of Horace* (Cambridge).

Woodman, A. J. and R. H. Martin (1996) *The Annals of Tacitus: Book 3* (Cambridge).

Woodman, A. J., and D. West, edd. (1974) *Quality and Pleasure in Latin Poetry* (Cambridge).

—— —— (1984) *Poetry and Politics in the Age of Augustus* (Cambridge).

Woolf, G. (2000) *Becoming Roman: The Origins of Provincial Civilization in Gaul* (Cambridge).

Wuilleumier, P. (1975) *Tacite: Annales livres IV–VI* (Paris).

Yardley, J. C. (1994) 'The Literary Background to Justin/Trogus', *AHB* 8: 60–70.

—— (2003) *Justin and Pompeius Trogus: A Study of the Language of Justin's Epitome of Trogus* (Toronto).

Yardley, J. C. and W. Heckel (1997). *Justin: Epitome of the Philippic History of Pompeius Trogus. Books 11–12: Alexander the Great* (Oxford).

Yarrow, L. M. (2006a) *Historiography at the End of the Republic: Provincial Perspectives on Roman Rule* (Oxford).

—— (2006b) 'Lucius Mummius and the Spoils of Carthage', *SCI* 25: 57–70.

Yellin, K. (2008) *Battle Exhortation: The Rhetoric of Combat Leadership* (Columbia, SC).

Zadorojnyi, A. V. (1998) 'Thucydides' Nicias and Homer's Agamemnon', *CQ* 48: 298–303.

Zagorin, P. (2005) *Thucydides: an Introduction for the Common Reader* (Princeton).

Zehnacker, H. (ed.) (2004) *Pline l'Ancien. Histoire naturelle livre III*, 2nd edn. (Paris).

Zuretti, C. O. (1922) 'La lettera di Nicia (Thuc. VII 11–15)', *RFIC* 50: 1–11.

Index Locorum

Index Locorum

General Index